The Complete
Kay Francis Career Record

The Complete Kay Francis Career Record

All Film, Stage, Radio and Television Appearances

LYNN KEAR and JOHN ROSSMAN

Foreword by
JAMES ROBERT PARISH

McFarland & Company, Inc., Publishers
Jefferson, North Carolina

Also by Lynn Kear

Laurette Taylor, American Stage Legend (McFarland, 2010)

Also of interest by
Lynn Kear and James King

Evelyn Brent: The Life and Films of Hollywood's Lady Crook (McFarland, 2009)

By Lynn Kear and John Rossman

Kay Francis: A Passionate Life and Career (McFarland, 2006)

Frontispiece: A pastel portrait from *Mandalay* (1934).

The present work is a reprint of the illustrated case bound edition of The Complete Kay Francis Career Record: All Film, Stage, Radio and Television Appearances, *first published in 2008 by McFarland.*

Library of Congress Cataloguing-in-Publication Data

Kear, Lynn.
The complete Kay Francis career record : all film, stage, radio and television appearances / Lynn Kear and John Rossman.
   p.   cm.
Includes bibliographical references and index.

ISBN 978-1-4766-7529-9
(softcover: acid free paper) ∞

1. Francis, Kay, 1905–1968. 2. Francis, Kay, 1905–1968 — Credits.
   I. Rossman, John, 1945–   II. Title.
         PN2287.F672K42   2018
   791.4302'8092 — dc22   2007050416

British Library cataloguing data are available

© 2008 Lynn Kear and John Rossman. All rights reserved

No part of this book may be reproduced or transmitted in any form or by any means, electronic or mechanical, including photocopying or recording, or by any information storage and retrieval system, without permission in writing from the publisher.

Cover photograph: An early shot of the promising Hollywood newcomer Kay Francis (courtesy James King)

Printed in the United States of America

McFarland & Company, Inc., Publishers
Box 611, Jefferson, North Carolina 28640
www.mcfarlandpub.com

To James King and the late Jimmy Bangley,
two of Kay's most devoted and enthusiastic fans

ACKNOWLEDGMENTS

Thanks to Charles Harthy for his research assistance on Homer, Michigan, and the Gibbs family. Mindy Hill and Jimmy Kirk provided invaluable library assistance.

Special thanks to Harold Sunners and Charles Stumpf for their recollections of Kay on stage. We also want to thank Dan Callahan for his insights into Kay's films.

James King graciously agreed to review and comment on the filmography. His insights, advice, and friendship were invaluable.

We're grateful to Mike Rinella who provided numerous reviews based on decades of research on Kay. Thanks also to the American Film Institute, Michelle Vogel, E.J. Fleming, Elizabeth Nocera, Gwen Serna at www.CaroleLandis.com, Eric Gans, Gayle Haffner, Robrt Pela, Dianna Everett, William J. Mann, John Cocchi, Marc Wanamaker, Christopher Nickens, Glenn McMahon, Michael Rinella, Jeanine Basinger, James Robert Parish, Allen Morrison, Joseph Yranski, senior film librarian at the Donnell Media Center, Larry Johnson, Oklahoma City Public Library, and Marty Jacobs, curator, Theatre Collection, Museum of the City of New York.

Very special thanks go to Kimber Herndon for editorial assistance, along with unwavering moral support. She sat through every Kay Francis film, offered advice, and never lost enthusiasm for the project.

Special thanks also to the kind people at the Wesleyan University Archives: Leith Johnson, Joan Miller, and Lea Carlson.

Others who deserve thanks include Sybil Jason, Marsha Hunt, Gloria Stuart, Chuck Tranberg, Joan Seaton, Sidney P. Bloomberg, R.C. Parediz, Susan Caputo, Ray Bean, Valarie Stewart, Ebony Showcase Theatre and Cultural Arts Center, Inc., Laura Wagner, Wade Ballard, Devin Herndon, Diane Hirschfield, Candace Rich, Bill Kizer, Dick Moore, and Rebecca Peters.

The following individuals and research centers and libraries provided able assistance: Andrew C. Jelen, librarian, Wichita Falls Public Library, Wichita Falls, Texas; Janis Ashley, William S. Hart Museum; Jane Klain, The Museum of Television & Radio; Alissa Cherry, Yellowstone Research Library; David M. Hardy, Federal Bureau of Investigation; Susan Halpert, Houghton Library, Harvard University, Cambridge, Massachusetts; Roger Stoddard; Erika Ingham, senior archive assistant, Heinz Archive and Library, National Portrait Gallery, London; Patricia H. Svoboda, research coordinator, CEROS/CAP, Smithsonian Institution, National Portrait Gallery, Washington, D.C.; Kathy Mortenson, Falmouth Public Library, Falmouth, Massachusetts; Falmouth Historical Society; Ellen Bailey, Pasadena Playhouse; Amarillo Library, Amarillo, Texas; Abbott Public Library, Marblehead, Massachusetts; Allentown Public Library; Atlanta-Fulton Public Library; Berkshire Athenaeum, Pittsfield Public Library; Beverly Hills Public Library; Bermuda National Library; Cedar Rapids Public Library; Central Library of Rochester and Monroe County, New York; Church of the Transfiguration, New York; City of St. Paul Public Library; Cleveland Public Library; Columbus (Ohio) Public Library; Deep River Public Library; Detroit Public Library; Enoch Pratt Free Library; Fitchburg Public Library; Fort Lee Free Public Library; Fort Worth Public Library; Grand Rapids Public Library; Hampton Bays Public Library; Houghton Library, Harvard University; Indianapolis Marion County Public Library; Jacksonville Public Library; Kalamazoo Public Library; Library of Congress, Washington, D.C.; Los Angeles City Historical Society; Louisville Free Public Library; Madison Public Library; Miami-Dade County Library; Museum of the City of New York; New Haven Free Public Library; New York Historical Society Library; New York Public Library; New York Public Library for the Performing Arts; Newport Public Library; Notre Dame Academy; Peoria Public Library; Princeton Public Library; Public Libraries of Saginaw; Public Library of Youngstown and Mahoning County; Reading Public Library; Rockville Center Public Library; St. Mark's School, Southboro, Maine; St. Paul Public Library; Santa Barbara Public Library; Saratoga Room, Saratoga Public Library; South Bend Public Library; Steele Memorial Library, Elmira, New York; Tompkins County Public Library; Wilmington Library, Delaware; Carol Davis, Woodland Public Library, Woodland, California; Worcester Public Library, Massachusetts; Kenneth Cobb, Director, New York City Municipal Archives; Ms. Wiggins, National Archives and Records Administration; Houston Public Library; Rosenberg Library, Galveston, Texas; St. Thomas Church, Fifth Avenue, New York City; Beaumont Public Library; and the Gwinnett County Library.

Contents

Acknowledgments   vi

Foreword by James Robert Parish   1

Preface   3

Biography   5

The Films of Kay Francis   17

Appendix A: Stage Appearances   205

Appendix B: Major Radio Appearances   222

Appendix C: Television Appearances   226

Appendix D: Selected Memorabilia   228

Appendix E: Residences   233

Appendix F: Katherine Clinton's Stage Appearances   234

Appendix G: The Players   237

Notes   263

Bibliography   265

Index   273

FOREWORD
by James Robert Parish

In recent years, 1930s Hollywood movie queen Kay Francis has enjoyed a terrific renaissance — thanks to repeated showings of her feature films on cable's Turner Classic Movies, to the release of DVDs of several of her pictures, and to new books such as this excellent volume covering in great detail the life and career of this glamorous, enigmatic cinema star. It is a well-deserved rebirth for this charismatic personality who was too often dismissed by contemporary film reviewers (and some later movie historians) as merely a beautiful, chic "clothes horse" whose trademarks were her severe widow's peak, a husky voice, and her (charming) lisp. Often overlooked by her critics was the fact that Francis, even when mired in undistinguished celluloid soap operas, boasted a special presence that made even these mundane offerings highly entertaining diversions.

I first discovered Kay Francis as an adolescent when a local TV channel in Boston, Massachusetts, began airing a package of 1930s and 1940s Warner Bros. pictures. One of the first entries I saw was 1932's *Man Wanted* in which Francis starred as a married business executive who becomes romantically attracted to her new personal assistant (played by David Manners). As I devoured other Francis entries aired on TV — such as *Jewel Robbery*, *British Agent*, *Wonder Bar*, and *One Way Passage*—I became hooked on the unique presence of this fascinating actress who so captured my imagination. It soon became a joke in my household of how infatuated I was with Miss Francis. In that pre–Internet, pre-cinema reference book era, I — living in a small town — was able to gather only scant data about the alluring Miss Francis.

However, each scrap of information I obtained (e.g., a few reprints of *New York Times* articles from the 1930s, brief biographical entries in encyclopedias) whetted my appetite to know more about this intriguing, exotic actress.

Once I discovered that Miss Francis had starred in a feature entitled *I Found Stella Parish* (1935), I knew the fates meant that one day I would, somehow, meet this sultry screen personality—even though I had little idea at the time of what had happened to her since she left films in the mid–1940s. In the 1960s, I was working as prop master at the Cape Playhouse, a star package summer theater located in Dennis, Massachusetts. Backstage, stapled to the walls and stretching up to the rafters, were posters of shows from each past season. Among these cardboard ads was one from the 1948 season in which Kay Francis starred in a tour of *The Last of Mrs. Cheyney*. If anyone ever wished for an H. G. Wells time machine in which he could jump back in time, it was me.

A few summers later, just before reporting for "duty" for a new season with the Cape Playhouse, I visited Los Angeles. While rummaging through show business books and film still shops on Hollywood Boulevard, I noted in one emporium a sign-in book, where one could write down requests for photographs. I listed my interest in Kay Francis material and gave my summer address. A few weeks later I was again back at the Playhouse. I received a letter from Gene Ringgold in Los Angeles; Gene was associated with the memorabilia shop where I'd left my request. He told me that Francis was staying at a Cape Cod resort some ten miles from where I was based. I immediately wrote

Miss Francis a note, expressing my great interest in her career and life. I received no response. Then one day during a dress rehearsal of the week's new show, I was called to the pay phone located in the green room.

"This is Miss Francis," said the caller. I still get goose bumps when I think of that moment. I brushed off my backstage duties for the rehearsal and listened in awe as Francis told me that her Hollywood career was long behind her, that she still had unpleasant memories of leaving Warner Bros. in the late 1930s, and that she was puzzled about why a person of my young years could possibly be interested in her past professional accomplishments. I was forced to abruptly end the conversation when I was called on stage to handle a momentary crisis regarding a misplaced prop. Miss Francis' final words to me were that she did not wish to meet me.

Undaunted, a few weeks later on my day off from the Playhouse, I drove over to the resort in Falmouth where Miss Francis was vacationing. I asked for her at the front desk, and, to my surprise, she was quickly summoned. Moments later, I stood facing the one-time Queen of Warner Bros. She was wearing a casual outfit — a white blouse, white shorts, and walking shoes. Except for her once jet black hair now salt-and-pepper, she might just as easily have been exiting from a film soundstage during her 1930s heyday. We spoke for a few minutes — during which she repeated her lack of interest in discussing her show business past — and then she excused herself.

Over subsequent years, my interest in Kay Francis remained high. Gene Ringgold and I collaborated on a career article on her for *Films in Review* magazine. I sent Miss Francis a copy of the issue. (At the time she was living across town from me in Manhattan.) I received a telegram from her thanking me for the article, but noting — in her usual brusque manner — that there were several errors within the piece.

Miss Francis and I never met again, although I continued to send her occasional notes. When she died of cancer in August 1968 I contacted her attorney's office to inquire where she would be buried. I heard the secretary yell across the room, "Hey, anyone know what happened to Kay Francis's ashes?" No one there at the time seemed to know.

Following her death, Kay Francis' screen work and once high ranking in Hollywood fell into yet another eclipse — with only a scattering of film buffs devoted to perpetuating her memory through screenings and word-of-mouth.

Today, a new generation of TV and DVD viewers have the golden opportunity to catch up with Miss Francis' extensive oeuvre of screen work, including such peaks as 1932's *Trouble in Paradise*, 1933's *The House on 56th Street*, 1937's *Confession* and the same year's *First Lady* (in which Kay demonstrated her adeptness at brittle comedy). Whether you initially admire Francis for her pulchritude, her deftness at being more soignée than Norma Shearer, Ruth Chatterton, or Lilyan Tashman in hip-clinging sophisticated gowns, or for her cinema acting trick of staring blankly at the camera in moments of high drama, she is a vivid screen personality well worth getting to know better both in her many films and in books such as this one.

PREFACE

This book is a celebration of Kay Francis' acting career. (For a detailed look at her fascinating life, please see our biography, *Kay Francis: A Passionate Life and Career*, McFarland, 2006.) In addition to a brief biography of Kay, we provide a complete record of her film, stage, radio, and television career.

The focus here is on her films. Each film entry includes cast, crew, opening dates, synopsis (with snippets of dialogue), production notes, trivia, and reviews. All of Kay's films were personally viewed by one or both of us, with the exception of *Illusion*; we did, however, have the opportunity to hear *Illusion*'s soundtrack, including dialogue.

Kay was also a remarkable performer on stage, radio, and television. Those performances are covered in appendices A, B and C, and we've provided dates, cast, reviews, production notes, and trivia. Appendix D lists Kay Francis memorabilia and Appendix E lists Kay's residences in New York and California. Appendix F documents Katherine Clinton's (Kay's mother) stage career. Finally, Appendix G presents brief biographies on Kay's and Katherine's fellow performers.

We hope you'll turn often to this reference book and use it as a companion when viewing Kay Francis' films.

BIOGRAPHY

After completing two films for Paramount in New York, 24-year-old Kay Francis came to Hollywood in April 1929. When Paramount asked the once-struggling stage actress to relocate to sunny California, she initially refused. Romantically involved with her *Gentlemen of the Press* director Millard Webb, she was reluctant to leave New York City. In truth, she was never comfortable living in California and eventually moved back to the East Coast after her film career ended.

By 1929, Kay had already endured a hardscrabble childhood followed by two marriages and divorces. Finally persuaded by her studio, the actress said goodbye to Millard, her mother and friends, and traveled by train to Los Angeles, along with her longtime girlfriend and occasional lover, Kattie Stewart. By 1932, Kay was one of Hollywood's top stars.

Born in Oklahoma City on January 13, 1905, Katharine Edwina Gibbs spent her early life moving across the United States with ne'er-do-well father Joseph Gibbs and stage actress mother Katherine Clinton. In her first few years she also lived in Santa Barbara, Los Angeles, Denver, and Salt Lake City as her father tried to support his family.

Gibbs, the son of a wealthy landowner, was born in Homer, Michigan, on January 16, 1862. Known in the farming community as an amateur actor and a bit of a playboy, he married Kay's mother on December 3, 1903, in New York. He'd been married twice before, and had recently deserted second wife Mary in Homer. Much to Joe's distress, Mary ended up with the family fortune after a judge ruled he'd abandoned her.

Quickly realizing that her husband was neither marriage nor father material, Katherine left him when Kay was still a toddler and headed east, hoping to resume her stage career. Kay had few memories of her father and probably never saw him again. Gibbs died penniless in St. Louis on January 20, 1919, leaving behind fourth wife Minnie and two young daughters, Virginia and Helen.

Katherine Clinton Franks, born on May 17, 1874, in Chicago, trained at the Chicago Conservatory. She later joined the esteemed Augustin Daly Company, America's top stock company at the time, using the stage name Katherine Clinton. While with Daly from 1898 to 1902, she acted with some of America's biggest stage stars, including Ada Rehan, Blanche Walsh, and Maude Adams. She left Daly in June 1902 and briefly joined Boston's Castle Square Company, which she left for an even briefer engagement with the Jessie Bonstelle Stock Company in Rochester, New York.

This might have been where she met Joseph Gibbs, who was twelve years her senior. After marrying Gibbs on December 3, 1903, Katherine moved with him to Oklahoma City, where she appeared in occasional plays and taught acting before and after Kay was born.

After leaving her husband, Katherine struggled to care for Kay. There were few acting jobs, though she did work for the Lindsay Morison stock company in 1909 and later, around 1914, toured in vaudeville with performer Harry Brooks. With her meager earnings, she and Kay often roomed in inexpensive boarding houses. Katherine sometimes sent Kay to live with friends, and, occasionally, scraped together enough money to send her daughter to boarding schools, including New York's Ossining School and the Cathedral School of St. Mary's.

Kay's early career ambitions ranged from circus performer to fashion designer to motion picture palace organist. However, her mother coolly decided that the best plan was for her pretty daughter to attend secretarial school. Kay took her mother's advice and attended the Katherine Gibbs (no relation) School of Secretarial Training.

Kay worked briefly in the business world until she met handsome James Dwight Francis, the son of a well-known Massachusetts family. After knowing each other for slightly less than a year, Kay and Dwight married on December 4, 1922. Kay was 17, and Dwight was 25 (they shared the same January 13 birthday). During her courtship and marriage, Kay became part of the smart set, and briefly enjoyed a life of leisure that included polo and tennis, attending the opera and Broadway plays, and dancing at the Waldorf Astoria.

The marriage, however, was doomed; both husband and wife were immature and unprepared for the sacrifices that a successful marriage required. Although Kay tried to be the dutiful housewife—they kept an apartment in New York City and one in Dwight's hometown of Pittsfield, Massachusetts—she soon realized her husband was not interested in working. When both became involved in affairs, the marriage ended. Kay had not yet turned 20.

Despite the split, Kay stayed in the good graces of Dwight's family, and they paid her way to Europe for the divorce. She spent her European visit sightseeing and engaged in several romances, ranging from socialite Kiki Whitney Preston to illustrator Charles Baskerville (a New York friend). Perhaps most important, Baskerville introduced her to Stuart Walker, the stage director who would eventually hire her for his stock company when she returned to the United States. Oh, yes, and Kay *did* obtain her divorce from Francis, though she kept his name.

She decided in Europe—some say on the ship returning home—to become a stage actress like her mother. Within a week after returning to the United States, Kay met with producer Edgar Selwyn and was cast in a modern-day production of "Hamlet." Her role, the Player Queen, was small, and the production closed after a brief run. But it got Kay's foot in the door and was her first role on stage since her school days.

Along with a new career, Kay also acquired a new husband. Massachusetts district attorney William Gaston swept her off her feet, and they impulsively—and secretly—married on November 19, 1925. She'd met him in New York before she went to Paris to divorce Francis. The couple opted for a "modern" marriage: he lived in Boston, and she in New York, but their short-lived marriage was marred by infidelity and a lack of desire on the part of either to settle down. Although they remained friends, the couple divorced on September 21, 1927.

Desperate to earn a living, Kay tried modeling. She was strikingly beautiful. Tall and dark, Kay was a natural in front of a camera. Before she left New York on her European divorce trip, she'd posed for English painter Sir Gerald Kelly, and while living in New York, she modeled for friend and occasional lover Charles Baskerville and for magazines including *Harper's Bazaar* and *McCall's*. When there were no modeling jobs, Kay tried her hand at public relations, but ultimately decided to put her energy into acting.

Her early stage roles were arguably dilettante efforts. In addition to "Hamlet," she had an uncredited part in a one-night production of "The School for Scandal." Despite countless reports to the contrary, she never understudied Katharine Cornell in "The Green Hat"; her diary clearly indicates that she failed the audition. She did, however, pass Stuart Walker's audition, and joined his theatre company in April 1926. The cast performed a grueling schedule until the fall of that year, appearing in Dayton, Cincinnati, and Indianapolis. This was where Kay learned her craft and became serious about her career. She later described it as her most important training. She also began to indulge in the heavy drinking that plagued the rest of her life. Nevertheless, Kay's work with Walker resulted in her first good notices. Now, she was not just noticed for her beauty but also for her talent.

When the tour ended in the fall of 1926, Kay returned to New York City with boyfriend and fellow Stuart Walker performer McKay Morris. They sometimes shared an apartment in New York, though the relationship was doomed because of McKay's homosexuality. Convinced she was in love with him, Kay often ended up drowning her sorrows in speakeasies and clubs, including Texas Guinan's, Club Alabama, and her favorite, Tony's.

This was a generation that lived hard, and Kay was no exception. She was in many ways the quintessential flapper—"the notorious character type who bobbed her hair, smoked cigarettes, drank gin, sported short skirts, and passed her evenings in steamy jazz clubs, where she danced in a shockingly immodest fashion with a revolving cast of male suitors."[1] One of Kay's roommates was Lois Long, a columnist who wrote about the flapper lifestyle for *The New Yorker*. Under the pseudonym Lipstick, Lois regaled readers with tales of a nightlife that Kay also enjoyed.

On a typical evening, just as the late-night crowd began crawling out of the midtown theaters and restaurants, amid the glow of electric streetlights and the steady din of car horns and subway rumblers, Long and her friends would catch a taxicab, "start at '21," and go on to Tony's after 21 "closed." ... Long and her friends often made their way uptown to Harlem, the storied center of black cultural life in 1920s New York, which was also a popular nighttime draw among middle class white New Yorkers. Often, Long and her entourage would arrive uptown after three a.m. and stumble home well after the stock exchange bell sounded the opening of business. Incredibly, she stuck to this routine almost every night. And she [like Kay] developed a titanium tolerance for liquor. "If you could make it to the ladies' room before throwing up," she chortled, you were "thought to be good at holding your liquor.... It was customary to give two dollars to the cab driver if you threw up in his cab." Which happened from time to time.[2]

Since acting jobs were hard to come by, Kay took an unusual position in husband William Gaston's play "Damn the Tears." Oddly, she was not a performer, but the costume designer. The ill-fated production, which garnered terrible reviews, opened on January 21, 1927, and closed after 22 performances.

Fortunately, a new, more successful play, "Crime," opened a month later on February 22. Kay also began dating Allan A. Ryan, Jr., grandson of millionaire Thomas Fortune Ryan. Theirs was a tumultuous relationship that included abortions, frequent arguments, breakups, and makeups. Ryan wanted Kay to marry him — and quit her career. She did consider marrying him, but refused to give up the stage.

She picked up another acting gig in October when she toured with actor-writer Gertrude Bryan in "Amateur Anne." Little attention was paid to the play or to Kay, and the show quickly folded. Before the end of the year, Kay played an airplane pilot in "Venus." Opening on December 25, 1927, it, too, quickly closed.

Finally, Kay was cast in the play that led her to Hollywood. "Fast Company," later renamed "Elmer the Great," starred Walter Huston and opened in Massachusetts on May 3, 1928. After some tweaking, it traveled to Chicago on June 18. The play finally opened on Broadway on September 24, and Kay and the play received good notices, though it closed before the end of the year.

Walter Huston is sometimes credited with getting Kay a screen test for *Gentlemen of the Press*; he also reportedly advised her against marrying Ryan. Writer Ward Morehouse also took credit for discovering Kay at Tony's and getting her the screen test that launched her film career.

Kay actually had her first screen test on February 19, 1926, when she tested for D.W. Griffith at the Famous Players studio in Astoria, New York. The test resulted in no contract and no jobs. Perhaps still feeling the sting of that rejection, Kay was reluctant — perhaps even terrified — to make her second test in 1928. However, this time Paramount liked what they saw and quickly signed her for *Gentlemen of the Press*.

A nice portrait of Kay that appeared in the *Philadelphia Record*.

Kay's first studio was Paramount Pictures.

While making this film, Kay began a serious relationship with director Millard Webb. Though she was erroneously reported to have married playwright John Meehan around this time, it was Webb who gave Kay a ring and came close to marrying the already twice-divorced Miss Francis.

After *Gentlemen of the Press*, Kay next worked on *The Cocoanuts*, a Marx Brothers comedy. Paramount then sent the budding actress to Hollywood. Once she arrived there, she worked steadily for the next seventeen years, eventually making more than sixty films.

Her early films immediately typecast her. Credited as one of the talking picture's first vamps, she played hard, shallow women in *Dangerous Curves, Illusion, The Marriage Playground*, and *Behind the Make-Up*. Then, in 1930, she appeared as a sympathetic wife to compulsive gambler William Powell in *Street of Chance*, produced by David O. Selznick and directed by John Cromwell. This was a breakout role for Kay.

Paramount recognized her as one of their new stars and included her in the revue *Paramount on Parade*. In that same year, she played the vamp extraordinaire in *A Notorious Affair*; Countess Balakireff proved to be one of Kay's sexiest roles. She followed this by playing the loving girlfriend of morally ambiguous attorney William Powell in *For the Defense*. United Artists borrowed her for the prestigious *Raffles* production with British star Ronald Colman. *Let's Go Native*, a silly comedy with Jack Oakie and Jeanette MacDonald, followed.

Her next film, *The Virtuous Sin*, was her only pairing with stage actor Kenneth MacKenna, who became her third husband. Kay had met him in New York, and they reconnected in Hollywood, finally marrying on January 17, 1931. Talented and handsome, MacKenna was in many ways Kay's best choice for a husband. He was stable, hard-working, and intellectual. He was also crazy about her. Their union, however, failed after a few short years when Kay began to stray. By the time she divorced MacKenna, she was already seeing French star Maurice Chevalier.

Kay received a significant salary increase when she signed with Warner Bros.

MGM borrowed Kay for *Passion Flower*. Though it provided the opportunity to work with friend Kay Johnson, wife of director John Cromwell, it was not a good picture. This was her last film released in 1930, and it was already Kay's thirteenth picture.

Kay appeared in seven films released in 1931, and movie magazines began covering the new star. This, however, came at a cost — her loss of privacy. Kay deeply resented the intrusion into her personal life and consequently developed a reputation for aloofness, coldness, and snobbery.

Scandal Sheet, her first picture released in 1931, was a gritty newspaper film that paired her with George Bancroft and Clive Brook. *Ladies' Man*, a mediocre film with William Powell and Carole Lombard, followed. Kay's role in *The Vice Squad* with Paul Lukas was minor, while *Transgression* again made her a leading lady, this time opposite Ricardo Cortez. She followed it with *Guilty Hands*, a fun mystery with Lionel Barrymore.

Perhaps her best film in 1931 was the moody, atmospheric *24 Hours*, again with Clive Brook. Though Miriam Hopkins stole the picture, Kay performed well as the jaded society wife, a role she was born to play. The last film in 1931 was George Cukor's *Girls About Town* with co-stars Lilyan Tashman and Joel McCrea.

In 1931 Kay left Paramount for Warner Bros. While her contract was lucrative, Kay would eventually become embittered at Warner Bros., and there were likely many times she regretted the decision. Her first two films released in 1932 were her last Paramount pictures — *The False Madonna* and *Strangers in Love*. She'd made 23 films for Paramount and was now rich and famous.

Her first film for Warner Bros. was *Man Wanted* with David Manners. This was followed by *Street of Women*. While these two films were unremarkable, *Jewel Robbery* was something special. Pairing her again with William Powell, the sophisticated comedy was one of Kay's best performances. To show her range, she followed it with the sublime drama *One Way Passage* (again with Powell), a Hollywood classic.

Paramount borrowed Kay for the even more brilliant *Trouble in Paradise*. Directed by Ernst Lubitsch, this, her 28th film, was the highlight of Kay's career. Co-starring Herbert Marshall and Miriam Hopkins, *Trouble in Paradise* is an important film. If Kay made no other film but this one, Hollywood would remember her for it.

Kay reteamed with Ronald Colman for United Artists' *Cynara*. Though a glossy production, it was a weak film that never came together. Still, without a doubt, 1932 was her best career year. However, as her career soared, her marriage was failing, though the official announcement did not come until December 19, 1933.

The Keyhole (1933) was her first — and one of her best — pairings with George Brent. *Storm at Daybreak*, with Walter Huston and Nils Asther, was next. It was one of her rare period pieces, which were not her strength; Kay was a modern woman, best at playing contemporary roles. In her next film, *Mary Stevens, M.D.*, Kay played a strong professional woman. This tearjerker set the stage for the melodramas Kay is best known for. Seeing Kay fall to pieces after losing her illegitimate child to illness in *Mary Stevens* is still moving.

I Loved a Woman, an Edward G. Robinson picture, was another period film that featured a miscast Kay as an opera singer. *The House on 56th Street* was one of her better Warner Bros. films. Although the first part is set in 1905 (the year of Kay's birth), the movie comes alive when Kay, released from prison after being unjustly convicted of causing a man's death, becomes a contemporary con artist.

Mandalay, the first film released in 1934, featured Kay in a sexy pre–Code role. *Wonder Bar*, with Al Jolson, was next. The film adaptation of the Broadway play was not successful. It also created one of the first strains in her relationship with Warner Bros. when the studio boosted Dolores Del Rio's role at Kay's expense. *Dr. Monica* and *British Agent*, the last films released in 1934, were mediocre. Kay, still in the midst of a tumultuous relationship with French singer and actor Maurice Chevalier, did, however, manage to have a one-night stand with *British Agent* co-star Leslie Howard.

Top: A rare shot of Kay wearing slacks (courtesy James King). **Bottom:** This photograph of Kay was published in a Spanish magazine (courtesy James King).

Left: Kay wears a revealing gown in a Paramount publicity shot. *Right:* Kay looking a bit Clara Bow–like in this publicity pose.

In 1935 Kay's first three films co-starred George Brent—*Living on Velvet*, *Stranded*, and *The Goose and the Gander*. Only the latter was the least bit clever. *I Found Stella Parish* was the last film released in 1935. Tellingly, Warner Bros. released only four Kay Francis films that year. She was falling out of favor with her studio, and the feeling was mutual. The last straw was when she was replaced by Claudette Colbert in *Tovarich*, a role that had been promised to her. It was around this time that Kay fell in love with screenwriter-director Delmer Daves.

Kay's first film of 1936, *The White Angel*, was one of her worst. Not only was it a period piece, but it was a biopic in which she was badly miscast as Florence Nightingale. Her second (and only other) 1936 film was *Give Me Your Heart*. This melodrama, one of her best roles, featured her as an anguished mother forced to give up her baby to her lover's invalid wife.

By 1937, Kay and Warner Bros. were at each other's throats. *Stolen Holiday* and *Another Dawn* did little to build Kay's reputation. *Confession*, however, was a good film, and Kay gave one of her better performances. It still resonates with viewers. The last film of 1937 was *First Lady*, a comedy that wasn't as funny as it could have been, though it did play to Kay's strengths.

Around this time, Kay's relationship with Daves was ending. Ironically, the Hollywood press had them on the verge of marriage when Kay met Erik Barnekow in October 1937 at the home of friend Dorothy di Frasso. The German-Scot had been a German World War I pilot and was supposedly heir to the Barnekow fortune, which included mines and castles. Al-

A selection of postcards used in the early 1930s to promote Kay and her films.

ready divorced at least once, Barnekow was not wealthy. Kay, who *was* quite wealthy by this time, fell madly in love with him. In fact, she announced that she'd marry him. The marriage never happened, however, due to a combination of Barnekow's reluctance, Kay's misgivings, and, most important, World War II. Eventually Barnekow returned to Germany, and a broken-hearted Kay pined for him for years. Finally, probably unknown to Kay, he committed suicide shortly after the United States joined the war effort. He was 44.

In 1938, Warner Bros. put Kay in some of the worst films of her career. The first, *Women Are Like That* with Pat O'Brien, was tedious, while *My Bill* was just plain awful. *Secrets of an Actress* and *Comet Over Broadway* had potential, but ended up being uneven melodramas.

By 1939, Kay was through with Warner Bros. and vice versa. The studio, in a move that could only be viewed as punishment, assigned Kay to a couple of B movies. *King of the Underworld* and *Women in the Wind* were the last two films Kay made for the studio, and it was a sad ending.

Her three best films while employed at Warner Bros. were *Trouble in Paradise* (made by Paramount), *Jewel Robbery*, and *One Way Passage*. All were made in 1932, and considering that she remained at the studio until almost 1940, an argument could be made that Warner Bros. lost sight of her strengths, which contributed to her career's decline.

After being released from her contract, Kay began happily freelancing. Her first role was *In Name Only* (1939) with friends Cary Grant and Carole Lombard. It wasn't a great film, but it did offer one of Kay's best performances. This time she was cast as a multi-dimensional bitter wife who outfoxes Cary and Carole for much of the movie. In 1940, Kay also made *It's a Date*, a Deanna Durbin film; *When the Daltons Rode*, her only western; and *Little Men*, a weak adaptation of the Louisa May Alcott novel.

Kay claimed to be thrilled that her leading lady days were over, but in truth, it was a blow to her ego. Still, she was relieved that she no longer had to work long days and beg Warner Bros. for her treasured European vacations.

In 1941, Kay made *Playgirl*, *The Man Who Lost Himself*, *Charley's Aunt*, and *The Feminine Touch*. None were remarkable. In the next year, she made only two films. *Always in My Heart* was abysmal. However, it represented a moral victory for Kay; her old studio, Warner Bros., was forced to hire her back — and pay what she demanded. *Between Us Girls*, a Diana Barrymore showcase, was also released in 1942. Sadly, it is almost unwatchable.

During the war years, Kay stayed busy with the USO, Red Cross, and other patriotic and charitable activities. She dated several men, including Rouben Mamoulian, Ivan Goff, Hugh Fenwick, and Otto Preminger, and was often seen at parties and dances. She did not make another picture until 1944 when *Four Jills in a Jeep* was released by Twentieth Century–Fox. The film, based on her USO tour with Mitzi Mayfair, Martha Raye, and Carole Landis, did not garner good reviews.

It wasn't long after this that Kay was presented with an unusual offer. Monogram Pictures, a small B studio, asked if she'd be interested in acting *and* co-producing. Kay, always looking for good investments, was intrigued by the idea of owning a piece of the films. The Monogram trilogy, *Divorce* (1945), *Allotment Wives* (1945), and *Wife Wanted* (1946), were low-budget films that often looked it — though *Allotment Wives* is an undiscovered film noir gem.

Kay had a well-deserved reputation for cheapness. Like many frugal people, she could also be impulsively generous. There are many accounts of Kay providing money and gifts to people, often anonymously — and then she'd turn around and be peculiarly tight-fisted. While co-producing the three Monogram pictures, she cut the budgets to the bone. There are even stories, perhaps apocryphal, that she provided costumes and makeup from home — and brought sandwiches to the set to feed the crew! What's definitely true is that the Monogram pictures were inexpensive quickies. Pricey talent and retakes were a luxury. Only *Allotment Wives* holds up. *Divorce* and *Wife Wanted* are stinkers.

It's little wonder that Kay decided to go back to the stage. The Kay Francis who returned to theatre was a much better actor than the 1920s novice. Still, she was nervous because she was now the star of the show, not merely a supporting actor. Her film experience, however, had turned her into a nuanced actor. Her fame also made her a box office draw.

One problem for theatre researchers is that we have to rely on others to give us a glimpse of the magic of a live performance. By all accounts, Kay was an absolute delight on stage. When she returned to theatre in the mid–1940s, she was, of course, a seasoned performer, and an actor learns tricks after years of steady work. Kay's early theatre training, as well as her Hollywood experience, combined to make her a successful and memorable stage star after her film career ended. Her name alone could get people in the seats. But her charismatic presence, warm personality, and unique charm made Kay a favorite.

Beginning in September 1945, Kay toured in Patsy Ruth Miller's "Windy Hill." The show closed when Kay's Monogram bosses insisted she return to fulfill her contract. In September 1946, Kay opened in "State of the Union," replacing a pregnant Ruth Hussey. She took the show on the road the following September.

Perhaps inspired by *It's a Date*, Kay sailed to Hawaii in November 1940 with lover Rouben Mamoulian.

She also had a new man in her life, stage manager Howard "Hap" Graham. Unfortunately, their relationship was marred by frequent drinking and bickering. By the time the show made it to Columbus, Ohio, in January 1948, Kay's life took a terrible turn. She was hospitalized in serious condition after taking too many sleeping pills and subsequently burning her legs on the hotel room's radiator. Recovery was long and difficult, but Kay decided the best cure was a return to the stage.

She made a comeback in "The Last of Mrs. Cheyney" in June 1948. She toured in this show for several months, and also started a relationship with co-star Joel Ashley. Young, handsome Ashley was an even worse drinker than Graham — and married. Their relationship was stormy and ill-conceived. Despite Kay's personal troubles, her appearances were always a treat for fans. Harold Sunners still has fond memories of seeing her in August 1948 at Brooklyn's Flatbush Theatre, though almost sixty years have passed. "I remember being excited about seeing a big movie star 'live' and that she performed extremely well. Her voice carried well and I heard her quite clearly. I remember thinking that here is this movie star performing live, here in Brooklyn."[3]

In December, Kay took "Favorite Stranger" on the road until April 1949. Her next engagement was in June when she was cast in "Let Us Be Gay," which toured until November, and then was briefly revived the following spring and summer. From May to July 1950, Kay appeared in "Goodbye, My Fancy." In August "The Web and the Rock" opened, but then quickly closed. In the following year, she toured in "Mirror, Mirror" from June to September. All of these productions featured her new leading man Joel Ashley.

Writer-researcher Charles Stumpf recalled seeing Kay in "Mirror, Mirror" on August 27, 1951, in Barnesville, Pennsylvania. The theatre was located in an amusement park, and the production was by the Kenley Players. Kay's injuries in 1948 had been so devastating that she often sat during the production. Still, Stumpf was wowed. "I was impressed because she was one of the first movie stars that I ever saw in person. I think I was struck mostly by her appearance. She was tall, and her hair was jet black. She had sort of a husky quality to her voice. Her presence was dynamic which always

Left: Kay Francis in a black-and-white evening gown. *Right:* A casual but glamorous Kay in a publicity photograph.

seems to add height. She was very impressive."[4] Stumpf also recalls that Kay traditionally gave a curtain speech where she greeted the audience, providing a great thrill for those who remembered her from her movies.

Kay played an actress in "Theatre" in March 1952, and was so popular that the play enjoyed numerous revivals over the next couple years. This was also around the time that she met her last lover, Dennis Allen, a young stage actor-director. With Allen, she'd enjoy her longest relationship, though it, too, disintegrated amid boredom and bickering, and Dennis moved out of Kay's New York apartment in 1961.

In between revivals of "Theatre," Kay also appeared in "Black Chiffon," which quickly closed in June 1954. Kay's last stage appearance was August 9, 1954, in "Theatre." At the time, she had no definite plans to retire, but her health declined, and she'd never go on stage again.

She also occasionally appeared on television. Kay did not enjoy this medium. She was an avid viewer, but she had a phobia about television, mainly because it was live, and she believed older women did not photograph well. She realized, of course, that it provided an excellent opportunity, but it was never a fun experience. Unfortunately, it's difficult, if not impossible, to find television footage of Kay today. No doubt, her vivaciousness and charm came through, especially on game shows.

Her first television appearance was on *This Is Show Business* on May 14, 1950. On November 7, 1950, she appeared on *Prudential Family Playhouse*, and on January 8, 1951, she guested on *Hollywood Screen Test*. Other television appearances included *The Betty Crocker Show* (May 24, 1951), *Lux Video Theatre* (June 4, 1951), *Beat the Clock* (October 20, 1951), *The Frances Langford-Don Ameche Show* (October 21, 1951), *Celebrity Time* (November 11, 1951), *The Stork Club* (April 22, 1952), *The Ken Murray Show* (May 10, 1952), and *Anyone Can Win* (September 1, 1952).

Kay's mother died at the age of 82 on January 29, 1957. She was still living in California,

Kay gave this watercolor self-portrait to friend and physician Dr. Bill Branch in the 1940s. Branch, who was also Joan Crawford's personal physician, was associated with Presbyterian Hospital in Los Angeles.

where her only daughter had bought her a lovely home. Kay, who was 52 when her mother died, spent her last years as a recluse. She rarely went out and spent much of her time watching television, drinking, and talking to old friends on the telephone.

Kay died of cancer in her New York apartment on August 26, 1968, at the age of 63. She had made excellent investments and left most of her million-dollar estate to the Seeing Eye organization in Morristown, New Jersey, which provides guide dogs for the blind.

When she died she'd been out of the news for years. Though most major newspapers ran her obituary, she was on her way to being forgotten. It's likely that the main reason Kay is known today is Turner Classic Movies. While film societies occasionally show her films, the cable television channel routinely shows Kay Francis films, introducing new generations to the one and only Miss Fwancis.

What is it about her that still captivates? For one thing, there is no one quite like Kay Francis. Her smoky voice and dark looks are unique. She was an original in her time, and even today there is no "Kay Francis type."

She was also a much better actress than critics gave her credit for. Many writers jumped on the "Kay Francis can't act" bandwagon, but that judgment was simply not true. Her best performances were in *Jewel Robbery*, *One Way Passage*, *Trouble in Paradise*, *24 Hours*, *The House on 56th Street*, and *Confession*. You'll note this list includes both comedies and dramas.

According to writer Dan Callahan, "Many people jeered at her leaning on wardrobe and her lisp, but those who watch Turner Classic Movies late at night know that Kay Francis movies can become an addiction — when you look at her, you know that all the most salacious stories about old Hollywood are based in truth."[5] Kay Francis fans are obsessive. They can tell you the first time they saw Kay and became a fan. For most, it's an important point in their lives, a time when something changed. That's the kind of power she has over viewers. And that is why she is — and always will be — a Hollywood legend.

THE FILMS OF KAY FRANCIS

Gentlemen of the Press

(Paramount, 1929) 75 min.
Released on May 11, 1929.

Credits: Producer, Monta Bell; director, Millard Webb; based on the play by Ward Morehouse; screenplay, Bartlett Cormack; dialogue director, John Meehan; camera, George J. Folsey; editor, Morton Blumenstock.

Cast: Walter Huston (Wickland Snell); Katherine [Kay] Francis (Myra May); Charles Ruggles (Charlie Haven); Betty Lawford (Dorothy Snell); Norman Foster (Ted Hanley); Duncan Penwarden (Mr. Higgenbottom); Lawrence Leslie (Red); Harry Lee (Copy Desk Editor); Brian Donlevy, Victor Kilian (Bit Parts).

WORKING LATE ONE NIGHT, newspaper editor Wick is visited by an angry woman. Kay Francis' first appearance in a motion picture is ... her shoes. Much was made of Kay's small shoe size so here's your chance to take a look. The camera tilts up to show the rest of Myra May. She looks fantastic in her fur-trimmed finery and sports a short, sleek, butch haircut.

"Are you the editor?" she brusquely asks. "I'm suing this dirty paper for $50,000. Libel. And I'll get it, too! You printed a vicious lie about me. Named me as co-respondent in that Cummings divorce suit. And I'm suing for $100,000. And unless you retract this story I'm suing for $150,000."

Wick, assuring Myra he'll take care of everything, gets her phone number — Trafalgar 5423 — and inquires about her occupation.

"I'm here from California doing secretarial work. Just temporarily, of course. I'm not an ordinary secretary."

After Myra departs, Snell learns that long-neglected daughter Dorothy has eloped with Ted Hanley. Within seconds, the happy couple arrives at his office and Wick discovers that Ted, too, is a newspaperman.

Wick quits the newspaper to take a $15,000-a-year position as director of publicity at the National Mausoleum Society. Myra becomes his secretary (Kay worked as a secretary after graduating from business school and gets to demonstrate her skills in this film), and Ted his assistant. Higgenbottom, Wick's boss, sets up a press conference. Snell urges him to provide food and alcohol. "Reporters always have to eat before they can listen. And since Prohibition they have to drink, too."

While Wick is out, Myra puts the moves on Ted, abruptly snatching a cigarette from his mouth. "Mind if I have a puff?" she suggestively asks. Later Ted offers her a drink. "I don't drink," she says, "but I'll have one with you."

There's a long sequence involving reporters at the party as they cavort, drink, eat, gamble, make telephone calls, and drink and eat some more. Every man who sees Myra makes a comment or leers at her. "Come up to my apartment sometime and fight for your honor," Charlie slurs at Myra.

The press conference turns out to be a non-story, and the newspapermen hurry out. Disgusted and embarrassed, Wick quits. When he learns that Dorothy and Ted are expecting a child, he concludes it's time to break up with Myra. He finds Myra with Ted at her apartment.

"All I've got to do is to look at Ted Hanley, and I've got him," she smugly tells Wick.

Wick decides to stay with Myra, fearing she'll ruin his daughter's marriage. He gets a job as the night city editor. Several months pass.

"Say, what's the idea?" Myra barks into the phone one night. "Did you forget to send up that gin? Say, listen, baby, you get that gin up here, and you get it up here quick or I'll come down with the gang and stage the party there." A weary Wick sends Myra and her drunken friends more liquor.

Meanwhile, Dorothy is in the hospital having the baby. Ted phones and explains she's had a boy, but Dorothy is ill. Snell starts to leave for the hospital, but stays to cover a story about a sinking ship. Dorothy's condition worsens. She calls for him from her hospital bed: "I want my Daddy." Ted puts Dorothy on the phone. Wick, however, is busy dictating the newspaper story. Dorothy tells him she's afraid, but Wick doesn't hear. Dorothy dies before Wick returns to the phone. Wick, shocked and grieving, puts down the phone. A young reporter approaches and asks the legendary editor for advice.

"Get out," Wick says. "Get out of it. Get a gun. Go on the highway, rob, steal, beg. Do anything, but get out of it quick before it poisons you. Get out of it. Get out of it." The final scene shows the newspaper staff readying an edition for distribution.

This film was produced at Paramount's New York studios. Billed as Katherine Francis, Kay has a great line when she first meets Wick.

Kay's first publicity photographs were taken in Chicago in 1928 when she was touring in *Elmer the Great*.

"You'll just love my Pekinese," she promises. Watch for his reaction. She plays a typical film vamp — a manipulative, bitchy man-trap — and is one of the best flirts on film, directing her considerable charm at virtually everyone.

Kay was very influenced by the flapper lifestyle. Indulging in smoking, drinking, and sexual experimentation, flappers were identified by a modern look — risqué clothing, a slouching posture, and an adrogenous, independent attitude. Looking like a subject in a Gordon Conway[6] illustration, Kay maintained this demeanor in her first film as well as future ones. Notice how she often places a hand on her hip, leans forward, and then to the side. Interestingly, critics of flappers were particularly incensed by this mannerism and cautioned young girls "that bad posture led to a 'defect of figure,' that is, the problem of an enlarged hip, which was 'nearly always the outcome of a bad habit of sitting, standing, leaning, or walking in a manner that naturally throws the hip out [akin to the threat that if you make a certain expression, your face will stay that way]. Miss E.K. Bertine, who supervised the exercise program at a women's health center in New York, complained, in fact, that young women had gotten the wrong idea about what it meant to be beautiful. Their posture, a 'lop-sided' stance characterized by 'sunken chests and round shoulders,' suggested fatigue, rather than beauty."[7] By the way, Kay's hair at this time was typically cut in a barbershop.

The film's original title was *News*. Marked by long, stagey scenes, it's typical of early sound pictures. Walter Huston, who once said, "Hell, I ain't paid to make good lines sound good. I'm paid to make bad lines sound good," has his work cut out for him in this one. Jesse Lasky saw Huston in "Elmer the Great," signed him for the lead in *Gentlemen of the Press*, and paid him $10,000 for the four weeks it took to produce the film. Huston complained about the long waits, bright lighting, and tedious details — but found the money more than compensated. Like William Powell, Ronald Colman, and a few others, Huston was one of the more natural acting performers in the early talkies.

The screenplay was based on Ward Morehouse's stage play, which opened on August 27, 1928, at the Henry Miller Theatre. Produced by George Abbott, it ran for 128 performances.

Cast members included John Cromwell (who would later direct Kay in numerous films), Granville Bates, Duncan Penwarden, Helen Flint, Carlotta Irwin, and Betty Lancaster. Director Milton Webb reportedly attended dozens of performances before starting the film.

Morehouse explained that he began writing the story in 1927: "The principal character, Wick Snell, veteran newspaperman, who'd been everywhere and seen everything, was inspired by a man who sat next to me on the rewrite desk at the *Tribune*—Arthur James Pegler, father of Westbrook Pegler. He fumed and he snarled about the injustices of newspaper life; he'd been in the business too long, he'd say, and he'd gotten too little out of it. He was hard and bitter and rasping but, underneath, there was a soft, kindly side, all of which went into the writing of the character of Snell."[8]

Brian Donlevy plays the reporter in the party scene who asks, "I wonder how old Snell landed this graft." At the time the picture was made, Betty Lawford and Monta Bell were dating. They later married and divorced. Kay began an affair with director Webb, but it ended when she moved to Los Angeles.

REVIEWS: "Mr. Millard Webb, free-swinging director, strode to the plate at the Paramount Eastern film foundry, grasped his wagon tongue firmly and smote out the first entirely successful newspaper picture in the history of the photoplay. In fact, successful isn't just *the* word to describe *Gentlemen of the Press*. It's a knockout.... Walter Huston is superb as the old star reporter, and a long-legged, dark girl named Katharine Francis is going to be a great film sensation in vamp roles of the new, slinky type...." (*Photoplay*, June 1929)

"Kay Francis, as the snaky secretary in 'Gentlemen of the Press,' has given one of the most astonishing first performances in the history of motion pictures. She appeared in a blaze of glory, as the first great vamp of the audible pictures, using a type of male-killing technique that is perfection itself for the new form of entertainment. Miss Francis will occupy a sizable place in the yet unwritten history of the talkies." (*Photoplay*, October 1929)

"Huston is supported by a fine cast of players, the two girls both looking and speaking well. With Katherine Francis as the seductive siren and Betty Lawford as the daughter photographing well and also recording, the major

Kay made her screen debut in *Gentlemen of the Press* (1929) at age 24 with stage co-star and friend Walter Huston.

difficulty in casting this talkie was over." (*Variety*, May 15, 1929)

"Rates fair entertainment with authentic newspaper atmosphere but lacks dramatic punch." (*Film Daily*, May 19, 1929)

"It is one the best of the talking comedy dramas, despite occasional bad recording and broken continuity ... Katherine Francis presents an unusual, intriguing appearance, but is handicapped by a somewhat ridiculous old-fashioned vamp role." (*Los Angeles Times*)

"The picture, which is all-talking, moves very slowly, and despite a few diverting moments, fails to hold one's interest because of the insincerity of the characterizations ... Katherine Francis, as the vampy secretary, is a real screen find; she's decorative and has a charmingly husky recording voice." (*New York Evening Journal*)

"The Eastman film makes only a motion picture of fair quality. Nor can it be said to tell a story that gives the audience much of an idea of the life of a newspaper man.... Fine work was done by Katherine Francis, who is quite unfamiliar to us in the movies, as the vamp,

Myra May. She was just the type of woman that a man like Snell would have fallen for." (*Rochester Evening Journal and Post Express*)

"A good deal of the entertaining quality of the picture derives from Katherine Francis' seductive portrayal." (*San Francisco Chronicle*)

"A splendid cast carries a variety of human characterizations with stirring effect ... Katherine Francis, another Broadway favorite, is charming and competent.... Taken altogether, 'Gentlemen of the Press' is truly enlivening entertainment. It reveals the real possibilities of the screen." (*Washington Post*)

The Cocoanuts
(Paramount Famous Lasky Corp., 1929) 90 min. Released on May 24, 1929.

Credits: Producers, Monta Bell, Walter Wanger; associate producer, James R. Cowan; director, Monta Bell; musical numbers directed by Joseph Santley and Robert Florey; based on the play by George S. Kaufman and Irving Berlin; adaptor, Morrie Ryskind; original music and lyrics, Irving Berlin; camera, George Folsey; editor, Barney Rogan; choreographer, Erna Kay; musical director, Frank Tours; art director, William Saulter. Songs: "Florida by the Sea," written by Irving Berlin, sung by chorus, danced by Gamby-Hale Girls and Allan K. Foster Girls; "When My Dreams Come True," written by Irving Berlin, sung by Oscar Shaw and Mary Eaton; "The Bell Hops," written by Irving Berlin, danced by Gamby-Hale Girls; "Monkey-Doodle-Do," written by Irving Berlin, sung by Mary Eaton, danced by Gamby-Hale Girls and Allan K. Foster Girls; "Ballet Music," written by Frank Tours, danced by Gamby-Hale Girls; "Tale of the Shirt," Music from Bizet's Carmen, lyrics by Irving Berlin, sung by Basil Ruysdael and chorus; "Gypsy Love Song," written by Victor Herbert, performed by Chico Marx.

Cast: Groucho Marx (Hammer); Harpo Marx (Harpo); Chico Marx (Chico); Zeppo Marx (Jamison); Mary Eaton (Polly); Oscar Shaw (Bob); Katherine [Kay] Francis (Penelope); Margaret Dumont (Mrs. Potter); Cyril Ring (Yates); Basil Ruysdael (Hennessey); Sylvan Lee (Bell Captain); Allan K. Foster Girls, Gamby-Hale Girls (Dancing Bellhops); Barton MacLane (Bather).

THE NEGLIGIBLE PLOT INVOLVES hotel jewel thieves Penelope and Yates. Penelope devises a plan to steal jewelry from Mrs. Potter, the mother of pretty Polly. The first impression of Kay is that she towers over almost everyone in the cast, except Margaret Dumont. In her first scene, Kay, fashionably dressed, wears a cloche hat and carries a walking cane. An obvious villain, she says her lines in a stagey, theatrical voice. Vamping it up, she flirts first with Chico and then Harpo. A typical line is: "You know, you look like the Prince of Wales. Tell me, what are you doing tonight? Well, don't you *dare* come to room 320 at 11:00."

A real estate auction is interrupted when Margaret Dumont announces that her jewels, worth $100,000, have been stolen. When Harpo locates them (he overheard where they'd be hidden) he's accused until attention turns to Bob. Kay pretends Bob confessed the crime to her. Bob is carted off to jail, though Harpo and Chico quickly help him escape. An engagement dinner is held for Polly and Yates that night. Penelope arrives in a huge, glittering headdress. Yates sputters through a terrible speech before he's fingered as the thief. At this moment, there's a brief but wonderful close-up on Kay (it's one of the film's few close-ups). In Kay's final scene, a detective lights her cigarette. She takes a puff and angrily blows smoke into Yates' face. The camera tilts down to show they're handcuffed together.

Probably the best Kay Francis scene involves adjoining hotel rooms. The rooms of Kay and Margaret Dumont are set up so we can simultaneously see inside both—a typical stage set. Three doors, three Marx Brothers—not to mention Kay, Margaret, and a detective—trust us, it's funny. It's an old trick, but can be amusing with good timing.

The film is simply a filmed stage musical-comedy. It is too long and often more tedious than funny, but there are a few laughs. This is the first film pairing of Groucho and Margaret Dumont, who appeared in both "The Cocoanuts" and "Animal Crackers" on the stage. Sometimes it doesn't seem they're in the same film, let alone the same scene. It would be difficult to find actors with two more different styles, but it often results in comedy. There are also a couple of good scenes between Kay and Harpo, slapping and shoving each other. Kay wasn't known for physical humor, but with Harpo's help she's an excellent straight man. The film also contains the "Why a Duck" sequence.

The most visually interesting shot occurs just before a song-and-dance sequence. In an overhead shot, the girls appear as designs, similar to what Busby Berkeley would do a few years later. Unfortunately, the other camerawork is uninspired.

There were special problems that plagued the studio in Astoria during the making of *Cocoanuts*. For one thing, the studio, constructed during the silent era, was not soundproof so to avoid recording an excessive number of city sounds, production started early in the morning. Also, the new microphones used for sound pictures had not been perfected. During the making of *Cocoanuts*, all paper had to be soaked because the crinkling sound was too distracting. Paper couldn't be "unfolded near a microphone without such an onslaught of crackles, rustles, and pops infecting the sound track that it sounded like the place was burning down." The solution, however, was imperfect: "For reasons we keep waiting to hear explained in the dialogue, every piece of paper that appears in the film is limp and soggy like it's just been retrieved from a kosher brine barrel."[9]

The biggest problem facing the directors was equipment failure and, well, the Marx Brothers. The brothers were chronically late and sometimes even disappeared from the set. Their horseplay and adlibs resulted in ruined takes because of off-screen giggling and confusion. Bemused director Florey plugged away: "Whatever happened, his reaction was always the same: 'This is funny?'"[10]

Little attempt was made to make the set lifelike. It was obviously an interior stage set with crudely painted backgrounds and artificial props. For example, the "lawn" used in the auction scene was made up of grass mats, covered with wood shavings, and a barrel of purple wood shavings added into the mixture.

Groucho Marx was a fan of neither director, claiming French director Florey didn't understand English, and that Santley didn't understand comedy. The reported budget for this picture, filmed in February and March 1929, was $500,000. William Saulter, Paramount's art director, built the largest sets up to that time for Astoria. The original stage production ran approximately 140 minutes. Musical numbers—not comedy bits—were cut from the movie production, which ran approximately 120 minutes.

The Marx Brothers were appearing in Broadway's "Animal Crackers" during the making of *Cocoanuts*. Like other stage actors who supplemented their incomes with occasional film work, they traveled by train to work at Astoria during the day, and then back to Manhattan for their live performances.

The Gamby-Hale Girls were a popular Broadway attraction. Originally formed by dancer-choreographer Chester Hale, they often performed in musical comedies. "Each week Hale devised some new spectacle to display them in — the 'Undersea Ballet,' set to Debussy music, was one of his most widely copied diversions; it was a marvel of sea-green chiffon, rubber octopuses, scrim, magic-lantern waves, and Chester Hale Girls drifting through a canvas-and-gauze Davy Jones Locker on wires."[11] At one time, they were named the Chesterettes, which caused snickering among the more adolescent crowd.

Advertising proclaimed the film as "Paramount's All Talking-Singing Musical Comedy Hit!" and "Paramount's All Talking Musicomedy Sensation."

REVIEWS: "All four of the boys provide insistent laughter and get along splendidly with the talkie apparatus ... Cyril Ring villains in interesting fashion, with Kay Francis capably egging him on in his dirty work." (*Chicago Tribune*)

An early shot of the promising Hollywood newcomer (courtesy James King).

"Kay Francis is a stylishly wicked vamp and puts [the role] across believably." (*New Bedford Evening Standard*)

"The antic quartet labors valiantly; the mad humors thought up by the Messrs. Kaufman and Ryskind ring out heroically; the Irving Berlin score is sung with desperation by Mary Eaton and Oscar Shaw, while Katherine Francis and Margaret Dumont strive to be helpful, but the resulting effort is a pretty sad imitation of a good Broadway musical show.... An additional handicap was the bad quality of the sound recording at the opening show, which made Miss Eaton and Mr. Shaw even less effective than their bad parts warranted and kept the handsome Miss Francis from registering with much success." (*New York Herald-Tribune*)

Dangerous Curves
(Paramount Famous Lasky, 1929)
73 min. Released on July 13, 1929.

Credits: Supervisor, B. F. Zeidman; production supervisor, Ernst Lubitsch; director, Lothar Mendes; story, Lester Cohen; screenplay, Donald Davis, Florence Ryerson; dialogue, Viola Brothers Shore; titles, George Marion, Jr.; camera, Harry Fischbeck; editor, Eda Warren; original music, W. Franke Harling.

Cast: Clara Bow (Pat Delaney); Richard Arlen (Larry Lee); Kay Francis (Zara Flynn); David Newell (Tony Barretti); Anders Randolf (Colonel P. P. Brock); May Boley (Ma Spinelli); T. Roy Barnes (Pa Spinelli); Joyce Compton (Jennie Silver); Charles D. Brown (Spider); Stuart Erwin, Jack Luden (Rotarians); Oscar Smith (Porter); Ethan Laidlaw (Roustabout); Russ Powell (Counterman).

THE FILM OPENS WITH A circus performance, where we're introduced to Pat Delaney, daughter of the great Pop Delaney, a high-wire legend who tragically died during a performance. Pat is in love with wire walker Larry, who's in love with Zara, who's in love with Tony, who is in love with ... Zara. However, Zara strings Larry along because she needs the job.

Larry finds Zara drinking before a performance and scolds her. "Oh, but I'm so cold, Larry," she demurs. "I've been shivering all evening. You don't want me to catch cold, do you, big boy? Oh, but one little bracer couldn't hurt anybody. Please, big boy?"

Larry, a fool for Zara, spends money on her and lets her take the day off from rehearsal. Zara gleefully runs off to spend time with Tony.

Mr. Brock, the show's producer, tells Larry that Zara is nothing but trouble. "Dangerous curves ahead," he warns.

Pat suggests Larry put her in his act, but Larry gently tells her he's in love with Zara. A deflated Pat joins her friend for a date with a couple of obnoxious, cheapskate circus fans, and sees Zara and Tony together. Pat tells Larry, and he confronts the couple, only to be told by Tony that they're in love.

It's time for Larry's act. While Zara and Tony make goo-goo eyes at each other, Larry loses his balance and tumbles from the wire. The circus moves on while Larry recovers from his broken rib. Brock tries to rehire him, but Larry, who's turned to drink, refuses. "A Jane gave you the works," Brock's assistant says, summing up Larry's woes. Pat visits Larry in Memphis and convinces him the show needs him. Larry returns and agrees to include Pat in his act. At first, Larry seems to have lost his nerve, but once he decides — with Pat's input — to change the act to one involving a clown and a

Paramount used this portrait of Kay for *Dangerous Curves* (1929) to promote her modern vamp image.

pretty woman, he improves—and decides to bring Zara back to the act. Zara returns, and tells Larry that she and Tony are through.

Pat finally loses her temper. "Ya ain't worth savin,' Larry Lee!" she tells him. Brock, who figures Pat's been through enough, gives her her own act. Meanwhile, Tony returns to Zara with the news that he's gotten them a contract, reminding her that she'd promise to return if he found steady work.

Larry shows up, learns that Tony and Zara are married, and goes off on a drunk. He sends for Pat, and tells her he has no intention of doing his act. He passes out. Pat skips her own act, overhears Brock say she's fired, and quickly dresses in Larry's clown suit, confident she'll be able to fool people into thinking she's Larry. She succeeds! Of course, she's a hit, and when Larry finds out what she's done for him, he falls in love and promises she'll be part of his act. No, really, he means it this time.

Supposedly one of Kay's childhood dreams was to grow up and become a circus performer. Well, she grew up to become an actress who played a high-wire artist in her third film. She plays a glamorous sophisticate who's in love with Tony, but the role doesn't require much. Still using a declamatory style of acting, her speech and mannerisms, including facial expressions, are unsubtle and unnatural, especially compared to the completely natural Clara Bow. This may be due to Kay's inexperience as well as to the difficulties in picking up voices on the recording equipment. However, Kay's exotic looks are unique.

Make no mistake, though—this is a Clara Bow film. She's the star, and she gets all the close-ups. See this film for her. She's charming and delightful, especially in the restaurant scene with Stu Erwin, Joyce Compton, and Jack Luden. She's also great in the breakfast scene with Larry—telling jokes, laughing, big eyes cutting. Handsome, rugged Richard Arlen says his lines awkwardly, though he's nowhere near as stiff as David Newell, who'd worked with Kay in the Stuart Walker Company.

The film was originally titled *Pink Tights*. Production supervisor Ernst Lubitsch assigned the property to Lothar Mendes. Production, which ran from April 17 to May 13, 1929, was delayed while Bow fought her microphone phobia: "During the shooting of one especially talky scene, Clara could endure no more. Frustrated and ashamed of her mistakes, she swore violently at the mike, then burst into tears and sank to the ground, sobbing and whimpering. Lothar Mendes summoned Lubitsch, who rushed to the set, calmed Clara, and ordered witnesses to keep silent. Though word of the incident never reached the press, details spread throughout the studio and fueled rumors that Clara could not cope with sound technology."[12]

Much of the film was shot indoors at night—or early morning—in order to avoid noise. There are no exterior shots. Kay was clothed in very chic clothing, not including a hideous circus outfit that proved Kay could literally wear anything—and also provided ample evidence she did *not* have ugly legs, as she claimed. She also wore a hand-me-down tailored suit from Bebe Daniels, apparently left behind in the wardrobe department. It seems odd since Kay and Bebe Daniels were quite different physical types.

A silent *and* sound version were produced. The silent version is apparently lost. You'll see vestiges of the silent school of acting when Clara, reacting to Larry's injury, flings her arms up in the air, opens her mouth and eyes wide, and holds the pose for several seconds. In addition, poor lighting and an occasionally shaky camera (particularly noticeable in Clara's boxcar scene) add to the film's technical weaknesses.

Kay was third-billed in this, the first film she made on the West Coast for Paramount.

REVIEWS: "Miss Bow, whose followers are numerically, at least, about as the sands of the sea, does not get much of a chance to add to her laurels; and circus-goers will be pained at certain of the liberties taken with circus ritual." (*New York Times*, July 21, 1929)

"Best shot: Kay Francis in front of a bedroom door." *Time* (July 29, 1929)

"The story has first rate incidental comedy angles leading up to the finish that has ... [Bow] performing a thrill stunt for the punch finale." (*Variety*, July 10, 1929)

"Clara Bow forsakes her flaming sex and tries to be coy. Result not so hot." (*Film Daily*, July 21, 1929)

"Between you and me and the much advertised gate post, this is the best picture Clara Bow has ever made.... It's an interesting film, brimming with human interest, suspense and laughs ... Kay Francis is stunning as Zara." (*Chicago Tribune*)

"Kay Francis ... gives a very finished performance and again shows perfect voice management. With continued wise direction, she should be an asset to the talkies." (*Rochester Times-Union*)

"Miss Francis is the possessor of one of the most charming voices yet to come through the microphone and she shows signs of becoming the vampire supreme of the screen." (*Washington Post*)

Illusion

(Paramount Famous Lasky, 1929)
80 min. Released on September 27, 1929.

Credits: Producer, B. P. Schulberg; director, Lothar Mendes; based on the play by Arthur Cheney Train; adaptor-dialogue, E. Lloyd Sheldon; titles, Richard H. Digges, Jr.; sound, Harry M. Lindgren; camera, Harry Fischbeck; editor, George Nichols, Jr. Song, "When the Real Thing Comes Your Way," written by Larry Spier; musicians, Abe Lyman and his "Californians" in "Believe It or Not."

Cast: Charles "Buddy" Rogers (Carlee Thorpe); Nancy Carroll (Claire Jernigan); June Collyer (Hilda Schmittlap); Regis Toomey (Eric Schmittlap); Knute Erickson (Mr. Jacob Schmittlap); Kay Francis (Zelda Paxton); Eugenie Besserer (Mrs. Jacob Schmittlap); Maude Turner Gordon (Queen of Dalmatia); William Austin (Mr. Z); Emilie Melville (Mother Fay); Frances Raymond (Mrs. Y); Catherine Wallace (Mrs. Z); J. E. Nash (Mr. X); William McLaughlin (Mr. Y); Eddie Kane (Gus Bloomberg); Michael Visaroff (Equerry); Paul Lukas (Count Fortuny); Richard Cramer (Magus); Bessie Lyle (Consuelo); Colonel G. L. McDonell (Jarman, the Butler); Lillian Roth (A Singer); Harriet Spiker (Midget); Anna Magruder (Fat Lady); Albert Wolffe (Giant); Virginia Bruce, Phillips Holmes (Bits).

CLAIRE AND CARLEE APPEAR IN a magic act together, but Carlee isn't satisfied. Social climber Zelda encourages Carlee to expand his horizons. "To be accepted socially, one doesn't have to be respectable, only amusing," she explains, and then introduces him to high society. He's quickly accepted into their circle — and couldn't be happier. "Any presentable young chap who plays bridge and has a decent-looking dress suit, he's in big demand nowadays," he tells a friend. "You know, I made over $400 playing bridge last week. Now I know what it means to have swell things. To have a place in this world. To know people. Real people. To be somebody."

Carlee is warned. "Everything looks great to us at a distance. That's illusion. We never know what's real until it's too late."

Carlee becomes infatuated with Hilda, a wealthy young socialite. "If I knew about you, all the glamour might go," she cautions, clearly not wanting to know his background. Carlee has a fit when Claire goes out with Eric, Hilda's brother, a cad who's had several young women sue him for breach of contract. "Keep your hands off a nice girl," Carlee tells Eric.

Eric refuses. Claire ends up performing with another magician, and Carlee realizes he's still in love with her. When he tells Hilda, she's relieved. "I couldn't have married a circus man, a vaudeville actor, a man who got into society doing card tricks and gambling," she explains, adding that she's the daughter of a daughter of a truck driver. Things might be different "if my family was secure socially, but they aren't."

Meanwhile, Claire performs in her new act. One part involves bullets. Claire, however, fails to switch the fake bullets with the real ones. Carlee is horrified when Claire is wounded. She's taken to the hospital, and Carlee promises never to leave her again "because you're the only one I care for."

Claire has the last line: "He didn't hurt me. In fact, I didn't feel a thing."

Kay is described as an "entrepreneuse" with a million-dollar personality. She arranges marriages between socially ambitious debutantes and titled European gentry.

This is one of the most difficult Kay Francis films to find, though the UCLA Film and Television Archive has at least a partial copy in its collection. Like many films of this period, it was filmed in both a silent and sound version. Kay still sounds very theatrical in her delivery. Lillian Roth sings "Revolutionary Rhythm," and Nancy Carroll and Buddy Rogers, separately, sing "When the Real Thing Comes Your Way." The film was based on a 1929 novel by Arthur Chesney Train.

REVIEWS: "Just a weak story that rambles aimlessly tied up to a lot of ritzy atmosphere. Weak entertainment." (*Film Daily*, September 29, 1929)

"June Collyer, Regis Toomey, and Kay Francis acquit themselves creditably in more or less character roles." (*Los Angeles Times*)

"...average entertainment. It tells a rather hackneyed story but it places the old situations

Kay played a minor role in *Illusion* (1929) with Charles "Buddy" Rogers.

in new settings and the direction is skillful.... Kay Francis plays the role of a sort of social mentor, and she does it with her usual ability." (*Rochester Evening Journal and the Post Express*)

"It is a pleasant enough little picture, but there is nothing original either in situation or treatment, and the interludes of dance and song are not spectacular enough to be amusing.... June Collyer is piquant and natural as the wealthy rival and Kay Francis all that could be desired in lesser role." (*Washington Post*)

The Marriage Playground

(Paramount Famous Lasky Corp., 1929) 70 min. Released on December 13, 1929.

Credits: Director, Lothar Mendes; based on the novel "The Children" by Edith Wharton; screenplay, J. Walter Ruben; adapter-dialogue, Doris Anderson; sound, M. M. Paggi; camera, Victor Milner.

Cast: Mary Brian (Judith Wheater); Fredric March (Martin Boyne); Lilyan Tashman (Joyce Wheater); Huntley Gordon (Cliff Wheater); Kay Francis (Zinnia La Crosse); William Austin (Lord Wrench); Seena Owen (Rose Sellers); Philippe De Lacy (Terry Wheater); Anita Louise (Blanca Wheater); Little Mitzi Green (Zinnie); Billie Seay (Astorre Wheater); Ruby Parsley (Beatrice [Beechy] Wheater); Donald Smith (Chipstone [Chip] Wheater); Jocelyn Lee (Sybil Lullmer); Maude Turner Gordon (Aunt Julia Langley); David Newell (Gerald Omerod); Armand Kaliz (Prince Matriano); Joan Standing (Scopy); Gordon De Main (Mr. Delafield).

MARTIN MEETS JUDY WHEATER — surrounded by a passel of children — on the Lido beach. At first mistakenly believing they're hers, Martin soon learns they're the assorted offspring of Martin's old friends — and Judy's parents — Joyce and Cliff Wheater. The children have come from various alliances of Joyce and Cliff, who play on the marriage playground — marrying and divorcing. The children live in fear that they'll be separated. One of their games is a (weird) "pretend version" of divorce court.

Kay plays Zinnia, a shallow, self-centered, golddigging movie actress, one of Cliff's exes. She shows up with yet another husband, an effeminate ninny named Lord Wrench, and plans to take her daughter, the not-so-darling Zinnie, played by Mitzi Green, who had a knack for playing brats.

"I was helpless then," Zinnia tells Judy, who reminds her that she didn't want Zinnie after the divorce. "I didn't have a big, strong man to take care of me. Now I can give her the sort of refined home that she needs."

For some reason, Judy doesn't want to give up Zinnie. Martin becomes involved, hoping to convince Zinnia to leave the brat with Judy. "You're the first man I've met who really understands me," Zinnia flirtatiously tells him.

Blanca flatters Zinnia out of a gift: "I think that's the prettiest dress I ever saw you wear. Isn't it from that Russian place where they won't sell you anything unless you've got a perfect figure?"

Judy falls in love with Martin—"You're just the type most any woman would like to have an affair with"—but Martin is engaged to Rose. After Judy lays a passionate kiss on Martin, he's taken aback. "See here, young lady, you don't kiss men like that, no matter how grateful you are. Someone's apt to, well, take advantage."

"But I might like that," Judy says. "After all, I'm Joyce's daughter."

Martin scolds her. "Why, Judy! Even grownups don't make such insinuations about their mothers. At your age, it's unmentionable."

Rose feigns illness, and Martin returns, but quickly realizes he can't live without Judy and the children. Judy kidnaps the kids and goes to Martin. He realizes he's in love with her and tells Cliff they plan to marry. Cliff informs Martin that he and Joyce have reconciled.

The best lines are reserved for Rose's brittle Aunt Julia: "Who's dead?" she growls. "I hope it's someone I don't like." She also adds pearls of wisdom: "A man always finds it easier to be faithful to another man's wife than to be faithful to his own."

This cynical film is supposed to be a cautionary tale about irresponsible, neglectful parenting, but it just kind of makes you not want children.

Kay's scenes are funny, and it's easy to see why comedy is her strength. She is humorous and light, even though the character is written with broad strokes. This is the first time Kay played a motion picture actress—and a mother—and it's also her best performance up to this point. Mary Brian is sweetly charming and natural, and it's clear why she was a huge star. She's playing a 17-year-old, and does indeed seem too young for Fredric March. Former silent star and beauty Seena Owen also does an excellent job as the savvy Rose.

All scenes, including those on the "beach," were shot indoors. Edith Wharton supposedly hated this film version of her 1928 novel.

Kay and Lilyan wear sophisticated clothing, especially beachwear that's designed to show lots of skin. The suntan craze was at its height in 1929; for the first time, young women went stockingless and tanned their legs. The fad was used as the title of a 1929 Radio Pictures musi-

Kay modeling in the Paris-decreed style for *The Marriage Playground* (1929).

cal with June Clyde, Ann Pennington and Arthur Lake — *Tanned Legs*.

Remade in 1990, *Marriage Playground* was retitled *The Children*. Directed by Tony Palmer, it starred Ben Kingsley, Kim Novak, Siri Neal, Geraldine Chaplin, and Joe Don Baker. Britt Ekland played Kay's role.

REVIEWS: "Although it has spasmodic lapses and the youngsters are a trifle too precocious, even for this generation, it is quite an intelligent production with well-woven strands of humor and sympathy, pathos and an appealing romance." (*New York Times*, December 14, 1929)

"A peach of a picture well above the satisfaction-giving average of a program release and the kind that leaves a sense of full-hearted, human pleasure behind it." (*Variety*, December 25, 1929)

"Splendid direction of Edith Wharton's story of children. Fine cast. Class picture with popular appeal." (*Film Daily*, December 15, 1929)

"[S]everal cuts above the usual film fare in its handling of character and atmosphere, in line with the truism that even the sloppiest movie made from a good writer's book will betray its literary origin despite the movie hacks' best efforts." (Lawrence J. Quirk, *The Films of Fredric March*, p. 52)

"...turns out to be one of those intelligent and sincere little film dramas that happens along only now and then.... You will find such pleasant players as Lilyan Tashman playing the modern mother, Kay Francis as a rival charmer and little Philippe De Lacy, the best of all child stars, as one of the poor little rich children." (*Liberty Magazine*)

"[A] fair photoplay that is a bit too confused in the handling of its many characters to be more than moderately effective.... Fredric March is a satisfactory hero, and Lilyan Tashman, Kay Francis and Jocelyn Lee add to the decorative qualities of the work." (*New York Herald-Tribune*)

"An agreeably gentle little story which will get you if you aren't careful.... It is directed by Lothar Mendes, who demonstrates here, for the first time since his arrival from Germany some five years ago, a talent for producing picture plays with genuineness and credibility.... Much of the film's beauty may be traced back to the individual performances of its players.... Other work of the first rank to be found in the course of the drama is turned in by Fredric March, Huntley Gordon, Kay Francis, and that finest of

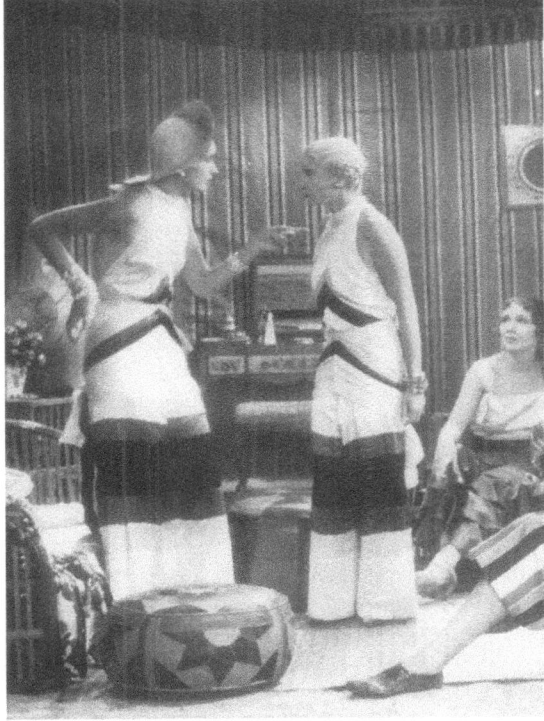

Kay and Lilyan Tashman wear beach pajamas in a tense moment from *The Marriage Playground* (1929).

all child actors of the screen at this time, Master Philippe De Lacy." (*New York World*)

"The jazz generation is composed exclusively of wayward mamas and papas, if we are to believe this picture, and all of the youngsters we have been so warned about are spending all their time trying to lead them into a straight and narrow path.... Kay Francis is hotsy-totsy as the vamp.... One of the best of the sophisticated pictures." (*Screen Secrets Magazine*)

Behind the Make-Up

(Paramount Famous Lasky Corp., 1930)
65 min. Released on January 6, 1930.

Credits: Directors, Robert Milton, Dorothy Arzner; based on the story "The Feeder" by Mildred Cram; adaptors-dialogue, George Manker Watters, Howard Estabrook; songs, Leo Robin, Sam Coslow, Newell Chase; original music, W. Franke Harling, John Leipold; sound, Harry D. Mills; camera, Charles Lang; editor, Doris Drought.

Cast: Hal Skelly (Hap Brown); William Powell

(Gardoni); Fay Wray (Marie Gardoni); Kay Francis (Kitty Parker); E.H. Calvert (Dawson); Paul Lukas (Boris); Agostino Borgato (Chef); Jacques Vanaire (Valet); Jean De Briac (Sculptor); Torben Meyer (Waiter); Bob Perry (Bartender).

HAP IS A STRUGGLING New Orleans vaudevillian. He's first seen in a clown outfit entertaining a crowd. The scene ends with a disolve on his makeup-less face. He is now dressed in street clothes, smoking a cigarette.

Hap finds Gardoni on the street, weak with hunger. "My friend," Gardoni tells Hap, "before you came along, I was ready to kill myself." Gardoni explains that he's the son of one of the most famous clowns in Italy. "To be a Gardoni is to be an artist." Hap explains his own act: "Songs, dances. I ride a bicycle, too"— and the secret to success—"You gotta give 'em hokum nowadays."

The two decide to team up. "You are good, but you are not good enough," Gardoni tells him, explaining that actually the key to success is subtle comedy. Their Baton Rouge performance is a disaster, and Gardoni disappears.

Hap returns to New Orleans and gets a job as a dishwasher at the restaurant where girlfriend Marie waitresses. "I've juggled lots of dishes, but I've never bathed any," Hap cracks. In love with Marie, he proposes. "I don't know how I feel about you," Marie demurs. "Sometimes it's like a sister, and sometimes it's like a mother." Ouch.

Hap soon finds Gardoni performing. He's stolen Hap's act, and quickly steals Marie. Hap remains a good sport and even travels with Gardoni and Marie—now married—on their way to success in New York. Hap is Gardoni's "feeder" (opening act).

Marie is deeply in love with Gardoni, but he's fallen for the slinky, gorgeous Kitty Parker, who toys with Gardoni, until he becomes heavily indebted to her for gambling losses. Kitty leaves him for Boris. "We're through," Kitty coldly tells him. "I don't need you, Gardoni."

Gardoni commits suicide by jumping into the river. Hap pays Gardoni's gambling debts with his remaining money, and convinces Marie that Gardoni was a saintly, great man who attempted to help with *his* gambling debts. Even when a devastated Marie finds Kitty's note to Gardoni detailing the amount he owes her, Hap takes the blame. Marie realizes Hap loves her a lot so when Hap gets a job in Dayton, Ohio, she follows him.

The final scene is a bookend finale. Hap again performs in his clown suit; one of the lines is "Never Say Die." Though it's a happy ending—sort of—it's clear that Marie stays with Hap because he's pathetic.

Hal Skelly was a circus, vaudeville, and Broadway performer, and this was his fourth film. He died in 1934 when the car he was riding in was hit at a railroad crossing.

William Powell was already a veteran film actor, having appeared in more than 40 films by 1930. Powell's a wonderful actor, but his accent sounds more Transylvanian than Italian. Dorothy Arzner co-directed, but received no credit. The last vestiges of silent film are seen in several title cards scattered throughout the film.

Kay, who was billed fourth, does not appear until around the thirty-seven-minute mark. Still, she gets to play charming and ice cold in this role, and is more comfortable in front of the camera, and/or the direction was better. Unfortunately, the lighting is poor, and she is not photographed well.

A charming Kay smiles in this still from ***Behind the Make-Up*** (1930).

Songs include "My Pals," "Say It With Your Feet," and "I'll Remember, You'll Forget." The picture was based on a short story by Mildred Cram, which appeared in the May 1926 edition of *Red Book*.

REVIEWS: "The characters are quite well delineated, but the story is rather limp and disappointing. The lighting of the scenes and the movements of the players are effectively done. Kay Francis does nicely as the adventuress." (*New York Times*, January 18, 1930)

"Only a fair program picture, despite good characterizations by both Mr. Skelly and William Powell, because of the familiar theme and of the draggy action. Kay Francis is good in her small part as the adventuress." (*Harrison's Reports*, January 25, 1930)

"Kay Francis is subtly convincing." (*Variety*, January 15, 1930)

"Very ordinary production with uninteresting story that fails to hold interest." (*Film Daily*, January 19, 1930)

"It has pathos, characterization, and a good plot but Robert Milton, the director, tried to make an artistic masterpiece out of it, when in reality it is neither smashing drama nor outstandingly artistic. Kay Francis plays her usual vamping role." (*Hollywood Daily Citizen*, February 7, 1930)

"As for Fay Wray and Kay Francis, they are two delightful actresses who do wonders with bad parts." *(London Times)*

"We wish we could say a very fine picture has come out of the efforts of the players and the director, Robert Milton. "Behind the Make-Up" does hold interest always, chiefly because of their able performances, and partly because it continues for some time to give promise of something fairly big. But it seems to us to be throughout a series of episodes devoid of dramatic or humorous conflict and never coming into focus in a clashing situation ... Kay Francis does fair work in a conventional and cruel siren role." (*Rochester Democrat and Chronicle*)

Street of Chance

(Paramount Famous Lasky Corp., 1930) 76 min. Released on January 31, 1930.

Credits: Director, John Cromwell; producer, David O. Selznick; story, Oliver H. P. Garrett; dialogue, Lenore J. Coffee; adapters, Howard Estabrook, Ben Hecht, Charles MacArthur; titles, Gerald Geraghty; sound, Harry D. Mills; camera, Charles Lang; editor, Otto Levering; original music, John Leipold; costume design, Travis Banton.

Cast: William Powell (John B. Marsden [Natural Davis]); Jean Arthur (Judith Marsden); Kay Francis (Alma Marsden); Regis Toomey ("Babe" Marsden); Stanley Fields (Dorgan); Brooks Benedict (Al Mastick); Betty Francisco (Mrs. Mastic); John Risso (Tony); Joan Standing (Miss Abrams); Maurice Black (Nick); Irving Bacon (Harry); John Cromwell (Imbrie).

THE SCENE IS New York City in the 1920s. Bond dealer J. B. Marsden is actually Natural Davis, one of the city's most notorious gamblers, a man who'll gamble on anything, including whether the next car's license plate number will be even or odd. Wife Alma has had it. His addiction has made her life a nightmare, albeit an affluent one, and she wants a divorce.

Marsden has financially supported brother Babe for years. He's also hired a detective agency to keep an eye on him, fearing Babe, too, will succumb to the gambling bug. Marsden receives a telegram informing him that Babe has married Judith, and promptly sends them a $10,000 wedding gift. Meanwhile, Mrs. Mastic shows up at his bond office, begging him to return the $2,150 her husband lost in a gambling game. Marsden agrees but secretly marks the bills. Later at the Hotel Avon, Mastic shows up to gamble, pretending he knows nothing about the woman who claimed to be his wife. Marsden kicks him out of the game. Mastic realizes Marsden's on to him and tries to apologize, telling him it was all a gag. "I don't cheat, frame, or double-cross," Marsden claims, and makes it clear he doesn't put up with anyone who does. Mastic is murdered, and though Marsden is suspected, he's cleared.

Meanwhile, Babe and wife Judith arrive in New York. Babe wants to gamble with Natural Davis, not realizing it's his brother. He's already parlayed the $10,000 gift into $50,000, and wants to turn it into $150,000 to invest in a real estate partnership. Then — he promises Judith — he'll quit. Marsden meets with Alma and asks for another chance. In the morning, he assures her, they'll leave town for a second honeymoon, and he'll never gamble again. Marsden pleads with Babe to return to San Francisco. When Babe refuses, Natural decides to teach him a lesson. First, he asks for the $10,000 gift to be returned, and then asks gambling buddy Dorgan to clean out Babe. Marsden meets with Judy, gives her the $10,000, tells her Babe has a gambling problem, and asks her to take him back to San Francisco after the game. Babe has a lucky streak and cleans out Dorgan, who now suspects Marsden set him up.

While Marsden and Alma pack, the newspaper boy arrives to tell Babe that Dorgan thinks he's been double-crossed. Marsden tells Alma he can't catch the train with her. "You begged for another chance," Alma angrily tells him. "I gave it to you. I opened up my arms to you." She unpacks. Marsden tells her he'll be back to take the noon train. Alma sobs when he leaves.

At the hotel, Babe realizes his brother is Natural Davis. He tries to leave, but Marsden stops him: "You'll play until one of us is broke." Babe keeps winning. Marsden cheats—and gets caught. "Natural Davis is a dirty crook, all right," Babe bitterly says before leaving. "Tonight is the first crooked deal I ever pulled," Marsden insists.

Dorgan reminds Natural about Mastic: "Returning the dough don't cut it." Natural telephones Judy, telling her to get Babe on the train. He returns at 11:15 to collect Alma, but she's left, canceling the tickets. Babe, safely on the train, turns down a poker game.

Marsden is lured back to the hotel and shot. Meanwhile, Alma, who realizes Marsden had arrived in time to take the noon train, frantically tries to locate him. Marsden, given a note by a desk clerk, stumbles outside and collapses. In the ambulance, a police officer asks who shot him. "Try and find out, copper. Try and find out." Marsden reads the note: "Mr. Marsden, please call your wife." He crumples it up. He places one last bet—whether he'll live or die. "You lose," he says, and promptly dies.

Kay's first scene is on the telephone after Marsden receives the motion to separate. Stiff in her telephone scene, Kay is much better when face to face with Powell. These two usually had great chemistry, and they have some nice scenes together in this film.

This was Kay's first real lead—she was second billed—and her first sympathetic role. It was also the first film in which she abandoned the ultra-short haircut for a less severe style. Her hair is still short, but the middle part softens it. Many point to this film as the one that made Kay a star.

Cromwell, husband of actress Kay Johnson, was known as an actor's director. Not terribly concerned with angles and style, he preferred to let actors make the film real and compelling. Producer Selznick insisted on Kay and Jean Arthur. He supposedly was infatuated with Arthur, and described this film as "my first really personal film, one I really worked on and cared about."[13] Producer and director successfully fought to keep the sad ending.

The William Powell character was said to be based on Arnold Rothstein. Nicknamed Mr. Big, Rothstein was a crime boss, bookie, habitual gambler, fraudulent stock broker, and Wall Street bond thief. He was even suspected of fixing the 1919 World Series. A wealthy man, who at one time ran a gambling house on West 46th Street, Rothstein was shot on November 4, 1928, in Room 349 at the Park Central Hotel—now the New York Sheraton—at Seventh Avenue and 55th Street. When police inquired as to his attacker, he said, "I'll take care of it myself." Rothstein died two days later. Although George McManus was acquitted of Rothstein's murder, many think he probably was guilty of killing Rothstein for unpaid gambling debts.

One of Kay's first appearances on a magazine cover (1930).

In 1930 Kay sported a sophisticated coiffeur as she started playing more sympathetic roles.

The film was remade by Fox in 1934 as *Now I'll Tell* and starred Spencer Tracy, Helen Twelvetrees, and Alice Faye. Paramount's 1937 version, titled *Her Husband Lies*, starred Gail Patrick and Ricardo Cortez.

Howard Estabrook was nominated for an Oscar for Best Writing Achievement for *Street of Chance*. Ben Hecht and Charles MacArthur were uncredited writers on this film. Background scenes were filmed on location in New York, and the picture offers some wonderful shots of the hustling, bustling city in the late 1920s as well as some great sets. Watch for the scene where a mike boom shadow can be seen on Powell.

REVIEWS: "Admirably acted and its incidents are so craftily devised that they compel attention. It is a picture charged with excitement growing out of the stealth suggested in its scenes of Times Square and other sections on Broadway. Kay Francis is believable as the gambler's wife." (*New York Times*, February 3, 1930)

"First rate gambling drama effectively told and skillfully played by top-notch cast." (*Film Daily*, February 2, 1930)

"Tense drama, full of realism." (*Los Angeles Evening Herald*, February 20, 1930)

"Oliver H.P. Garrett has written a thrilling story, but even so, much of the credit must go to John Cromwell, who directed the story with finesse and with a fine regard for detail. No woman on the screen could be more stunning than Kay Francis as 'Natural's wife. She wears her clothes like a thoroughbred and she adds interest to a story in which men are featured." (Louella O. Parsons, *Los Angeles Examiner*, February 21, 1930)

"The big gambler has his day in Paramount's *Street of Chance*, a fine picture, that without doubt will be a candidate for the 'ten best' of 1930. As William Powell's first starring picture, the film at the Paramount Theater is an impressive debut. It has photographic realism, taut suspense, unobtrusive sentiment and superb acting. In addition to Powell's, excellent performances are given by Kay Francis as 'Natural's wife; Regis Toomey as his brother; John Risso as the one-armed newsboy and tipoff man; Stanley Fields as the gambler, Dorgan; Brooks Benedict as the double-cross artist, and Jean Arthur as the brother's wife. Each of these players have given more than a good performance." (Harrison Carroll, *Los Angeles Evening Herald*, February 21, 1930)

"Powell gives a powerful portrayal as the gambler. Regis Toomey as the young brother is good as is Jean Arthur as his little wife. Kay Francis as Powell's wife is delightful. John Cromwell directed this picture for all the thrills and suspense he could get out of it." (Doris Denbo, *Hollywood Daily Citizen*, March 28, 1930)

"'Street of Chance' has all the earmarks of being the best melodrama of 1930.... Regis Toomey, the grinning boy detective of 'Alibi,' is gorgeous as the kid brother, and sleek Kay Francis is superb as Natural's wife." (*Liberty Magazine*)

"Kay Francis ... is terribly fetching and her acting gives a sympathetic touch to an unsympathetic character.... The director, John Cromwell, has composed a picture of the liveliest, most convincing kind, well-knit, crammed with incident and replete with clever characterizations." (*London Times*)

"Here's a punchful racketeer picture that is going to give rival producers jaundice until they get a carbon copy in the can. Bill Powell's finesse and Kay Francis' sincere emoting would be highlights in any picture." (*Photoplay Magazine*)

"Next to Powell's fine work comes the playing of Kay Francis. This girl, one of the smartest appearing actresses on the screen, more than justifies the very laudatory things I have said about her in other pictures. She doesn't get much to do in this film, but she certainly makes her role stand out." (*Rochester Evening Journal and the Post Express*)

"Kay Francis, as the wife, is fully equipped to lend distinction to a character that has been taught to distrust even the truth." (*Washington Post*)

"Tremendously gripping.... Kay Francis displays histrionic finesse." (*Screen Secrets*, April 1930)

Paramount on Parade

(Paramount Famous Lasky Corp., 1930) 101 min. Released in New York on April 19, 1930, Rialto Theater.

Credits: Supervisor, Elsie Janis; producers, Albert S. Kaufman, Jesse L. Lasky, Adolph Zukor; directors, Dorothy Arzner, Otto Brower, Edmund Goulding, Victor Heerman, Edwin H. Knopf, Rowland V. Lee, Ernst Lubitsch, Lothar Mendes, Victor Schertzinger, A. Edward Sutherland, Frank Tuttle; writer, Joseph L. Mankiewicz; songs, Elsie Janis and Jack King; Ballard MacDonald and Dave Dreyer; Leo Robin and Ernesto De Curtis; L. Wolfe Gilbert and Abel Baer; Richard A. Whiting and Raymond B. Eagan; Whiting and Robin; David Franklin; Sam Coslow; Samuel Pokrass; incidental music, Howard Jackson; dance-ensemble director, David Bennett; set designer, John Wenger; camera, Harry Fischbeck and Victor Milner; editor, Merrill G. White.

Cast: Iris Adrian, Richard Arlen, Jean Arthur, Mischa Auer, William Austin, George Bancroft, Clara Bow, Evelyn Brent, Mary Brian, Clive Brook, Virginia Bruce, Nancy Carroll, Ruth Chatterton, Maurice Chevalier, Gary Cooper, Cecil Cunningham, Leon Errol, Stuart Erwin, Henry Fink, Kay Francis, Richard "Skeets" Gallagher, Edmund Goulding, Harry Green, Mitzi Green, Robert Greig, James Hall, Phillips Holmes, Helen Kane, Dennis King, Jack Luden, Abe Lyman & His Band, Fredric March, Nino Martini, Mitzi Mayfair, Marion Morgan Dancers, David Newell, Jack Oakie, Warner Oland, Zelma O'Neal, Eugene Pallette, Joan Peers, Jack Pennick, Russ Powell, William Powell, Charles "Buddy" Rogers, Lillian Roth, Rolfe Sedan, Stanley Smith, Fay Wray, Jane Keithley, Rosina Lawrence, Jeanette MacDonald, Al Norman, Ernst Rolf, Jackie Searl.

THIS WAS PARAMOUNT'S most prestigious 1930 film. Production began on August 19, 1929, and ended February 19, 1930. "Every contract player in the studio had been spending weeks and weeks preparing for his or her sequences for the picture. They were all carefully fitted for wardrobes that would suit the elegance they were to represent."[14] This film was typical of revues of the period. With the introduction of sound, studios were eager to show their stars singing, dancing — and talking. Fay Wray, one of the stars, explained how the studio developed the film: "There was a roster of stars at Paramount and there was a roster of management. The roster of management made decisions for and about the roster of stars. It was difficult for them to make choices once the added factor of sound was involved. In a film called *Paramount on Parade*, they lumped every star, major and minor, into one musical under the guidance of eleven directors. The cast numbered almost fifty. The decision may have advanced sound and proved that Paramount could make a lot of it, but it did little for any individual."[15]

Unfortunately, a complete print does not exist. Paramount threw away the original

Kay played a sultry Carmen in a musical number filmed in early Technicolor. This was one of her two sequences in *Paramount on Parade*.

Kay Francis in a rare publicity photo shot in February 1930. The Hollywood Dog High School trained many movie star pets.

negative with the Technicolor sequences; in fact, until 1996, available prints excluded all Technicolor sequences, except the finale with Maurice Chevalier singing "Up on Top of a Rainbow," which existed only in black-and-white. After making the black-and-white television prints, Paramount tossed the Technicolor sequences and negatives. (This happened frequently and explains why many of the Technicolor musicals from 1929–1930 have been lost.) Fortunately, the UCLA Archive has partially restored the film, including the Technicolor sequences. The even better news is that two of Kay's appearances have been added to the restored print.

During the title credits, Kay appears with George Bancroft, standing behind the letter "M," as the title—*Paramount on Parade*—is shown. In the restored sequence, the title is displayed one letter at a time in black-and-white stills while the song "Paramount on Parade" is played in the background and the words displayed on the screen.

After the credits, the opening number is "Showgirls on Parade." In the restored version, stills of the chorus girls are shown. The next sequence includes Jack Oakie, Skeets Gallagher, and Leon Errol singing "We're the Masters of Ceremony." This is followed by "Love Time," with Charles "Buddy" Rogers and Lillian Roth on a cuckoo-clock set singing "Any Time's the Time to Fall in Love." The next scene is "Murder Will Out," a parody of detective mysteries with William Powell as Philo Vance, Clive Brook as Sherlock Holmes, Eugene Pallette as Sergeant Heath, Warner Oland as Dr. Fu Manchu, and Jack Oakie as the victim. The best sketch follows: "Origin of the Apache"—a slapstick vignette directed by Ernst Lubitsch with Maurice Chevalier and Evelyn Brent in a bedroom. The next offering is the Technicolor sketch "Song of the Gondolier," with Italan tenor Nino Martini singing "Torna a Sorrento." This is followed by "In a Hospital," a comedy sketch with Leon Errol, David Newell, and Jean Arthur. Then Jack Oakie and Zelma O'Neal appear in "In a Girl's Gym," singing "I'm in Training for You."

Kay appears in the next scene, "The Toreador," another restored Technicolor number. The scene opens with the Marion Morgan Dancers in ruffled dresses performing a typical Spanish dance. When it ends, Kay appears as Carmen in an arched doorway at the top of a flight of stairs, smoking, and wearing a gorgeous ruffled silver Spanish outfit with a long train and a huge red cabbage rose on her left shoulder. A long orange Spanish shawl, trimmed with silver brocade, is draped over her shoulders, and she wears a black flat-brimmed hat with another huge red cabbage rose behind her ear. Kay languidly leans against the arch and blows a huge cloud of smoke. She then struts down the stairs, hands on hips, and parades and twirls for a several moments in front of the chorus. A trumpet fanfare then accompanies chorus boys, dressed as matadors, who line up on each side of the steps. Harry Green descends, covering his face with his cape and gets a laugh — even in silence — when he uncovers his face to show he's wearing huge glasses. The chorus asks, "Who is he?" Kay answers with her one line of dialogue: "Who are you?" Harry then sings "I'm Isidore the Toreador," while Kay leans against a table, hands still on hips. A dance by a man and woman — dressed in white costumes — follows, and the finale features everyone facing the camera as if they were on a stage. Kay is in the center, next to Harry Green. Kay looks lovely but gets only one semi-close-up, as does Harry Green. These numbers were recorded live, and photographing close-ups would have required special lighting and makeup, which was done only for big stars at that time.

This is the only time you'll see Kay in Technicolor, and she's lovely, though the color is a bit faded. The sound does not exist for the number; the song lyrics are shown as titles on the screen, as is her line. She neither sings nor dances, but struts in the Spanish costume.

"The Toreador" is followed by Ruth Chatterton in "The Montmartre Girl." Complete with French accent, she sings "My Marine" to Stuart Erwin, Stanley Smith, and Fredric March in a Paris cafe. Maurice Chevalier appears in the next sketch, "Park in Paris." He's a police officer, patrolling the park, and singing "All I Want Is Just One Girl." Little Mitzi Green then does an impersonation of Chevalier singing this song, just after she's impersonated Charlie Mack of Moran and Mack warbling the same song. "The Schoolroom" features Helen Kane as a teacher, singing "What Did Cleopatra Say?" while the students answer, "Boop Boopa Doop." Skeets Gallagher and Dennis King appear in "The Gallows Song," a Technicolor musical number featuring the song "Nichavo!" The sound is missing for most of this sequence, which was filmed on the set of the Technicolor operetta, "The Vagabond King." Fortunately, the song by Dennis King has been restored. Next, Nancy Carroll and chorus appear in "Dance Mad," singing and dancing to "Dancing to Save Your Sole," accompanied by Abe Lyman's Band. "Dream Girl," a Technicolor sketch with Jean Arthur, Richard Arlen, Mary Brian, Gary Cooper, James Hall, Fay Wray, and others, features the song "Let Us Drink to the Girl of My Dreams." The sound is missing, so the song's words are shown on the screen. The next number is "The Redhead," featuring Clara Bow, with Jack Oakie, Skeets Gallagher, and 42 sailors singing along to "I'm True to the Navy Now."

Kay's last scene is part of an amusing George Bancroft sketch titled "Impulses." "Last night I went to a party," George explains at a golf course. The scene cuts to the previous evening when George arrives. Hostess Cecil Cunningham points out Kay and a female companion.

"My dear," Kay gushes to her friend, complimenting her jewelry. "What exquisite pearls."

A moment later, she flatters George. "Mr. Bancroft, I think you're simply marvelous. Why do they always make you play a bad man?"

The party is civilized, polite, and deadly dull. Back at the golf course, Bancroft shakes his head. "Now, I don't know how you feel about it, but my impulse was not to conduct myself as I did. There's an idea! Now, if everybody there had followed their impulse, I imagine the party would have been somewhat different."

The scene dissolves to the party. "You ever see such a funny-looking crowd?" Cecil asks, and caustically refers to Kay and companion as "drugstore beauties." The pearls, this time, enrage Kay. "Those are lovely pearls," she says, fingering them. "What are they strung on? *Telephone wire?*" She yanks the necklace, sending the pearls clattering to the floor, and stalks off. "Hey, Bancroft!" she barks. "Come here!" She takes a vase, removes the flowers, and yells again: "You heard me! Come here!" Kay hides the vase behind her. "I've got something for you," she teases. Bancroft spies the flowers, bends down, and Kay smashes the vase over his head. She gives him the flowers, dusts him off, and sends him on his dazed way.

The Technicolor finale, which exists only in black and white, is "The Rainbow Revels," with Chevalier and a female chorus. They're chimney sweeps who sing "Sweepin' the Clouds Away."

According to Edward Baron Turk, Jeanette MacDonald filmed two numbers for *Paramount on Parade*. The first was a comedy episode, "It's Tough To Be a Prima Donna," in which she sang "Il Bacio," a song from "The Mikado," and "That's My Weakness Now." Copyright issues led the studio to cut the scene. She also sang "Music in the Moonlight" in a gondola. This scene was also cut from the U.S. version. In the version recently restored by UCLA, Jeanette is seen in a gondola for a few seconds in the background at the very beginning of Nino Martini's number, "Torna a Sorrento"—but in the medium shots and close-ups which follow, the woman in the gondola is not Jeanette.

For years, rumors incorrectly suggested that Jeanette appeared as mistress of ceremonies in Spanish and French versions; Paramount released different versions in other countries, inserting popular stars from Scandinavia, France, Germany, Japan, South America, etc.[16] *Galas de la Paramount* was the only foreign version that was released in the United States. This film's masters of ceremonies included Ramon Pereda, Rosita Moreno, and Barry Norton. According to the American Film Institute, the Spanish version includes the following numbers: "Any Time's the Time to Fall in Love"; a scene with Spanish actor Ernesto Vilches; the Apache dance; Nino Martini singing to Rosita Moreno from the gondola; the Albertina Rasch dancers; "Dancing to Save Your Sole"; "I'm Isadore, the Toreador"; Juan Pulido singing popular Spanish songs; "All I Want Is Just One Girl"; Mitzi Green's impersonations; "Let Us Drink to the Girl of My Dreams"; "La Argentinita" and guitarist Luis Yance perform Spanish songs; "I'm True to the Navy Now"; "Nichavo!"; Rosita Moreno; and "Sweeping the Clouds Away."

REVIEWS: "A bright and imaginative film. This jovial satire is beautifully staged, and virtually all the sketches are endowed with wit, surprises, competent acting and tuneful melodies." (*New York Times*, April 21, 1930)

"With its smashing lineup of popular personalities, plus a load of comedy and specially enjoyable performances by Maurice Chevalier, little Mitzi Green, and Nino Martini, an unusually promising singer from abroad, this revue should get over everywhere with a bang." (*Film Daily*, April 20, 1930)

"Rialto audiences applauded each of the skits, sketches and musical numbers." (*Variety*, April 23, 1930)

"Harry Green, the kibitzer, is howlingly funny in a song in which he introduces himself as 'Isadore the Toreador' to the refrain of the Toreador's song from 'Carmen.' This act opens with some excelling singing of choruses from 'Carmen' by a large group of singers whose movement about the scene, photographed in color, gives a sense of fluency and cinematic quality. This is one of the most elaborate and brilliant of the spectacles and is a fine example of the manner in which comedy has been blended with music and dramatic action...." (*Rochester Democrat and Chronicle*)

"Seen today, the total effect is wearisome after a while." (Lawrence J. Quirk, *The Films of Fredric March*, p. 58)

A Notorious Affair

(First National Pictures, 1930) 70 min. Released in New York on April 25, 1930, Strand Theater.

Credits: Producer, Robert North; director, Lloyd Bacon; based on the play "Fame" by Audrey Carter and Waverly Carter; adaptor-dialogue, J. Grubb Alexander; set designer, Anton Grot; assistant directors, John Daumery, Irving Asher; costumes, Edward Stevenson; original music, Cecil Copping; conductor, Leo S. Forbstein; sound, Oliver S. Garretson; camera, Ernest Haller; editor, Frank Ware.

Cast: Billie Dove (*Patricia Hanley Gherardi*); Basil Rathbone (*Paul Gherardi*); Kay Francis (*Countess Olga Balakireff*); Montagu Love (*Sir Thomas Hanley*); Kenneth Thomson (*Dr. Allen Pomroy*); Philip Strange (*Lord Percival Northmore*); Malcolm Waite (*Higgins, the Butler*); Ellinor Vanderveer (*Society Lady*); Blanche Frederici (*Lady Keon*); Wilson Benge (*Briggs, Sir Hanley's Butler*); Gino Corrado.

THE FILM OPENS IN Surrey, England at the estate of Sir Thomas Hanley. We're quickly introduced to horsewoman Countess Olga Balakireff (there's *no* question they used a stunt double for Kay's riding scenes). Dressed very stylishly in a mannish riding outfit, complete with top hat and spit curls on each cheek, she spends quality time in the stable with the stable hand, and then asks him how old he is. "Twenty-eight, your ladyship. Six years in your service."

"I always thought you were a lot older," Kay replies, before immediately casting her smoldering glance toward a younger male servant feeding the dogs.

At the dinner party later that night, Hanley's daughter, Patricia, arrives with poor but talented violinist Paul Gherardi, and promptly announces they're married, making her father unhappy. "When you were a child, it was stray cats you brought home," he scolds.

"But I'm older now, Father," Patricia explains.

"Patricia," Dad says, "remember, if you do this thing, you'll not only cut yourself off from me, but from all decent society."

Meanwhile, Paul awkwardly joins the party, horrifying the snobs. Only the Countess seems charmed. When he announces that he plays the violin, one of the upper class women exclaims, "Oh! How awful!"

In *A Notorious Affair* (1930), Kay played a sultry Russian countess who steals violinist Basil Rathbone from his wife.

"I had always hoped that I am not," Paul offers.

"I'm sure you aren't," the Countess gently says.

Paul later asks Patricia about the Countess. "London's most daring horsewoman," she explains. "The Countess is very versatile."

The next scene shows the Countess in her London mansion. The dog feeder is now her butler-companion. "Higgins," the Countess says, "I never knew you had pale blue eyes. I hate pale blue eyes. Funny, I never noticed it before. I think I'll send you back to the kennels where you belong." You get the feeling she runs hot and cold. The Countess becomes Paul's "sponsor," and quickly launches him on a successful career. Patricia remains devoted to Paul — but suspicious. After a concert, she returns home alone, while Paul fibs, saying he has an appointment. He goes home with the Countess.

"A bottle of champagne and two glasses," the Countess orders her new butler. "In my boudoir." While Paul plays the violin, the Countess erotically nibbles on a rose.

"How can I play when you are looking at me like that?" Paul asks.

The Countess' seduction literally gives Paul a nervous breakdown. Returned home by ambulance, his physician turns out to be Dr. Pomroy, one of Patricia's old suitors. "Too much popularity," the doctor solemnly tells Patricia when asked for the diagnosis. He recommends rest, a good diet, and no excitement. Patricia, who's found the Countess' handkerchief on her husband, ignores a whining Paul when he calls to her, "My milk is cold, and my room is too hot."

In the next scene, Patricia has left him, and Paul and the Countess are in southern France. A bored Countess sits on the balcony. Paul begins to play the violin. "Is that necessary at this hour?" she complains. He reminds her that he doesn't want his fans to forget him. "How will they ever forget you? When you make such a terrible noise?" she asks. Paul seeks reassurance about his career, asking, "What if I should lose my technique?" The Countess replies, "I'm afraid you already have, my dear," and then proceeds to flirt with a man on the lower patio.

Meanwhile, Dr. Pomroy has unsuccessfully tried to see Patricia. When she finally relents, they're interrupted by a telegram informing her that Paul has collapsed and may never be able to play again. He is in a hospital asking for her. Patricia goes to him, along with Dr. Pomroy. "You'll need my help," he says.

"If you can give it generously," she replies.

"Under the circumstances, anything but generosity would be impossible."

That's typical dialogue. Anyway, Paul has an operation, but remains paralyzed. He is suspicious about his wife and Dr. Pomroy. "Do you think I don't know why you stand out there in the wind?" he asks Patricia. "No matter what happens, I will always be lying here between you."

Dr. Pomroy tells Patricia there is nothing more that can be done for Paul — and he also acknowledges that he and Patricia have no future. When Patricia returns to the doorway to gaze upon the sea — she does that a lot — she hears Paul's violin. He's been faking his paralysis. "My heart, too," he tells her, "was paralyzed with fame, and I cannot expect you to live here any more among all my ghosts. You are free, Patricia."

Believe it or not, she forgives him. "Perhaps we are both free, Paul." He urges her to go to Dr. Pomroy. "It must have taken something more than mere selfishness to make you lie motionless between me and my happiness," she says.

"Just cowardice," he replies. "Imagine my trying to hold you with pity."

"When love was all that was necessary," Patricia answers. They embrace and kiss.

Although many point to *Street of Chance* as making Kay a star, an argument could be made that *A Notorious Affair*, her ninth film, made her unforgettable. She exudes total sexual confidence in this one; the boudoir scene with the rose is worth the price of admission. Although third-billed, she has her largest number of scenes to date, is comfortable in front of the camera, and completely believable as the hottie nymphomaniac. Cameraman Ernest Haller photographed Kay beautifully and gave her several great close-ups.

This very adult drama used title cards for several scene shifts. It also used beautifully painted scenery for London's skyline — shades of Anton Grot's European background. The film was based on a stage play that opened in London in March 1929. The music, by German-born Felix Mendelssohn-Bartholdy, included "Hark! The Herald Angels Sing" and the Second Movement from Violin Concerto (Op. 64).

This was not one of Billie Dove's favorites. "I never said anything about the pictures at the time. They told me what to do and I made the picture period. I did one where Basil Rathbone played the violin, *A Notorious Affair*, and I thought that was a terrible picture. Basil was very nice, though, and so was Montagu Love who played my father in it."[17]

Kay had previously worked with Rathbone in a 1926 Stuart Walker production, "Love Is Like That." Rathbone's biographer, Michael Druxman, wrote that the actor "was not at his best. His foreign accent was inconsistent and, at times, he delivered his speeches too broadly."[18]

REVIEWS: "Kay Francis, too, as the scheming countess, puts Miss Dove somewhat in the shade." (*New York Times*, April 26, 1930)

"Kay Francis, whose upward rise has been very rapid since last summer, is limited in scope here, but sufficiently supports, merely by her presence, the story's suggestion of a seductive countess of definite nymphomaniacal tendencies." (*Variety*, April 30, 1930)

"Routine drama rather stereotyped in story but moderately sophisticated, aided by prominent cast. Billie Dove manages to be sweet, but hasn't a chance for much else. Basil Rathbone does better than might be expected in the stereotyped role of the violinist. Kay Francis plays the countess well." (*Film Daily*, April 27, 1930)

"A thoroughly entertaining picture. One of the most subtle husband-stealing 'vamps' of the screen is Kay Francis. It is quite obvious that once she makes up her mind to 'get' a man, there is no way out. She plays her role with the cool assurance becoming her type. There is no undue eagerness displayed on her part, which is especially pleasing to the opposite sex." (Kenneth R. Porter, *Los Angeles Examiner*, June 28, 1930).

"*A Notorious Affair* is one of the best pictures seen in Warners' Downtown in months. Its chief characters are Billie Dove, Basil Rathbone and Kay Francis, who gives the Cleopatra touch to the proceedings. The Russian countess with the emotional habits of Catherine the Great is given a smoking enactment by Kay Francis. She provides Hollywood's most disturbing portrayal since *Hell's Angels*." (W.E. Oliver, *Los Angeles Evening Herald*, June 28, 1930)

"An interesting, well acted play. The vampire in the story is Kay Francis, who marks her men — then goes after them in a systematic way." (*Los Angeles Record*, June 28, 1930)

For the Defense

(Paramount-Publix Company, 1930)
62 min. Released on July 18, 1930.

Credits: Director, John Cromwell; story, Julius Furthman; screenplay-dialogue, Oliver H.P. Garrett; camera, Charles Lang; editor, George Nichols, Jr.; recording engineer, Harold M. McNiff.

Cast: William Powell (William Foster); Kay Francis (Irene Manners); Scott Kolk (Jack De Foe); William B. Davidson (District Attorney Stone); John Elliott (McGann); Thomas E. Jackson (Daly); Harry Walker (Miller); James Finlayson (Parrott); Charles West (Joe); Charles Sullivan (Charlie); Ernest Adams (Eddie Withers); Bertram Marburgh (Judge Evans); Edward Le Saint (Judge); George "Gabby" Hayes (Ben, the Waiter); Billy Bevan (Drunk); Robert Homans (Lineup Lieutenant); Kane Richmond (Young Man at Speakeasy); Syd Saylor (Evening Sun Reporter).

BILL FOSTER IS A successful — if disreputable — lawyer who defends the worst sort of criminal. Police officer Daly considers him a nemesis. "You're the fifteenth of mine he's sprung in the last year," he tells one perp on the street. "Someday," he adds, "I'll get him and get him plenty."

There's a marvelous courtroom scene where Foster, defending a man charged with murder, throws down a bottle of nitroglycerin (the state's chief piece of evidence). When order is restored, Bill explains that he'd smelled the bottle's contents and satisfied himself the material wasn't explosive. The district attorney admits the contents were removed as a safety precaution. The trick wins Foster's client an acquittal.

"I've met a lot of men in this town who built themselves up to look like the Woolworth Tower," he tells girlfriend Irene Manners, a beautiful stage actress. "In twenty-four hours, down they came."

"That'll never happen to you," Irene reassures, but she's agitated, wanting to talk about marriage. He laughs it off, but Irene's serious. Within this scene, there's a weird jumpcut when Kay suddenly talks to the camera. The scene must have been added later, but there's no attempt to match the lighting, and the effect is jarring, to say the least. Irene explains how she feels about marriage: "It means so much more to a woman. I'd like being married."

Meanwhile, Jack desperately wants to marry Irene. While Irene's out driving with him, Jack drunkenly reaches over, causing her to go off the road and hit a bystander. Irene leaves the scene, and Jack is charged with the man's death. Irene convinces Bill to defend him. The district attorney presents evidence that a woman was in the car — and a ring was found. When Bill discovers it was a ring he gave Irene, he assumes she cheated on him. Irene finally admits she was with Jack that night — and that she was driving.

Bill thinks she's protecting Jack. "You must be hot for him to pull that." Still, he tries to get Jack acquitted, and goes so far as to bribe a juror. The result is a hung jury, but Bill is soon arrested and put on trial. Irene tells the district attorney the truth, and agrees to testify, knowing it'll ruin her reputation. She gives Bill a note: "Please — if you ever loved me — if you ever believed I loved you — let me tell them the real reason you did it — Let me tell the truth for you if not for Jack."

A blasé Kay was often shown with two accessories — pearls and a cigarette — an appealing complement to her "butch" haircut.

Kay Francis in an early publicity photograph.

Bill, however, refuses to read the note and pleads guilty, with the stipulation that Jack's charges be dismissed. Bill takes the train to Ossining — Kay's real-life stomping grounds when she was a teenager — and prison. In the last scene, there's a hard rain. Bill's car drives up to the prison gates. Irene pops her head in the window. "Bill, if I'm here waiting for you when you come out, won't you believe me then?"

"I think I would," Bill admits.

"I'll be here."

"I'll be looking for you." The car drives through the gates.

Kay received second billing in this film, which used background shots photographed on location in New York. It was part of a genre called shyster films, focusing on lawyers and courtrooms. This one was based on a real person: New York defense lawyer William Fallon.

Cromwell, who was usually an adept director, seemed to shorthand this one. There are few close-ups, and the sound and lighting are often mediocre. He also does not do a great job of directing Kay. For example, Kay's reaction shots in the courtroom when Bill examines the ring are weak. She's capable of much better acting than is seen in this picture.

Kay on an early cigarette card.

REVIEWS: "Mr. Powell carries on his role well, as does Kay Francis as the lady of the case." (*New York Times*, July 19, 1930)

"William Powell puts over strong characterization of slick attorney for racketeers in cleverly told story. Fine programmer." (*Film Daily*, July 20, 1930)

"Adding to his remarkable collection of portraits in a great city, William Powell now gives us a gripping picture of the shyster lawyer. Miss Francis is capable as the actress and Scott Kolk creates sympathy for himself as the lover." (W.E. Oliver, *Los Angeles Evening Herald*, August 15, 1930)

"Powell gives a satisfying characterization, with customary finish and sophistication. Kay Francis is interesting and varied in her portrayal of the actress who indirectly and unwittingly brings him to his downfall. So compactly and skillfully have the situations been built up with dramatic effect that one is inclined to overlook the fact that some of them are so utterly unbelievable as to be slightly ridiculous." (Rachel Rubin, *Hollywood Daily Citizen*, August 15, 1930)

"There's a crisp, businesslike polish to this production. It holds attention from start to finish. Opposite Powell is seen Kay Francis, remembered for her effective work in *Street of Chance*. Miss Francis gives a good account of herself. She has been well photographed and wears some smart clothes." (*Los Angeles Illustrated Daily News*, August 16, 1930)

"The plot almost creaks with age. Every obvious theatrical device has been employed in the name of drama, and the continual courtroom scenes, jail corridors and bridge of sighs grow monotonous. But Powell, by the force of his performance, has made the picture interesting and human. Kay Francis again is asked to fill the role of a smart clothes horse, but she does so with dignity and a certain amount of feeling. Furthermore, she possesses one of the few musical feminine voices heard in pictures." (Elizabeth Yeaman, *Hollywood Daily Citizen*, September 12, 1930)

Raffles

(Samuel Goldwyn, Inc., United Artists, 1930) 70 min. Released on July 24, 1930.

Credits: Producer, Samuel Goldwyn; directors, Harry D'Arrast, George Fitzmaurice; based on the novel "The Amateur Cracksman" by Ernest William Hornung and the play "Raffles, the Amateur Cracksman" by Hornung and Eugene Wiley Presbrey; screenplay, Sidney Howard; assistant director, H. Bruce Humberstone; technical directors, Gerald Grove, John Howell; art directors, Park French, William Cameron Menzies; sound, Oscar Lagerstrom; camera, George S. Barnes, Gregg Toland; editor, Stuart Heisler.

Cast: Ronald Colman (A.J. Raffles); Kay Francis (Lady Gwen); David Torrence (Inspector MacKenzie); Frederic Kerr (Lord Harry Melrose); Alison Skipworth (Lady Kitty Melrose); Bramwell Fletcher (Bunny Manders); John Rogers (Crawshaw); Wilson Benge (Barraclough); Frances Dade (Ethel Crowley); Virginia Bruce (Debutante).

A MAN GIVES HIS opinion of the amateur cracksman who's been terrorizing England: "He's a common burglar!" A newspaper headline screams: "Amateur Cracksman Again! Robbery of British Museum!" In a beautifully photographed scene with radiant shadows, someone robs a safe of a bracelet, replacing it with a note: "The Amateur Cracksman his farewell appearance."

Raffles and Lady Gwen are at a fancy party when he asks her to marry him.

"Why not?" she answers.

He gives her the bracelet.

"I'm going to be married to the loveliest creature on God's green earth," Raffles tells his butler when he returns home. "I'm starting a new life tonight." However, he quickly learns old friend Bunny, waiting in another room, has attempted suicide.

"I'm a thief!" he tells Raffles.

"One way or another, we're all thieves at times," Raffles says consolingly. Even his friends don't know his true identity is the amateur cracksman.

"They'll treat me like a common cheat," Bunny tells Raffles, admitting to writing a bad check to pay for gambling losses. "I know what honesty and honor mean to you," he adds, not wanting to involve Raffles.

In *Raffles* (1930) Kay had her first screen pairing with Ronald Colman. She found Ronnie exciting both on and off screen.

Raffles, deciding to help repay Bunny's debt, sees a photograph of the Marchioness of Melrose wearing the famous Melrose necklace—a priceless piece that once belonging to the Empress Josephine. He accompanies Bunny to the Melrose estate. At dinner, Inspector MacKenzie of Scotland Yard arrives to see Lord Melrose. "I've come here to inform you that there are burglars in your neighborhood," he announces. "More particularly, *a* burglar." Melrose gives Raffles, MacKenzie and others a tour of the home, including the burglar alarm, which he inadvertently sets off and scares the fire out of Lady Melrose.

Complicating matters, amateur crooks try to break into the Melrose mansion. Another complication occurs when Gwen arrives, much to Raffles' surprise. "Didn't expect me here, did you?" she asks.

Lady Melrose's necklace is ostensibly locked in the safe. While MacKenzie guards it, Raffles disengages the burglar alarm. Crawshaw, one of the bungling burglars, comes through an upstairs window and steals the necklace—from Lady Melrose's neck. Raffles stops Crawshaw before he makes his escape and demands the necklace. Crawshaw agrees to give it up in return for getting away safely. MacKenzie finds the disengaged alarm and resets it. When Raffles and Crawshaw open the window, the alarm goes off, and Crawshaw is caught. The authorities are unable to find the jewelry. They see the necklace case in the safe, assume the necklace is inside, and arrest the burglar for breaking in.

The next morning Raffles announces he's returning to London. Privately, he tells Gwen he isn't worthy of her. He tells her about a man he knows. He wanted to lead a new life for her sake. But he's found he can't do it. "On the first possible excuse, he's gone wrong again."

While Gwen tries to talk him out of leaving, Lady Melrose announces that her necklace is missing. "I want somebody arrested," she demands. Turns out it was Raffles' suggestion to put the necklace case, *not* the necklace, in the safe. Lord Melrose offers a reward—coincidentally, the same amount of Bunny's debt—for its return.

Gwen, realizing Raffles is probably guilty, overhears MacKenzie discuss his plan to capture Raffles. "It isn't too late. I love you. I love you," she says to herself as Raffles drives away.

She follows him to his apartment. "I don't care what you are," she says. "I don't care what you've been. I love you. I love the man you really are." She wants to go away with him.

They hide the necklace in the tobacco tin when MacKenzie arrives. He's expecting Crawshaw, who's been released. Just as the inspector prepares his pipe, digging his hand into the tin, Gwen distracts him, and Raffles swiftly removes the necklace. Meanwhile, Crawshaw has been spotted. When the inspector goes to the roof to look for him, Crawshaw comes into the room, gun drawn. He wants the necklace. Raffles overpowers him, and then gallantly helps him escape out the window. Raffles chloroforms himself, but when the inspector finds him, he also finds tickets to Amsterdam, suggesting he planned to escape. "Aren't you the amateur cracksman, Mr. Raffles?" MacKenzie asks.

Raffles admits it, and instructs Bunny to remove the necklace from the tobacco jar; he'll get the reward and be able to pay off his debt. Lord Melrose asks that no charges be brought. Gwen gives MacKenzie the bracelet from the previous robbery. "Well, MacKenzie, you've got your necklace," Raffles says. "You've even got your bracelet." He lights a cigarette. "But you haven't got me!" Fast motion is used to show his quick flight.

"I'll meet you in Paris!" Gwen calls after him.

"They'll nab him downstairs," the inspector confidently says.

"I wonder," Gwen says.

Raffles has indeed escaped, dressed in the inspector's coat and hat. The inspector smiles. "One can't help liking him."

Kay was second billed. This was not a good role for her as there's little to do but stiffly stand around, wring her hands, and remain devoted to Colman. The movie, too, is slow-moving. Harry D'Abbadie D'Arrast was first hired to direct, but immediately had conflicts with producer Goldwyn, who told the director he didn't like his rushes. "'You and I don't speak the same language, Mr. Goldwyn,' D'Arrast responded. 'I'm sorry, Mr. D'Arrast,' Goldwyn snapped, 'but it's my money that's buying the language.'"[19] George Fitzmaurice, who'd directed Colman before, was hired to replace D'Arrast.

Bette Davis was considered for the role of Lady Gwen, but Goldwyn failed to see her charm in her screen test. He reportedly shouted, "What are you guys trying to do to me?"[20] Goldwyn complained of "her pop-eyed looks, as well as her clipped way of speaking."[21] Davis, who learned of Goldwyn's unflattering comments, paid him back in 1941 when she requested $385,000 for *The Little Foxes*. Goldwyn reluctantly agreed.

F. Scott Fitzgerald was an uncredited screenwriter. Sound director Oscar Lagerstrom received an Academy Award nomination for sound recording.

According to Colman's biographer, "It was made purely as a star vehicle to showcase Colman's poise and charm. But, unlike Joan Bennett and Fay Wray in *Bulldog Drummond* and *The Unholy Garden*, respectively, Francis's warm acting is a match for Colman's. You can believe they're in love."[22] Goldwyn specifically requested that this version of *Raffles* be a glamorous love story. Not surprisingly, Kay and Ronald had a brief fling during the filming.

Versions of this story were produced in 1905, 1910, 1914, 1917, 1920, 1932 and 1960. Others who played Lady Gwen include Gwendolyn Amersteth and Olivia de Havilland. Actors who have played Raffles include J. Barney Sherry, Gerald du Maurier, John Barrymore, Kyrle Bellew, House Peters, and David Niven. The character was originally included in Ernest William Hornung's short stories, and then Hornung used Raffles in full-length novels. Goldwyn needed to secure more than 45 different rights before the motion picture could be produced. The character was conceived by Hornung in 1899 as a counterpoint to brother-in-law Arthur Conan Doyle's Sherlock Holmes.

In the October 1930 issue of *New Movie Magazine*, a letter from a fan praised the new star. "May I express my very great admiration for one of Hollywood's successful newcomers, 'the elegant Kay Francis,' who arrived without trumpet blare of advance publicity and quietly and steadily has come into her own? Through sincere and skillful interpretation of every role, however small, she has established herself as an actress of unquestionable talent and ability. Witness her splendid performance in 'Raffles.'"

REVIEWS: "In Kay Francis the caster has made a happy choice — an actress with that suggestion of reserve vitality that makes her stand out strongly in a part that is intrinsically pale." (*Variety*, July 30, 1930)

"Entertaining screen fare. Ronald Colman is ideally cast as Raffles, and handles the serio-comic role with a deft touch that makes it one of his best roles to date. He is given beautiful support by the alluring Kay Francis, whose sophistication and charm make her an ideal team-mate for the star. The film carries plenty of suspense and action." (*Film Daily*, July 27, 1930)

"Sleek brunette Kay Francis adorns the picture with stunning gowns and ultra sophistication in which she revels. However, her appearance suggests a siren rather than one who would sacrifice everything to become a fugitive from justice with Colman." (Elizabeth Yeaman, *Hollywood Daily Citizen*, July 24, 1930)

"Probably the most colorful role next to that of Raffles himself is played by Kay Francis. Miss Francis is always getting herself married or engaged to fascinating crook characters on the screen. She is an interesting personality and a talented actress." (Louella O. Parsons, *Los Angeles Examiner*, July 24, 1930)

Let's Go Native
(Paramount Publix Corp., 1930) 75 min. Released on August 20, 1930.

Credits: Executive producer: Adolph Zukor; producer and director, Leo McCarey; screenplay-dialogue, George Marion, Jr., Percy Heath; songs, Richard A. Whiting, George F. Marion; dances-ensembles director, David Bennett; sound, Harry D. Mills; camera, Victor Milner.

Cast: Jack Oakie (Voltaire McGinnis); Jeanette MacDonald (Joan Wood); Skeets Gallagher (Jerry); James Hall (Wally Wendell); William Austin (Basil Pistol); Kay Francis (Constance Cooke); David Newell (Chief Officer Williams); Charles Sellon (Wallace Wendell Sr.); Eugene Pallette (Deputy Sheriff Careful Cuthbert); Iris Adrian (uncredited); Earl Askam (Mover); Harry Bernard (Mover); Virginia Bruce (Secretary); E.H. Calvert (Diner); John Elliott (Captain); Charlie Hall (Mover); Pat Harmon (Policeman); Oscar Smith (Cook); Rafael Storm (Argentine Producers' Representative); Grady Sutton (Diner).

KAY RECEIVED SEVENTH billing in this musical comedy. There's more gags than plot in this one, but the gist of it involves a Broadway show being sent to Buenos Aires. Costume designer Joan Wood is in love with Wally Wendell, a millionaire's grandson. Wally is in love with

Kay, Jack Oakie, and Jeanette MacDonald in *Let's Go Native* (1930). Poor Jeanette.

her, but Grandfather Wendell — the Polecat of Wall Street — wants him to marry Constance Cooke, the heir to a laundry soap fortune. Before Joan leaves for Argentina, there's a funny scene with Joan and the deputy sheriff. She thinks his comments are about her, but they're actually about her repossessed car.

"I don't know when I've seen a nicer paint job," he says.

"It'll be all right when I'm finished," she says, applying her makeup.

"It's unusual to find a body like yours. Not a scar on it," the deputy marvels.

"Well, you see, I've never had an operation," she explains.

Joan gets Wally a job on the ship, along with cabbie Voltaire and pal Basil. Voltaire explains how he got his name. "Well, see, when I was born, my ma told the nurse to tell the doctor my name was Walter. The nurse was Jewish, so the doctor wrote it down the way it was pronounced 'Voltaire.'"

Meanwhile, Constance ends up on the same ship. She was actually trying to escape Wally, but now that she's seen him she's changed her mind. "You look a lot better than you did at 16. You're not bad." Soon after, there's a shipwreck. Wally, Joan, Constance, Voltaire, and Basil end up on an island.

"Strange-looking place," Basil says. Indeed. The unusual natives are wearing Joan's costumes, which washed up after the wreck, and their king is a guy from Brooklyn. The newcomers eat from a buffet, and break their teeth on oysters (or "orsters," as the king calls them). There are pearls in abundance. When Basil tries to mark off a tennis court, he hits oil. The king generously gives Joan the island to repay her for the costumes.

Voltaire seduces Constance, and then sings to her. Kay sings, too, on "I've Got a Yen for You." Part of it's talk-singing, but there's some actual singing, too, and she's remarkably good. A ship finds them, with Wally's dad on board. Joan sells him the island for $1 million. When the contract is signed, an earthquake begins rumbling. Constance, wearing a skimpy costume (Kay again gets to show off her legs), is carried off by Voltaire. Well, at least he tries. She's too heavy, and they end up sprawled on the ground. Basil and Voltaire awkwardly take her arms and legs and tote her off. Everyone is finally on the boat when the island blows up and sinks into the water.

"The pearls and the oil are still there. You'll have to dig a little deeper," the island's new owners are told.

Jeanette MacDonald, charming as usual, was unhappy about the script and asked for revisions. She didn't get them. Paramount's Leo McCarey hurried through the shooting, completing it in three weeks. Other songs include "It Seems to Be Spring," "Let's Go Native," "My Mad Moment," and "Joe Jazz."

This movie is an excellent example of how misguided studios could be when sound arrived. What *were* they thinking? The early scenes are quite good, but once they get to the island it disintegrates. The odd pairing of Jack Oakie and Jeanette MacDonald also hurts the picture; it's as though they're in different films. Jack Oakie is actually better paired with William Austin — yes, the ninny from *Marriage Playground*. Not every gag works, but their antics are often amusing. The editing is quick, using many close-ups of legs, faces, and dancers.

Kay, vamping again, does not appear until around the thirty-eight-minute mark. Her comedic talents, sadly, are wasted in this one.

Jack Oakie complained about the difficulty of filming musical numbers. "Whenever we made a musical picture, we had to sing every number over and over, time and time again," he explained. On *Let's Go Native*, "they brought in 40 musicians who took up more than half of the stage and also a group of experts called music coordinators to oversee the music through a specially-built soundproof glass cage. The day I was singing 'I've Got a Yen For You,' those experts kept tapping on that glass cage all day and all night. Every time I finished the number, they tapped on the glass wall; and through a speaker they constantly gave direction. Some of their reasons didn't make good sense to us but, after all, they were the expert musicians. 'The saxophones were too loud. We'll have to move them back a little,' they'd explain. Well, when the saxophones weren't too loud, the oboes were too quiet. I had been on the set since 8:00 A.M. and must have gone through that song almost a hundred times. At 8 o'clock that night Sam Jaffee, head of the studio at that time, came down to the set and asked, 'What's holding you up?'"[23] Later Oakie discovered the musicians were simply bucking for overtime pay. "When the studios finally stopped the live act, took the musicians off the set, and started to prerecord all music, you should have heard those musicians and glass tappers holler!"[24]

Promotional materials called it "Paramount's wild, merry, mad hilarious farce!"

REVIEWS: "A ludicrous audible film hodgepodge. Miss MacDonald gives as pleasing a performance as is possible in such a mélange. Mr. Oakie, William Austin, James Hall, Kay Francis and others add to the wild gayety." (*New York Times*, August 30, 1930)

"Grand entertainment for anybody's theater. Whatever story has been inserted into this picture is inconsequential. The gags — rapid-fire ones — are the ingredients that make it audience stuff." (*Film Daily*, August 31, 1930)

"There are sufficient ridiculous, brilliant and hilarious moments throughout *Let's Go Native* to furnish laughter to please all types of humor senses. [A]n exceptionally well-made production that doesn't let up for a second in entertainment interest. At times one tires slightly of laughing, but then come moments of romance or of dancing — and by a very pretty chorus, too." (Jerry Hoffman, *Los Angeles Examiner*, September 12, 1930)

"Although the plot is a nonsensical one, the film presents a cast of favorites, some exciting scenes, much singing and dancing and hilarious comedy. Kay Francis was attractive in becoming costumes and is heard in an alluring song." (Marjorie Ross, *Hollywood Daily Citizen*, October 10, 1930)

"There are songs, dances, gags that make you grin in spite of your more intellectual self. And that's about all. Director McCarey has crowded too much into one little picture to keep his audience always interested. However, we'll grant that there are more chuckly moments than boring ones." (*Screen Book*, November 1930)

The Virtuous Sin

(Paramount Publix Corp., 1930) 80 min. Released on October 24, 1930.

Credits: Directors, George Cukor, Louis Gasnier; based on the play "A Tabornok" ("The General") by Lajos Zilahy; screenplay, Martin Brown; scenery, Louise Long; original music, Sam Coslow, Karl Hajos, Howard Jackson, Ralph Rainger, Leo Robin, Max Terr, Richard A. Whiting; sound, Harold M. McNiff; camera, David Abel; editor, Otto Lovering.

Cast: Walter Huston (General Gregori Platoff); Kay Francis (Marya Ivanova); Kenneth MacKenna (Lieutenant Victor Sablin); Jobyna Howland (Alexandra Stroganov); Paul Cavanagh (Captain Orloff); Eric Kalkhurst (Lieutenant Glinka); Oscar Apfel (Major Ivanoff); Gordon McLeod (Colonel Nikitin); Youcca Troubetzkov (Captain Sobakin); Victor Potel (Sentry).

IT'S ST. PETERSBURG IN January 1914, and Marya has just returned from Moscow. She meets Victor for dinner. It's been a year since they've seen each other.

"Perhaps I ran away because we were such good friends," she tells him. Victor hasn't been working. "Oh, I'm disappointed, Victor," Marya scolds. "I thought the thousands of Russians dying of tuberculosis would mean much more to you than any girl."

Victor tells her he's in love with her and asks her to marry him. Marya is reluctant. "Your father has a title. Mine has a little shop. It just wouldn't work out. It isn't only that. I have a great affection for you, Victor. But it isn't love. I don't know what love is. I may never know."

Victor is persistent. "Our marriage need be nothing more — well, how shall we say it — than a scientific union."

Marya reluctantly agrees—just the first of many times when Kay agrees to marry a man she doesn't love, which you'd think she'd learn is *always* a bad idea. Victor returns to the lab and makes a great discovery. "I couldn't have done it without the help of my wife," he says. Unfortunately, he soon receives orders to report for military duty.

Distressed that he can't continue his work, Marya decides to see General Platoff. The line is long, and the general rebuffs all who ask for favors. "Don't bother to turn on the tears," he says. "I want all the men I can get, and I mean to have them."

Meanwhile, Victor is proving to be a poor

Kay wore this 1914-era evening gown (a Travis Banton design) in *The Virtuous Sin* (1930).

soldier, and is ultimately ordered to face a firing squad. "Well, General Platoff cannot be touched by tears," Marya says, realizing she must save Victor. "There'll be no tears this time." She finds a club the general frequents. "Is that a restaurant next door?" she asks.

"Well, they have food there." Pause. "I don't think you'd like it. It's no place for a lady."

Undaunted, Marya meets with Alexandra, the mistress of the house. This is a delightful scene, and offers another opportunity to hear Kay sing in her own voice. Jobyna Howland is one of the few women you'll see towering over Kay Francis. In the scene, the six-foot former stage star asks Marya for a brief audition. If you listen closely, you can hear one barely audible piano note before Kay begins singing. She apparently needed the prompt before she went into her song. Kay's voice is a deep vibrato. She doesn't have a lot of range, but does very nicely in this small number.

Alexandra hires Marya, changing her name to Carmina. The men are rowdy, and Marya, not wanting to go through another night of being nearly pawed near to death, comes up

Kay and husband Kenneth MacKenna in an intimate scene from *The Virtuous Sin* (1930) (courtesy James King).

with a plan to meet the general. She pretends to be interested in the sentry, and then, upon seeing the general approach, calls for help. "He kissed me, that beast!" The general agrees to let her accompany him, and she walks alongside. "Oh, I've heard all about you," she says. "They call you Iron Face. You're not quite human because you have no heart." She charms him and tells him where she works. That night at the brothel — probably the largest brothel you'll ever see on film — the general arrives. Alexandra offers them a room upstairs, but Marya prefers a walk.

"You'll be cold," she says, as he gives her his coat.

"No. Not tonight." He kisses her. She tells him to stop. "I thought that's why walks in the moonlight were invented," he protests.

Amidst all this sexual tension, Marya suddenly suggests they ride a seesaw. No kidding. It has some effect because when the general returns to his office, he softens, agreeing to a mother's request to have her son return home. The general sends Marya flowers and a note, requesting she dine alone with him that night. Platoff tells her he's in love with her. "This is something I've never felt before," he tells her. "It makes me terribly happy, and yet it makes me angry."

"I think love is like a wave," Marya says. "If it comes on you unawares, nothing can stop it from sweeping over you. Of course, if you're a good swimmer —"

"I want to drown. Carmina, I love you."

Marya spends the night with the general. The next morning, Marya asks her favor. "I want the life of Lt. Victor Sablin."

"What is he to you?" the general asks.

"I'm his wife."

"Yes, now, I understand it all, from the beginning on that dusty road," the general says. "Just one more, only cleverer than the rest." He orders her out.

At noon, a guard brings a note to Victor. "I'm free!" he exclaims. However, an ungrateful Victor is angered when he realizes how Marya won his freedom.

The general arrives for an inspection. When Victor realizes the general is the guilty party, he pulls a gun, but the general easily takes it away. Suddenly, the military forces are under attack. Victor tries to commit suicide, but the general prevents it.

"A few weeks later ... on the threshold of what had been a home," Victor returns and treats Marya coldly. "I'm alive," he says, "because you broke your promise to me."

"That promise was beyond my strength to keep."

Victor explains he'll return to his work and give her a divorce.

"To be loyal, I had to be disloyal," she says. "To find love, I had to go where no love should have been."

Marya returns to the general and tells him Victor has left her.

"He doesn't realize how fine you are, how loyal?" the general asks, surprised. "Can there be any room for misunderstanding between us? Can misunderstanding ever separate me and you?"

"Not if you hold me very close," she replies. They embrace and kiss.

Though second-billed, this is Kay's first real starring role. She'd come a long way in little more than a year since vamping with the Marx Brothers. Kay looks splendid in the 1914 costumes and hairstyles, and this film offers her best acting up to this point.

The Virtuous Sin (the British release title was *Cast Iron*) starts slowly. It's not until Marya cooks up the plan to seduce the general that the film becomes interesting. For the most part, the Cukor touch is missing. Oddly, there is little chemistry between Kay Francis and future husband Kenneth MacKenna. However, she has wonderful chemistry with Walter Huston, who chased her around a bit in her early Hollywood days. She also has interesting chemistry with Jobyna Howland. In fact, the film is worth watching for Jobyna. At one time, Mrs. Patrick Campbell was considered for her role, but her salary request was too high. As for MacKenna, it's easy to see why he abandoned an acting career for work behind the scenes. Although attractive, his acting style lacks subtlety. Huston, however, is quite good in his scenes, and shows a more sophisticated style than in the stilted *Gentlemen of the Press*.

According to writer Ivor Montagu, "Its origin was a play called 'The General,' the sort of play which is put on and runs for three nights in Budapest and, so far as I could learn, something of that sort had been its fate. It had the kind of plot which, when you read it, you imagine must be turned down immediately by every management in stage and film, but, apparently, no."[25] Montagu, a filmmaker and critic, described the two actors cast in the lead roles: "Huston, an oldish actor at the time, was a man of outstanding personality and dignity, [and] Kay Francis was a woman also dignified and handsome, radiating intelligence and poise."[26]

In the play, Kay played a nurse who ended up attending the cold general after he was injured. The original setting was Budapest, Hungary; however, producer B.P. Schulberg claimed that Americans thought Hungary was a city — if they'd even heard of it — and that Russia was much more in the news. The film's first director was Rowland V. Lee, who balked at the casting, especially Kay. He made this rather implausible comment: "Kay Francis is wrong for the woman. Who would want to hump Kay Francis?"[27] At first the studio agreed. They changed their minds, however, when Lee's newest film premiered — and the results were disastrous. Lee was promptly taken off *The Virtuous Sin*.

Cukor and Louis Gasnier co-directed the film. Cukor, an Oscar winner, directed classics like *The Women* and Gasnier's work included movie serials as well as the cult favorite *Reefer Madness*. Hollywood doesn't get much stranger than the decision to combine these two directors. Cukor later told an interviewer that while he enjoyed working with Francis and Huston, he was embarrassed by the movie, found it dated, and hoped it would disappear.

Gustaf Bergman adapted Zilahy's play and directed a Swedish version, *Generalen* (1931). Edvin Adolphson and Paul van der Osten played the male leads, and Inga Tidblad played Kay's role.

Film historian William K. Everson did not believe the movie needed to be "rediscovered," pointing to its slow pacing and some heavy-handed performances among the supporting cast." He did like the cinematography and the "handsome scene design (although the brothel appears to be the size of the czar's Winter Palace.)"[28]

REVIEWS: "Clever comedy. There is a constant fund of interest in this picture's action. It is one of those rare offerings in which youth takes a back seat and the General wins the bright-eyed Marya." (*New York Times*, November 2, 1930)

"A strange effort toward sophistication in the manner of Sardou, *The Virtuous Sin* falls between burlesque and melodrama.... [I]ts single virtue is that it provides the first important vehicle for the alluring and competent Kay Francis. Best shot: interior of a house of ill-fame patronized by high tsarist military officials." (*Time*, November 10, 1930)

"Good dramatic story, well acted.... Here is a story, that by virtue of its compelling situations and excellent acting should have made a great picture. However, poor direction and mediocre dialogue have succeeded in spoiling any hopes along those lines.... To the actors belongs the glory of the picture. Kay Francis, despite the fact that the photography in many of the scenes was most unkind, gives a splendid portrayal of the wife, and Walter Huston as the General does a fine piece of acting." (*Hollywood Daily Reporter*, September 29, 1930)

"Average program flicker for business purposes but one that should do much to help Kay Francis on her way." (*Variety*, October 29, 1930)

"Trite story material and dialogue put this Russian melodrama in weakling class, slow and obvious stuff." (*Film Daily*, October 26, 1930)

"The role of sacrifice is undertaken by Kay Francis, and while she is playing the gay coquette she is very acceptable too." (*Los Angeles Evening Herald*, October 31, 1930)

"The greatest credit belongs to Walter Huston and Kay Francis, and, by all means, Kenneth McKenna, who, naturally, have the greatest number of scenes." (Jerry Hoffman, *Los Angeles Examiner*, October 31, 1930)

Passion Flower
(Metro-Goldwyn-Mayer, 1930) 78 min.
Released on December 19, 1930.

Credits: Director, William C. de Mille; based on the novel by Kathleen Norris; adaptor-dialogue Martin Flavin; additional dialogue, Laurence E. Johnson, Edith Fitzgerald; art director, Cedric Gibbons; gowns, Adrian; sound, J. K. Brock, Douglas Shearer; camera, Hal Rosson; editor, Conrad A. Nervig.

Cast: Kay Francis (Dulce Morado); Kay Johnson (Cassy Pringle Wallace); Charles Bickford (Dan Wallace); Winter Hall (Leroy Pringle); Lewis Stone (Antonio Morado); ZaSu Pitts (Mrs. Harney); Dickie Moore (Tommy Wallace); Ray Milland; Ellinor Vanderveer (party guests).

"I'M IN LOVE," Cassy announces to Cousin Dulce. Turns out she's in love with her chauffeur Dan. Her father disapproves. "If you leave this house with that man, you'll leave for good."

Dulce is married to the much older and very rich Tony. She and Tony give Dan and Cassy a wedding gift—a little farm across the road. Dan refuses it. Instead, he and Cassy rent a room from the always-complaining Mrs. Harney. "The hot water spigot is the cold water spigot. The cold water spigot is the hot water spigot. But it don't make much difference. There's no hot water, anyway."

Cassy and Dan quickly have a boy and girl. They are still living in the tiny apartment, and it's now their fifth wedding anniversary. Dan has just been laid off. Dulce lays into him. "You think you're standing on your feet. You're not. You're standing on your foot." *Huh*?

Kay was on loan to MGM for *Passion Flower* (1930), where she was costumed by legendary designer Adrian.

A beautiful shot of Kay Francis in *Passion Flower* (1930). This is an atypical look for Kay.

Anyway, Dan changes his mind, and agrees to take the farm. Six weeks later, Dulce and Dan start an affair. They've been riding horses, and upon returning to her home, she convinces him to stay. "Please stay, Dan. I want you to." He kisses her hand and agrees.

Tony has seen everything. When Dulce comes downstairs, decked out in a beautiful gown, Tony meets her. She admits she's in love with Dan. He tells her she'll ruin her life. "My life couldn't be any more ruined than it already is," she says. "It hasn't been heaven living like this. Oh, I'm sorry, Tony. I didn't mean to hurt you."

"You're letting yourself in for a lot of heartache, Dulce."

"I'm so unhappy," Dulce complains to Dan. "Tony accused me of being in love with you. You see, it's true. I do love you."

Meanwhile, when Dan is out, the telephone rings. "Somebody's dead, I suppose," Mrs. Harney says. "If it ain't the wrong number, it's bad news." Cassy gets word that her father is very ill, and has to borrow Dulce's car.

"I can't smash up my home," Dan tells Dulce before Cassy arrives. "I came tonight to tell you that."

"I had no right to dream of happiness," Dulce says. "Well, I'll always have the memory, Dan."

Cassy has watched the scene from outside the window, and later confronts Dulce.

"I did fight against it," Dulce claims. "Love isn't a thing that you can control."

"You've already left me," Cassy tells Dan. "Go back to her. Tell her I sent you."

Time passes, and Cassy's father has died and left her money. One night she and Mrs. Harney are talking about men. "He didn't run away. I sent him," Cassy admits.

"They're kind of handy in the daytime, and they're sort of entertaining in the evening," says Mrs. Harney. "But as far as I'm concerned, I'd just as soon have a good radio."

Cassy writes a letter to Dan asking him to come back. Meanwhile, Dan is living it up with Dulce. The letter is delivered, just as Dulce gets word that Tony is dead. "Poor Tony. Oh but darling, don't you see what this means for us. Everything is different now. I'm free. We can be married now, darling."

After they return home, Dulce tells Dan she's talked to Cassy about a divorce. "Cassy agreed. I think she'd rather like to have her freedom. Perhaps there's somebody else." Cassy does agree, but only if Dan asks for the divorce himself.

Dan visits Cassy and the children. "It's funny, isn't it? That I should go on loving you when you love someone else," Cassy admits. "I suppose I ought to be ashamed of it, but I'm not."

Dan tells her he's read her letter "a thousand times." Cassy asks for a kiss before he leaves. Dulce shows up.

"My husband loves me. *Me!*" Cassy tells her. Dan admits to Dulce that he regrets leaving his family.

"It's over," Dulce says. "You're not leaving me. I'm leaving you. Don't blame yourself. You never really wanted to leave Cassy." She tries to maintain her dignity. "The only thing you can do for me, Dan, is to go on here. You owe it to me."

"You're a grand person," he says.

"No. Don't spoil it. Don't spoil my noble gesture by making me cry. I don't want you to remember me with mascara running down my cheek. You know, I'm really taking advantage of you. You can't ever forget me if I leave you like this. Goodbye, Dan."

This was the first time Kay received top billing, which is odd because Bickford and Johnson are the real leads. This is not Kay's best acting. When people say she couldn't act, they're talking about performances like this. Paramount loaned Kay to MGM for the role. The film was based on a story by Kathleen Norris that was serialized in the March–September 1929 issues of *Delineator*.

Leila Hyams was originally cast in the Kay Johnson role. Johnson is very good, as are Bickford and Lewis Stone. The two Kays were friendly during Francis' early years in Hollywood, and enjoyed a brief flirtation. At one point in her diary, which clearly detailed her bisexuality, Francis reported Johnson had told her she'd always love her.

ZaSu Pitts has the best lines—and knows what to do with them. "Dishes, dishes. Dirty dishes. But what's the use? They'll only be dirty again tomorrow."

Charles Bickford, often described as difficult and temperamental, minced no words in his autobiography about the "horrific" film. Other studios had tried borrowing Bickford for leads, but MGM refused. When Bickford desperately wanted to appear in *Cimarron*, MGM told him they had an important film ready for him. "This little dilly was to be produced by [Irving] Thalberg, directed by William de Mille, Cecil's brother, and was to co-star Kay Johnson, Kay Francis and myself. After reading the script I screamed my protests to Thalberg. I threatened to walk out of the studio rather than play in the thing. He pleaded with me to calm down and trust him. Mr. Mayer, it seemed, had his heart set on my playing in this one, and I mustn't jeopardize the big plans that were being made for me by refusing to do it. I should have told him to shove the big plans, and walked. But my trust in Thalberg prevailed and once again I was outsmarted. Of all the bad pictures I have appeared in, and there were many, 'The Passion Flower' takes the cake. As I had warned Thalberg, it had exactly nothing to commend it and turned out to be the big daddy of all stinkeroos. It was but one of the Thalberg productions that you never heard about."[29]

REVIEWS: "Kay Francis does exceptionally well as the fashionably-clad Dulce." (*New York Times*, December 22, 1930)

"The picture version of Kathleen Norris' novel is not as fundamentally true as the book, though audiences not familiar with it will like the film tremendously. Kay Johnson and Kay

Charles Bickford and Kay Francis are lovers in *Passion Flower* (1930).

A stunning Kay Francis in *Passion Flower* (1930).

Kay played the wife of a metropolitan newspaper publisher and the mistress of his banker friend in *Scandal Sheet* (1931).

Francis handle difficult roles well, but Charles Bickford, while physically like Dan, lacks romantic appeal." (*Photoplay*, January 1931)

"Charles Bickford does his best work to date, but seems a bit miscast as the vacillating type." (*Screen Play*, January 1931)

"The picture is really interesting and Kay Johnson does a beautiful piece of natural acting. Miss Francis, who uses her beauty, wit and charm to win Dan away from Cassie, enacts the role with realistic fervor and ZaSu Pitts gives her unusually excellent performances as the landlady." (Marjorie Ross, *Hollywood Daily Citizen*, February 27, 1931)

"Kay Francis is coming along. However, having several pictures to her credit now, it's doubtful if this brunette will ever achieve stardom but that she's an invaluable featured player is something the Coast has already found out." (*Variety*, December 24, 1930)

"Kay Francis handles her role — rather a thankless one — in her usual excellent style, while Kay Johnson is cast to better advantage than she has been in any of her recent films." (*Billboard*)

Scandal Sheet

(Paramount Publix Corp., 1931) 75 min.
Released on February 6, 1931.

Credits: Director, John Cromwell; story, Oliver H.P. Garrett; screenplay, Vincent Lawrence, Max Marcin; sound, J. A. Goodrich; original music, Karl Hajos, W. Frank Harling; camera, David Abel; editor, George Nichols Jr.

Cast: George Bancroft (Mark Flint, the Editor); Clive Brook (Noel Adams, the Banker); Kay Francis (Mrs. Flint); Gilbert Emery (Franklin, the Publisher); Lucien Littlefield (McCloskey, the City Editor); Regis Toomey (Regan, the Reporter); Mary Foy (Mrs. Wilson); Harry Beresford (Arnold); Jackie Searl (Little Boy); James Kelsey (Malloy); Irving Bacon; William Arnold; Vince Barnett; Davison Clark; Monte Collins; Adrienne D'Ambricourt; Robert Dudley; Perry Ivins; Broderick O'Farrell; Leslie Palmer; Robert Parrish; Victor Potel; Jack Richardson; Syd Saylor; Nick Stuart; Frederick Sullivan.

MARK FLINT, A RUTHLESS, cynical editor, wants news — the more lurid and sensational the better — and doesn't care who gets hurt. He shows a softer side when dealing with his wife. "I've never disappointed her yet," he says. "I guess that's why we're the championship lovers." That's what *he* thinks.

Flint's banker, Noel Adams, asks Mrs. Flint to go away with him. She requests twenty-four hours to make up her mind. Meanwhile,

Kay on the cover of *Silver Screen* (March 1931).

a financial scandal arises involving Adams and the bank. Flint visits Adams, sees packed bags, and assumes Adams is planning a getaway. Mrs. Flint later tells Adams she's decided to stay with her husband. "I don't think we'd be happy," she tells him. "We'd regret it." She doesn't believe her husband could recover. "I mean too much to him. I just couldn't forgive myself."

Adams tells her he's in trouble at the bank, and that her husband is printing the story. Mrs. Flint starts to call her husband, but hears a newsboy—the story has already been printed. A photographer takes a shot of Mrs. Flint and Adams standing at the window. Mrs. Flint changes her mind and decides to leave her husband. "I'm glad he printed the story, and I'm glad you're in trouble because now, dear, just because you need me, it's the one little thing I needed in all this world to fall in love with you with all my heart."

Flint sees the photo of his wife and Adams. He insists it be printed and dictates the story. "... The woman, young, handsome, is Mrs. Mark Flint, wife of a prominent newspaper man at whose home Adams was a frequent visitor. Adams in the guise of financial advisor wormed his way into the confidence of the newspaper man's w–newspaper man." Flint leaves the office and finds his wife packing at home.

"I always like to give a woman a chance to make a statement," he explains. "That's why I'm here." He shows her the photo. She implores him not to print it. He grabs her and insists she give a statement.

"Here's my statement. I love Noel Adams. Do you hear! I love him!"

Flint visits Adams' apartment at 1046 Park Avenue and then returns, dazed, to the newspaper office. He dictates the story: "Slug this new lead. Adams Bank Fraud Story.... At 11:15 this morning Mark Flint, managing editor of the *Bulletin*, walked into the apartment of Noel Adams, president of the Standard and Trust Bank, and shot him dead. Thereafter he returned to the office of the *Bulletin* and wrote this story. He then went to the nearest police station and gave himself up." Flint starts to walk out of the office. "Wait a minute. Let me see that. Change 'gave himself up' to 'surrendered.' Using three words when one is enough. I must be cracking up."

Flint is convicted and sent to prison, where the warden makes him the prison newspaper's editor. A reporter visits and finds Flint happily barking orders. The warden stops by, asking him to tone down the sensationalism. "He's a good warden," Flint explains. "But what does he know about the newspaper business? Why, listen, if they'd leave me alone, I'd give the *Sing Sing Herald* the biggest circulation in this country!"

Third billed, Kay appears in few scenes as the well-dressed society woman. Kay's acting is better in this one than *Passion Flower*, though she has some clunky lines and is a little cross-eyed in the scene where Mark confronts her. The two go eyeball to eyeball, and Kay apparently couldn't decide which eye to look at. She's also a tad overwrought in this emotional scene, but the overall direction, again by John Cromwell, is clever and fast-paced. There are also lots of great art deco interiors. A large newsroom was built for the film. In addition, scenes were shot in the *Los Angeles Illustrated Daily News* press room.

The original American title was *Unfit to Print*. At one time, it was also known as *Rich Man's Folly*. The British release was titled *The Dark Page*.

The story was based on Charles Chapin, former editor of the *New York Evening World*, who referred to his reporters as "cogs." In real life, he killed his wife in a botched murder-suicide. After being sentenced to Sing Sing, Chapin not only started a prison newspaper, he also became known as the "Rose Man" because of his work on an extensive landscaping project, including a bird sanctuary. He died in prison on December 12, 1930.

Promotional ads proclaimed: "The screen's greatest artists George Bancroft, Clive Brook, Kay Francis in *Scandal Sheet* ... Greatest Newspaper Scandal of the Talking Screen!"

REVIEWS: "Kay Francis gives a steady performance as Mrs. Flint." (*New York Times*, February 9, 1931)

"It is not the relentless grind of the presses that make *Scandal Sheet* good entertainment, it is the sincerity with which John Cromwell directed the story and the intelligent cast in leading roles who lift the tone immeasurably, for the story is thin in spots, even though the dialogue is bright copy. Kay Francis plays the wife with that sirenic, intriguing manner that has marked her earlier screen efforts. Women admire her immensely for her ability to wear lovely clothes faultlessly. With a new hairdress, Miss Francis loses some tailoredness and gains in softness and charm." (Eleanor Barnes, *Los Angeles Illustrated Daily News*, January 16, 1931)

"Miss Francis has what can be most nearly described as 'sensible seductiveness' in this part.... She has an emphasized femininity that is charmingly human, and as natural and unaffected as the wind. Besides that she has been given lines to say that are extremely clever in their extreme simplicity." (Llewellyn Miller, *Los Angeles Record*, January 16, 1931)

"One saving grace is an occasional touch of humor and another is the presence of Kay Francis ... because of her suave playing of an impossible role." (*Variety*, February 11, 1931)

Ladies' Man

(Paramount Publix Corp., 1931) 76 min. Released on April 30, 1931.

Credits: Director, Lothar Mendes; story, Rupert Hughes; screenplay, Herman J. Mankiewicz; sound, Harry Lindgren; camera, Victor Milner. *Cast:* William Powell (*James Darricott*); Kay Francis (*Norma Page*); Carole Lombard (*Rachel Fendley*); Gilbert Emery (*Horace Fendley*); Olive Tell (*Mrs. Fendley*); Martin Burton (*Anthony Fendley*); John Holland (*Peyton Weldon*); Frank Atkinson (*Valet*); Maude Turner Gordon (*Therese Blanton*); Hooper Atchley (*Headwaiter*); Richard Cramer (*Private Detective*); Edward Hearn (*Maitre D'*); Lothar Mendes (*Lobby Extra*); Bill O'Brien (*Elevator Starter*); Frank O'Connor (*News Clerk*); Lee Phelps (*Desk Clerk*); Clarence Wilson (*Jeweler*); Wilbur Mack; Bess Flowers.*

THE PICTURE BEGINS WITH Mrs. Fendley and James in a chauffeur-driven car on a busy New York street. An older woman, and wife of a wealthy man, Mrs. Fendley has taken James as her gigolo. James lives at the Hotel Metropole, and enjoys the finer things in life, partially financed by Mrs. Fendley. In order to avoid suspicion, she gives him jewelry — instead of cash or a check — which he then pawns for cash.

Rachel, Mrs. Fendley's daughter, also takes a romantic interest in James. "I've been looking forward to substituting for Mother for months," she tells him. For some reason, she wants to marry him.

The Fendleys have a birthday party for Rachel, and Norma is one of the guests.

"Who's that man?" Norma asks her aunt.

"That's Jamie Darricott, this year's ladies' man."

Later James asks Norma if he can show her New York. "Somehow I think your New York and my New York are different," she says. He makes a date, but when he arrives at her hotel, he's told she's checked out and left a note for him. "Mr. Darricott — You didn't really believe you could order me around, did you? I'm leaving for home, as I told I would, at seven thirty. Au revoir — or is it goodbye? N.P."

He hurries to the train station. She's waiting. "Now," she tells him, smiling, "if you still want to show me your New York...." They go off, arm in arm.

"Is this an automobile or a bedroom?" Norma asks as they drive around New York in Mrs. Fendley's car. When Mrs. Fendley and Rachel realize he's seeing Norma, they get steamed and make a few scenes. For some reason, this doesn't scare off Norma. She asks James about his background.

"Norma, since I can remember anything, I remember being picked up by women. By and by, I learned that I could make money by it." He tells Norma he loves her. "I've fallen into the clouds. Heaven help me when I start to drop," he tells her.

"You don't have to drop if you don't want to."

Meanwhile, Mr. Fendley learns about his wife's jewelry, and then Rachel shows up at his office. "It's Mother and Jamie Darricott," she tells Dad. "You've got to do something about them. They're making a fool out of you. Dad, you ought to kill Jamie Darricott."

Mr. Fendley explains that he trusts his wife, but becomes angry when he discovers James has also romanced Rachel. Meanwhile, James promises Norma he'll tell Mrs. Fendley he's through, and repay her for all the gifts.

"When you tell her, don't be unkind, will you?" Norma asks.

There's one last ball James needs to attend with Mrs. Fendley. He's playing Potemkin to Mrs. Fendley's Catherine. After that, he and Norma will marry. Mr. Fendley arrives when his wife is dressing for the ball. "I have an idea that I owe him something for what he's done for you," Fendley says darkly.

Mrs. Fendley phones Darricott and warns him. The elaborate ball begins, complete with ridiculous costumes, powdered wigs, and other hoopla.

Mrs. Fendley arrives at James' apartment, and finds Norma there.

"Miss Page and I are going to be married," he tells Mrs. Fendley. "Goodbye, dear," James tells Norma, "just this once, and then it'll never be goodbye again."

After Norma leaves, Mrs. Fendley threatens to kill him if he marries Norma. Mr. Fendley arrives, and asks his wife to leave. He shows James the pawned jewelry. Norma phones James from the lobby. Fendley pulls a gun. "I can conceive of nothing, Mr. Darricott," Fendley says over the ringing telephone, "that could come to you over the telephone that would be of importance to you. Nothing."

James turns off the light and tries to escape. There's a struggle for the gun. The fight continues to the balcony until James is thrown to his death. Mr. Fendley, shaken, arrives at the ball. He slowly approaches his wife and puts a bracelet on her wrist. "I will lead the grand march, Mrs. Fendley. Mr. Darricott has found it impossible to appear." Fendley motions for the orchestra to begin.

Meanwhile, a crowd has gathered outside the hotel. An ambulance arrives, and police find Mr. Fendley at the march. "Wait," one says to the other. "Let him have his fun. He can't get away."

Norma stands outside, crying over James' body. "What's the matter with you, sister?" someone asks Norma. "Were you in love with him, too? I'm sorry."

"You don't have to be sorry for me. He loved me. They can't ever take that away from me," she says, looking directly into the camera.

Kay started working on this film on November 17, 1930. The studio called her in for retakes in late February 1931. Second-billed, she plays another society woman amidst trashy upper class. The movie is fairly slow-moving until Kay's character hits the scene (at around the twenty-two minute-mark), immensely helping this tawdry tale. She's very good in this role, and the bantering between her and Powell is entertaining. Unfortunately, there are few close-ups, and her hairstyle is sort of a helmet-do, which, *fortunately*, didn't last long.

The film was based on a 1930 Rupert Hughes novel. The society family's name was Alexander,

Kay Francis in beige chiffon and gold lace in *Ladies' Man* (1931).

This is a price list from the pressbook for *Ladies' Man*. Exhibitors used this to order publicity materials. Today these cards, posters, and stills are worth a small fortune.

not Fendley, in the novel. Director Lothar Mendes, who'd been brought from New York to make this movie, also appeared as an extra. Paul Lukas was originally slated for the William Powell role. Then he was to play a supporting role. Finally, he was removed from the cast altogether to star in *Buy Your Woman*—which would have co-starred Kay, but apparently was never made.

REVIEWS: The review in *Time* (May 11, 1931)

explained that this was Powell's last film for Paramount, and it appeared the studio put little effort into the production. "The scene in which he [Powell] lies crushed to death on the pavement is the end of his life in Paramount pictures. From now on he will work for Warner and there are indications in *Ladies' Man* that the deal had already been completed and that the producers had lost interest in Powell — indications in the dialog, construction and directing of a carelessness rare in Paramount pictures, usually so exacting in the matter of craftsmanship."

"William Powell's intelligent performance as the fashionable gigolo and some comparatively grown-up dialogue by Herman J. Mankiewicz save the picture." (*New York Times*, May 1, 1931)

"Beautiful settings, an unusually adroit cast, and no end of lovely gowns give the picture a high production value. It entertains, too, but there are so many pleasant subjects which could have been just as entertaining. Kay Francis completes the feminine triumvirate as the woman Powell really loves. Her role, the least showy of all, is the most human in the story." (Marquis Busby, *Los Angeles Examiner*, May 1, 1931)

"Unsympathetic motivation and disagreeable theme makes this poor entertainment. It's all very depressing, disagreeable and lacks logic." (*Film Daily*, May 3, 1931)

"There is not one sympathetic character in the entire picture. William Powell's portrayal of the gigolo is contemptible from start to finish. Kay Francis is an object of disgust because she permits the gigolo to pick her up and then falls in love with him like all the other women." (Elizabeth Yeaman, *Hollywood Daily Citizen*, May 29, 1931)

The Vice Squad
(Paramount, 1931), 78 min.
Released on June 5, 1931.

Credits: Director, John Cromwell; story, Oliver H.P. Garrett; original music, Rudolph G. Kopp, Ralph Rainger; sound, E. C. Sullivan; camera, Charles Lang; second camera, Robert Pittack, Frank Titus; assistant camera, Cliff Shirpser, Russell Harland; still photographer, Ray Jones.

Cast: Paul Lukas (Stephen Lucarno/Tony); Kay Francis (Alice Morrison); Judith Wood/Helen Johnson (Madeleine Hunt); William B. Davidson (Magistrate Tom Morrison); Rockliffe Fellowes (Detective Sergeant Mather); Esther Howard (Josie); Monte Carter (Max Miller); G. Pat Collins (Pete); Phil Tead (Tony); Davison Clark (Doctor); Tom Wilson (Court Attendant); James Durkin (Second Magistrate); William Arnold (Prosecutor); Lynton Brent (Court Clerk); Juliette Compton (Ambassador's Wife); Irving Bacon.

THE FILM OPENS WITH this notice: "This story attempts to show how Vice Squads, designed to make our communities more moral, have in many American cities done the very opposite. The methods of old-fashioned Vice Squad must go! The great majority of policemen resent its ruthless treatment of women and girls, trapped by paid 'stool pigeons' in situations which appear to justify their arrest."

Stephen is in a parked car with an ambassador's wife, explaining to her that he's marrying someone else. During their rendezvous, a police officer tells them he's going to take their names. The woman panics and runs him down. Stephen refuses to identify the woman. At a party at the embassy, where he's supposed to announce his engagement to Alice, he instead tells her they'll have to put off the engagement.

A crooked cop offers a deal. He'll call the incident an accident if Stephen agrees to be a stool pigeon who entraps young woman. Two years pass. A judge in one of the cases turns out to be Tom, Stephen's friend, and Alice's brother. A girl on trial accuses Stephen of being a stool pigeon. Tom laughs and asks Stephen into his chambers, hoping to find out why he vanished two years ago and also to arrange a meeting with Alice. Stephen sneaks out. The crooked cop scolds him for being seen in court.

"I don't want your money," Stephen says. "Keep it. I've had enough. Dirty, stinking business."

The cop threatens him with a murder charge if he stops cooperating. "Go on," the cop says, "and get drunk like you usually do."

Madeleine, an aspiring writer, lives in the Village with her bohemian artist girlfriend, Josie. She befriends Stephen and prevents his suicide. "I'm afraid I'm not worth all this," he tells her.

Madeleine is horrified at his living conditions. "Of all the bare, desolate holes," she mutters, seeing his room.

Kay with Paul Lukas in *The Vice Squad* (1931). His romantic advances were unappreciated by Kay when they first met on the set of *Illusion* (1929).

Meanwhile, Josie brings a doctor. "He's half-starved. He's been drinking his meals too long."

When Madeleine leaves, she runs into the dirty cop. He assumes she's a prostitute and makes a pass at her. "It would pay you to play ball with me, sister. In your business." She slaps him. The cop assigns Stephen to 21 Cristobal Street — Madeleine's apartment. When Stephen arrives, they're both surprised.

He immediately leaves and tells the cops. "This girl. She's not that kind. No evidence."

The cops tell him he's through for the night. After he leaves, they arrest Madeleine for vagrancy. Stephen runs into the judge again, and this time Tom makes him come inside where he sees Alice, who tries to help Stephen, but he tries to leave again. "You can't keep doing this sort of thing to me," she tells him. There's a beautifully filmed scene in the shadows when she tells him she loves him. "I always have." She convinces Stephen that Tom will not convict Madeleine, and begs him not to go to court. Stephen tells her he must, and they go together. Madeleine tells her story in court, but because the supporting witness — Stephen — won't testify, the judge states, "I have no alternative except to find her guilty. Step down, please."

Stephen steps forward. Shocked, Tom asks Stephen to take the stand. He admits he was a stool pigeon. Alice lowers her head and stalks out; she's through. Stephen identifies all the police officers he's worked with. Maddy is released.

Stephen disappears from the courtroom, but Maddy finds him in a cab and climbs in with him. "I'd love to go nowhere," she says, after asking him where he's going. "I've always wondered where that was."

Josie looks into the cab. "Hey, stop that," she says and then tells the cabbie to take them to a park. The taxi drives off.

Kay is second-billed — and again paired with director John Cromwell — but this isn't a big role. Cromwell was an excellent director for her, but the juicy part in this picture is Judith Wood's. This film marked the first time the actress formerly known as Helen Johnson used her new name. Sort of a cross between Kim Novak and Ann Harding in the looks department, her performance was subtle and interesting. She's very good, and it's difficult to understand why she never became a big star, though it might be blamed on a 1931 car accident which required months of recuperation. Wood herself later suggested it was due to her romantic adventures. She was involved with many men, including Franchot Tone, William Powell, and Robert Montgomery. "I was what we'd now call a liberated woman. Of course, they called it something else, much less polite, in those days." After Hollywood, she married a British diplomat (the son of *Beau Geste* author R.C. Wynn) and was a spy in Japan just before World War II started. After her divorce, she acted on radio and considered becoming a film director but found the door closed to women. Eventually, Wood found yet another career, this time as a costume designer — "everything from operas to porno films." In an interview late in life, Wood struck a melancholy tone. In regards to men, she said, "You might call them my real career — certainly wasn't a sideline. I never played this part on screen, but I was a strong, intelligent woman searching for a man to look up to. My entire life has been a near-miss!"[30]

Paramount briefly considering starring Fay Wray in Kay's role — this was shortly after Kay signed her Warner Bros. contract, and Paramount was not happy. Lilyan Tashman, too, was considered for Kay's role.

A question that lingers: Why did Stephen have to ring in order to gain entrance to Madeleine's apartment, but the vice squad simply showed up at her door?

REVIEWS: "Kay Francis does well as Alice Morrison." (*New York Times*, June 6, 1931)

"The picture reveals a new actress of much merit — Judith Wood, formerly known on the screen as Helen Johnson. Here is a young lady who is destined to go far — if given half a chance. Paul Lukas, although his role is extremely difficult, manages to put a sincere note to everything he does. He is aided by Kay Francis in her most splendid fashion, but seen much too briefly on the screen." (*Los Angeles Evening Herald*, June 5, 1931)

"Miss Francis' new coiffure is again a handicap, otherwise she stands up as always." (*Variety*, June 9, 1931)

Transgression
(RKO, 1931) 72 min.
Released on June 12, 1931.

Credits: Producer, William LeBaron; director, Herbert Brenon; based on the novel, "The Next Corner" by Kate Jordan; adaptation, Elizabeth Meehan; dialogue, Benn Levy; original music, Max Steiner; sound, John E. Tribby; camera, Leo Tover; assistant director, Ray Lissnerr; assistant to assistant director, Sammy Fuller; costumes and set design, Max Ree; editor, Arthur Roberts.

Cast: Kay Francis (Elsie Maury); Paul Cavanagh (Robert Maury); Ricardo Cortez (Don Arturo); Nance O'Neil (Honora Maury); John St. Polis (Serafin); Adrienne d'Ambricourt (Julie); Cissy Fitzgerald (Countess Longueval); Doris Lloyd (Paula Vrain); Agostino Borgato (Carlos); Ruth Weston (Viscountess); Alphonse De Cruz; Alphonse Ethier; Chris-Pin Martin; Rolfe Sedan.

THE PICTURE BEGINS AT an English mansion. Dowdily dressed, Elsie brings husband Robert a flower from their garden. "Lest you forget."

Mining engineer Robert travels to Bombay, while Elsie waits in Paris. While there, Elsie goes from dowdy to delightful. She gets the glamour treatment, and the hausfrau is turned into a hottie who drinks and flirts with Don Arturo.

"In exactly four minutes," she tells him, "you'll vanish. Just like that." She holds a cigarette to a balloon and pops it.

"Even after last night?" he asks. "That ride in the dawn? And your lips for the first time?"

"It all seems so ugly this morning." Elsie receives word that her husband is arriving that night. When Robert arrives — they've been apart for a year — he's shocked at her glamorous appearance. She's also become cold and aloof. They agree to return to England in a week.

Elsie travels to Don Arturo's house in Spain, intending to meet friend Paula. However, Paula never arrives, and Don Arturo uses the opportunity to seduce her. She likes it. "Oh, Arturo, love me like this always."

After the seduction, Elsie decides to leave

Robert and sends him a letter. "I've asked him to divorce me. That letter should be sufficient evidence."

After dinner, Don Arturo gives her a ring and starts to lead her upstairs. They're interrupted by an old man, the father of Maria, a 16-year-old girl who died having Arturo's child. There's a struggle, and the old man kills Arturo.

"That letter! I must get that letter!" Elsie is frantic. Ashamed of her behavior, she throws away the ring, and tries to return to England before the letter reaches Robert.

"Separations are dangerous things, my dear," Robert tells her, noticing her odd behavior. "We've both changed. We've grown apart. It isn't too late to start again, is it? I couldn't bear to lose you."

She asks him to be patient. Honora, Robert's spinster aunt, who doesn't like Elsie, notices Elsie eagerly awaiting the mail. Elsie receives a letter from Paula, but accidentally drops a newspaper clipping.

Honora finds it:

Mystery Woman in Marques' Murder
Dark English Beauty Escaped From Villa
Nobleman's Relatives Hush Scandal

Honora stalks off with a determined look and hands the clipping to Robert. "Read this."

"My wife is not that sort of woman," Robert claims. Honora accuses Elsie of being the dark beauty. Robert asks Honora to apologize.

"It's not the kind of house any decent woman would want to stay," Honora says, announcing that she's leaving.

Don Arturo's servant Seraphin arrives and asks Elsie to convince Robert to go in on a financial deal with him — or he'll tell Robert about the affair. Seraphin has the letter. "It has never left my wallet."

Elsie refuses. "You can threaten me with a dozen letters like that before I'll let you cheat my husband! Oh, I've been wrong. I know that. This may break up my home! It probably will! But he shall know who you are the moment he enters this room!"

Robert has been listening. "I'll take that letter, señor," he says, forcibly taking it. Robert hands it to Elsie.

She gives it back. "I want you to read it," she says. Robert opens it. It's blank. Elsie realizes

In this scene from *Transgression* (1931), Kay has returned to husband Paul Cavanagh and been forgiven for a brief but torrid affair with Ricardo Cortez.

Arturo burned her letter. "Robert, I want to tell you what was in that letter."

He shushes her, shakes his head. "No, my dearest, that's all over. It never was. Like the letter that tortured you. Nothing. Nothing at all."

She leans her head on his shoulder. "I love you so," she says.

The picture is melodramatic claptrap, but it doesn't try to be something it's not. Though Kay is top-billed, this is not her best acting. It is, however, a typical Kay Francis performance: She suffers, wears gorgeous gowns, is radiantly beautiful, makes a tragic mistake, and is ultimately loved by a wonderful man.

Based on Kate Jordan's 1921 novel, the film was a remake of *The Next Corner* (1924), directed by Sam Wood. That cast included Conway Tearle, Ricardo Cortez, and Lon Chaney.

Dorothy Mackaill played Kay's part. There was also a 1924 French film based on the same source, *Nuit d'Espagne*. Before *Transgression* was decided upon, the working titles included *The Next Corner* and *Around the Corner*.

Kay was borrowed from Paramount, and Cavanagh from Fox. There's a discrepancy about who played Countess Longueval. Some sources claim it's Cissy Fitzgerald, while others credit Ruth Weston. Nance O'Neil was a close friend — and rumored lover — of Lizzie Borden in the early 1900s.

REVIEWS: "Miss Francis gives a clear portrayal." (*New York Times*, June 15, 1931)

"Kay Francis' display of beautiful gowns and negligees, Ricardo Cortez's smooth reading and Herbert Brenon's distinguished direction give this production audience appeal, notwithstanding the familiar theme and talkative story." (*Film Daily*, June 7, 1931)

"The pangs of this illicit passion call upon Kay Francis, as the wife, for distraught emotions all through the picture. The pain of it all was never more vividly set forth. If you have known her chiefly for gay, seductive parts, the novelty of this overemotionalized role might intrigue." (W.E. Oliver, *Los Angeles Evening Herald*, July 31, 1931)

"Herbert Brenon has provided the most lavish of backgrounds for his directorial effort, and lovers of exquisite architecture and scenic beauty will revel in the Spanish and English settings that enhance this piece." (Eleanor Barnes, *Los Angeles Illustrated Daily News*, July 31, 1931)

"Cast is average as a group, except for a tendency to underact, an unusual fault. Kay Francis, aside from other things, was also given opportunity in situations and dialog. But even she seemed held down." (*Variety*, June 16, 1931)

Guilty Hands

(Metro-Goldwyn-Mayer, 1931) 60 min.
Released on August 28, 1931.

Credits: Producer-supervisor, Hunt Stromberg; directors, W.S. Van Dyke, Lionel Barrymore; story-screenplay, Bayard Veiller; camera, Merritt B. Gerstad; editor, Anne Bauchens; wardrobe, Rene Hubert; musical director, William Axt; recording director, Douglas Shearer; assistant director, Al Shenberg; art director, Cedric Gibbons; original music, L. Andrieu, Domenico Savino.

Cast: Lionel Barrymore (Richard Grant); Kay Francis (Marjorie West); Madge Evans (Barbara Grant); William Bakewell (Tommy Osgood); C. Aubrey Smith (Reverend Hastings); Polly Moran (Aunt Maggie); Alan Mowbray (Gordon Rich); Forrester Harvey (Spencer Wilson); Charles Crockett (H. G. Smith); Henry Barrows (Harvey Scott); Sam McDaniel (Jimmy); Robert McKenzie (Second Man on Train); Blue Washington (Johnny).

THE PICTURE STARTS WITH Richard Grant discussing the morality of murder. "I believe that under certain circumstances, murder is justifiable." For ten years, he was a New York district attorney, and is now in private practice. He meets with Gordon Rich, who wants a new will. Gordon, a cad who's gone through a string of young girls, also announces that he's getting married — to Richard's daughter.

Richard tells him he won't allow his daughter to marry him. "You ought to have been killed years ago. You're no good, you know. The world would be much better off without you."

Gordon threatens to retaliate if Richard tries to stop him. "After I'm dead, I'll get you," Gordon prophetically warns him.

"Meet you in Hell," are Richard's parting words.

Turns out Babs, Richard's daughter, has become obsessed with Gordon and broken things off with Tommy, a more suitable, if bland, suitor. Richard tries to talk Babs out of marriage with Gordon. "Barbara, this man you want to marry is a beast about women. I mean that literally. He's just like an animal. So your wedding night, instead of being a thing of beauty that you'll remember all your life long with great happiness, will be a horror and a shame!"

She doesn't believe him and won't change her mind. Meanwhile, Marjorie, Gordon's girlfriend, is unhappy to learn of the marriage. "That child. A mere child," she scolds.

Gordon tells her he must marry Babs in order to have her. "In her case, it's got to be marriage." Gordon reminds Marjorie that he's always returned to her.

Before Gordon retires for the night, he meets with his servants and asks them to inform him if Richard leaves his bungalow. A storm (of course) begins raging. Richard enters his bungalow, and the servants watch his shadow pace in the window. When Gordon says goodnight to Babs, he manhandles her, making her cry. After everyone has gone to their rooms,

Richard jumps out of his bungalow window. The servants, however, continue to watch the "shadow" in the window.

Gordon is at his desk writing a note: "To the Police, My life has been threatened by Richard Grant. If I am found dead, he has killed me. Gordon Rich."

Richard comes through Gordon's window, takes the gun from the desk, and shoots him. A crack of thunder obscures the sound. Richard places the gun in Gordon's hand. Richard spies the letter to the police and picks it up.

"Darling, I want to see you," Marjorie says, outside the locked door. In a matter of moments, someone screams, "Murder!"

After the body is discovered, Richard leads the investigation. He concludes that Gordon committed suicide.

"I say he didn't kill himself! I say he was murdered!" Marjorie screams. (Kay, like Constance Bennett and Ruth Chatterton, often used a professional screamer named Alice Doll.)

The servants come in, explaining that while instructed to watch Richard's bungalow, they heard Marjorie scream. "It certainly sounded like you, Miss," one says. "Goodness knows, I heard you often enough."

They further attest to the fact that Richard paced all night. Babs later Babs asks her father if he killed Gordon. "Gordon Rich was entirely responsible for his own death," he tells her. He also informs Babs of a 16-year-old who committed suicide because of Gordon. "I think he killed himself to rid himself of the memory of those women."

Babs confides that she'd changed her mind about marrying Gordon that night. Richard laughs ruefully. "Just a little joke of my own. You wouldn't understand it."

Meanwhile, Marjorie goes to Richard's bungalow and finds Richard's phonograph ingenuously rigged up with a light and paper so it appears a person's shadow is in the window. She returns to Gordon's room. "Gordon," she says, "I've got him! I just had to come back and tell you. Bye, my dear." She sobs, and then reapplies her makeup at the desk. A loud clap of thunder — yes, it's *still* storming — causes her to spill her makeup. She wipes it away, revealing the indentation of Gordon's letter to the police. Triumphant, she grabs up the blotter.

Suddenly, Richard is behind her, covering

Kay Francis comfortably resting in her "favourite room" in the early 1930s. This illustration was featured in the book *The Film Lovers Annual*.

her mouth. "It's true. I killed him." He tells her she's a beneficiary in the will, and he intends to convince the police she's the murderer. "I swear I'll send you to the electric chair!"

A police boat siren sounds. It's dawn. Richard sends her out of the room, and tears up what remains of the blotter. The chief of police, a friend of Richard's, examines the body. An accompanying doctor explains rigor mortis. "It's a medical term for the hardening and stiffening of muscles after death. You can almost see the fingers tighten. In this case, it's very far advanced. In a few minutes, I couldn't bend the arm like this." Everyone agrees Gordon committed suicide. Marjorie tries to tell her story, but the gun, still clutched by Gordon, goes off. The bullet strikes Richard's chest.

"You did it, Rich. I didn't think you could," Richard utters before collapsing.

The police chief asks what Marjorie was going to say. "I don't know, chief. I just can't remember ... now." She smiles and gleefully throws back her head.

Kay Francis appeared in *Guilty Hands* (1931) with Lionel Barrymore, Madge Evans, C. Aubrey Smith, and Alan Mowbray. This illustration was featured in the book *The Film Lovers Annual*.

Though second-billed, Kay's part is small. It's a nice role, though, as Marjorie is smart, morally questionable, knowing, sophisticated, and grief-stricken when evil boyfriend Gordon Rich is murdered. A little too many crazed looks from Kay in a less-than-subtle performance, but still an interesting role as the bad girl. (She does *not*, however, convincingly play "Believe Me If All Those Endearing Young Charms" on the harp in the after-dinner scene.) Madge is beautiful as the virginal, sweet girl seduced by Gordon, but her character is less complex than Kay's. The role was a tour de force for Barrymore, though he could be a bit hammy.

The film's original title was *Shadows on the Wall*. Production started June 4 and concluded June 22, 1931. No wonder director Van Dyke's nickname was One-Take. Advertising proclaimed: "They both knew how he had met his death! Why didn't they tell?" and "Mystery ... chills ... an ending that you'll never guess!"

REVIEWS: "Kay Francis plays well." (*New York Times*, August 29, 1931)

"Murder theme with unusual plot makes strong dramatic fare, with Lionel Barrymore giving splendid performance." (*Film Daily*, August 30, 1931)

"One of the best murder yarns produced, in which Lionel Barrymore gives an excellent and polished performance.... Kay Francis and Madge Evans also contribute excellent performances." (*Photoplay*, September 1931)

"Kay Francis is splendid as the friend of the murdered man. It is not an easy role, but Miss Francis is always believable in the emotional fireworks." (Marquis Busby, *Los Angeles Examiner*, September 3, 1931)

"Barrymore stands out all over, never once permitting anyone to chisel in an inch near him. Nearest is Kay Francis who flounders for a few minutes, but is quickly rescued by Barrymore's biggest scene." (*Variety*, September 1, 1931)

"Kay Francis ... is hardly surpassed by Mr. Barrymore in her remarkably convincing performance as the dead man's champion, and Madge Evans is perfectly delightful as the daughter." (*Picture Play*, December 1931)

24 Hours

(Paramount, 1931) 65 min.
Released October 2, 1931.

Credits: Director, Marion Gering; associate director, Dudley Murphy; based on the novel by Louis Bromfield and the play by William C. Lengle, Lew Levenson; screenplay, Louis Weltzenkorn; camera, Ernest Haller.

Cast: Clive Brook (Jim Towner); Kay Francis (Fanny Towner); Miriam Hopkins (Rosie Dugan); Regis Toomey (Tony Bruzzi); George Barbier (Hector Champion); Adrienne Ames (Ruby Wintringham); Lucille La Verne (Mrs. Dacklehorst); Wade Boteler (Pat Healy); Minor Watson (David Melbourn); Charlotte Granville (Savina Jerrold); Bob Kortman (Dave the Slapper); Malcolm Waite (Murphy); Thomas E. Jackson (Police Commissioner); Charles D. Brown (Detective); Mary Gordon (Nurse); Robert Homans (Police Official); Nicholas Kobliansky (Extra); Imboden Parrish (Extra); Virginia Pickering (Baby); Ben Taggart (Detective).

THE FILM BEGINS IN front of a clock in snowy New York City. We're taken inside a luxurious city house and a society party. Fanny looks bored, jaded. Husband Jim is also bored, jaded—and drunk. Fanny complains about their marriage and his drinking. "Nothing we can say to each other any more. We wore marriage out at the elbows," she comments when Jim takes another drink.

"Just where did it go off the track?" he asks.

"Oh, so much has happened, Jim. You've done so much to me. Oh, I guess I've done rotten things to you."

Jim leaves without Fanny and talks to doorman Pat, who mentions his wife will have the baby any day. He also mentions that Rosie Dugan is his sister—he doesn't realize she's Jim's mistress—and the baby, if a girl, will be named after her. The wind is whistling, the snow blowing.

After a shooting outside a speakeasy, Jim walks up to the building and sees blood in the snow. He goes inside and has a quick drink.

Fanny has left the party with David. In the cold taxi, she writes "David" with her finger on the window condensation, and then writes her name underneath it. "You know," she says, "I thought I was in love with you. I find I'm really in love with Jim." She writes Jim's name in the window. "I'm damaged goods. I won't hand bargains across the counter to my husband. As for you, that's as finished as last year's snow." She tells David she saw him pass a note to Mrs. Wintringham at the party. "She's your kind," she adds.

At the speakeasy, Jim overhears men talking

about the murder, identifying the killer as Tony. Back home, Fanny knocks on Jim's door but finds he's not in. She stands in front of her wedding picture. "Here Comes the Bride" comes on the soundtrack. Fanny cries out for Jim. This mawkish touch is unusual for the usually subtle film.

Jim goes to Rosie's, a speakeasy. Rosie sings "I'm Yours for the Taking," and then sits with Jim. "It's a funny world," Rosie tells him. "You've got everything people want. I've got everything I wanted to have. Both of us ain't got nothing. Let's have another drink!" She asks him to come home with her, and then excuses herself to talk to no-good husband Tony. He wants her to take him back. She discovers a gun on him and keeps it. "I know what happened at Jake's Place tonight. I know the snow was red," she says. She has a bouncer toss Tony out, sings another torch song, and goes home with Jim.

Rosie leads a drunken Jim to the sofa where he stretches out. While he sleeps, she puts on a loud record. Rosie calls to check on her brother and wife, and asks to be called when the baby's born. Tony comes in. They struggle, and Tony kills her. The music keeps playing. When the phone rings, Tony runs out of the apartment.

Jim awakens, breaks down Rosie's door, and discovers her body. He hurriedly leaves, but is seen by Pat. Meanwhile, Tony is holed up at the Valparaiso Hotel. He asks Mrs. Dacklehorst to deliver a note — and bring back a hot meal. "When I come back, I'll bring you something hot. Real hot. Something that'll warm you up," she tells him. She returns, hands him a cup, and says, "There, Tony. Here's something hot for you." He takes the cup and is shot in the face.

Fanny reads a newspaper headline: "Millionaire Arrested on Charge of Killing Noted Night Club Girl." She tosses it down. The rest of the headline reads:

James Morton Towner, Wealthy Clubman, Held in East 22nd Street Police Station
Clue in Emerald Shirt Studs
Official Believe He Strangled Rosie Dugan, Night Club Singer

Fanny hurries to the police station to support her husband.

When fingerprints found on a liquor bottle in Fanny's room match Tony's, Jim is released, but sends Fanny away. "When I sent her away just now, I sent away the greatest woman I've ever known," he says.

In the final scene, Fanny arrives on Jim's ship. "I'm drunk, Fanny," he tells her.

"I know. I don't care if you're drunk or sober, Jim. I want to tell you this. If Rosie Dugan loved you drunk, I love you drunk. If Rosie Dugan loved you sober, I love you sober. I love you always, Jim." She agrees to have a drink with him. "We were so happy once, Jim. So beautifully happy. I just want to ask you one question. Do you love me?"

Jim quotes Rosie: "The one that gets there first is always first. Let's drink to my last drink," Jim says. The glasses clank together, the ship's horn sounds, and the clock chimes.

Kay was second-billed in this film about remarkably unhappy people. It contains sharply written dialogue, and is beautifully filmed. It's a good film to watch on a hot, humid day as the snowy scenes will definitely chill you. It also offers an opportunity to see beautiful art deco buildings and sets. By the way, the clock that plays such a prominent role in the film is

Kay models an elegant hostess gown designed by Travis Banton for *24 Hours* (1931).

modeled after the one that sits atop the Paramount Building in Times Square.

Unfortunately, the film has a pretty bad ending after an hour of excellence. One of the best performances is given by Miriam Hopkins; this is a good one to see her in.

This film (titled *The Hours Between* in the United Kingdom) was based on popular Ohio novelist Louis Bromfield's 1930 novel. Bromfield became a close friend of Kay's; she stopped at his farmhouse in 1948 on her way back to New York after her burn injuries. Lucille LaVerne, who played Mrs. Dacklehorst, was an actress Kay admired from her New York stage days.

In April 1931, when it was announced that *24 Hours* would go into production, Wynne Gibson was cast in Miriam Hopkins' role, and David Burton, George Abbott, and Dudley Murphy were slated as directors. Kay's first day on the set was July 2, 1931.

Advertising copy proclaimed: "A lifetime of thrills in two turns of the clock! New York ... where life says, 'Hurry, Hurry!' and no man knows today what woman will be swept into his arms—and out again—tomorrow! Where cruelty and love, hatred and romance do double time! Where a generation of excitement is packed into *24 Hours*."

REVIEWS: "Makes an interesting diversion. Those who hope to see more ideas from the book may be disappointed, but they will not be disappointed in the acting." (*New York Times*, October 3, 1931)

"Miriam Hopkins, as the cabaret entertainer, walks away with the entire picture in our opinion." (Dan Thomas, *Los Angeles Record*, September 12, 1931)

"Kay Francis is not the charmer she used to be. Perhaps that isn't fair. It is obvious she is minus the good roles in which she first attracted attention." (Jimmy Starr, *Los Angeles Evening Herald*, October 2, 1931)

"The picture is not as forceful and gripping as its potentialities promise. Kay Francis as the society woman is alluring and poised as ever, and brings great sincerity and feeling in her role." (Harriet Parsons, *Los Angeles Examiner*, October 2, 1931)

"Clive Brook, Kay Francis and Miriam Hopkins give well-toned performances." (*Time*, October 12, 1931)

"Her part doesn't give Miss Francis much of an acting opportunity, but the very vividness of her style and personality somehow manage to make her a positive individuality." (*Variety*, October 6, 1931)

Girls About Town

(Paramount, 1931) 80 min.
Released on October 30, 1931.

Credits: Associate producer, Raymond Griffith; director, George Cukor; story, Zoë Akins; screenplay, Raymond Griffith, Brian Marlow; camera, Ernest Haller; costumes, Travis Banton; second camera, Don Keyes, Frank Titus; assistant camera, George Bourne, Ellsworth Fredericks; still photography, Frank Bjerring.

Cast: Kay Francis (Wanda Howard); Joel McCrea (Jim Baker); Lilyan Tashman (Marie Bailey); Eugene Pallette (Benjamin Thomas); Alan Dinehart (Jerry Chase); Lucile Webster Gleason (Mrs. Benjamin Thomas); Anderson Lawler (Alex Howard); Lucille Browne (Edna); George Barbier (Webster); Robert McWade (Simms); Judith Wood (Winnie); Adrienne Ames (Anne); Katherine DeMille (Girl); Patricia Caron (Billie); Claire Dodd (Dot); Hazel Howard (Joy); Louise Beavers (Hattie); Sheila Bromley, Veda Buckland (Girls).

THE CREDITS RUN OVER a montage of fashionable girls partying, accompanied by upbeat, jazzy music. Jerry sets up men with female escorts—you probably know where we're going here. Wanda and Marie are two of his best girls. We see lots of dancing, drinking, laughing, and an occasional grim face from the girls. At the end of the evening, the girls are beat and convince the men it's not a good idea to come up. Their maid puts on a wig and sits by the window, pretending to be their elderly mother.

"I'm getting pretty fed up with all this," Wanda tells her friend. Lilyan still likes the money—they've each received a check from Jerry for $500. When the maid awakens them at 5:30 in the afternoon, they each have special requests.

"Grapefruit juice and some aspirin," Wanda orders, climbing into bed with Marie.

"Bromo Seltzer and the evening paper," Marie requests.

Jerry invites Wanda and Marie to his yacht where they're introduced to Jim Baker and Benjamin Thomas. Wanda pairs off with Jim, and Marie with Benjamin. Jim tells Wanda he knows being nice to him is part of her racket. They play around and kiss. Soon she's lying in his arms. "I might go serious on you, Jim." He asks her to go away with him, and then explains he was only kidding. They pretend some more. "I love you!" they shout back and forth until it becomes painful.

Wanda finds she has fallen in love. They're paid, and Wanda tears up her check. "Imagine getting a thousand dollars for falling in love," she says. When Jim asks her to marry him, she tells him she's already married, but will ask for a divorce. Husband Alex — played by Kay's old friend Anderson Lawler — agrees.

Meanwhile, Benjamin's matronly wife pays Marie a visit. She and Marie bond, and Marie resolves to make Benjamin less stingy. Marie throws a birthday party for Benjamin. Alex shows up at the party, and tells Jim he'll name him as co-respondent in the divorce unless he gets $10,000. Jim writes a check and then punches Alex. The marriage, of course, is off. Wanda visits Alex in Brooklyn to get the money back, but Alex shows her his wife, sick in bed. There's a baby, too.

"You're even lower than I thought," she tells Alex. "Do you think I could hurt those two?" she asks.

Alex admits he got a divorce two years before in Mexico. Wanda lets Alex keep the money, but still wants to pay Jim back. She and Marie decide to have a clothing and jewelry auction. There's a great scene when they sell off their stuff. Judith Wood, the star of *Vice Squad*, plays one of the bidders.

Wanda gets the $10,000, and Marie agrees to return the jewels to Benjamin *if* he agrees to give them to Mrs. Thomas.

"I want to find out how you do it," an intrigued Mrs. Thomas says to Marie.

"Now, Daisy, listen," Benjamin cautions, "you carry on like this, and the first thing you know you'll just turn out to be another one of those girls about town."

Jim asks Wanda to forgive him. They kiss. Benjamin and Mrs. Thomas reconcile, too.

Marie calls Jerry. "My telephone number is still the same. But from now on, I work alone."

Joel McCrea and Kay on location in *Girls About Town* (1931).

Kay Francis and Lilyan Tashman were announced as the stars in March 1931. Kay, who started working on the film on August 14, received top billing. Some scenes were filmed in Catalina, and the film also includes stunning art deco buildings and interior design.

Kay and Lilyan are marvelous in this one. It's a deft comedy, and they work well together, often exchanging knowing looks. Tashman is much more endearing than in *Marriage Playground*, though, according to Kay's diary, Lil was often drunk on the set. Lil's flirtation with Pallette is wonderful — they make a great pair. Kay is completely charming. Cukor should have directed her in dozens of films.

There's a nice scene where Joel and Kay swim. It's an opportunity to see two of Hollywood's most attractive actors in swimwear. In fact, if you look closely, you'll see that Kay's bathing suit is *quite* revealing. There are also scenes where Kay and Lilyan trounce around in pretty lingerie. The Hays Office warned the studio about the excessive use of lingerie as well as the implication that Wanda would not mind being his mistress.

Louise Beavers, Leatrice Joy's maid before she started her film career, has the best lines, but you need to listen closely. "Just a minute, my little lump of coal," she sweetly says to Marie.

Cukor, who directed Zoë Akins' play, "The Furies," on Broadway, had to be careful about the girls' occupation because of the Production Code. "As a result," Cukor commented, "these girls seemed to exist in a kind of never-never land. Although Zoë Akins portrayed them as the high-class tarts that they really were, they were made to appear on the screen as virtuous young ladies rather than as sinners." To that extent, he joked, *Girls About Town* might have been better titled 'The Virtuous Sinners.'"[31]

Advertising copy proclaimed: "A picture for people who call a spade a spade. Unwed but not unwanted ... riding in limousines, but not paying the chauffeurs ... shopping with married men's check books ... beautiful and beguiling ... dancing and flattering ... Goldiggers!— but they DO fall in love! An inside look at life and love as it rages in today's seemingly crazy fashion.... Not a lesson on Modern Morals ... but a story as true and real as next month's rent ... refreshing in its spontaneous humor ... thrilling in daring drama ... inspiring in its love story!"

REVIEWS: "It is burdened in the latter stages by highly improbable serious sequences. George Cukor is responsible for the compelling direction. In some respects it is an excellent fashion show, for both Miss Tashman and Miss Francis avail themselves of every opportunity to appear arrayed in the glory of the latest creations, which include gowns, pajamas and bathing suits. And these actresses, representing the blonde and the brunette, look very attractive." (*New York Times*, November 2, 1931)

"Kay Francis shows off her figure in undies while explaining she's through with the gold-digger racket and intends going straight because she's found love with a rich rube. The undie pose and that bit about going straight all in one has its own satirical kick." (*Variety*, November 3, 1931)

"Amusing but unimportant yarn of gold-diggers gets over principally because the four principals are good. The sets are extravagant, the four principals are clever, and with adroit direction the piece looks far better than it really is on a cold analysis. It will amuse the uncritical and the flappers." (*Film Daily*, November 1, 1931)

"If I had had the scissors I would have trimmed the picture and kept only the fast-moving comedy." (Louella O. Parsons, *Los Angeles Examiner*, October 31, 1931)

The False Madonna

(Paramount, 1931) 72 min.
Released on December 5, 1931.

Credits: Director, Stuart Walker; associate director, Edward D. Venturini; based on the story "The Heart Is Young" by May Edginton; screenplay, Arthur Kober, Ray Harris; dialogue, Arthur Kober; camera, Henry Sharp; camera operators, Otto Pierce, Daniel Fapp; assistant cameras, Paul Cable, Arthur Lane; still photographer, Bert Lynch; original music, Herman Hand, W. Franke Harling, Bernhard Kaun, John Leipold; song, "Roamin' in the Gloamin'" by Sir Harry Lauder.

Cast: Kay Francis (Tina); William "Stage" Boyd (Doctor Ed Marcy); Conway Tearle (Grant Arnold); John Breeden (Phillip Bellows); Marjorie Gateson (Rose); Charles D. Brown (Peter Angel); Julia Swayne Gordon (Dowager); Almeda Fowler (Mrs. Swanson); Kent Taylor (Extra).

ONE RAINY NIGHT, Tina, Ed, Rose, and Peter are asked to leave town. "My order is to get you birds on the 9:30 train," a police officer tells them. Tina announces that she's giving up the criminal life. Her friends scoff, reminding her that she's quit before and returned. "I'm sick of all this cheapness and bickering," she insists. "I want rest and peace."

A train porter asks Ed, a medical doctor, to attend to a sick woman. He discovers she's a Bellows, from a rich banking family. Before the woman succumbs to her illness, Marcy determines that she'd left her husband and child fourteen years before for a Mr. Swanson. Armed with this information, along with a necklace, letters, and photographs, Marcy persuades Tina to pretend to be the woman. "Tina's gonna double for that woman," he explains. "She's going to play the long, lost Madonna to the Bellows' kid." He sees it as a winning proposal all around. "If the millionaire kid doesn't want you, he pays you off. If the boy likes you, all you've got to do is grab as much dough as you can carry."

He finally convinces Tina, and she writes to the son, now 17, and asks if he'd be willing to see her. Phillip eagerly requests that she come to the family home. Tina, dowdily dressed but wearing the necklace, meets Phillip and quickly discovers he's blind from an airplane accident two years before. She also meets the boy's guardian, Grant Arnold, who is the family lawyer. He reminds her they'd met once before, and is suspicious from the start.

Tina tells Ed she's having second thoughts. "Ed, I'd like to drop this. It's the boy," she pleads.

"It's a natural," he insists. "Prepare for the big scene tomorrow," he tells her.

Arnold tells Tina that Phillip is dying. "Any shock, no matter how slight, might finish him," he explains. (One of *those* Hollywood illnesses that is always fatal but with no real symptoms.) Tina and sickeningly sweet Phillip take a tour of the house and gardens, and then Phillip plays the piano and they sing "In the Gloaming" together — Kay sings in her own voice. One of the lines is "When the lights are dim and low...." It bums out Tina, and she stops.

Phillip insists Arnold write Tina a check for

A reflective Kay played an unwilling member of a team of blackmailers in *The False Madonna* (1932).

$50,000. When Phillip leaves the room, Arnold takes the check from Tina and wordlessly tears it up.

Tina concludes she can't go through with the con. Phillip has an attack—"the worst he's ever had"—and asks for his mother. Tina rushes to his bedside.

Arnold begins to have second thoughts about her. "They're very strange," he tells Phillip about Tina's eyes. "At first I thought they were black. There's something mysterious about them. They make you wonder what she's thinking about, and whether you'll ever be allowed to know."

Ed shows up at the estate, and orders her to get the money from Phillip or he'll tell the boy of their scheme. "I'm not grabbing, and I'm not running," Tina says. "As long as I can stay and be what that boy thinks I am, I'm not running." Ed explains he'll return at 10:00 the next morning, which he does. However, by that time, Phillip has died. Tina tells Ed she no longer wants anything to do with him.

Arnold shows up, and tells Ed he knows about his past—he was barred by the medical association, and is wanted for other offenses. He also explains that the real Mrs. Bellows was his former secretary so he knew all along Tina was an imposter.

Ed pulls a gun. "What would you do, Ed?" Tina asks. "Shoot me? Go ahead. I have nothing more to live for now. When I came here, I believed your code. I believed that life was a racket. That it was 'get mine first' because the world owed me what I could grab. I let you talk me into this last job." She goes on a rant. "That boy believed in me. He trusted me. Why, I forgot that such things existed."

Arnold tells Ed that the police are on their way. After a knock on the door, Arnold helps Ed escape out the window. Arnold, however, tells Tina that no police are coming. He also tells her he's fallen in love with her and offers her the proverbial house and garden. "Sometimes the blind can see so much more clearly than we can. Tina, you want a home and peace and love, don't you?" he asks.

"Every woman wants that in her heart."

"I've got a home, too, and a garden and ... well, you know what I mean. Tina, you could make me very happy."

They embrace. It doesn't seem like a recipe for a happy marriage, but there you are.

Kay received top billing, playing a world-weary dame with more of a heart than she knew, but it's a B movie, probably meant to punish her for signing with Warner Bros. This movie has some of her best acting as she gets to play tough and tender. An argument could be made that Kay was miscast. The role called for someone older, and her performance, perhaps as a result, is uneven. Her middle scenes, especially, seem stiff. She does better with the hardened woman scenes early in the picture and the bereaved mother figure near the end.

This is a very tough crowd she hangs out with. In one scene, Peter wins a kewpie doll and asks Rose what he should do with it. "What's the use?" she answers. "You wouldn't do it if I told you."

The film was released as *False Idol* in the United Kingdom. The original working title was *The Heart Is Young*, which was the name of the May Edginton short story that appeared in the March 15, 1930 issue of *Collier's*. Director Stuart Walker is the same Stuart Walker for whom Kay toured in the 1920s.

Kay attended a showing at the newly opened Paramount Theatre in Oakland on December 16, 1931. More than 10,000 arrived for the gala, which included speeches by George Bancroft, John Breeden, Elissa Landi, John Boles, and Frances Dee. In addition, between showings, audience members heard Lou Kisloff's orchestra accompany Fanchon & Marco's stage show. Other acts on the program included Brock and Thompson, Patsy Marr, Sam Hearn, the Seven Arconis, dancer Lavonne Sweet and the Sunkist Beauties chorus line.

REVIEWS: "Miss Francis plays nicely but is miscast." (*Variety*, January 26, 1932)

"If the film were not acted with such quiet sincerity, you'd feel the boy was about to regain his sight and fall in love with the pseudo mother at any moment. *The False Madonna* is not startling melodrama. But it will please wherever it is seen." (W.E. Oliver, *Los Angeles Evening Herald Express*, January 8, 1932)

"Miss Francis, always smartly costumed, and convincing in parts of this type, is up to her standard." (Eleanor Barnes, *Los Angeles Illustrated Daily News*, January 8, 1932)

"Fairly good crook drama with a somewhat touchy story and excellent performances." (*Film Daily*, February 7, 1932)

Strangers in Love

(Paramount, 1932) 68 min. Released on March 5, 1932.

Credits: Director, Lothar Mendes; based on the novel "The Shorn Lamb" by William J. Locke; screenplay, Grover Jones, William Slavens McNutt; camera, Henry Sharp; assistant camera, Al Smalley, Francis Burgess, Warner Cruze; second camera, Warren Lynch; original music, Rudolph G. Kopp, John Leipold, Stephan Pasternacki; still photographer, Earl Crowley; sound, Harold C. Lewis.

Cast: Fredric March (Buddy Drake/Arthur Drake); Kay Francis (Diane Merrow); Stuart Erwin (Stan Keeney); Juliette Compton (Muriel Preston); George Barbier (Mr. Merrow); Sidney Toler (Detective McPhail); Earle Foxe (Mr. Clarke); Lucien Littlefield (Professor Clark); Leslie Palmer (Bronson); Gertrude Howard (Snowball); Ben Taggart (Crenshaw); John M. Sullivan (Dr. Selous).

EGYPTOLOGIST ARTHUR DRAKE employs childhood friend Diane as his secretary. She suspects Arthur has swindled her good-natured father and asks Detective McPhail to help her get the goods on him. Buddy, Arthur's long lost twin, visits him to ask for money. "Doesn't seem possible that two people so physically alike as you and I," Buddy laments, "could be so utterly different in every other respect."

Arthur, who inherited their father's fortune, gives Buddy $1,000 and asks him to leave. When Buddy becomes suspicious, Arthur tears up the check, becomes agitated, and dies from a chronic heart condition.

Buddy decides to become Arthur. Buddy's friend Stan becomes suspicious when he sees Buddy's death notice and investigates. Buddy admits what he's done. "It's a dangerous game, pal," Stan tells him.

"How can they put me in jail? I'm dead?"

Diane finds herself charmed by the "new" Arthur.

"From now on, I'm going to be known as the late Mr. Drake," he announces, explaining he wants to become more spontaneous. Buddy lets his old beloved mammy, Snowball—don't expect racial sensitivity in this one—in on the secret. "I'm back, and I'm Mr. Arthur now."

Snowball tells him that his father called for him before he died. When Muriel, Arthur's girlfriend, shows up at the Drake estate, Buddy asks Snowball for the lowdown. "She's one of them 'come and pleases and go as you pleases' kind," she explains.

Muriel becomes frustrated with "Arthur" and threatens to talk. She asks for a check, which Buddy gives her—and then promptly sends Stan to 141 East 25th Street to get it back. Stan pretends to be an automobile crash victim to get in her apartment. He tells the epic story of his auto accident, gets the check in hand, and hurries out of the apartment. Shortly thereafter, the detective shows up and arrests Muriel and her cohort, Clark. They implicate Arthur in a financial scandal. "We've got enough on him to send him up for life," the detective tells Diane.

Conflicted, Diane gives Drake a heads-up. They kiss. "I'm not Arthur Drake," Buddy admits. Diane and her father plead with him to escape. The detective arrives to arrest him, but Diane turns out the lights, and she, Stan, and Drake escape. A boat chase ensues.

"I've always wanted to be shot at!" Diane gleefully says, enjoying the excitement.

Back at the estate, they dry off in front of the fire, and Buddy learns that he was supposed to have been left half the estate. No charges are filed. Diane and Buddy embrace and kiss.

Kay was second-billed in this last film on her Paramount contract. Hollywood loves twins. In this delightful, charming picture, Fredric March is brilliant in a dual role. This was his first picture after his Oscar-winning *Dr. Jekyll and Mr. Hyde*, and Paramount was eager for him to again play two characters.

Kay appears in many outfits and smokes lots of cigarettes. Too bad March and Francis didn't appear in another film together. Good chance to see Juliette Compton, who didn't get the breaks she deserved. The film was also tentatively titled *The Black Robe* and then *Intimate*. It was based on William J. Locke's *The Shorn Lamb*, which appeared in *Ladies' Home Journal* in the May through August 1930 issues.

REVIEWS: "Miss Francis gets everything possible out of her sec role. She works with a nice restraint throughout, pacing her part with just the proper shading." (*Variety*, March 8, 1932)

"It would be too much to say that the finished product is brilliant or surprising, but it is consistently enjoyable." (*Time*, March 14, 1932)

"Besides the charming and ingratiating Mr. March, who punctuates every scene with

Lobby card for *Strangers in Love* (1932) with Kay, Juliette Compton, and Fredric March (courtesy James King).

thorough deftness, there is Kay Francis adding vividness to an ordinary heroine role. This combination of Francis and March is successful. Both being tall, brunette and somber, they are nice to look at, although neither one has much of a chance to be somber in this." (Harry Mines, *Los Angeles Illustrated Daily News*, February 26, 1932)

"March and Kay Francis ideal team in clever story that has laughs ripping through it." (*Film Daily*, March 6, 1932)

"The star's acting, as well as that of the supporting cast, makes a most interesting picture from this otherwise commonplace melodrama. Kay Francis as the girl is charming. The blonde menace — and what a menace! — is played very effectively by Juliette Compton." (Harry Mines, *Los Angeles Illustrated Daily News*, February 26, 1932)

"Kay Francis as the girl is charming. The dialogue is exceptionally good." (Vance King, *Hollywood Citizen News*, March 18, 1932)

"Though it was pretentious and essentially lightweight fare, the picture did give March a chance to get in some clever characterizational nuances." (Lawrence J. Quirk, *The Films of Fredric March*, p. 83)

Man Wanted
(Warner Bros., 1932) 60 min.
Released on April 15, 1932.

Credits: Director, William Dieterle; story, Robert Lord; screenplay, Charles Kenyon; camera, Gregg Toland; editor, James Gibbon; musical director, Leo F. Forbstein; original music, Bernhard Kaun; gowns, Earl Luick; art director, Anton Grot; second camera, Bert Shipman; assistant camera, Perry Finnerman; sound, Oliver Garretson; still photography, Homer Van Pelt.

Cast: Kay Francis (Lois Ames); David Manners (Tommy Sherman); Una Merkel (Ruthie Holman); Andy Devine (Andy Doyle); Kenneth Thomson (Fred Ames); Claire Dodd (Ann Le Maire); Elizabeth

Patterson (Miss Harper); Edward Van Sloan (Manager); Junior Coghlan (Youngster in Store); Betty Farrington (New Secretary); Bess Flowers (Party Guest); Douglas Gerrard (Mr. Orca); Charlotte Merriam (Receptionist); Lee Phelps (Waiter); Eric Wilton (Extra); Robert Greig.

THE MOVIE OPENS AT the *400 Magazine*. Behind the editor's door — Private In Conference — editor Lois and husband Fred are making out. She's thrilled with her career and seems to be in love with her playboy husband.

"Don't you ever resent having a rich loafer for a husband?" he asks. Which, it turns out, is exactly what he is — only worse.

Tommy, who works for French & Sprague Sporting Supplies, is sent to the magazine to demonstrate a rowing machine. He's unhappily engaged to Ruthie. Tommy sees old, homely Miss Harper and assumes she's Mrs. Ames. When Lois does arrive, he takes over for Miss Harper, who's fired when she refuses to work late.

That night Lois is awakened from her sleep when her husband has yet another party downstairs. "I don't see how she does it," someone says. "She works all day and sleeps all night."

Lois hires Tommy at $50 a week. Soon, he's making $250 a week. Ruthie is jealous. "Well, I've seen your boss," she complains to Tommy. "I looked through the hedge. When I asked what she looked like, you certainly gave me a fine description."

"That was when I first met her, she's been reducing," Tommy explains. He joins Lois at the Bar Harbor Polo and Hunting Club.

Lois falls asleep, and he kisses her. "It can be forgotten because it has no meaning," she explains.

Fred is at the club, too, planning a tryst. Lois finds another room key in Fred's pocket. She places it on his pillow, and pretends to be asleep when he comes in. Finding the key, he's puzzled and a tad frantic.

"I'm quitting," a frustrated Tommy tells friend Andy when he returns. He decides to marry Ruthie.

"You're stuck on your boss," Andy tells him. "That's why you're quitting your job and that's why you're marrying this other Jane."

Left: Warner Bros. chose a new look for Kay in Man Wanted (1932). *Right*: Perhaps Kay was smiling because she'd just signed a lucrative contract with Warner Bros.

When Lois returns to the office, Tommy tells her he's resigning to marry Ruthie and work for her father. He agrees to stay on a bit longer.

There's a very nice shot of Lois' sad, poignant face looking through wrought iron gates waiting for Fred to return home. "I was going to write you a letter when I got to England," he says, finally returning.

"Divorce. Oh, it's been all my fault," she says. Before she leaves his room, he finds a note she'd slipped under the door: "Darling, I've been waiting up to see you. Somehow we've drifted apart and it's chiefly my fault. Let's make up. Lois."

On Tommy's last day at the office, he works late and ends up dining with Lois. Ruthie arrives at the office for a confrontation. "You've humiliated me for the last time!" she yells, threatening to tell Lois' husband.

"He's on his way to Paris for a divorce," Lois smugly replies, and then dictates a letter to Tommy: "My dear Mr. Sherman, in regard to our recent conversation, I regret that I did not inform you of my pending divorce. However, I promise it will never happen again. Yours forever, Lois." They kiss.

Kay received top billing in her first movie at Warner Bros. The most striking difference is the increase in close-ups. Cameraman Gregg Toland shot this film beautifully, and Kay and David Manners are one of the most attractive couples you'll see in 1930s films.

Though lacking Paramount's sophisticated dialogue, the film offers beautiful set design with great examples of art deco interiors. German-born director William Dieterle believed wife Charlotte was psychic. She determined when productions started and ended. He was also known for wearing white leather gloves on the set.

Elizabeth Patterson knew Kay from their Stuart Walker days. Una Merkel was one of the best comediennes—and scene stealers—in the business.

It's an interesting role reversal picture—and the first of many professionals Kay would play at Warner Bros. Working titles included *A Dangerous Brunette*, *Working Wives*, and *Pleasure First*.

The Andy Devine shower scene was a sticky, messy ordeal. Glycerine was used to make it appear Andy had just stepped out of a hot shower. Ironically, the glycerine itself necessitated a real shower after its application!

David Manners later described Kay as temperamental. According to his website (David-Manners.com), "Francis was difficult to work with and even walked off the set until he and fellow co-star Andy Devine 'quieted down.'" Apparently Devine and Manners clowned around on the set too much for Kay's taste.

The advertising copy read: "He Fell in Love with His Boss. Tom Sheridan was afraid of himself—afraid of what he might do. He had fallen hopelessly in love with his young and attractive employer, Lois Ames! What right had he to adore this devastating woman who was already married ... what right to interfere, even if her husband was cruel to her? Would it not be better for him to resign his position and marry pretty Ruth Holman to whom he was engaged? He had been determined to do this, but then—one evening the two women met—and the soul of each was laid bare... This entrancing story, 'Man Wanted,' with Kay Francis and David Manners." Another shouted: "She took what she wanted! She was beautiful ... wealthy ... impetuous ... spoiled ... and she took whatever she wanted in life ... so she turned to love ... and found ... Man Wanted."

REVIEWS: "Miss Francis suffers slightly in comparison with Manners. His youth emphasizes a maturity in her screen personality which, charming as it is, should not be so endangered." (*Variety*, April 19, 1932)

"This is good, light material which has the benefit of some luxurious settings, pleasing dialogue, rather clever situations and some good performances. Miss Francis photographed well and, wearing stunning costume creations, as usual, creates a smooth, svelte delineation as the wife who found happiness in the world of business rather than in the smart set." (Harry Mines, *Los Angeles Illustrated Daily News*, April 1, 1932)

"Considering the slimness of the story, director Dieterle and the players have done exceedingly well with it." (*Film Daily*, April 17, 1932)

Street of Women
(Warner Bros., 1932) 59 min.
Released on May 26, 1932.

Credits: Supervisor, Hal B. Wallis; director, Archie Mayo; based on the novel by Polan Banks; screenplay,

Mary McCall, Jr.; adaptation & dialogue, Charles Kenyon, Brown Holmes; art director, Anton Grot; settings supervised by W.& J. Sloane; music director, Leo F. Forbstein; original music, W. Franke Harling; camera, Ernest Haller; editor, James Gibbon.

Cast: Kay Francis (Natalie Upton); Alan Dinehart (Larry Baldwin); Marjorie Gateson (Lois Baldwin); Roland Young (Link Gibson); Gloria Stuart (Doris Baldwin); Allen Vincent (Clarke Upton); Louise Beavers (Mattie, the Maid); Adrienne Dore (Frances); William Burress (Doctor); Wilbur Mack (Mayor).

THE FILM OPENS WITH a shot of a building site. "On this site is being constructed the world's tallest structure The Baldwin Building, Linkhorne Gibson, Architect." Larry Baldwin is one of the builders. His secret mistress for three years has been fashion designer Natalie, owner of Madame Natalie, a deluxe dress salon. The two can see the building from her marvelous high-rise apartment. "There never would have been a Baldwin Building if it hadn't been for you," he tells her. They seem a happy couple, perfect partners in business and marriage. "Three years ago, I was nothing," he tells her. Larry has been married for seventeen years to a social butterfly who agrees to talk to him only "between parties."

Link, a mutual friend, is in love with Natalie. "Behind every skyscraper is a woman," he tells Natalie. "All those streets lined with skyscrapers were built by women." Natalie asks about the alleys. "A woman," he replies.

When Natalie finds out brother Clarke is coming to visit, she tells Larry she can't see him any more. "We haven't hurt anybody, and we haven't done any wrong. But with Clarke, it's different." Natalie adores Clarke and has paid for his education in Europe.

Meanwhile, Link hires Clarke to work on the Baldwin Building. It turns out that Clarke is an old friend of Doris Baldwin — Larry's daughter — and Clarke and Doris strike up a romance, making tentative plans to marry.

Larry meets Natalie at Tea Shoppe Antiques, promising to ask his wife for a divorce. He later

Marjorie Gateson, the wife of Kay's lover, visits Kay's dress salon in *Street of Women* (1932).

tells daughter Doris about his plans. "Our affair is not a trivial one," he says. "Her name is Natalie Upton."

Doris runs away in tears. Mrs. Baldwin refuses to give Larry a divorce. "You would upset my scheme of things considerably," she says, referring to Natalie as "a cheap chorus girl." She then calls on Natalie at her salon, gives her a once-over, and asks to see her fashions. "Something men like," she requests. A modeling show follows. "You're to be congratulated on giving people exactly what they want," she concludes.

When Natalie returns home, she finds Doris waiting for her. "Miss Upton, I've come to ask you to give up my father."

Natalie tells Doris they've kept the affair secret to protect her. "Our love is beautiful, and we're proud of it," she adds.

Doris tells Natalie that she and Clarke are engaged. "Can't you see that this would ruin it?"

Natalie agrees to stop seeing Larry. "That's the way it has to be, Larry. I've promised Doris. We've had our happiness, and now we have to pay for it."

Larry agrees. "It was too good to last, wasn't it?" he asks.

Clarke finds out about the affair, and angrily confronts Natalie. "Who do I thank for my Paris education? The lady who gave her services, or the gentlemen who paid for it?" He promises to pay back Larry for the money spent on his education and leaves for a job in Argentina.

Natalie suffers. Doris and Larry commiserate because they're separated from the Upton they love.

It's Christmas. Link tries to reconcile Natalie and Clarke, but Clarke is still cold. "Nat, dear," Link says, "even if you don't love me, marry me." Natalie admits she's in love with Larry Baldwin.

Doris and Clarke run into each other at a supper club. Upon seeing Clarke, Doris quickly departs. Clarke runs after her and gets in her car. Doris speeds, and the car crashes. Doris is injured.

When Natalie arrives, Clarke apologizes, and then promises Doris he won't leave again. In the next scene, Doris and Clarke are in a church reciting their marriage vows. Link talks Mrs. Baldwin into getting a Reno divorce, tells Larry about his wife's departure to Reno—and mentions that Natalie is leaving for Europe. In the final scene, Larry and Natalie embrace and kiss in front of the Baldwin Building.

Kay received top billing again — and it's one of her best roles. She's photographed well and wears splendid costumes. There are several close-ups of her eyes tearing up — we'll see a lot of *that* in the coming Warner Bros. films. The film was based on the 1931 novel *The Street of Women* by Polan Banks.

Advertisements for the picture proclaimed: "The secret port of misunderstood men! Where every address is the 'right' number ... where every woman was once a lady ... where passion masquerades as love and adventure answers every phone call."

REVIEWS: "Kay Francis going in for sobby emotion, is not as effective as in the brilliantly metallic parts in which she won recognition. Her playing is apathetic and only infrequently appealing." (*Variety*, May 31, 1932)

"Roland Young and Kay Francis deliver with distinction in a play that should please all intelligent patrons of the films. The production is punctuated with many clever situations, and some unusually intelligent and witty dialogue." (*Film Daily*, May 29, 1932)

"It is an exceedingly well-done drama, both from a directorial and acting standpoint. This is Miss Francis' second Warner film. The studio is giving her good vehicles and evidently spending money on her production, judging by the exquisite setting and the lineup of talent in the supporting cast. Miss Francis wears some stunning clothes and has been photographed advantageously. Her performance is warm, sincere, and charming." (Harry Mines, *Los Angeles Illustrated Daily News*, June 17, 1932)

"Kay Francis, since she went to Warners, has been working hard and fast, turning out pictures rapidly. The chief trouble is that the result is they look like it. Her first Warner film wasn't any wow; neither is this." (*Movie Mirror*, July 1932)

Jewel Robbery
(Warner Bros., 1932) 63 min.
Released on July 21, 1932.

Credits: Director, William Dieterle; associate director, William Keighley; based on the play, "Ekszerrablas a Vaci-uccaban" by Ladislaus Fodor; screenplay, Erwin Gelsey, Bertram Bloch; camera, Robert Kurrle; editor, Ralph Dawson; music director, Leo F. Forbstein; original music, Bernhard Kaun; art director, Robert Haas.

Cast: William Powell (The Robber); Kay Francis (Baroness Teri von Hohenfels); Helen Vinson (Marianne Horne); Hardie Albright (Paul, Undersecretary of State); Andre Luguet (Count Andre); Henry Kolker (Baron Franz von Hohenfels); Spencer Charters (Johann Christian Lenz, the Night Watchman); Alan Mowbray (Fritz); Lee Kohlmar (Hollander, the Jeweler); Lawrence Grant (Professor Bauman); Harold Minjir (Jewelry Clerk); Ivan Linow (Chauffeur); Charles Coleman (Charles, the Butler); Ruth Donnelly (Berta, the Maid); Clarence Wilson (President of Police); Leo White (Assistant Robber); Don Brodie, Eddie Kane (Robbers); Gordon "Wild Bill" Elliott (Girl-Chasing Gendarme); Herman Bing (Alpine Tourist); George Davis (Polachek); Robert Grieg (Henri); Sheila Terry (The Blonde); Jacques Vanaire (Manager); Harold Waldridge (Leopold); Al Hill, John Davidson.

THE SETTING IS VIENNA. A jewelry store has just installed a new burglar alarm system. The inventor explains how the system works when he's interrupted by a clerk — "It's too late! The store has just been robbed!"

We now move to a beautiful mansion. "Madame is awake. Hurry, hurry!" A procession of maids line up to service Teri, wife of a rich, old baron. Marianne visits while Teri gets dressed, and tells her news of the jewel robbery. Teri discusses her marriage woes: "For a month, marriage was thrilling and exciting, but then it became dull. Unbearably dull."

Teri and Marianne go to the jewelry store to see the Excelsior diamond. The two women discuss what they'd do for the diamond. "I'd deceive my husband with pleasure," Marianne says. "Oh, a woman would do much more than that," Teri says. "She would *tolerate* her husband."

While her husband meets with the jeweler, her former lover hassles her. "You're a coquette," Paul accuses.

"Sometimes," she agrees. "I'm not a fine woman. In my own eyes, I'm shallow and weak." She laughs in his face when he tells her she needs him.

Her rich husband buys the ring, just as the robber enters the store. "Will you kindly put up your hands?" he asks. His men gather up the jewels while he plays a medley of waltzes— including "The Emperor Waltz" and "The Blue Danube"— on his portable record player.

"This is becoming delightful," Teri says, charmed.

"I studied in Paris," he explains.

The robber passes a cigarette to Hollander, the store's owner. In a few minutes, Hollander gets the giggles. When asked what he gave Hollander, the robber replies, "A pleasant, harmless smoke. He'll awake up in the morning fresh and happy, with a marvelous appetite." When the others refuse the cigarettes, they are locked in the safe. He asks Teri with which gentlemen she'd prefer to stay.

"I prefer not to be locked up at all. With either of them."

Thus, the two men are locked in the same safe, while she flits about.

"You're so lovely," he tells her. "It's hard to be brutal with you."

"You do strike a fresh note. Up to now, men have always been brutal because I am lovely." She smiles and asks him to join her in the safe. "What do you expect me to do in there alone?" she coyly asks.

"Madame, this is business," he says, trying to be serious. He sees her ring and takes it. She slaps him.

"A souvenir of the lady who was willing to share a safe with me," he concludes before leaving.

Teri returns home to find roses. While she undresses behind a screen, it appears she's coming out nude, but is actually wearing an extremely low-cut gown — a great trick on the audience! Teri suddenly realizes the safe is open. Suspecting he's stolen her jewels, she investigates but finds he didn't take anything — but left something. "He gave me a gift of my ring."

Marianne has had enough. "Teri, it's immoral. This is one night I should be very glad to be with my husband."

Marianne leaves, a recording begins playing, and the robber makes his entrance. "You were everything I anticipated," he says when she finds out he'd been watching her. Worried she'll be implicated now that the ring has been

Opposite, top: Kay Francis in *Jewel Robbery* (1932). She's just received a bouquet from the dashing robber. **Bottom:** Kay Francis and Helen Vinson in *Jewel Robbery* (1932). Kay's suggestive gown defied physics and the censors.

returned, she points a gun at him. "If you don't steal back that ring immediately, I'll shoot you," she says.

She drops the gun when he kisses her. Detectives arrive. They find not only the ring but the stolen jewels in her safe. Teri's in a panic. The robber pulls a gun, but he's quickly overcome. They all head to the police station.

"Do they examine you here in this room?" she asks, after they reach their destination.

"Examine," the robber says, "and cross-examine. You get to like it after a while."

It turns out to be a ruse. The "detective" and "police" are the robber's accomplices. "Whatever you do must be done by force," she tells him after dinner. He picks her up, carries her off, and drops her to pillows on a lower level.

"Show me your jewels, will you?" she asks. He opens his safe and shows his prizes. The robber tells her he's leaving Vienna that night and invites her to Nice. They kiss. While he gets her coat, she steals his jewels, and then leaves. Teri turns back at the bottom of the stairs, realizing she can't leave him. Just then, the police arrive. The robber ties her to a chair. "This is the only way to return you to respectability. Auf wiedersehn, dear. I love you," he says as he leaves, just after returning her ring.

Teri cries for help. The robber escapes, driving away in a stolen police car.

"My nerves are shattered," Teri says. "Simply shattered. I must get away for a long rest. At once. I think I'll go to Nice. Yes, Nice. Nice. On the first possible train." Smiling, she approaches the camera and puts a finger to her lips, asking for our silence.

This was Kay's first real comedic lead, and she's brilliant. Kay's opening scene in the movie is memorable. From frolicking in a bathtub to being carried by an Amazon, there's a lot to like. She wears one dress that seems to defy physics. It must have been taped on or surely would have fallen off her shoulders.

The picture, a delight, has a Lubitsch feel to it. It's obviously pre–Code and includes kinky sexuality, drugs, adultery, and more. The sets are in the German expressionist style. Dieterle directed several other Kay Francis films, including *Man Wanted*, *Dr. Monica*, *The White Angel*, and *Another Dawn*, but none more effectively than *Jewel Robbery*. During the making of the film, set visitors included D.W. Griffith and his wife, Anita Louise and Maureen O'Sullivan.

This was the film debut of Helen Vinson, who had previously acted on Broadway. Often typecast as the heroine's shallow girlfriend, Vinson was tall (5 feet 7½) like Kay, which may have hindered her career at Warner Bros. "That studio seemed to me like an absolute sea of short men.... When I played with Jimmy Cagney, who is a lovely man but a little man, he had to stand on a box. Paul Muni was small and didn't like it a bit that I wasn't smaller. You should have seen what I had to go through when George Raft and I danced in *Midnight Club!* Even the production chief, [Darryl F.] Zanuck, was little. He didn't know how to cast me. I got my release after a year and freelanced very happily from then."[32] More than a decade after *Jewel Robbery*, Vinson appeared in *In Name Only* as another shallow girlfriend.

Background music included "Auf Wiedersehn, My Dear," a hit song from 1932, recorded by Bing Crosby, Rudy Vallee, and Russ Columbo, among others. The tagline of this gem was "He stole her jewels—but that wasn't all."

The movie was based on Ladislaus Fodor's 1931 play "Ekszerrablas a Vaci-uccaban." Bertram Bloch provided the adaptation for the 1931 New York play, "The Jewel Robbery."

REVIEWS: "This thing is meant to be very gay, very light, frothy. It misses the achievement by several miles. It runs across what should be slender, silver threads of the plot, with the feet of a rhinoceros. It's heavy. Kay Francis is adequate in her role." (Relman Morin, *Los Angeles Record*, February 29, 1932)

"Amusing crook drama, fantastic in plot, but made very enjoyable by good production and smart acting. Powell gives another of his deft portrayals, while Miss Francis displays some intriguing new gowns in addition to holding her own histrionically opposite Powell. The work of the two together is always keenly interesting." (*Film Daily*, July 23, 1932)

"Here, I am afraid, is an unmoral tale, but one so completely tongue in cheek and so continental in flavor that who shall condemn it. Both Kay Francis and William Powell enter thoroughly into the spirit of the occasion and William Dieterle adds the proper touch to the direction. It's a daring but amusing picture."

Kay Francis and William Powell share an intimate moment in *Jewel Robbery* (1932).

(Harrison Carroll, *Los Angeles Evening Herald Express*, July 29, 1932)

"In striving to inject a Lubitsch touch, Dieterle has gotten rather muddled up with the treatment of this picture. Kay Francis is required to speak lines of sophistication. But they sound pretty unnatural coming from her. For some reason Miss Francis seems to have forgotten how to act. She is self-conscious, and a little silly. At no time can you believe in her or her type. Helen Vinson reveals charm, beauty and acting ability. Perhaps if she did not handle her sophisticated dialogue so well the deficiencies of Miss Francis would not be so apparent." (Elizabeth Yeaman, July 29, 1932)

"The picture wavers between light comedy and farce, William Powell straining toward the first, Kay Francis relaxing in the second." (*Time*, August 1, 1932)

"William Powell is ideally cast. The same may be said for Kay Francis as the beautiful but bored and eccentric wife of an elderly banker." (*Variety*, July 26, 1932)

One Way Passage
(Warner Bros., 1932) 67 min.
Released on October 13, 1932.

Credits: Producer, Robert Lord, Hal B. Wallis; director, Tay Garnett; assistant director, Robert Fellows; story, Robert Lord; screenplay, Wilson Mizner, Joseph Jackson, Tay Garnett; camera, Robert Kurrle; editor, Ralph Dawson; lyrics, Al Dubin; conductor, Leo F. Forbstein; original music, Bernhard Kaun, W. Franke Harling; orchestrator, Bernhard Kaun, Ray Heindorf; costumes, Orry-Kelly; art director, Anton Grot.

Cast: William Powell (Dan Hardesty); Kay Francis (Joan Ames); Frank McHugh (Skippy); Aline MacMahon (Barrel House Betty/The Countess); Warren Hymer (Steve Burke); Frederick Burton (Doctor); Douglas Gerrard (Sir Harold); Herbert Mundin (S.S. Maloa Steward); Wilson Mizner (Singing Drunk); Mike Donlin (Hong Kong Bartender); Roscoe Karns (Bartender on S.S. Maloa); Dewey Robinson (Honolulu Contact); William Halligan (Agua Caliente Bartender); Stanley Fields (Captain); Willie Fung (Hong Kong Curio Dealer); Heinie Conklin (Singer of "If I Had My Way"); Harry Seymour (Ship's Officer); Glen Cavender (French Bartender); William Gould (Singing Drunk); Jane Jones (Singer); Ruth Hall, Allan Lane (Joan's Friends); Charles Sherlock (Man Listening to Betty).

THE FILM BEGINS IN a Hong Kong bar, the kind of place where the piano player has carved a hole in a piano key to hold his cigarette. The bartender is making a special drink, the Paradise Cocktail. "You can tell your grandchildren about that one," the bartender proudly says as he hands it to Dan. However, just as Dan is about to drink it, he's bumped from behind, spilling much of the drink. He turns to face Joan. Their eyes meet.

"I'm so sorry," she says.
"I'm so glad," he responds.

They toast. He breaks the glass against the bar and lays down the stem. Joan does the same, and the stems intertwine.

"Known him long?" a friend asks.
"Ever so long," Joan says.
"Where?"

Joan thinks. "I can't quite remember."

Dan, an escaped prisoner, is arrested by Steve. They board the *S.S. Maloa*, which is sailing to San Francisco with a stopover in Honolulu. Handcuffed to Steve, Dan tries to escape by jumping off the boat. Dan pulls Steve to safety. In gratitude — not knowing Dan pushed him into the water — Steve leaves the handcuffs off while they're at sea.

Meanwhile, Joan is in her room being scolded by her doctor. "No more parties. No more cigarettes. No more dancing. And no more cocktails. You're cutting your months into weeks, your weeks into days." This is Joan's last trip before she ends up in a sanitarium. She doesn't look the least bit sick — another one of those Hollywood illnesses that has no real symptoms.

"Funny how we cling to life even after it's worthless," Joan says. Spying Dan, she defies her doctor and decides to live it up.

Steve becomes infatuated with the sophisticated countess. However, she drops her high-class act when she sees Skippy, an amusing crook with a high-pitched laugh. She's actually Barrel House Betty, a con artist and friend of Skippy and Dan. She tells Skippy this will be her last con, explaining she wants a chicken ranch.

Skippy tells Betty that Dan is headed to San Quentin where he'll be hanged. Betty owes Dan a favor, and is able to repay it when Joan plans a day in Honolulu. Betty and Skippy scheme to get Dan out of the brig after Steve becomes suspicious of Dan's trip to Honolulu. Meanwhile, Dan writes a note: "Joan — I am running away — a fugitive condemned to death. I've tried to tell you but couldn't. I will attempt to reach Mexico. If you can forgive me, come to me there. If not, know that I understand, and love you always. Dan." He asks that it to be delivered after they've docked in Honolulu.

Dan plans to escape, but Joan sees him. Not wanting to disappoint her, he accompanies her to Honolulu where he makes arrangements to smuggle himself on a boat. Dan brings Joan a lei. Hawaiian music is playing. "I could stay here forever," Joan says. Dan tries to talk to her about his plans. "Dan, if it's serious, I don't want to hear it," she complains.

They smoke cigarettes and kiss. In a moment, he tosses his cigarette. Hers rolls onto his. We now see that the cigarettes have burned themselves out, and Joan is in Dan's arms. "We belong to each other always," Dan says. He tells her he won't be returning with her.

Joan faints. Dan returns Joan to the ship and takes the unopened note. "Her condition is desperate," Joan's doctor tells him. "She must have absolute quiet and rest if she's to reach the mainland alive. She survived this attack, but it isn't humanly possible for her to survive another. The slightest excitement might kill her. A shock, surely would."

Meanwhile, Betty has fallen for Steve. "Copper lover!" Skippy accuses. "I'm ashamed of you."

It's now the 24th day of the voyage. San Francisco is in the distance. A telegram comes to the ship: "Woman masquerading on ship as Countess Barilhaus positively identified as Barrel House Betty Notorious Confidence Woman Stop Investigate. Chief of Police." Steve tells Betty he doesn't want to be a cop any more. "I got a chicken ranch in Petaluma."

Betty admits her past. "I'm not any of the things you think I am," she says. "I've been a long way and I've left a wide trail." They agree to start over together.

"Four glorious weeks," Joan says, sharing a drink with Dan. She tells him she wants to be

Kay Francis and William Powell in *One Way Passage* (1932). This shows the genuine chemistry between the two stars.

in Agua Caliente on New Year's Eve, a month away.

"Here's to Agua Caliente New Year's Eve," he says.

"Nothing could keep me away," she responds. "Nor me."

They drink, smash the glasses, and entwine the stems. The ship arrives in San Francisco, but when Joan goes to Dan's room, the steward tells her that Dan is facing a murder charge. Joan staggers out, finds him before he's taken off the ship with Steve, and tearfully gazes into his eyes, saying goodbye.

"Not goodbye, dear," he corrects him. "Auf weidersehn. Until New Year's Eve."

"Auf weidersehn," she replies.

They kiss. Dan is taken away. Joan watches, smiling, waving, crying. Her face changes, her eyes roll back, and she collapses into the crowd.

In the final scene, we see "Agua Caliente Happy New Year" written on a balloon just before it's popped. People are celebrating. A somber Skippy sits alone at the bar. Two bartenders hear the sound of breaking glass. "Hey, look out for them glasses with your elbow!" one says to the other.

"I never touched any glasses," the other says.

There, on the bar, are two broken glass stems, lying atop each other, intertwined. The glasses slowly disappear.

This charming film was originally titled *S.S. Atlantic*. The plot sounds trite and sentimental, but this picture absolutely works. It's one of the most romantic movies ever made. There is great chemistry between Francis and Powell, and both give delightful, subtle performances. On June 1, 1932, Kay recorded in her diary that she and Powell got drunk in her dressing room while waiting to be called to the set. The production ended on June 9 at 3:30 in the morning.

Kay pointed out that the white organdy dress she wore in an important scene "was absolutely the wrong dress for the occasion. One doesn't get off at Honolulu in a white organdy. But it happened to be the only dress that would do for the scenes I had to play. In one of the scenes William Powell had to pick me up and carry me. At first I tried to wear the right dress for the boat — a sports dress, but when Powell lifted me up, the skirts came way up. In another scene I was supposed to look very fragile, as a woman who has only a few days to live would look. Now I'm a pretty hale and hearty creature, and I couldn't look as if I were dying in a sports dress. I had to wear organdy to create an illusion. And so the dress, though terribly wrong for the boat, was right for the scenes I had to play. We had to trust that people would forget all about the dress as the picture went on."[33]

On March 6, 1939, Kay and Powell recreated their roles in a radio adaptation on *Lux Radio Theatre*. The cast also included William Gargan and Marjorie Rambeau. The film was remade by Warner Brothers in 1940 and titled *Till We Meet Again*. Directed by Edmund Goulding, it starred Merle Oberon and George Brent, and also featured Geraldine Fitzgerald, Pat O'Brien, and Binnie Barnes. Frank McHugh (and his high-pitched laugh) repeated, but this time his character was named Rocky. Tito Davison directed a 1954 Mexican film, *El Valor de vivir (The Price of Living)*, with a cast including Arturo de Cordova, Rosita Quintana, Maria Douglas, and Julio Villarreal. The *Lux Video Theatre* television program presented a teleplay of *One Way Passage* on March 7, 1957. James Coco and Carol Burnett did a parody of the classic on *The Carol Burnett Show* on September 28, 1974 (skit titled "One Way Ticket").

Co-star Warren Hymer was the son of "Crime" playwright John B. Hymer, a drama which featured Kay during the 1927 theatre season. The younger Hymer suffered from alcohol problems and died in 1948. The song "If I Had My Way" was written by James Kendis and Lou Klein. Robert Lord won an Oscar for Best Original Story. Director Tay Garnett had refused a writing credit.

Advertising proclaimed: "What would you do with only four weeks to love? The best picture this team has ever made! William Powell and Kay Francis in the kind of story only these two could bring to the screen. A trip to paradise with no returning." According to another ad, "Romance ... reaching the Heights of Heaven!"

REVIEWS: "In its uncouth, brusque and implausible fashion, 'One Way Passage,' ... offers quite a satisfactory entertainment." (*New York Times*, October 14, 1932)

"Kay Francis has made me an even more ardent worshipper of her beauty and her skill, notably in *Trouble in Paradise*, but more especially in *One Way Passage*. This, I contend, was one of the best six films of 1933 [sic]. It was beautifully handled by the players; it was directed expertly and it weaved a story fascinating and poignant. The breaking of those wine glasses at the end of the film, on New Year's Eve, will live long in the memory. Kay Francis and William Powell excelled themselves in this production." (*Film Pictorial*, December 30, 1933)

"Polished acting by William Powell and Kay Francis in a fascinating melodrama which has a credible plot and a strictly logical ending. Very good entertainment of some distinction. The stars are brilliantly in harmony — smooth and sympathetic in their performance." (Irene Thirer, *New York Daily News*, October 14, 1932)

"Tay Garnett has directed the picture with sympathy and superior skill, and he has evoked excellent performances from the players." (*New York Evening Post*)

"Clicks with unusual love story and fine work of Powell and Francis." (*Film Daily*, August 23, 1932)

"Tay Garnett's direction is excellent. Although the story occasionally seems to be a little undecided about itself and is not always plausible, *One Way Passage* is a picture that holds the interest." (Harrison Carroll, *Los Angeles Evening Herald Express*, December 2, 1932)

"A quiet, sharp, romantic tragedy. *One Way Passage* was directed with the sense of pace and compression it required by Tay Garnett." (*Time*, October 24, 1932)

"The casting from Powell and Miss Francis down is excellent." (*Variety*, October 18, 1932)

Trouble in Paradise

(Paramount, 1932) 81 min.
Released on November 8, 1932.

Credits: Producer-director, Ernst Lubitsch; based on the play "The Honest Finder" by Aladar Laszlo; screenplay, Samson Raphaelson; adaptation, Grover

Jones; gowns, Travis Banton; song, W. Franke Harling, Leo Robin; camera, Victor Milner; still photographer, Earl Crowley; camera operator, William Miller; assistant camera, Guy Roe; sound, M.M. Paggi; art director, Hans Dreier.

Cast: Miriam Hopkins (Lily Vautier/Mlle. La Vautier); Kay Francis (Mariette Colet); Herbert Marshall (Gaston Monescu/La Valle); Charlie Ruggles (The Major); Edward Everett Horton (Francois Filiba); C. Aubrey Smith (Adolph Giron); Robert Greig (Jacques, the Butler); George Humbert (Waiter); Rolfe Sedan (Purse Salesman); Luis Alberni (Annoyed Opera Fan); Leonid Kinskey (Radical); Hooper Atchley (Insurance Agent); Nella Walker (Mme. Boucher); Perry Ivins (Radio Commentator); Larry Steers (Party Guest); Tyler Brooke (Commercial Singer); Fred Malatesta (Hotel Manager); Eva McKenzie (Duchess Chambreau); Hector Sarno (Prefect of Police); Gus Leonard (Elderly Servant).

EVEN THE CREDITS are cool: Old English type appears over muted scenes, accompanied by a sprightly song. The opening is one of the most famous first scenes in cinema — a Venice garbageman collects early in the morning, and then suddenly bursts into "O Sole Mio."

Meanwhile, the delicious tale begins with Francois being robbed of 20,000 lira by a man pretending to be a doctor interested in his tonsils. On the balcony, Gaston gives the waiter an order. "Beginnings are always difficult," he laments, then glances down at Lily floating by in a gondola. "It must be the most marvelous supper," he says. "We may not eat it, but it must be marvelous. And, waiter, you see that moon? I want to see that moon in the champagne. And as for you, waiter, I don't want to see you at all."

Lily, pretending to be a countess, arrives for dinner. A wonderful scene ensues between Lily and Gaston. "Baron," Lily asserts, "you are a crook. You robbed the gentleman."

"Countess," Gaston politely responds, "you are a thief." He informs her that she stole Francois' wallet from him. "In fact, you tickled me." Gaston shakes Lily until the wallet falls to the floor.

"I like you, baron," she says. "I'm crazy about you."

He returns her pin — he's stolen it from her dress. She asks the time. He realizes she's taken his watch. "It was five minutes slow," she explains, "but I regulated it for you."

Gaston's not finished. "Hope you don't mind

Kay wears a Travis Banton frock in *Trouble in Paradise*, a 1932 Lubitsch masterpiece.

if I keep your garter," he says. Surprised, she reaches down.

"*Darling!*" Lily jumps into his lap.

"I love you," he tells her as they lie upon the sofa together. The two slowly disappear, and a "Do Not Disturb" sign goes up on the door.

Rich widow Mariette Colet owns Colet & Company. "Remember," their slogan states, "It doesn't matter what you say. It doesn't matter how you look. It's how you smell."

Mariette refuses Francois' marriage proposal. "Marriage," she says, "is a beautiful mistake which two people make together. For you, Francois, I think it would be a mistake."

The major also wants to marry Mariette. "Don't be so downhearted, major, you're not the only one I don't love. I don't love Francois, either," she says comfortingly.

The rivals take her to the opera where Gaston steals Mariette's jeweled bag.

Gaston and Lily are reminiscing — they've been together for almost a year — when Lily finds a newspaper ad: "Handbag Lost — Twenty Thousand Francs Reward — Twenty Thousand Francs Reward for person who delivers handbag lost last night at Opera Comique. Handbag decorated with diamonds and sapphires."

"I'd be honest about it, and return it to the lady," Lily says, after quickly figuring the reward is greater than its pawn value. Gaston returns the bag and shortly becomes indispensable to Mariette.

"If I were your father," Gaston scolds, "which fortunately I am not, and you made any attempt to handle your own business affairs, I would give you a good spanking. In a business way, of course."

"What would you do if you were my secretary?" Mariette asks.

"The same thing."

"You're hired," she coos.

Lily becomes Gaston's assistant. There's a wonderful scene with Lily and Mariette. Mariette has breakfast in bed, and Lily tells her she takes care of her little brother, adding that her mother is dead. (Miriam Hopkins was Kay's friend, but she was ruthless when it came to scene stealing. In this one, Miriam's chair had to be nailed down because of her persistent attempts to upstage Kay.)

Kay and Herbert Marshall on the art deco set of *Trouble in Paradise* (1932) (courtesy James King).

"Yes," Mariette says, "that's the trouble with mothers. First, you get to like them, and then they die."

Lily is jealous of Mariette and suspects Gaston is infatuated with her. "This woman has more than jewelry," she complains to Gaston. "Did you ever take a good look at her ... um ..."

"Certainly."

"They're all right, aren't they?"

"Beautiful."

Gaston and Mariette do indeed become closer, causing others to gossip "She says he's her secretary. He says he's her secretary. Maybe I'm wrong. Maybe he is her secretary."

Adolph, Mariette's advisor, is suspicious of Gaston, which leads Gaston to tell Lily they need to clear out. There's a great scene with Lily packing, singing a nonsensical song. It's hard to know how much of this was scripted, and how much was Miriam Hopkins.

Gaston, for his part, can't bear to leave just yet. There's a great shot of Mariette and Gaston kissing in the mirror, their shadows on the bed.

At a party, Francois suddenly realizes Gaston was the doctor in Venice. "*Tonsils!*" he says with great meaning. Mariette refuses to believe him. Adolph confronts Gaston, and Gaston counters by accusing Adolph of cheating Colet & Company for years. Lily, angry and jealous, runs off after stealing cash from the safe.

Mariette returns to her house and Gaston's room. "When a lady takes her jewels off in a gentleman's room, where does she put them?" she asks.

"On the night table."

"But I don't want to be a lady." Mariette starts to open the safe.

"You have been robbed ... for years," Gaston interrupts, explaining about Adolph. He admits that he, too, is a crook. "I came here to rob you," he says, "but unfortunately I fell in love with you."

Lily arrives and tells Mariette *she* took the money — not Gaston. "You paid 125,000 francs for a handbag. You can pay 100,000 for him!"

Gaston says goodbye to Mariette.

"But it could have been glorious," Mariette says.

They kiss.

"Do you know what you're missing?" he asks. She nods. "No," he corrects. "*That's* what you're missing." He pulls out a necklace. "Your gift to her," he explains.

Miriam Hopkins, Herbert Marshall, and Kay Francis in *Trouble in Paradise* (1932). This was Kay's finest film.

"With the compliments of Colet & Company," Mariette says.

In the final scene, Gaston and Lily sit quietly in the back seat of a cab. Lily is still angry. Gaston suddenly searches his pockets. Lily calmly brings out the necklace. She looks in her purse. Mariette's money is missing. Gaston shows her it's in his pocket. They embrace and kiss.

This was Kay's second major comedy role. It was her 28th film, and probably her greatest one. She was paid $4,000 a week, with a six-week guarantee. She *doesn't* smoke in this one — a rarity as she smoked in almost every other film, except the period ones. *Trouble in Paradise*, selected for the National Film Registry, is a masterpiece, one of the greatest film comedies ever produced. From beginning to end, it's clever, adult, and an utter delight. The only thing better than watching this film is watching it for the *first* time. Unlike *24 Hours*, which cannot maintain its excellence, *Trouble in Paradise* never falters.

British actor Herbert Marshall, one of the last debonair Hollywood actors, had been wounded in France in World War I and lost his right leg. In the scenes of him running up and down the stairs, a double was used. "I thought I had never seen a lady so thoroughly and convincingly loved," Norma Shearer said of him. "He is both manly and wistful. He wins the sympathy of women because his face expresses tenderness and silent suffering." Gloria Swanson, who had a long affair with him, wrote, "In those few words Norma caught perfectly the essence of Bart Marshall."[34]

Ernst Lubitsch checked in daily with numerologist Mrs. Thomas Platt. Sets included Busch Gardens, UA's Venice Canal, the newly built Los Angeles hospital, and specially built scenery at Paramount. In addition, Hans Dreier designed Kay's mansion as an art deco–Bauhaus mix, using some of his own furniture. As a result, the *mise en scene* can be thought of as a fourth character. The budget was $519,706.

Kay had this to say about one particular costume: "One of the loveliest gowns I wore in *Trouble in Paradise* was a black beaded dress. But I wouldn't have worn it on a bet off the screen. It was utterly impractical. It had a train four yards long and it weighed forty pounds."[35]

This was one Lubitsch's favorite films: "As to pure style, I think I have done nothing better or as good as *Trouble in Paradise*."[36] (Lubitsch also named *The Patriot*, *The Love Parade*, and *Ninotchka*. His favorite was *The Shop Around the Corner*.) Writer Raphaelson, however, wasn't quite so pleased with the finished product: "It was just another job and it never occurred to me that I was making history. I much more enjoyed and had much more respect for *Heaven Can Wait* and *Shop Around the Corner* which dealt with sentiment, with emotions, with backgrounds, clerks— their slavishness, the tensions between them, their insecurity, romance on a level that I felt and respected ... that had more body to me. I cared more about those people than I did about the people in *Trouble in Paradise*. I thought the people in *Trouble in Paradise* were just puppets."[37] Raphaelson earned $750 a week writing this film.

Nobody dithers better than Edward Everett Horton. A brilliant character actor, Horton enjoyed working with Lubitsch, and appreciated the week of rehearsals before filming started. "No matter what you thought or what you wanted to do, Mr. Lubitsch had gone over it in his mind and had come to a conclusion. Just as soon as you could put yourself *en rapport* with him, you were very happy. He knew actors very well, and he wanted something from them that even they didn't know they had. He was a genius, you see."[38]

Surprisingly, the film did little business, grossing only $475,000. Initially, it lost money, though this was recouped in the European market. Although Lubitsch based the movie on a play, he advised screenwriter Raphaelson not to read it: "No use reading the play, Sem [sic]. It's bad." Lubitsch also enlisted the help of contract writer Grover Jones; though Jones received a credit, he provided little to the finished script. "Jones sat there amiably spinning anecdotes at lunch while Lubitsch and Raphaelson wrote the script, and was rewarded with an 'adaptation' credit."[39] The Aladar Laszlo play, which opened in Budapest in December 1931, was based on George Manolescu, who wrote about his criminal life in the 1907 *Memoirs*. Two silent films resulted. By the way, the credits reverse Laszlo's name and make him Laszlo Aladar.

Obviously a perfectionist, Lubitsch's hard work resulted in elegance and simplicity. For example, the opening scene took three days. "He wouldn't be content unless we got a brilliant opening shot," Raphaelson said. "We wanted to introduce Venice. Now, pictorially, the conventional way of saying that is to open on a long shot of Venice, medium shot of wherever you want to be, and close shot on the canal and the house, and then you go inside the house or hotel or whatever it is. That's the conventional way. Now, Lubitsch would sit and say, 'How do we do that, without doing that?' What Lubitsch and Raphaelson finally came up with was the famous opening where the singer of a glorious operatic air turns out to be a trash collector. Even in glorious, romantic Venice, someone has to pick up the garbage but, this being Venice — and Lubitsch — they must do it with panache. This sardonic undercutting of the ordinary is perhaps the quintessential 'Lubitsch touch,' but the director was careful not to overdo a good thing."[40]

Raphaelson finished his script on July 15, 1932. Paramount wanted Lubitsch to consider Adrienne Ames, Phillips Holmes, Charles Starrett, Irving Pichel, and Cary Grant. Lubitsch ignored the suggestions and cast the picture with his choices, including Kay.

Lubitsch didn't decide on the final title until almost a month after production shut down. Working titles included *The Golden Widow*, *Thieves and Lovers*, *The Honest Finder*, and *A Very Private Scandal*. In an early script, Kay's character's name is Marianne. If you're not sure what is meant by "The Lubitsch Touch," check this one out.

The Hays Office objected to the portrayal of Venice and its police. More specifically, the emphasis on Venice's garbage was frowned upon, as were the comical scenes involving the police. Furthermore, the Hays Office objected to lines such as, "Oh to hell with it" and "I like to take my fun and leave it." In addition, some eagle-eyed censor noticed a shot of C. Aubrey Smith mouthing "son of a bitch." The film was refused re-issue in 1935 when the Production Code was strengthened. In July 1943, Paramount submitted the script to the Motion Picture Producers and Distributors Association (MPPDA), hoping to produce a musical version, but the request was denied. It was many years before the film could be seen again. Kay attended an August 26, 1953, showing at the Museum of Modern Art with boyfriend Dennis Allen.

REVIEWS: "It is a shimmering, engaging piece of work.... Kay Francis is attractive and able as Marianne." (*New York Times*, November 9, 1932)

"It is far from being the best Lubitsch." (*New York Herald Tribune*)

"One of Lubitsch's best productions." (*Photoplay*)

"Well, this *is* a joy! A delightfully suave, sophisticated, technically perfect picture in which the directorial genius of Lubitsch is mingled with the exciting personalities of Mr. Marshall, Miss Francis and Miss Hopkins to provide superb entertainment for any adult mentality. The director hasn't overlooked a single detail, and as every part is close to perfection, so is the whole production. Assisting Lubitsch is the imperious, provocative Kay Francis, the sprite-like Miriam Hopkins and that new-come beau ideal of the cinema, Herbert Marshall. No more attractive trio ever graced the screen." (*New York American*, November 9, 1932)

"As full of merit as 'Trouble in Paradise' is, one feels that it might have been a bit more satisfactory. Mr. Marshall is as finished and as likeable as can be. Miss Hopkins is, as usual, amusing, appealing to the eye, and entirely an asset. Kay Francis, under Lubitsch's direction, is, of course, better than she has been in months." (*New York Sun*, November 9, 1932)

"Mr. Marshall is in every way a magnificent player here and quite as much may be said of his two leading ladies, Miriam Hopkins and Kay Francis." (*New York World* Telegram, November 9, 1932)

"Again Ernst Lubitsch triumphs as a director, carrying with him everyone concerned. Many, including the present reporter, consider it the finest of all his pictures. Mr. Marshall realizes for the first time on the screen precisely the opportunities that have made him extraordinarily successful on the stage. The picture is a triumph too for Miriam Hopkins, whose roguish humor and pervasive charm have never been so evident, while Kay Francis is gorgeously handsome and suavely alluring in the most smartly effective gowns worn by any actress this season." (*Los Angeles Times*, November 13, 1932)

"Civilized, suave, enchanting and light-minded. It is pictures like this which make people like me decide that a life spent in theaters is worth while after all. Credit must be given to the whole cast." (Llewellyn Miller, October 10, 1932)

"Once again Herr Ernst Lubitsch, that master megaphonist, has taken his cute cinematic egg-beater and whipped up a very frothy celluloid dish — a movie that is highly nonsensical, perfectly charming in its fun and just naughty enough to cause an endless amount of chuckles. Miriam Hopkins may receive first billing on the credit card, but Kay Francis, borrowed from Warner Brothers, steals the honors. And what a lovely little thief she is!" (Jimmy Starr, *Los Angeles Evening Herald Express*, October 22, 1932)

"*Trouble in Paradise*, as compared with the average motion picture, is as the comparison of diamonds to paste. Kay Francis is lovely as the rich woman. Her gowns are smart and she is extremely convincing as the attractive woman who turns down all her admirers for her charming, if not reliable secretary." (Louella O. Parsons, *Los Angeles Examiner*, November 4, 1932)

"*Trouble in Paradise* is a film in which scenes rather than the whole stand out sharply. Of the several fine performances in the picture, I like best those of Herbert Marshall, as Gaston, and of Miriam Hopkins as Lily. They are near perfection. For that matter, Kay Francis is excellent as the heiress and all the others are good." (Harrison Carroll, *Los Angeles Evening Herald Express*, November 4, 1932)

"Unconventional both in theme and handling, this satirical comedy of master crooks in the upper strata makes choice entertainment. The acting of every role is perfectly in harmony with the sophisticated nature of the story." (*Film Daily*, November 10, 1932)

"It is a blithesome comedy, interspersed with delightful music, injected as only Lubitsch can do, rich dialogue and some of the funniest scenes of recent films. There cannot be enough said about Miriam Hopkins, Kay Francis, Herbert Marshall, Charles Ruggles, and Edward Everett Horton, the principals, in praise of their workmanship in this film." (Vance King, *Hollywood Citizen News*, December 12, 1932)

"A triumph of direction and decor which could have been accomplished only by that scowling, heavy-jowled Teuton who is Paramount's chief contribution to the civilized cinema, Ernst Lubitsch." (*Time*, November 21, 1932)

Cynara
(United Artists, 1932) 78 min.
Released on December 24, 1932.

Credits: Producer, Samuel Goldwyn; director, King Vidor; screenplay, Lynn Starling, Frances Marion; from the play by H. M. Harwood and R. Gore-Brown and Brown's novel "An Imperfect Lover"; photography, Ray June; art director, Richard Day; film editor, Hugh Bennett; musical score, Alfred Newman; assistant director, Sherry Shourds; sound, C. Noyer, Frank Maher; song, "Blue Skies" by Irving Berlin (1926), sung by Phyllis Barry; Charlie Chaplin footage from A Dog's Life (1918).

Cast: Ronald Colman (Jim Warlock); Kay Francis (Clemency Warlock); Phyllis Barry (Doris Lea); Henry Stephenson (John Tring); Viva Tattersall (Milly Miles); Florine McKinney (Garla); Clarissa Selwyne (Onslow); Paul Porcasi (Joseph); George Kirby (Mr. Boots); Donald Stuart (Henry); Wilson Benge (Merton); C. Montague Shaw (Constable); Charlie Hall (Court Spectator); Halliwell Hobbes (Inquest Judge).

THE PICTURE BEGINS IN Naples as Jim packs, planning to leave the country. His career as a barrister has been ruined following a scandalous affair.

Wife Clemency has no plans to go with him. "Jim, if I could really understand," she pleads. "I have to imagine everything, and that's so much worse."

Jim is reluctant, hoping to spare Clemency the sordid details. However, he explains, "It started the night you left." In a flashback to London, it's the day before their seventh wedding anniversary. Clemency makes a sudden decision to accompany Garla, who's involved in a romantic misadventure, to Venice, planning to return in four weeks. Jim joins his despicable friend John for dinner, where they meet two girls—Doris and Milly. Jim and Doris go to a Charlie Chaplin film and then he escorts her home. Although Doris gives him her phone number, Jim tears it up. "I'm only interested in one woman, and her name's not Doris."

A few days later, Jim judges a swimsuit contest and meets Doris again; it turns out this second meeting was arranged by John. Doris wins, but promptly collapses, and Jim takes her home. "I've always dreamed of someone like you," she tells him, and promises to leave when he tires of her. They kiss.

In the next scene, they're on vacation together. In a rowboat Doris sings "Blue Skies," a song that is played throughout the movie. Jim tells Doris his wife will be returning soon.

When Jim returns home, Garla and Clemency have indeed returned. "I've been miserable away from you," Clemency says. "You too?"

Doris calls him at home, and Clemency becomes suspicious. Jim meets Doris in a park, trying to break it off.

"I want you all the time," Doris tells him. She also tells him she's been fired from her job. "I'm no good any more. I keep thinking about you." She begs him to continue the affair.

They agree to meet on Wednesday at five. Instead of meeting her, however, Jim writes a letter, telling her he can't see her any more. He sends it with his assistant, and he and Clemency go for a walk. Meanwhile, Doris goes out looking for him, and misses the letter.

When Jim and Clemency return home, Milly is waiting for him. She scolds him for his treatment of Doris and threatens to tell his wife. A policeman arrives and asks if he knows Doris. "Will you be surprised to hear that the young woman is dead?" She's taken poison and committed suicide.

There's an inquest. When Jim takes the stand, he admits to the affair and says he ended it because of his wife. However, he refuses to discuss Doris's past (she'd told him of a previous affair). The judge brings no charges but concludes, "It is unfortunate that he cannot be held criminally responsible for his conduct."

The scene shifts back to Naples. "Then you weren't the first?" Clemency asks, apparently thinking this important.

"It was her secret," Jim says. "What's done is

done," he adds. "She's paid her bill. And I've paid mine."

Clemency and Jim say goodbye. The devilish John shows up, and tells Clemency it was Doris' fault. "She broke the rules," he says. Then he plants the idea in her head that she might never see Jim again — perhaps something might happen on the ship.

Clemency arrives at the boat and rejoins Jim. They cry, hug, and wave goodbye to a smiling John. The boat departs.

Working titles for this slow moving, tawdry film included *I Have Been Faithful* and *Way of a Lancer*. Goldwyn originally didn't want to use *Cynara* because he didn't think anyone would know how to pronounce it. The reissue title was *I Was Faithless*.

In a scene in a movie theatre, director King Vidor was allowed the rare opportunity to use a clip from Chaplin's *A Dog's Life*. According to Vidor, "Chaplin and Goldwyn were part of United Artists, and in a way, they were friends.... It was rather difficult to get one of Chaplin's films, or even a clip from one of them. He watched them very closely, more so than anyone else. I was quite surprised myself to see that it got into the film. I didn't think it would happen."[41]

This is really Ronald Colman's film. Kay has few scenes. Interestingly, Colman sued Goldwyn for $2 million, claiming defamation of character. The lawsuit was filed in November 1932 after production ceased, but before the film's opening.

The *Fatal Attraction* of its time, it was a cautionary tale for husbands who considered straying. The title was taken from an 1896 Ernest Dowson poem, "Non sum qualis eram," which included the line: "I have been faithful to thee, Cynara, in my fashion." The story was originally in Robert Gore-Brown's 1928 novel *An Imperfect Lover*. Gore-Brown and E.M. Harwood adapted the novel into a stage play starring Philip Merrivale and Phoebe Foster. One important difference between film and play was that the film used flashbacks. The production cost $697,958, and was made at the urging of Arthur Hornblow Jr., who was certain that the hit British stage play would make a blockbuster American picture.

Although it's not a great film, it does have solid production values. Vidor gave credit to Goldwyn. "I think Goldwyn was always striving for very high quality.... I suppose all of his films had a certain slickness. He had Richard Day, one of the best art directors.... There was an air of perfection around the studio."[42]

Newcomer Dorothy Hale was cast as Clemency, but replaced the first week. Hale, who'd only had two months of stage experience — and that in the chorus — was let go when Goldwyn decided they needed an experienced actress to complement newcomer Phyllis Barry. Hale, born in Pittsburgh in 1905, committed suicide on October 21, 1938, when she leaped to her death from the Hampshire House in New York City. Mexican artist Frida Kahlo commemorated her death with the painting "El suicidio de Dorothy Hale" (The Suicide of Dorothy Hale). It was commissioned by Clare Boothe Luce, Hale's friend, who was horrified at the finished piece. Her plan to give it to Dorothy's mother was quickly discarded.

Kay Francis was borrowed from Warner Bros. This was Phyllis Barry's first American film role, and she did not distinguish herself. According to Vidor, he was initially disappointed by her performance after being wowed by her audition. "I particularly leaned toward the unknown young girl because this part seemed to call for that. We made tests, and I can't remember how many we did. The problem is that a girl, an aspiring actress, will give quite a bit of effort in a test, as much as Lillian Gish would give you every day for the duration of a picture. You see the test, are quite surprised, and you put her in the part because she seemed to work so hard. Later on you see that they never give you that same amount of energy during the rest of the picture."[43] Years later, however, Vidor watched the film again, and concluded, "In seeing it again, I didn't feel as let down as I did the first time. I thought that she was absolutely competent, pleasant, and right for the part."

Eddie Cantor was filming *The Kid from Spain* at the same time and on the same lot. According to a movie magazine, Eddie wandered over to Kay's set and was chased off but not before creating a madcap scene. "The director's chair was upturned, lights were overturned, and without knowing why Eddie ran for his life. Out of the corner of his eye, he spied a bed on the set and made one leap under the covers. Instantly there was a scream. A yell. And there was Eddie gazing bug-eyed at Kay Francis. In the same bed. And to cap the climax, like the third act of a play, the stage door opened and there was Mrs. Cantor and the five Cantor girls. 'Papa,' screamed the girls. 'My heavens, look at papa.'"[44]

Advertising proclaimed: "Back to the arms of his wife after a hectic weekend with his mistress!"

REVIEWS: "Mr. Colman gives an ingratiating portrayal.... Kay Francis is efficient as the wife and Phyllis Barry is sympathetic and natural as Doris." (*New York Times*, December 26, 1932)

"Regardless of what kind of stage show 'Cynara' was, it is now a motion picture depending on familiar but fine romance and drama, with Ronald Colman's artistic acting always predominant." (*Motion Picture Herald*, November 5, 1932)

"Stage play has been put on screen with beautiful balance of directness and simplicity. It finds Ronald Colman in probably the best clean-cut acting he has done since 'Raffles,' not excepting 'Arrowsmith.'" (*Variety*, January 3, 1933)

"Triangle story with new angle. Ronald Colman, Kay Francis and Phyllis Barry have the leading roles. Very good — but it will bore the kids." (*Modern Screen*, June 1933)

"Mr. Colman is ingratiating and dignified in 'Cynara,' but somehow or other he doesn't project the rather deep emotional quality that Mr. Merrivale did. Nor is Kay Francis as the wife exactly right. 'Cynara' is a nice, sentimental, tasteful little film, nicely written and with only a few lapses from its mood." (*New York Sun*, December 27, 1932)

"Strikingly done drama appealing principally to class audiences. Sophisticated and adult fare. Dialogue is smart and yet natural." (*Film Daily*, November 12, 1932)

"*Cynara* is a most unusual picture.... Because [it] presents, with sombre thoughtfulness, a situation which the cinema almost always handles blatantly; and because the values which it involves, while not particularly subtle, are wholly unlike those which U. S. cinema audiences are usually called upon to comprehend." (*Time*, December 26, 1932)

"A great team, Ronald Colman and Kay Francis. She is particularly charming and effective as the wife. No one on the screen can play the lady with more finesse and more realism than Miss Francis." (Louella O. Parsons, *Los Angeles Examiner*, December 30, 1932)

The Keyhole

(Warner Bros., 1933) 70 min.
Released on March 30, 1933.

Credits: Director, Michael Curtiz; based on the story "The Adventuress" by Alice D. G. Miller; screenplay, Robert Presnell; dialogue director, Arthur Greville Collins; art director, Anton Grot; gowns, Orry-Kelly; music director, Leo F. Forbstein; orchestrator, Ray Heindorf; original music, W. Franke Harling; camera, Barney McGill; editor, Ray Curtiss.

Cast: Kay Francis (Ann Brooks); George Brent (Neil Davis); Glenda Farrell (Dot); Allen Jenkins (Hank Wales); Monroe Owsley (Maurice Le Brun); Helen Ware (Portia DeWitt Brooks); Henry Kolker (Schuyler Brooks); Ferdinand Gottschalk (Brooks' Lawyer); Irving Bacon (Grover, the Chauffeur); Clarence Wilson (Weems, Head of the Acme Detective Agency); George Chandler (Joe, the Desk Clerk); Heinie Conklin (Mr. Smith, Room 210); Renee Whitney (Cheating Wife); Gordon "Wild Bill" Elliott (Dancing Man); George Humbert (Hotel Metropole Waiter); Gino Corrado (Hotel Metropole Waiter); Maurice Black (Cuban Jewelry Salesman); Leo White (Porter); John Sheehan (Bartender); Walter Brennan.

THROUGH A LARGE KEYHOLE, we see a man sitting at a table examining press clippings

Posing for endless costume shots, such as this one for *Cynara* (1932), often put Kay in a sour mood.

Kay's first pairing with George Brent was in *The Keyhole* (1933), a romantic drama.

illustrating the career of a famous dance team. The man throws down the notebook, eyes a poison bottle, and writes a note: "Dearest Ann: Life holds nothing for me but humiliation and poverty. I prefer to die by my own hand." He signs it "Maurice."

Ann hurries to the apartment. "In the nick of time," Maurice says. "Come in." A disgusted Ann reminds him she gave him $10,000 six months ago. He now wants $50,000 and takes her necklace for security. "I might give it back if you'll stay," he leers.

She slaps him hard. "And the next time you try to kill yourself, let me know," she says. "I'd love to help you."

She returns to her mansion — more like a palace than a house — and her suspicious, rich old husband Schuyler. Later, Ann tells her story to sister-in-law Portia, explaining she'd met Maurice when she was 17, fell in love, and married him. "It didn't take me long to find out what he really was. It was pretty awful." He left her for another woman. Ann, assuming they were divorced, went to America and married Schuyler. Maurice showed up six months later and started blackmailing her (it turns out they weren't divorced).

Portia advises Ann to leave the country for a vacation. Meanwhile, Schuyler hires the ACME Detective Service to follow Ann to Havana. Hank, one of the detectives, has a romance with Dot (played by the wonderful Glenda Farrell), while Neil, the other detective, tries to entrap Ann.

Maurice follows and confronts Ann. She promises to cash a check when they land. Meanwhile, Neil, unaware of Maurice, keeps Schuyler abreast of the situation with telegrams. When they arrive in Havana, Ann tells Neil she can't see him any more. Neil is persistent, and Ann finally agrees to spend the day with him in Old Havana.

Portia tells her brother why Ann really went away. Schuyler flies to Havana. Ann admits to Neil that she's married and that Maurice is blackmailing her. Later that night, Neil confesses to Ann that he was hired by her husband. "All the while we've been together, I've been a paid spy in the employ of that man." He tells her he's supposed to take her in his arms when Schuyler comes in the room so she'll be caught, but he can't go through with it. "I'm not a private detective any more. I'm not a sneak. I'm just someone who loves you. Believe me. I do love you."

Maurice knocks on the door. Neil goes out

the back, but returns when Maurice. gets rough with Ann. Schuyler knocks on the door. Maurice escapes out the window. Ann takes Neil in her arms and kisses him as Schuyler walks in. "This was what you paid your money to see, wasn't it?" she bitterly asks. "I wouldn't disappoint you for anything, Schuyler." She tells him the marriage is over. "You've destroyed what little there was between us. I tried to be fair, but you've hounded me and spied on me since the first day we married. Then you deliberately put someone in front on me who you thought I might fall in love with, hoping that I wouldn't because you still wanted to keep me. And yet down in your dirty little mind, wondering if I would."

"I picked you up out of nothing," Schuyler angrily tells Ann. "You can go back to nothing, for all I care."

Ann and Neil hear a siren. Maurice has—conveniently—fallen to his death from the balcony. Neil takes Maurice's suicide note—which Ann fortunately kept—and places it on the desk. The music swells. They kiss. The camera zooms out until we're looking through another large keyhole.

Kay received top billing in this opulent picture, made during the Depression's height. Shooting began in late November 1932 and took 25 days. The production cost was $169,000. The film was based on Alice D.G. Miller's story "The Adventuress." At one point, the title was changed to *Isle of Fury*—but was changed back to *The Keyhole* before the picture was released. *Isle of Fury* was later used for a Humphrey Bogart film in 1936. Kay reportedly wore 23 costumes in the film. Antonio Moreno was originally cast at Maurice, and William Powell was the first choice for the George Brent character. This was Kay's first pairing with Brent.

The picture is worth seeing for Glenda Farrell, a remarkably gifted actress who threatened to steal every scene she was in. In an interview, she explained the typical work week for a nonstar at Warner Brothers. "Not many actors could talk," she said. "So they shoved the ones who came from Broadway into everything. It all went so fast. I used to ask myself, 'What set am I on today? What script am I supposed to be doing—this one or that one?'" She was up at 5:00 A.M., at the studio by 6:00 A.M. She worked six days a week, sometimes getting home at 9:00 P.M., sometimes midnight. "All I shouted for was a day off. We got it Sunday. But I had to stay in bed that one day to get ready for the next six days of shooting. I wonder if Jack Warner really appreciated his movie-acting family?" At Warner Bros., where she made 22 pictures her first year, Glenda never achieved real stardom. But that didn't bother her. For one thing, Warner Bros. had a kind of repertory theatre approach to its contract players. The studio rotated many of them between leading and supporting roles and bit parts. "So you weren't Kay Francis," she said. "You were still well paid and you didn't get a star complex."[45]

Romance on the High Seas (1948) was a Warner Bros. film that shared similarities with *The Keyhole*. It was a Doris Day musical, directed by Michael Curtiz.

Advertisements for the film proclaimed: "He was paid to learn the worst! He ruined reputations for a wage ... But he paid for it all when he saw the woman he loved through *The Keyhole*."

REVIEWS: "George Brent, as the detective, is still a bit too stiff to look human. Kay Francis grabs most of the honors. Glenda Farrell and Allen Jenkins furnish hilarious comedy. Photography is only fair. It's just so-so." (*Modern Screen*, June 1933)

"Entertainment is confined to the personal performances of the lead pair and the generous wardrobe worn unaffectedly by Miss Francis." (*Variety*, April 4, 1933)

"There is some excellent and ingratiating humor contributed by Glenda Farrell and Allen Jenkins, and though it is the fringe of the story which they are supposed to occupy, the effect of their scenes together is to dominate." (*New York Evening Post*)

"Miss Francis acts her role with the desired lightness. But, even so, the story is a little too obvious to be much more than a good-natured piece of work." (*New York Times*, March 31, 1933)

"What makes *The Keyhole* acceptable entertainment is the charm of Kay Francis' acting, good settings by Anton Grot and a few amusing sequences in which Allen Jenkins, as a brash and dipsomaniac assistant detective, pursues a mercenary blonde (Glenda Farrell) under the delusion that she is an heiress." (*Time*, April 10, 1933)

"It is only mildly satisfactory. Mr. Brent,

Miss Francis and Monroe Owsley play satisfactorily if not brilliantly." (*New York Sun*, March 31, 1933)

"Poor Miss Kay Francis is beset by unworthy males—and, it might be added, by an unworthy story—in the new picture at the Radio City Music Hall. Miss Francis makes the wife as real as her dialogue will permit." (*New York Herald Tribune*, March 31, 1933)

"Light entertainment saved by grace of Kay Francis' charming personality. Miss Francis is gorgeous and makes the film entertaining through sheer personality." (*Film Daily*, March 31, 1933)

"Once more Miss Francis is given the opportunity to display the finest wares of the studio dress designer. Allen Jenkins and Glenda Farrell are drawn in for comedy relief. Miss Farrell, by the way, must have been understudying Ruth Chatterton, or else she has developed her talent for mimicry to an amazing extent." (Elizabeth Yeaman, *Hollywood Citizen News*, April 14, 1933)

"Aside from the usual display of wardrobe given Kay Francis, there is Kay herself, as warm and appealing a personality the screen has to offer. There is a lack of artificiality about Miss Francis that makes her refreshing." (Jerry Hoffman, *Los Angeles Examiner*, April 14, 1933)

Storm at Daybreak
(Metro-Goldwyn-Mayer, 1933) 78 min.
Released on July 21, 1933.

Credits: Associate Producer, Lucien Hubbard; director, Richard Boleslavsky; based on the play "Black-Stemmed Cherries" by Sandor Hunyady; adaptor, Bertram Millhauser; original music, Dr. William Axt; lyrics, Gus Kahn; camera, George Folsey; editor, Margaret Booth; art director, Alexander Toluboff; interior decorator, Edwin B. Willis; costumes, Adrian; sound, Douglas Shearer; sound mixer, William N. Sparks. Song: "Two Lips Like Cherries."

Cast: Kay Francis (Irina Radovic); Nils Asther (Captain Geza Petery); Walter Huston (Dushan Radovic); Phillips Holmes (Csaholyi); Louise Closser Hale (Militza Brooska); Jean Parker (Danitza); Charles Halton (Villager); Leonid Kinskey (Serbian Villager); Akim Tamiroff (Gypsy Fiddler); Mischa Auer (Assassin); Frank Conroy (Archduke Franz Ferdinand); Eugene Pallette (Janos); C. Henry Gordon (Panto Nikitch); James Bell (Peter); Clarence Wilson (Captain); Oscar Apfel (Counselor Velasch); Hal Boyer (Mitry, Deserter); Frankie Burke (Jankovitch); Richard Cramer (Stepan); Allan Fox (Greg, Deserter); Etienne Girardot (Hungarian Officer); Ferdinand Munier (Party Guest with White Beard); Russ Powell (Man); Lucien Prival (Hungarian Soldier); Harry Semels (Serbian Villager); Milton Wallace (Colonel Patou); Wilhelm von Brincken (Hungarian Officer).

THE FILM BEGINS WITH an explanation of the setting. "Before the World War, Austria-Hungary was made up of people of many races, loosely held together as one nation. Among these were Serbs and Hungarians, bitter enemies since time immemorial. Their hatred for each other grew with the years. By June 28, 1914, it hung like a black cloud over the little town of Sarajevo, gaily decked for a state visit from the Archduke Ferdinand and his consort." Ferdinand is assassinated, and war is declared against Serbia.

Serbian mayor Dushan is the voice of reason and calm. Wife Irina helps Peter and other Serb deserters from the Hungarian army. Meanwhile, Geza, an old friend of Dushan's, arrives at Dushan's estate with his Hungarian soldiers. Still trying to hide the deserters, Irina invites Geza into their home for wine. She plays the piano and sings (obviously dubbed), while Geza watches the deserters escape. "You must be tired," he tells Irina. "You needn't play any longer. Your deserters are well away by this time."

Six weeks pass, and Geza and Irina have become friendly. However, Geza and his soldiers are sent to the front. Before they leave, there's a celebration. Geza tells Dushan that Panto, one of his workers, has reported him to the authorities for helping the deserters escape. Dushan makes Panto sign a retraction, fires him, and sends him on his way.

"The woman gets a wrong man, and the right one comes along too late," Irina laments to Geza before he rides off. There's a montage of battle scenes superimposed over Irina's tragic face. Later, Irina finds that Geza has been wounded. Dushan brings his injured friend back to his farm.

"Dear God," Irina prays. "you brought him back safely to me. Thank you. Thank you. Now, save me."

Dushan confides to Geza about his marital troubles. "She doesn't love me. Not the way I love her. She loves me as you love a child or a pet dog." Dushan further explains that "something or somebody is standing between us. I wish I knew what."

A peace treaty is signed, the area returns to Serbian rule, and the evil Panto is now in charge. When Geza tells Irina he must leave, she asks to go with him. He reminds her of Dushan. "He'll always be with us. Between us. Between every kiss."

Dushan sees the two together and becomes suspicious. A Serb official arrives at Dushan's house on a rainy night. He has a search warrant for Geza. Irina begs Dushan to warn Geza. "You love him!" he accuses and refuses to help. Irina hurries out into the wind and rain to warn Geza.

Dushan is right behind her. "Let's hear it from your own lips," he tells Geza. "That she is your mistress!"

"That question is too filthy to be answered," Geza answers.

Dushan attacks Geza, but then stops, ashamed and beaten. "It's no use. I'm done," he says.

Irina tells him she loves Geza, but it's over. "You love each other," Dushan says. "I'm out of it. From now on, we'd be strangers, dressing in front of each other. And at night beside me, your eyes closed, I know you'd be thinking of him."

When Panto arrives to arrest Geza, Dushan kisses Irina one final time, walks downstairs with a strange look in his eyes, and tells Panto that Geza has left with his wife. He and Panto head off into the driving storm. Dushan drives the horses like a madman. "Love is a funny thing, Panto," he says. "I don't think I'll get my wife, Panto. I don't think you'll get my friend."

Panicked, Panto tries to grab the reins, but the carriage crashes off a cliff. The music swells. Irina and Geza visit Dushan's grave, and Irina makes the sign of the cross. They bow their heads.

Historical romances may not have been the best vehicles for Miss Francis' talents. This is one of the rare films where you'll see Kay with long hair. In this one, she's married to brutish

Kay Francis and Nils Asther in *Storm at Daybreak* (1933). It's hard to tell who's prettier.

Walter Huston, but obviously more suited to the gentle, almost feminine Hungarian Nils Asther. There's lots of chemistry between these two. Swedish-born Asther was often cast as Russian, Asian, and other ethnic roles.

The film was based on Sandor Hunyady's 1931 play "Fekete szaru Csereszyne" (Black-Stemmed Cherries). Believe it or not, this property was originally bought for Greta Garbo. At various times, it was titled *Rhapsody*, *Black Stemmed Cherries*, and *Strange Rhapsody*. Wallace Beery was at one time considered for a lead role.

The soundtrack included Johannes Brahms' Hungarian Dance No. 6 in E Flat Minor, Ludwig von Beethoven's Symphony No. 3 in E Flat, "Eroica" (Op. 55), Second Movement "Marcia Funebre," Franz Liszt's "Les Preludes," Brahms' "Hungarian Dance No. 5 in A," Johann Strauss' "Roses from the South" and "Artist's Life, Op. 316." In addition, the song "Two Lips Like Cherries," was written by Dr. William Axt and Gus Kahn.

Boleslavsky is an able director, perhaps influenced by Sergei Eisenstein. Note his use of quick editing, montages, and close-ups. Film production began in late April 1933.

REVIEWS: "Beautiful photography of Kay Francis in Central European costumes distinguishes 'Storm at Daybreak.'" (*Newsweek*, July 29, 1933)

"Although Miss Francis is as attractive as always, she hardly seems suited to the enigmatic and mysterious qualities demanded in the role of the wife." (*New York Times*, July 22, 1933)

"Romantic drama with Hungarian setting has a love story that the femmes will like." (*Film Daily*, July 22, 1933)

"Miss Francis looks appealing, tearful at times and usually very unconscious of her exotic frocks and negligees." (Eleanor Barnes, *Los Angeles Illustrated Daily News*, August 12, 1933)

"Undeniably *Storm at Daybreak* ... holds together well and the skill of its actors makes its gaudy situations credible." (*Time*, July 17, 1933)

"Kay Francis, Nils Asther and Walter Huston are the leading characters, all giving splendid performances. I'm anxious to know whether it was Kay who actually sang, or was the voice doubled? Merely to discover whether Kay adds a fine singing voice to her other accomplishments." (Jerry Hoffman, *Los Angeles Examiner*, August 12, 1933)

"... one of the most gripping screen-tales you'll see this year. To its excellence contribute many factors—sincerity of portrayals by brilliant actors, and 'realness' of lines, rather than staginess. More beautiful than ever is Kay Francis, herein particularly smartly photographed." (*Movie Mirror*, September 1933)

Mary Stevens, M.D.

(Warner Bros., 1933) 71 min.
Released on August 3, 1933.

Credits: Supervisor, Hal B. Wallis; director, Lloyd Bacon; assistant director, Chuck Hansen; based on the story by Virginia Kellogg; adaptors, Rian James, Robert Lord; dialogue director, William Keighley; gowns, Orry-Kelly; music director, Leo F. Forbstein; original music, Bernhard Kaun; camera, Sid Hickox; assistant camera, Wesley Anderson; second camera operator, Thomas Brannigan; editor, Ray Curtiss; sound, Robert B. Lee; props, Pinky Weiss; art director, Esdras Hartley.

Cast: Kay Francis (Dr. Mary Stevens); Lyle Talbot (Dr. Don Andrews); Glenda Farrell (Glenda); Thelma Todd (Lois Rising); Una O'Connor (Mrs. Arnell Simmons); Charles C. Wilson (Walter Rising); Hobart Cavanaugh (Alf Simmons); Harold Huber (Tony); George Cooper (Pete); John Marston (Dr. Lane); Christian Rub (Gus); Reginald Mason (Hospital Superintendent); Walter Walker (Dr. Clark); Ann Hovey (Miss Gordon, the Receptionist); Constantine Romanoff (Dynamite Schultz); Harry Myers (Nervous Patient); Grace Hayle (Wealthy Lady); Edward Gargan (Cop); Sidney Miller (Sanford Nussbaum); Wilfred Lucas (Barry); Lloyd Ingraham (Ship's Captain); Harry Seymour (Ship's Officer Bringing Serum); Wallace MacDonald (Purser); Joseph E. Bernard (Steward Bringing Purse); Andre Cheron (French Official); Cora Sue Collins (Jane Simmons); Theresa Harris (Alice, the Maid); Milton Kibbee (Deck Steward); Chuck Hamilton, Henry Otho (Firemen); Inez Palange (Tony's Wife); Lee Phelps (Station Master).

AN ALARM SOUNDS, and a Manhattan Hospital ambulance is dispatched to the second floor of 1110 Orchard Street. A woman is having a baby in a crowded, working-class part of town. "I'm the doctor," Mary announces at the door.

"I've got to have a man doctor," the Italian father insists. Although he threatens her with a huge knife, Mary is calm and professional. She delivers twins, and the father faints.

Pediatrician Mary and boyfriend Don open a practice together. Don breaks a dinner date with Mary to go out with a politician's daughter, Lois Rising. Don tells her Walter, Lois' dad, might get him a great job. "Some people work for a career, and some people marry one," Mary comments. Indeed, Don gets a job at the City Compensation Bureau and marries Lois. Don buys a Duesenberg and other expensive items. When he takes her to lunch, Mary asks where he's getting his money. He admits he's cheating the city. "You've changed so in the last six months," she tells him.

After lunch, Don reports for surgery, but Mary knows he's had too much to drink. She has to take over for him. "I'm disgusted with you!" Meanwhile, Mary's pediatrician practice is thriving. She's ably assisted by her tough-talking nurse, Glenda. Mary keeps a scrapbook on Don's career, and admits to Glenda that she misses him. When Don is caught up in a scandal and leaves town, Mary takes the same train, arriving in White Sulphur Springs, West Virginia, where they stay at the Green Brier Hotel. It's been more than a year since they've seen each other, and they dance, dine, and romance. She tells him she's still in love with him, but "you belong to Lois, and I'm getting out before we do something both of us will regret."

Glenda calls and tells Mary the grand jury has indicted Don. Don explains that Walter Rising will fix it, and soon receives a telegram saying the indictment is off. Mary and Don plan to marry. Don will resign his job and get a divorce. However, Walter won't let him quit and convinces Lois to stymie the divorce. Mary refuses to see Don until he's free. Finally, Don calls to meet with her, and Mary assumes it's good news about the divorce. They agree to meet that night for dinner.

"Now, take a good grip on that desk," Mary tells Glenda. "Plant your feet firmly, and prepare for the shock of your life. I'm going to have a baby." Mary is thrilled and plans to tell Don at dinner.

However, Don has other news. "Lois is going

Glenda Farrell brought hard-boiled humor to *Mary Stevens, M.D.* (1933), a drama about the struggles of a woman physician.

to have a baby." The divorce is off for at least a year. He asked what news Mary had.

"Oh, I've forgotten. It didn't amount to much, anyway." Mary plans to go overseas with Glenda, and come back with an adopted baby. "I'm glad what ails you isn't catching," Glenda quips.

Mary has the baby in France. Don phones from New York. It turns out Lois tricked him. "She wasn't going to have a baby any more than you were," he explains. Ha ha.

Mary, Glenda, and baby sail back to New York. A sick child on board requires Mary's attention. The child has infantile paralysis, and they need serum. An exposed child plays with Mary's purse and puts a pen in her mouth. The purse is returned to Mary. Baby Donald picks up the pen and sucks on it.

While Mary cares for the sick children, Glenda tells her the baby is running a fever. Mary realizes he's sick, too. The serum finally arrives, but Donald dies before she can inject him. "My own baby," Mary cries. "I couldn't save him. Give the serum to the other children. My baby won't need it."

When they arrive in New York, Glenda tells Don the whole story. In the next scene, Don visits Mary at her apartment. She's still grieving, won't eat or sleep. Her hair is streaked with gray. "No dinner last night," Glenda reports. "A cup of black coffee and three cigarettes for breakfast."

Mary doesn't want to go on living, let alone practice medicine. Hours pass. She dreams of the baby, suddenly awakens, and realizes she was having a nightmare. Glenda is asleep. Mary's eyes grow large as she gazes at the window. She opens it, looks down, and moves toward the ledge. Just as she leans over, the doorbell buzzes.

Gus hurries into her room. Baby Karl has swallowed a safety pin and is choking. Mary tells him she doesn't practice any more. Glenda insists she help. Mary uses a mirror, a spoon, and a lamp's light ... but it's her *hairpin* that does the trick. "I *got* it!" she proudly says, fishing out the safety pin. "They say medicine is a man's game," Mary says. "I wonder what a man would have done in a case like this."

Mary and Don open a practice together. A Jewish mother brings son Sanford to Mary's office. Glenda opens the door to see Mary and Don kissing. "Just a second," Glenda says, "Dr. Stevens is working on a man."

"Oh yeah?" says a smiling Sanford.

To prepare for the role, Kay saw an operation at the Los Angeles County Hospital on March 3, 1933. Production started March 18. Again top-billed, Kay is very convincing as an attentive, then grieving mother in this gripping drama, even if she does look like an Anne Geddes baby in her surgical outfit.

Thelma Todd, known as the Ice Cream Blonde, died mysteriously in 1935 outside her restaurant, Thelma Todd's Sidewalk Café. The official cause of death was carbon monoxide poisoning. Some believe she was murdered, and that her ghost now haunts the site. George Brent was originally slated to play Lyle Talbot's role, but the newlywed asked for permission to honeymoon with wife Ruth Chatterton. Una O'Connor was borrowed from Fox.

The film was reissued in 1936, but denied the Seal of Approval from the Legion of Decency. An unmarried woman having a baby was just too, *too* much.

Advertising stated: "'I'm going to forget the advice I gave to other women!' Here's drama torn from the very heart of womankind! Don't miss the screen's first daring story of a woman doctor." Another proclaimed: "Why didn't this woman physician take the same advice she gave to other girls? See why she told her lover to marry another woman! See why she went to Paris when she didn't have to! See how she paid for the sin she taught other women to laugh at!"

REVIEWS: "Both Kay Francis and Lyle Talbot perform competently, and there is one brief and excellent bit of acting by Una O'Connor." (*New York Times*, August 5, 1933)

"Kay Francis and Lyle Talbot turn in excellent performances." (Eleanor Barnes, *Los Angeles Illustrated Daily News*, July 28, 1933)

"Marred by signs of haste in production, it contains, like many recent Warner pictures, bits of first-class writing. Dr. Stevens' assistant Glenda (Glenda Farrell), an energetic girl with a warm heart and a sharp tongue, is an expertly invented character." (*Time*, August 14, 1933)

"Kay Francis is always dignified, yet very personable, as Dr. Stevens." (*Variety*, August 8, 1933)

"Imagine Kay Francis as a doctor, in fact a baby specialist! That's a new kind of role for our fascinating and glamorous Kay, but, take our word for it, she gives a moving, convincing performance that will make you laugh and cry. Three cheers for our Kay!" (*Silver Screen*)

I Loved a Woman
(Warner Bros., 1933) 80 min.
Released on September 21, 1933.

Credits: Director, Alfred E. Green; based on the book by David Karsner; screenplay, Charles Kenyon, Sidney Sutherland; camera, James Van Trees; editor, Hubert Levy; costume design, Earl Luick; art director, Robert M. Haas; original music, Leo F. Forbstein.

Cast: Edward G. Robinson (John Hayden); Kay Francis (Laura McDonald); Genevieve Tobin (Martha Lane Hayden); J. Farrell MacDonald (Shuster); Henry Kolker (Sanborn); Robert Barrat (Charles Lane); George Blackwood (Henry); Murray Kinnell (Davenport); Robert McWade (Larkin); Walter Walker (Oliver); Henry O'Neill (Farrell); Lorena Layson (Annette, the Maid); Sam Godfrey (Warren); E. J. Ratcliffe (Theodore Roosevelt); Paul Porcasi (Hotel Proprietor); William V. Mong (Bowen); Davison Clark (Doctor); Wallis Clark (Banker); Charles Coleman (Hayden's First Butler); James Donlan (Voting Returns Announcer); Douglass Dumbrille (U.S. Attorney Brandt); Claude Gillingwater (Banker); DeWitt Jennings (Banker); Howard C. Hickman, Edward Keane, Edwin Stanley (Businessmen at Meeting); Milton Kibbee (Lane's Secretary); Wallace MacDonald (Hayden's First Secretary); Edwin Maxwell (Gossiper); Amy Rayan (Gypsy); Phil Tead (Reporter); Harry Walker (Hayden's Second Secretary); Morgan Wallace (Pollock); William Worthington (Jefferson).

THE PICTURE OPENS IN Athens in 1892. Hayden's father owns the largest meat packing plant in the world. Hayden, however, is different. He's an art lover, a man who enjoys music and beauty. Called back to Chicago when his father dies, he marries Martha Lane, daughter of a rival meat packer, and quickly finds he's not the businessman his father was.

By 1897 Hayden's company has gone from number one in sales to six. Hayden is forced to borrow money from his father-in-law's company. His marriage, too, is failing. He meets aspiring opera singer Laura McDonald who wants him to be her sponsor. "I'm as sure of success as I am of death," she tells him. "The top and nothing but the top" is her definition of success. She asks him to her flat for an audition. He asks her to sing "Home, Home on the Range." She does (obviously dubbed).

Kay played an opera singer who sang "Home on the Range" to soothe the nerves of tycoon Edward G. Robinson in *I Loved a Woman* (1933).

He's charmed. "This will always be a lovely memory," he tells her. Laura goes to Europe for training, and John tells her he loves her, wants to marry her. "I've been a man without talent, perpetually trying to create something beautiful."

He decides to focus on her career. She refuses to marry him, not wanting the "dull domesticity" he now has. She encourages him to build his business, "make it the world's greatest industry. That's art. That's beauty. Enough for any man." She also wants him to be ruthless. "Promise to be ruthless, ruthless as our love."

Hayden, who'd not wanted to profit from the Spanish-American War, changes his mind. He cuts corners, risking the food's safety. There's a montage of war footage, intermixed with soldiers eating Hayden beef. We see a newspaper headline: "More soldiers died from embalmed beef than from Spanish bullets." Although an investigation is ordered into his business practices, Hayden is able to return the $5 million he borrowed from father-in-law Lane. "I made $50 million out of this war," he crows.

Colonel Teddy Roosevelt threatens to ruin

Hayden: "You packers murdered my boys in Cuba!"

Hayden is cocky and arrogant. "I'll take those words to heart when you come into power," he replies. He and others work behind the scenes to make sure the McKinley-Roosevelt ticket wins—they figure they can handle Roosevelt if he's the vice-president. However, McKinley is assassinated; Roosevelt becomes president, and promises to prosecute the packers.

Martha's father suggests she divorce Hayden. Embittered, Martha expects Laura to leave him. "Then he'll come crawling back to me. I shall wait until then."

Laura returns to the United States. "No matter what happens, no matter how we or the course of our lives may change, here's to our eternal friendship," she toasts Hayden.

"Friendship? Don't you love me, Laura?"

"John, of course, I love you. Passionately. But I can only promise friendship. Let's drink to it." She sits on his lap and kisses him.

Hayden is tried for manslaughter for the tainted meat. Martha begins to write him a letter. "John—I know now what the jury's verdict will be. Your punishment is inevitable." The verdict comes in. "The verdict of the jury is—" Martha continues to write: "I've hidden my humiliation and waited for the day when your well deserved disgrace would catch up with you, and this woman who took my place would desert you. Call my leaving you at this time revenge if you like, but—" Martha stops writing when she hears a boy announce a newspaper extra. She sees the headline: "Hayden Acquitted!"

Martha tears up the letter, and hires a detective to create a nasty scandal. "I've been waiting with the patience of a very bitter woman," she explains. Laura's butler is paid $2,000 to entrap Laura and Hayden. However, Laura returns with another man. "You imbecile!" Martha says to the detective. But, just as they're about to leave, John arrives. He becomes jealous when he sees Laura with the other man.

"I'm sorry, John," Laura coldly, unapologetically says. "It had to happen. You've lost nothing because you never were the only one. Oh, John, I'm trying in my way to be honest with you." A calm, reasoned Laura explains that by "believing in you, I made you believe in yourself." She concludes that he won't be able to forget her. Hayden leaves in a huff. Laura shrugs, and takes a drink.

Hayden returns to his wife. Martha takes off his hat, kisses his head. "I ordered cocktails," she says. "I thought you'd need one."

He leans into her shoulder. "It's been my fault," he says. "I'm just beginning to realize how thoughtless I've been. But I'm going to do better by you, Martha. I'm half mad with ambition, but I'm going to make you part of it. I'm going down in history as the world's greatest merchant. I'll be a king of our times. And I'm going to make you a queen." Martha doesn't react. "Don't you care for me a little bit?" he asks. She laughs. "I wouldn't touch that second cocktail if the first affects you that way." She leaves with a satisfied look on her face.

Meanwhile, the packers' trust is broken up by the courts. Then John sees a newspaper headline—"Laura McDonald Rumored Engaged to German Prince. Nuptials to Take Place Next Month in This City."

War is declared in Europe. Hayden Packing enters into agreements to supply the beef. He goes on a buying frenzy, but the war ends, and all contracts are cancelled. Hayden is ruined. Martha's father tells him to go into receivership. "Mr. Hayden, we can't do anything for you," the bank tells him.

He knocks on Martha's door and tells her the banks have turned him down. He needs $10 million and begs her to get the money from her father. He's been juggling the books and will be arrested if found out.

Martha smiles. "So it's finally here," she says. "The time when you'd come crawling."

He's taken aback. "I never realized it before, but I can see it now, how much you hate me."

"What do you think kept me living with you for twenty years, after I'd known about that other woman?" Martha isn't finished. "I've given up the best part of my life waiting to pay you back for the humiliation I've suffered. Now you're a broken-down old man, facing disgrace, and I'm all you've got to turn to."

Hayden goes to bed. Martha places a blanket on him. "You're a great comfort, Martha."

She turns up the heat register. "Your room will be warm shortly. Tomorrow I'm leaving you," she concludes.

Hayden is indicted. We see a newspaper

clipping—"10 Years Ago Today"—describing how Hayden fled to Athens after his indictment. Now an elderly man, Hayden rests on the balcony. He confuses the past and present, and speaks of his father letting him stay in Athens for three years. "I'm an old man now," he says, suddenly clear.

Laura has come to see him. "A very old friend is here to see you," he's told. "A lady. A singer. Her name's Laura McDonald."

Hayden struggles to remember. "Who? Oh, yes. A dark young lady. She was beautiful. I used to run around with her."

He refuses to see her. Laura plays "Home on the Range" on the piano and sings. "I'll see you in Paris in six months," he mumbles. Laura, now elderly and gray herself, but still beautiful, appears in the doorway.

"Who is this woman?" he asks.

Laura tears up and shakes her head.

"Just a friend," he's told.

"I'm sleepy," John complains, leaning back. The music swells—"Home on the Range."

The original title of this period romance was *Red Meat* and then *Raw Meat*. The movie was a thinly veiled biography of businessman Samuel Insull. At least one writer, Bill Collins, found similarities to *Citizen Kane* in plot, theme, and characters. Writer Sidney Sutherland would later work with Kay on all three of her Monogram films in the 1940s. Edward Gargan was the brother of William Gargan, who starred with Kay in two films.

Edward G. Robinson didn't like the script and argued with writers throughout production. He later wrote this about the film and Kay: "I saw it the other night on Channel 52 (the Edward G. Robinson network), and I was astonished to find it pretty good. Let me give a small bow to Kay Francis. Despite her lisp, despite her background as a model, despite her inexperience in the theater, she had that indefinable presence that somehow enabled her to be convincing as well as beautiful. Another night, on that same relentless channel, I saw her play Florence Nightingale. You cannot imagine a more ludicrous piece of casting—Miss Francis with her Upper West Side New York accent playing an English nurse in the Crimean War and defying British field marshals. And, by God, she made it stick. Hurrah for her!"[46]

Kay's singing voice was dubbed by Rose Dirman, who also dubbed voices for Marion Davies and Miriam Hopkins. This is an example of a movie that had great talent and lots of money, but still ended up being a dud. Slow moving and nonsensical, it makes you wonder what they—the studio, crew, actors, etc.—were thinking.

This film also has some of Edward G. Robinson's worst acting. The normally reliable Robinson is all over the place in the role of a wealthy man who, yes, loved a woman. Genevieve Tobin is marvelous as the devoted wife who becomes bitter and vindictive after spending years with the cruel, indifferent Robinson. She's a woman who truly believes in the adage that revenge is a dish best eaten cold. Tobin bides her time, waits till her husband is at his most vulnerable, and then leaves him. Still, the film doesn't make a lot of sense, and when it finally ends with an aged, dying Robinson not recognizing a graying and perhaps remorseful Kay, one is glad it's finally over.

The two most compelling characters are Laura (Kay always maintained that her best scenes were cut) and Martha. A film focusing on one or both might have been more interesting. Compared to them, John is a weak, impressionable man who never figured out what to do with his life.

REVIEWS: "Mr. Robinson, Miss Francis, and Genevieve Tobin have all been seen to better advantage than in 'I Loved a Woman.'" (*Newsweek*, September 30, 1933)

"Kay Francis is a grateful and sympathetic opera singer who holds interest even when she is caught double-crossing her benefactor." (*Variety*, September 26, 1933)

"[It] is for the most part unusually interesting.... Miss Francis is distinctly pleasing as Laura McDonald." (*New York Times*, October 1, 1933)

"There is tremendous production value, lavish sets, a large cast, effective photography, excellent timing and an interesting story." (Eleanor Barnes, *Los Angeles Illustrated Daily News*, September 15, 1933)

"*I Loved a Woman* has an originality and a method of directorial handling that endows it with a fascinating interest for those of us who grow tired of ga-ga love stories with syrupy endings." (Louella O. Parsons, *Los Angeles Examiner*, September 15, 1933)

The House on 56th Street

(Warner Bros., 1933) 69 min. Released on December 1, 1933.

Credits: Supervisor, James Seymour; director, Robert Florey; story, Joseph Santley; screenplay, Austin Parker, Sheridan Gibney; art director, Esdras Hartley; dialogue director, William Keighley; gowns, Orry-Kelly, Earl Luick; assistant director, Russell Saunders; second assistant director, Arthur Lueker; camera, Ernest Haller; assistant camera, Ellsworth Fredericks; editor, Howard Bretherton; conductor, Leo F. Forbstein; original music, W. Franke Harling, Bernhard Kaun; grip, Dudley Slausson; hair stylist, Emily Moore; props, Keefe Maley; still photographer, Charles Scott Welbourne.

Cast: Kay Francis (Peggy Martin Van Tyle/ Mrs. Stone); Ricardo Cortez (Bill Blaine); Gene Raymond (Monte Van Tyle); John Halliday (Lyndon Fiske); Margaret Lindsay (Eleanor Burgess); Frank McHugh (Chester Hunt); Sheila Terry (Dolly); William "Stage" Boyd (Bonelli); Hardie Albright (Henry Burgess); Phillip Reed (Freddy); Philip Faversham (Gordon); Henry O'Neill (Baxter); Walter Walker (Dr. Wyman); Nella Walker (Mrs. Eleanor Van Tyle; Symona Boniface (Blackjack Player); Frank Darien (Justice of the Peace); George Davis (French Waiter); Lester Dorr (Ship's Steward); Jim Farley (District Attorney); Mary Gordon (Justice of the Peace's Wife); Samuel S. Hinds (Curtis); Olaf Hytten (Peggy's Butler); Lorena Layson (Sextet Girl); Wilfred Lucas (Prosecuting Attorney); John Marston (Ship's Captain); Dennis O'Keefe (Extra); Russ Powell (Tom, the Bartender); George Reed (James, the Butler); Leo White (Beautician); Renee Whitney (Sextet Girl); Pat Wing (Sextet Girl).

THE FILM OPENS ON the stage of the 1905 Gotham Theatre Follies. The chorus girls parade about, singing "Strolling Through the Park One Day." Monte and Lyndon, two men who love Peggy, are in the audience. After the show, Peggy does card tricks backstage. "My grandfather managed to make a living at it," she explains. "Then they caught him holding five aces. He died. Lead poisoning. I learned everything from my father. He could make cards talk."

Peggy decides to marry Monte, though she worries about Lyndon. "He doesn't deserve to be hurt, Monte. He's been too good to me."

"You almost make me wish that I were a marrying man," Lyndon says when she tells him. "But I'm not."

Monte and Peggy marry and travel to Europe, taking in the Moulin Rouge, Venice, and the gambling houses. Monte notices that Peggy has a gambling problem and asks her to stop. "When you gamble, you seem to forget everything, including me," Monte tells her.

"If it upsets you one little bit, I promise never to do it again."

Upon their return to the United States, Monte takes her to the corner of Park Avenue and East 56th Street. "Welcome home, darling. It's all yours," he says, carrying her across the threshold.

"Monte," Peggy says, "I never want to leave this house. I want to live here always."

They quickly have a baby. According to a newspaper clipping, "The baby is the granddaughter of Mrs. Eleanor Van Tyle, widow of the late Aubrey Van Tyle and long prominent in New York society."

At first, Eleanor has nothing to do with the couple because Peggy was a showgirl. However, she comes to see the baby, and is pleased that Peggy named her daughter after her.

A few years later, Lyndon sends Peggy a note: "Convalescence is a dreary business. The doctor threatened to send me to Europe and I may never return. Won't you drop in some afternoon for old time's sake?" Out of guilt, Peggy visits Lyndon. "I made one great mistake in my life," he tells her. "Ever giving you up. I could have asked you to marry me. That was my great mistake. Peggy, I need you. I should never have let you go, my darling. Never. You're the one person on Earth I've loved." He grabs her.

"You're being unfair," she complains, and tells him she's leaving. He takes a gun out of the drawer. They struggle, the gun goes off, and Lyndon collapses. The butler sees Peggy holding the gun.

The newspaper headlines scream: "Fiske Shooting Stirs Society ... Prominent Society Woman Arraigned For Murder!... District Attorney Scores." Peggy is convicted of manslaughter and given twenty years. Monte continues to support her. She begs him to go on with his life and focus on the baby. "Don't tell her unless you have to," she insists. Time passes. The house is boarded up. Peggy ages as she plays cards in her cell. Gray-haired, she receives news that Monte has been killed in the war. More time passes.

Finally, it's 1925. Peggy, now out of prison,

stands at the corner of Broadway and 38th Street. The world is fast-moving and frightening. Cars have replaced carriages, the buildings tower, the streets are busy. Meanwhile, Monte's mother has left Peggy $5,000, and Eleanor has been raised to think her mother dead.

Before she leaves New York, Peggy gets a makeover at a beauty salon. A montage sequence shows her transformation from a graying, middle-aged woman to ... *Kay Francis*! On a ship, she meets Blaine, a con artist and professional gambler. After she beats him at cards, he suggests they team up. "Why not?" she says. "It's a gamble, like everything else in life."

Although they try to keep it professional, Blaine admits he loves her. "You mustn't, Bill. I seem to hurt anybody who ever cares for me."

After much traveling, they end up in New York. Now a distinguished silver-haired lady, she sees a photograph in a magazine: "Mr. and Mrs. Henry Burgess, who are leaving this week for an extended European trip.... Mrs. Burgess is the daughter of the late Monte Van Tyle and popular in the younger set of New York and Newport."

Margaret Lindsay and Kay play mother and daughter in *The House on 56th Street* (1933) (courtesy James King).

Peggy wants to leave New York, but Blaine tells her that Bonelli, who's taken over a house and made it into a speakeasy, wants her to be the blackjack dealer. They arrive at Bonelli's— it's Peggy's old mansion. Peggy hesitates, but Blaine convinces her, reminding her they're broke. One night, while Peggy works upstairs, Eleanor Burgess— Peggy's daughter — is downstairs. Eleanor, who has a gambling problem, promised her husband she wouldn't gamble again. "I better stay down here where I'm safe and the gambling bug can't bite me," she tells a friend, adding that she and her husband are leaving the following night for Europe.

Eleanor is finally convinced to go upstairs, where Peggy immediately recognizes her. Eleanor has a winning streak. Peggy wants her to stop, but Eleanor keeps playing. "I'll teach her a lesson to stop her gambling for the rest of her life," Peggy decides.

Indeed, Eleanor is soon $5,000 in the hole. Still, she won't stop. Quickly, she's $15,000 down. Finally, Eleanor puts her head down and sobs. Blaine tells Eleanor to come back the next day to pay her debts.

"Let's tear them up," Peggy says to Blaine, referring to Eleanor's IOUs. "This might ruin that girl's whole life," she says.

When Eleanor returns, Blaine tells her she must pay the debt or he'll call her husband. Eleanor's frantic. He phones Eleanor's husband, and Eleanor picks up a gun. "Stop it, I tell you!" We hear a gun shot.

Peggy finds Blaine dead. "He was telephoning my husband," Eleanor says.

Peggy removes the IOUs from Blaine's pocket. While Eleanor sobs, Peggy comforts her.

"That's what my mother did!" Eleanor hysterically tells her. "She shot a man, killed him, and went to prison! Died there!"

Peggy tells her she'll take care of everything. "I'm not going to have your life ruined the way your mother's was."

Eleanor is surprised. "I never expected you to be my friend," she says.

"Perhaps some day," Peggy says, "you'll look back and see that I was the best friend you ever had."

Eleanor leaves, and Peggy locks the door to Blaine's office. That night Bonelli finds Blaine's body. He eyes Peggy. She nods. "I did it."

Bonelli tells her he'll take care of it. "I can't

afford to lose you, and you can't afford to go. You and I can make plenty of real money together. And I'd like to have you stay here.... Always."

We see a flashback of Peggy and Monte. "I never want to leave this house," Peggy tells him. "I want to live here always."

"So you shall," Monte says.

"And so I shall," she tearfully repeats. "So I shall."

This is a great role for Kay. She has numerous costume changes and is photographed beautifully. The film was a Ruth Chatterton reject. Kay, too, resisted the role, but Warner Bros. convinced her it was worthy of her attention. Adolphe Menjou was originally cast in the Ricardo Cortez role.

It was remade in England as *The Return of Carol Deane* (1938) with Bebe Daniels and Arthur Margetson — and written by John Meehan, Jr., son of the writer Kay supposedly married in the 1920s. This British film was produced at Teddington Studios, whose distributor was Warner Bros. Lorena Layson, who also appeared in *The House on 56th Street*, became Louis B. Mayer's second wife in 1948.

Advertisement copy proclaimed: "Again I was to be the mistress of the House on 56th Street. The first time I came to the house on 56th Street, I came as a bride. Now I had come back to it — *come back after all those unhappy years*. It was too late to turn back ... no way to escape the cruel irony that forced me to preside as mistress in the *very rooms* that were so sacred to the memory of Monte and my little girl! It was Fate ... I knew that what had happened in the past was merely a prologue — that the great drama of my life was yet to be played..."

REVIEWS: "[Q]uite an original and intriguing pictorial drama. Miss Francis, as Peggy, gives an adequate performance. She looks charming in the costumes of the Nineties." (*New York Times*, December 2, 1933)

"'The House on 56th Street' has more than the ordinary quota of originality, even though it does not sustain the motif in the deliberate and restrained manner one might wish. Miss Francis does quite well by her role." (*New York Times*, December 10, 1933)

"Combination romance and gambling yarn makes engrossing entertainment, chiefly for adults." (*Film Daily*, December 2, 1933)

"For swell acting and a good dramatic and logical story you mustn't miss this one." (*Silver Screen*, January 1934.

"Miss Francis, who is generally unemotional, appears to best advantage in the latter part of the picture wherein she portrays a hard, disillusioned professional gambler." (Elizabeth Yeaman, *Hollywood Citizen News*, January 5, 1934)

"Ruth Chatterton is said to have refused [*The House on 56th Street*] as a vehicle. Kay Francis finds in it an opportunity to do some of the best dramatic work of her career." (Jerry Hoffman, *Los Angeles Examiner*, January 5, 1934)

"Miss Francis gives the role of the heroine a certain aplomb that it doesn't deserve, wears a wealth of gorgeous clothes and looks interesting." (*Variety*, December 5, 1933)

Mandalay

(Warner Bros., 1934) 65 min. Released on February 15, 1934, Strand Theater.

Credits: Producer, Robert Presnell Sr.; director, Michael Curtiz; based on the story by Paul Hervy Fox; screenplay, Austin Parker, Charles Kenyon; art director, Anton Grot; gowns, Orry-Kelly; camera, Tony Gaudio; editor, Thomas Pratt; technical director, Don Taylor; grip, William McNally; still photographer, Mac Julian; assistant camera, Stuart Higgs; conductor, Leo F. Forbstein; original music, Sammy Fain, Irving Kahal, Heinz Roemheld; sound, W.S. Brown; props, G.W. Bernstein; assistant director, Frank Shaw; hair stylist, Ruth Pursley.

Cast: Kay Francis (Tanya Borisoff/Spot White/Margaret Lang); Ricardo Cortez (Tony Evans); Lyle Talbot (Dr. Gregory Burton); Warner Oland (Nick); Ruth Donnelly (Mrs. Peters); Reginald Owen (Police Commissioner); David Torrence (Captain of the Sirohi); Etienne Girardot (Mr. Abernathie); Rafaela Ottiano (Countess); Lucien Littlefield (Mr. Peters); Halliwell Hobbes (Colonel Dawson Ames); Bodil Rosing (Mrs. Kleinschmidt); Herman Bing (Professor Kleinschmidt); Lillian Harmer (Louisa Mae Harrington); Torben Meyer (Mr. Van Brinken); Harry C. Bradley (Henry P. Warren); James Leong (Ram Singh); Shirley Temple (Betty Shaw); Leonard Mudie (Police Lieutenant); Frank Baker (First Mate); Olaf Hytten (Cockney Purser); Eric Wilton (English Agent); Otto Frisco (Fakir); George Herrera (Second Steward); Desmond Roberts (Police Sergeant); Hobart Cavanaugh (Purser); Henry Otho (Second Sergeant); Lottie Williams (Peters' Friend).

THE FILM IS SET in Rangoon. Tanya knows little about Tony's financial affairs, but is madly in love with him. "Life didn't mean a thing to me until I met you," she tells him. "Now it means everything."

Tony hints that something may be afoot. "No matter what happens, I want you to promise to keep your chin up," he says.

They eat at Nick's supper club. Tanya checks out the women. "All these girls, what are they?" she asks.

"Just like café girls anywhere."

"You mean...?"

"I mean exactly that, my dear."

Nick invites Tanya and Tony upstairs where he's entertaining business associates. Tanya sits at the piano and sings (obviously dubbed). Tony makes a deal with Nick, and Tanya is unknowingly part of it. Nick hands Tanya a note from Tony. "Tanya — Forgive me if you can. There was nothing else I could do without losing everything. Goodbye — Good luck and chin up. Tony."

Nick explains that Tony has traded her. "It was a question of you or a cargo of guns, and you lost."

Depressed, Tanya pouts and doesn't eat. The countess counsels her. "You're making such a fool of yourself. If I had your beauty and my experience, what I could do. You'll find out that it's easier to make men do what you want them to, than it is to fall in love and have them make a fool of you."

Tanya agrees this makes sense, and quickly becomes hardened but savvy. Wearing a shimmering gown, her jet black hair plastered down, she makes an entrance down the wide staircase.

"So they call her Spot White, eh?" one customer says.

"She should be called Spot Cash."

There's a montage of bar shots — Tanya smokes, drinks, dances, accepts jewelry, etc. Time passes. Nick and Tanya are called to the Superintendent of Police.

"She's so playful, so full of spirit," Nick explains.

The colonel sees Spot alone. "I've had more complaints about you than any other woman in town. Two officers were court martialed on your account." He tells her she's being deported. "Why the devil haven't you behaved yourself? You seem intelligent."

"I am." She boldly sits on his desk and reminds him of a dalliance they had. "I'm being deported, you know. Oh, I may leave Rangoon. But I'm leaving with 10,000 rupees of your money." She offers him a cigarette — it's his cigarette case. "You called me your itty, bitty baby," she reminds. "Well, colonel?" He pays, and Tanya gets on a boat out of Rangoon.

Dressed conservatively, she tells the purser her name is Margaret Lang and that she's going to Mandalay. While unpacking, she drops Tony's photograph. The glass shatters, and she cuts her hand. The steward tells Dr. Burton about the incident, and he tends to her wound. Burton tells her he's going to black fever country to help with an epidemic. Later, the doctor gets drunk, is asked to check on a sick child, but never shows up. Tanya finds him and tells him the child is already dead. Burton explains he resigned from the Army and ran away when a 19-year-old West Point cadet died under his care; his drinking was blamed. "I've got to do something decent," he explains.

"Decency isn't in bottles," she says.

The doctor makes an effort to remain sober. Meanwhile, Tony comes aboard and knocks on Tanya's door. "I thought you might be glad to see me," he actually says. He tries to embrace her, but she pulls away. "Why do you call yourself Miss Lang?" he asks.

"Under that name, I have no market value," she says.

He wants her to forget what happened. "Everything has gone wrong for me since that night at Nick's," he tells her. "Everything. Let's have a drink of old times. Just you and I."

They have a drink, and Tony tells her he loves her. "I'll never let you go again, Tanya. Never." He kisses her.

"I've earned my freedom," she tells him. "I'm a human being again!"

Tony gets a coded message that warns of his imminent arrest. Meanwhile, Dr. Burton has gotten drunk again. The wonderful Ruth Donnelly plays Mrs. Peters, an American traveling with her husband. She and Tanya have a brief conversation about men. "You certainly can wear clothes!" Mrs. Peters says. "You know, I bought a dress in Paris, but I'm afraid to wear it. My husband made me take it off. Said I looked nude. You know, like a wet seal. It's funny how men are. They like to see other women wear things like that. But they want their own wives to wear Mother Hubbard's. Haven't you noticed?"

Kay Francis as the tragic Tanya (Spot White) in *Mandalay* (1934).

"Well, I've never been a wife," Tanya says.

"Well, you've got something coming to you, my dear."

Tanya returns to her cabin, hoping to avoid Tony. The crew receives a telegram requesting they arrest and hold Tony. They discover an open window and a poison bottle. "We have a case of suicide on board," they conclude.

Tanya is questioned by the captain. She first says she didn't know him, but finally admits she lied because she was ashamed. "He was friendly enough at first, and then I ... I found that he wasn't." Dr. Burton defends her.

"Have you ever heard of Spot White?" Tanya later asks Dr. Burton. "Have you ever heard of Nick's place in Rangoon? If you'd ever been there, you'd have seen me."

"*You*?"

"Do you want to know the rest? Or is that enough?"

Burton tells her he still loves her. She asks him to take her up to black fever country when they arrive in Mandalay. "I can't do that. Don't you realize there isn't one chance in a hundred of coming out of it alive."

"Listen," she says, "we're two wrecked people. We need one another."

Kay Francis and Ricardo Cortez enjoy a romantic moment on the cover of the *Mandalay* (1934) sheet music.

"You mean, if we come through, perhaps together we can make something of ourselves?"

"Isn't that our only hope?"

He asks if she'd feel that way if Tony were still alive. She doesn't know, but doesn't want his name brought up again. "He's gone now. There's only you."

Tony returns. He tells her he ransacked her cabin for money, couldn't find any, but did find the poison bottle. He set up the scene and then hid. He wants to form a partnership and open up a joint together.

"You want to put me back into that?" she asks.

"Why not? I think it's a swell idea. Don't you?" She spies the poison bottle and pours him a drink. "You're my girl no matter what happens," he says. She gives him the drink. "We'll drink to our future success in Mandalay," he says. Tony embraces her. She pulls away. Tony reels from the effects of the poison.

"I loved you, Tony. I loved you more than life. And what did you make of me? Spot White. I couldn't go back to that. I couldn't! Forgive me."

He reaches out for her throat, and then, rather conveniently, jumps out the window, into the water. The ship arrives in Mandalay. Tanya is stone-faced as she and Dr. Burton walk away from the ship and head for black fever country.

Production started October 17, 1933, and ended November 17. Kay is top-billed again, and is a must-see. Her hair has grown out some, and she's photographed beautifully. Ruth Chatterton turned down Kay's role, supposedly because she was tired of playing "bad ladies." At one time, Chatterton's husband George Brent was slated to play the male lead, but refused in October 1933 because of a salary dispute. Donald Woods and Kathryn Sergova were at one time the leads. An exasperated Elsie Janis wrote, "By the time you read this, *Mandalay* will probably have become *Labrador*. Janet Gaynor may be playing the over-advertised heroine while Baby LeRoy replaces George Brent as the leading male interest. Such is the ever-changing Hollywood crazy quilt of casting."[47]

Like *Mary Stevens, M.D.*, this film was re-issued in 1936, but denied the Seal of Approval from the Legion of Decency. The bath scene before Tanya and Tony leave for dinner was censored and almost completely cut. This scene was filmed at night, and Kay complained that it was very chilly. During production, she also took a tumble down the stairs and severely bruised herself. Patricia Keats, a writer for *Silver Screen*, witnessed the accident. "Hollywood's best dressed actress started down the steps, looking languidly toward the dance floor. One heel got caught in the train of her gown, and down she came, bumpity bump BUMP.... But Kay refused to let a little thing like that make her call off work for the day. She really was considerably bruised, but as she remarked to me, 'The bruises aren't where they show.'" By the way, the stairs were supposedly modeled after similar ones in a Shanghai nightclub.

The boat landing scenes were filmed on the Sacramento and San Joaquin Rivers near Stockton, California — popular places to film steamboat scenes. The paddle-wheel steamer, supposedly belonging to the Irrawaddy Flotilla Company — a legendary name in colonial Burma — was actually the *Capital City*, named after Sacramento. Other scenes were filmed on Catalina Island.

This was one of Shirley Temple's first film roles. She later wrote, "*Mandalay* was a steamy, sensual tropical yarn, but my fleeting part was as a homey prop, held for an instant in someone's arms."[48] Actually, some film viewers have gone slowly mad trying to find her. According to Anne Edwards, Shirley played the child of Mr. and Mrs. Peters. Her part was so small that her name didn't appear in the credits when the film was first released. It was added during its re-release.

Notice the bandage on Lyle Talbot's head? He had injured himself in a car accident, and the screenplay had to be rewritten to explain the bandage.

The song, "When Tomorrow Comes," was written by Sammy Fain and Irving Kahal. Virginia Verrill dubbed Kay's singing voice.

Fans love this picture — sometimes for the wrong reasons. According to Jerry Vermilye, "[T]his unlikely tale of a mistreated lady's survival becomes an unintentionally amusing sixty-five minutes of constant drinking, smoking, and incredible conversation.... *Mandalay* offers pure, foolish escapism, and for 1934's Depression-weary moviegoers, what could have been more welcome?"[49]

Ricardo Cortez (born Jacob Krantz) seemed to make a career of playing murder victims. Kay appeared in four films with him, and he's bumped off in each.

Advertising copy proclaimed: "When the dawn comes up like thunder ... to end bewitching nights. Kay Francis in a land where beauty is a girl's misfortune!"

REVIEWS: "Poor story material for Kay Francis, miscast as shady lady, and Ricardo Cortez. However, Rangoon and Mandalay atmosphere perfect." (*Photoplay*, October 1934)

"They moved Kay Francis to the other side of the world, around Rangoon, for a story laid in the Far East that's duck soup to the star. Miss Francis is an intriguing and interesting figure." (*Variety*, February 20, 1934)

"Miss Francis is highly decorative and Lyle Talbot plays the young physician pleasantly." (*New York Times*, February 15, 1934)

"This particular road to Mandalay is a hackneyed one. Miss Francis, in spite of her handicaps, manages to prove that she is still one of the most intelligent actresses on the screen." (*London Daily Telegraph*, July 2, 1934)

"Kay Francis miscast in rather poor story that is too much for the good cast to overcome." (*Film Daily*, February 15, 1934)

"Lovers of lurid melodrama should be pleased with the plot. The cast is competent enough." (Elizabeth Yeaman, *Hollywood Citizen News*, March 2, 1934)

"*Mandalay* is her most melodramatic to date. She creates a real illusion as the seductive Spot White, charmer of all races, with a few overtones of that flamboyant humor lately regarded as Mae West territory. Make no mistake, you'll like Kay Francis in her clothes, her rich, exotic lure, her drama, no matter how you quarrel with the over-wrought story." (W.E. Oliver, *Los Angeles Evening Herald Express*, March 2, 1934)

Wonder Bar
(Warner Bros., 1934) 85 min.
Released on February 28, 1934.

Credits: Producer, Robert Lord; director, Lloyd Bacon; based on the play by Karl Farkas, Robert Katscher, and Geza Herczeg; screenplay, Earl Baldwin; songs, Harry Warren, Al Dubin; music director, Leo F. Forbstein; musical numbers created and directed by Busby Berkeley; camera, Sol Polito; editor, George Amy; art direction, Jack Okey, Willy Pogany; costumes, Orry-Kelly; assistant camera, L. De Angelis; electrician, Frank Flanagan; second camera operator, Mike Joyce; still photographer, B. Longworth.

Cast: Al Jolson (Al Wonder); Kay Francis (Liane Renaud); Dolores Del Rio (Inez); Ricardo Cortez (Harry); Dick Powell (Tommy); Guy Kibbee (Henry Simpson); Hugh Herbert (Corey Pratt); Robert Barrat (Captain Von Ferring); Ruth Donnelly (Mrs. Emma Simpson); Louise Fazenda (Mrs. Panzy Pratt); Fifi D'Orsay (Mitzi); Merna Kennedy (Claire); Henry Kolker (Mr. R.H. Renaud); Henry O'Neill (Richard); Kathryn Sergava (Ilke); Gordon De Main, Harry Woods (Detectives); Emile Chautard (Pierre, the Concierge); Pauline Garon (Operator); Alphonse Martell (Doorman); Jane Darwell (Baroness); Gordon "Wild Bill" Elliott (Norman); Michael Dalmatoff (Russian Count); Renee Whitney, Amo Ingraham, Rosalie Roy (Chorus Girls); Alfred James (Night Watchman); Clay Clement, William Stack (Businessmen); Grace Hayle (Fat Dowager); Hal LeRoy (Himself); Spencer Charters (Pete); Demetrius Alexis (Young Boy); William Anderson (Call Boy); Louis Ardizoni (Leon, the Cook); Hobart Cavanaugh (Drunk); Gino Corrado (Second Waiter); Dick Good (Page Boy); William Granger (First Bartender); Robert Graves (Police Officers); Lottie Woods (Wardrobe Woman); Mia Ichioka (GeeGee); George Irving (Broker); Bud Jamison (Third Bartender); Eddie Kane (Frank); Edward Keane (Captain); John Marlowe (Young Man); Bert

Kay played the minor role of a banker's unfaithful wife in *Wonder Bar* (1934).

Moorhouse (Joe); Marie Moreau (Marie, Liane's Maid); Mahlon Norvell (Artist); Dave O'Brien (Chorus Boy); Dennis O'Keefe (Man at Bar); Henry Otho (2nd Bartender); Gene Perry (Gendarme); Paul Power (Chester); Rolfe Sedan (First Waiter); Miriam Marlin (Chorine)

INEZ AND HARRY ARE the top-billed act at Al Wonder's Montmarte nightclub. Tommy's in love with Inez, who's in love with Harry, who's in love with Liane, who's in love with Harry. Further complicating matters is owner Al Wonder — he's in love with Inez, too.

Detectives tell Liane Renaud's disbelieving banker husband that she's having an affair with dance teacher Harry. "Mr. Renaud, every detective knows that when married women start taking dancing lessons from gigolos and begin to lose expensive jewelry, the results are not always so amusing."

Liane denies she's having an affair, claiming, "I'm so bored I could scream."

Meanwhile, Captain Von Ferring closes out his bank account. Financially ruined, he decides to spend one last night at the Wonder Bar and then kill himself.

A nervous Liane arrives at the club without her husband, hoping to see Harry. The show begins. Inez and Harry arrive late and perform their dance act. The production turns into an elaborately staged platinum-blonde chorus-girl dance ensemble, beautifully choreographed with pillars as only Berkeley could do, complete with aerial crane camera.

"Why can't this go on forever?" Inez asks, when the number concludes with her and Harry kissing.

Liane wants to send a note to Harry, but is interrupted by her husband's arrival. When Mr. Renaud is called away from their table, Liane quickly tells Tony he must return her necklace — that's how she pays for her "dancing" lessons — because detectives are inquiring about it. He lies, telling her he's sold it, and informs her he's leaving for America. She wants to go with him. Harry tells Inez the same news. She, too, wants to follow him. He's cold to both women.

Al gives Harry 100,000 francs for the necklace and tells him he's fired. Meanwhile, Liane waits for Harry in the car, planning to rendezvous with him after his act.

"If you run away with Harry tonight, you'll regret it the rest of your life," Al tells her. He gives her the necklace, telling her Harry sold it to him. "A little present from me to you. Now if you still think he's on the level, go away with him."

Harry and Inez perform the Gaucho Dance, a fast-paced number where "he whips her and he whips her and he whips her. But she loves it!" Harry tells Inez he's leaving for good — without her. Inez, eyes on fire, grabs his knife and stabs him. They hurry off stage. Al sees the bloody knife. "Just a little scratch," Harry says.

Inez apologizes and faints. Harry dies.

Al, told the captain is planning to drive off a cliff, carries Harry's body to the captain's car, and the drunken, suicidal captain drives away.

Meanwhile, Liane has returned to her husband's table. "Your decision has made me very happy," Al tells Liane. She thanks him and shows her husband the necklace, explaining she's found it. "Are you going to scold me?" she asks.

A rare smile from Kay in *Wonder Bar* (1934) (courtesy James King).

"Don't be silly. But you ought to be spanked for being so careless."

Inez wakes up, believing she's killed Harry. Al tells her he's fine, and that the captain has taken him home.

Tommy makes a date with Inez, while Al gets a phone call from the police: The captain and Harry were killed in an auto accident.

Al whistles, gathers his things, and leaves his dressing room. "Well, I guess it's home," he says, getting in his car. The Wonder Bar carpet is rolled up.

Kay hated this production. She's a sullen little girl. No smiles in this one. Kay and Al weren't speaking. Neither were Ricardo and Al. In the scene when Al has to carry his body, Ricardo, the Latin heartthrob did the "I weigh 500 pounds" routine. Henry Kolker made a part-time career out of playing Kay's cuckolded husband; this was his third time.

Kay's role had been turned down by Genevieve Tobin, and had been considered as a possible comeback by Norma Talmadge. The biggest problem Kay had, besides not liking Al, was her role was cut at the expense of the beautiful Dolores Del Rio. If you look closely, you'll see that a double is used in some of Dolores' dancing scenes.

Among the stars considered for leads in the film were Adolphe Menjou, Bette Davis, Ruby Keeler, Ann Dvorak, and Barbara Stanwyck. At one time, Frank Borzage was up for the director job. Irving Kahal and Sammy Fain were the original choices for songwriting.

The film, structured like *Grand Hotel*, was based on Al Jolson's Broadway show. The play opened on March 17, 1931, at the Nora Bayes Theatre, and ran for 76 performances. An adaptation of a German play, it was described as "a revolutionary show. It had no curtain and the café staff moved back and forth on the stage throughout the performance to add a touch of realism."[50] Jolson wisely negotiated his contract so he'd receive ten percent of the film's grosses — and *Wonder Bar* was one of the top-grossing films of the year.

The sets are wonderful — better than the picture. Berkeley proudly described one of the production numbers: "I had them build me sixty tall white movable columns, to move against a black background. The columns were on separate tracks, independent of each other and all controlled electrically. I had a hundred

Ricardo Cortez, Dolores Del Rio, Al Jolson, Kay Francis, and Dick Powell at the *Wonder Bar*.

dancers dance with the columns. Then they all disappeared and in their place was a huge forest of silver trees with a white reindeer running around. To get the effect I wanted, I built an octagon of mirrors — each twenty-eight feet high and twelve feet wide — and inside the octad a revolving platform twenty-four feet in diameter. When I was drawing up my plans for this, everyone at the studio thought I had lost my mind. Even Sol Polito, one of the best cameramen I ever worked with, couldn't figure out how I was going to photograph a production from the inside without the camera being seen. Actually, when I figured it out in my office using eight little compacts — the kind girls carry in their handbags — I discovered there was a way of moving at the center of the mirrors without being reflected."[51]

Merna Kennedy, who played one of the flirtatious hostesses, was married to Berkeley at the time. A comic sidelight is the four American tourists — two married couples — played by great character actors. The men want to play around, and the wives want to keep track of their husbands, and maybe play around themselves.

Don't miss the legendary gay scene, either. After Al's act, there's a dance number. A man asks to cut in on a couple. "Certainly," the young woman says. The man, however, dances with the male partner. She stalks off. "Boys will be boys!" Al exclaims with an effeminate swing of his hips.

Al's performance is high energy. While he's an acquired taste, you get an idea of his appeal. He performs the final act, "Goin' to Heaven on a Mule," in blackface. This number has to be seen to be believed. We could explain it to you, but you still wouldn't understand. "Ever since I was a little picaninny" is just one of the lines.

This film could not have been made after the Production Code went into effect. For one thing, Dolores Del Rio murders her straying lover — and gets away with it. Another problem is the sado-masochistic relationship between Del Rio and Cortez. Then there's the scene where the gay man happily dances off with the male. And don't forget the overtly racist musical number, "Goin' to Heaven on a Mule." The script was submitted to the SRC in October 1933, and came back with thirteen requested changes. Producer Hal B. Wallis mostly ignored the changes but ran into trouble when local censor boards in Ohio and Pennsylvania cut some of the scenes.

According to Wallis, the production was costly: "The huge set of a London nightclub was so expensive, I was forced to caution Berkeley. When I told him he couldn't have more than a hundred dancers (a fantastic extravagance at the time), he groaned with disappointment — then went on to make a hundred look like a thousand with the use of mirrors. Somehow, he managed to hide the cameras in a mirrored room."[52]

Ironically, one of the *Wonder Bar* mirrors was used during the making of *Tovarich*, the Claudette Colbert picture that led to Kay's lawsuit with Warner Bros. Director Anatole Litvak and special effects designer Byron Haskin put their heads together to solve a problem: "A lesson in patience and ingenuity was learned by all during the filming of the Bastille Day celebration in *Tovarich*. Three hundred extras were milling around a real street when fog drifted in to prevent further filming. Litvak moved a process screen rooftop to a sound stage, but he couldn't achieve the proper camera angles at the new location. Special effects man Byron Haskin finally came to the rescue with a mirror borrowed from the set of the musical [*Wonder Bar*]. Litvak and Haskins set up a 75-foot cloth tunnel. At one end a rear projection machine was placed, focused on the glass at the other end. The mirror was tilted to reflect on the screen erected at the edge of the roof set. The camera on the roof ridge filmed the necessary shot of [Charles] Boyer and Colbert on the rooftop as they gazed down in bewilderment at the celebration in the street."[53] Movie magic!

Advertisements proclaimed, "Warner Bros.' parade of stars marches to greater glory! Sensation of two continents on the stage, it comes to the screen in a blaze of unrivalled splendor to give you a gloriously new conception of musical screen spectacle!"

REVIEWS: "Suffice it to say that those who are partial to this type of entertainment will probably relish 'Wonder Bar,' especially during those interludes where Mr. Jolson lifts his voice to vehement singing." (*New York Times*, March 1, 1934)

"'Wonder Bar' is a dazzling medley of music, laughs, lavish display, and action." (*Newsweek*, March 3, 1934)

"Chock full of entertainment elements and eye and ear production values pleasing to both exhibitors and patrons." (*Motion Picture Herald*, February 17, 1934)

"Like other recent Warner Brothers productions, *Wonder Bar* contains more than its quota of obscenity." (*Time*, March 5, 1934)

"Miss Francis plays her faithless wife role with a superciliousness and condescension not in keeping with the assignment." (*Variety*, March 6, 1934)

Dr. Monica
(Warner Bros., 1934) 75 min.
Released on June 20, 1934.

Credits: Executive producer, Jack L. Warner, Hal B. Wallis; producer, Henry Blanke; director, William Keighley, William Dieterle; based on the play by Maria Morozowicz-Szczepkowska; screenplay, Charles Kenyon; English adaptation, Laura Walker Mayer; art director, Anton Grot; gowns, Orry-Kelly; music director, Leo F. Forbstein; original music, Heinz Roemheld; camera, Sol Polito; editor, William Clemens; assistant director, Lee Katz.

Cast: Kay Francis (Dr. Monica Braden); Warren William (John Braden); Jean Muir (Mary Hathaway);

Verree Teasdale (Anna Littlefield); Phillip Reed (Bunny Burton); Emma Dunn (Mrs. Monahan); Herbert Bunston (Mr. Pettinghill); Ann Shoemaker (Mrs. Hazlitt); Virginia Hammond (Mrs. Chandor); Hale Hamilton (Dr. Brent); Virginia Pine (Louise); Pauline True (Betsey, Anna's Maid); Leila McIntyre (Elizabeth, Monica's Maid); Norma Drew (Anna's Second Maid); Edward McWade (Janitor); Harry Seymour (Taxi Driver); Eric Wilton (Spike, Chandor's Butler); Gordon "Wild Bill" Elliott (Rutherford, the Horseback Rider); Reginald Pasch (Mr. Swiegart); Marion Lessing (Mrs. Swiegart); Helen Jerome Eddy (Miss Gelsey); Louise Beavers (Sarah, Mary's Maid); Stanley Mack (Bob, Airplane Mechanic); Claire McDowell (Miss Bryerly); Paul Power (Clerk); Sam Rice (Extra at Dock).

MONICA IS A DOCTOR, and husband John a writer. However, they don't spend much time together because of Monica's busy career. John's been having a secret affair with young aspiring pilot Mary Hathaway. One night at a party, Monica confides to Mary that John is going to Europe for six months. She won't be joining him because she plans to use the time to meet with a doctor—Monica desperately wants to have a baby.

Mary faints at the party and then hurries off, returning to her apartment. John meets her there and explains the European trip is partly to break off the affair. "It'll be easier with the ocean between us," he explains. Mary tells him she loves him, but knows he's still in love with Monica.

While John's in Europe, Monica stays with friend Anna. Monica tells Mary that she wants a baby because "it'll make John happier."

Meanwhile, Mary drinks too much and is obviously miserable. "Who is he, Mary?" Monica asks, realizing someone's broken her heart. "Darling, you're young," she consoles. "You'll get over it."

Later, Monica learns Mary is pregnant. She counsels Mary to talk to the man, but is told he is married. Mary becomes desperate.

"Monica, you've got to help me!" Mary pleads, hinting she'd like an abortion. Monica scolds her, and assures Mary everything will be fine.

John returns after two months. However, Monica gets bad news about the procedure that might enable her to have a baby. "There's no use my going to the hospital. Ever."

Meanwhile, Monica arranges for Mary to go to the country to have the baby. While preparing for childbirth, Monica overhears a

In *Dr. Monica* (1934), Kay played an obstetrician with marital and fertility problems.

hysterical Mary call John. She haltingly walks down the stairs. "The man is John," she tells Anna. "Get another doctor."

"She's your patient," Anna says. "Right now her life and reputation are in your hands."

"Do you think I'd touch her?" Monica asks. "I'd kill her. I have the right."

Anna slaps her (watch Kay flinch before Anna raises her hand). "Go upstairs, Monica."

"Thanks."

Monica delivers the baby, though not without glaring bigtime at Mary. She returns to New York and John, though she doesn't tell him she knows about the affair. She and John have a two-week second honeymoon. When it's over, Monica decides to leave John so he and Mary can be together. "They love each other and it's their child. Those two weeks of happiness may be all I have for the rest of my life."

Monica gets a job in Vienna. John thinks he'll be joining her, but Monica writes him a letter, explaining why she must leave.

Meanwhile, Anna visits Mary and tells her that Monica is leaving John because of the baby. "What a splendid thing for her to have done," Mary says. "Giving me my baby, knowing it was—I've simply got to do something." Mary thinks, looking up towards the heavens. An idea occurs to her. "Anna, I have an idea. I haven't had many in my life. Good ones. Leave it to me, will you? Everything will turn out all right for Monica."

Mary writes a note to Monica, holds the baby, kisses her, and sobs. "Goodbye, darling." She hurries out of the house, goes to the airfield, and jokes with the mechanic that she's headed for Paris. The plane takes off.

The baby has been dropped off at Monica's with a note: "Forgive me Monica—I'll never bother you again. The baby is yours and John's. Can't you forgive me, and be happy. Mary."

Anna phones. "Monica, something dreadful has happened. Mary's flown a plane out over the ocean, and they have no trace of it. They're afraid she's lost."

Monica grimly hangs up and leads John to the baby. "I've adopted her, John."

"I think it'll be the most wonderful thing in the world. We've always wanted one. Where did you get it? Whose is it?"

"I thought it better we didn't know who the parents were. Then we can think of it more as ours. The mother died. I know it comes from splendid people." Monica picks up the baby.

"I swear I've never seen you look so lovely," he says.

She hands the baby to John. "She's yours," Monica says, not kidding. They smile.

Joel McCrea and Barbara Stanwyck were at one time considered for the leads. Kay received top billing, but this was *not* a good movie. In fact, it's probably the worst film of her career up to this point, though the sets are lovely. This was yet another role turned down by Ruth Chatterton. Production began February 24, 1934, and ended March 15, 1934. Working titles included *The Affairs of Monica* and *When Tomorrow Comes*.

The film was based on a successful Polish play by Maria Morozowicz-Szczepkowska. An English-language adaptation by Laura Walker Mayer was produced on Broadway with Alla Nazimova playing Kay's role. The American production opened November 6, 1933, but ran for only two weeks.

The film ran into plenty of problems with the Legion of Decency and the Production Code because of adultery and the hint of abortion. Joseph Breen wanted any mention of abortion removed. According to Mark A. Vieira, the following exchange between Mary and Monica was in the original script:

Mary: This is hideous! You're got to help me.
Monica: Of course I will.
Mary: When? Right away?
Monica (sternly): Just what do you mean?
Mary (desperately): You know!
Monica (angrily): Don't you ever talk that way again—don't you ever think that way again![54]

The abortion reference was removed, resulting in a jump cut.[55] However, even with the cut, the Legion of Decency *still* condemned it.

Warren William sent Warner Bros. into hysterics when he returned for retakes. He'd already started work on *Cleopatra*—he was playing Caesar—and Cecil B. DeMille had requested he get a haircut and shave off his mustache. Warner Bros. thus had to spend much time and money making a wig and finding a suitable mustache.

Kay, who attended the premiere with boyfriend Maurice Chevalier, realized this picture was a dud. "Kay Francis, looking perfectly

In this publicity photograph from *Dr. Monica* (1934), Kay wears an Orry-Kelly design.

Kay Francis and Jean Muir in *Dr. Monica* (1934).

stunning in a green sports suit, brown hat with a feather stuck in it, and brown accessories, attended the preview of *Dr. Monica* with Maurice Chevalier. Unfortunately, the audience laughed in the wrong places at this preview. And believe it or not, no one laughed any harder than Kay. Now there's what we call a sense of humor!"[56]

Advertising was interesting for this controversial movie: "Only a super–woman could have lived this story.... Only a super-star could bring it to the screen! You'll marvel as you watch the supreme artistry of Kay Francis sweep triumphantly through a role only the greatest dare to play! You'll thrill as four great personalities from Warner Bros. famed star ranks re-create the story critics warned could not be screened! You'll applaud it as the finest dramatic achievement of the present year!"

REVIEWS: "It moves apace and the acting is excellent. Miss Francis is believable in her role and Miss Teasdale adds to the general interest of the film." (*New York Times*, June 21, 1934)

"There is little to interest men. It is far too deep and heavy for even the more mature adolescents." (*Motion Picture Herald*, May 26, 1934)

"A trivial contribution to the cinema's dossier on bastardy, *Dr. Monica* serves to demonstrate the versatility of Warner's latest star, Jean Muir." (*Time*, July 2, 1934)

"Even in her best moments Miss Francis in this film is mostly a well-dressed lady who is acting: always acting." (*Variety*, June 26, 1934)

British Agent
(Warner Bros., 1934) 75 min.
Released on September 20, 1934.

Credits: Director, Michael Curtiz; supervisor, Henry Blanke; suggested by the novel by R.H. Bruce Lockhart; screenplay, Laird Doyle; British dialogue, Roland Pertwee; dialogue, Pierre Collings; art director, Anton Grot; music director, Leo F. Forbstein; original music, Bernhard Kaun, Heinz Roemheld;

camera operator, Al Roberts; assistant camera, Bob Davis, Ernest Haller; editor, Thomas Richards; assistant editor, Warren Low; dialogue director, Frank McDonald; technical director, Nicholas Kobliansky; gowns, Orry-Kelly; recording engineer, Dave Forrest; electrician, Claude Hutchinson; grip, Owen Crompton; props, Scotty Moore; still photographer, Homer Van Pelt.

Cast: Leslie Howard (Stephen Locke); Kay Francis (Elena); William Gargan (Bob Medill); Phillip Reed (Gaston LeFarge); Irving Pichel (Pavlov); Walter Byron (Undersecretary Stanley); Cesar Romero (Tito Del Val); J. Carrol Naish (Commissioner for War); Ivan Simpson (Evans); Gregory Gaye (Kolinoff); Halliwell Hobbes (Sir Walter Carrister); Arthur Aylesworth (Farmer); Mary Forbes (Lady Catherine Trehearne); Doris Lloyd (Lady Carrister); Alphonse Ethier (DeVigny); Paul Porcasi (Romano); Addison Richards (Zvododu); Marina Schubert (Maria Nikolaievna); George Pearce (Lloyd George, Cabinet Officer); Tenen Holtz (Lenin); Walter Armitage (Under Secretary Armitage); Frank Reicher (Mr. X); Donald Crisp (Marshall O'Reilly); Lew Harvey (Suspect); Olaf Hytten (Undersecretary); Frank Lackteen (Suspect); Leonid Snegoff (Russian Diplomat); Wyndham Standing (Englishman); Basil Lynn, Thomas Braidon, Winter Hall, Fred Walton (Cabinet Members); Robert Wilber (Suspect); Claire McDowell (Woman); Zozia Tanina (Dora Kaplan, Woman who shot Lenin); Vesey O'Daveren (Secretary).

"In 1917 the eyes of the world were on Russia, where revolution had swept the czar into exile and the provisional government into power. The aim of this government was to keep Russia in the war, but the people in the streets and the soldiers in the trenches wanted only bread and peace. War and a second revolution were in the balance. In London, as in all diplomatic centers, the situation was regarded as a crisis. For if Russia quit the war and signed a separate peace with Germany, it meant the release of thousands of German troops which would be thrown against the allies on the western front."

Diplomat Stephen Locke, meeting with British government officials, advises that England recognize the Russian government. Otherwise, he fears the government will align with Germany. Although Russian officials assure the British there will be no revolution, riots break out in the city. Elena, Lenin's assistant, caught up in the crowd, engages in a shooting battle with a soldier. Stephen rescues her.

"The Soviet under Lenin was established overnight. It seemed that the outcome of the war was in the hands of the new government. Would they go on fighting, or sign a separate peace with Germany, was the question. The allied world fearfully awaited the answer." The embassy is closed, and Stephen is bored, having little to do. While he and his buddies are at a gypsy café, Elena comes in with associates, including Pavlov, the head of the secret police. "We just don't speak the same language, do we?" she asks Stephen when they can't agree politically. Still, they leave the café together and go back to his apartment. "Stephen, our lives lead in opposite directions, away from each other."

Stephen tells her he loves her, and they kiss. He receives a letter from the home office and decodes it. "For your private information, you are instructed to act as unofficial representative in Russia. We look to you to do all in your power to prevent signing of a separate peace with Germany. This does not convey recognition of Russia but commissions you to act only as an individual. We cannot be responsible for your safety or your decisions but await your recommendations."

A smoldering image of a gun-toting Kay from *British Agent* (1934).

Elena leaves, telling him she doesn't know when they can see each other again. Later at a political meeting, Stephen promises English trade if they continue to fight. Elena, who knows about the secret letter, passes a note, explaining that Stephen has no official role. Accused of buying time, Stephen is given three weeks to meet Russian demands.

When Stephen returns to his flat, Elena is waiting for him. He accuses her of betraying him. This is a typical Elena statement: "You're clever, Stephen. But not clever enough. Weak, but not weak enough. Strong, but not strong enough." Does that make *any* sense? Weird ... but not weird enough.

A couple weeks pass. Elena tells Stephen the British troops have decided to fight the Russians. Stephen's devastated. "England hasn't let me down," he says. "I've let her down."

Elena tells him she's leaving for Moscow, and, *again*, they won't be able to see each other. In Moscow the government releases a proclamation: "The Soviet government has negotiated and signed a peace with Germany."

Stephen, acting as a private citizen, joins with others who seek to overthrow the Soviets. "The Soviet had enemies within as well as without. Royalists, the White Army, and dissatisfied Reds joined forces and fought the Soviet in the dark. The Soviet fought back to make a hidden but grim civil war."

The Soviets, believing Stephen is supporting the White revolt, ask Elena to find evidence. She refuses, but is told she can save his life; if arrested, he'll only be deported, but if he continues his actions he'll be shot. An assassination attempt is made on Lenin. While he lingers near death, Elena tells Stephen to leave Russia. He refuses. "I promise you," she says, "that if you stay, tomorrow our love will be dead."

"What have you done to me now?" he whines.

"You're to be deported tomorrow on evidence that I got by representing myself as your agent." Elena provides the evidence, and Stephen goes into hiding. One by one, his colleagues are discovered and killed. Stephen's last buddy is captured. Though tortured, he won't give up Stephen's location.

"Find out where Locke is," Elena is told. "That is your only duty." She gets the information, repeats it in a monotone, and returns to Stephen. "I want to be alone with you. Forever. I haven't the courage to go on being a patriot or an idealist any longer, Stephen. I tried to, but I'm too much of a woman." She knows they will be killed shortly. "There's only you and I now," she says.

He holds her, talking about the future, describing the village where they'll live. The bells chime. Stephen steps toward the window. There's gunfire. He realizes she's betrayed him *again*.

"Hold me closely," she requests. "Forever."

A car drives up just before soldiers destroy the building. Lenin has regained consciousness. The Soviets celebrate. Lenin has pardoned all political prisoners. Stephen and Elena embrace. In the final scene, they're on a train together, smiling and waving goodbye to Stephen's buddy.

Legend has it that Jack Warner wanted to send a film crew to Russia; his request was denied. Still, this was a big-budget picture. It required more than 40 sets, and the riot scenes used more than 1,500 cast members and 3,000 ammunition rounds.

Barbara Stanwyck turned down Kay's role. Film production began March 26, 1934, and ended June 11. Kay, who severely injured her arm during production in an accident at home, wore a smock to hide the 25 stitches she received. Her injury, which may have been a suicide attempt, delayed production.

Kay, who had a brief affair with Howard during the making of this film, also appeared in a radio drama on *The Gulf Screen Guild Show* with him on March 26, 1939.

The picture is long, uninvolving — at least until the final scene — and unrelentingly depressing. It's also much more of a Leslie Howard than a Kay Francis film. Co-star William Gargan, in his autobiography, referred to Kay as "that glorious creamy beauty."[57]

Kay admitted to an interviewer that shooting a gun made her nervous. "There are not so many things I fear in the world but a gun is one of them. I am frightened to death of a pistol and in this scene [when she fires a gun outside the embassy] my imagination works overtime. I am deadly afraid that by some mistake they may have put a real bullet into the gun instead of a blank! That thought paralyzes me and I am no good for hours. When I take the thing in my hand, I shake like a leaf, as you can see, and it takes me half an hour to stop. I shall be so happy when these sequences are over; it is like a nightmare. Supposing I should shoot somebody, because the gun is loaded!"[58]

In the same interview, Kay expressed relief that costumes for *British Agent* were less glamorous. "'For once, I'm allowed to do a picture in which the wardrobe mistress doesn't have to follow me about with a needle and thread ... I am a Bolshevist, you know, and Bolshevists at the time of the revolution were not well dressed. For a long time I've been wanting to wear clothes that didn't distract from the characterization. I have never wished to become a clothes horse but it happens that several of my roles have called for expensive gowns and I am glad if I have been able to wear them pleasingly.... It is very distracting to have the wardrobe department require more of your time than the script. To be properly dressed in films and out is an exceedingly trying business. It takes hours and hours of time and concentration and the fashion trends change so rapidly it is almost impossible to keep up with them. Whoever is responsible for publicizing me as one of the better dressed women in Hollywood has caused me a lot of trouble. I have never tried to startle or amaze with my clothes. I wear what I like and I employ experts to design my clothes. I detest fittings but they are necessary. It seems to me important that all of us should look as well as we can. Putting the best foot forward is an art but, when the public comes to the theater to see certain stars because of their gowns, it does not inspire or encourage an actress to give of her best.'"[59]

Author Lockhart was arrested and accused of being Dora Kaplan's accomplice in the attempted murder of Lenin. He was released when England and Russia exchanged prisoners. His novel *British Agent* was based on his experiences and published in London in 1932.

Researchers suggest Pierre Collings was an uncredited writer on the script. Some sources claim that Corinne Williams—not Zosia Tanina—played Dora Kaplan. Frank Borzage was slated to direct the film, but Michael Curtiz ended up with it.

A movie ad proclaimed: "Two great Warner Bros. Stars bring you the screen version of the best-seller that rocked the chancelleries of Europe. The story of one man against a million—and of the woman who loved him, yet was his enemy to the death. Told by the man who lived this astounding romance. Leslie Howard, Kay Francis appear together for the first time in *British Agent*." Another shouted: "A world gone mad with terror divided them.... [H]e taught her how to love—she taught him how to die!" And "Her country demanded she take a man's life, while her heart demanded his lips, his love!"

REVIEWS: "Masterly direction and photography." (*Photoplay*, October 1934, p. 53)

"Michael Curtiz has staged the drama capably.... [T]he dark-eyed and vibrant Miss Francis makes a handsome undercover agent for the Cheka." (*New York Times*, September 25, 1934)

"Excellently acted by Miss Francis and Leslie Howard." (*New York World-Telegram*, September 20, 1934)

"This is an excellent vehicle for Leslie Howard and Kay Francis, and it should please audiences generally." (*Film Daily*, August 2, 1934)

"Miss Francis is more handsomely photographed than in several previous pictures, and Howard gives the sensitive performance that we have come to expect from him." (Elizabeth Yeaman, *Hollywood Citizen News*, September 15, 1934)

"*British Agent* is lifted a notch above the level of run-of-the-mill spy pictures by the eloquent dialog by Laird Doyle, by expert performances by Howard and Francis. Good shot: a firing squad dealing with one of Locke's confreres." (*Time*, September 17, 1934)

"Miss Francis' straight, breezy charm is well suited to the role of Elena..." (W.E. Oliver, *Los Angeles Evening Herald Express*, September 15, 1934)

Living on Velvet
(Warner Bros., 1935) 77 min.
Released on March 2, 1935.

Credits: Producer, Edward Chodorov; director, Frank Borzage; assistant directors, Lew Borzage, Lee Katz, John Gates; story-screenplay, Jerry Wald, Julius Epstein; art director, Robert M. Haas; gowns, Orry-Kelly; music director, Leo F. Forbstein; original music, Al Dubin, Harry Warren, Bernhard Kaun, Heinz Roemheld; camera, Sid Hickox; editor, William Holmes.

Cast: Kay Francis (Amy Prentiss); Warren William (Walter "Gibraltar" Pritcham); George Brent (Terrence C. "Terry" Parker); Helen Lowell (Aunt Martha Prentiss); Henry O'Neill (Thornton); Samuel Hinds

(Henry L. Parker); Russell Hicks (Major); Maude Turner Gordon (Mrs. Parker); Martha Merrill (Cynthia Parker); Edgar Kennedy (Counterman); Austa (Max, the Dachshund Dog); Lee Shumway (Officer); Walter Miller (Pilot, Formation Leader); Emmett Vogan (Officer); May Beatty, Mrs. Wilfrid North (Dowagers); Frank Dodd (Minister); David Newell (Jim Smalley); Bud Geary (Aunt Martha's Chauffeur); William Wayne (Butler); Gordon "Wild Bill" Elliott (Commuter); William Bailey (Ted Drew); Wade Boteler (Police Sergeant); Harry Bradley (Talkative Man at Party); Eddy Chandler (Policeman at Carnival); John Cooper (Messenger Boy); Jay Eaton (Man at Amy's Party); Frank Fanning (Doorman); Paul Fix (Intern); Sam Hayes (Air Show Announcer); Grace Hayle (Talkative Woman at Party); Harry Holman (Bartender); Selmer Jackson (Officer); Stanley King (Soldier); Jack Mower (Policeman in Park); Harold Nelson (Sexton); Jack Richardson (Taxi Driver); Niles Welch (Major's Aide); Lloyd Whitlock (Man at Amy's Party); Eric Wilton (Lawton, Walter's Butler); Neal Dodd (Minister).

In this scene from *Living on Velvet* (1935), Kay awaits husband George Brent on the front porch of their Long Island cottage.

IN FEBRUARY 1933, a small plane flies through fog with four passengers on board: pilot Terry, his sister, and parents. The plane crashes, and only Terry survives. After this, Terry travels around the world, living recklessly and flying dangerously. At the Benton Field Long Island Aviation Day on June 10, 1934, an intruder airplane creates havoc with the formation. "He's either a practical joker or he's just insane," someone says. It's Terry horsing around. His friend Gibraltar rescues him from being arrested, and then scolds him.

"I suffered three scratches and a headache." Terry says about the crash that killed his family. "I really shouldn't have lived. I really died with them that moment. Every minute since then, every minute from now on, is pure velvet."

Gibraltar takes him to his home and then to Amy's party. "Who's Amy Prentiss?" Terry asks.

"The girl I might marry."

Terry makes the rounds at the party, passing a couple of pretty lesbians having an intimate conversation. "It's the most interesting book, exactly like *The Well of Loneliness*," one says.

"Nice going," he casually says to them.

From across the room, Terry sees Amy. Their eyes meet. It's a moment. They leave the party together, which is followed by a cute scene (don't miss this one!) that makes fun of Kay's speech impediment.

"I like the sound of your voice," Terry says.

"I want to hear more of it. Won't you say something nice and long?"

"Thirty days hath September, April, June —"

"What?"

"Thirty days hath September, April, June —"

"Apwil? Apwil? Hmm. I see. Repeat after me, please. Around the rugged rocks, the ragged rascals ran."

"Awound the wugged wocks, the wagged wascal wan. There, see? Now you know everything." She beams.

He's charmed. They end up in Central Park in front of General Sherman's statue. He's devastated to learn she's Amy Prentiss. "Your Gibraltar's Amy."

"Just Amy," she corrects. "I don't belong to anyone. I'm just Amy, that's all."

"He loves you."

"Not too much."

"And you love him."

"Not enough."

Terry disappears. When he turns up drunk at a police station, Gibraltar takes him home. Amy wants to marry Terry, though Aunt Martha is strongly opposed to the idea. "Scoundrel without a single saving grace" is her description of Terry.

Terry, too, tries to convince Amy it's a bad idea. "Gibraltar can give you everything."

"But I don't want anything."

"You'll never know a minute's rest or a day's contentment."

She looks dreamily at him. "Oh, it all sounds so wonderful," she coos.

"All right," he finally says, "get your hat."

They're married, and of course, Gibraltar is the best man. He also rents them a house in Patchogue.

Terry, moody and reluctant to work, receives some good news. According to Gibraltar, he and Amy own stock that is worth $8,000. Terry spends the money — and more — on an airfield, hangar, and airplane without discussing it with Amy.

"I'm leaving you, Terry. But before I go, there's something I want to say to you. I'll try to be simple and straightforward. Terry, this attitude of yours toward life, this contempt that you have for people in the world, all this dashing around of yours, all the flying about, the happiness, the unrest, mean just one thing.

Kay Francis in a fashion shot for *Living on Velvet* (1935).

There's a void in your life, Terry. A distinct and terrible void." She moves in with Aunt Martha and discovers the stock was worthless — Gibraltar *gave* them the $8,000. "You're such a grand person," Amy tells him.

Terry begs Amy to come back. "What do I have to do to get you back?" he asks.

"I don't know, Terry. One day you'll come to me and something in the way you stand, something in the way you speak, just something about you. I'll know that you're no longer running on a ragged precipice."

He tells her he can't change and leaves in the car Gibraltar left for him (this Gibraltar guy is so nice it's creepy). Amy pretends to be happy and carefree. "*I'm* living on velvet now!" she announces at a party.

Gibraltar receives a call — his car's been in an accident. He and Amy go to the amusement park where Terry wrecked the car.

"You mustn't die, Terry," Amy tearfully pleads.

In the next scene, they're back on the park bench next to Sherman's statue. It's snowing. "Amy, there's something I've been saving to tell you at this moment," Terry says. "You've been a grand nurse and certainly a grand companion, but the job's over. You're free, Amy."

"But I don't want to be free. Freedom's overrated."

"You mean that, darling? Do you?"

"Do whatever you like, be whatever you want to be. I want you. I love you."

"Amy, if you love me, you'll stop talking about a Terry Parker that doesn't even exist any more." The camera tilts up to the statue.

The working title was *Tragedy with Music*. This dud was supposedly handpicked for Kay by Jack Warner. There are some nice aerial scenes, and good chemistry between Brent and Kay, especially during their first meeting. Orry-Kelly designed seventeen outfits for Kay, who helped with examples she'd brought back from a European trip.

Watch for the last scene where Kay and George sit in a snowy park — not one flake falls on either. There's another flub when George Brent, who's supposedly on Long Island, takes his plane into the sky — and we see snow-capped mountains.

The original screenplay ended with Terry's death in an automobile accident, and Gibraltar getting the girl. However, Jack Warner did

Kay Francis in a scene from *Living on Velvet* (1935). Warren William is on the right.

not want to renew Warren William's contract so Brent's character lived and reconciled with Kay.

On January 4, 1935, Kay and George Brent appeared on the radio show *Hollywood Hotel* to re-enact scenes and promote the film. Following the program, Kay and George had a one-night stand.

This is one of the few films where Kay's speech impediment plays a role. Interestingly, on May 8, 1933, a Warner Brothers employee (Frederic Macalpin) in the recording department wrote an interesting letter to *Time* in which he applauded the advancements in recording technology. "Sound apparatus nowadays records just what is spoken in the way it is spoken with a high average of measured accuracy, and individual words are no difficulty. However, often adjustments of various kinds have to be made to counteract individual peculiarities of voice or inflection. On our own lot: George Arliss' sibilants are especially strong. Richard Barthelmess' vowels have a tubby-throaty effect. When Kay Francis says tomowow, wobber, twouble, however, we must record it that way."

Advertising copy proclaimed: "It's reckless ... riotous, romantic! Come along on a fast and furious romp ... with this threesome who had a new design for loving!"

REVIEWS: "Miss Francis displays not merely a new collection of gowns (which had the feminine members of the audience cooing) but somewhat surprising talent for comedy in the earlier sequences." (*New York Times*, March 8, 1935)

"I want to be among the first to say that *Living on Velvet* is one of the better pictures and that at last Kay is given a sort of play she deserves. Kay is delightful and her gowns will be copied all over the world." (Louella O. Parsons, *Los Angeles Examiner*, March 2, 1935)

"Kay Francis giving her usual facile performance as the girl. It is an interesting story and well told by director Borzage." (Harrison Carroll, *Los Angeles Evening Herald Express*, March 2, 1935)

"Miss Francis, who wears flashy clothes, contributes some bizarre costumes to this season's already bizarre collection. One gown she wears, which has an overgrown muffler swung around her neck, is a quaint blend of shawl and bath towel effect." (Eleanor Barnes, *Los Angeles Illustrated Daily News*, March 2, 1935)

Stranded

(Warner Bros., 1935) 76 min.
Released on June 20, 1935.

Credits: Supervisor, Sam Bischoff; director, Frank Borzage; based on the story "Lady with a Badge" by Frank Wead, Ferdinand Reyher; screenplay, Delmer Daves; additional dialogue, Carl Erickson; assistant director, Lew Borzage; art directors, Anton Grot, Hugh Reticker; gowns, Orry-Kelly; music director, Leo F. Forbstein; original music, Bernhard Kaun, Heinz Roemheld; camera, Sid Hickox; editor, William Holmes.

Cast: Kay Francis (Lynn Palmer); George Brent (Mack Hale); Patricia Ellis (Velma Tuthill); Donald Woods (John Wesley); Barton MacLane (Sharkey); Robert Barrat (Stanislaus Janauschek); June Travis (Jennie Holden); Henry O'Neill (Mr. Tuthill); Ann Shoemaker (Mrs. Tuthill); Frankie Darro (Jimmy Rivers); William Harrigan (Updyke); Joseph Crehan (Johnny Quinn); John Wray (Mike Gibbons); Edward McWade (Tim Powers); Gavin Gordon (Jack); Mary Forbes (Grace Dean); Emmett Vogan (Officer on Ferry); Sam McDaniel (Porter); Joan Gay (Diane Nichols); Edwin Mordant (Surgeon); Wilfred Lucas (Pat, a Worker); Mia Liu (Japanese Girl); Richard Loo (Groom); Rita Rozelle (Polish Girl); Louise Seidel (Danish Girl); Frank LaRue, (Immigration Officers); Adrian Morris (River Boss); Milton Kibbee (Pat, the Timekeeper); Vesey O'Davoren (Tuthill's Butler); Spencer Charters (Boatman); Jessie Arnold (Scrubwoman); Harry Bradley (Train Conductor); Mae Busch (Lizzie); Burr Caruth (Old Man); Stan Cavanaugh (Second Taxi Driver); Glen Cavender (Immigrant); Walter Clyde (Hospital Assistant); Frank Coghlan Jr. (Page); Claudia Coleman (Madame); Georgie Cooper (Floor Nurse); Nick Copeland (Bridge Worker at Meeting); Don Downen (Clerk); Ralph Dunn (Bridge Worker); Florence Fair (Miss Walsh); Dick French (Clerk); Harrison Greene (Blustery Man); Shirley Grey (Marvel Young); Lillian Harmer (Desk Attendant); Edward Keane (Doctor); John Kelly (Sailor); Joe King (Dan Archer); Eily Malyon (Old Maid); Frank Marlowe (Agitator at Meeting); Pat Moriarty (Steve Brodie); Henry Otho (Bridge Worker); Sarah Padden (Workman's Wife); Paul Panzer (Updyke Agitator); Jack Richardson (First Taxi Driver); Adrian Rosley (Headwaiter); Cy Schindell (Bridge Worker); Frank Sheridan (Boone); Edwin Stanley (Police Surgeon); Harry Tenbrook (Rollins, Updyke's Agitator); Zeffie Tilbury (Old Hag); Wally Wales (Peterson); Niles Welch (Safety Engineer); Eleanor Wesselhoeft (Mrs. Young); Leo White (Haines, the Drunken Worker); Tom Wilson (Immigrant); Lillian Worth (Blonde); Marbeth Wright (Switchboard Operator); Emma Young (Chinese Girl).

LYNN IS A TRAVELERS AID worker at the railway station, helping the lost, lonely, and pathetic. Grace convinces Lynn to let Velma move in with her. Velma's mother is a major donator, and Velma claims she wants to volunteer. Lynn soon learns that Velma is only pretending to be interested in humanitarian work; she really wants to be able to see her boyfriend without her mother knowing.

Mack Hale, a rude and unfriendly contractor, comes looking for a worker who he fears was sent back to Wisconsin. Lynn recognizes Mack. "You were the first man who ever kissed me," she tells him, reminding him that they grew up together, but haven't seen each other in nine years. He warms up and asks her out.

Meanwhile, back at the site where Mack is building a bridge, Sharkey visits, threatening to cause problems if Mack doesn't pay protection money. "Five thousand dollars before the first of the month or else!" Mack refuses.

Mack doesn't respect Lynn's work and asks her to take a vacation so she can spend time with him. "From now on, your job comes second," he tells her.

Meanwhile, Sharkey pays men to cause trouble on the bridge. Mack fires the workers who show up drunk. One night Lynn has to work late for Immigration Services. Mack tags along. Velma, who's been after Mack, tells him she's not as devoted as Lynn. "I find it's very stupid work," she tells Mack.

"Well, I guess you get out of it what you put into it," he responds.

That night at dinner, Mack disparages the people Lynn helps. "Human beings aren't muck," she argues.

Back at the site, Mack is injured in a fight with Sharkey. Lynn takes him home. The next

Warner Bros. used this remarkably unflattering portrait for *Stranded* (1935).

Candid shot of the ever-beautiful Kay at a Pickfair party in 1936. She attended the Mary Pickford gathering with boyfriend Delmer Daves (screenwriter of *Stranded*).

morning, he again tells her to quit her job. "From now on, you're just the wife of a construction engineer," he tells her.

"I like my job. It's part of me."

"You mean, you want your work and you don't want me."

"We just don't see things the same way."

"You've wasted every hour you've given them," he tells her. "I guess this is goodbye. For keeps," he says.

Sharkey continues to sabotage the bridge. An inebriated worker falls to his death — "They won't need an ambulance for Johnny now. They'll need a shovel." A rumor spreads that Mack caused the death. The bridge workers call a meeting to decide if they should walk out. Lynn tries to find Mack, but he's with Velma, whose father Mr. Tuthill is helping finance the bridge.

Velma asks Mack what he thinks of her.

"Well, you'd be okay with a spanking or two."

"I've never met anyone who could give me one. Think you could?"

Tuthill requests that Mack attend the workers' meeting. Before he arrives, Lynn bravely works her way through the rowdy crowd. Angry by the time she reaches the front, she tells them about Sharkey and the protection money, silencing their boos and jeers. Meanwhile, Sharkey is on the verge of killing one of the workers until others intervene and bring him to the meeting. Mack arrives, explains what's happened, and turns Sharkey and the agitators over to the workers, who (we assume) beat the fool out of them. Mack apologizes to Lynn.

"We're practically in the same business, Mack.

You build with steel, and I try to build with people."

He has a change of heart about her work, and agrees to accept her under her terms.

"Don't be humble," she says. "It'll break my heart if you're ever humble. Never lose your arrogance. That's the you I love."

As they kiss, the city's skyline is the backdrop.

It's not Kay's best acting — she's lost the subtlety. Kay was so impressed by June Travis' acting in this picture that she personally recommended her to her bosses. "Up to Jack Warner's office, and over to Hal Wallis' and back to Warner's she flew one day for the sole purpose of telling these bewildered gentlemen about a little girl who had a minor part in her picture. 'I tell you that girl has something. Give her a chance. Give her better roles.'"[60] The gesture helped Travis win a leading role in *Ceiling Zero*, with James Cagney and Pat O'Brien.

The production began filming March 6, 1935, and concluded April 15. The working title was *Lady with a Badge*, but the studio feared audiences would think the movie was about a policewoman. More attention was paid to the sets than the script. A replica of the Golden Gate Bridge, then under construction in San Francisco, was created by the Warner Brothers technical department. "Plans had to be drawn exactly as though the real bridge were to be erected: every girder, every brace, the placement of every rivet had to be a precise copy of the original. And it took the studio technicians four days of round-the-clock work to do a job which in reality required more than eight months to accomplish."[61] Borzage also filmed at the bridge site. Furthermore, the extras who appear as bridge workers were actual steelworkers. Director Borzage thought they'd provide a more realistic look. The expensive production also required the construction of a railway terminal. "The railway terminal built to order for the production took six 24-hour working days to complete. The main portion of the set is a lobby covering 45,000 square feet and was fully equipped with information booths, ticket windows, telegraph counters, magazine stands, clocks, redcaps, scurrying people, train callers and all the rest. The station was built in the Gothic style, framed in columns of Carrara marble and otherwise constructed to appear as though it could withstand the ravages of centuries."[62]

The tag line was "See For Yourself Why Women Marked 'Missing' Would Rather Die Than Be Found!" Huh? Other advertising included this: "Why do a million girls leave home?... Only a woman's ears should hear the stories poured from painted lips by America's 'missing' girls! Kay reveals them as no one else could as she triumphs again in the most unusual role of her career!" And "The screen's exotic star and filmdom's fastest-rising favorite ... in a dynamite-packed drama of a man's pride — and a woman's heart." Yet another advertisement proclaimed: "Kay Francis faces a woman's greatest problem in 'Stranded.'"

REVIEWS: "Miss Francis gives a smooth and sensitive performance but she is wasted in an uninteresting role as a girl who takes her job too seriously." (*Variety*, June 26, 1935)

"Possibly the real excuse for *Stranded*, beyond the individual fashion show which Kay Francis contributes throughout, was Warner Brothers' remorse for not including in *Black Fury* the scene in which a beautiful girl harangues a group of striking workers." (*Time*, July 1, 1935)

"Miss Francis, more becomingly photographed and costumed than ever before, finds an excellent screen partner in George Brent." (*New York Sun*, June 21, 1935)

"'Stranded,' like its predecessor, 'Living on Velvet,' hardly merits the talents of its two leading players. Its chief distinction is found in the style show put on by the well-dressed Miss Francis." (*New York Daily News*, June 21, 1935)

"Clothes, as usual, do most of Miss Francis' acting for her." (Elizabeth Yeaman, *Hollywood Citizen News*, June 28, 1935)

The Goose and the Gander
(Warner Bros., 1935) 65 min.
Released on September 12, 1935.

Credits: Supervisor, James Seymour; director, Alfred E. Green; story-screenplay, Charles Kenyon; art director, Robert M. Haas; gowns, Orry-Kelly; music director, Leo F. Forbstein; original music, Bernhard Kaun, Heinz Roemheld; assistant director, Chuck Hansen; camera, Sid Hickox; editor, Bert Lenard; camera operator, Wesley Anderson.

Cast: Kay Francis (Georgiana Summers); George Brent (Bob McNear); Genevieve Tobin (Betty Summers); John Eldredge (Lawrence Thurston); Claire Dodd (Connie Thurston); Helen Lowell (Aunt Julia

Hamilton); Ralph Forbes (Ralph Summers); William Austin (Arthur Summers); Spencer Charters (Winklesteinbergher); Eddie Shubert (Sweeney); John Sheehan (Murphy); Charles Coleman (Jones, the Butler); Wade Boteler (Sprague, Hotel Detective); Davison Clark (Detective at Train Station); Nick Copeland (Mike, the Detective); Cliff Saum (Detective Snyder); Glen Cavender (George, the Detective); Al Woods (Bellboy); Milton Kibbee (Hotel Garageman); Edward McWade (Justice of the Peace); Jane Buckinham (Mrs. Burns); Gordon "Wild Bill" Elliott (Teddy); Olive Jones (Miss Brent); Carlyle Blackwell (Barkley); Eddy Chandler (Policeman); Eddie Graham (Beach Casino Guest); David Newell (Hotel Clerk); Guy Usher (Police Sergeant); Tom Wilson (Baggageman); Helen Wood (Violet).

THE FILM OPENS ON a beach. Good news for those who find George Brent and/or Genevieve Tobin attractive — they're in bathing suits. The bad news? So is William Austin, whose body is almost as soft and feminine as Genevieve Tobin's.

Georgiana overhears Betty planning a fling with Bob. Later that night at the nightclub, she sees ex-husband Ralph Summers. "He used to be my husband," she explains to Teddy, her dance partner.

"We haven't met since then," Ralph says.

"You're happy, I hope," she cordially says, and gives him some advice "Ralph, I have no reason to like your wife. In fact, I've never even laid eyes on her, but don't hurt her the way you hurt me."

In a moment, Georgiana realizes she *does* know Ralph's wife. Betty, the woman who broke up her marriage, is the same woman who's planning the tryst with Bob. Georgiana comes up with a plan to get back at Betty *and* get Ralph back.

She fixes it so Bob and Betty end up at her house — and unwittingly also arranges it so the Thurstons, jewel thieves who have taken some of her own jewelry, also arrive at Twin Pines. Things become complicated when the

Helen Lowell and Kay share a suspenseful moment in the delightful comedy *The Goose and the Gander* (1935) (courtesy James King).

Thurstons pretend to be Bob and Betty — and Bob and Betty pretend to be married. Bob explains that he and his "wife" will require separate bedrooms.

"Why, I think that's scandalous," Aunt Julia says. "Is the world coming to an end?"

That night, Bob and Georgiana take a stroll. He tells her that he and Mrs. McNear are separating in the morning. Georgiana drops the news that Ralph is coming for luncheon the next day.

The next morning, Bob tells Betty that Ralph is coming for lunch. She asks what it means. "It means the old gander is putting over a fast one on the little goosie."

When Ralph and his tattletale brother Arthur eventually show up, they're captured by the thieves. Meanwhile, Bob has fallen in love with Georgiana and wants to marry her. Betty invites the thieves into her room, explaining she's the real Betty Summers. They tell her that Ralph and Arthur are tied up, and ask her to wait in the car for a fast getaway. Bob tells her he won't leave Georgiana.

The police arrive. Confusion reigns supreme when Georgiana tries to explain. The thieves convince the officers they are the real Mr. and Mrs. Ralph Summers, and Georgiana and Bob are taken away to jail, handcuffed to each other.

When the police finally release Georgiana and Bob — they've captured the real crooks — Bob asks for a justice of the peace. Georgiana advises Betty to tell Ralph she'd secretly gone to the lodge to be a witness for Georgiana's marriage to Bob, but the crooks came and spoiled everything. Bob and Georgiana get married, and Ralph finally shows up. Georgiana listens as Ralph and Betty accuse each other. "They'll get along," she knowingly says, and kisses Bob.

This clever comedy is probably the best Brent-Francis pairing. Kay is delightful — confident and charming — and the role plays to her strength for comedy. Genevieve Tobin, so good in *I Loved a Woman*, is too broad in this comedy. The two male leads, George Brent and Ralph Forbes, were both ex-husbands of actress Ruth Chatterton. During production, the two rarely spoke.

REVIEWS: "Its chief impediment to an evening pleasantly unimportant in the cinema comes from its insistence on cramming the dialogue with r's, which has an embarrassing habit of becoming w's when Miss Francis goes to work on them." (*New York Times*, September 12, 1935)

"The brunette actress's parts generally receive special attention from the script department. Writers go over them to eliminate as much R's from her lines as possible because Miss Francis's R frequently becomes W. This evidently didn't happen in 'The Goose and the Gander.'" (*Newsweek*, September 21, 1935)

"Miss Francis is pleasant, but not outstanding as the first wife with Brent, who seems to be copying E.E. Horton, a good feeder." (*Variety*, September 18, 1935)

"The statuesque Miss Francis and the Greek, godlike Mr. Brent make a combination at once cinematically happy and exciting." (*New York Daily News*, September 12, 1935)

"Brent is outstanding, while Kay Francis is quite lovely as the heroine." (Jimmy Starr, *Los Angeles Evening Herald Express*, August 3, 1935)

"Dandy domestic farce with good cast and director making most of comedy situations. Kay Francis does well." (*Film Daily*, September 12, 1935)

I Found Stella Parish
(Warner Bros., 1935) 84 min.
Released on November 4, 1935.

Credits: Producer, Harry Joe Brown; director, Mervyn LeRoy; story, John Monk Saunders; screenplay, Casey Robinson; music director Leo F. Forbstein; original music, Heinz Roemheld; art director, Robert M. Haas; gowns, Orry-Kelly; camera, Sid Hickox; editor, William Clemens; grip, Rudy Mashmeyer; still photographer, James Manatt; special effects, Fred Jackman, Willard Van Enger; sound, Robert B. Lee; props, Eddie Edwards; assistant director, William H. Cannon; hair stylist, Jane Romaine.

Cast: Kay Francis (Stella Parish/Elsa Jeffords/Aunt Lumilla Evans); Ian Hunter (Keith Lockridge); Paul Lukas (Stephan Norman); Sybil Jason (Gloria Parish); Jessie Ralph (Nana); Joseph Sawyer (Chuck); Eddie Acuff (Dimmy); Walter Kingsford (Reeves, the Editor); Robert Strange (Jed Duffy); Ferdinand Munier (Andrews); Rita Carlyle (First Waiting Woman); Shirley Simpson, Elspeth Dudgeon, Tempe Pigott (Waiting Women); Charles Evans (Old Actor); Lotus Liu (Lotus, Stella's Theatre Maid); Olaf Hytten (Robert, Stephen's Butler); Elsa Buchanan (Stella's Maid); Vesey O'Davoren (Deck Steward); Lotus Thompson (Reeves' Secretary); Milton Kibbee (Costumer); John Dilson (Charles Einfeld, Producer's Assistant at the Joe Barnes Company); Harlan Briggs (Theatre Manager); Alice Keating (New York

Operator); Marie Wells (Hotel Operator); Phyllis Coghlan (London Operator); Emmett Vogan (Reporter); Lew Harvey (Reporter); Gordon "Wild Bill" Elliott (Reporter); Crauford Kent (Lord Chamberlain); Edward Cooper (Caligula); Hugh Huntley (Cemellus); Ralph Bushman (Eric); Vernon Downing (Slave); Vernon Steele (Slave); Mary Treen (Sob Sister); Barton MacLane (Clifton Jeffords); Harry Beresford (James); Harry Allen (Driver to Steamship); Nick Copeland (New York Taxi Driver); Bess Flowers (Party Guest); Sam Harris (The Major, Aboard Ship); Dell Henderson (Actor in Prison Scene); Charles Irwin (Purser); Wilfred Lucas (Customs Official); Eily Malyon (Ship's Clothing Clerk); Alphonse Martell (Waiter); Wedgwood Nowell (Extra Leaving Ship); Lee Phelps (Photographer); John Graham Spacey (Reeves' Reporter); Will Stanton (Messenger); David Thursby (Tontan, Curtain Operator).

THE PICTURE OPENS IN London. On a marquee we see "Stephan Norman Presents Stella Parish in 'This Brief Hour.'" American actress Stella Parish has become successful in England, and producer Stephan wants to marry her. Stella is a recluse, and though they've known each other for three years, Stephan finds her behavior strange. "It seems that you have a deep mistrust of every living soul, even of me."

After that evening's show, Stella returns to her dressing room, where she's met by a man. "You can't scare me," she says not very convincingly.

"On the night of her greatest triumph, she's disappeared," a dumbfounded Stephan tells his friend, newspaperman Keith, after he discovers that Stella's vanished. Keith thinks it's a publicity stunt. "You've grown up to be quite a little gentleman of the press, haven't you?" Stephan scolds, and then lets Keith read the note: "My dearest Stephan, tonight I am leaving the theatre and England forever. I cannot tell you why. I'd only ask you try to forgive me. To try to balance our few but precious years of friendship against this final wrong. Goodbye, Stephan, and thank you for your sweetness. I am too miserable to write more."

Ace reporter Keith follows Stella to the docks. Traveling with Nana and daughter, she's disguised as an old woman with makeup, wig, and dowdy clothing. Daughter Gloria has been instructed to call her Auntie. Keith develops a friendship with Gloria. It isn't until the boat docks in New York, however, that he realizes Auntie is Stella. When he says goodbye, he

Kay models an Orry-Kelly gown in *I Found Stella Parish* (1935).

kisses her hand — and sees the hand of a young woman.

Keith sends a telegram to his editor: "I have found Stella Parish Stop Withhold publication until I secure all details Lockridge."

Stella, no longer in disguise, is now introduced as Gloria's mother. When they have lunch, Keith tells her how much he admires Auntie. "Very clever woman, your aunt. She's fascinating. To begin with, she's that rare combination of real beauty with brains."

Stella is amused. "What a pity you and auntie weren't born in the same generation so you could fall in love with each other."

"A great tragedy," he agrees.

Six weeks later, Keith is still working on the story. "I can see him working on Parish now," his editor tells colleagues. "Dining, taking her dancing, gaining her confidence. That's the way to gain a story from a woman." The editor scoffs when someone suggests he might fall in love. "A reporter never falls in love, except with his typewriter."

Keith gets Gloria alone and pumps her for information. She shows him trunks containing Stella's stage costumes, and he spies one stamped

Gotham Warehouse and Storage Company with claim ticket #80397. When Stella and Nana return, he asks Stella about her stage career. "Well, I never was much of an actress. But every girl at one time or another thinks she's a Bernhardt."

Keith investigates the ticket. "That dress was made for Elsa Jeffers in 'The Lady Misbehaves,'" he's told. Keith sends another telegram: "The following is authentic story of Stella Parish Stop Parish left the stage in terror when appearing in 'The Lady Misbehaves' Stop she carried with her a guilty secret...."

Stella, who's fallen in love with Keith, tells him she needs to come clean about her past. He discourages her confession. "Surely if I can stand to tell it," she says, "you can stand to listen. You see, I love you."

"I didn't know that," he says.

Stella tells her story. She was married to Clifton Jeffers when they were in vaudeville. They drank too much, and he was insanely jealous. She'd gone to her leading man's dressing room, fearing she was pregnant, needing to talk to someone. Clifford killed the actor and was sent to prison. She was implicated and served time as well.

"My baby was born in prison. *Born in prison.* Do you know what that means? Place of birth: Auburn Penitentiary, New York. Daughter of a convicted murderess. Swell start to give a kid. Her first sight of the world — prison bars. The nursery — stone walls."

She didn't stay in prison long. "After all, a parole board is made up of men, and by this time, I knew all there was to know about men."

Stephan found her working in a road show and made her a success. Her husband tracked her down and threatened blackmail.

After Stella leaves, Keith calls the *London Bulletin.* "We've got to kill it, sir!"

Too late. The story's already published. Keith hurries to Stella, but there are dozens of press cars outside. Angry and defiant, Stella is being interviewed. She's offered large sums for an exclusive interview. "Looks as though I won't have to make the best of the situation, boys. Looks as though I can make the most of it," she cynically says, looking and sounding like Mae West, seated on the sofa, hands on hips. Keith arrives. "Pull up a chair and join the inquisition," she barks at him. She accuses him of using her and her child. "You see before you, boys, a true gentleman of the press."

Keith tries to explain. "I didn't know how you felt. Until tonight, you were only a headline to me. You were playing a clever game, and I was trying to outwit you. I was after a story. I'm a reporter."

She doesn't buy it. A booking agency calls, offering her jobs. She's hardened, cynical. "I don't give a hoot what I do or where I do it as long as I get paid from the spot where the greenbacks are the thickest," she spits.

She tells Nana to take Gloria away. She'll take care of Gloria financially but have no contact with her. "I tried to build a wall of love around her, to protect her. Well, they pushed that over. Now I'll build a wall of gold and silver."

Stella goes on tour in a show about her life — "Stella Parish in Person." It's tawdry, sensationalist. In one scene she flirts with the head of the parole board. "Sure, I want out!" she snarls, slouched over in a jail cell. "I've got a yen for some sunshine and fresh air. The stench of so much repentance in here is too much for my nostrils. You're on the parole board. You run it. You can get me out of here.... I'm still young. I'm not hard to look at."

Keith sees it and walks out. Of course, the show's a hit, and there's a montage of theatres where she plays. Finally, she's at the Jed Duffy Theatrical Agency, asking for more work. "The gold rush is over," her agent tells her. "You're yesterday's news, baby. And the suckers ain't gonna ladle out their dough to read old headlines. Come back when you've shot yourself another man."

She gets bug-eyed. The not-so-classy agent suggests burlesque. Needing the money, Stella appears on a burlesque program as "The Woman Who Tells Everything."

When Stephan shows up backstage, Stella sobs. "You are a first-rate actress who is hiding her talents in cheap burlesque," he says, adding that he has a play for her. "No one else could play it. And no one else will."

Stephan, who was sent by Keith, sends Keith a telegram: "Have persuaded Stella to return against her better judgment and mine Stop You had better be right."

Nana reads it in France. Keith is there, too. "I love her, Nana," he admits. "I found it out too late."

Gloria falls into Keith's arms, crying, asking for her mother. "Is she lost?" she asks.

"In a way," Keith says.

Some petition against Stella's return because of the scandal. Stella is frightened, afraid she can't do the role. Stephan consoles her, but tells Keith, "She's unbelievably bad."

We see a marquee: "Stephan Norman Presents Stella Parish in 'This Brief Hour.'" Stephan's a nervous wreck, and Stella, too, is frazzled, nervous. She begs him not to send her out on stage.

"You say you have no friends out there," Stephan says. "Look in the first upper box." She sees Nana and Gloria.

Keith shows up. "Haven't you done enough to me?" she asks.

Keith tells her he loves her. "He does love you," Stephan explains. "His love is stronger than mine. He sent me to America after you."

Keith gives Stella a pep talk. Stella blows a tearful kiss to Gloria, kisses Keith, and tells Stephan, "I'm not afraid any more." She wipes away her tears and steps onto the stage, amid much applause. The final shot is a close-up on Stella's face. A tear rolls down her smiling face.

This is not Kay's best work. She actually makes a fist and bites her fingernail to indicate distress in one scene. Also, the idea that she's a famous classical stage actress unfairly sets her up to look foolish in the play within a play. Mervyn LeRoy is certainly a more than capable director, but this one never comes together.

Filming began on August 19, 1935. Perc Westmore designed a blue-white wig for Kay's Grecian play scene. Orry-Kelly promptly threw together a blue-white gown, and then director Mervyn LeRoy got in on the act when he asked the set be made blue-white. Seems like a lot of work for a black-and-white film.

LeRoy liked to use the number 62 on screen in every one of his films; in this movie, you'll see it when Keith rides in New York cab #562. The film was based on John Monk Saunders' story "The Judas Tree," and that was the working title. Mary McCall, Jr., was hired to write the screenplay but was replaced by Casey Robinson.

On November 1, 1935, Kay, Sybil Jason, and

Paul Lukas and Kay Francis in *I Found Stella Parish* (1935).

Ian Hunter appeared on the radio show *Hollywood Hotel* to re-enact scenes and promote the film.

The advertisement proclaimed: "Hurling defiance at society. Kay daringly discloses the story you never knew about that frontpage beauty who bared the secrets of her double life to the one man with the power to break her."

Kay claimed to have never set foot in Homer, Michigan, her father's birthplace. This didn't stop the local newspaper from printing a review of *Stella Parish* with this title: "Former Homer Girl Appears on Local Screen." The *Homer Index* (January 9, 1936) raved about Kay's performance: "Kay Francis, who once lived only a mile from Homer [sic], is now one of the screen's most brilliant stars. She gives the best performance of her career in the intensely emotional drama, *I Found Stella Parish*.... In this picture Miss Francis is given an unusual opportunity to express emotional feeling, and she rises to it with the flair of a real artist." The movie played at the local Majestic Theatre.

REVIEWS: "Miss Francis's unfortunate lisp continues to plague this corner; it makes even more unbelievable the notion that London could regard her Stella Parish as the Duse of the day." (*New York Times*, November 4, 1935)

"Splendidly directed and played by an unusually strong company." (*New York Daily Mirror*, November 4, 1935)

"That ceaseless search of Warner Brothers for a worthy Kay Francis vehicle has not ended. Miss Francis, a handsome woman who has still to prove herself a great actress, deserves a good deal better than this hour and a half of heroics." (Eileen Creelman, *The New York Sun*)

"Powerful story of an actress and mother love. For Kay Francis *I Found Stella Parish* is an ideal vehicle. She is one of the screen's most charming women, and as the Stella Parish of the London stage she is always a cameo of film loveliness." (*Variety*, November 6, 1935)

"Despite a basic theme that is of familiar design, this attraction is a generally satisfying affair, especially for the women fans, chiefly because of the good performance by Kay Francis in a role that covers a wide range." (*Film Daily*, November 2, 1935)

The White Angel
(Warner Bros., 1936) 75 min. Released on June 25, 1936.

Credits: Producer, Henry Blanke; director, William Dieterle; based on a biographical sketch in "Eminent Victorians" by Lytton Strachey; screenplay, Michael Jacoby, Mordaunt Shairp; dialogue director, Stanley Logan; art director, Anton Grot; special photography, Fred Jackman; musical director, Leo F. Forbstein; original music, Heinz Roemheld; orchestrator, Hugo Friedhofer; camera, Tony Gaudio; editor, Warren Low; gowns, Orry-Kelly.

Cast: Kay Francis (Florence Nightingale); Ian Hunter (Fuller); Donald Woods (Charles Cooper); Nigel Bruce (Dr. West); Donald Crisp (Dr. Hunt); Henry O'Neill (Dr. Scott); George Curzon (Sir Sidney Herbert); Phoebe Foster (Mrs. Elizabeth Herbert); Charles Croker-King (Mr. Nightingale); Georgia Caine (Mrs. Nightingale); Billy Mauch (Tommy); Lillian Kemble-Cooper (Parthenope Nightingale); Ara Gerald (Mrs. Ella Stevens); Montagu Love (Mr. Bullock); Halliwell Hobbes (Lord Raglan); Frank Conroy (Mr. LeFroy); Eily Malyon (Sister Colombo); Egon Brecher (Pastor Fliedner); Barbara Leonard (Minna); Fay Holden (Queen Victoria); Ferdinand Munier (Alexis Soyer, the Cook); Tempe Pigott (Mrs. Waters, the Nurse); Daisy Belmore (Nurse); Alma Lloyd (Nurse); May Beatty (Nurse); Kathrin Clare Ward (Nurse); Dorothy Arville (Nurse); Lawrence Grant (Colonel); Nelson McDowell (Superintendent of Hospital); Eric Wilton (Servant); Robert Bolder (Doctor); James May (Doctor); Arthur Turner Foster (Doctor); Harry Allen (Soldier); Clyde Cook (Soldier); Harry Cording (Storekeeper); Neil Fitzgerald (Officer in Barracks); Charles Irwin (Soldier); George Kirby (Soldier); Lowden Adams (Secretary); Jimmy Aubrey (Sentry); Frank Baker (Customs Official); Lionel Belmore (Captain); George Broughton (Corporal); George Bunny (Coachman); Rita Carlyle (Mrs. Mellon); Fay Chaldecott (Praying Child); Silvia Vaughan (Praying Child's Mother); E.E. Clive (Surgeon); Vesey O'Davoren (Thompson, the Butler); Edith Ellison.

"TOWARDS THE YEAR 1850, England was at peace with the world. Her men were following her ships to the four corners of the earth, building the great empire that is Queen Victoria's monument. Women were only permitted to nod meek approval. In all England, only Her Majesty had the right to express herself with the independence of a man."

Florence is not like the other girls. She has no interest in marriage, children, or leisure. "Half our life," she laments, "is spent in waiting and

Kay Francis as Florence Nightingale in *The White Angel* (1936) (courtesy James King).

doing nothing. That's supposed to be the whole duty of a woman."

Her father serves on the welfare committee, and discovers that hospitals and nursing in England are in a scandalous condition. When he shares the information with Florence, they both want reform. "Father," she says, slamming her fist down, "how can you go to dinner parties, while these scandals continue?"

"It's worse than anyone can imagine," he tells her.

Though Florence is devastated, her mother isn't concerned: "I'm only thankful, Flo, that I lead a well-ordered life in pleasant places and in beautiful surroundings."

Florence decides to study nursing. "There was only one school in Europe where modern nursing methods were understood and taught. Florence Nightingale went there determined to equip herself for the new career she had chosen." Florence returns to England. "Her schooling completed, Florence Nightingale hurried home, happy in the thought that perhaps through her — a new era might dawn for ailing humanity."

She sees Dr. West, but he tells her that her skills are best used in the home, suggesting she marry. "It will take more than a Dr. West to stop me," Florence says, then looks towards the heavens.

When England goes to war, she offers assistance to the War Office. "The idea of female nurses is repellant," is the consensus. Her friend Sidney apologizes. "I'm sorry, Flo. They won't even consider the idea."

A reporter writes stories illustrating the problems of the wounded and sick, which leads to Florence being sent to Scutari, along with 38 nurses she personally interviewed. "The voyage of the *Vectis* was a succession of dangers and discomfort. But Florence Nightingale and her brave band ignored all hardships, in anticipation of the great work to which they had dedicated themselves."

Once they arrive, they find the conditions are terrible — filth, rats, moaning, etc. Although discouraged, Florence gets to work. The reporter publicizes Florence's work, making her a folk hero to the English. "At Scutari, the death rate was greatly reduced. Men lived, where previously they would have died. But Florence Nightingale was not content. She carried her merciful work directly to the scene of battle."

Florence is sent to Balaklava where she meets resistance. Finally, worn down, she becomes sick with cholera. As she's carried away, the grateful soldiers pay tribute to her. All of England prays for Florence to get well. When she regains her health, she's promoted to general superintendent of nurses.

When Florence returns to England, she has a meeting with the queen. "You are dangerously progressive," Bullock, a member of the War Office, tells Florence. He sees the queen first. While waiting, Florence rehearses her speech in front of a portrait: "I thank your Majesty, for the high honor you have conferred upon me by inviting me here today. I left for Scutari sustained and inspired by your Majesty's sympathy for my cause and with a clear knowledge of the difficulties of the task that lay before me. But the actual difficulties that I and my loyal nurses had to face were the unbelievable apathy and negligence of the hospital staff. Whatever else I may have accomplished in the war, I have shown beyond doubt that nursing is woman's highest vocation and it is for the future of nursing that I am pleading."

She continues, reciting the nurses' pledge. When she finishes, the queen applauds, having heard it all. The queen gives Sidney a box — all we see of the queen is her hand. The box contains a brooch, commemorating her work: "Blessed are the merciful."

Kay was terribly miscast, and the weak script didn't help. Sometimes creative people get caught up in the details and forget the big picture. In this case, the result was a deadly dull picture. Producer Hal Wallis had his staff conduct extensive research: "We cabled London,

It's not easy to find a glamorous shot of Kay in *The White Angel* (1936), but this one comes close (courtesy James King).

Kay Francis tends to a lame dog in *The White Angel* (1936).

seeking information on characters and atmosphere of the era 1850–1860. We wanted pictures (contemporary photographs, where possible) of St. Thomas's Hospital; uniforms of the Crimean War; photographs of Queen Victoria, Dr. John Hall, Sidney Herbert, John Sutherland, Andrew Smith, and Lord Raglan. They sent back an enormous number of lithographs, drawings, and photographs, and art director Anton Grot did unusually fine sketches for us based on them. Sir Edward Cook's excellent book *The Short Life of Florence Nightingale* informed us that Crimean War soldiers wore unattractive uniforms of gray tweed, with ugly scarves of brown holland. They had to be modified, of course."[63] Of course.

The studio also faced censorship problems. For one thing, the Hays Office told them they couldn't present brutality on film, which made things difficult since they were making a movie about one of the most brutal wars in history. Then British censors told them they couldn't show royalty on film. The studio was finally allowed to show long shots of the queen. The American print shows close-ups, but those shots were cut from the British version.

Another problem arose. The actress found to play Queen Victoria was a perfect resemblance. However, she had a Brooklyn accent so her voice was dubbed by British actress Doris Lloyd. Director Dieterle received numerous memos concerning one actor, a bearded friend, who kept appearing as an extra. Apparently his face appeared so much it became distracting. Wallis' memos kept insisting the man be used as a background extra only. Wallis also "objected to Dieterle's old trick of cutting in the camera, giving us nothing to cut later."[64] He also complained that Dieterle changed a day scene into a night one without permission.

Production started March 2, 1936, and ended April 22, 1936. The Balaklava scenes were filmed at the abandoned Civilian Conservation Corps camp about 40 miles from Hollywood.

Extras, paid $6.50 a day, were recruited for the hospital scenes. Actual amputees were used. "Aren't they pitiful?" Kay asked in an interview. "Yesterday, after we finished work, many of them walked all the way over Cahuenga Pass to save the 40 cents carfare. That is, those who could. Out of the men they hired from the streets yesterday, 45 failed to show up today. They got their money and I suppose they don't want to work any more until they spend it."[65]

Snow, made from cornflakes, made life diffcult on the set. Some flakes went down Kay's neck, while others flew in her mouth when she tried to talk, causing coughing fits. In addition, the production schedule was upset by bad weather, and Kay sometimes had to change makeup three times a day. Each time the application took two hours. Needless to say, Kay blew her stack more than a few times, and rumor has it that the bloopers from this film were quite profane.

On May 29, 1936, Kay, Ian Hunter, and Donald Woods appeared on the radio show *Hollywood Hotel* to re-enact scenes and promote the film.

In June 1936 Kay and director William Dieterle addressed a nurses' convention at the Hollywood Bowl. The audience numbered more than 10,000, and Kay admitted she suffered from stage fright.

The original title was *Angel of Mercy*. Josephine Hutchinson was first considered for Kay's role. A 1915 film, *Florence Nightingale*, starred Elisabeth Risdon. *The Lady with the Lamp* (1951) was a British production with Anna Neagle. A 1995 television program, *Florence Nightingale*, featured Jaclyn Smith (!) as Nightingale.

Watch for the scene where George Curzon tells Florence that government officials are opposed to her being sent to help in the Crimean War. Although it's supposed to be winter in London, through the window you see flowers blooming.

REVIEWS: "Miss Francis's performance is sincere and eloquent, however we may regret its reverential tone." (*New York Times*, June 25, 1936)

"The direction of William Dieterle is imaginative and the acting is uniformly excellent. Kay Francis plays with a rapt intensity that does wonders in establishing a rather shadowy figure without stamping it with compelling power. Here is a plausible performance which never reaches the heights of Paul Muni's in 'The Story of Louis Pasteur.'" (*New York Herald*, June 25, 1936)

"The title role gives Kay Francis a fine opportunity to present a great screen performance and the star takes every advantage the part offers to project the character of the famous heroine of the Crimean War with intelligence, sympathy and force." (Kate Cameron, *New York Daily News*, June 24, 1936)

"It is as entertaining as it is powerful and sincere, skillfully written, forcefully directed, playing by an inspired actress, 'The White Angel' is a film you mustn't miss. Miss Francis never before has attempted a role as Florence Nightingale. She plays it magnificently, with dignity, tenderness, intelligence and passion." (Bland Johaneson, *New York Daily Mirror*)

"In their effort to honor the memory of Florence Nightingale, they have quite killed whatever personality that great lady may have had. Her screen biography is incredibly lifeless. Kay Francis's Florence Nightingale is a two-dimensional figure, a beloved saint too revered by her biographers to make her portrait a human being." (Eileen Creelman, *New York Sun*, June 23, 1936)

"Kay Francis does one of her grandest serious roles. It's an epic in compassion, a companion piece for *The Story of Louis Pasteur*." (Harrison Carroll, *Los Angeles Evening Herald Express*, May 29, 1936)

"Kay Francis' work in the title role is easily the best she has done and will deserve much consideration in the Academy voting for the best actress." (*Film Daily*, June 2, 1936)

"The picture bears the mark of reverence for the theme and respect for the historical setting. Carefully produced and directed, 'The White Angel' deserves a place only slightly below 'The Story of Pasteur' as an achievement in biographical drama. With a more impassioned actress than Kay Francis in the principal role 'The White Angel' might have risen to the heights. The fact that it sustains a rare atmosphere throughout is a tribute to the production rather than to any individual performance, for Miss Francis's contribution is largely on the decorative side." (*New York Evening Post*, June 25, 1936)

"Warner Brothers have produced a film that must take its place high in the ranks of the year's outstanding motion pictures.... [D]irected with a touching simplicity and a fine appreciation of the fanatical passion with which Florence Nightingale devoted herself to the cause of hospital nursing, 'The White Angel' recreates this wax-work celebrity in flaming incidents and rich, strong writing. Miss Francis does a magnificent job as the Lady of the Lamp." (*New York World-Telegram*, Jun 25, 1936)

"'The White Angel' is a beautiful picture, an intensely stirring and inspiring document. It is in every respect a magnificent production, splendidly written and directed, the picture has been expertly cast even to the most minor of parts." (*New York Evening Journal*, June 25, 1936)

"The film not only brings us close to a famous figure and one of history's greatest humanitarians, but it tells her story in such dramatic phrases that the picture stands forth as ennobling, inspirational entertainment. Kay Francis has captured the spirit of the character she recreates for one of the finest portrayals, indeed, the very best, that she has contributed." (*New York American*, June 25, 1936)

"A credible but overly sentimental account of the career of Florence Nightingale. What is missing in the production is a performance as distinguished as that of Paul Muni. Miss Francis fills her role pictorially, but she never allows you to forget that she has nobly dedicated herself to the service of humanity." (*Brooklyn Daily Eagle*, June 25, 1936)

"*The White Angel* ... is not only a worthy but often a fascinating study of the past, reviving handsomely the glory of bygone days and deeds." (*Time*, July 6, 1936)

"There may be a quarrel about Kay Francis in the title role. She handles herself well and the part might ordinarily be considered a plum for any actress. But there seems too much restraint. A more passionate attitude might have made for greater emotional voltage from the spectator's viewpoint." (*Variety*, July 1, 1936)

Give Me Your Heart

(Warner Bros., 1936) 87 min.
Released on September 17, 1936.

Credits: Executive producers, Jack L. Warner, Hal B. Wallis; Supervising producer, Robert Lord; director, Archie L. Mayo; based on the play "Sweet Aloes" by Jay Mallory (Joyce Carey); screenplay, Casey Robinson; gowns, Orry-Kelly; music director, Leo F. Forbstein; songs, Harold Arlen, E.Y. Harburg; incidental music, W. Franke Harling, Heinz Roemheld; camera, Sid Hickox; editor, James Gibbon; sound recordist, Robert B. Lee; props, Pat Patterson; assistant director, Sherry Shourds; art directors, C.M. Novi, Max Parker.

Cast: Kay Francis (Belinda Warren); George Brent (James Baker); Roland Young (Edward "Tubbs" Barrow); Patric Knowles (Robert "Bob" Melford); Henry Stephenson (Edward, Lord Farrington), Frieda Inescort (Rosamond Melford); Helen Flint (Dr. Florence "Bones" Cudahy); Halliwell Hobbes (Oliver Warren); Zeffie Tilbury (Aunt Esther Warren); Elspeth Dudgeon (Alice Dodd); Russ Powell (Cab Driver); Dick French, Ethel Sykes (Departing Guests); Bruce Warren (Harry, the Young Man); Elsa Peterson (Young Woman); Velma Wayne and Charles Teske (Dance Team); Tockie Trigg (Edward, the Baby); Helena Grant (Nurse); Louise Bates (Mrs. Ethel Hayle, the Hostess); Demetrius Emanuel (Waiter); Bess Flowers (Carleton Bar Extra); Phyllis Godfrey (Grace, the Maid); Mitchell Ingraham (Bartender); Alphonse Martell (Dining Room Captain); Carlyle Moore Jr. (Elevator Operator); Edgar Norton (Jenkins, the Servant); Edmund Mortimer (Mr. Hayle, the Host); Eric Wilton (Johnson, the Butler).

TUBBS BARROW FINDS A car with women's gloves lying inside. Soon we see Bob and Linda coming back from a "walk in the woods." Bob, married to invalid Rosamond, has been having a secret affair with Linda. Tubbs confronts Linda and asks her what she's going to do. Linda leaves for Naples to get her father's advice.

"I've got a problem I can't solve," she starts to tell him, but he collapses and dies (we're not joking—he literally *dies* when she says this). By the time Linda returns to England, she learns she's pregnant with Bob's child. Tubbs arranges a meeting between Linda and Bob's father, who wants her to give him the child. She refuses.

"My dear," he tells her, "you don't stand on firm enough moral ground to be able to say I will do this or I will not do that. You have committed a wrong, a terrible wrong." He explains the things he can give the child. "I'm offering it a home and a name, a succession to a title, and the fortune that rightly belongs to Bob's child. A family tradition of character and honor. A father and a mother. What are you offering?"

Linda reluctantly agrees and returns to America. A couple years pass, and she's living in New York, married to Jim Baker. However, she has bouts of melancholy. "Happiness isn't a chronic state," Linda explains. Jim's worried about her, and is losing patience with her moodiness. He wants her to go with him to England, but she's on edge.

Tubbs and Florence, Linda's doctor, meet at the Baker household. Tubbs is there, pretending to see Jim about a tax matter. "You're smoking too much," Florence tells Linda. Boy, that's the truth. Linda smokes non-stop throughout the movie.

Tubbs invites Linda and Jim to dinner. When Linda sees Bob and Rosamond at another table, she becomes a nervous wreck. The Farringtons join them, and Linda asks to be taken home. Jim has a fit, and Linda sits down, smokes a ton of cigarettes, and orders a couple martinis. Jim asks her to slow down.

Rosamond tells Linda she reminds her of someone. "There's something about the brow," she says, scrutinizing Linda, and then talks about baby Edward, bringing out his photo.

"Lovely eyes," Jim says. Linda refuses to look at the photo. Finally, Tubbs forces her to. She smiles, touches the photo, and starts crying.

Kay was gorgeous in *Give Me Your Heart* (1936), as a woman compensating for separation from her baby with furs, gowns, and cigarettes.

Linda leaves the room, and Rosamond follows her. "It is you, isn't it?" Rosamond asks.

"Yes."

"You don't like me very well, do you?"

"Like you? I hate you. You didn't suffer to have him. Why you couldn't even — why should I be talking to you like this? You probably hated me just as much as I have you."

"No. Oh, a little at first. And Bob more than you. I tried not to. I kept saying to myself I'm a civilized woman. This mustn't make any difference. But it did. Oh my dear, you don't realize what you did for me. You gave me something I could never otherwise have had. Happiness I'd never dared to hope for. I felt so guilty. I've been tremendously happy and all at your expense."

She invites Linda upstairs to see Edward. He's asleep. Linda leans down, and kisses his cheek. Rosamond leaves her alone with the baby. Linda rests her cheek against Edward's and then strokes his cheek and neck. When she leaves the room, she thanks Rosamond, and asks if she can send Edward a rocking horse.

"Oh, I do wish we could be friends," Rosamond says. "See a lot of each other, I mean. Funny that our greatest bond makes that impossible, isn't it?"

"You've taken a great weight off my heart. I know I'll never have to worry about him again."

Jim and Linda take a walk. He scolds her for her behavior that night. She apologizes and says she's changed, even suggesting she's ready to have children.

"I think I'm going crazy," he says, surprised she's so agreeable.

"Oh, darling, don't do that. Not just when I've gotten sane again." They walk arm in arm, with Jim whistling.

Production started May 4, 1936. Kay probably set a record for cigarette smoking in one film. Roland Young gives a somewhat annoying performance, though Helen Flint is very good in a supporting role.

Jay Mallory was a pseudonym of actress Joyce Carey. The film was based on Mallory's 1934 hit London play that starred Diana Wynyard. The American version was less popular — Evelyn Laye's Broadway play closed after only 24 performances. The film's original title was *Sweet Aloes*, and some publicity materials, including posters and lobby cards, can still be found with this title. The title was changed to avoid confusion with *Sweet Alice*. Other working titles included *I Gave My Heart* and *I Give My Heart*.

Others considered for Kay's role included Ann Harding, Claudette Colbert, and Bette Davis. Although Kay worked with Archie Mayo on several pictures, they didn't like each other. He went so far as to tell her she couldn't act. After one argument on this picture, Kay walked off the set.

Cosmopolitan was a production company set up by William Randolph Hearst to make films starring his lover Marion Davies. Uncredited extra Pauline Garon was a former star who'd fallen on hard times. Her throaty laugh was said to rival Kay's. The bar used on the set was so attractive that a local nightclub offered to buy it.

On September 25, 1936, Kay and George Brent appeared on the radio show *Hollywood Hotel* to re-enact scenes and promote the film.

The movie ad proclaimed it as "The Picture Every Woman Will Want Some Man to See. To all the women of all the world who know — as no man can ever know — the anguish that is the glory of love, the despair that is its ecstasy. Warner Bros. give this amazing exploration of the heart of a girl faced with a fatal infatuation — then driven by a tragic fate to share her baby's love with the woman who should have been its mother! See it and you will understand why famous feminine critics unite in calling this the finest picture of its type in recent years. Only to a world of advancing social ideas would the screen dare present so fearlessly candid a drama. And only for a public whose tastes have been keyed to a higher entertainment level could Warner Bros. have planned the remarkable expression of exceptional new-season pictures which are inaugurating a new Golden Age of the screen." Another ad proclaimed: "Kay at the peak of her loveliness and George at the top of his form reward you with performances that will make you thank them from the bottom of your heart!" And yet another: "My baby calls another woman Mother! Her baby ... or a life of ease.... Which did she choose?"

REVIEWS: "*Give Me Your Heart* is a conventional tear-jerker, aimed especially at female cinemaddicts for whom its sentimental appeal will theoretically be reinforced by Kay Francis' clothes." (*Time*, September 28, 1936)

"An affecting, mature and sophisticated drama of mother love and applied psychiatry. Miss Francis, still amazingly gowned and handicapped by that distressing difficulty with her 'r's, plays Belinda with pathos and reticence." (*New York Times*, September 17, 1936)

"Kay Francis does the mother role well, but not as well here as in 'Parish.' Her part doesn't afford the opportunities of that picture, it's true, but too frequently sympathies aren't with the actress in her latest endeavor. Miss Francis doesn't make the part as real as it might have been." (*Variety*, September 16, 1936)

"Cosmopolitan Productions have turned out an intensely absorbing drama, well devised for the talents of the handsome Kay Francis, who has in this one her best modern characterization to date. Miss Francis gives an outstanding performance, handling the variety of emotions called for by the script with considerable skill." (*New York Evening Journal*, September 17, 1936)

"The star extracts from the situation of the heroine every ounce of feeling that the part calls for. It is no easy role that Miss Francis portrays. She is called upon to project a highly neurotic woman on the screen and she accomplishes this task with a finesse that is both subtle and delicate." (*New York Daily News*, September 17, 1936)

"Despite the fact that it is done with becoming gravity, and peopled by characters who conduct themselves like ladies and gentlemen, 'Give Me Your Heart' is a well-nigh perfect target for the film censors, now newly aroused by an encyclical from the Vatican." (James Francis Crow, *Hollywood Citizen News*, July 10, 1936)

"This will appeal especially to women. Its delicate subject has been handled with good taste and intelligence. It gives Kay Francis a strong emotional role and she does unusually good work." (*Film Daily*, July 14, 1936)

"Kay Francis, who has that rare gift of playing a suffering heroine, keeping herself attractive and interesting at the same time, has never given a better performance. Believe me, with all the tears that she has to shed, it is indeed a feat. As for the famed Francis clothes, Orry-Kelly has given her some stunning creations." (Louella O. Parsons, *Los Angeles Examiner*, September 25, 1936)

"In her day, Kay Francis has drawn many

good roles but no other so warmly sympathetic as the heroine in *Give Me Your Heart*. It is characteristic of the film's adult treatment that none of the characters is made out as a heavy. They are nice people who have gotten involved in a mess." (Harrison Carroll, *Los Angeles Evening Herald Express*, September 25, 1936)

Stolen Holiday

(Warner Bros., 1937) 76 min. Released on February 1, 1937.

Credits: Executive producer, Hal B. Wallis; associate producer, Harry Joe Brown; director, Michael Curtiz; story, Warren Duff, Virginia Kellogg; screenplay, Casey Robinson; musical director, Leo F. Forbstein; original music, Al Dubin, Werner R. Heymann, Heinz Roemheld, Harry Warren; art director, Anton Grot; dialogue director, Stanley Logan; gowns, Orry-Kelly; special effects, Fred Jackman; camera, Sid Hickox; editor, Terry Morse.

Cast: Kay Francis (Nicole Picot); Claude Rains (Stefan Orloff); Ian Hunter (Anthony Wayne); Alison Skipworth (Suzanne, the Fortune Teller); Alexander D'Arcy (Leon Anatole); Betty Lawford (Helen Tuttle); Walter Kingsford (Francis Chalon); Charles Halton (Mayor Marcel Le Grande); Frank Reicher (Charles Ranier); Frank Conroy (Dupont, the Crooked Cop); Kathleen Howard (Mme. Delphine); Nowell Wedgwood (M. Borel, the Swiss Printer); Robert Strange (Prefect of Police); Egon Brecher (Deputy Bergery); Eddie Foster (Agitator); Leonard Mudie (Wedding Guest); George Beranger (Swiss Waiter); Albert Conti (Photographer); Holmes Herbert (Nicole's Dance Partner); Brandon Hurst (Police Detective); Houseley Stevenson (Minister); Leo White (Taxi Driver).

THIS IS THE FIRST Kay Francis movie that begins with the disclaimer: "The names of all characters—The characters themselves—The story—all incidents and institutions portrayed in this production are fictitious—And no identification with actual persons, living or deceased, is intended or should be inferred." So, of course, you immediately know this one's based on a real person.

The film opens in Paris in 1931 at the Delphine Summer Fashion Show. Two women discuss Nicole Picot, one of the models. "She's that American. Nicole something or other," one says.

"What a fantastic coiffure," the other responds.

"Rather shocking. So ... mannish," she says with an admiring tone, obviously checking her out.

In fact, Kay's hairstyle is similar to the one she wore in her first pictures in the late 1920s. After the show, Suzanne asks Nicole what she wants to do. "Something I can do better than anybody else in the world. But what?"

"You've got a body," Suzanne says. "That's why you're here."

"Clotheshorse," Nicole complains.

"Find yourself a rich husband with it," Suzanne suggests.

"And write the life history of a parasite. So that's your opinion of my ability."

Creepy Stefan Orloff takes Nicole to a beautiful mansion, pretending that she'll be modeling clothing. Nicole quickly realizes they're alone in the house. "This is a trick," she says. "I'm not going to stay to find out what kind."

He explains he wants to borrow money and needs Nicole as a prop to pretend he's rich. He convinces her to participate in his plan. Four years later, we see an announcement: "The House of Picot ... invites you to a showing of New Fall and Winter Models on the afternoon of August first, 1936 at four o'clock. Admission by card only."

Nicole now owns a fancy shop and credits

Kay wore so many different costumes in *Stolen Holiday* (1937) one critic devoted her whole film review to the fashions.

Stefan for her success. "Everything I am, you've made me," she says.

Stefan sponsors a charity ball in the White Room of the Hotel Eugenie. British diplomat Anthony and Nicole meet when he insults her dress, calling it "frightful." Meanwhile, Stefan, preoccupied with a financial scam, asks Nicole to accompany him to Switzerland.

Anthony is on the same plane. Nicole insults his coat, and then snubs him when he apologizes. Suzanne, however, becomes friendly with him, and tries to play matchmaker (she detests Stefan). Soon, Anthony and Nicole become a twosome, and Nicole falls in love.

There's a cute scene when their car breaks down, and they break into a country house to fix a meal. He finds squab, and she explains what will happen next. "I think you're supposed to wring their necks. Don't be rough!"

He can't do it. Nicole plays with the other squab as though it were a pet. They have eggs instead.

"They're together constantly," Suzanne gleefully tells Stefan. Investigators begin closing in on Stefan and his band of swindlers. He tells Nicole that his friends have been thieves, he trusted them, and they betrayed him. His solution is for them to marry. He plans a huge wedding with important people. "It will publicize them as my closest friends. It will work, Nicki."

Anthony is livid. Nicole lies and says she loves Stefan. "You always said I'd trip over my heart didn't you?" she says to Suzanne, "You didn't say I'd break it at the same time."

She marries Stefan and is one of the saddest brides you'll ever see. After the ceremony, the investigators arrive. Nicole tells Stefan she won't run away with him. "I've always believed it's rather nice for a husband and wife to keep in touch with one another," she coldly tells him.

The scandal finally breaks, and Stefan is sought by the authorities. A hostile crowd vandalizes Madame Picot's shop, blaming her for financial losses resulting from Stefan's dealings.

Stefan sends Nicole a message: "Do not worry about me. I am Monsieur Conte, safe in an isolated chalet near Chamonix. If you have changed your mind, come secretly. All my devotion."

Before Nicole leaves, Anthony arrives. "I don't love him," Nicole tells him. "I love you." Still, she insists she must go to Stefan. "You can't discount the value of friendship, Tony.

Kay Francis and Ian Hunter in *Stolen Holiday* (1937). Kay is wearing an Orry-Kelly gown.

This is all part of a chapter that began long before you came into it. It can only be finished between Stefan and me."

Upon arriving at Stefan's hideout, he tells her that the first night she was with him she actually helped perpetuate a swindle. "How could you take the best and the most unselfish in me and use it?" she asks. He asks her to go away with him. "I can't hate you," she says. "I'm too sorry for you."

Stefan sees men coming up the walk and knows it's the end. Nicole says she'll help him. "Will you teach me the words to beg your forgiveness?" he asks, leaving her in the room.

She hears a gunshot and runs downstairs. The investigator tells her Stefan put a gun to his head and killed himself. She's told to leave so she won't be involved. We find out that Stefan was actually murdered. "You idiot!" the investigator says. "Since this man is supposed to have committed suicide by shooting himself in the right side of his head, it might be more convincing in the photograph if you do not place the gun in his left hand." They promptly switch the gun.

Nicole writes a check to help those who lost

money. "Well, Suzanne, it's all gone. Furs, jewels, home, Picot Incorporated. We're right back where we started."

Anthony wants to marry her. She refuses. They walk outside together, get in a cab, with him repeatedly asking her to marry him. When he threatens to yodel (don't ask), she agrees. She smiles, and they kiss.

Kay began filming on July 20, 1936. The production was partly shot in Lake Arrowhead, California. Kay is particularly well lit in this film and, as in *Give Me Your Heart*, smokes a lot of cigarettes. She does remarkably well with some clunky lines. Ian Hunter, who almost never gets the girl in his movie roles, is a tad more animated in this one — and ends up getting the girl.

The film was based on a French scandal involving a man named Serge Alexandre Stavisky. Arlette Simon was a Coco Chanel model who'd married Stavisky. He committed suicide, but the Production Code insisted that the crook appear to be murdered. In real life, Simon became a showgirl at New York's French Casino club. The original title was *The Mistress of Fashion*. *Stavisky*, a 1974 French film directed by Alain Resnais, starred Jean-Paul Belmondo, Francois Perier, and Anny Duperey.

REVIEWS: "Miss Francis has again put the studio gown designers to work creating a lot of fancy clothes. The gowns fit both the star and the story." (*Variety*, February 3, 1937)

"As film entertainment it moves listlessly, freighted as it is with leisurely assemblages in incredibly lavish surroundings and conspirators who play hide-and-seek with a frock-coated prefecture. Kay Francis parades the most striking wardrobe that Hollywood's couturiers can conceive in the Paris manner." (*New York Times*, February 1, 1937)

"Kay Francis, fresh from a trip to Europe, hides her acting ability under a series of fantastic clothes, which as usual bring sighs from women, snorts from men. Most fantastic: a white evening gown, half Escape from the Seraglio, half Visit to the Turkish Bath." (*Time*, February 8, 1937)

"Absorbing drama gives Miss Francis opportunity to wear stunning gowns should please her following. Beautiful gowns will appeal to women, and Kay Francis wearing them will appeal to men, and the spirited dialogue will attract the higher intellectual registers." (*Film Daily*, December 22, 1936)

Another Dawn
(Warner Bros., 1937) 73 min.
Released on June 18, 1937.

Credits: Executive producers, Jack L. Warner, Hal B. Wallis; associate producer, Harry Joe Brown; director, William Dieterle; screenplay, Laird Doyle; based on "Caesar's Wife" by W. Somerset Maugham; dialogue director, Stanley Logan; art director, Robert Haas; gowns, Orry-Kelly; wardrobe, Henry West, Ida Greenfield; hair, Ruby Felker; makeup, Ward Hamilton; technical advisor, Major Sam Harris; musical director, Leo F. Forbstein; music, Erich Wolfgang Korngold; orchestrators, Hugo Friedhofer, Milan Roder; assistant director, Frank Heath; sound, Robert B. Lee; camera, Tony Gaudio; assistant camera, Frank Gaudio; editor, Ralph Dawson; choreographer, Michael Kidd; production manager, Tenny Wright; special effects, Willard Van Enger, James Gibbon; unit manager, Al Alleborn; grip, Glen Harris; props, Pat Patterson; still photographer, Madison Lacy.

Cast: Kay Francis (Julia Ashton); Errol Flynn (Captain Denny Roark); Ian Hunter (Colonel John Wister); Frieda Inescort (Grace Roark); Herbert Mundin (Wilkins); G. P. Huntley, Jr. (Lord Alden); Billy Bevan (Hawkins); Clyde Cook (Sergeant Murphy); Richard Powell (Henderson); Kenneth Hunter (Sir Charles Benton); Mary Forbes (Mrs. Benton); Eily Malyon (Mrs. Farnold); Charles Austin (Yeoman); Joseph Tozer (Butler); Ben Welden (Mr. Romkoff); Spencer Teakle (Fromby); David Clyde (Campbell); Charles Irwin (Kelly); Reginald Sheffield (Wireless Operator); Martin Garralaga (Ali, the Servant); George Regas (Achaben); Jack Richardson (Lang); Edward Dew (Glass); Robert M. Simpson (Lloyd); Will Stanton (John's Caddy); Neal Kennedy (Julia's Caddy); Sam Harris (Guest); Stefan Moritz (Arab Horseman); Tyrone Brereton (Soldier); Leonard Mudie (Doctor); Yorke Sherwood (Station Master); Claire Verdera (Innkeeper); E.L. Fisher-Smith (Steward); Alec Harford (Steward); John McCallum (Nurse)

A REMOTE OUTPOST — a long, long way from Tipperary — where a handful of the King's best preserve a precarious peace amongst the warring natives, at the cost of much British blood spilled in the desert sand.

Colonel John Wister is the commander. He goes on vacation, leaving Denny Roark in

Opposite: **A selection of postcards showing Kay's different hairstyles.**

charge. On a cruise, Wister meets the lovely American Julia Ashton. We first see her shoes — shades of *Gentlemen of the Press* — and then the camera tilts up. Later, Wister and Julia find themselves at the same estate.

Julia is still in love with inventor Duncan Hitchen, who died in a plane crash. "He died clean and young," she says of Duncan, "before anything could grow older or dimmer. Although they're ashamed of it, every honest woman knows that her life has but one love, and however long it lasts, it's hers forever. Mine was three years. Three ecstatic years."

"The hopes we have for tomorrow die today," he chimes in. Wister falls in love with her and asks her to marry him.

"I feel very flattered," Julia says. "Because I admire and respect you so much. I'd give anything in the world if I could love you. I want to, but I just can't, that's all. See, I still love him."

Wister somehow convinces Julia to return with him. Upon arrival, Roark spies Julia, comes on to her, and is rebuffed. Wister soon introduces them. "I can't tell you how happy I am for both of you," Roark's sister Grace says, sounding like she's going to cry — she's in love with Wister.

An uprising forces Wister to leave, which leaves Roark and Julia alone. Turns out Roark's laugh is like Duncan's. They listen to bedouin music. "Somehow it seems to go with the desert and the night," Roark explains. "Sort of a melodic will-of-the-wisp that dares your emotions to follow it."

This strikes a chord with Julia. "That's *it*. That's it exactly." Julia tells Roark about Duncan.

"Wish I was like him."

"I'm afraid you are."

Later, they kiss. "It was just one of those things that happens without a cause and has no meaning," she tells him. Wister returns, but tells her he has to leave again almost immediately. "I just don't want you to leave," Julia says, suggesting he send Roark instead.

Roark and his men run into trouble. "The Northern Desert — stronghold of Achaben — powerful, warring native Sheik — who controls the river water that is life and livelihood to the peaceful tribes in the valleys below him." Ambushed, Roark sends a report to Wister. "He's got one chance in a hundred," Wister tells a panicked Julia.

Roark sends another message: "Running out of ammunition but not arrows. Five of us left. Good fight. Can't win all the time." A man accused of previous cowardice saves Roark and one other man. Roark, however, is wounded.

When Julia visits him during a sandstorm, Roark tells her he's in love with her. "Oh, it's all so futile," Julia says. "We can't be blamed for what we want, only for what we do. One can't stop loving. I've tried. I thought I never could love again."

"The hopes we have for tomorrow die today," Roark says.

They agree nothing can be done because of Wister. Roark applies for a transfer.

"You love Julia, and you're trying to escape it," Grace tells her brother, adding that she's been in love with Wister for years. "I've learned another kind of love than that which comes from wanting and having. A quiet kind that watches and shares in someone's life without that someone knowing." You know, the *creepy* kind.

Meanwhile, Wister needs a dam destroyed. Although Wister knows about Roark and Julia, he refuses to grant Roark's transfer. "If I could only blame them, it'd be easier," Wister tells Grace, "but I can't."

Julia decides to leave the outpost and both men. Wister overhears their conversation. "One of us must go," Julia says. "If we don't, something terrible will happen. You and I aren't strong enough. I'll still keep on loving you. That won't end. But I can't stay here, Denny. I can't! Respecting him, loving you, hating myself! It's just not possible."

Wister tells Roark he's decided to take Roark's plane, loaded with explosives, and destroy the dam. Roark tells him there's not enough fuel to return. It's a suicide mission. Roark and Wister argue about who'll go. They flip a coin, and Roark "wins." However, Wister sneaks off, while Roark says goodbye to Julia, and takes the plane.

"He's gone out there to die ... for me," Roark tells Julia. "Not even a miracle can save him." They receive word that the dam has been destroyed, and the plane went down in flames.

"Why'd he do it, Denny?" Julia asks.

"To give us that," Roark says, pointing at the sky. "Another dawn."

"Leaving us all his tomorrows to live out," she adds. "He knew that we three could always be together, only if he went away." Julia leans into Roark.

This melodramatic claptrap was originally titled *Caesar's Wife*. And don't count on any cultural sensitivity, either. This film was bought for Bette Davis, but she turned it down during her contract dispute. On July 16, 1935, Louella Parsons reported that Tallulah Bankhead was being tested for the role, and would likely be signed. Screenwriter Laird Doyle died in an airplane crash on November 2, 1936 — a few days after finishing his script. Kay rode a horse for the first time when making this film.

Grace loves Wister, who loves Julia, who loves Roark, who loves Julia. The solution? Wister flies off on a suicide mission, leaving the two lovers to face "another dawn." We're supposed to believe that all three are honorable. "If they were less honorable, there would be a solution," Grace laments in a melancholy voice. If they were the *least* bit honorable, they wouldn't find themselves in beautifully lit and photographed scenes, gazing lustily at each other.

Locations included Yuma, Arizona; Imperial County, California; and Lasky Mesa in Agoura, California. Production started September 26, 1936, but wasn't finished until February 1937 when Kay returned from her European vacation. The film was shot with two endings. In one, Ian Hunter died, and in the other, Errol Flynn is killed. Preview audiences decided Hunter had to go.

The studio spent a small fortune on palm trees used for one scene. The insured plants could only be photographed for three minutes at a time because of the camera's hot lights. Kay and Errol narrowly escaped serious injury when a prop tree toppled, almost crushing them.

Supposedly, the title came from Warner Brothers' use of *Another Dawn*— a fictitious title — that often appeared on "fake" movie theater marquees in films. When a suitable title couldn't be found for this film, they apparently decided *Another Dawn* was just as good as any. The line of dialogue at the end, which doesn't make a whole lot of sense anyway, was apparently added to the script.

Advertising copy read: "A woman trying to escape her past.... An adventurer with a scorn for death and a lust for life. A love thrill you will never forget."

REVIEWS: "This one rings no changes, follows the old pattern faithfully; generates no suspense and no excitement because it is always and completely predictable." (James Francis Crow, *Hollywood Citizen News*, April 1, 1937)

"Flynn and Miss Francis, playing together for the first time, have keyed their performance nicely to the mood. It has the lure of adventure in strange places and of a love theme that scratches deeper than the surface." (*Los Angeles Evening Herald Express*, June 24, 1937)

"Trapped in so painfully trite a triangle, *Another Dawn*'s cast coolly do their theatrical best. Ian Hunter, in what is apparently an air-conditioned oasis, is properly stoic. A raging sirocco does not discourage Miss Francis from exhibiting her usual sweeping evening gowns and Grecian neckline." (*Time*, July 5, 1937)

"William Dieterle's direction is sentimentality confused." (Elizabeth Yeaman, *Hollywood Citizen News*, June 24, 1937)

Confession

(Warner Bros., 1937) 91 min.
Released on August 19, 1937.

Credits: Executive producer, Jack L. Warner; producer, Hal B. Wallis; supervisor, Henry Blanke; director, Joe May; based on the screenplay "Mazurka" by Hans Rameau; English adapters, Julius J. Epstein, Margaret LeVino; dialogue director, Stanley Logan; art director, Anton Grot; gowns, Orry-Kelly; music director, Leo F. Forbstein; piano, Max Rabinowitz; original music, Peter Kreuder, Heinz Roemheld, Jack Scholl; camera, Sid Hickox; editor, James Gibbon; publicist, Arthur J. Zellner; grip, Dudie Maschmeyer; women's wardrobe, Ida Greenfield; men's wardrobe, Rydo Loshak; assistant camera, Vernon Larson; still photographer, Madison S. Lacy; assistant editor, Rudi Fehr; best boy, Walter Burris; gaffer, Paul Burnett; script clerk, Fred Applegate; second camera operator, Wesley Anderson; sound, Oliver S. Garretson; props, Emmett Emerson; assistant directors, Sherry Shourds, Fred Tyler; production manager, Al Alleborn; hair, Ruby Felker; makeup, Ward Hamilton.

Cast: Kay Francis (Vera Kowalska); Ian Hunter (Leonide Kirow/Koslov); Basil Rathbone (Michael Michailow); Jane Bryan (Lisa Koslov); Donald Crisp (Presiding Judge); Dorothy Petersen (Mrs. Koslov); Laura Hope Crews (Stella); Mary Maguire (Hildegard); Robert Barrat (Prosecuting Attorney); Ben Welden (Defense Attorney); Veda Ann Borg (Xenia); Helen Valkis (Wanda); Anderson Lawler (Reporter); Michael Mark (Russian Interpreter); Sam Rice, Albert Lloyd, Perc Teeple, Jack Richardson (Men at Station); Lyle Moraine (Usher at Theatre); Ferdinand

Munier (Bald Man at Theatre); Peggy Keys, Jewel Jordan (Autograph Fans); Sam Ash (Waiter); Edward Keane (Cabaret Manager); Dawn Bender (Lisa as a Baby); Janet Shaw, Jody Gilbert, Evelyn Mulhall, Symona Boniface, Elsa Peterson (Actress Friends); Edward Price, Jeffrey Sayre, John Mather, Lane Chandler, John Davidson, Maurice Brierre (Actor Friends); Lawrence Grant (Doctor); Maurice Cass (Music Professor); Glen Cavender (Bailiff); Gennaro Curci (Extra); Don Downen (Young Man in Court); Alan Gregg (Extra); Herbert Heywood (Porter Carrying a Letter); Leyland Hodgson (Leading Man in Opera); Stuart Holmes (Policeman in Court); Matty King (Dancer); Rolf Lindau (Clerk at Candy Counter); Theodore Lorch (Man in Court); Alphonse Martell (Maitre D'Hotel); Paul Panzer (Man Bringing Suitcase); Henry Roquemore (Fat Man in Court); Cliff Saum (Reporter); Ferdinand Schumann-Heink (Man in Court); Harry Semels (Porter on Train); John Shelton (Actor); Bernard Siegel (Theatre Doorman); Adele St. Mauer (Koslov's Maid); Myrtle Stedman (Nurse Maid); Don Turner (Man Leaving Theatre); Dale Van Sickel (Diner in Cabaret); Emmett Vogan (American Frontiersman in Show); Patricia Walthall (Frontiersman's Assistant); Pierre Watkin (Lawyer Stagoff); Tom Wilson (Man in Court Sitting Next to Mrs. Koslov); Jack Wise (Reporter); John Harron.

"THIS FILM IS A dramatization of the facts revealed in the legal documents of a law suit which caused a sensation in a European city in the year 1930."

While Lisa sees her mother off at a train depot, she's being carefully watched by concert pianist Michael. Lisa and friend Hildegarde receive tickets to his concert that night, and Michael sends her a note during his performance. "I am so glad you came! I should like to see you after the concert at Entrance IV. If this is agreeable, when I look up at you, please nod to me." Lisa inadvertently nods to something Hildegarde says, and after the concert tries to explain the miscommunication to Michael.

He's persistent, even though she tells him she can't see him. When she arrives at her music lesson the next day, Michael is waiting for her. "I had to see you again," he says, pulling her to him, kissing her. She hurries away.

Meanwhile, Lisa's mother has returned from her trip. While Lisa opens a present her mother brought back for her, a woman appears at their apartment. Lisa calls out, thrilled with her new dress, but her mother awkwardly tells her she's busy with the woman.

Michael telephones, asking Lisa to meet him. She refuses, but finally relents and meets him at a rowdy nightclub. The curtain opens, and a woman stands onstage. It's Vera, a heavily made-up blonde cabaret singer. She wanders into the audience. Michael takes Lisa's hand and kisses it. Vera sits on a man's lap, takes a drink, and then gets up. Lisa and Michael kiss. Vera sees them and stops singing. Michael stands, and he and Vera share a glance. Vera faints. Michael takes off, dragging Lisa with him.

"*Michael Michailow!*" a woman shouts in the lobby as Michael hustles Lisa away. He turns, sees her, and turns his back. Two shots are fired. Michael falls to the floor, rolls down the stairs, and lands not far from Vera's feet. Vera throws the gun down.

In the next scene, we're in a courtroom. Lisa and her mother are in attendance. "I have nothing to say," Vera says in court.

The judge pleads with her to tell her side of the story. "It is a question of your life," he explains.

"What do you all want of me?" Vera cries. "I

In *Confession* (1937), Kay went from opera to cabaret and, finally, to a courtroom on trial for murder.

killed him." She's hardened, bitter, and weary. When Vera's suitcase is brought into court, an anxious Vera suddenly claims she'll talk — if they promise not to open the suitcase.

Her attorney asks that her statement be heard behind closed doors. "What she is about to say may be a violation of public decency."

The courtroom is cleared. Vera rises. "It was in 1912 in Warsaw," she begins, and we go into a flashback. The scene is the Warsaw Opera House on Wednesday, February 12, 1912. The performance is "Mazurka, an Opera in One Act" by Michael Michailow, conducted by Michael. Opera star Vera Kowalska returns to her dressing room, bubbly and happy. She's giving up her career to marry soldier Leonide.

Michael tells her he's in love with her. She laughs and tells him she knows his kind. Leonide comes backstage. Obviously in love, they kiss — one of Hollywood's longest kisses up to that point.

Leonide and Vera marry and have a child. We're next shown war footage for 1914 and 1915. While Leonide is away, Vera receives Michael's invitation to a charity ball. After the ball, the party continues at Michael's. Vera drinks too much. Michael wants her to rejoin the opera. "In the end, I shall win," he says.

Vera becomes dizzy, and Michael offers to take her home, but, instead, takes her to a room. When she awakens, she hurries home, ashamed. When Leonide returns, she embraces him, ready to tell him what happened, but realizes he's lost an arm in battle. Leonide misunderstands, thinking she's upset about his injury. "I love you more than you'll ever know," she guiltily tells him.

Michael continues to pester her. She receives a letter: "Vera!" Michael writes. "You haven't answered a single one of my letters. I must see you again. I shall be waiting for you at two o'clock. Don't fail! M."

She hurries out, telling Leonide she's going out to see a sick friend. Vera pleads with Michael to stop. "Let me alone! I love my husband. I love my child."

Vera leaves, only to find that Leonide has followed her. Leonide divorces her and gets custody of the baby. After a hospitalization, Vera can't locate Leonide and Lisa. Only able to find work at cheap cafes, she continues looking for her husband and child. She'd finally found a telephone listing for Leonide Kozlov — he'd changed his name after the divorce. That was the day Vera showed up to speak to Lisa's mother.

Vera, after learning that Leonide died three years before, peeked into the room and saw Lisa hugging her mother. Lisa was never told of Vera and the scandal. "I had seen my daughter again," Vera tells the court. "I could give her nothing. My life would disgust her. My love would only frighten her."

Vera explains that that same night she saw Michael kissing Lisa, and felt she had to stop him from ruining her daughter. The suitcase holds her papers, proving her story. "If you examine them in open court, Lisa, the whole world, would have known that I was her mother. She must never know."

Vera sits. The public is re-admitted. The prosecutor, moved by the story, asks the court to sentence her to five years in prison for second degree murder.

"Accused, the law gives you the last word." Vera stands.

"Nothing," she replies.

The jury finds her guilty of murder in the second degree, and sentences her to three years. The judge explains the leniency: "It became clear to all of us that the actuating motive of the crime was the desire, the determination I might say, of the accused to save a young girl from the seductions of a man who only can be regarded as morally degraded."

After the verdict, Lisa approaches Vera in the hall. "I just wanted to tell you that — I just had to tell you, that I want to wish you the best of everything," Lisa says.

A transparent, ghostly Vera comes forward and embraces Lisa; the physical Vera remains rooted, looking blank.

"Thank you, Miss Lisa."

Vera walks down the corridor, looks out the window, and sees Lisa and her mother, strolling arm in arm toward a car. She smiles, tears in her eyes. The car drives away. Vera continues down the corridor, standing straighter now.

Kay gives one of her best performances in, arguably, her last great film. There's plenty of range as she goes from playing a cheap, overly made-up cabaret singer, to an effervescent young bride in flashback, and then, finally, a world-weary shell of a woman on trial for her life. It seems a role that Dietrich would have been offered, though it is disconcerting to first spy Kay in a frizzy blonde wig suggestively dancing and singing in a deep, European-accented voice. Still, it's Kay's movie, and she shines in scene after scene.

This film was previously made in Germany with the exact same screenplay. In fact, Joe May did not direct but recreated *Mazurka* shot-by-shot.

The premiere of *Mazurka* was in Berlin on December 10, 1935. Directed by Willi Forst, it starred Pola Negri (a favorite of Kay's from the time she was a youngster), who sang in her own voice in her cabaret scenes but was dubbed by soprano Hilde Seipp for the opera scenes. Warner Brothers bought distribution rights with the stipulation that *Mazurka* could only be shown in Germany. Pola bitterly complained that the move hurt her career. "When the picture was released, the press was unanimous in declaring my performance the greatest of my career and calling *Mazurka* the best talkie ever made in Germany. Word of its extraordinary quality rapidly spread through Europe and overseas to America. Unfortunately for me, the reports were so superlative that Warner Brothers bought up all American rights as a vehicle for their star Kay Francis. This meant that the Forst-Negri version would never be shown in the United States, and that there would be no new offers from Hollywood." Pola added that her version was "a triumphant success" while the remake "turned out to be a complete fiasco."[66] Negri's words sound like hyperbole. However, after viewing *Mazurka* it turns out she was partly right. *Mazurka* is a masterpiece and a must-see by anyone interested in great filmmaking. The performances by Pola and Garbo-lookalike Ingeborg Theek are excellent, and Forst's direction (he was a former lover of Dietrich's) is original, compelling, and masterful.

After seeing *Confession*, but before we saw *Mazurka*, the authors thought Joe May was a forgotten genius. Now we think he's weird and Willi Forst is a genius and want to watch every film he's ever made. Hollywood apparently thought so, too, because an earlier Forst film, *Maskerade* (1934), was also remade shot by shot and retitled *Escapade* (1935). As for May, why in the world would a creative person want to replicate something another creative person did? He even used actors and extras who resembled their counterparts in *Mazurka*. In addition, May apparently drove everyone nuts by running scenes of *Mazurka* on the set. What actor would be comfortable watching another play his/her role during filming? Considering the nightmarish set, it's amazing that Kay, Rathbone, and Bryan are as good as they are — a credit to their talent.

Associate producer Henry Blanke also was no fan of May: "The original German version was excellent and quite innovative. My director, Joe May, who I had not wanted to hire in the first place, was so impressed with the earlier film that he decided that *his* production would be an exact duplicate. He spent weeks in an editing room studying the Negri picture on a Movieola, frame-by-frame. When the production began filming, May sat on the set with a stop-watch to be sure that each scene ran the exact length as the original. The whole thing was a disaster."[67]

Jane Bryan, who gave an excellent performance, hated working on the film. Calling the direction "ridiculous," she recalled, "We were all marching through the film like sleepwalkers. There was absolutely no spontaneity."[68] Kay openly argued with May on several occasions. In one instance, she sparred with him over a line. She wanted to say, "I won't," while Joe wanted "I can't." The difference, according to the undiplomatic May, was "the difference between you and a good actress."[69] It was well-known in the film community that actress and director did not get along. According to one magazine, "the best dialogue in *Confession* will not be heard on the screen. It was between Kay and Joe May. The picture resolved itself into one long fight between star and director."[70] Kay overcame the poor direction and gave a remarkable performance. Needless to say, May did little to help her confidence.

A March 25, 1937, memo written by a studio production manager tattled on director May, complaining that he'd made only six camera set-ups for the entire day. Furthermore, May, who'd hired Basil Rathbone at $5,000 a week, refused to use a double for the scene where Michael is shot on the stairs. Poor Basil, who was perfectly willing to do the scene, had to fall down the stairs *ten* times over a period of two hours. May did not work again for Warner Brothers.

The two-story set for the Vienna café scene was a bit unusual. Normally, Hollywood sets partially built the second story and then used camera tricks to help create the illusion.

Kay sings "One Hour of Romance." Part of it is talked—and that's Kay—but the actual singing is dubbed. Kay's not terribly believable as a renowned opera diva. It might have been wiser to make her a popular singer.

The film was originally titled *One Hour of Romance*. A March 1937 studio memo suggested changing the title to *Confession* because the studio wanted to rename *The Great Lie* to *One Hour of Romance*. By the time *The Great Lie* was released in 1941, *One Hour of Romance* had been abandoned as a title. Other working titles included *One Hour to Live* and *Mazurka*.

Kay started working on the film on February 23, 1937, and requested a closed set. She was reportedly horrified when she saw the rushes of herself in the blonde wig. During production, she was also grieving the loss of her dog Weenie, who died on March 7.

Songs included the Mazurka theme and "One Hour of Romance." Fredric March was the original choice for the male lead, but became unavailable. Producer Henry Blanke unsuccessfully lobbied for Bette Davis and Warner Baxter as the leads. Lola Lane was considered for the role of Xenia; the wonderful character actress Veda Ann Borg ended up playing Xenia, and would also appear in Kay's last film, *Wife Wanted* (1946). Kay was unhappy with Warner Bros. during production and became involved in a lawsuit, which columnists referred to as "The Battle of the Century."

Movie ads proclaimed: "A New Kay ... in her most endearing role!" And "Kay Francis confesses ... and you hear the throbbing of a woman's heart ... see a mother's soul stripped bare!"

REVIEWS: "The Strand's current 'Confession' is, however, the first film that has discovered Miss Francis performing that neatest of tricks, darkly brooding in a blond peruke." (*New York Times*, August 19, 1937)

"Well acted and directed mother-love story has clever treatment. Kay Francis' work is her best in some time, while Basil Rathbone, Donald Crisp and Ian Hunter are fine in their roles." (*Film Daily*, July 20, 1937)

"Kay Francis sheds her glamour for a role of heavy dramatic sacrifice and mother love. Miss Francis is thin and bedizened for her portrayal of this mother who suffers unjustly. And when she gives forth song the effect is startling. The songs which emanate are both torchy and operatic! The only time she looks like Kay Francis is in the brief scenes of her heyday as an opera star, when she is glamorously attired. Bereft of her dazzling wardrobe, she is pitiful rather than tragic. Her personality does not embrace sacrificial motherhood gracefully." (*Hollywood Citizen News*, October 1, 1937)

First Lady

(Warner Bros., 1937) 82 min.
Released on December 23, 1937.

Credits: Executive producers, Jack L. Warner, Hal B. Wallis; associate producer, Harry Joe Brown; director, Stanley Logan; based on the play by George S. Kaufman, Katharine Dayton; screenplay, Rowland Leigh; art director, Max Parker; music director, Leo F. Forbstein; original music, Max Steiner; gowns, Orry-Kelly; assistant director, Sherry Shourds; camera, Sid Hickox; editor, Ralph Dawson.

Cast: Kay Francis (Lucy Chase Wayne); Anita Louise (Emmy Page); Preston Foster (Stephen Wayne); Walter Connolly (Carter Hibbard); Victor Jory (Senator Gordon Keane); Verree Teasdale (Irene Hibbard); Louise Fazenda (Mrs. Lavinia Mae Creevey); Marjorie Gateson (Sophie Prescott); Marjorie Rambeau (Belle Hardwicke); Eric Stanley (Tom Hardwick); Henry O'Neill (George Mason); Lucile Gleason (Mrs. Ives); Sara Haden (Mrs. Mason); Harry Davenport (Charles); Gregory Gaye (Gregoravich); Olaf Hytten (Bleeker); Jackie Morrow (Boy); Jack Mower (Halloran); Joseph Romantini (Senor Ortega); Grant Mitchell (Ellsworth T. Banning); John Harron (Waiter); Elizabeth Dunne, Lillian Harmer, Robert Cummings, Sr., Wedgwood Nowell (Extras).

THE SETTING FOR THIS picture is Washington, D.C. "The policies of a great nation are molded by prominent men, but behind these men stand women, guiding their husbands' destinies—using the same devices that the feminine sex has always used throughout the ages. The hand that rocks the cradle rocks the Capitol, which only goes to prove that wives are women in Kankakee or Washington, D.C. While this story and all names, characters, and incidents portrayed in it are fictitious, and no identification with actual persons, living or deceased, is intended or should be inferred—it may have happened!—It could have happened!"

Lucy Chase Wayne, granddaughter of former President Andrew Chase, is married to Secretary of State Stephen Wayne. Irene, her rival, is married to an old Supreme Court Justice. Both have set their sights on Senator Keane. In fact, Lucy helped Keane with a speech.

"You know, dear," Lucy's husband says, "I'd feel a lot more comfortable if you'd just take to drinking, gambling, or shoplifting. They're much safer vices than ghostwriting for senators."

Irene's interest in Keane is of a more romantic interest. She hopes to divorce her husband, marry Keane, and steer him toward the White House.

When Lucy and Irene get together, the fur really flies. "How I envy your knack with older men," Lucy says. "Oh, that reminds me. How is your husband?"

Irene has a few zingers, too. "You're so fortunate in having a past, my dear. It gives you something to talk about."

Lucy comes up with a plan to make Irene think that husband Carter Hibbard is a presidential nominee; if convinced, she'll drop her pursuit of Keane. She enlists the aid of Mrs. Creevey, the president of the WPPP — Women's Peace, Purity, and Patriotism League. Irene, contemptuous of her husband, is bored, brittle, and frustrated. Some of the best scenes are between Irene and Carter.

"I'm leaving you because I cannot stand it one minute longer!" Irene finally tells him. Carter agrees to give Irene a divorce. However, before she leaves, she gets wind of the fact that Carter might run for president. That changes everything.

Irene shrugs upon learning the news. "Well, what can I say? My husband's interests are mine."

Lucy is devastated to find that Carter — not her husband — is actually being considered for the Presidency. "There just seems to be a lot of Hibbard sentiment, Lucy. We don't know how it started," Stephen tells her. Even worse, Lucy discovers that her husband *would* have been the candidate — if not for her meddling in the Hibbard business.

Lucy talks to her grandfather's portrait and vows to beat Irene. Fortunately, she discovers that one of Irene's previous husbands, a charming Slovanian Prince, is in the United States—and that they're still married.

"Tomorrow our divorce will become legal in America," he tells Irene.

"To think all these years you've been living with Carter without being married to him. Though why you should ever want to do that, I haven't any idea," Lucy says.

"You're nothing but a dirty politician," Irene accuses.

"You bet I am!"

A defeated Irene pulls Carter aside. "You may have to alter slightly that impromptu speech you've been preparing so carefully."

Carter pulls out of the race, and Lucy gets her wish — Stephen becomes the candidate.

Production started May 7, 1937. Kay received top billing, and it's a real departure for her. The problem is the character lacks depth. Kay does much better playing complicated women, using her tragic eyes that show she's experienced much. This character is shallow and superficial. Kay's still fun to watch, and probably provides us with a good idea of what she did on stage in the so-so comedies after her film career ended. The picture's just not as clever as it wants to be. The dialogue isn't consistently sharp, though Verree Teasdale is quite good.

Notice Kay knitting in an early scene. Off the set, Kay was an avid knitter.

Orry-Kelly tried to tone down the glamour in this picture. "So many pictures have to be overdressed to get character, but we felt that the heroine should symbolize good taste —

Kay checks her makeup on the set of *First Lady* (1937), a film version of a popular Broadway hit.

Candid shot of Kay Francis and Preston Foster in *First Lady* (1937).

what well-bred American women really wear."[71] During the production, an observer noticed that for a close-up, Kay stood next to a table — wooden blocks elevated the table at least a foot. "Miss Francis is the screen's tallest actress and the elevated table gives the cameraman the correct composition necessary for good photography."[72]

The play by Kaufman and Dayton starred Jane Cowl and opened at the Music Box Theatre in New York on November 26, 1935; it closed the following June after 236 performances. The property was originally bought for Norma Shearer. The Lucy character was based on Alice Roosevelt Longworth, daughter of Teddy Roosevelt and wife of House Speaker Nicholas Longworth.

The Washington, D.C., premiere included wives and girlfriends of many prominent politicians. Eleanor Roosevelt was invited, but did not attend.

This was British stage director Stanley Logan's first feature-length film. He wisely surrounded Kay with veteran theatre performers.

On November 26, 1937, Kay, Preston Foster, and Verree Teasdale appeared on the radio show *Hollywood Hotel* to re-enact scenes and promote the film.

Louise Fazenda, a former Mack Sennett silent screen comedienne, was married to producer Hal Wallis. Jokesters called him the Prisoner of Fazenda.

REVIEWS: "There is an art of insult, and Miss Francis has not mastered it. She delivers her lines with the self-conscious unction of an actress who had just discovered how good they were when rereading the script that morning." (*New York Times*, December 23, 1937)

"Her performance is splendid and witty, and her costumes striking." (*Variety*, September 1, 1937)

"As the smoke of battle clears, there has been

little action, and no romance, in this excellently acted comedy. For these conventional elements, 'First Lady' substitutes witty dialogue and a memorable sketch of a backstage Washington, dominated by its womenfolk, that brews its storm in its afternoon teacups." (*Newsweek*, December 13, 1937)

"Rich in comedy and satire, pix nets a full quota of laughs. Kay Francis does fine work, and Verree Teasdale, in her best role to date, gives a superb performance." (*Film Daily*, September 3, 1937)

"It's all good fun and Kay is at her best as the charming Washington hostess. Kay has a chance at comedy and she does it so well that I am hoping we will see her more often in gay adventures of this type. Moreover, she has a chance to wear the gowns for which she is justly famous, although her clothes are by no means the chief attribute of this excellently produced Warner picture." (Louella O. Parsons, *Los Angeles Examiner*, December 13, 1937)

"Miss Francis contributes an interesting portrait of the feminine meddler-in-politics, and her gowns, thanks to Orry-Kelly, are the kind that a well dressed American woman in the heroine's position might wear." (Harrison Carroll, *Los Angeles Evening Herald Express*, December 13, 1937)

"*First Lady* is carried off with an unusual vivacity by Kay Francis. Its main drawback — that, as in most Kaufman plays, its crises are epigrammatic rather than emotional — is counteracted by its novel background and its general impudence." (*Time*, December 13, 1937)

"As Lucy Chase Wayne, wife of the Secretary of State, the regal but unanimated Miss Francis was outacted by Verree Teasdale, biting and venomous as the wife of a Supreme Court Justice." (Ted Sennett, *Lunatics and Lovers*, p. 275).

Women Are Like That

(Warner Bros., 1938) 78 min.
Released on April 11, 1938.

Credits: Associate producer, Robert Lord; director, Stanley Logan; from the Saturday Evening Post story by Albert H.Z. Carr, "Return From Limbo"; screenplay, Horace Jackson; art director, Max Parker; gowns, Orry-Kelly; musical director, Leo F. Forbstein; original music, Heinz Roemheld; sound, Stanley Jones; camera, Sid Hickox; editor, Thomas Richards; unit manager, Lew Baum.

Cast: Kay Francis (Claire Landin); Pat O'Brien (Bill Landin); Ralph Forbes (Martin Brush); Melville Cooper (Leslie Mainwaring); Thurston Hall (Claudius King); Grant Mitchell (Mr. Franklin Snell); Gordon Oliver (Howard Johns); John Eldredge (Charles Braden); Herbert Rawlinson (Avery Flickner); Hugh O'Connell (George Dunlap); Georgia Caine (Mrs. Amelia Brush); Joyce Compton (Miss Hall); Sarah Edwards (Mrs. Hattie Snell); Josephine Whittell (Miss Douglas); Loia Cheaney (Miss Perkins); Edward Broadley (Holliwell, the Butler); Sam McDaniel (Porter); Symona Boniface (Lady Behind Claudius on Boat); Harry Bradley (Mr. Frazier); Allan Cavan (Jimmy, the Bartender); George Humbert (Waiter); Anderson Lawler (Freddie); Lillian Harmer (Landlady); Bernice Pilot (Maude); Renie Riano (Hotel Maid); William Worthington (Minister); Harvey Clark (Salesman); Carole Landis (Lady at Claire's Party); William Hopper.

THE FILM OPENS WITH an invitation: "Mr. Claudius King requests the honour of your presence at the marriage of his daughter Claire to Mr. Martin Brush on Friday, the first of April at twelve o'clock, King Manor, Blue Waters, Long Island."

At the wedding, however, Claire and usher Bill Landin elope. "This is an awful thing we're doing to poor Martin," Claire says. Martin, who works with Bill and Claudius at the Brush-King ad agency, predicts the marriage won't last a week.

We see another invitation: "Come to our paper wedding anniversary. The first year is the worst but nary a cloud in the Landin Sky. Tuesday at 8 they celebrate and sincerely hope that you'll drop by." Claudius, Claire's eccentric father, gives Bill a "present" at the party. "My dear Willie: Just to inform you that your darling Claudius has been a very naughty boy. You think the firm has a bank balance of $100,000, don't you? Well it did before I borrowed about $85,000 to play the stock market. It grieves me to...."

Bill burns the note and tells board members that Claudius has swindled the company. He offers to make restitution with the condition that Claire not be told. He'll stay at the agency, but work for a minimal salary until the money is repaid. The pressure gets to Bill, and he starts drinking, creating tension in his marriage.

Bill sends his secretary to beauty salons to get ideas for a new ad campaign. "Well, I certainly hope her looks are considerably approved," Claire bitchily snaps.

"Claire," Bill scolds, "don't you think that was rather unkind?"

"Yes. Yes, I guess it was. Oh, I admit that I was petty, and I bitterly resent being petty. But you're making me so!"

Claire does her own research to help Bill. There's a montage of scenes showing Claire's beauty treatments. In the last one, a salon worker slaps Claire's face repeatedly until Claire hauls off and slaps her back. (Play it back slowly, and you'll see the woman start to smile before the scene fades out.)

Claire helps Bill with the campaign, but when Bill submits it to Martin, who's now the boss, he has a fit at Martin's flippancy and throws the sketches out the window. Bill tells Claire he's quit Brush-King.

Claire suggests she present it at another agency. He laughs. "That's the dirtiest laugh I've heard since "Way Down East" played the Opry House," she says.

Claire and Martin put a presentation together for "The Spirit of Bel-Angel," and then Claire successfully pitches the campaign to Mainwairing. Once Bill learns of it, he's upset. "Why are you so sour?" she asks. He accuses her of flirting with Mainwairing. "One more dig like that and you're going to get the fight you seem to be looking for, my darling."

Bill leaves Claire. "I intend to make the break before we get to a point where we want to kill each other. This way it's sharp. Clean, quick. No regrets."

"The only thing I see clearly is that I'm almost beginning to hate you," she tells him.

Bill takes a trip around the world, while Claire becomes a success at Brush-King. Months pass. Martin wants Claire to divorce Bill and marry him. Claire reluctantly agrees.

Meanwhile, Bill gets an advertising job at Dunlap and ends up ruining Brush-King. "Since your firm has bought out this Brush-King Agency and you personally may become my boss, it gives me great pleasure to offer my resignation," Claire writes. "You may be a wonder boy to others, but to me you are a severe pain in the neck."

They meet at a divorce lawyer's office on a Saturday afternoon. Martin has a cold, and quickly falls asleep. Bill turns on music and starts reminiscing.

Artist Marland Stone created one of Kay's loveliest covers for the January 1936 *Picture Play*.

"I think of you as an experience that I had," Claire tells Bill, "one which I don't regret but I never want to have again."

Bill and Claire dance, and Martin wakes up, agitated. "If there's any explanation for this disgraceful, outrageous, idiotic behavior, I don't want to hear it," he says. "I'm sorry for you, Claire. When you're dancing with Bill, you have the same hopeless expression on your face as a drunkard has when an open bottle of whiskey is left near him. I think I'm very lucky to have found you out in time. In my opinion, marrying you would be downright dangerous." He stomps out.

When the lawyer arrives, Bill and Claire are kissing on the sofa. "Mrs. Landin, Mr. Landin, your divorce.... Wh-wh-wh-what in the world is this?" the lawyer asks.

"This is lovely," Claire dreamily says, before returning to kissing.

Though the movie is a dud, Kay has good chemistry with fast-talking Pat O'Brien. Although O'Brien (whose head appears to be abnormally large in this film) is charming at times, his character is unlikable: short-tempered, immature, and irresponsible. In addition, Martin and Claire's father are no prizes, either. A better title might have been *Men Are Like That*. Kay's Claire is actually a strong character who has integrity. This would be a great film to use in a Women and Film class.

O'Brien wrote fondly about Kay: "One of the most glamorous leading ladies I played opposite was Kay Francis. Not only was she a big dark beautiful creature, but she was endowed with a wonderful sense of humor. I saw Kay a few years ago when I was playing in Falmouth, Massachusetts. She and Eloise [Mrs. O'Brien] and I dined together and I reminded her how completely uninhibited she was." He recalled that during love scenes she removed her shoes. "I was taller than most of the men I played with,"[73] Kay replied. Kay, like Jeanette MacDonald and Greta Garbo, often wore bedroom slippers on the set.

George Brent rejected the Pat O'Brien role. Carole Landis received no on-screen credit but is in the movie and has one line. The scene occurs a little over the hour mark when Mrs. Snell arrives at Claire's with Bill. Mrs. Snell announces that the atmosphere at Claire's is "positively pagan," and Bill asks about Mr. Snell's whereabouts. Landis, wearing an attractive hat and dress, stops smoking long enough to answer: "Why, I think he's over there in the bedroom with our hostess."

Production started August 29, 1937. Working titles included *Return from Limbo* and *This Woman Is Dangerous*. The film was based on Carr's short story, published in the February 22, 1936, issue of *The Saturday Evening Post*.

Watch for the scene where Kay mispronounces fascinating. "Tell me more about Peoria. It's fastinating."

REVIEWS: "Another disappointment for Kay Francis. Her speech at a business forum is a bit touching." (*Variety*, March 30, 1938)

"Misses essential light mood of theme and settles into dull routine piece. Kay Francis wears charmingly a different costume in almost every scene, and this will be the principal attraction in the picture for the femmes. She displays no particular histrionics worth mentioning, and along with Pat O'Brien, walks through scenes rather indifferently." (*Film Daily*, April 13, 1938)

"Pat O'Brien and Kay Francis, cast as the man and wife, help along this conception very ably.

Pat is his usual admirable screen self [and] Miss Francis, who wears her usual quota of nice clothes, does another of her self-possessed, gay, not too emotional heroines." (W. E. Oliver, *Los Angeles Evening Herald Express*, June 3, 1938)

"[It] dawdles drearily with the problem of getting Actor Pat O'Brien off a Scotch-&-soda diet and back into the advertising game. Droopy Actress Kay Francis models a few notable Orry-Kelly costumes, drops innumerable r's." (*Time*, April 18, 1938)

"There is only one question I must ask the authors of 'Women Are Like That.' It is, 'Like what?'" (*New York Times*, April 11, 1938)

My Bill
(Warner Bros., 1938) 65 min.
Released on July 9, 1938.

Credits: Producer, Bryan Foy; director, John Farrow; based on the play "Courage" by Tom Barry; screenplay, Vincent Sherman, Robertson White; art director, Max Parker; gowns, Orry-Kelly; musical director, Leo F. Forbstein; original music, Howard Jackson; sound, Charles Lang; camera, Sid Hickox; editor, Frank Magee; assistant director, Russell Saunders; dialogue director, Vincent Sherman.

Cast: Kay Francis (Mary Colbrook); Dickie Moore (Bill Colbrook); Bonita Granville (Gwen Colbrook); John Litel (Mr. John C. Rudlin); Anita Louise (Muriel Colbrook); Bobby Jordan (Reginald Colbrook); Maurice Murphy (Lynn Willard); Elisabeth Risdon (Aunt Caroline Colbrook); Helena Phillips Evans (Mrs. Adelaide Crosby); John Ridgely (Mr. Martin, the Florist); Jan Holm (Miss Kelly, Rudlin's Secretary); Sidney Bracy (Jenner, Aunt Caroline's Butler); Bernice Pilot (Beulah, the Colbrook Maid); Tommy Bupp (Football Player); Glen Cavender (Mr. Perry); William Gould (Dr. Judd); William Haade (Piano Mover); John Harron (Bank Clerk); Stuart Holmes (Passerby); Henry Otho (Piano Mover); Billy Wayne (Taxi Driver); Tom Wilson (Onlooker); Jack Wise (Man Who Buys Newspaper).

THE SETTING IS COLBROOK, Massachusetts. We see a statue of William Colbrook, the city's founder, and then arrive at the home of Mrs. Reginald Colbrook and family. Mary Colbrook, Reginald's widow, has four children and serious financial troubles. Furthermore, three of the four kids are greedy brats. The fourth, Bill, is the youngest and refers to his mother as "sweetheart."

Mary gets a loan from banker John, a former boyfriend, and goes on a spending spree for the children. She also tries to teach them some values. "Anyone can be normal in normal times. That's no test. It's when everything goes against us, that we have to show our true colors."

While playing football, Bill accidentally breaks old Mrs. Crosby's window. She scolds him, but they soon become friends.

Mean Aunt Caroline Colbrook arrives. "I wanted to observe this particular branch of the Colbrook family in their natural, wild state." She badmouths Mary to the children. "Your mother has squandered every cent your father left you. You're paupers." She's unkind to Mary. "You're stupid," Aunt Caroline tells her. "A stupid, impractical woman."

The children, except Bill, turn on their mother. Aunt Caroline insinuates that Bill isn't a Colbrook, and convinces the three oldest to move in with her. Meanwhile, Mary's daughter Muriel changes her mind about marrying boyfriend Lynn because he doesn't make enough money. "I won't humiliate myself," she tells him. Muriel also finds out that Mary borrowed money from John, and suspects her mother did something immoral. She plans to marry a rich man and repay the debt. "I won't be the first daughter that's had to pay for her mother's indiscretion," she dramatically says.

The children quickly learn that living with Aunt Caroline is no Sunday school picnic. She's strict and controlling. "Freedom and laxity lead to moral disintegration," she tells them at dinner. She also announces that they'll be moving back into their old house — and Mary and Bill will be asked to leave.

Mary decides to leave Colbrook with Bill. However, that night, when Bill tries to say goodbye to Mrs. Crosby, he finds that she's become quite ill. Upon finding that Mary and Bill have been kicked out of their house, Mrs. Crosby asks them to move in with her. Mrs. Crosby soon takes a turn for the worse, and Mary has to explain death to Bill. "There comes a time when our friends have to leave us. And like those ships, even though we can't see them any more, they're still there ... in our minds, in our hearts, and we're in theirs."

When Caroline finds out about Mary's loan from John, she's quick to judge. "A woman like your mother will always be able to get along. Stripes on the zebra — you can't change 'em.'"

Muriel and Reggie meet with John, and he scolds them. "In a few years you'll realize just

Kay Francis on the cover of *Movie Mirror* in April 1936. She's wearing one of her favorite emerald rings.

how much your mother knows. Then you'll be ashamed of yourselves." He describes Mary as "one of the finest women that ever bore a thoroughbred and three ungrateful brats! I don't care what you two unnatural children think about me. I lent that money to your mother without thought or hope of repayment. I could tell you many things — fine things — about your mother, but I'd only be wasting my time."

John tells Bill that he's sole heir to Mrs. Crosby's estate. The other children write their mother: "Dearest Mother, We have been fools and no matter what happens we want to be with you. Please forgive us. Your loving children, Reginald, Muriel, and Gwen."

The family is gathered around the dinner table when Aunt Caroline arrives. "My Bill's inherited more money than the Colbrooks stole from the Indians!" Mary gleefully announces. John tells Caroline that her brother — Mary's husband — made Mary's life a living nightmare because he found out that John had once been in love with her. "But she gave up her life for him. And he never once understood nor appreciated." He adds that he's still in love with Mary.

"I met your father when I was very young," Mary tells the children. "He had money and position while my family were poor and pretty much on the rocks. When he asked me to marry him, I felt it was my duty, even though I was in love with John, although he was just a struggling bank clerk at the time. Later, your father learned that I'd been in love with him. He became jealous and cruel and bitter. He taunted me day and night for no earthly reason. When Bill was born, he didn't veil his words any longer, but threatened to turn me out." She explains that she avoided John for years. "Make no mistake. Bill is a Colbrook. I've loved John Rudlin for years, and I'm going to marry him."

Aunt Caroline leaves, and they toast Mrs. Crosby: "Who will never be forgotten in this family."

Muriel toasts her mother: "For her loyalty and devotion to all of us."

"You're okay, sweetheart," Bill says.

"My Bill!" Mary says.

Although Kay is playing the mother of four children, including one only a few years younger than herself, she looks quite beautiful in this awful film. She's also refreshingly cheerful, though she couldn't have been happy working on this stinker. The working title was *Every Woman's Life*.

It was based on Tom Barry's play "Courage," starring Janet Beecher. It opened in New York on October 8, 1928, and ran for 280 performances. In this version, there were eight children — one illegitimate. The first film adaptation was made in 1930 by Warner Brothers. Directed by Archie Mayo, it starred Belle Bennett as Mary Colbrook, and also featured Rex Bell and Marian Nixon. Robert and Gwendolyn Nowlan didn't particularly like either version: "The performances in *Courage* are nothing special, although Belle Bennett as the widow tries hard. It was the youngsters who played her children that let the production down. Leon Janney as the ever-loyal Bill was something of a pain. Worse yet was Dickie Moore in the title role in the remake. He talked to Kay Francis more as if she were his sweetheart than his mom. In *My Bill*, the number of children were reduced to four [from seven], this time all legitimate. Kay Francis dressed a bit too well for a woman of desperate straits."[74]

The film started production on March 31, 1938, and wrapped April 25. In the opinion of writer Vincent Sherman, "The performances were good, and so was Farrow's direction, but the story was old hat and the film one I would like to forget."[75]

On May 13, 1938, Kay, John Litel, and Bonita Granville appeared on the radio show *Hollywood Hotel* to re-enact scenes and promote the film. On March 3, 1941, Kay, Warren William, and Dix Davis appeared in a *Lux Radio Theatre* adaptation.

REVIEWS: "The hollow sound currently audible almost to the sidewalk in front of the Strand Theatre is the dialogue and incident in 'My Bill,' both of which hit the soggy bottoms of sentimentality and unadulterated phoniness. Theoretically such a cast ought to be able to do something with the most difficult material. But 'My Bill' is the triumph of material over human efforts. Again, they have burdened poor Kay Francis, long time a sufferer with her pronunciation of 'r's, with a line which reads, 'Stop wrinkling your pretty brows.'" (Archer Winsten)

"Kay Francis [is] less glamorously gowned than usual, ..." (*Time*, July 18, 1938)

"John Farrow has done a smart job of the direction, and under his shrewd guidance the players make parts of this reasonably diverting. In case you like to laugh a little and cry a little and don't care how brazenly it is done you'll probably have a good enough time at 'My Bill.'" (William Boehnel)

"It is all too pat, too incredible, too unimportant." (*New York Times*, July 7, 1938)

Secrets of an Actress
(Warner Bros., 1938) 70 min.
Released on October 8, 1938.

Credits: Producer, David Lewis; director, William Keighley; based on the screen story "Lovely Lady" by Milton Krims; screenplay, Milton Krims, Rowland Leigh, Julius J. Epstein; art director, Anton Grot; gowns, Orry-Kelly; musical director, Leo F. Forbstein; original music, Heinz Roemheld; sound, Charles Lang; camera, Sid Hickox; editor, Owen Marks; assistant director, Chuck Hansen.

Cast: Kay Francis (Fay Carter); George Brent (Dick Orr); Ian Hunter (Peter Snowden); Gloria Dickson (Mrs. Carla Orr); Isabel Jeans (Marian Plantagenet); Penny Singleton (Miss Reid); Dennie Moore (Miss

Blackstone); Selmer Jackson (Thompson); Herbert Rawlinson (Harrison); Emmett Vogan (Joe Spencer); James B. Carson (W.P. Carstairs), Jerry Fletcher (Theater Usher); Theresa Harris (Blanche, the Maid); John Harron (Party Guest at Bar); Grace Hayle (Fat Visitor in Dressing Room); Leyland Hodgson (Man in Theater Lobby); Arthur Housman (Drunk Who Keeps Turning Off Lamp); Olaf Hytten (Reynolds, Peter's Butler); Anderson Lawler (Thompson's Assistant); Clayton Moore (Theater Usher); Jack Mower (Purser); Wedgwood Nowell (Man in Theater Lobby); Spec O'Donnell (Call Boy); George O'Hanlon (Delivery Boy); Jack Richardson (Man in Theater Lobby); Cliff Saum (Man in Audience); Leo White (Florist); Peggy Moran (Actress Waiting to See Carstairs).

THE PICTURE OPENS WITH a clever use of credits: We see a woman unlocking and opening a diary. Fay Carter tells her agent she doesn't want to go on the road again. In particular, she doesn't want to go to Sioux City, even though she has nothing against Sioux City. "I've played it. I was carried on in my mother's arms in Sioux City. I was Little Eva in Sioux City. I've done Desdemona to my father's Othello in Sioux City." A tour holds no appeal. "There's no road any more. What used to be a road is now a double feature movie, a newsreel, a travelogue — and try to get in on bank night! No. I'm either going to see my name in lights in New York or quit the profession entirely."

A producer offers her a tour, but Fay turns it down. "Tell him the road is dead. Fay Carter helped to kill it. She has no intention of returning to the scene of the crime."

Fay shares a room with Marian, who's comically drunk in almost every scene. They're running out of money, and Fay isn't getting many offers. "They say I'm too sophisticated to play a milk maid."

Marian goes on a drinking binge and swings at a man at the bar. She hits an innocent bystander, architect Peter Snowden. He helps Fay take Marian home, and sees a photograph of Fay's father. It turns out that years before Peter had a small role on stage with Fay's legendary actor father, Henry Carter, in Rutland, Vermont.

Fay explains her dilemma to Peter and tells him she has a good play with a good part, but no one will produce it. He reads it and wants to produce it. Business partner Dick Orr attended Carnegie Tech and studied scenic de-

Romantic Movie Stories featured Kay on the cover of the December 1935 issue.

sign, so Peter asks him to help with the sets. Dick doesn't think Peter should invest in a show. There's a cute scene at the restaurant when Dick and Fay debate whether producing a play is a good business investment.

Fay Carter Productions starts rehearsing "Springboard" at the Mayflower Theatre. Dick's estranged wife, Carla, wants a part in the show. He refuses and instead asks for a divorce. "If I don't love you enough to live with you," Carla says, "I certainly don't dislike you enough to divorce you. Just being separated from you is my happy medium, thank you."

The play opens at the Hammond Theatre. Overheard conversation in the lobby at the premiere: "I believe she's the daughter of an old actor who used to trail around the country putting the ham in 'Hamlet.'"

The play is a success. Fay is thrilled. "No dark glasses for me. I want everyone to know who I am. Any actress who doesn't, never should be allowed inside a theatre."

Dick admits that he was wrong. "I wanted to show you your city," he says on the balcony, showing her the New York skyline. "You took possession of it tonight when the curtain rang down on the last act."

They kiss. "I thought I hated you," she says. They kiss again.

Peter tells Dick he's making him full partner at the architectural firm so he can direct his energies into working full-time with Fay. Marian reads a review: "It's a long time since Broadway has had the opportunity to discover an actress who actually knows how to act. Fay Carter is unique."

Meanwhile, Peter mentions to Fay that Dick is married, and tells her he wants to build her a theatre — and marry her.

"I love you, Peter, but I'm not in love with you. Besides, I wouldn't give up work for married life. The theater and my job would always have to come first." When he tells her it would be more of a business partnership, she agrees.

Dick apologizes for not telling her about Carla, and also asks for her hand in marriage. "It's over, Dick. It's too late. I promised Peter I'd marry him."

Peter hosts a reception to announce their engagement. Dick and Carla show up, and Peter finds out from Carla that Dick asked for a divorce because he's madly in love with Fay and vice versa.

On the drive back home, Peter awkwardly kisses Fay. Later, Peter arranges a dinner date for Dick and Fay. Dick tells Fay he's leaving on an ocean liner for Norway in 45 minutes. "I just stuck a pin in the map, and up came Norway."

Peter has drinks with Carla and lies to her, telling her he's firing Dick from the firm. "It's easy to forgive a woman, don't you think?" he asks, explaining why he's still going to marry Fay.

As Dick goes down one elevator, Peter comes up another. "I've just come from Carla," Peter tells Fay. "She's agreed to go to Reno."

"But I want to marry you," Fay says.

"No, you don't. You want to be decent. Now that's no good for marriage. We've got to live our lives, my dear. Not pretend them."

Peter and Fay hurry to Dick's ship. Fay calls out to Dick, "Carla is going to get a divorce!" He can't hear. She borrows a woman's lipstick and writes "Carla Divorce" on two trunks. But one trunk is taken and carried on to the ship. Dick shrugs, not understanding. The trunk is carried past Dick. He sees the word "Divorce," jumps off the boarding plank, and rushes into Fay's arms. Peter waits in the car. Fay and Dick embrace.

Production started February 17, 1938, and ended in mid–March. Working titles included *Lovely Lady* and *The Woman Habit*. Gloria Dickson, married at one time to makeup artist Perc Westmore, does a great job of playing a world-class bitch. "In the Middle Ages, they'd have burnt you at the stake as a witch," Peter tells her at one point. Margaret Lindsay was originally cast in the Gloria Dickson role.

This is the second time Kay played a woman who agreed to marry poor Ian Hunter, though she didn't love him. You'd think he'd learn.

A couple years after this film, George Brent identified the most glamorous women in Hollywood for a magazine. He named Kay, along with Dolores Del Rio, Greta Garbo, Marlene Dietrich, Joan Crawford, Loretta Young, Norma Shearer, Irene Dunne, Joan Blondell, and little-known Margaret Carthew. He did not, however, name his lover at the time, Bette Davis. Once she discovered the omission, she reportedly flew into a rage and left him.

REVIEWS: "A diverting little back-stage story, the picture casts Miss Francis in the role of an actress and consequently gives her a chance to wear an assortment of interesting costumes. The film is spun out at a lively clip and the players are satisfactory in their roles." (Rose Pelswick)

"Very swank, with good dialogue and handsome settings." (*Los Angeles Illustrated Daily News*, October 7, 1938)

"There is absolutely no excuse for releasing such a picture as this one proved to be. If Vitagraph wants to kill off Kay Francis, they are doing a swell job of it. More walkouts than we have had for some time, and I'd have walked out too if I could have left the theatre unattended. Boresome; extremely so." (*Motion Picture Herald*, March 4, 1939)

"Nothing in 'Secrets of an Actress' is surprising, except possibly the realization that its plot still is making the rounds and getting away with it." (*New York Times*, October 8, 1938)

"It has the aid of some bright writing, even performances and William Keighley's facile direction; but nothing much can be done with it. It's old hat, no matter how it's worn." (*New York Times*, October 16, 1938)

Comet Over Broadway
(Warner Bros., 1938) 65 min.
Released on December 16, 1938.

Credits: Executive producers, Jack L. Warner, Hal B. Wallis; associate producer, Bryan Foy; director, Busby Berkeley; based on a Hearst's International Cosmopolitan magazine story (March 1937) by Faith Baldwin; screenplay, Mark Hellinger, Robert Buckner; contributor to screenplay, Frank Cavett; contributors to treatment, N. Brewster Morse, Fritz Falkenstein; musical director, Leo F. Forbstein; original music, Ray Heindorf, M.K. Jerome, Heinz Roemheld; gowns, Orry-Kelly; art director, Charles Novi; sound, Charles Lang; camera, James Wong Howe; editor, James Gibbon; grip, Warren Yaple; still photographer, Madison S. Lacy; assistant director, Russell Saunders; makeup, Robert Cowan; hair stylist, Ruby Felker; props, Bud Friend.

Cast: Kay Francis (Eve Appleton); Ian Hunter (Bert Ballin); John Litel (Bill Appleton); Donald Crisp (Joe Grant); Minna Gombell (Tim Adams); Sybil Jason (Jackie Appleton); Melville Cooper (Emerson); Ian Keith (John Banks); Leona Marical (Janet Eaton); Ray Mayer (Tommy Brogan); Vera Lewis (Mrs. Appleton); Nat Carr (Haines, Burlesque Manager); Chester Clute (Willis); Edward McWade (Harvey); Clem Bevans (Benson); Dorothy Comingore [Linda Winters] (Mrs. McDermott); Jack Mower (Hotel Manager); Edgar Edwards (Walter); Alice Connors, Fern Barry, Susan Hayward (Amateur Actors); Owen King (Actor); Janet Shaw (Woman); Kay Gordon, Jessie Mae Jackson (Chorus Girls); Frank O'Connor (Officer); Henry Otho (Baggage Man); Frank Orth (Cab Driver); Sidney Bracy (English Porter); Jimmy Conlin (Comic); Charles Seel (Jury Foreman); Mitchell Ingraham (Court Clerk); Raymond Brown (Judge); Emmett Vogan (Prosecutor); Edwin Stanley (Doctor); Howard M. Mitchell (Court Officer); Dudley Dickerson (Porter); Lester Dorr (Performer); Jerry Fletcher (Bellhop); Jan Holm (Ticket Booth Girl); Victoria Elizabeth Scott (Jackie, age 18 months); Jack Wise (Stage Manager); Loia Cheaney.

PAY CLOSE ATTENTION TO the first scene because it's the only time you'll ever see Kay Francis chewing gum on film. Eve Appleton, Bill's wife and Jackie's mother, works at a Burnsdale newsstand in 1928. She's a huge show business fan and learns that notable actor John Banks is coming to town. Once he arrives, he's invited to an amateur production, "The Golden Era," which stars Eve.

A drunken Banks attends the play. (Watch for a very young Susan Hayward playing one of the actors.) "You were superb, simply superb!" he tells Eve. "I could do a great deal for you if you'd let me."

Bill is unimpressed with Banks, especially when Banks tells him, "I offered to improve your wife's technique." Later, Eve lies to Bill and meets Banks in his room. Banks passes off his valet as his manager. "My dear young lady, if you can act, New York is at your feet." He pretends to send a telegram: "Found another Katharine Cornell." Banks gives Eve some tips. "You know you have a perfect face, wide, liquid eyes, maturity, poise. You have everything but experience."

Just as he's about to kiss her, Bill arrives and orders Eve to the car. When Banks asks for an apology, Bill hits him, accidentally killing him. Bill is charged with murder. "In my opinion, John Banks died of concussion of the brain, caused by a sudden and severe blow on the left temple," the medical examiner testifies.

Bill's defense attorney places the blame on Eve: "Bill Appleton, an innocent man, is going to pay for the murder of John Banks. And do you want to know who's really guilty of the crime? You are. You lied, Eve. Calmly and deliberately you lied to Bill, and that lie killed John Banks. Bill loves you. It's the kind of love I don't think you understand. It's dumb, patient, and trusting like a dog." He blames her theatrical dream — she wanted fame more than she wanted her husband and child.

Bill is found guilty of murder in the first degree and sentenced to life. Before he's imprisoned, Eve kisses him and makes a promise. "I haven't been the best wife in the world ... I haven't been a lot of things I should have.... Today, after I leave here, Jackie and I are going away from Burnsdale ... but I might not see you again till after my job's done, and my job is to get you out of here! When the work's done and you are free, then I swear that I'll come back as your wife, and I'll try to make you as happy as I can."

Eve changes her name to Eve Wilson and joins a stage troupe, taking along Jackie. She works burlesque, carnivals, and finally vaudeville. When Brogan wants to take their act on the road, he encourages her to leave Jackie with someone else. Minna Gombell is great as Tim, a tired show biz pro who's seen it all but still has a heart of gold. Although she swears she won't do it, Tim finally consents to take care of Jackie. "I had a kid once ... years ago," Tim says. "Pretty little monkey, just like Jackie. She was fine one morning. She was dead that night."

There's a gratuitous harem scene with Kay and the girls scantily clad. "Don't they ever have any men in a real harem?" one girl asks. "Yeah," another answers. "In a way."

It's now September 1933, and Eve auditions for a role in a Bert Ballin play, "None So Blind," starring Janet Eaton. Bert hires her, and Eve and Bert become close. Too close. Janet wants her fired. "Good sport, wasn't it?" Eve angrily asks. "Swell fun. Tossing her heart into the clouds and watching it bounce back into the cellar."

"Wait a minute," Janet tells her. "I'm the star around here. If there are any scenes to be played, I'll play them."

Eve rushes out, crying. She sees a poster, advertising a trip to London for $135, and leaves America. Meanwhile, Bill's lawyer meets with Tim. He needs $10,000 to help free Bill. Tim and Jackie visit Eve in England after Eve has become a star.

Eve is devastated to learn that Jackie thinks Tim is her mother. "Six years I've been waiting to see her, and what do I get?" Eve asks. "'How do you do, Miss Wilson?'"

Tim apologizes, but says she was afraid it'd hurt Jackie too much. Meanwhile, Bert's been frantic to find Eve. "I knew that if I saw any more of him or be anywhere near him, that I'd forget the one thing I'd sworn to remember," she tells a friend. However, after four years, Bert sees her in a production of "Shadowed Love" and comes backstage to offer her a New York play. She asks for $10,000 as an advance.

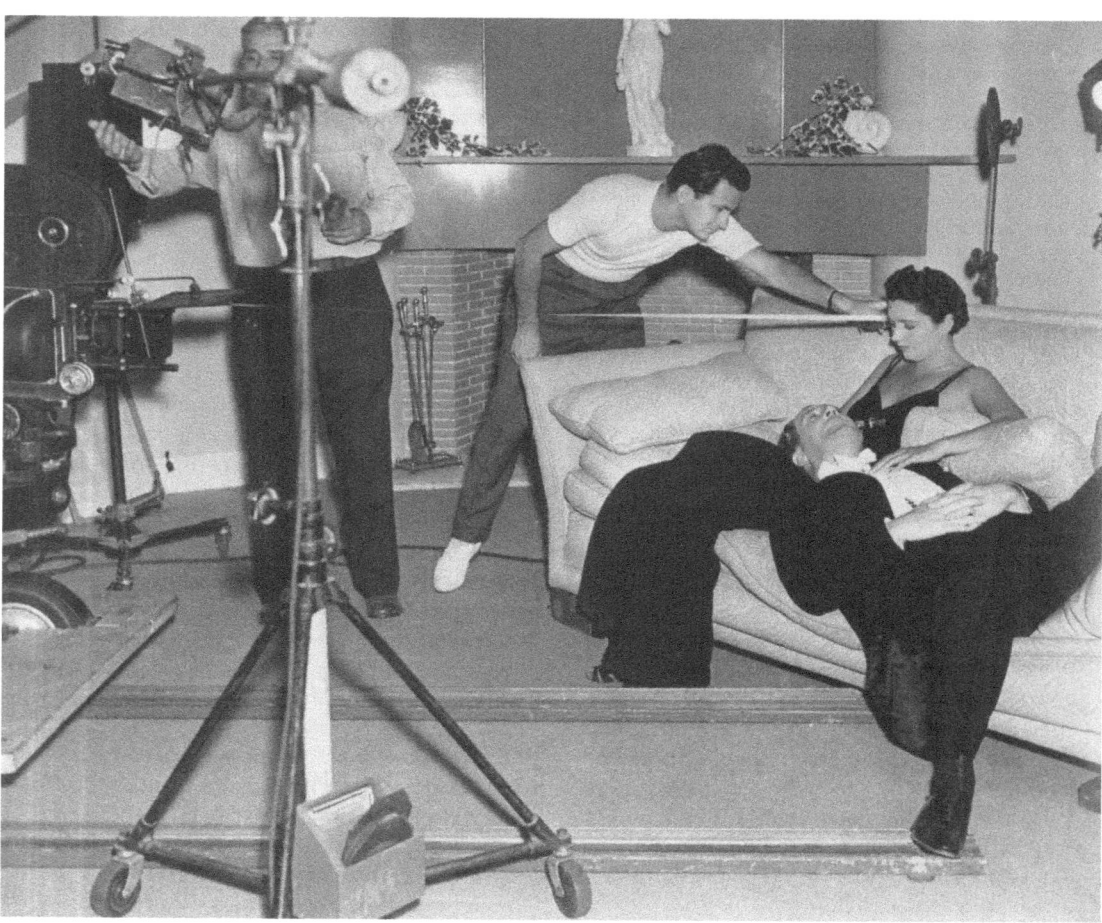

Candid shot of Kay Francis and Ian Hunter taking a break on the set.

Eve appears in "Those Who Trespass" in New York and is a big hit. "I know that life will never hold so much for me again or be so beautiful," she tells Bert that night.

He gives her the money, and she suddenly remembers her imprisoned husband. "You look as though you've seen a ghost," Bert says.

"Yes. I have." Bert wants to marry her, but Eve tells her story. She insists she must keep her promise to Bill.

Bert convinces her to talk to Bill to see if he'll let her go. Eve goes to the prison to tell him he'll be free in a few months. He professes his love for her, and thinks of nothing but her and Jackie.

Eve backs out of the play, and Jackie is finally told the truth. She sobs and doesn't want to leave Tim, the only mother she's known. Eve tells her to pretend she's playing a role. "You'll have to be a great little actress, Jackie."

Bert sees off Eve and Jackie, and tells Eve he'll never give up hope. When they walk off towards the prison, hand in hand, Jackie calls her "Mommy."

Eve stops. "What did you say?" she asks.

"I said Mommy."

"*Yes*. Yes, darling? What is it?"

"Keep your head up, Mommy," Jackie says. Eve clutches Jackie, and they continue walking.

Kay received top billing in a film that has a terrible ending. It's depressing and shows how bad judgment can ruin people's lives. The only one happy at the end is Eve's husband Bill, who *did* start off the whole tragedy by losing his temper and hitting a man. Who in the world thinks this marriage and family will be a happy one?

Bette Davis turned down the role. Offended to even be offered such a picture after winning her second Oscar, Davis called it "old-fashioned dribble" and "junk."[76] Davis' nemesis Miriam Hopkins was then offered the role, but when she became ill Kay was slated.

Still, some of Kay's fans remember this one fondly. "I would hear my father say: 'I'll go if there's a Kay Francis movie playing.' I don't believe he ever missed one of her films. I know what he was trying to say. Movies were more than movies when she was in the cast. And it wasn't too long before I, too, caught the Kay Francis fever. I particularly remember one wintry day in 1938 when I left high school at 2:30 P.M., ventured into the Garde Theatre at the top of State Street in New London, Connecticut, and stayed there until the theatre closed at 11 P.M.. The film was Warner Brothers' *Comet Over Broadway*. I thought at the time that it was one of the greatest films ever made. Time and common sense have since altered my opinion. But forty years ago Kay Francis could do no wrong — with the possible exception of failing to properly pronounce her r's. She was, in my opinion, not only the finest actress in films but also the most beautiful."[77]

Directors Edmund Goulding and William Keighley both refused to work on the picture. The working title was *Curtain Call*. Production started July 14, 1938, and ended on August 11. On the second day of filming, director Busby Berkeley was briefly hospitalized, and John Farrow substituted until July 19. Footage from *I Found Stella Parish* was supposedly used in some scenes. Watch for the scene when Sybil does a great impression of Kay Francis! Jason replaced Janet Chapman.

In her 2005 autobiography, Sybil Jason complained about George Eells' 1976 book, *Ginger, Loretta, and Irene Who?*, though she did not mention the author or title. Specifically, Jason found fault with the information about Kay. "A number of years ago, I read a book on famous leading ladies of the screen and one of the author's subjects just happened to be a star, Kay Francis, who portrayed my mother in two different movies. Coincidentally, the writer chose those very same two movies to describe the back-of-the-scenes stories and the horrendous actions and attitudes of the lady star during the making of these films. Absolutely none of it was true. She was a complete professional at all times, generous to everyone within her sphere, and certainly one of the nicest ladies I have ever had the privilege of working with and knowing on a personal basis."[78]

REVIEWS: "When a Kay Francis production reaches the Palace for its New York premiere as the lesser portion on a double bill which features 'Hard to Get,' it's a sorry state of affairs. In spite of the definite B stamp, Kay is as ever the statuesque star who wears any old clothes with distinctive style. The tale moves along well, but it isn't particularly moving, in spite of Kay's constant hardships." (Irene Thirer, *New York Post*)

"I do wish, before Kay Francis leaves the

screen for her marriage [Kay had recently announced her ill-fated engagement to Erik Barnekow], that Warner Bros. would give her a light role so we could remember her in a gay mood and smiling. But not bravely, through her tears." (Wanda Hale, *New York Daily News*)

"[T]he picture is notable for three reasons: Stately, usually fashionably gowned Kay Francis in the spangles of a burlesque queen, 12-year-old Sybil Jason's murderous impersonations of Kay Francis, and a story certain to tug at the heartstrings of every mother's heart." (*Los Angeles Examiner*, December 12, 1938)

King of the Underworld
(Warner Bros., 1939) 69 min.
Released on January 14, 1939.

Credits: Executive producer, Jack L. Warner; associate producer, Bryan Foy; director, Lewis Seiler; based on the serialized novel "Dr. Socrates" by W.R. Burnett; screenplay, George Bricker, Vincent Sherman; dialogue director, Vincent Sherman; musical director, Leo F. Forbstein; original music, Heinz Roemheld; assistant director, Frank Heath; art director, Charles Novi; gowns, Orry-Kelly; technical adviser, Dr. Leo Schulman; sound, Everett A. Brown; camera, Sidney Hickox; editor, Frank Dewar.

Cast: Humphrey Bogart (Joe Gurney); Kay Francis (Carole Nelson); James Stephenson (Bill Stevens); John Eldredge (Dr. Niles Nelson); Jessie Busley (Aunt Josephine); Arthur Aylesworth (Dr. Sanders); Raymond Brown (Sheriff); Harland Tucker (Mr. Ames, the Head G-Man); Ralph Remley (Mr. Robert, the Grocer); Murray Alper (Eddie); Charley Foy (Slick); Joe Devlin (Porky); Elliott Sullivan (Mugsy); Alan Davis (Pete); John Harmon (Slats); John Ridgely (Jerry); Richard Bond (Intern); Paul MacWilliams (Anesthetist); Richard Quine (Medical Student); Stuart Holmes (Doorman); Vera Lewis (Woman); William Gould (Chief of Police); Clem Bevans, Carl Stockdale, Nat Carr (Villagers); Jack Mower, John Harron (G-Men); Sherwood Bailey (Boy); Jimmy O'Gatty, Frank Bruno, Paul Panzer, Cliff Saum, Doc Stone (Gangsters); Sidney Bracy (Farmer); Lottie Williams (Farmer's Wife); Tom Wilson, Glen Cavender (Deputies); Davison Clark (Foreman); Pierre Watkin (District Attorney); Charles Trowbridge (Dr. Ryan); Ed Stanley (Dr. Jacobs); Ralph Dunn (First Policeman); Jerry Fletcher (Young Man); Lew Harvey (Chic, a Gangster); Herbert Heywood (Clem); Max Hoffman Jr. (Second Policeman); Al Lloyd (Drug Store Clerk); Peggy Moran (Young Man's Wife); Jack Richardson (Townsman Running); Ann Robinson (Second Nurse); Francis Sayles (Furniture Store Proprietor); Janet Shaw (Blonde Nurse); Charles Sullivan (Gangster).

PHYSICIANS CAROLE AND NILES Nelson operate on a gunshot victim. Meanwhile, Joe Gurney (the gangster who ordered the shooting) waits to hear how the operation turns out while thumbing through a book about Napoleon. When Joe gets word that the thug is going to make it, he kills the gunman. "A good general has got to know when to be just, severe, or mild," he says, quoting Napoleon.

Joe pays a visit to Niles, thanks him, and pays him $500. Carole figures Niles got the money from gambling—a habit she doesn't approve of. "A physician playing the horses—it's cheap and petty. It doesn't add up," she scolds him.

Niles wants to move uptown. She agrees as long as he stops playing the horses. She keeps her part of the bargain, but Niles doesn't. He has a nice car, beautiful office and home, but spends most of his time gambling.

Joe requests Niles' help with a wounded man. Suspicious, Carole follows him to the West Side. Niles tells Joe it's his last job. The police raid the room, and Carole is brought in for questioning. They tell her Niles has been working for Joe for some time—and they think she knows where Joe is. They finally tell her Niles is dead, killed in the raid.

Carole is tried, but there's a hung jury. She's given three months to prove she had nothing to do with Joe's gang or lose her license. Carole opens a practice in an area where Joe's gang might be hanging out. "You're putting your head right in the lion's mouth," Aunt Josephine warns her.

Joe and his gang pick up writer Bill on their way to a jailbreak. Joe's intrigued to learn Bill wrote *The Material Causes of Napoleon's Collapse*. They arrive at the sheriff's office, and there's a shootout. Bill is shot. Carole treats him in the jail cell, and tells her story. Later, Joe and his gang show up at Carole's house, wanting her to treat Joe, who was also wounded. "I got a soft spot in my heart for you since the cops knocked off your husband," Joe tells Carole.

"Some people aren't sensitive to pain, especially moronic types," she explains to him. Pleased, he gives her $100 and runs around telling everyone, "I'm a moronic type."

Carole spends the money at the grocer's. Bill

is released, and Josephine and Carole convince him to stay until he's well enough to travel. However, Joe's men kidnap Bill and take him to their hideout. Joe wants Bill to help write his autobiography. "What you want is a ghost writer."

"No," Joe corrects. "Not mystery stuff. Just plain facts."

They come up with a title—*Joe Gurney: The Napoleon of Crime*. Bill overhears Joe tell his cohorts that he'll be killed when the book is finished.

Meanwhile, Carole is taken to the hideout when Joe's wound becomes infected. Carole sees Bill, and Joe explains that Bill's working on his book. "You know," Joe tells Carole, "I don't go for dolls as a rule. I mean, they're just something nice to have around the house like cats and dogs and pets and things. You've got brains." He wants her to be his queen.

The grocer shows up at Carole's to warn her—the $100 bill she gave him was traced to a robbery, and the police are on their way to arrest her. Carole leaves instructions with Josephine on what to tell the police. She takes medicine that will temporarily blind Joe—he's complained of eye trouble—and goes back to his hideout. She tells Joe his eye is badly infected, and he'll go blind in six hours if he doesn't take the medicine. She warns the boys that they, too, might be infected.

Suspicious, Joe asks Carole to put the drops in Bill's eyes first. Carole complies, and Joe and the boys line up for their drops. Meanwhile, Josephine tells the police where to find the hideout. The boys open their eyes and panic when they realize they can't see. Carole guides Bill though the house, trying to escape Joe. The police begin shooting. The cat and mouse game continues with Carole and Joe. Finally, a policeman shoots Joe, and he falls down the stairs, clutching his chest.

"Where's my writer?" he asks.

"I'm here, Joe."

"I guess you'll have to finish my book without me."

"The finish was written long ago."

"Heh. Heh. Yeah. I get it. Hey, pal. Do me a favor, will you? Don't tell 'em that a dame tripped me up. Will you? I–" Joe collapses.

In the next scene, Bill is typing away. Carole comes home, and they kiss. They have a child who's pretending to read a medical book, but

In *King of the Underworld* (1939), one of Kay's last films at Warner Bros., she did her best in a role originally played by Paul Muni.

he's actually reading *The Napoleon of Crime*. Heh. Heh.

The working title of this remake of *Doctor Socrates* was *Unlawful*. Production started May 25, 1938. Ann Dvorak was originally slated for Kay's role. In the original film, the doctor convinced the gangsters they had a fatal illness and required injections. The "medicine" actually induced sleep, and the men were captured. According to writer Vincent Sherman, "I felt that we could not use the same device, putting them to sleep, so I had Kay give them shots [actually drops] to distort their vision. It was, I thought, more filmic and would allow for some gunplay at the finish to give us a better climax."[79]

A 1942 remake, titled *Bullet Scars*, starred Regis Toomey, Adele Longmire, and Howard Da Silva. Produced by Warner Bros., it was directed by D. Ross Lederman.

Advertisements proclaimed: "Beware of this man! At his command cities are raided and plundered.... An army of killers is turned loose.... Don't Kill This Killer! Bring Him Back Alive!... Drop That Gun, Killer!... If he lives, hundreds will die!"

REVIEWS: "Kay Francis is only featured and gives a poor performance, though her characterization, that of a medico, detracts much of the glamour with which she has been identified. And it gives her little chance to strut the latest fashions." (*Variety*, January 11, 1939)

"No matter how the credits read, Miss Francis is the protagonist of this piece. In plain words, 'King of the Underworld' is nothing to go out of your way to see." (Wanda Hale, *New York Daily News*)

"Miss Francis, although by no means a standout, handles a thankless role capably, and deserves better than the secondary billing the Warners have given her in this last of her pictures under the Warner contract." (James Francis Crow, *Hollywood Citizen News*, January 13, 1939)

"Kay Francis handles this role of the wronged woman and turns in a convincing performance, better than many of her recent efforts." (George Jackson, *Los Angeles Evening Herald Express*, January 13, 1939)

Women in the Wind
(Warner Bros., 1939) 63 min.
Released on April 13, 1939.

Credits: Producer, Mark Hellinger; associate producer, Bryan Foy; director, John Farrow; based on the novel by Francis Walton; screenplay, Lee Katz, Albert DeMond; assistant director, Marshall Hageman; art director, Carl Jules Weyl; dialogue director, Jo Graham; technical adviser, Frank Clark; musical director, Leo F. Forbstein; gowns, Orry-Kelly; camera, Sid Hickox; editor, Thomas Pratt; sound, Charles Lang.

Cast: Kay Francis (Janet Steele); William Gargan (Ace Boreman); Victor Jory (Doc); Maxie Rosenbloom (Stuffy McInnes); Sheila Bromley (Frieda Boreman); Eve Arden (Kit Campbell); Eddie Foy, Jr. (Denny Corson); Charles Anthony Hughes (Bill Steele); Frankie Burke (Johnnie); John Dilson (Sloan); Spencer Charters (Henry, the Farmer); Vera Lewis (Farmer's Wife); Sally Sage, Alice Connors, Marian Alden, Iris Gabrielle, Diana Hughes (Aviatrixes); John Harron (Process Server); John Ridgely, Jack Mower, Frank Mayo (Salesmen); Lucille De Never, Marie Astaire (Women); Steven Darrell, David Kerman (Photographers); Emmett Vogan (Radio Announcer); George O'Hanlon (Bellboy); Eddie Graham (Microphone Man); Milton Kibbee, Sidney Bracey, Wilfred Lucas (Burbank Officials); William Gould (Palmer); Gordon Hart (Drew, Air Races Official); Ila Rhodes (Joan); Rosella Towne (Phyllis); Raymond Bailey (Attendant); Richard Bond (Salesman); Nat Carr (Salesman); Allan Cavan, Lew Kelly, Al Lloyd, Lee Phelps (Wichita Officials); Joe Cunningham (Telegraph Office Attendant); Ralph Dunn (Policeman on Field); Edgar Edwards (Wichita Starter); Hudson Fausset (Attendant); Frank Faylen (Chuck, the Mechanic); Paul Panzer (Mechanic); Jack Gardner (Mechanic); George Guhl (Bartender); John Hiestand (Radio Announcer); Reid Kilpatrick (Voice of Announcer); Alexander Leftwich, Wedgwood Nowell, Pat O'Malley (Cleveland Officials); Carlyle Moore Jr. (Cleveland Radio Operator); Will Morgan (Intern); Cliff Saum (Policeman); Tom Wilson (Attendant); Jack Wise (Welcoming Official); David Newell (Man in Crowd).

PILOT ACE BOREMAN SETS the record for circling the world. Janet and invalid brother Bill listen to the radio reports, and Janet gets an idea: She wants to fly Ace's plane "Polly" in a Los Angeles women's air derby. Bill used to be a flyer ... until the accident. If she wins the derby, she'll get $15,000, which she'll use to pay for Bill's specialist.

While trying to find Ace at the airfield, Janet runs into Kit, a pilot and frequent divorcee. Ace, Kit explains, almost became one of her husbands.

"What happened?" Janet asked.

"He said no."

Janet, an experienced pilot, pretends she doesn't know anything about flying and gets into "Polly" with Ace. While he retrieves her purse, which she "accidentally" dropped out the window, she takes off in "Polly." We're not flyers, but we'd have to say she was incredibly reckless, almost crashing a few times and coming dangerously close to hurting someone.

An angry Ace reads her the riot act when she lands. Janet flirts with him, and then asks to use "Polly" for the women's air derby. Ace agrees. Later, she overhears Ace telling his buddy Stuffy he was only pretending. "Feed 'em, fly 'em, and forget 'em," he says.

Janet takes him home. "I feed 'em, fry 'em, and forget 'em," she tells Ace, referring to her chickens. Ace tries to leave, but Doc, who's in love with Janet, stops him, and tells him Janet wants to win the race for his old friend Bill.

"Your brother gave me my wings," Ace tells Janet. "He can have anything I've got."

Meanwhile, Ace gets a call from ex-wife Frieda, who tells him they're still married, and *she* wants to fly "Polly" in the derby. In addition, Ace's record is broken by Denny Corson, who beats Ace's time by 41 minutes. When Janet arrives at the airfield and finds Frieda working on "Polly," she gets some bad news. "This plane belongs to me," Frieda tells Janet. "He was in my apartment when he telephoned you last night. He realized he'd made promises he couldn't keep. See, his plan is to let you down as gently as possible. It's an old custom of his. I'm Mrs. Ace Boreman."

Ace reluctantly confirms the news, and Janet walks away without hearing his explanation. "Do you realize what you've done to that family?" Doc asks Ace. "You're pretty low."

Ace convinces Denny to let Janet fly his plane. "There's only one plane that can beat 'Polly,'" he tells Doc. Denny agrees, though Ace doesn't want Janet to know he arranged it.

Frieda finds out. "First Ace. Now Corson. What are you doing? Collecting flyers?" Frieda asks Janet.

"No. And I'm not collecting from them, either." *Meow.*

The race begins. The first stop is Wichita, and Janet is the first to reach it. Frieda is in second place. Frieda pays a mechanic $2,000 to sabotage Janet's plane. Meanwhile, Kit's plane starts smoking, and soon starts on fire. Oil pours out. The plane goes into a tailspin, and then corkscrews headfirst into the ground. There's a ball of flames, and nothing but the tail fin left. Emergency workers bring Kit out on a stretcher. She has an oil streak on her forehead and some smudges.

"Sure. I'm okay," she says. "That can't break me up. Haven't I been married four times."

Before Janet goes back in the air, Kit gives her a letter from Doc. "Dear Janet: It was Ace Boreman who got Corson to give you his plane. He was willing to sacrifice his motor — and his whole future, perhaps — because of his love for you. Go on and win for Bill. But when you get to Cleveland, hang on to Ace. All my love, too. Doc."

Janet's fuel gauge indicates she's almost out of gas — a result of the sabotage. She lands in a cornfield, buys gas from a farm couple, and is back in the air, but can't quite clear a tractor —

Candid shot of Kay at home.

she loses a wheel. It's a race to the finish line, but Janet's landing gear is wrecked. Radio control can't contact Janet to warn her.

Frieda sees the problem and warns Janet. "Ladies and gentlemen," the announcer says, "Mrs. Foreman is deliberately sacrificing her own chances for victory in an attempt to warn Miss Steele of her danger. You are seeing, ladies and gentlemen, a great exhibition of sportsmanship."

Janet lands on one wheel, winning the race. Frieda and Janet shake hands. "That was pretty swell what you did up there," Janet says.

"You don't know it, but I owed you that one." Frieda hands Ace a telegram explaining that their Mexican divorce was upheld.

Turns out Denny Corson borrowed one of Ace's motors when he built his plane. "Hope you're not mad at me," he says.

"Mad at you?" Janet says. "I could kiss you!" She starts to kiss him.

"You're going the wrong way," he says and points her toward Ace. Janet and Ace kiss. The music swells.

This loser was based on Francis Walton's 1935 novel. Production started September 2, 1938, and ended September 27. Additional filming took place in December 1938. A film crew was sent to Cleveland, Ohio, for air derby location shots. This was Kay's last film for Warner Brothers. It's pretty bad, but the flying sequences are fun. Eve Arden wrote about the film — and Kay — in her autobiography: "I made *Women in the Wind* with the lovely 'Kay Fwancis,' who couldn't pronounce her r's. Directed by John Farrow, Mia's father, it concerned the first Powder Puff Derby, and I was the girl who crashed. I had a very dramatic scene in the plane, struggling with the controls, oil spurting in my face, and then the plane crashed. Finally, I was carried on a stretcher past Kay Francis and urged her to 'go on and win for me!' It was one of the few premieres I was 'requested' to attend and, to my horror, after the oil-in-the-face scene, I saw them cut to a plane in a completely vertical dive, flames shooting from every angle, ending in a crash to forecast the atom bomb. A little fanciful work by the special-effects man who had not watched the rest of the scene! As they carried me on a litter across the screen, virtually untouched and every hair in place, the audience howled!"[80]

Notice the oil smudge on Kay's face changes every time the scene is cut. Also, there's a rather jarring jump cut in the last scene. Kay declares "I could kiss you!" to Eddie Foy, Jr., but before she does just that, there's an awkward cut, and you suddenly see Kay facing and kissing William Gargan instead. All in all, a fairly sloppy editing job on this picture.

The character of Denny Corson was perhaps based on Douglas "Wrong Way" Corrigan.

REVIEWS: "Story is rather slight, but unfolds rapidly and smoothly. Picture is last for Kay Francis after several years under contract to Warners. Gargan breezily handles the top assignment, and Miss Francis is adequate." (*Variety*, April 19, 1939)

"Underneath her groomed and stylish exterior, Kay Francis is a sky rider, a 'woman in the wind,' a racer through black storms, and everything you have in the way of gall and courage. I am sorry to have to add that she and her picture are bald-faced imitations of 'Tailspin,' the picture of lady flyers that Twentieth Century-Fox flew around the country a couple of months ago." (Archer Winsten)

"An aviation action picture that was very good. Good shots of speedy planes that the audience liked a great deal." (*Motion Picture Herald*, June 24, 1939)

"Never quite gets off the ground." (*New York Times*, April 13, 1939)

In Name Only

(RKO, 1939) 94 min. Released on August 4, 1939, Radio City Music Hall.

Credits: Executive producer, Pandro S. Berman; producer, George Haight; director, John Cromwell; based on the novel "Memory of Love" by Bessie Breuer; screenplay, Richard Sherman; original music, Roy Webb; art directors, Van Nest Polglase, Perry Ferguson; set decorator, Darrell Silvera; Miss Lombard's gowns by Irene; other gowns, Edward Stevenson; assistant director, Dewey Starkey; sound, Hugh McDowell, Jr.; special effects, Vernon L. Walker; camera, J. Roy Hunt; editor, William Hamilton.

Cast: Carole Lombard (Julie Eden); Cary Grant (Alec Walker); Kay Francis (Maida Walker); Charles Coburn (Mr. Richard Walker); Helen Vinson (Suzanne Duross); Katharine Alexander (Laura Morton); Jonathan Hale (Dr. Edward "Ned" Gateson); Maurice Moscovich (Dr. Muller); Nella Walker (Mrs. Grace Walker); Peggy Ann Garner (Ellen Eden); Spencer Charters (Fred, the Gardener); Alan Baxter (Charley, the Drunk); Harriet Mathews, Sandra Morgan (Women on Boat); Harold Miller (Man on Boat); John Dilson (Head Train Steward); Douglas Gordon (Steward); James Adamson (Black Waiter on Train); Tony Merlo (Waiter); Frank Puglia (Tony, Café Manager); Alex Pollard (Butler); Charles Coleman (Archie Duross); Florence Wix, Clive Morgan, Major Sam Harris, Kathryn Wilson (Party Guests); Grady Sutton (Paul Graham, Suzanne's Escort); Bert Moorhouse (College Man Asking About Game); Mary MacLaren (Nurse at Desk); Robert Strange (Hotel Manager); Jack Chapin (First Bellhop); Allan Wood (Joe, a Bellhop); Harold Hoff (Bellhop Bringing Bottle); John Laing (John, the Chauffeur); Frank Mills (Bartender); Byron Foulger (Owen, an Office Clerk); Arthur Aylesworth (Farmer on Truck); Fern Emmett (Hotel Chambermaid); Edward Fliegle (Night Clerk); Gus Glassmire (Yawning Hospital Attendant); Lloyd Ingraham (Hospital Elevator Operator); George Rosener (Dr. Hastings, at the Hotel).

THE FILM BEGINS IN Ridgefield, Connecticut. While fishing, commercial artist Julie Eden meets Alec Walker. Julie has a 5-year-old daughter, Ellen, and tells Alec her husband died four years ago. Her bitter sister also lives with them. "Your husband died while you still had faith in him," she says, warning Julie about Alec.

As it turns out, Alec is married to Maida. When he shows up late for a social gathering at his mansion, his parents are unhappy with him. "As for your not showing up this afternoon," Maida tells Alec, "all I want to say is that I understand perfectly."

"Even when we're alone, you can do it," he accuses.

"Do what, dear?"

"Make it look as if I'd beaten you. Make me feel I want to."

He tells her he won't join them for dinner and suggests his parents wouldn't be happy if they knew the truth about them. "You wouldn't want that to happen, would you?" he asks.

"They wouldn't believe it, dear."

"Yes. You've seen to that, haven't you?"

Alec goes alone to a restaurant and runs into Maida's friend, Suzanne. She's been after him for years. He rebuffs her, but she insists he take her home. On their way, they argue over the radio, Alec loses control, and the car crashes through a fence. Alec is unconscious, and Suzanne runs to get help — to Julie's house.

Suzanne explains the delicate situation. "Mr. Walker's wife is my best friend, and if people should discover I've been out with him, there might be talk." Suzanne leaves, and Maida shows up at the accident scene.

Alec returns home, and Maida has a talk with him. "Alec, you must admit that things have been rather difficult for me for some time. I know you feel that I failed you in certain ways. But it doesn't seem to me that you've done much to help. I don't mean to complain, but there is a limit."

"You said you loved me when you married me, didn't you?"

"Yes."

"It wasn't true, was it?"

"Of course it was."

He reminds her of David, a man who killed himself when Maida and Alec were on their honeymoon. Alec hands Maida a letter she'd written to David: "David darling, You know what money and social position means to me — I must go thru with it — but I love only you and always will." Alec received the letter from David's mother after his death.

"All right," Maida admits. "It's true. I did love him. I was mad about him. What of it?"

"How could you do it?"

"I had a choice. I could take David and love

In Name Only (1939) featured Kay as a conniving wife. Kay out-acted Cary Grant and Carole Lombard and earned her best reviews in years.

and nothing else or I could take you and what went with you. I took you."

Julie doesn't want to see Alec any more now that she knows he's married. "I don't think there should be any more picnics," she tells him.

Maida visits Julie with flowers, welcomes her to the neighborhood, and invites her to a garden party. Meanwhile, Maida lets family and friends know that Alec is carrying on with Julie. When Julie arrives, she's treated to icy glares and snubs.

Alec takes Julie home, and explains about Maida. "I didn't know there were women like that," Julie says. Alec tells Julie he loves her. Julie, however, doesn't want to break up his marriage.

Alec asks Maida for a divorce. "I thought I could keep you somehow. Didn't care how I did it," she sadly says. "And now I've lost. Now that it is over, I suppose I ought to wish you happiness. But I don't. I hope you'll be miserable. I hope you'll both be miserable."

She plans to go to Paris with Alec's parents on Labor Day. "Oddly enough, they consider me rather a satisfactory daughter-in-law. I'd like to be the one to tell them that I haven't been." Alec is suspicious. "I'm selfish in a lot of ways, Alec. But even my worst enemy couldn't say that I'm stupid. I know when I'm beaten."

"You know, Maida, in certain respects I admire you a great deal."

"You needn't bother. I'd do the same thing again if I thought I could win."

"That's what I mean."

Meanwhile, Julie has left for New York. Alec arrives to tell her of the divorce. Julie is offered a job in Paris, but turns it down to marry Alec. Suzanne sees Maida before she departs for Europe. "Now, honestly, Maida, you're not going to let that girl take Alec away from you, are you?"

"What do you think?"

"Really, Maida, you're marvelous!"

Maida keeps delaying the divorce. Julie becomes impatient. It's almost Christmas, and still no divorce. Alec is surprised when Maida and his parents return to celebrate the holiday with him. Alec says he has other plans. Before he leaves, Julie calls, and Maida explains to her that Alec is with his family.

Julie goes to Alec's. "This is Christmas Eve," Maida tells her. "Alec understands he should spend it with his wife. Why can't you?" Julie asks if she's going to give Alec a divorce. "I should think by this time it should be quite obvious what my intentions are."

Maida threatens to turn the divorce into a scandal. She also threatens to call Ellen to testify. Julie gives up. "You know there's nothing too cruel, too vicious.... We never had a chance, Alec. From the very beginning. Go now while we still love each other. At least let's not give Maida that satisfaction."

Alec leaves. It's a cold, snowy night. He goes off on a drinking binge and ends up at the Hotel Pierce. He complains it's too hot, opens some windows, keeps drinking, and finally passes out. A doctor is called. Julie is also contacted.

Alec's condition worsens, and Julie calls his family doctor, Gateson. Alec is hospitalized with pneumonia. The specialist tells Alec's father that the patient "shows no desire to get better," and mentions that he keeps calling for Julie. They allow Julie to see him. "Tell him whatever you think he wants to hear," she's told.

Maida arrives, but Julie won't let her in. "You'd rather see him dead than with me, wouldn't you?" Julie asks. "You don't love him. You don't love anybody except yourself."

"I gave up love for what I've got," Maida says. "Do you think I'm going to let you or anyone else get it away from me? If Alec gave me every cent he has, it still wouldn't be enough. Some day his father is going to die–"

Alec's mother gasps. She's at the door with Alec's father, watching the scene. "Maida," Alec's father says, "you might as well take what you can get from Alec because you won't get anything from me."

Alec asks for Julie. The door slowly closes until we can't see Maida any more.

"Oh, Alec, darling, everything is going to be all right," Julie tells him.

"I thought you told me that before. I must have been dreaming."

"We were both dreaming, darling, but now it's true." She rests her head on his chest.

Kay was hired in February 1939, and started working on April 17. John Cromwell directs her very sympathetically — not sure if it was intentional — but the result is one of Kay's best performances. Her character is much more interesting than Alec's or Julie's. An intriguing movie, in fact, could be made, based on Maida Walker. Kay explained the film's plot in this way: "Cary Grant and I are married but we do not love each other and I have married him for position. I am an ambitious woman, and when he falls in love with Carole Lombard I refuse to let him go. You see, it is a natural situation, such as springs up in a thousand homes in the land. For people are only human, after all, filled with foibles and frailties. And it is mighty hard for a woman who has worked hard to get a man to give him up. Nobility comes hard."[81]

Kay also rightly pointed out that her role was not the type the studio would have assigned her: "Every tendency would be to prettify the character until the writer's original conception would finally be altogether lost. I want to be an actress, capable of portraying many differently pitched roles, not just a woman who dresses up and speaks noble lines."[82]

The production was filmed in San Marino, California. The first title was *Memory of Love*, which was changed to *The Kind Men Marry*, before they finally settled on *In Name Only*. Douglas Fairbanks, Jr., was originally cast to play Alec. On December 11, 1939, Francis, Lombard, Garner, and Grant recreated their roles for the *Lux Radio Theatre* adaptation.

Fourth-billed actor Charles Coburn organized the summer Mohawk Drama Festival through Union College in Schenectady, New York. In this program, drama students worked side by side with professional actors, presenting new plays weekly. Dennis Allen, Kay's last boyfriend, apprenticed at one of the summer sessions.

The Hays Office turned down the first script because Julie became pregnant. Finding out he has only six months to live, Alec accuses her of blackmail and makes her leave in a weird attempt to protect her. Joseph Breen and Co., and the final script made no mention of a pregnancy and offered a happy ending of sorts.

Watch for the scene when Alec shows up at the hotel. He clearly opens room 1522. However, the manager breaks down the door to Room 1524.

Advertising copy proclaimed: "Whose arms should be denied? His wife's or the woman's he loves!"

REVIEWS: "Miss Francis does well, shading her role well. She does not photograph as well here, however; makeup, mayhaps, somewhat a fault, unless the idea was to make her less glamorous than she has been in the past." (*Variety*, August 9, 1939)

"Of the three principal performances, that of Miss Francis is to this department the most noteworthy, for she has been sadly mishandled in recent films, and it is gratifying to report the compelling nature of her work. The Kay Francis role is really the key role in the film, although this is no disparagement to the excellent performances of Grant and Miss Lombard." (*Hollywood Citizen News*, August 2, 1939)

"What impressed preview critics most forcibly about *In Name Only* was the performance of Kay Francis, who has been delivering good performances for years, but hardly anyone was aware of it because her abilities were stifled in inferior picture products and her frantic efforts to assert herself were without avail. In this case, she is the root of much evil, and by this role wherein she inflicts the position of a hateful woman on her luckless victims, she will call attention to herself again as an actress of first rank." (Carl Combs, *Hollywood Citizen News*, August 26, 1939)

"Kay Francis, as the wife, has her most hateful screen assignment to date, with which she does her best to aid the plot. It's a diverting picture, in spite of some near to yawny moments." (W.E. Oliver, *Los Angeles Evening Herald Express*, August 26, 1939)

"K. Francis takes role of gold seeker to perfection. Splendid performances by Carole and Cary." (*Motion Picture Herald*, November 4, 1939)

"Kay Francis, on the other side of the fence this time, is a model cat, suave, superior and relentless. And a generally excellent cast contribute in making this one of the most adult and enjoyable pictures of the season." (*New York Times*, August 4, 1939)

"Surprising to many cinemaddicts ... will be the effectively venomous performance, as Alec's mercenary wife, of Cinemactress Kay Francis.... [S]leek Cinemactress Francis in her first freelance job shows that she still belongs to the A's, that, properly encouraged, she can pronounce the letter r without wobbling." (August 14, 1939, *Time*)

"The picture is made quite creditably, by three people — Miss Carole Lombard, Mr. Cary Grant and Miss Kay Francis. Both actresses break new ground.... Miss Francis, 'the best-dressed woman in Hollywood,' who used to step unresilently, with a lisp, through glamorous parts, for the first time grips our attention as the hard unscrupulous wife, who is after something more valuable than alimony, her father-in-law's money. I liked this wholeheartedly unpleasant character...." (Graham Greene, *The Spectator*)

It's a Date
(Universal, 1940) 103 min.
Released on March 22, 1940.

Credits: Producer, Joseph Pasternak; director, William A. Seiter; story, Jane Hall, Frederick Kohner, Ralph Block; screenplay, Norman Krasna; orchestrator, Frank Skinner; musical director, Charles Previn; music, Lucien Denni ("Oceana Roll"), Prince Leleiohaku ("Hawaiian War Chant"), Queen Liliuokalani ("Aloha Oe"), Felix Mendelssohn-Bartholdy ("The Wedding March"), Pinky Tomlin and Harry Tobias ("Love Is All"), Ralph Freed and Frank Skinner ("It Happened in Kaloha"), Hans J. Salter (incidental music); Eddie Cherkose, Jacques Press, Leon Belasco ("Rhythm of the Islands"), Giacomo Puccini

("Musetta's Waltz Song"), Franz Schubert ("Ave Maria"); Lyrics, Ralph Freed; camera, Joseph Valentine; editor, Bernard W. Burton; sound supervisor, Bernard B. Brown; sound technician, Joseph Lapis; art director, Jack Otterson; associate art director, Martin Obzina; assistant director, Frank Shaw; gowns, Vera West; set decorator, R.A. Gausman.

Cast: Deanna Durbin (*Pamela Drake*); Kay Francis (*Georgia Drake*); Walter Pidgeon (*John Arlen*); Samuel S. Hinds (*Sidney Simpson*); S. Z. Sakall (*Carl Ober*); Lewis Howard (*Freddie Miller*); Cecilia Loftus (*Sara Frankenstein*); Henry Stephenson (*Captain Andrew*); Eugene Pallette (*Governor Allen*); Joe King (*First Mate Kelly*); Fritz Feld (*Headwaiter*); Charles Lane (*Mr. Horner*); John Arledge (*Newcomer*); Romaine Callender (*Evans*); Virginia Brissac (*Miss Holden*); Leon Belasco (*Captain*); Anna Demetrio (*Cook*); Mary Kelley (*Governor's Wife*); Eddie Acuff (*Ship's Steward*); Fay McKenzie, Linda Deane, Phyllis Ruth, Virginia Engels (*Young Girls*); Eddie Polo (*Quartermaster*); Mary Shannon (*Wardrobe Mistress*); Mark Anthony (*Officer*); Harry Owens and His Royal Hawaiians (*Themselves*); Randy Oness (*Singer*); John Daheim (*Sleepy-Eyed Man*); Landers Stephens (*Business Executive*); William Ruhl (*Ship's Officer*); David Oliver (*Officer*); Louis Natheaux (*Party Guest*); Eddie Lee (*Captain Andrews' Servant*); Jennifer Gray (*Cable Office Girl*).

THE FILM OPENS IN New York City with Georgia Drake on stage, appearing in "Gypsy Lullaby." As Georgia sings, daughter Pamela, an appreciative audience member, mouths the words. Pamela wants to be a big star like her mother.

Georgia plans to travel to Honolulu for six weeks, and then return and do a play. After producer Ober meets her, however, he explains to Sidney that the part is for a 20-year-old. Sidney reminds him that Georgia played 15-year-old Juliet the year before.

Pamela convinces Sidney and Ober to visit an amateur stage camp. Once there, Ober gets the idea of having the young actors rehearse the second act of his new play about Saint Anne. Pamela wows them. She thinks she's up for a maid role, but Ober and Sidney tell her they have a different role in mind. "We want you to play Saint Anne."

Pamela doesn't think she's ready. "I know I'm forward and fresh sometimes, but that's just to get attention." To get Georgia's advice, she travels to Hawaii on the same ship as wealthy businessman John. He sees Pamela rehearsing, and mistakenly thinks she's broken-hearted. In an effort to cheer her up, he hides in a lifeboat and pretends to be a stowaway. She brings him food and plots to get him off the boat. John fixes it so he's "found out," but she jumps in the ocean in order to provide a distraction for John to get away. John rescues her. "I think what you did," she gushes, "exposing yourself because you thought I was in danger, is the smartest, most unselfish thing I've ever heard of."

The captain lets it slip that it was all a game. Pamela pushes John back into the ocean. They finally make up, and Pamela mistakenly thinks he's developed a crush on her. "You've been very sweet, but it's impossible," she tells him. "I want to remember you just like this," she tells him, giving him a little peck on the cheek.

"She not only imagined a proposal out of me, but she turned me down!" a bemused John tells the captain.

"I need you so much," Pamela tells Georgia when she meets the ship, explaining she not only got a big role but also had a shipboard romance. Pamela describes the part to Sara: "Well, I play everything. I'm happy, and I'm sad. My heart's broken. I want to kill myself. I go crazy. I recover. I go crazy again. Oh, Sara, it's the real me."

Georgia starts reciting lines from the play — it's the same role Pamela has won. "I've been waiting all my life for a part like this," Georgia says. Pamela, sickened by the discovery that she's taken her mother's part, gives the plot synopsis to Georgia and Sara, but changes details so they don't realize. The result is a strange-sounding part.

"There's no disgrace in having a failure, but you mustn't have a part that makes you look bad," Georgia warns.

Meanwhile, Sidney sends a message to Georgia that Pamela intercepts. "Just found out Pam on her way to you. Am calling you 8 o'clock tonight, your time, to explain everything."

Pamela doesn't want Georgia home when Sidney calls so she tells Georgia they're having dinner with the man she met on the boat. "I can't possibly get out of it now. It's a date," Pamela explains.

Pamela then goes to John and *makes* the date. At dinner, Pamela excuses herself so she can go home and take the phone call. This gives Georgia an opportunity to talk to John. "She isn't as old as she looks," she tells him, concerned about the possible romance between the two.

Kay Francis and Walter Pidgeon in *It's a Date* (1940).

"Why didn't you tell me it was Mother's play?" Pamela asks Sidney. Pamela refuses the role so it won't be taken away from Georgia.

"I feel I'm at the crossroads, frankly, of life's highways," Pamela explains, telling Georgia and Sara that she's thinking of marrying John.

For some time, there's confusion about which Miss Drake John is interested in. John invites Georgia to the ball. Pamela thinks she's invited, too, and plans to propose to John. John whisks Georgia outside while Pamela sings. "I'm so in love I can't even see straight," he says. Georgia misunderstands, thinking he wants to marry Pam. "Georgia, won't you marry me?" he finally asks.

Meanwhile, Sidney and Ober show up at the ball. "I'm not going to play St. Anne," Georgia announces. "I'd like a few years of just being married."

Sidney and Ober are relieved, especially when Georgia suggests Pamela play St. Anne. "I've been rehearsing her. She's almost as good as I am."

John tries to tell Pamela, but she thinks he's proposed. "I'm going to try and make you awfully happy and be a good wife to you."

The governor announces that John and Georgia are to be married. Pamela blinks, looks at John, glares, and then makes a long, impassioned speech. "I'm through with men," she concludes.

"She can play that part," Ober says as Pamela stalks off.

In the final scene, Georgia and John are in the audience as Pamela sings "Ave Maria" at the conclusion of "St. Anne." There's a final close-up on Pamela's face as it blends into a shot of the chorus and set.

Kay received second billing in what is really a Deanna Durbin picture. Durbin is annoying as Pamela, a spoiled brat if there ever was one. She does, however, sing beautifully, and this is a real showcase for her. There are also some charming scenes between Kay and Walter, two experienced actors who play knowing adults.

Production began in late December 1939,

and was completed in a speedy fifty-four days. Locations included Honolulu and Sherwood Lake, California. The original title was *It Happened in Kaloha.*

Deanna Durbin sang "Love Is All" (one of the most beautiful songs ever written), "Ave Maria," "Musetta's Waltz Song," and "Loch Lomond." Kay "sang" "Gypsy Lullaby" (obviously dubbed). Harry Owens and His Royal Hawaiians performed "It Happened in Kaloha" and "Rhythm of the Islands." Background music included "The Oceana Roll," "Aloha Oe," "Hawaiian War Chant," and "The Wedding March."

A 1950 MGM remake, titled *Nancy Goes to Rio,* starred Jane Powell and Ann Sothern, and featured Carmen Miranda.

REVIEWS: "The cast is uniformly excellent. Walter Pidgeon does his usual suave, unhurried dream prince job, and Kay Francis, who still avoids an 'r' as if it were a social error, never looked better — or younger — in her entire career. Cecelia Loftus is fine as the companion, Sara, or, as Miss Francis calls her throughout the picture, 'Thawah.'" (Dorothy Kilgallen)

"Kay Francis is capital as the mother whose career prevented time for romance." (*Variety,* March 27, 1940)

"He [Pasternak] has also taken soulful-eyed, sirenic Kay Francis, given her her best part for many a long picture.... There are a lot of bright dialogue [sic], a lot of amusing situations, a lot of amiable people who have such a good time together that everybody else does too." (*Time,* April 8, 1940)

"It is, in the main, a charming, if highly improbable entertainment..." (*New York Times,* March 23, 1940)

When the Daltons Rode
(Universal, 1940) 81 min.
Released on August 23, 1940.

Credits: Director, George Marshall; based on the book by Emmett Dalton, Jack Jungmeyer; screenplay, Harold Shumate; musical director, Charles Previn; original music, Frank Skinner; art director, Jack Otterson; associate art director, Martin Obzina; assistant director, Vernon Keays; camera, Hal Mohr; editor, Ed Curtiss; sound supervisor, Bernard B. Brown; sound technician, Robert Pritchard; gowns, Vera West; set decorator, R.A. Gausman.

Cast: Randolph Scott (Tod Jackson); Kay Francis (Julie King); Brian Donlevy (Grat Dalton); George Bancroft (Caleb Winters); Broderick Crawford (Bob Dalton); Stuart Erwin (Ben Dalton); Andy Devine (Ozark Jones); Frank Albertson (Emmett Dalton); Mary Gordon (Ma Dalton); Harvey Stephens (Rigby); Edgar Dearing (Sheriff); Quen Ramsey (Clem Wilson); Dorothy Granger (Nancy); Bob McKenzie (Photographer); Fay McKenzie (Hannah); Walter Soderling (Judge Swain); Mary Ainslee (Minnie); Erville Alderson (District Attorney Wade); Sally Payne (Annabella); June Wilkins (Suzy); William Gould (Deputy on Train); Jack Clifford (Deputy); Pat West (Pete, the Restaurant Owner); Dorothy Moore (Girl); George Guhl (Deputy in Baggage Car); Robert Dudley (Juror Pete Norris); Edward Brady (Deputy); Walter Long (Deputy on Train); Bob Reeves (Henchman); Kernan Cripps (Freight Agent); Tom London (Lyncher); Mary Cassidy (Girl); Lafe McKee (Doctor); Russ Powell (Engineer); John Beck (Native); James C. Morton (Juror Ed Pickett); Edgar Buchanan (Narrator/Old-timer); Harry Cording (Jim Osburn); James Flavin (Annabella's Brother).

Kay Francis in a Vera West costume from *It's a Date* (1940).

"TOWARDS THE END OF the 19th century in America, civilization surged ever west and, in its wake, came that inseparable pair, Injustice and Crime. In the history of reckless violence that seized Kansas and Oklahoma, no name carried more terror than Dalton. There were more famous outlaws, but none more daring, none more desperate. This, then, is the story of the Dalton brothers, based, to a large extent, on the tales that the old settlers still tell of them — woven together with strands of fiction. But, so incredible were the Daltons, that no man can say where fact ends and fancy begins."

Attorney Tod Jackson arrives in town looking for his old friends, the Daltons. He finds the ruffians while they're having a family photograph taken with their mother. Tod also meets telegraph operator Julie, who turns out to be Bob Dalton's girlfriend.

Tod decides to stay and help the Daltons with troubles they're having with a land development company. While Bob's out of town, Julie and Tod become close, and Tod tells her he can't stay. "If you think I'm going to stick around and watch you and Bob Dalton raise a family, you're crazy. I can't help it if I'm in love with you."

Julie wants Tod to tell Bob the truth about them. "If you loved this girl, you'd do something about it," she says.

After an altercation with land surveyors, Ben Dalton is charged with murder. Tod defends him. Bob shows up for the trial and gives Julie a sapphire ring, but when he realizes Ben can't get a fair trial, the Daltons take Ben and escape after a gun battle.

There's a montage of headlines indicating they've gone on a crime spree. The Daltons hide out in a barn. When they learn their house has been burned, Emmett Dalton goes to town. Julie harbors him, but men overpower her and try to lynch him. Tod intervenes and takes Emmett to jail for safety. They're met by Bob and the other Daltons. A mob tries to break into the jail, but the Daltons escape. Another crime spree results. The reward for their capture rises from $1,000 to $20,000.

"No matter what happens to Bob, we have our own lives to live," Tod says, but Julie insists they tell Bob before they marry. Meanwhile, Bob sends a message: "Tell Julie I haven't forgotten." He finally returns and tells Julie he's taking her to South America.

"I'm not going with you! Has it ever occurred to you that I might have changed? I don't love you, Bob."

Bob goes off to find Tod. Meanwhile, Tod has discovered that local banker Caleb is behind the land developers. Bob tries to kill Tod, but Julie stops him. "You beast! Have you no decency left in the world. You can't control our lives!"

Ma, too, scolds Bob, though he raises his hand to her before finally settling down. "Funny how things get twisted, ain't it?" Bob asks, kind of apologizing.

There's shooting outside — the other brothers have tried to rob the local bank. The Daltons are shot one by one. Caleb, pointing a rifle from an upstairs window, draws a bead on Tod. Right before dying, Bob kills Caleb.

The family portrait in the beginning of the movie is now in a photographer's store window; authentic Dalton raid photos and Death Alley photos are $1.00 each; family group photos, $2.00; and postcards, fifty cents.

Julie and Tod plan to go to Guthrie. "That reminds me of a couple that hung around here for a week once waiting for the Guthrie stage," the old-timer narrator says. "Do you know what they finally did?"

"Uh," Julie says, "they took the train."

Tod and Julie walk off arm in arm, chuckling. "Now, who do you suppose told them?" the old-timer asks. *Who cares?*

This tedious film started production May 27, 1940, and wrapped July 3. It's strictly formula, using many — if not all — western cliches. There's actually a scene when Tod, on the verge of being ambushed by the villain, is saved by a former friend, still loyal, who manages to squeeze off a bullet, killing the villain before succumbing to his injuries. There's also a running gag about the Andy Devine character being a ladies' man — a little bit goes a long way. Still, Bill Collins thought it was a minor masterpiece and named it as one of his favorite westerns. "You rarely see stagecoach chases, lynchings, courtroom scenes and gunfights presented with such 'punch.'"[83] Stuart Anthony and Lester Cole also may have worked on the script. Mrs. Emmett Dalton was hired as a consultant.

Odd that no one thought of putting Kay Francis in a western before, huh? *Joking*! Kay, however, was disappointed that the first script didn't allow her to ride or shoot. Director Marshall rewrote the scene where Bob finds out about Julie and Tod so she at least got roughed up a bit. Walter Pidgeon was originally cast in the Scott role, but was replaced when he became ill.

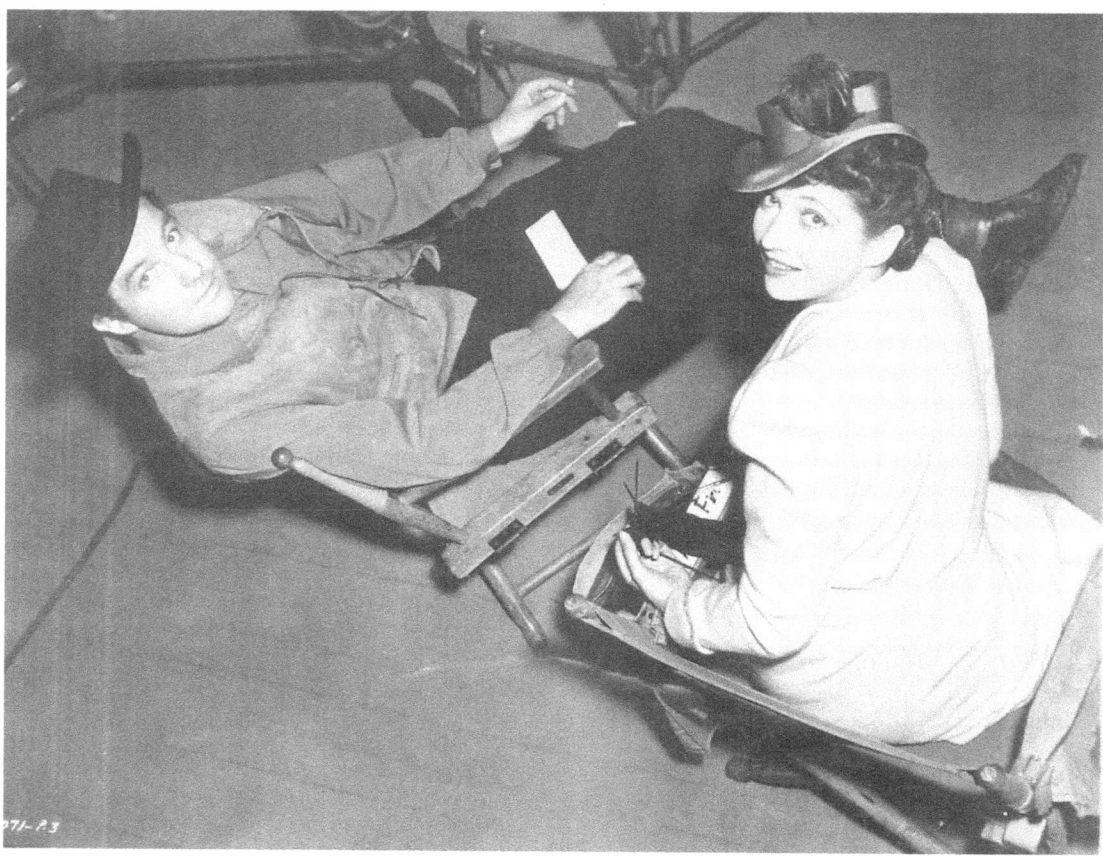

In this candid shot from *When the Daltons Rode* (1940), Kay relaxes on the set with Broderick Crawford.

The Dalton brothers' demise came on October 5, 1892, when they attempted to rob two banks in Coffeyville, Kansas. All the brothers were killed, except Emmett, the youngest, who was wounded. Imprisoned for fifteen years, he became a writer and movie consultant upon his release from prison. The story of the Dalton brothers was first filmed in 1918. *Beyond the Law*, directed by Theodore Marston, was based on Emmett Dalton's book of the same name. It starred Emmett, Harris Gordon, and Ida Pardee.

Another version filmed in 1945, *The Daltons Ride Again*, featured Kent Taylor, Lon Chaney Jr., Noah Beery Jr., and Martha O'Driscoll. In 1957, Reginald LeBorg directed Merry Anders and Penny Edwards in United Artists' *The Dalton Girls*.

REVIEWS: "Randolph Scott and Kay Francis ... are of secondary importance to the adventures of the Dalton outlaws." (*Variety*, July 31, 1940)

"The action is fairly convincing, although the ability of the Daltons to pass unwounded through hails of bullets becomes increasingly difficult to accept. The best points of the picture are its fast pace and good casting." (Archer Winsten)

"*When the Daltons Rode* is no sly *Destry* but a fairly conventional Western whose big-city actors often are merely incongruous.... [I]it is good in precisely the ways hundreds of Westerns have been good before: the train robbery, the chase through the sagebrush, the last great scene where false men and true shoot it out until the gun finally drops from the villain's luckless hand." (*Time*, August 9, 1940)

"The picture is straight, fast Western fare, and for folks who like plenty of shootin', here is your gunpowder." (*New York Times*, August 23, 1940)

Little Men

(RKO, 1940) 84 min. Released on December 7, 1940.

Credits: Producers, Gene Towne, Graham Baker; associate producer, Donald J. Ehlers; director, Norman Z. McLeod; based on the novel by Louisa May Alcott; screenplay, Mark Kelly, Arthur Caesar; art directors, Van Nest Polglase, Al Herman; musical director, Roy Webb; original music, Roy Webb; camera, Nicholas Musuraca; editor, George Hively; special effects, Vernon L. Walker; sound recordist, John E. Tribby; assistant director, Sam Ruman; costumes, Edward Stevenson; set decorator, Darrell Silvera.

Cast: Kay Francis (Jo); Jack Oakie (Willie, the Fox); George Bancroft (Major Burdle); Jimmy Lydon (Dan); Ann Gillis (Nan); Carl Esmond (Professor); Richard Nichols (Teddy); Elsie, the Moo Girl of the New York World's Fair (Buttercup); Casey Johnson (Robby); Francesca Santoro (Bess); Johnny Burke (Silas); Lillian Randolph (Asia); Sammy McKim (Tommy); Edward Rice (Demi); Anne Howard (Daisy); Jimmy Zaner (Jack); Bobbie Cooper (Adolphus); Schuyler Standish (Nat); Paul Matthews (Stuffy); Tony Neil (Ned); Fred Estes (Emmett); Douglas Rucker (Billy); Donald Rackerby (Frank); William Demarest (Constable); Sterling Holloway (Reporter); Isabel Jewell (Stella); Bud Jamison (Cop); Sarah Edwards (Landlady); Duke York (Poker Player); Howard Hickman (Doctor); Stanley Blystone (Bartender); Charles Arnt (Drunk); Nora Cecil (Matron); Hal K. Dawson (Telegraph Operator); George D. Green (Poker Player); Jack Henderson (Drunk); Bill Irving (Bartender); George Irving (Truant Officer); Lew Kelly (Postman); Russ Powell (Railroad Conductor); Clarence Wilson (Reynolds); Nella Walker.

THE CREDITS BEGIN WITH someone looking through a stereoscope—that's the most creative thing in this movie. The actual film starts with scam artist Major Burdle being presented with a baby. Old pal Willie explains that the baby is Lefty's; his final wish was for the Major to raise it.

The Major grows to love the boy he calls Dan. Together, they travel and work cons. Years pass, and the major is now selling a booze cure tonic for a dollar, with Dan as his assistant. Authorities insist Dan be put into school, and suggest Plumfield, a boarding school. Meanwhile, Willie shows up again (years ago, he'd escaped from prison and made people think he'd drowned). Together, they take Dan to Plumfield.

Before they arrive, Jo tells her husband they're having financial problems and will probably lose the farm. The Major pretends to be a rich man, and the professor pulls him aside, asking him to invest their remaining $2,500 so they can keep the school.

Meanwhile, Dan has trouble fitting in with the other children. "Dan doesn't know our ways yet," Jo explains. "He's come to learn." Dan wants to smoke, play cards, shoot pool, and sing naughty shanties, but the family's activities run more toward checkers, storytelling, dominoes, and Old Maid.

Jo tries to teach Dan to milk the beloved cow, Buttercup. "You're the only one in school who's been shirking their farm duties," she tells him. Danny is obstinate. "You have no respect for anyone," she concludes, deciding he must be punished. "We don't punish people here," she explains. "We let them punish themselves."

"You want me to spank myself?" he asks.

"No. In Plumfield, we do it this way. We never hurt the other fellow." She holds out her hand.

"You mean you want me to hit you?"

"Yes." He throws down the stick. "Pick it up," she orders. "Now do what you're told. Give me six good strokes."

"I can't."

"Daniel Burdle, do as you're told!" He hits her once. "Harder!"

"I'll hurt you!"

"I want you to hurt me! Go ahead!" He hits her a couple times. "Again!"

He throws down the stick, crying. "I can't hurt you!" Not sure what lesson was imparted there, but it seemed to work, even though the movie threatened to turn into a different kind of film entirely!

Anyway, Jo asks the professor about the money. He proudly tells her he gave the money to Major Burdle to invest. "You've been swindled," she laments, noting they haven't heard from the Major since he left. Meanwhile, the Major and Willie have traveled all over America, trying to make a living. The Major finds out that the bank where he deposited the money has failed, and the professor's money is gone.

Jo and the professor get a letter from the bank, dated September 2, 1880, telling them they will need to leave Plumfield at the end of the month—and the banker wants to buy their beloved Buttercup, too. Another boy at Plumfield tells the other children that they're being forced to leave and sell Buttercup and her new calf because Danny's father stole their money. Danny hits him. A newspaper reporter writes a story: "Father Called Thief; Student Attacks Chum."

Desperate to help, Willie and the Major scam $2,500 from a bank and return to Plumfield. However, the constable arrives and arrests the Major for forgery. Jo tells them they need $5,000 to keep Plumfield open. Willie, who's a wanted man, turns himself in so Jo can collect the $5,000 reward and save the school. Willie and the Major go to jail, though Danny is told they're hitting the road again. They ride off with the constable, and when he tells them they're going to the state penitentiary, Willie is thrilled. "That's me alma mater. The warden will be so happy to get his ticker back [Willie had stolen the warden's watch when he escaped] he'll probably give us the bridal suite!"

Production started July 29, 1940. Producers Towne and Baker wanted Edward G. Robinson for Bancroft's role and Jean Hersholt for Oakie's. Towne and Baker were probably uncredited screenwriters. Kay received top billing, but is not photographed well and has an unflattering hairstyle, complete with unfortunate bangs. There are entirely too many cow reaction shots.

This was a remake of a 1935 RKO film, starring Ralph Morgan, Dickie Moore, and Erin O'Brien-Moore — the same actress who replaced Kay in "State of the Union" in 1948. According to *Cinema Sequels and Remakes*, "The two film versions were teary, insignificant stories with nothing memorable about them."[84] There's also a 1997 version with Mariel Hemingway as Jo.

Kay was given the opportunity to work with old pal Jack Oakie on this one, which had to make the weak script more palatable. Oakie, an old vaudevillian, kept the crew amused with clowning and practical jokes. He also makes the film watchable.

Director Norman Z. McLeod used an abundance of stick figure drawings for storyboards

George Bancroft, Kay, and Carl Esmond in *Little Men* (1940) (courtesy James King).

Lobby card for *Little Men* (1940) (courtesy James King).

until the cast and crew took to calling him The Stick Man. McLeod also had to sit in a medical doughnut during much of the production because of a painful cyst on his bottom.

Jimmy Lydon, then an experienced 16-year-old stage actor, liked and respected Kay. "Kay was a wonderful gal. We worked together as two professionals. She did a lot of heavies before *Little Men*. This was a tender part, which she liked."[85]

According to RKO promotional materials, the film was marketed to adults and children. "Made primarily as adult entertainment, full of drama, romance and comedy, it still retains for children the great appeal of the original novel, and should be especially seen by them." An instructor's guide was published by Educational and Recreational Guides to assist teachers in using the film in classrooms.

Elsie was loaned to the producers in the summer of 1940 — the film was produced in July and August—and Kay helped lead a Los Angeles parade when the cow arrived on the Super Chief. Publicity also required Elsie attend a garden party at the Ambassador Hotel with cocktails at Ciro's. Still, conflict resulted. Producer Gene Towne was disappointed in Borden's promotional campaign. Meanwhile, Borden's felt the producers didn't give Elsie enough publicity. Kay never worked with Elsie again.

REVIEWS: "I rather doubt whether the author herself would have recognized her work in the form it now takes. 'Little Men' is a pedestrian, heavy handed sort of picture. Everybody works very hard in it, including Miss Francis and Master Oakie, its two nominal stars, but I'm afraid the whole thing just doesn't quite come off. Museum pieces should be shown in museums—not movie theaters." (Leo Mishkin)

"There's not much point in criticizing the performances. The performers must have done what they were told to do. However, Carl Esmond as the Professor is decidedly youngish, and Kay Francis as Jo leaves something to be desired. Her favorite expression, 'Christopher Columbus!' is cannily chosen to bring out her weakest consonant. She doesn't quite say 'Chwistopher,' but it's close enough to make you keep wondering for a long time." (Archer Winsten)

"Instead of the sentimental and simply story which Miss Alcott's original was, this one is maudlin and smarty-smart, too obviously rigged for tears and laughs. Kay Francis is just too sweet and good as Mrs. Jo." (*New York Times*, December 9, 1940)

Play Girl
(RKO, 1941) 76 min. Released on January 29, 1941.

Credits: Executive producer, Lee Marcus; producer, Cliff Reid; director, Frank Woodruff; story-screenplay, Jerry Cady; camera, Nicholas Musuraca; editor, Harry Marker; art director, Van Nest Polglase; set decorator, Darrell Silvera; assistant director, Sam Ruman; associate art director, Albert D'Agostino; sound recordist, Theron O. Kellum; special effects, Vernon L. Walker; musical director, Paul Sawtell; Miss Francis' gowns, I. Magnin & Co.; wardrobe, Edward Stevenson.

Cast: Kay Francis (Grace Herbert); James Ellison (Thomas Elwood Dice); Mildred Coles (Ellen Daley); Nigel Bruce (William McDonald Vincent); Margaret Hamilton (Josie); Katharine Alexander (Mrs. Dice); George P. Huntley (Van Payson); Charles Quigley (Lock, the Polo Player in Montage); Georgia Carroll (Alice Sawyer, Girl with Tom at Concert); Kane Richmond (Don Shawhan); Stanley Andrews (Joseph Shawhan); Selmer Jackson (Uncle Fred Dice); Dick Hogan (Bellhop); Ralph Byrd (Miami Doctor); Cecil Cunningham (Dowager, Next to Payson at Concert); Charles Arnt (Grady, the Private Detective); Marek Windheim (Dr. Alonso Corvini, the Orchestra Conductor); Oliver Cross (Cashier); Eddie Dew (Bartender); Douglas Evans (Concert Radio Announcer); Charles Flynn (Football Player); Boyd Irwin (Mike Kilroy, Man in Steam Bath); Frank Meredith (Brakeman); Joey Ray (Usher); Gwen Seager (Miss Seager, Vincent's Secretary); Larry Steers (Dance Extra); Gayne Whitman (Jeweller); Theodore von Eltz (Mr. Hunter, the Hotel Manager).

GRACE HERBERT IS AT Lake Placid—check out Kay's ski togs, a rare example of her wearing slacks—romancing handsome, young Don. Don's father, however, arrives to tell Grace he's researched her list of broken engagements, cash settlements, and scandals. Don, he says, has no money.

"I'm a very sensible woman, Mr. Shawhan. Will you have a cocktail?" the aging golddigger asks.

He escapes before she can get her hooks into him. Grace and maid Josie have been together for 17 years. Josie informs her they're almost broke, and they travel to Miami so Grace can go to "work." A newspaper item describes Grace's plight: "Grace Herbert has found the fishing verra, verra poor in Florida this season. Grace has not caught one sucker yet. Maybe she has lost her bait."

A reflective Grace explains what she's learned about men: "At 16, they're crazy about girls of 19. At 25 they want girls their own age. At 30, they'll settle for a girl of 25. And at 40, they're right straight back where they started—chasing the 19-year-olds. What's a gal to do when she's past 30?"

Meanwhile, Grace meets 19-year-old Ellen and decides to train her. "I wish I were 19 again, knowing what I do now. I could be rich inside of a year." Ellen isn't sure, but Grace takes her to Chicago. Along the way, they meet Texan cowboy Tom Dice, who helps them change a tire. Ellen is smitten.

Grace, however, suggests she meet Bill Vincent in Chicago. Grace gives her a kind of script—and does a great impression of Vincent. When Vincent shows up, he indeed repeats Kay's lines just as she'd said them. Her plan works, and Bill starts giving Ellen furs, cars, jewelry, and more.

Grace suggests it's time to move on to New York, and Ellen finally lets Bill kiss her. "I'll be such a good wife to you," she says.

"See here," he stammers, "I'm not the marrying kind."

Ellen storms out, and Grace negotiates a $50,000 settlement. "And all you did was kiss him good night," Grace reminds Ellen.

In New York, Ellen begins dating auto manufacturer Van Pasen but drops him when she finds Tom again. Grace isn't happy—until she finds out Tom's worth $11 million.

Ellen, however, is disappointed. "This spoils everything."

When Grace suggests she marry Tom, Ellen turns on her. "Nothing would give you greater pleasure than to get your hands on $11 million!" Ellen leaves town, telling Grace she can't marry Tom for his money.

Grace decides to go after Tom herself. "There's

A lobby card from *Play Girl* (1941) featuring yet another stunning hat. Nigel Bruce looks stunned.

nothing easier to catch than a man on the rebound," she tells Josie.

Meanwhile, Bill, in town from Chicago, tells his story in a steambath. Van overhears the conversation. They end up comparing notes and realize they have Grace and Ellen in common. Notice in this scene how Bill impersonates Grace/Kay: "If you *weally, weally* want to do something nice for her, I've seen the most gorgeous mink coat. I'm sure Ellen will be wild about it."

Van and Bill confront Grace. She plays them for fools — Van ends up giving her a check for $3,200, and Bill pays her $3,019.50.

Meanwhile, Grace is very close to hooking Tom when his mother comes to visit. "I hate to spoil your breakfast, but it's your future mother-in-law," Josie announces.

Mrs. Dice, a warm and gracious woman, wants to make sure Grace loves Tom. She nicely tells Grace that she's investigated her.

"Then you know all about me?" Grace asks.

Mrs. Dice nods, but explains that as long as Tom's happy, she's okay with the marriage. When Tom arrives, Grace tells him he's still in love with Ellen. "She ran away not because she didn't love you, but because she did love you," she says, giving him Ellen's Miami address.

"If you approve of her, I'm sure I will," Mrs. Dice says. Tom hurries off to Miami. "I've just seen the most magnificent thing a woman could do," Mrs. Dice says. She has a favor to ask. Tom's unmarried Uncle Fred is downstairs, and she wants Grace to show him around New York. "He's never met a woman that interested him. I know he'll think just what I do. That you're the finest woman we've ever met."

Grace hurries off to dress while Mrs. Dice phones for Fred to come up.

"Here we go again!" Josie says, spraying perfume on Grace.

"For the last time, Josie. *The last time.*"

Production started September 23, 1940, and

ended in late October. Though not consistently funny, the film does give Kay a chance to do what she does best — light comedy. Margaret Hamilton, always a joy, has some great lines, including this one about her boss: "Why, she's said goodbye to more men than most women have said hello to."

The working title was *Debutantes, Inc.* Sheila Ryan and Elyse Knox were both up for the role of Ellen, but Mildred Coles was eventually borrowed from Warner Bros.

REVIEWS: "Miss Francis is still the glamour girl who displays an eye-arresting figure in either negligee or smart fashions. She's still plenty poised and attractive regardless of story requirements. Miss Francis capably handles the role of the fading glamour girl." (*Variety*, December 18, 1940)

"The cast is efficient, and Frank Woodruff's direction is peppy — his script (by Jerry Cady) accentuated by occasional bright pieces of dialogue." (Irene Thirer, *New York Post*)

The Man Who Lost Himself

(Universal, 1941) 72 min. Released on March 21, 1941.

Credits: Producer, Lawrence W. Fox, Jr.; associate producer, Ben Hersch; director, Edward Ludwig; based on the novel by H. De Vere Stacpoole; screenplay, Eddie Moran; camera, Victor Milner; special photographic effects, John P. Fulton; musical director, Hans J. Salter; original music, Charles Previn, Hans J. Salter, Frank Skinner; editor, Milton Carruth; art director, Jack Otterson; associate art director, Richard H. Riedel; set decorator, R. A. Gausman; gowns, Vera West; sound supervisor, Bernard B. Brown; assistant director, Seward Webb; technician, Hal Bumbaugh.

Cast: Brian Aherne (*John Evans/Malcolm Scott*); Kay Francis (*Adrienne Scott*); S. Z. Sakall (*Paul*); Henry Stephenson (*Frederick Collins*); Eden Gray (*Venetia Scott*); Wilson Benge (*Butler*); Nils Asther (*Peter Ransome*); Sig Ruman (*Dr. Simms*); Marc Lawrence (*Frank De Soto*); Henry Kolker (*T.J. Mulhausen*); Janet Beecher (*Mrs. Milford*); Dorothy Tree (*Mrs. Van Avery*); Russell Hicks (*Mr. Van der Girt*); Frederick Burton (*Mr. Milford*); Selmer Jackson (*Mr. Green*); Henry Roquemore (*Bartender*); Sarah Padden (*Mrs. Cummings, the Maid*); Ethel Clifton (*Maid*); Paul Bryar (*Bar Waiter*); Irene Coleman (*Office Girl*); Cyril Ring (*Relative*); Frank O'Connor (*Cab Driver*); Lloyd Whitlock (*Attendant*); William "Billy" Benedict (*Messenger Boy*); Billy Engle (*Newsboy*); William Gould (*Mr. Ryan*); Margaret Armstrong (*Mrs. Van der Girt*).

THE FILM'S PREMISE IS that Malcolm Scott and John Evans are doppelgangers. Scott, a wealthy man married to Adrienne, is generally thought of by all as a bad egg. He escapes from a mental hospital and manages to run into Evans at a hotel bar. Meanwhile, Evans gets some bad news from partner Philips in Porto Rico (that's how it was spelled in those days) and goes on a bender. Scott gets Evans even drunker, puts him in a cab, and orders him taken to the Scott home.

Upon awakening the next morning, Evans realizes everyone thinks he's Scott — and quickly understands that Scott is not liked. "I'm ashamed to be known as your sister!" Venetia says, storming out of the house, accusing him of terrible things.

Evans sees a newspaper headline: "A man identified as John Evans from Porto Rico, was instantly killed early this morning when he either fell or was pushed in front of an on-rushing subway train. The body is being held for coroner's investigation."

Evans announces that Malcolm Scott is dead,

On the set of *The Man Who Lost Himself* (1940), Kay socializes with co-star Brian Aherne.

Stylish lobby card from *The Man Who Lost Himself* (1941). If only the movie were as good as the set.

but everyone assumes he's trying to tell them that he's changed. "I know you too well," Adrienne tiredly says. "How often have I heard that? 'I'm not Malcolm Scott. He's dead. I'm a new man!'" She asks him if he has anything else to say.

"I think you're wonderful," he says, dreamily. Evans learns that Scott is being blackmailed because of a woman's letters. Meanwhile, insurance investigators pay a visit, asking about Evans. While Evans deals with other messy details of Scott's life, he finds he's falling in love with Adrienne.

She feels something, too, but wants to fight it. "You haven't given me a minute's peace or happiness in the past five years," she tells him. Evans takes her in his arms and kisses her. Her mouth remains open in surprise for several moments. She returns to the house later that night, much warmer, even flirtatious, lighting his cigarette, pinning a flower on his coat. She reminds him the flower is their signal for when they're through fighting. "The real reason I came back," she admits, "was because I've been so lonely for you. The new you." She passionately kisses him. "I don't know where you got your new technique," she tells him, dazed, "but rather than be jealous, I'm grateful!" Adrienne leads him upstairs. "From now on, you and I are together," she says. "Till death do us part."

Evans, panicked when she wants him to unzip her, escapes with loyal servant Paul. "I'm doing the wrong thing, but I feel right doing it," he says. In the morning, he finds that Adrienne has left with her bags.

Scott's family and psychiatrist arrive. Evans plans to finally announce the truth. However, Paul has given Scott sleeping pills (don't ask). The family and doctor conclude that Malcolm needs to be hospitalized again, and he's put in a straitjacket.

Adrienne receives news that it was indeed her husband who died; it's not clear if he committed suicide or was murdered, but at this point we don't care, and neither will you. "That makes me a widow," Adrienne says, not unhappily. She hurries home to find that Evans has been taken to a mental hospital. Adrienne laughs. "The man that you sent away is a perfect stranger. His name is John Evans."

Adrienne and Paul retrieve Evans from the hospital. Paul drives recklessly because he, too, has taken sleeping pills (don't ask). This offers a rare example of Kay Francis doing physical comedy when she's forced to drive from the back seat. She hadn't been asked to do this since *The Cocoanuts*.

Evans wakes up and insists he be called John Evans from now on — no more Mr. Scott. "Soon I hope you'll be able to call me Mrs. John Evans," Adrienne says, putting herself in the straightjacket with John. "You're stuck for the rest of your life," she says, kissing Evans.

The final shot is a reaction shot of Paul, smiling, and then falling asleep.

Kay started work on the picture on January 6, 1941, and the production wrapped on February 15. The movie is not clever, and Brian Aherne is an unsubtle comedy actor. Some might even call him a bad, hammy actor.

The film was a remake of a 1920 silent film, starring William Faversham and Hedda Hopper. It was based on H. De Vere Stacpoole's 1918 novel. Stacpoole also wrote *The Blue Lagoon*. In the late 1930s, Leslie Howard acquired the rights and planned to produce and star with Wendy Hiller. However, the production was cancelled when the war began.

Lawrence Fox originally wanted Cary Grant or Melvyn Douglas, but settled for Aherne when the project ended up at Universal. Silent stars Gertrude Astor and Charles Ray are supposed to be in the film, but this remains unverified. Nils Asther had not been in an American film since 1934.

Ads proclaimed: "They Looked Alike ... But Didn't Make Love Alike!"

REVIEWS: "A somewhat preposterous comedy.... Besides the engaging efforts of Aherne and the pleasant Miss Francis, S.Z. Sakall lends comedy aid as the perplexed butler of the household." (Gerard Gaghan)

"Aherne competently handles the farcical assignment, with Miss Francis also neatly fitting into her role as the wife." (*Variety*, March 26, 1941)

Charley's Aunt
(Twentieth Century–Fox, 1941) 81 min.
Released on August 1, 1941.

Credits: Producer, William Perlberg; executive producer, Darryl F. Zanuck; director, Archie Mayo; based on the play by Brandon Thomas; screenplay, George Seaton; additional dialogue, Morrie Ryskind; original music, Alfred Newman; art directors, Richard Day, Nathan Juran; set decorator, Thomas Little; costumes, Travis Banton; camera, J. Peverell Marley; editor, Robert Bischoff; matte artist, Chesley Bonestell; sound, Joseph E. Aiken, Roger Heman.

Cast: Jack Benny (Babbs Babberly/Lord Fancourt); Kay Francis (Donna Lucia); James Ellison (Jack Chesney); Anne Baxter (Amy Spettigue); Edmund Gwenn (Stephen Spettigue); Reginald Owen (Mr. Redcliff); Laird Cregar (Sir Francis Chesney); Arleen Whelan (Kitty Verdun); Richard Haydn (Charley Wyckham); Ernest Cossart (Brassett); Morton Lowry (Harley Stafford); Lionel Pape (Babberly); Claud Allister, William Austin (Spectators); Russell Burroughs, Gilchrist Stuart, John Meredith (Teammates); Bob Conway, Bob Cornell, Basil Walker, Herbert Gunn (Students); Will Stanton (Messenger); C. Montague Shaw (Elderly Man); Maurice Cass (Octogenarian); Brandon Hurst (Coach); Stanley Mann (Umpire).

THE FILM IS SET at Oxford University in 1890. Charley is expecting his aunt, Donna Lucia, a woman who married a Brazilian and inherited millions. He's never met her, and he and his chums assume she's old and hideous-looking.

Meanwhile, Donna Lucia meets with the law firm of Hogarth, Hawks & Babberly Solicitors. She's curious about the young lady her nephew Charlie plans to marry. In order to avoid suspicion, it's agreed she'll use the alias of Mrs. Beverly Smythe.

Oxford student Babbs Babberly — nephew of one of the law partners — is enlisted to escort her. Charley receives a note informing him that Donna Lucia has been delayed. Meanwhile, Babbs tries on a woman's costume for a play, and ends up being talked into serving as chaperone for Amy and Kitty, whose evil guardian Spettigue is trying to prevent marriages to Jack and Charley.

That's how Babbs becomes Donna Lucia, and this sets the stage for Babbs becoming the object of affection of Jack's father and Spettigue. Meanwhile, the real Donna Lucia arrives, pretending to be Mrs. Smythe.

Babbs has to make a quick change to entertain her. However, there's a new complication. Charley and Jack have had their marriage proposals accepted by the girls, but they need to get the guardian's permission in writing. They figure Babbs/Donna Lucia can get the letter. Babbs changes back to Donna Lucia.

The real complication arises when Mrs. Smythe goes to a garden party, and is quite surprised to learn that Donna Lucia will be there. "What sort of lady is she?" she asks.

"Oh, a horrible old thing."

Mrs. Smythe toys with Babbs/Donna Lucia, but finally admits the ruse when she catches Babbs/Donna Lucia smoking a cigar. "Lord Babberly, I've known who you were for hours."

Babbs tells her the whole story. For some reason, Donna Lucia has fallen for Babbs, and insists he handle her affairs when he joins his uncle's firm.

"Do you solemnly promise to be my first client?"

"I do."

Meanwhile, Jack's father sees Babbs/Donna Lucia and Mrs. Smythe smooching on the park bench, and notices Babbs/Donna Lucia's pant leg. He heartily congratulates Spettigue, and has a good belly laugh.

Spettigue agrees to sign the letter but insists that Babbs/Donna Lucia seal the deal with a kiss. Babbs makes Spettigue close his eyes, dips his hand into the goldfish bowl, touches his fingers to Spettigue's lips, and then makes a smacking sound. He gets the letter, but his wig falls off.

Spettigue claims the letter isn't valid because it's addressed to Donna Lucia. The real Donna Lucia snatches it and announces who she is. Spettigue fumes.

"Say, I wonder if he can sue me for breach of promise?" Babbs asks.

Donna Lucia laughs and kisses him.

Kay's Donna Lucia is an older, beautiful woman, knowing, wise, and sophisticated — the kind of role Kay could easily pull off. The film includes some funny gags, but it is more than a bit hoary. It was, after all, based on an 1892 play. Fox paid $125,000 for the film rights. Part of the five-year lease included the stipulation that no changes be made. Still, the company made two significant changes — the romance between Babbs and Donna Lucia and how Babbs is talked into impersonating Donna

Kay Francis in a rare publication titled "Pictures of Movie Stars" (1938).

Lucia. Broadway producers Carly Wharton and Martin Gabel sued Fox claiming ideas were stolen from their 1940 adaptation. Nothing further is found about this case so it likely was settled out of court. Jose Ferrer played the role in the successful Broadway production. Benny and director Mayo reportedly attended at least one performance before working on the film.

Believe it or not, Tyrone Power was originally considered for the Babbs role. In a more believable casting decision, Bob Hope was also up for it.

Production began May 12, 1941, and ended June 24. Kay reported to the set May 24. Kay appeared as Donna Lucia on Jack Benny's radio show on May 18, 1941.

An earlier silent film version (1925) starred Sidney Chaplin as the crossdresser (director Archie Mayo is reported to have been a gag man on this production), with Eulalie Jensen playing Donna Lucia. A 1926 Swedish film was also produced, along with a 1930 version starring Charles Ruggles and Doris Lloyd. A British version, *Charley's (Big Hearted) Aunt* was released in 1940 and starred Arthur Askey and Jeanne de Casalis. Warner Brothers remade the film *again* in 1952, with Ray Bolger and

Margaretta Scott playing Donna Lucia. This one, titled *Where's Charley?*, was based on a 1948 stage adaptation starring Bolger with music by Frank Loesser and a book by George Abbott. A German film, *Charley's Tante*, was produced in 1956, and starred Walter Giller. A March 28, 1957 television adaptation starred Art Carney, Jeanette MacDonald, and Richard Haydn (as Spettigue). *La Marraine de Charley*, a 1959 French film, starred Fernand Reynaud. In 1963 *Charley's Tante* was released in Austria. A 1967 Spanish version was titled *Charley's Aunt in a Mini-Skirt*. In 1970 the BBC presented female impersonator Danny La Rue in a play adaptation.

An unusual trailer was produced for the film in which Benny talked about the movie with Tyrone Power and Randolph Scott while sitting in the studio café. Written by George Seaton, the trailer did not use any film footage and, of course, did not reveal any surprises. Power discussed *A Yank in the R.A.F.* and Scott *Belle Starr*.

At the 1942 Academy Awards show, Benny was presented with a mock Oscar by Bob Hope. The statuette was dressed in a skirt and smoking a cigar. Benny accepted, saying: "I've been waiting around for so long for an Oscar that I'm ready to accept anything from anybody."

UCLA cricket players participated as extras. Richard Haydn and James Ellison were borrowed from RKO, and Reginald Owen was borrowed from MGM. Although character actor Laird Cregar was six years younger than Ellison, he played his father in the movie. Cregar died of a heart attack a few years after the film, caused by an overzealous attempt to lose weight.

Benny's dress was a replica of the one worn by Etienne Girardot in his 1893 stage production. Girardot's was a copy of the dress worn in 1892 by W.S. Penley in the London production. Benny's dress was eventually auctioned by a British charity.

REVIEWS: "Kay Francis, the real aunt, is much more pleasant than she has been in longer roles of recent years." (Archer Winsten)

"The audience at yesterday morning's first screening was all but rolling in the aisles in expressive appreciation of Benny and the old [Brandon] Thomas gags that have withstood with remarkable sturdiness a half century of constant use. Assisting Benny in the cast are Kay Francis in a slim but effective role." (Kate Cameron)

"There seemed to be little doubt yesterday but that this new screen version of the age-old comedy will stand out as one of the biggest smashes of the season. In addition to Mr. Benny, of course, the film also features a number of other players, despite the fact that they have very little to do. There is Kay Francis in a minor role as the veritable aunt, but Benny's the boy who puts it over." (Leo Mishkin)

"The wealthy Donna Lucia is portrayed by Miss Kay Francis, upon whom the years seem to be sitting lightly. This is a first-rate cast, and, as shrewdly directed by Archie Mayo, they don't let the spectators down." (Gilbert Kanour)

"Only Kay Francis, as the lady from Brazil, seems oddly colorless. Although it is breezily played, it has the dubious gayety of an old gentleman cutting a caper. We could almost hear the joints creak." (*New York Times*, August 2, 1941)

The Feminine Touch
(Metro-Goldwyn-Mayer, 1941) 97 min.
Released on December 12, 1941.

Credits: Producer, Joseph L. Mankiewicz; director, Major W.S. Van Dyke II; screenplay, George Oppenheimer, Edmund L. Hartmann, Ogden Nash; original music, Franz Waxman; song "Jealous" composed by Jack Little; lyrics, Dick Finch, Tommie Malie; art director, Cedric Gibbons; special effects, Warren Newcombe; camera, Ray June; editor, Albert Akst; set decorator, Edwin B. Willis; gowns, Adrian; hair stylist, Sydney Guilaroff; assistant director, Tom Andre; associate art director, Paul Groesse; recording director, Douglas Shearer.

Cast: Rosalind Russell (Julie Hathaway); Don Ameche (John Hathaway); Kay Francis (Nellie Woods); Van Heflin (Elliott Morgan); Donald Meek (Captain Makepeace Liveright); Gordon Jones (Rubber-Legs Ryan); Henry Daniell (Shelley Mason); Sidney Blackmer (Freddie Bond); Grant Mitchell (Dean Hutchinson); David Clyde (Brighton); Gino Corrado (Party Waiter); Robert Homans (Subway Cop); Harold Minjir (College Official); Bernard Nedell (Subway Snake); Jack Norton (Drunk at Party); Anne O'Neal (Lady on Subway); Dennie Travis (Piano Player), Robert Ryan.

JOHN HATHAWAY IS A psychology professor at Digby College, where he's writing a manuscript, *Jealousy and All Its Aspects and Universal*

Applications. When he's asked to give a meaningless test to a cretin athlete, John quits and leaves with wife Julie for New York, where they visit the publishing house of Elliott Morgan, Inc., and meet Morgan's able assistant, Nellie.

She likes the book but wants it to be about marital jealousy. Meanwhile, Elliott Morgan becomes infatuated with Julie. For her part, Julie is desperate for John to became jealous, but he believes it a stupid emotion. In fact, he insists Elliott and Julie spend even more time together.

Meanwhile, Nellie and John collaborate on the book. She wants to change the title to *The Female of the Species*. Julie is worried about Nellie and John because they seem to have a lot in common. "You're more like I am," she tells Elliott. "Not very clever and sort of unmental."

For her part, Nellie is in love with Elliott, but he's a womanizer who won't settle down. Still, Nellie longs for domesticity. "Show me a woman that's free, and I'll show you a woman that sits home at night ... alone," she says.

John is arrested on the subway after a prank goes awry (John pretended to be a masher, and Julie pretended to be offended). Julie goes to Elliott for help, but Elliott only pretends to call his attorney. He actually plans to seduce Julie.

Meanwhile, Nellie, who's discovered Julie at Elliott's apartment — check out his cool bachelor pad! — calls his friends and tells them that Elliott's having a come-as-you-are party. The guests arrive, including the attorney. Julie asks about John, and discovers Elliott never made the call. "It was just a cheap trick," Julie accuses.

Nellie arrives, fully dressed. "I thought this was a come-as-you-party," Elliott says to Nellie. "Why haven't you a telephone in each hand and a knife in your teeth?"

"My knife is busy elsewhere. It's in your back." Nellie tells him she's leaving the publishing house — and him. "I've been riding on that merry-go-round long enough, and I'm dizzy. Little Nellie wants to get off."

Elliott tells her he feels foolish, embarrassed. "I'm terribly ashamed of myself," he admits.

"If you're lying, I'll kill you and go to the chair with a song on my lips," she warns.

Nellie returns to work with John, and comes in humming "Happy Days are Here Again." She tells John that she and Elliott plan to marry. John receives a telegram from Julie — she's gone

The 1924 hit song "Jealous" was sung in a nightclub sequence in *The Feminine Touch* (1941).

to Elliott's cottage. Nellie suggests they follow her.

"How can you marry a man you don't trust?" John asks.

"I'd only marry a man I couldn't trust. How could I know that I wanted a man if I didn't hate everybody else who wanted him? How could I be jealous if I couldn't be jealous?"

John decides to go to the island so he can cancel the book contract. Meanwhile, when Elliott finds Julie there, he asks her to leave, telling her he plans to marry Nellie. John and Nellie arrive, and John tells Elliott he won't allow him to publish his book because "you just see it as a chance to make a lot of money. Quick."

"What? Is that bad?" Nellie asks.

Julie refuses to leave, but John drags her out of the house. He accidentally walks into the water, and when the boat floats away, he swims after it, inadvertently starting the motor. He gets his tie caught and is rapidly dragged through the water.

In the next scene, John is in bed, sneezing — one of those Hollywood colds that actors get when they fall in water.

"I'm leaving you," Julie tells John. "I'm not as smart as you are, and I've made up my mind not to let you change it."

John pleads with her to stay. Nellie announces that she and Elliott have reconciled, and they'll publish John's book just as he wrote it.

Elliott's beard is shaved. This is trouble because John was convinced Julie had no interest in Elliott because he had a beard (don't ask). Suddenly jealous with rage, John chases Elliott around a tree. There's an awkward fistfight, and both men fall to the ground.

The women start to argue. The argument escalates to shoving, and then slapping. Quickly, it turns into a catfight.

In the final scene, all four come out of City Hall. Wedding music plays. The men have black eyes. A man calls out "Hello, Sugar," and John chases after him and hits him. He happily returns to the others.

Kay sports one of her worst hairstyles and also wears one of the most ridiculous hats you'll ever see. It looks like she's wearing Mouseketeer ears—but worse. Beware of movies that have dream sequences—Julie dreams John beats up several guys. And beware of movies that have a scene where a character "comically" falls into water. Still, Roz, Kay, and Don—all professionals—are charming, even if this is the only film where you'll hear Kay call someone "dearie." Hard to believe that Woody Van Dyke was the same guy who directed the sublime *Thin Man* films with William Powell and Myrna Loy. He again lived up to his nickname of One Take Woody on this one. Production began on July 1 and ended July 29, 1941.

Poet Ogden Nash received a writing credit. Notice the framed photo still of Kay Francis at Elliott's cottage. It appears to be from one of her earlier films. Working titles included *Female of the Species*, *Heartburn*, and *All Woman*. John Carroll was originally cast in Van Heflin's role.

REVIEWS: "'The Feminine Touch' contains some of the smartest dialogue ever recorded on a sound track. It's all very light but it's gay. And Rosalind Russell gives one of her finest performances. Miss Francis, too, is well cast...." (Edgar Price)

"Rosalind Russell and Kay Francis [are] as attractive a pair of movie gals as you're apt to see on any screen.... Some of the dialogue is glib, but for the most part the action is feverishly padded. Miss Francis does O.K. with her material." (Irene Thirer, *New York Post News*)

"It starts out to be sophisticated, ends in a giddy spell of slapstick and is generally amusing in between. Certainly it won't win any prizes, but it will take your mind off your troubles. Ladies, you should see the little models worn by the Misses Russell and Francis. Some stuff." (Richard Peters)

"Rosalind Russell and Kay Francis, two women with a flair for wearing tweeds, trick hats and ultra evening attire, are exceptionally good. They completely overshadow the pathetic males and come across with some of the neatest, most zestful acting of their two careers." (Virginia Oakey)

"Around a much-used topic Oppenheimer, Hartmann and Nash have dropped some chortling repartee, and Miss Russell swings through it with glee. She receives able assistance from Kay Francis." (*New York Times*, December 12, 1941)

Always in My Heart
(Warner Bros., 1942) 92 min. Released on March 13, 1942.

Credits: Producers, Walter MacEwen, William Jacobs; director, Jo Graham; suggested by a play ("Fly Away Home") by Dorothy Bennett, Irving White; screenplay, Adele Comandini; dialogue director, Frank Fox; music, Heinz Roemheld; "Una voce poca fa" from "Barber of Seville" by Gioacchino Antonio Rossini and Cesare Sterbini; "Always in My Heart" by Ernesto Lecuona and Kim Gannon; "Carnival of Venice" by Nicolo Paganini and Barclay Grey; musical director; Leo F. Forbstein; vocal arrangements, Dudley Chambers; orchestrator, Frank Perkins; camera, Sid Hickox; editor, Thomas Pratt; art director, Hugh Reticker; gowns, Orry-Kelly; makeup, Perc Westmore; sound, Francis J. Scheid; special effects, Edwin A. DuPar, Byron Haskin; assistant director, Phil Quinn.

Cast: Kay Francis (Marjorie Scott); Walter Huston (MacKenzie Scott); Gloria Warren (Victoria Scott); Patty Hale (Booley); Frankie Thomas (Martin Scott); Una O'Connor (Angie); Sidney Blackmer (Philip Ames); Armida (Lolita); Frank Puglia (Joe Borelli); Anthony Caruso (Frank); Elvira Curci (Rosita); Herbert Gunn (Dick); Harry Lewis (Steve); John Hamilton (Warden); Borrah Minevitch and His Rascals (Blackie and His Musicians); Leon Belasco (Violinist); Cliff Saum (Trusty); Lester Sharpe (Tuba Player); Frank Mayo (Tom, the Guard); Hank Mann

(Truck Driver); Lon McCallister (Boy); Jean Ames, Juanita Stark, Mary Brodel (Girls); Frank Lackteen (Pedro); Bob Stevenson (Fisherman); Pat O'Malley (Cop); Russell Arms (Red); Glen Cavender (Second Truck Driver); George Guhl (Café Proprietor); Herbert Heywood (Sailor); Jack Mower (Ames' Chauffeur); Spec O'Donnell (Ice Cream Vendor); Leo White (Studio Manager); Lottie Williams (Lady Buying Bread).

INTERIOR DECORATOR MARJORIE SCOTT lives in Santa Rita with two children, Vicky and Marty; housekeeper Angie; and Angie's granddaughter Booley. Mr. Ames is trying to convince Marjorie to marry him. Before she agrees, she meets with ex-husband Mac, serving time in prison. She talks about the kids, shows him photos, and then announces that she's met someone. "Someone who wants to marry me. I couldn't give him his answer until I talked to you." She tells Mac that if there's any chance of him getting out, she'll wait.

Although he knows he's being paroled, he tells her there's no chance, thinking she—and the children—will have a better chance without him. Marjorie hears the prison orchestra playing a tune and asks the warden about it. He tells Marjorie they're playing one of Mac's compositions, "Always in My Heart."

Mac is released in a rainstorm and goes to the Santa Rita wharf where he works with local musicians. He finds Marjorie's house on Maple Avenue. Vicky, who hopes to go to music school, is singing scales—which should have been enough to send him away. Marty has a new car, courtesy of Mr. Ames. When Marty drives off, Mac knocks on the door and tells Vicky he'll tune the piano. She tells him the piano belonged to her late father. He refuses payment, but asks for a song.

Ames and Marjorie return home, and Mac sneaks out the back. Later, at a birthday party for Vicky, Ames gives her a new piano. Vicky has a fit when she discovers the old piano was junked. She also receives a gift from Joe, a music teacher whom Ames doesn't approve of because he lives in Fishtown. When Vicky visits Joe to thank him, she hears someone playing the piano, and, upon investigation, finds Mac—and her old piano. Mac teaches her to play "Always in my Heart."

Meanwhile, Marty is dating a fast, loose girl named Lolita. When Lolita's ex-boyfriend picks a fight, Mac intervenes, telling Marty to stay away from that type of girl. "What right has he got butting into my business?" Marty asks.

Marjorie hears Vicki singing "Always in My Heart" and asks where she learned the song. Marjorie, realizing Mac's in town, goes to see him at the wharf. "You said there wasn't a chance. Can't you see this changes everything?" Mac tells her he's leaving that night. "You should have been more honest," Marjorie complains. She tells him she was supposed to marry Ames that night.

"Marge, I want you to marry this man."

Meanwhile, there's trouble at home. Ames forbids Vicky to sing in public with the Fishtown orchestra. He also tells her that he and Marjorie have registered her in an Eastern school, and she'll be leaving the next week.

Marjorie returns, and tells Ames her story. "Thirteen years ago my husband went to jail. He made me divorce him immediately. For the children, I let everyone believe that he was dead. Even you. He was innocently involved by a man in a crooked deal. There was a fight. The man died. Mac was sent up for life. I didn't even know that he'd been pardoned till tonight. He's here, and I've just seen him."

Ames still wants to marry her. "I love you, Marjorie. I don't want to lose you."

Vicky goes to Mac's and finds photographs and news clippings. She realizes Mac is her father. Mac tells her that he wants Marge to marry Ames—and that he's leaving for San Diego on Callahan's boat. "I just found out about it, and I have to lose you again," she cries, clinging to him.

Meanwhile, Marty is out with Lolita, and her ex-boyfriend attacks him with a knife. Mac gets involved and is stabbed. Vicky, deciding to run away, misses Callahan's boat, and takes a speedboat to catch it. Mac and Marty go after her.

Marjorie and Ames show up, also looking for Vicky. Mac saves Vicky, and there's a family reunion. Marty is very impressed. "Oh, boy, is he hot stuff. Fight, swim—Gee, Mudge, what a man."

Mac apologizes to Ames for the trouble he's caused. "You're a very fortunate man," Ames tells him.

"Goodbye, Marjorie. And the best of luck to all of you." Mac starts to leave.

"No use, Mac," Marjorie tells him, "we're going to start all over again. The four of us. Whether you like it or not."

In the final scene, Mac is at the piano wearing a suit. Vicky leans against the piano and sings. The Fishtown orchestra plays. Marty and Marjorie are in the audience, as are Angie and Booley. The final shot is Vicky hitting the last high note.

This weeper isn't too bad if you fast-forward through the music scenes. Walter Huston and Francis are two old pros who make this bad film watchable. Una O'Connor, too, is quite good. The song "Always in My Heart" was nominated for the Academy Award for Best Song in 1943. Production began in mid–October 1941 and ended in late November. Some scenes were filmed in Monterey, California.

Raymond Massey was originally slated to play MacKenzie Scott. Replacement Huston sang for the first time in a motion picture, though he had previously sung on stage.

Based on the 1935 play "Fly Away Home" by Dorothy Bennett and Irving White, the film was originally made by Warner Brothers in 1939. Directed by Michael Curtiz, *Daughters Courageous* starred John Garfield, Claude Rains, Fay Bainter, Donald Crisp, and the Lane Sisters. This version was a vehicle for recently signed 15-year-old Gloria Warren, a competitor — Warner Bros. hoped — to Deanna Durbin. It didn't work out, and Warren faded into obscurity: "She never caught on with the public, which was growing tired of sweet young girls with operatic voices."[86] We're sure Gloria Warren was a lovely person, and it's sad her career didn't work out, but her singing ruins this movie. This was also Patty Hale's film debut.

Always in My Heart was Kay's first film with Warner Bros. since she'd left the studio after her contract dispute. The studio obviously wanted veterans surrounding their young protégé, and Warner Bros. was forced to hire Kay back at her asking price. The film was Jo Graham's first directing effort after years of

Frankie Thomas, Kay, and Sidney Blackmer in *Always in My Heart* (1942) (courtesy James King).

working as a dialogue director. Borrah Minevitch and His Rascals were former vaudeville stars.

REVIEWS: "In spite of all its obvious merits, despite the performance of Mr. Huston, and the classy clothes worn by Miss Francis, and the singing and acting of a young newcomer named Gloria Warren, who looks very pretty and sings songs with a coloratura voice, 'Always in My Heart' stacks up pretty much as a magazine piece written more for the *Ladies Home Journal, Good Housekeeping* or *The Women's Home Companion*, rather than as a movie over which we can all get excited." (Leo Mishkin)

"Miss Warren's voice can go so high that it positively tickles your spine. Whether or not this effect is enjoyable is beside the point. The performances are pretty good, certainly good enough for the highly sentimental and not too likely story. Walter Huston, as always, is solidly satisfactory. Gloria Warren seems like an entirely normal kid, except for her piercing voice. Warner Brothers ought to be able to turn out a picture like this with their eyes closed, and maybe they have." (Archer Winsten)

"Gloria really clicks in a scene in which her really rich young voice flirts cheerily with a flute-like harmonica. In an extremely hifalutin' arrangement of Liszt's *Hungarian Rhapsody* at the finale, however, she just squeaks, poor kid." (John T. McManus)

"The potential star is flanked by the veteran Walter Huston on one side and by Kay Francis, who has had a good deal of experience in these tearful dramas, on the other. The drama follows a familiar course and that it holds the audience at all is due to its unfussy direction and the sincerity of the players, who give its familiar twists and turns a validity that makes one almost believe in the artificial tale." (Kate Cameron)

"'Always in My Heart' is a homely romantic drama that moves leisurely but steadily. It brings Kay Francis back to a top Warner role, gives Walter Huston a part he can play with assurance, provides young Gloria Warren with a debut for her clear but still-thin coloratura soprano and her attractive personality, and puts little Patty Hale — blond, toothless, cute and a chatterbox — up at the top of the list of screen brats." (Herbert Cohn)

"Mr. Huston plays the father with such ease and sincerity that the defects of his associates — especially Kay Francis — and of the script stand out in embarrassing prominence when he is not on the screen." (*New York Times*, March 14, 1942)

Between Us Girls

(Universal, 1942) 89 min. Released on September 4, 1942.

Credits: Producer-director, Henry Koster; associate producer, Philip P. Karlstein (Phil Karlson); based on the play "Le Fruit Vert" by Regis Gignoux, Jacques Thery; adapters, Hans Jacoby, John Jacoby; screenplay, Myles Connolly, True Boardman; art directors, Jack Otterson, Richard H. Riedel; gowns, Vera West; musical director, Charles Previn; camera, Joseph A. Valentine; editor, Frank Gross; sound director, Bernard B. Brown; gaffer, Warren Munroe; set decorators, R.A. Gausman, Ira Webb; property boss, Robert Laszlo; sound technician, Joe Lapis; special makeup, Bud Westmore; makeup, Jack Pierce.

Cast: Diana Barrymore (Caroline Bishop); Robert Cummings (Jimmy Blake); Kay Francis (Christine Bishop); John Boles (Steven Forbes); Andy Devine (Mike Kilinsky); Ethel Griffies (Gallagher); Walter Catlett (Desk Sergeant); Guinn "Big Boy" Williams (Father of the Boys); Scotty Beckett (Leopold); Andrew Tombes (Doctor); Peter Jamerson (Harold); Mary Treen (Mary Belle); Lillian Yarbo (Phoebe); Irving Bacon (Soda Dispenser); Aileen Pringle, Charles Coleman, Virginia Engels, Earle Dewey, Tommye Adams (Guests); Jack Chefe, Jack Mulhall, Leon Belasco (Waiters); Billy Lenhart (Boy); Bennie Bartlett (Kid); Walter Woolf King (Duke); Ed Gargan (Cab Driver); Edgar Licho (Ambassador); Bobby Barber (Waiter); Edgar Dearing, Wade Boteler (Police Officers); Herbert Heyes (Lieutenant).

CAROLINE BISHOP, DAUGHTER OF Christine Bishop, is a young actress. When the movie opens she's in a play — "Long Live the Queen" — and plays the ancient queen with old-age makeup and crackly voice. After the play's over, agent Mike tells her she'll next play Sadie in "Rain."

Before rehearsals start, Caroline visits her mother, who lives in a huge modern house. Christine has been seeing Steven, and she wants to introduce them, but Steven misunderstands when she says she has a daughter, assuming Caroline is very young.

"What happens when he finds out you're the mother of a 20-year-old daughter?" Caroline asks. She convinces her mother she might lose Steven if he finds out the truth.

When Steven and friend Jim arrive, Steve

brings a gift for Caroline. Chris laughs when she sees it's a doll. "Thank heavens, it isn't a rattle." Just as she's about to spill the beans, Caroline comes whistling and sliding down the banister, dressed in pigtails and a sailor suit. Caroline hides a photo of herself, pretending it's an aunt who has a drinking problem.

"Your sister, Christine?"

"More or less."

Caroline locks beloved housekeeper Gallagher in a closet to keep her quiet. After the men leave, Chris and Caroline are totally amused. Gallagher isn't. She slowly packs.

"We'll beat her," Chris suggests as punishment for Caroline. "Give her the beating of her life." Chris starts reminiscing about Gallagher—she's been with her since Caroline was born, etc. Gallagher stays.

Meanwhile, Caroline is rehearsing for "Rain" when Jim comes in. She pretends to be the alcoholic aunt, waving a bottle around.

"Where's the little girl?" he asks.

She runs upstairs to "find" Caroline, trips, and screams in pain. Jim thinks the drunken aunt is beating Caroline so he races up the stairs and slaps her. Caroline, sore jaw and all, finally shows up.

Jim has brought Caroline roller skates. Caroline pretends she can't keep her balance and has to hang on to him. Gallagher sees them, and Caroline puts her back in the closet. Jim takes Caroline out for ice cream where she gets into a fight with a kid at the soda counter, eventually causing a brawl. Caroline then drives the car to get away, but suddenly remembers she can't drive. A mad driving episode ensues, and then a trip to jail. Caroline faints, and a doctor is called. He examines her, and asks if she's wearing a costume.

Caroline suddenly "wakes up." Chris and Steven arrive. Order is restored, but Gallagher leaves the house because she's been locked up

Kay Francis and co-stars in *Between Us Girls* (1942). Kay looks serious despite her dip bowl hat. Left to right: Robert Cummings, John Boles, Diana Barrymore, Kay, Walter Catlett, Andrew Tombes.

again. For hours. They hire another maid, but are sad, sad, sad without Gallagher.

Caroline tells Mike she's not going to play Sadie. Mike convinces them to go to a night club, and Chris leaves word for Steven to join them. The maid calls the wrong guy, and Jim shows up. He thinks Caroline is the drunken aunt. She starts "playing" drunk again, but Jim sees a bandage on her arm that he'd put on Caroline after the ice cream brawl. He walks away, and she follows, climbing into his car. He drives away, unspeaking.

She says Mr. Blake way too many times (a sign of bad writing is the frequency that characters say other characters' names). Caroline finally confesses everything. He speeds until she screams and cries. He stops the car, gets out, and opens the door for her. She talks on and on, but he remains silent. Jim finally throws her in the water.

Caroline gets *another* one of those colds Hollywood actors get when they fall into water, and decides to play Joan of Arc rather than Sadie. Steve tells Christine he wants to marry her. She tells him the truth about her daughter's age. Meanwhile, she's caught Caroline's cold.

In the next scene, Caroline is playing Joan of Arc on stage. Christine and Steven watch from a box. *Steven* has a cold now—that's the kind of movie this is. On stage, there's a soldier having a costume problem. It's not really an actor at all, but Jim, trying to apologize.

"We'll answer *yes*! We'll answer *yes*!" she says, looking at him, smiling. She concludes the play and walks off stage. Only Jim remains, looking bewildered. He chases after her, calling her name.

A previous adaptation had been produced in Germany in 1934. *Fruchtchen* starred Frankziska Gaal and Hermann Thimig, and was directed by Richard Eichberg.

It's hard to imagine what it must have been like to work with the tempestuous, immature Diana Barrymore. Still, Diana seemed fond of Kay, even inviting her to a housewarming party at the former residence of Basil and Ouida Rathbone, along with Van Heflin, Jon Hall, Frances Langford, John Loder, Eddie Albert, and others.

The original title of this bad comedy was *Green Fruit*. Working titles also included *Boy Meets Baby*; *Caroline*; *Boy Meets Girl*; *What Happened, Caroline?*; and *Love and Kisses*. Production began April 17, 1942, and ended July 17. Some background footage was shot in New York City. This was director Koster's first film with Universal since signing a contract which allowed him and colleague Phil Karlstein to produce films. Koster specified that the same film crew he used on *Three Smart Girls* be hired to work on *Between Us Girls*.

Others considered for Diana's role included Ginger Rogers, Katharine Hepburn, and Deanna Durbin. Barrymore tested for the role in February 1942, but the producers did not find her a convincing teenager. They unsuccessfully attempted to borrow Olivia de Havilland from Warner Bros. Briefly, the producers considered scuttling the movie, but eventually signed Barrymore in March. She was paid $1,500 a week. During production her father John died. In addition, Diana married actor Bramwell Fletcher before the film opened, though the studio had requested she wait.

In her autobiography, Diana Barrymore described her experience on the film: "I had worked hard in that picture. Each morning I dashed down to the studios, to emerge as a twelve-year-old girl in pigtails, middy blouse, and short skirts. Tourists gaped when they saw me nervously puffing a cigarette on the set. I learned to roller-skate for harum-scarum scenes with Bob Cummings. In one scene he couldn't get himself to slap me hard, as the script required. Just as he was about to try for the seventh time, I kicked him sharply in the shins. He swatted me. It stung madly, but director Koster beamed. I sat for three hours while Perc Westmore magically made me into Queen Victoria. I stewed in Joan of Arc's armor. Everyone played up to me—Bob, Kay Francis, John Boles. Koster was magnificent. He even had the grips applaud me after each scene to give me the feeling of theater."[87]

Diana had not learned how important subtlety can be. She needed a good director. Koster wears out the jokes, letting them go on too long. To be honest, the whole premise is a bit creepy—Jim finding himself attracted to the teenager.

The maid who replaces Gallagher has some good lines, always complaining and muttering. "Stairs is all right as long as they on the ground, but stairs that go up and down...."

Cinematographer Joseph Valentine "introduces a new method of photography which contributes to the war effort by photographing flat white sets with colored lights as a paint substitute, thereby saving valuable paint chemicals."[88] Kay wears a very chic pantsuit near the end of the movie — another opportunity to see her costumed in slacks.

REVIEWS: "Kay Francis plays the mother with rare understanding and is ever a beautiful figure." (*Hollywood Reporter*)

"This is Miss Barrymore's starring debut, and the dexterity with which she handles her role indicates that another name has been added to showdom's Royal Family. Henry Koster, who directed Deanna Durbin to stardom, becomes a full-fledged producer-director with this film — which he has expertly designed to make the most of Miss Barrymore's bright new talent. His directorial ability is also apparent in the fine performances registered by Robert Cummings, who is starred with Diana, and by Kay Francis as the too-young mother." (Lee Mortimer)

"A wacky farce ... was apparently devised to give Diana Barrymore an acting workout. During the hour-and-a-half running time of the film, she appears as a 21-year-old ingénue, as the aged Queen Victoria, as Sadie Thompson, as Joan of Arc and chiefly, as a 12-year-old cut-up. It's practically all slapstick, and much of the piece is out-and-out burlesque." (Rose Pelswick)

"Kay Francis, adequately, does the youthful mother. Better looking than so many younger actresses, she is still good to look at." (Wanda Hale, *New York Daily News*)

"Henry Koster, who successfully directed many of the Deanna Durbin hits, was responsible for this one which now and then flashes a bright spark of witticism and whimsy. Mostly, however, it's just so much dressed-up hokum — and when we say dressed up, we mean that the production is lavishly mounted, and that the Misses Barrymore and Francis are exquisitely costumed." (Irene Thirer, *New York Post*)

"With an unabashed zeal hardly equaled by Mickey Rooney himself, Miss Barrymore runs the gamut of her limitations. In supporting roles, Robert Cummings portrays an amusingly baffled young man and Andy Devine, Kay Francis and John Boles are adequate. But inasmuch as the picture frankly sets out to exploit Miss Barrymore's talents, it stands or falls upon them. It falls, we fear, with a rather heavy thud." (*New York Times*, September 25, 1942)

Four Jills in a Jeep
(Twentieth Century-Fox, 1944) 89 min.
Released on April 6, 1944.

Credits: Producer, Irving Starr; director, William A. Seiter; story, Froma Sand, Fred Niblo, Jr.; based on the actual experiences of Kay Francis, Carole Landis, Martha Raye, Mitzi Mayfair; screenplay, Robert Ellis, Helen Logan, Snag Werris; orchestrator, Maurice De Packh; music and lyrics, Jimmy McHugh, Harold Adamson, Leo Robin, Harry Warren; choreographer, Don Loper; musical directors, Emil Newman, Charles Henderson; art directors, James Basevi, Albert Hogsett; set decorator, Thomas Little; associate set decorator, Al Orenbach; camera, Peverell Marley; editor, Ray Curtiss; costumes, Yvonne Wood; assistant director, William Eckhardt; second unit director, John Brahm; sound, Jesse Bastian, Murray Spivack; special effects, Fred Sersen; makeup, Guy Pearce; technical advisers, Colonel Phillip W. Booker, Major Ralph J. Watson; production manager, R.L. Hugh; unit production manager, Charles Hall.

Cast: Kay Francis, Carole Landis, Martha Raye, Mitzi Mayfair; Jimmy Dorsey & His Band; John Harvey (Ted Warren); Phil Silvers (Eddie); Dick Haymes (Lieutenant Dick Ryan); Alice Faye, Betty Grable, Carmen Miranda (Guest Stars); George Jessel (Master of Ceremonies); Glenn Langan (Captain Stewart); Lester Matthews (Captain Lloyd); Miles Mander (Colonel Hartley); Frank Wilcox (Officer); Paul Harvey (General); Mary Servoss (Nurse Captain); B. S. Pulley, Dave Willock (Soldiers); Ralph Byrd (Sergeant); Renee Carson (French Maid); Edith Evanson (Swedish Maid); Betty Roadman (Housekeeper); Mary Field (Maid); Mel Schubert (Pilot); Winifred Harris (Lady Carlton-Smith); Crawford Kent (British Officer); Frances Morris (Surgical Nurse); James Flavin (M.P.); Jimmy Martin (Aide); Eddie Acuff (Sentry); Kirk Alyn (Pilot); Martin Black, Lester Dorr, Mike Killian, George Tyne, Gordon Wynn, Buddy Yarus, Joel Allen, Joe Haworth (Soldiers); Alex Pollard (Butler); Alec Harford (Priest); Larry Thompson, Harry Strang (Sergeants); Roger Clark (Captain), Clarence Straight (Corporal); David Essex (Navigator) Donald Stuart, Bernie Sell (Sentries); John Whitney (Lieutenant); Warren Ash (Lieutenant Colonel).

"THIS STORY IS BASED on the experiences of four of the many performers who take entertainment to America's men in uniform in the theatres of war, as well as in the camps at home. Actors who serve in this global entertainment program consider it a privilege to lighten a little the hardships endured by your fighting men and to share, in a measure, their experiences in combat zones. The producers gratefully acknowledge the work of USO-Camp Shows, Inc., the Hollywood Victory Committee and the special service division of the war department."

At the CBS Studios, Kay Francis serves as mistress of ceremonies, and introduces Betty Grable who sings "Cuddle Up a Little Closer." Her number is interspersed with footage of soldiers on active duty listening to the radio. Later, Kay says good night as do Jimmy Dorsey and his band, Martha Raye, Mitzi Mayfair, and Carole Landis. "From your mistress of ceremonies, Kay Francis, who doesn't sing, dance, or recite but is willing to stick our her neck ... if necking is entertainment."

After the show, Kay tells Jimmy she's planning a trip to London–she's responsible for putting an entertainment unit together. Raye, Mayfair, and Landis accidentally volunteer, and they travel from Hollywood to New York to Lisbon, and then to an airport about 60 miles from London. Kay and Colonel Hartley of the British Foreign Office strike up a romance. It's also in England where Carole meets Captain Ted Warren, who's headed out on a mission. Meanwhile, the producers give Mitzi a romance: She runs into old boyfriend Dick.

The women perform at a Red Cross Benefit in London, and Kay gets a chance to become better acquainted with Colonel Hartley. He's a pediatrics doctor who enlisted. "You know, I've been a mother so often," Kay tells him. "Dozens and dozens of times. Week in and week out. I just loved it. I've even been Deanna Durbin's mother. Of course they were just motion picture babies. Sort of like Charles Lamb's dream children."

Martha accidentally volunteers them for Africa. Before they go, there's a scare when Ted hasn't returned from a mission. While they wait, they hear a special radio broadcast, emceed by Georgie Jessel and featuring Alice Faye singing "You'll Never Know." Kay and the girls are mentioned, too. "If you're listening in, girls, we're proud of you," Jessel says. "Yes, indeed. Mighty proud." The fiery Brazilian singer-dancer Carmen Miranda is next on the program, singing "I, Yi, Yi, Yi, Yi."

Ted finally returns, and a relieved Carole decides to marry him. Shortly after the wedding, they take off for North Africa. A radio operator receives a message and reluctantly passes it on. "The corporal's gone nuts. He just phoned and he saw Kay Francis there ... on a camel."

Sure enough, the girls come riding in on camels. One soldier warns them about the jerries and suggests they get in the trenches if bombing starts. "You can't entertain anybody with your brains knocked out," he points out.

"He's never been to Hollywood," Martha quips.

The nurse in charge is not happy to see them. "We're short doctors, we're short nurses, we're short Red Cross workers, and they send us you queens from Hollywood." Kay leads them inside, and the conditions are grim. Mitzi tells Kay she doesn't think she can do it. "Pretend that you're in Hollywood, that you're working on a picture," Kay suggests.

Hartley is there, too. He doesn't recognize Kay and asks her to scrub the floor, which she does. "Ever since I first saw you," he tells her, finally realizing who she is, "I've wanted to tell you that you're the most wonderful person I've ever known."

"Well, for goodness sake!" Kay says. "Couldn't you have found a better place to tell me?!"

"You're about the hardest working batch of wenches I've ever met," the nurse finally admits.

During one performance, there's a blackout. Carole finishes her song, and then they're led to the trenches where they endure a bombing run. Finally, they're ordered to return to the rear line. In the final scene, the women happily wave goodbye to the soldiers who have been ordered to counterattack.

Production began on October 18, 1943, and ended in December. Working titles included *Camp Show* and *Command Performance, U.S.A.*—named after the popular radio show. Ultimately, the title was changed to *Four Jills in a Jeep* after Carole Landis' autobiographical book became successful. Landis collaborated with a ghost writer, Edwin Seaver, on the Random House book, which was contracted after Carole had written several newspaper and magazine articles detailing her experiences. Carole's book was released in 1944 after being serialized in four installments (December 14, 1943, through January 15, 1944) in *The Saturday Evening Post*.

The trip began on October 16, 1942, and the women traveled for about three months, visiting England, Ireland, Scotland, and Wales. Several shows a day were performed each day, and the highlight was the performance before the Queen of England. The next leg of the trip was to North Africa, and they were the first USO tour to perform there. Almost a month was spent in this area.

Kay received top billing. At one time, it was reported that Carole and Kay would receive writing credits, but Kay's name did not appear on the final credits. The women quickly realized that no one was interested in their opinions about how to make the film, and the final effort was going to be in no way representative of what they'd gone through. According to Landis, "'Now, every time we make a suggestion someone tells us to go sit in the corner. When the boys we entertained in Africa see the picture, I hope they know the meaning of dramatic license.'" One writer quoted the girls, "If the four jills have their way, the picture *Four Jills in a Jeep* will be released with an introduction reading: 'Any resemblance between this picture and trip to Africa is purely coincidental.'"[89]

Researchers suggest that Lew Irwin, Mitzi Mayfair's agent, pitched the idea to the studio, while others believe Landis' articles were key to getting the film produced. Mayfair's last feature film appearance before this had been *Paramount on Parade* in 1930. She did not appear in any feature films after this, though she did make appearances in Vitaphone musical shorts, often with Hal LeRoy. Waldo Salt may have been an uncredited writer on the script. Islin Auster was the original producer, and John Sutton was the first choice to play Captain Lloyd. Jack Oakie was originally slated to play the Phil Silvers role, and Cornel Wilde was also a possible cast member. This was Dick Haymes' film debut.

The talented and lovely Landis actually did

Kay Francis, Mitzi Mayfair, Martha Raye, and Carole Landis in *Four Jills in a Jeep* (1944) (courtesy Liz Nocera).

Glenn Langan, Phil Silvers, Kay Francis, Carole Landis, and Mitzi Mayfair in *Four Jills in a Jeep* (1944) (courtesy Liz Nocera).

marry a man she met on the tour. This union, to Captain Thomas C. Wallace, was brief. Married on January 5, 1943, they separated in October 1944, and divorced in the summer of 1945. Both regretted the marriage. "I've had enough of being the guy Carole Landis married," he said, while she added, "It was a marriage which, I believe, we would have discovered was not meant to be had we disciplined ourselves and waited."[90] How true.

This was Martha Raye's first USO tour, but she later became famous for her devotion to entertaining troops of other wars. Her many awards included a Purple Heart, the Distinguished Service Award from the USO, and the Presidential Medal of Freedom. Martha wrote a song for the film titled "Jeep, Jeep, Listen the Soldiers Sing," but it does not appear in the final version.

The romance between Kay and the British officer is handled clumsily and seems unnecessary. This is also the case for the romance between Mitzi and Dick Haymes' character—and the supposed comedic pairing of Martha Raye and Phil Silvers. Even the Carole Landis romance is heavily fictionalized, though she did wear her actual wedding dress in the film.

The Hays Office insisted that none of the women wear sweaters in the film, though they were part of their wardrobe on the tour. Apparently the censors found the clothing too revealing. Another change involved the circumstances under which the four women ended up on the tour. In the film, they are reluctantly recruited after Martha brags about how well they'd do. In reality, they'd listened to Merle Oberon and Al Jolson talk about their experiences, and pleaded for permission to go on tour. After many delays, the women were finally given the go-ahead.

"How Blue the Night" and "How Many Times Do I Have to Tell You" became hit songs. Another song in the movie, "You'll Never Know," had an interesting genesis. Songwriter Harry

Warren once told Jack Oakie that the melody was actually "Oh What a Pal Was Mary"—played backwards.

Fox cynically re-released *Four Jills in a Jeep* in July 1948 within days of Landis' suicide. The newspaper ads included this notation: "This is a special Booking in tribute to the late Carole Landis."[91]

REVIEWS: "Kay Francis handles the role of emcee and boss of the party agreeably." (*Variety*, March 15, 1944)

"Viewed strictly as a movie, 'Four Jills in a Jeep' is a curiously makeshift affair. The good things it has are very, very good and the bad things it has—well, the hell with 'em. The four girls themselves are so very nice and the boys over in England and North Africa liked 'em so much we can forgive a whole lot of minor technical flaws." (*New York Morning Telegraph*, April 6, 1944)

"Though heavy with lightness, beauty and sex appeal, the film is only moderately entertaining. Apparently overlooked was the chance to portray the really fine, brave and heroic work the people of the screen and stage are doing to entertain the troops on all fronts." (*New York Daily Mirror*, April 6, 1944)

"'Four Jills in a Jeep,' wasting all its possibilities, is a dreary, badly made musical. Something went wrong in the writing....' Direction and acting are no better. The production looks thrown together as though it had been written on the set and photographed in a few days. 'Four Jills in a Jeep' is third-rate stuff." (*New York Sun*, April 6, 1944)

"The girls of the picture and all the other girls who cheerfully face the tough going of a trip to battlefronts are entitled to more respect than this picture gives them. None of them come back with any such tales of endless gaiety and excitement as this picture relates." (*New York World-Telegram*, April 5, 1944)

"No offense intended to those four famous camp-touring jills but the new film ... is strictly from Hollywood, and very routine Hollywood at that. About the only documentary note in the film is Carole Landis's wedding to her Air Force captain, an event which really happened. The rest is a patchwork of routine entertainment turns and stock romantic situations, ending up for all practical purposes with a series of close-up kisses in an African slit trench." (John T. McManus, April 6, 1944)

"If 'Four Jills in a Jeep' had stuck closer to the record, as outlined in Carole Landis' book of the same name, the picture might have been a livelier and funnier account of the historic USO tour. The fictional part of the story isn't as interesting as if an honest-to-goodness record of the frictions, comic blunders and contretemps of the tour had been added to the general sweetness of the girls toward each other and their good-natured acceptance of the inconveniences and setbacks of the trip." (Kate Cameron, April 6, 1944)

"The claptrap saga is just a raw piece of capitalization upon a widely publicized affair. It gives the painful impression of having been tossed together in a couple of hours." (*New York Times*, April 6, 1944)

Divorce

(Monogram, 1945) 71 min.
Released on August 18, 1945.

Credits: Executive director, Trem Carr; producers, Jeffrey Bernerd, Kay Francis; director, William Nigh; story, Sidney Sutherland; screenplay, Harvey H. Gates, Sidney Sutherland; original music-musical director, Edward J. Kay; technical director, Dave Milton; set decorator, Vin Taylor; assistant director, Richard Harlan; sound recorder, Tom Lambert; camera, Harry Neumann; supervising editor, Richard Currier; production manager, William Strohbach; stylist, Lorraine MacLean; gowns, Odette Myrtil; hats, Keneth Hopkins.

Cast: Kay Francis (Dianne Hunter Carter); Bruce Cabot (Bob Phillips); Helen Mack (Martha Phillips); Jerome Cowan (Judge Jim Driscoll); Craig Reynolds (Bill Endicott); Ruth Lee (Liz Smith); Jean Fenwick (June Endicott); Mary Gordon (Ellen, the Housekeeper); Larry Olsen (Michael Phillips); Johnny Calkins (Robby Phillips); Jonathan Hale (Judge Conlon); Addison Richards (Plummer, the Lawyer); Leonard Mudie (Harvey Hicks); Reid Kilpatrick (Dr. Andy Cole); Virginia Ware (Secretary); Napoleon Simpson (Train Porter); Pierre Watkin (John B. Carter).

"MARRIAGE—ENTERED INTO WITH such high hopes—such promise of happiness. Then—too often—DIVORCE—which solves no problems—merely creating new ones—And—in its wake, leaves disillusionment, heartbreak, despair—Of such is our story."

The first scene is inside a courtroom where a divorce proceeding is underway. The judge scolds the woman and suggests she reconcile with her husband. The next case involves John and Dianne Carter. They've been married for only a year — in fact, it's their wedding anniversary — and John admits that he's still in love with his wife, but says she has treated him cruelly and inhumanly. He says she slapped him and threw a glass at him. The judge notes that John's been very generous in his settlement, and also observes that Dianne has been divorced many times. She's not in the courtroom so the judge reluctantly grants the decree by default. Meanwhile, Dianne is traveling on a train headed to Hillsboro, Illinois, when she receives a telegram from her attorney: "Decree and settlement in the bag."

Meanwhile, Martha and Bob Phillips are celebrating their tenth wedding anniversary. Bob, just back from military service, holds a fake court martial for his kids. The brats are charged with refusing to brush their teeth (Robby) and kicking Ellen (Michael). Dad "dismisses" the charges.

Later that night Martha and Bob host a party, and Dianne arrives with friends. She not only once lived in Hillsboro, but had a "thing" with Bob. Bob's thrilled to see Dianne, and ends up spending most of the night with her.

"Maybe I wanted to see you again," Dianne says when Bob asks why she came back.

Martha asks about Dianne. "At one time or another, she gave every male in this town a fever of 110," a guest says.

Dianne visits Bob at work — he's in real estate — and he helps her find an apartment. Dianne calls Martha and asks her for help decorating her apartment.

A newspaper headline announces a business success for Bob: "Robert Phillips Heads Big Hillsboro Realty Project: Old Landon Estate Will be Purchased and Developed." (By the way, check out another headline on the same page: "Plane Is Flown Without Tail: Control Perfect.") Martha overhears Bob tell someone that Dianne helped finance the deal.

A lobby card from *Divorce* (1945). This was one of Kay's last films, but she still looked radiant.

"Do you think there's a price tag on Bob?" Martha angrily asks.

Michael comes down with the mumps, and Dianne sends him an expensive electric train with a note for Martha: "I must talk to you. Meanwhile, perhaps this toy will carry Michael through his mumps a little happier."

Martha meets Dianne at her apartment. "I think it's about time that you and I put our cards on the table," Dianne tells her. She explains she's working with Bob because she thinks the land deal is a good investment. She offers to withdraw her financing, and warns Martha about holding Bob back from success.

Bob, Dianne, and the kids go on a picnic. The kids take off on their bikes—gifts from Dianne—and Michael is slightly injured.

"I'm more than annoyed," Martha tells Dianne, and orders her to stay away from the children. "You're not interested in my children. You're interested in Bob." Martha asks Bob if he's in love with Dianne.

A poster for *Divorce* (1945).

"Okay, you asked for it. I am."

"If you keep on being as stupid and nagging as you are," Dianne chimes in, "you can't blame Bob for wanting to walk out on you."

Martha agrees to give Bob a divorce. Martha's friends try to help. "Martha," Jim begins in a slight variation on the introduction, "marriage is entered into with such high hopes—such promises of happiness. Then—too often—DIVORCE. In its wake, disillusionment, despair, heartache." That's an example—a great example—of just how—clunky—the—script—is.

Martha throws in the towel. "I had a husband. I lost him."

At the divorce court, Jim is the judge (seems like a conflict of interest, doesn't it?). The divorce is granted. Martha gets $150 a month, and Bob gets visitation on the last Saturday of each month.

One day Bob doesn't show up to pick up the boys because he's gambling with Dianne. A newspaper headline describes the resulting scandal: "Hillsboro Pair in Big Gambling Raid: Robert Phillips and Mrs. Dianne Carter in Police Raid." (Another headline reads: "Meteorite Falls Near Baby.") Martha sends her alimony check to Bob—torn up—and gets a job at Green's Department Store.

Dianne holds up the newspaper. "Would you rather be respectable or successful?" she asks. She and Bob argue about the future of their company. "We can't sit around here in Hillsboro," Dianne complains. "We've got the whole country to play around in, and after the War the whole world."

He tells her if they travel, it'll be with his money, not hers. See, he's got pride. Meanwhile, Dianne has become jealous of Bob's kids. "I've always been on the top side of the fence. It's kind of funny playing second fiddle," she says, mixing metaphors.

Dianne goes to Martha's house, and listens in as the kids have a court martial for Bob. He's charged with desertion. "Guilty as charged." The brats, now crying, reduce him in rank to a private and order him to leave the house and never come back.

Dianne runs into Martha on her way out. "I'm leaving town on the first train," she says. "Tell Bob I don't know anything about children's games."

Dianne is back on the train. The porter tells her she's changed since the last time he saw her.

"I guess I have. And I don't think I'm going to like it very much." The final shot is the back of the train as it leaves Hillsboro.

Kay received top billing in this weak melodrama. She did what she could with the character, but the script didn't allow for much development. When it was shown on television in 1953, the title was changed to *The Hillsboro Story*.

Johnny Calkins name is misspelled "Johny" in the credits. Researchers suggest the story idea came from newspaper cartoonist Percy Crosby whose cartoon "Break Up" showed a child being fought over by mother and father.

Alfred Zeisler was originally named director but was replaced by William Nigh. Paul Kelly was the first choice for Bruce Cabot's role. Production began on February 19, 1945, and ended in early March.

Bruce Cabot stipulated in his contracts that he would not work on the 13th of any month. This was his first movie role since being released from the Army — he wore his own uniform in his scenes. Overseas for seventeen months, he served in Africa and Italy.

Promotional materials took a tawdry approach: "Now! The other woman sought only to satisfy her selfish desires. The wife wanted only her husband's love and her children. The husband. An ex-veteran, the victim of a footloose divorce. The daring story of a divorcee who turned husband stealer.... Homewrecker. A surprise revelation of the 'Other Woman.' The wife, and the husband who was considered 'safe.'"

REVIEWS: "No less subtle than story presentation is Kay Francis' performance as siren. She stops short of actual bludgeoning, but bears so heavily on intimidation by gesture and dialogue that both she and Bruce Cabot look ridiculous." (*The Daily News*, October 11, 1945)

"Miss Francis and Miss Mack turn in creditable performances but Cabot appears to have lost his usual spark." (*Variety*, October 17, 1945)

"The story ... is not particularly novel and the outcome is quite obvious; however, one's attention is held because it directs some human appeal and it has good performances." (*Harrison's Reports*, June 9, 1945)

Allotment Wives

(Monogram, 1945) 80 min. Released on December 29, 1945.

Credits: Executive director, Trem Carr; producers, Jeffrey Bernerd, Kay Francis; director, William Nigh; story, Sidney Sutherland; screenplay, Harvey Gates, Sidney Sutherland; art director, Dave Milton; set decorators, Vin Taylor, Charles Thompson; assistant director, Richard Harlan; sound, Tom Lambert; camera, Harry Neumann; Second camera, Al Nicklin; editor, William Austin; Miss Francis' gowns, Odette Myrtil; Miss Francis' hats, Keneth Hopkins; stylist, Lorraine MacLean; production manager, Glenn Cook; musical director, Edward J. Kay; technical directors, David Milton, E.R. Hickson; mixers, Joseph I. Kane, William H. Wilmarth; special effects, Bob Clark; special optical effects, Larry Glickman; transparency projection shots, Glenn Cook.

Cast: Kay Francis (Sheila Seymour); Paul Kelly (Pete Martin); Otto Kruger (Whitey Colton); Gertrude Michael (Gladys Smith); Teala Loring (Connie Seymour); Bernard Nedell (Spike Malone); Matty Fain (Louie Moranto); Anthony Warde (Joe Agnew); Jonathan Hale (General Gilbert); Selmer Jackson (Deacon Sam); Evelyn Eaton (Ann Farley); Reid Kilpatrick (Philip Van Brook); John Elliott (Police Doctor); Terry Frost (George Shields); Doris Lloyd (Alice Van Brook); Marcelle Corday (Madame Gaston); Michael Browne (Grey); Elizabeth Wright (Helen Keefe); Sarah Edwards (Sadie), Paul Bradley; Cosmo Sardo, Parker Gee (Henchmen), Larry Steers (Head waiter); Nolan Leary, Frank Mayo, Phil Hegland, Roy Butler (Businessmen); Marie Harmon (Girl); Glenn Charles (Soldier); Rune Hultman (Connie's Soldier); Les Bennett (Technical Sergeant), Mary Arden (Police Matron); Vela Lehmann (Landlady); Laura Corbay (Tough Girl); Peggy Leon (Dowager); Betty Sinclair (Hostess); Karen Knight (Telephone Operator); Henry Vroom, (Soldier); John Gannon (Soldiers); Jean Andren, Louise Frye (Fashionable Women); Pat Gleason (Police Sergeant); Winnie Nard (Receptionist); Gertrude Astor (Marilyn); Edgar Caldwell (Marine); Billy Vernon (Sailor).

"TO THE WAR DEPARTMENT Office of Dependency Benefits and to the Navy Department — Monogram Pictures Corporation wishes to express its appreciation for the co-operation given in the filming of this production."

We next see an establishing shot of the New Jersey War Department Office of Dependency Benefits (ODB). The brief documentary explains the reasons for — and procedures of — the ODB. "Never in history was there such a gigantic stream of gold accessible to avaricious criminal elements. It looked easy. And the scramble to dip greedy fingers into the stream was on. The ODB, always alert to such a danger moved swiftly."

Colonel Pete Martin reports to General Gilbert and learns that women have been committing bigamy in order to get servicemen's ODB benefits. "Someone has organized this thing into a major racket of huge proportions. So far we haven't been able to find the head of it. But it must be stopped."

Newspaperman Pete is reluctant to get involved until the general tells him that his friend Fred was a victim of the scam. "You'll find him in Arlington Cemetery," the general says.

"When do I start, sir?"

Beautiful, vivacious Sheila Seymour has lunch with businessmen, seeking contributions to her canteen. Meanwhile, at another table, a woman — one of the wives — passes money to a man. The man introduces her to another soldier, but they're interrupted by a cop. "Beat it, soldier," the cop says, "this gal's got three husbands already." The soldier skedaddles. The man tries to pull a gun, but Pete, who's sitting at the bar, stops him.

Pete and Sheila meet. "You see, I had to butt in," he says. "The gun was pointed in your direction."

"Do you expect me to believe that?" she asks.

"No."

Sheila owns the Seymour Beauty Salon, a front for her criminal activities. Literally. Behind her office wall is a secret room where she meets with her cohorts. Whitey (his name *could* be Righty — we can't be sure) is her most trusted man. Moranto tries to buck her. "You're through!" Sheila tells him. "Get out!"

Moranto, who planned to take over the racket, is killed in a drive-by shooting. Whitey warns Sheila that Pete is working for the ODB, and suggests she quit, that the ODB is breathing down their necks. "A hot breath on my neck is sometimes more stimulating than a cold shower," she tells Whitey.

He mentions Connie, Sheila's kid. "You considering her?" he asks.

"The only decent thought I ever had in my

A lobby card from *Allotment Wives* (1945). Kay wore many hats during her career, and this one is a beaut.

life was for her," Sheila says, adding she'll quit in the spring when Connie graduates. She promises a long trip — the three of them — when it's all over.

Later, Whitey and Sheila see a drunken Connie at a bar. "It's just the way I started," a horrified Sheila says, watching Connie kiss a military man. Whitey takes Connie to Sheila's home. Meanwhile, Sheila goes to the canteen.

"I just saw a soldier trying to kiss one of our girls," someone complains.

"Did he succeed?" Sheila asks.

"No."

"Then it wasn't one of our girls."

Gladys, a Moranto associate, is at the canteen, too. "Hello, Edna," she says to Sheila. Sheila pretends not to know her. Later, Gladys visits Sheila's home. She's turned away at the door but watches a scene through the window between Sheila and Connie. "It's her all right," Gladys tells boyfriend Spike, "and she's got her brat with her."

Sheila and Connie argue. "I'm tired of your preaching!" Connie rages. "I'm tired of being just another stupid mother's daughter. I'm tired of *you*!" Sheila slaps her. Hard.

Sheila apologizes. "I never want you to go through what I did," she tells Connie, and asks her to return to school for the last two months, and then they'll go away together. Connie asks for a drink.

"Soda or water?" Sheila asks.

"Just straight for me," Connie says.

Sheila lunches with Pete, who tells her about the investigation. "I may turn out to be your ace in the hole," she tells him.

Gladys returns to Sheila's house. It turns out they're old friends. "You always wanted to go big time, even when we were kids together in that filthy slum," Gladys says, reminiscing. "You always said 'I'm gonna be a swell dame some day.'"

"I always said that I hated the poverty, and the dirt, and the hunger," Sheila says.

Gladys reminds her that they ended up in reform school together.

"Stealing was a stupid way to get up in the world," Sheila says.

"I'd heard you married some guy with a lot of dough. I even heard you had a baby. Is your husband dead?"

"Africa," Sheila vaguely says.

Gladys reminds her that they used to share things, and Sheila offers her a job at the beauty salon. That's not quite what Gladys had in mind.

After Gladys leaves, Sheila has Whitey arrange it so Gladys is arrested. She's put in the same cell with a woman who worked for Moranto. The cops try to listen in on their conversation, but Gladys is too smart for that, and the two write messages in lipstick. Wouldn't the cops have taken their lipstick?

The woman tells Gladys she's waiting for Moranto to spring her. Gladys writes "Dead." The despondent woman is on the verge of yelling out the name of the person she holds responsible. Gladys covers her mouth and gives her the lipstick. "Sheila Seymour," the woman writes.

"Well, well, well," Gladys says.

Later, the woman hangs herself in the cell. Gladys is released on a technicality. Although she wasn't aware of it, she married the second husband *after* the first husband was killed in action.

Gladys and Spike take Connie out for a good time. There's a montage sequence beginning August 1 and ending August 15 with scenes of the three drinking, gambling, clubbing, etc.

Whitey informs Sheila that Connie left school and has been seen with a blonde woman. "I want Connie and I want her quick. And also I want Gladys Smith. I want her all to myself. Tell the boys to bring her here to me. There's $5,000 for the one who gets her. Trouble for all if they don't."

That night, Spike and Gladys show up at Sheila's. On the phone with Whitey, Sheila says: "We can't extend any more credit. The book's are closed."

"Something's wrong!" Whitey says to the boys. "There's our secret code! Get the boys." They hurry off.

Spike and Gladys tell Sheila they have Connie, have told her about her past, and — even worse — have added her to their racket. "She has everything it takes," Gladys says. "Just like her mother."

Spike goes down to the safe, and Gladys calls the ODB — kind of strange they're open so late. "Hello, ODB. St. Claire Apartments. Ask for a Mrs. Baxter. She's one of the allotment wives. Here's another little tip. Her mother is—" Sheila shoots Gladys.

Whitey and the boys run upstairs. (Notice

how the light switch is turned on — the room has suddenly gone dark.) "Get rid of that," Sheila says, glancing at Gladys' body. Though injured, Spike gets away.

Meanwhile, Connie, now arrested, suffers from shock. "It's psychohysteria," Pete tells Sheila, and explains she's being held at the OBD.

Sheila volunteers to talk to the girl. Pete leaves Sheila alone with Connie, and Whitey and the boys soon break in and "kidnap" Connie — but not without a gunfight.

Gladys is found floating in the river with a bullet in her heart. Pete goes to Spike's apartment and finds a Gauloises Caporal Ordinaire box (he saw the same cigarette box when he lunched with Sheila).

Sheila returns home, and learns that Whitey's been killed in the shootout. "Always deny that Connie was my daughter," Sheila tells Deke. "Oh, say anything, but never say that she belonged to me."

Sheila tells Connie they're leaving on a trip. "Mother, I think you're wonderful," Connie tells her.

"You've never said anything like that to me before. But don't call me Mother. From now on, I'm Sheila."

Connie apologizes for the trouble she's caused. "Oh, Mother, I've been so wrong."

"You never would have been wrong if I hadn't been wrong before you. You've got an awful lot of me in you. You're going to have to fight it. Just remember, I always loved you."

Pete and the cops arrive at Sheila's. He waits for her at the bottom of the stairs and shows her the cigarette box. "I took these off a half-dead mug called Spike."

Sheila pulls a gun and is shot. "Nice shooting," she says, before falling down the stairs. Connie sobs on Deke's shoulder.

In the final scene, the general who started the investigation meets with Pete. "Sheila Seymour was an amazing woman," Pete tells him. "One had to know her to appreciate how she could establish a service canteen for criminal purposes and make it one of the most popular on the West Coast."

"I see they convicted Mrs. Seymour's adopted daughter," the general says.

"She was the least guilty of all, General. Unfortunate victim of a vicious woman who was fighting her mother for control of the syndicate."

Only Deke and the ODB know that Connie was Sheila's own child. "Don't worry. It'll be buried in the files."

"I knew you'd understand, sir," Pete says.

Kay received top billing in this very good film noir. It was the first and only time she was murdered in a film. Production started June 19, and the wrap party for the crew was July 2, 1945. Too bad *this* wasn't Kay's last film.

She wore a rolled bang hairstyle in the beginning of the movie, a style reminiscent of Joan Crawford circa 1940s. Later, in the scene where she's confronted in bed by Gladys and Spike, her hair hangs loose and looks great. By the way, Gertrude Michael, who played tough-talking Gladys, made her stage debut in the late 1920s with Kay's onetime mentor Stuart Walker.

The film is also known as *Allotment Wives, Inc.* and *Woman in the Case.* Writers George Sayre and Neil Rau may have helped with the script. Production started in mid–June and ended in the early part of July 1945.

REVIEWS: This is one of those movies where the reviews improve with age. According to John Cocchi, the movie "was a surprisingly good crime melodrama which allowed Kay to be totally unsympathetic and fascinating at the same time. Otto Kruger is ever suave and ever crafty as Kay's highly supportive associate and Selmer Jackson, usually a solid citizen, has a colorful role as a cultured member of the crime ring. Anthony Warde also goes against type as a law officer, while Bernard Nedell and Matty Fain are true to their typecasting as criminals. Although she comes to a well deserved end, Kay Francis rewards herself with a memorable exit line."[92]

Mick LaSalle was even more effusive in his praise of Kay: "It's surprising that Francis didn't become one of the top noir women. She's as tough as Crawford and as cool as Stanwyck, with an ironic fatalism that's more like Robert Mitchum than any femme fatale."[93] He also wrote that the movie "qualifies as a major rediscovery. It's another film that confirms that historians just can't make assumptions about movies they haven't seen. For years, *Allotment Wives* has been written off as an embarrassing coda to the career of '30s diva Kay Francis. Guess what? It's one of her best movies. The plot has echoes of another 1945 feature, *Mildred Pierce,* for which Joan Crawford won an

Oscar. But *Allotment Wives* is tougher, harder and stronger, and Francis' performance outshines anything Crawford ever did. In retrospect, it's amazing that Francis didn't go on to have a great second career. Notice the way she gets off her last line in the picture. It's classic."[94]

"As the co-producer of the picture and its distaff Fagin and mob chief, Kay Francis wears an assortment of impressive gowns and accessories, and appears far too genteel for her job." (*The New York Times*, November 22, 1945)

"Miss Francis, being cast with increasing frequency as a heavy, walks through her well-gowned but incredible part in a not too convincing fashion. Adequate for straight duties, she fails to express the high-key emotions sometimes demanded of her." (*Variety*, January 2, 1946)

"Paul Kelly ... is believable, but Kay Francis, as the head of the ring, and Otto Kruger, as her lieutenant, fail to make their characterizations convincing." (*Harrison's Reports*, November 10, 1945)

Wife Wanted

(Monogram, 1946) 73 min.
Released November 2, 1946.

Credits: Producers, Jeffrey Bernerd, Kay Francis; director, Phil Karlson; suggested by the novel ("Wife Wanted: An Unusual Human Story") by Robert E. Callahan; screenplay, Caryl Coleman, Sidney Sutherland; technical director, Dave Milton; assistant director, Doc Joos; production manager, William Calihan; musical director, Edward J. Kay; sound, Tom Lambert; "There Wasn't a Moon" by Edgar Hayes; camera, Harry Neumann; editor, Ace Herman; stylist, Lorraine MacLean; production manager, Glenn Cook; Miss Francis' gowns, Athena.

Cast: Kay Francis (Carole Raymond); Paul Cavanagh (Jeffrey Caldwell); Robert Shayne (Bill Tyler); Veda Ann Borg (Nola Reed); Teala Loring (Mildred Hayes); John Gallaudet (Lee Kirby); Barton Yarborough (Walter Desmond); Selmer Jackson (Lowell Cornell); Bert Roach (Arthur Mayfield); John Hamilton (Judge); Jonathan Hale (Philip Conway); Anthony Warde (Man); Sara Berner (Agnes); Charles Marsh (Tenant); Claire Meade (Tenant); Will Stanton (Squint); Paul Everton (Toland); Buddy Gorman (Newsboy); Shelby Payne (Secretary); Mabel Todd (Florist); Tim Ryan (Bartender); Barbara Woodell (Miss Shelton); Maurice Prince; Bob Alden (Messengers); Valerie Ardis (Nurse); *Wilbur Mack (Doctor); Budd Fine (Cop); Joseph J. Greene (Hector); Elaine Lange (Mrs. Wiley); George Carleton (Arthur Mayfield); Margo Woode (Miss Sheldon).*

THE FILM BEGINS WITH a newspaper ad: "WIFE WANTED — I have about $15,000 yearly income — don't drink, don't gamble, smoke, cuss or flirt. Age 33; 5 ft. 11; weigh 170. No children. I want good, kind mate who likes music, home and travel. Am seeking companion the usual way. State color eyes, hair. Send photo. Al Newman, Box XX-46, Hollywood, California." This has absolutely nothing to do with the rest of the movie.

Carole Raymond is a movie star whose agent has turned down two recent roles— they weren't right for her. He suggests, however, that she hook up with sleazy real estate agent Jeff Caldwell, who wants to form a partnership with a Hollywood star.

Carole takes Walter Desmond to look at some beachfront property. "A woman as lovely as you are shouldn't work at anything," he tells her, adding that he's fallen in love. She rebuffs him. "Carole, how much do you think you and your crooked partner have taken me for?" he suddenly asks.

She's puzzled. He tells her about an Arizona oil swindle that cost him $50,000 and a girl from the Friendship Club — a separate company that's next door to the real estate office — who tried to blackmail him. "Carole, I wanted you, and I didn't care what it cost me. Can't you understand that?"

He hands her a $40,000 certified check. Carole tries to call Jeff to see if things can be straightened out. A shadowy figure approaches Desmond, pushes him off the balcony, and steals the check. When Carole can't get in touch with Jeffrey, she returns to the balcony and finds Desmond has fallen to his death on the rocks.

A newspaper headline reveals that Desmond died in a "suicide leap." Jeff tells Carole to say and do what he asks or he'll implicate her. "I might suggest to the D.A. that you pushed him off of the cliff."

"I'm getting out," Carole says, but Jeff tells her he's already mixed her up in lots of crooked deals. "From now on, my dear, you're also a partner in the Friendship Club. You have some talents I can use in that line very, very profitably."

Carole gets drunk in a bar. When she wakes up, she finds Mildred Hayes—she'd once worked on a picture with her—in her room. "You were very kind to me last night, Miss Raymond. I'm in an awful lot of trouble, and, well, you told me I could come here and stay until things straightened out." Mildred's broke, has no friends, and is suicidal.

"That's the wrong way," Carole warns her. "It doesn't end troubles. It just makes greater ones for other people."

Meanwhile, newspaper reporter Bill Tyler, assigned to do a story on the Friendship Club, goes undercover as a Utah sheep rancher. Jeff sets up Bill with Carole. At dinner, Bill brings up the Walter Desmond incident, telling her he almost didn't come to the Friendship Club because of it.

Back at Carole's apartment, Mildred has some kind of a fit. She opens the window and looks down. It's a long way. She pulls herself away and begins to write something.

We're back at the nightclub. "I want you to go back to Utah before you get hurt," Carole warns him. She returns to her apartment to find Mildred having another fit. Carole sees the note: "Dear Carole: I'm sorry, but I'm too great a burden. Please forgive me, it is the only way out. Goodbye, Mildred." Carole calms Mildred.

Bill tells his editor that he thinks Carole knows something, and gives him an article that appears in the next day's paper: "A new angle to the mysterious death was uncovered today with rumors of an unidentified woman he met in a matrimonial agency."

Nola is the meanie who runs the Friendship Club. "When are you going to learn there's only one woman you can trust—your wife. And if you try any more smart stuff, I'll tell the whole world that I'm Mrs. Jeffrey Caldwell." She's jealous of Carole. "You're not falling for this dime store edition of a woman, are you?"

Jeff and Nola want to find Mildred, thinking

Kay still looked quite glamorous while playing a former movie star in *Wife Wanted* (1946).

Robert Shayne and Kay in *Wife Wanted* (1946).

she might be the mystery woman. When Mildred sees the newspaper article, she tells Carole about her connection to Walter Desmond — she'd fallen in love, got hurt, and asked for a refund, making a scene at the agency.

Jeff tells Carole to convince Bill to buy into the Arizona oil deal. She pitches the deal to Bill, but realizes she's falling in love with him. "Sometimes you set out to act a part, and then all of a sudden you're not acting," Carole tells Mildred.

Bill goes in on the deal, but while Carole's gone, Mildred has another fit. Nola tries to call Carole, but Mildred answers. "Oh, Carole, I knew you wouldn't forget me," she says before knowing who it is.

"Hello. Who is this?" Nola asks.

"Why, it's Mildred."

"Mildred? Mildred who?"

Mildred, who's a real honest-to-God dummy, finally hangs up. Nola tells Jeff that Mildred is at Carole's apartment. Guess what? Mildred has *another* fit. Carole can't get in touch with Mildred because when she calls, Mildred just stands there, *having a fit*, talking to herself. Mildred runs to the door, opens it, and it's Jeff.

He tries to get information from Mildred, but *she's having a fit*. Nola calls Jeff — why he answers Carole's phone we'll never know — and tells him Bill is a fraud. While Jeff's on the phone, Mildred tries to escape. She falls — well, actually *flings* herself down the stairs. While she lies unconscious at the bottom of the stairs, Jeff sneaks away.

Carole can't find Mildred in the apartment, but sees the phone off the hook — and Jeff's hat. Mildred has been taken to a hospital and has brain surgery — we're not kidding. "She'll be all right," the surgeon announces. He obviously doesn't know her.

When Carole shows up at Bill's room, he tells her he's on to her. "I happen to love you," she tells him.

"I am thinking of you as you really are," he

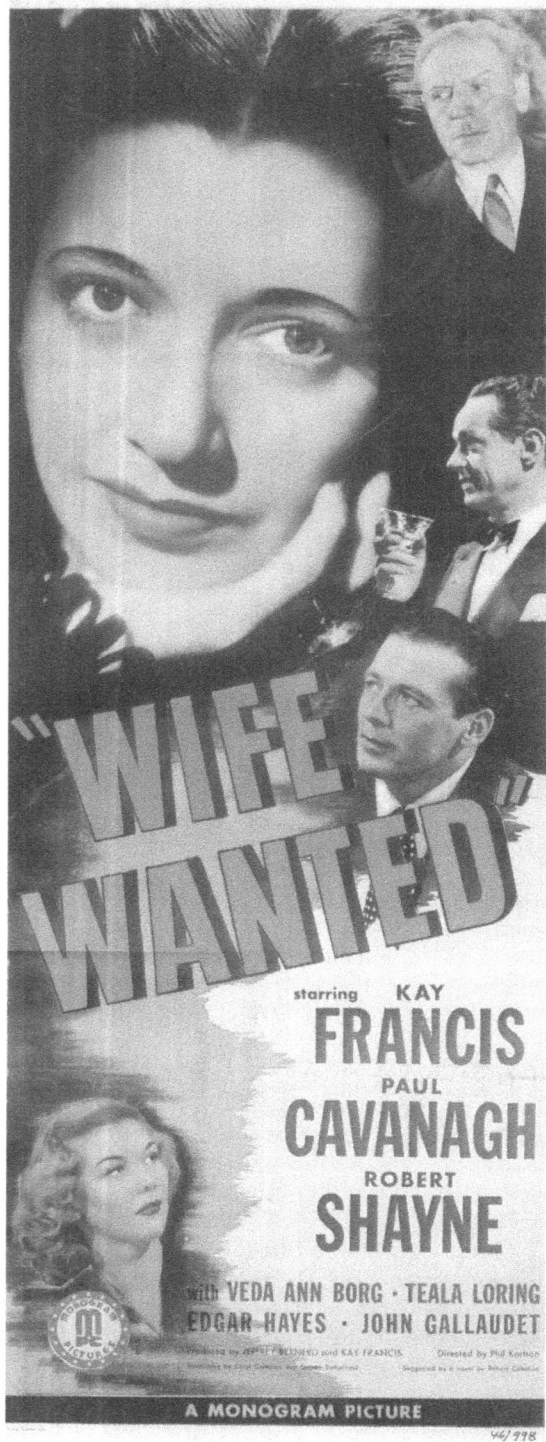

Kay Francis and cast featured on a half sheet movie poster for *Wife Wanted* (1946).

says. "One of Jeff Caldwell's come-ons. A very beautiful bait for suckers with bankrolls." (That couldn't have been an easy line to deliver.)

"Whatever I did to you, I did for just one reason," Carole says. "To get enough on Jeff Caldwell to put him behind bars."

Carole goes to see Jeff at the beach house, hoping to find Mildred. "You lied to me, Jeff. Mildred isn't here, is she?"

He tells her to endorse the Desmond check for $40,000. "You threw him over that balcony," she accuses.

"How very clever of you," he says, pointing a gun at her.

Before he can push her off the balcony, the police arrive. "I'm sorry, Carole, for the things I said to you," Bill says. "You see, I'm a reporter. I round up news, not sheep."

"We're both a couple of phonies, aren't we?" she asks.

"No, Carole. There's one thing about me that wasn't phony."

"Me, too. It's going to be sort of fun getting acquainted with the real us and not through a friendship club." They embrace on the balcony.

Production started June 19, 1946, and was completed July 3. The film is also known as *Shadow of Blackmail*. It was based on Robert E. Callahan's 1940 novel, *Wife Wanted: An Unusual Human Story*.

Kay received top billing in this bad, bad film—her last. It looks cheaply and quickly made. According to Ted Okuda, "One would be hard-pressed to defend the Monogram output; most were dull, shoddy efforts produced by those whose sole interest was to obtain a fast buck."[95]

This was the first and only time Kay's played dead drunk in a film. The performances are uniformly poor. This isn't to say, however, that it's unwatchable. In fact, this picture comes very close to being so bad it's good. Teala Loring was apparently trying out different acting exercises. Or something. Even Kay goes bug-eyed and short-hands this one. There are several obvious errors, such as the time when the telephone rings at the wrong cue. Kay says her line, and then pretends to be interrupted by the phone call. Kay was always a pro. Director Phil Karlson ended up having a long career—and certainly did improve. His other films included a (kind of) remake of *Scandal Sheet* (1952), *Kansas City Confidential* (1952), *Ben*

(1972), *Walking Tall* (1973), and his last, *Framed* (1975).

This was only the second time Kay played a movie star. The first was in 1929's *Marriage Playground*.

Promotional materials screamed: "Here's the Whole Shocking Story of So-Called 'Friendship Clubs' That Sell Marriage, Companionship and Romance, But Deliver Shame and Extortion!"

REVIEWS: "Too many divergent story lines in the screenplay by Caryl Coleman and Sidney Sutherland, and direction by Phil Karlson, which suffers from the same lack of cohesion, make this the least satisfying of the Bernard-Francis productions to date." (*Motion Picture Herald*, October 26, 1946)

"The story, which is not unusual, is too long drawn out, and the connection of some of the characters to the main plot is somewhat vague and confusing." (*Harrison's Reports*, October 26, 1946)

"This is an unsavory piece about silly older women who are easy victims for confidence men out to get their money. Kay Francis is miscast as a victim." (*Parents Magazine*)

APPENDIX A: STAGE APPEARANCES

1920/1921?—"Let's Not and Say We Did." Also known as "You Never Can Tell." Catholic School of St. Mary, Garden City, Long Island. Written by Katherine (Katty) Stewart and Katie Gibbs.

NOTES: Kay, then known as Katie Gibbs, attended the Catholic School of St. Mary in the fall of 1920, leaving in the spring of 1921. The musical play was so popular it was performed twice — once for students and then an encore performance for alumni. Kay, the tallest girl at school, was the male lead, and Katty played the female lead. Katty and Kay remained friends, and Katty accompanied Kay to Hollywood in 1929. One of Kay's lovers, Katty eventually moved to New Orleans.

November 9, 1925—"Shakespeare's Hamlet (In Modern Dress)" opened at the Booth Theater, New York. Staged by James Light, settings by Frederick S. Jones III, costumes by Aline Bernstein, produced by Horace Liveright. Cast included Charles Waldron, Basil Sydney, Ernest Lawford, Percy Waram, Stafford Dickens, Harry Green, Lawrence Tulloch, James Meighan, Julian Greer, Gordon Standing, John Burr, Herbert Ranson, Elmer Cornell, Walter Kingsford, John Burr, Bernard Savage, Adrienne Morrison, Helen Chandler, and Katharine (Kay) Francis, who appeared as Player Queen.

NOTES: The play ran for 88 performances. The Booth Theatre, located at 222 West 45th Street, opened on October 16, 1913. Designed by Henry B. Herts in the Beaux Arts style, it seated approximately 783. The theatre featured such stars as George Arliss, Jane Cowl, Ruth Gordon, Leslie Howard, Helen Hayes, Shirley Booth, Cornelia Otis Skinner, Julie Harris, Estelle Winwood, Melvyn Douglas, Rex Harrison, Alfred Lunt and Lynn Fontanne, James Cagney, and many others.

REVIEWS: "Shorn of the patterned trappings of tradition and squeezed into the tight and tailored clothes of today, 'Hamlet' ... seems neither better nor worse for the novel change.... Last billed, Katharine Francis did not rate a mention, unless one wants to include her in this comment: 'Some of the minor roles are not well played. The eccentricity of the modern 'Hamlet' is apparent chiefly when they repeat their lines clumsily.'" (*New York Times*, November 10, 1925)

NOTES: Kay had a one-night stand with fellow actor Basil Sydney in January 1926.

December 2, 1925—"The School for Scandal" opened at the Knickerbocker Theatre for one performance. Written by Richard Brinsley Sheridan. Produced by Basil Dean and George C. Tyler. Cast included Romaine Callender, May Collins, Henrietta Crosman, Joseph Dale, Jefferson De Angelis, Ben Field, O.P. Heggie, Mary Hone, Julia Hoyt, Ian Hunter, Anthony Kemble Cooper, Arthur Lewis, Neil Martin, Brian O'Neil, William Seymour, Harold Thomas, Philip Tonge. The Sunday performance was intended to preview the cast of the road show. Although she was not listed in the credits, Kay indicated in her diary that she appeared in this production. Kay later appeared in several motion pictures with Ian Hunter. Julia Hoyt was one of Kay's best friends.

April–September 1926—Kay Francis toured with the Stuart Walker Stock Company. (name spellings have been left as they appeared in playbills.)

Week of April 26, 1926, "White Collars" by Edith Ellis. Katherine Francis played Sally Van Luyn. Grand Opera House, Cincinnati, OH.

Week of May 3, 1926, "White Collars" by Edith Ellis. Katherine Francis played Sally Van Luyn. B.F. Keith's Theatre, Indianapolis, IN.

Week of May 10, 1926, "The Outsider" by Dorothy Brandon. B.F. Keith's Theatre, Indianapolis, IN.

Week of May 17, 1926, "Seventh Heaven" by Austin Strong. Kaye Francis played Arlette. B.F. Keith's Theatre, Indianapolis, IN.

Week of May 24, 1926, "They Knew What They Wanted" by Sidney Howard. Katharine Francis played Second Italian Mother. B.F. Keith's Theatre, Indianapolis, IN.

Week of May 31, 1926, "The Goose Hangs High" by Lewis Beach. B.F. Keith's Theatre, Indianapolis, IN.

Week of June 14, 1926, "Polly Preferred" by Guy Bolton. Katharine Francis played A Young Lady. B.F. Keith's Theatre, Indianapolis, IN.

Week of June 21, 1926, "White Collars" by Edith Ellis. Katherine Francis played Sally Van Luyn. Victory Theatre, Dayton, OH.

REVIEWS: "Katharine Francis as Sally Van Luyn, the rich sister of the hero of our story is splendid." "Quite the most stunning actress in the company is Katherine Francis, who plays the small role of Sally Van Luyn. We hope she may have more to do later."

Week of July 5, 1926, "Puppy Love" by Adelaide Matthews & Martha Stanley. Katherine Francis played Ivy. B.F. Keith's Theatre, Indianapolis, IN.

REVIEWS: "Katherine Francis also has the first real opportunity afforded her this season as the snappy stenographer, who doesn't indulge in necking parties and is 'pure as the snow,' but not drifting."

Week of July 12, 1926, "Puppy Love" by Adelaide Matthews & Martha Stanley. Katherine Francis played Ivy. Victory Theatre, Dayton, OH.

Week of July 19, 1926, "The Fall Guy" by James Gleason and George Abbott. Katherine Francis played Lottie. Victory Theatre, Dayton, OH.

Week of July 26, 1926, "The Old Soak" by Don Marquis. Cast included George Alison, Judith Lowry, Vivian Tobin, Larry Fletcher, Ernest Cossart, Victor Hammond, Margaret Douglass, John Thorn, Katherine Francis. Katherine Francis played Ina Heath. Grand Opera House, Cincinnati, OH.

REVIEWS: "Katherine Francis ... complete a cast that is uncommonly well balanced and singularly well qualified to bring forward all the good quality that 'The Old Soak' possesses." (*Cincinnati Enquirer*)

"A flash of genuine ability coupled with a magnetic personality was exhibited by Katherine Francis in her bit."

Week of August 2, 1926, "Maid Errant" by Robert Housum. Cast included George Alison, Ben Smith, Judith Lowry, Vivian Tobin, Ernest Cossart, George Meeker, Gertrude Rivers, Katherine Francis, Regina Stanfiel, Larry Fletcher, Elliot Cabot, Paul Wright, David Newell, Pauline Breustedt. Katherine Francis played Janet Wickham. Grand Opera House, Cincinnati, OH.

REVIEWS: "Almost a dozen charming young men and young women are included in the cast and contribute to the prevailing atmosphere of youthful animation." (*Cincinnati Enquirer*)

Week of August 9, 1926, "Justice" by John Galsworthy. Grand Opera House, Cincinnati, OH.

Week of August 16, 1926, "Dancing Mothers" by Edgar Selwyn & Edmund Goulding. Cast included Ben Smith, Teresa Dale, Ann Davis, Regina Stanfiel, Paul Wright, George Alison, Katherine Swan, Harry Ellerbe, Ernest Cossart, Adelaide Chase, Katharine Francis, Aldrich Bowker, Elizabeth Taylor, George Kinsey, David Newell, Owen Phillips, McKay Morris, Allen Steppler, Adelaide Kendall, Elliot Cabot, Boyd Agin. Katharine Francis played Irma Raymond. Grand Opera House, Cincinnati, OH.

REVIEWS: ... "Last night's audience at the Grand Opera House has the pleasure of witnessing one of the smoothest first-night performances of the season." (*Cincinnati Enquirer*)

Week of August 23, 1926, "Love Is Like That" by S.N. Behrman & Kenyon Nicholson. Cast included Aldrich Bowker, Teresa Dale, Ann Davis, Elizabeth Taylor, Elliot Cabot, Basil Rathbone, Ernest Cossart, Regina Stanfiel, Katherine Francis, Boyd Agin. Katherine Francis played Kay Gurlizt. Grand Opera House, Cincinnati, OH.

REVIEWS: "Teresa Dale, Elliot Cabot, and Katherine Francis do very clever work in the other principal roles." (*Cincinnati Enquirer*)

"Katherine Francis proved herself an accomplished vampire;" "She handles the cold and sophisticated touch with delightful finesse."

Week of August 30, 1926, "Beatrice and the Blackguard" by Ernest Goodwin. Cast included Harry Ellerbe, Edward Forbes, Katharine Frances, Ben Smith, Ellis Baker, George Alison, David Newell, Pauline Breustedt, Regina Stanfiel, Boyd Agin, Jack Storey, Owen Phillips, George Kinsey, Katherine Randolph, Perry Ivins, Elizabeth Taylor, Katherine Swan, Adelaide Chase, McKay Morris, Paul Wright, Aldrich Bowker, Malcolm Parker, Elliot Cabot, Gilbert Ornelas, Edward Forbes, George Somnes. Katharine Frances played Francesca. Grand Opera House, Cincinnati, OH.

NOTES: Kay rehearsed three additional roles for the Stuart Walker Stock Company: "Applesauce" by Barry Conners, "Candida" by George Bernard Shaw, and "The Swan" by Ferenc Molnar. However, she didn't appear in the productions.

January 21, 1927—"Damn the Tears" opened at the Garrick Theatre, NY. Produced by Alexander McKaig. Staged by Sigourney Thayer. Written by William Gaston. Cast included Reginald Barlow, Joyce Benner, Halliam Bosworth, Jean Bourdelle, Frederic A. Bryan, Elmer Cornell, Eleanor Griffith, Seth Kendall, Hugh Kidder, James Martin, Ralph Morgan, William S. Rainey, Florence Rylander, Joan

Storm, John Washburne, Harry Winston, Edwin Philips, Virginia Farmer. Settings by Norman Bel Geddes. Music by Ruth Warfield. Puppets by Remo Bufano. Portrait by Neysa McMein. Costume for Miss Griffith designed by Julia Hoyt. Other costumes by Kay Francis.

NOTES: Kay was briefly married to William Gaston. They married November 19, 1925, and the divorce was granted on September 21, 1927. The play ran for 22 performances. The Garrick Theatre, located at 65 W. 35th Street, was built in 1890 by Edward Harrigan. Named Harrigan's Theatre, the name was changed in 1895 to Garrick Theatre. In 1917, it was briefly known as Theatre du Vieux Columbier, before changing its name back to the Garrick Theatre. It was demolished in 1932.

REVIEWS: Alexander Woollcott described it as "confused and ... pitiable." Burton Davis wrote that it was "the queerest play of the season" and admitted that he was bewildered by it.

February 22, 1927 — "Crime" opened at the Eltinge Theater, NY. "Crime," a melodrama of 'New York's underworld,' in four acts, by Samuel Shipman and John B. Hymer. Cast included Sylvia Sidney, Douglass Montgomery, Mary Smith, Charles P. Mather, Clifton Self, Chester Morris, Earle Mayne, Kay Johnson, Gustav Yorke, Katherine Francis, Josephine Deffry, Walter D. Greene, James Rennie, Claude Cooper, Marvin Oreck, Jack LaRue, Michael Markham, Walter Power, Philip M. Sheridan, Barbara Barondess, Spurr K. Gould, Cleve Delland, Irving H. Rapper, Neill Bridges, Eddie Kelly, Jess Romer, Marie Cole, Jack Thomson, William Boulias, Carol Baldwin, John O'Meara, Charles P. Mather, E. F. Bostwick, John Ward, De Lancy Cleveland, R.H. Irving. Katherine Francis played Marjorie Grey. Staged by A. H. Van Buren; settings by P. Dodd Ackerman; produced by A. H. Woods. Costumes by Russeks. Lancaster Console Radio furnished by A. H. Grebe & Co., New York. Curtains and furniture upholstery by I. Weiss & Sons, New York. Hosiery by Van Raalte.

NOTES: Kay co-starred with playwright Hymer's son Warren in *One Way Passage* a few years later. She also remained friendly with actress Kay Johnson and co-starred with her in *Passion Flower*. Originally titled "The Crime Wave," the play was first produced with a different cast in Philadelphia in February 1925. In New York, it ran for 186 performances. Located at 236 West 42nd Street, the Eltinge opened on September 11, 1912. It was also once known as the Laff Movie, and is now a movie theatre known as the Empire Theatre. The architect was Thomas A. Lamb. It's been used for drama, vaudeville, burlesque, and movies. Other stars who appeared there include Jane Cowl, Pauline Frederick, Florence Reed, Estelle Winwood, Lionel Barrymore, Claudette Colbert, Laurence Olivier, Cecilia Loftus, Alice Brady, and Clark Gable. Seating capacity is almost 900.

Kay Francis in a sexy satin gown. Theater audiences expected Kay to be glamorous on stage.

REVIEWS: *The New York Times* reviewed the play on February 23, 1927, and described it as "four acts of a spectacular and fast-moving melodrama....A rowdy, amusing piece in which all the old hokum of crook drama has been excellently put together and well acted in a rapid performance." Billed as Katherine Francis, Kay's performance is not singled out. However, the reviewer does point out that "all of the cast are well selected and drilled."

"A melodramatic hippodrome." (Percy Hammond, *Herald-Tribune*)

"It poured out a hoard of thrills." (Frank Vreeland)

"Thumping melodrama." (Alexander Woollcott, *World*)

"Another exciting adventure in the theatre." (Burns Mantle, *Daily News*)

"A landslide." (Gilbert Gabriel, *Sun*)

"It appears to offer every promise of being a long time running mate to the galloping show called 'Broadway' and is as tightly and strongly knit." (E.W. Osborn, *Evening World*)

"A vivid, gripping and absorbing melodrama. I

confess that I enjoyed it as I haven't enjoyed a melodrama in seasons. It was such a complete expose of the art of crime." (Alan Dale)

October 1927—"Amateur Anne" opened. A New Comedy by Bayard Veiller and G.M. Fair. Cast included Sidney Eliot, A.J. Herbert, Katharine Francis, Dorothy Cox, Bennett Southard, James Hart, Gertrude Bryan, Allan Brooks, John Handley, Harry Bulger, Jr., Maurice Freeman, Jane Kennett, Isabel Dawn, Dora Kashinska, James B. Linhart, Fred Verdi, A.O. Huban, John Hanley. Katharine Francis played Lele Davis. Miss Bryan's song lyric by Frank Conlan. Music by Roy Webb. Gowns for Miss Bryan, Miss Francis and Miss Cox by Lord and Taylor's, The Misses Shop. Shoes for Miss Francis from Saks & Co.

NOTES: A handbill for the Bronx production advertised the play's virtues: "8 Snappy Broadway Night Club Girls .... A modern comedy half a step ahead of the front pages, telling the story of a girl who may be a queen on Long Island but is only a lady-in-waiting on Broadway. Featuring Gertrude Bryan, star of many musical comedies, and Allan Brooks, vaudeville headliner, movie star and stage leading man. Requiring three sets and more than 25 persons, including eight of the prettiest moths to be found in the glare of Broadway's night club lights." The tour included at least three play dates: **Week of October 5, 1927,** Shubert Theatre, Wilmington, DE [billed as Katherine]; **Week of October 10, 1927,** The Bronx Opera House, NY; **Week of October 17, 1927,** Parson's Theatre, Hartford, CT.

SYNOPSIS: "A Long Island society woman plays golf alone, takes morning walks, enjoys the air while her husband makes love to her woman house guest. The wife is pleasingly tolerant of her partner's love making and gin drinking. An actor is a week-end guest at her home. She likes him, seeks a divorce and aspires to the stage. She gets a part despite efforts of her actor friend to keep her out of the theatre. Of course she loves this actor. Her husband didn't want to get divorced, but finally is glad of it when his erstwhile wife bungles up her first appearance on stage. He marries the woman house guest who likes gin even as he [sic]. Then the actor marries the society woman now turned actress."

REVIEWS: According to the *Wilmington Every Evening,* "'Amateur Anne' is good entertainment for an evening." Other reviewers were less kind.

"The amateur quality of the work goes something beyond its title. Dialogue that supplies neither forward movement of the plot nor stimulus for the mind makes the first act a rather long drawn-out affair.... The members of the cast struggle with none too gracious roles." (*Hartford Daily Times,* October 18, 1927).

Another reviewer described Kay as "quite blase."

December 26, 1927—"Venus" opened at Theatre Masque, NY. "Venus," a comedy in three acts, by Rachel Crothers. Cast included Cecilia Loftus, Charles Hampden, Arnold Lucy, Tyrone Power, Patricia Collinge, Katharine Francis, Edward Crandall. Katharine Francis played Diana Gibbs. Settings by Livingston Platt; staged by Miss Crothers; produced by Carl Reed. "The Aviation costumes worn by Miss Loftus, Miss Francis and Mr. Crandall designed and furnished by Abercrombie & Fitch Co., New York City. Miss Loftus' and Miss Collinge's gowns designed by Evelyn McHorter. Executed by Lucile, of New York. Miss Collinge's and Mr. Power's flying clothes by Brooks Costume Company. Boots and Miss Collinge's shoes by I. Miller. Miss Loftus' shoes by Delman, New York City. Act One painted by Louis Kennett. Act Two painted by Oden Waller."

NOTES: The play had a preview on Sunday, December 25, and ran for eight performances. Tyrone Power's wife, Bertha Knight, died a few days before the opening. Married in 1917 to the great actor, she died on December 22, 1927. "Every one in the invited audience last evening was filled with sympathy for Mr. Power, whose wife died on Thursday. Cast in a frivolous, almost silly role, his task must have been peculiarly ungrateful. He played his part willingly and well." The Theatre Masque was built by the Chanin brothers in 1927. Designed by Herbert J. Krapp, its name was changed to the John Golden Theatre in 1937. The theatre became a movie house in the mid–1940s, but returned to legitimate theatre in the mid–1940s. It is located at 252 W. 45th Street.

SYNOPSIS: The plot concerns a magic pill containing pure intelligence. "Under the influence of the compound those who are preponderantly masculine turn feminine with a vengeance, and vice versa. Those who naturally come close to representing sex equality — in other words, the two young aviators, Diana Gibbs and Ross Hurst—change the least. As the doctor explains, they naturally tend toward pure intelligence. In the superadvanced state of life in Venus they have already witnessed beings who progress in terms of mind or of spiritual perception."

REVIEWS: *The New York Times* reviewer was not impressed: "Writing on an uncommonly imaginative theme, Rachel Crothers has put together an unimaginative play.... Her questions of sex equality and pure intelligence ... questions rather than answers.... The unfinished performance of the actors made for scanty enjoyment." Katharine Francis' performance is not mentioned in the review.

"The acting is satisfactory excepting in two particular instances. Katherine Francis and Edward Crandall could limber up considerably. They are not strong at any time, particularly in the first act." (*Billboard*, January 7, 1928)

"One of the stupidest. Far fetched yet unimaginative.... It is a comedy without laughs; a puerile, pseudo-intellectual creation.... Katherine Francis and Edward Crandall, for the purpose of the play, are presented as much alike as it is possible for two human beings of opposite sex to be that it kills interest." (*Variety*)

May 3–5, 1928—"Fast Company" [will be renamed "Elmer the Great"] played in Worcester, MA.

May 7–June 16, 1928—"Fast Company" played at the Tremont Theatre in Boston, MA.

June 18–September 22, 1928—"Elmer the Great" played at the Blackstone Theatre, Chicago. "Elmer the Great," a comedy in three acts, by Ring Lardner. Cast included Walter Huston, Lida MacMillan, Thomas V. Gillen, Nan Sunderland, Kate Morgan, Edith Luckett, Mark Sullivan, Tom Blake, Katharine Francis, Harold Healy, Rodney Hildebrand, Barney Thornton, Gordon Hicks, George Sawyer, Bill Bender, Henry Shelvey, Dan Carey, Charles Johnson, Jack Williams, Jack Clifford, Ted Newton, Fred de Cordova, Edgar Eastman, Everett Surratt, D.J. Hamilton, John Pierson, Arthur Finnigan, Edwin Walter, Mary Lohman. Katharine Francis played Evelyn Corey. Staged by Sam Forrest; produced by George M. Cohan. "Uniforms, Shoes and other baseball paraphernalia by A.G. Spaulding and Bros. Miss Sunderland's gowns by Sava Cola, New York. Miss Francis' gowns by Jenkins, New York. Fur coat worn by Miss Luckett furnished by Bonwit, Teller & Co. Miss Luckett's gowns by Saks, Fifth Ave., New York. Panatrope and records by courtesy of Brunswick-Balke-Collender Co., 623 So. Wabash Ave., Chicago."

NOTES: Kay had a tumultuous affair with fellow actor Harold Healy. Edith Luckett was the mother of Nancy Davis Reagan.

REVIEWS: "The entire cast, the baseball nine and the personages of the home town were carefully selected and the entire performance was most convincing. Nan Sunderland as Nellie Poole, Elmer's sweetheart, and Katherine Francis as Evelyn Corey, his actress friend, share honors in the juvenile feminine parts." (*Boston Globe*)

"Far and away better than the average summer fare.... The most refreshing comedy that has come to Chicago in many months.... A play abounding in keen satire, zestful humor and here and there touches of melodrama ... Katherine Francis as a show girl and Harold Healy as manager of the ball club were very good." (*Billboard Magazine*)

"'Tis a plain tale, told shrewdly and well told.... The play is acted to the nines by the performers.... Mr. Huston is ... just immense! ... [T]here is a new brunette beauty in Miss Francis." (*Chicago Tribune*)

September 24, 1928—"Elmer the Great" opened at the Lyceum Theatre, NY. It closed on October 27, 1928.

NOTES: The play ran for 40 performances, generally eight shows a week. Before the show opened on Broadway, it traveled to Worcester and Boston, MA, and Chicago; it played at the Blackstone for at least 11 weeks. Walter Huston was paid $1,000 a week, plus a percentage of the gross. Nan Sunderland was Walter Huston's mistress at the time and eventual wife. Unfortunately, he was still married to wife Bayonne, which resulted in at least one stormy backstage episode. "Elmer the Great" was used as the basis for three Hollywood films. The first was *Fast Company* (1929), directed by Edward Sutherland, and featuring Jack Oakie, Richard "Skeets" Gallagher, and Evelyn Brent in Kay's role. *Elmer the Great* (1933) was directed by Mervyn LeRoy and featured Joe E. Brown, Patricia Ellis, and Frank McHugh; Claire Dodd played Evelyn. *Cowboy Quarterback* (1939) was directed by Noel M. Smith with a cast including Bert Wheeler, Marie Wilson, and William Demarest. Gloria Dickson played Evelyn in this version. The Lyceum Theatre opened on November 2, 1903. Impresario Daniel Frohman had a peephole built into his private box upstairs so he could watch the stage. Located at 149 West 45th Street, it was designed by Herts and Tallent in the Beaux Arts style. Always used for legitimate theatre, it's also been known as the New Lyceum. Performers have included Billie Burke, Ethel Barrymore, Jeanne Eagels, John Garfield, Leslie Howard, Ina Claire, Judy Holliday, Maurice Chevalier, Alan Bates, John Gielgud, Sam Levene, Robert Preston, and Burgess Meredith.

REVIEWS: Billed *this* time as Katharine Francis, Kay received no individual mention in the review. However, the reviewer added, "With the assistance of an able cast, ably directed, Mr. Huston keeps 'Elmer the Great' on an even keel through all the story waters of Mr. Lardner's writing. In staging the comedy, Sam Forrest has shrewdly placed the burden of entertainment upon the acting." (*New York Times*, September 25, 1928)

"'Elmer the Great' is entertaining and amusing, thanks to the bitter and unrelenting humor of Ring Lardner and an unusually deft characterization by Walter Huston. As a play it is a trite and hackneyed piece of hokum ... Katherine Francis is attractive as the show girl." (*Billboard*, October 6, 1928)

"Woven about the vicissitudes of a thick-skulled baseball player, the new piece is intended to be a reflection of the comic highlights incident to the national game. Instead, it turns out to be a pleasantly animated comic strip.... Delightful characterizations are contributed by Kate Morgan, Katherine Francis, George Sawyer, Henry Shelvey, and Dan Carey." (*New York American*)

"Walter Huston's characterization of Elmer found great favor with last night's audience, and other parts were well played by Katherine Francis, Nan Sunderland and Harold Healy." (*New York Daily News*)

"These two are the cast's mainstay [Huston and Sunderland], plus Katherine Francis making her level-headed show girl stand up, as does Harold Healy with his assignment as the manager." (*Variety*)

September 20, 1945 — "Windy Hill" opened at the Shubert Theatre, New Haven, CT. A Comedy in three acts by Patsy Ruth Miller. Cast included Eileen Heckart, Donald McClelland, Lawrence Fletcher, Ruth Conley, Roger Pryor, Eulabelle Moore, Kay Francis, Grant Gordon, Earle Mayo, James Hagen. Kay played Antonia Connors. Produced by Ruth Chatterton in association with J.J. Leventhal. Staged by Miss Chatterton; Setting by Edward Gilbert.

September 20-22, 1945 — Shubert Theatre, New Haven, CT

September 24-October 6, 1945 — Forrest Theatre, Philadelphia, PA

October 8-13, 1945 — Ford's Theatre, Baltimore, MD

October 15-20, 1945 — Nixon Theatre, Pittsburgh, PA

October 22, 1945 — Colonial Theatre, Akron, OH

October 23, 1945 — Shea's Theatre, Jamestown, NY

October 24-25, 1945 — Auditorium, Rochester, NY

October 26-27, 1945 — Park Theatre, Youngstown, OH

October 29-November 3, 1945 — Davidson Theatre, Milwaukee, WI

November 5-10, 1945 — American Theatre, St. Louis, MO

November 12-17, 1945 — Cox Theatre, Cincinnati, OH

November 18-19, 1945 — Memorial Auditorium, Louisville, KY

November 20-21, 1945 — Memorial Hall, Dayton, OH

November 22-24, 1945 — Town Hall, Toledo, OH

November 26-28, 1945 — English Theatre, Indianapolis, IN

November 29-December 1, 1945 — Hartman Theatre, Columbus, OH

December 2-15, 1945 — Cass Theatre, Detroit, MI

Tour shut down for rewrites, resumed on December 25 in Buffalo, NY.

December 25-29, 1945 — Erlanger Theatre, Buffalo, NY

December 31, 1945-January 5, 1946 — Royal Alexandra Theatre, Toronto, Ontario

January 7, 1946 — Calurah Temple, Binghamton, NY

January 8, 1946 — Karlton Theatre, Williamsport, PA

January 9, 1946 — Rajah Theatre, Reading, PA

January 10, 1946 — Community Theatre, Hershey, PA

January 11-12, 1946 — Playhouse, Wilmington, DE

Tour shut down again for rewrites, resumed on January 25 in Norfolk, VA.

January 25-26, 1946 — Center Theatre, Norfolk, VA

January 28-February 2, 1946 — National Theatre, Washington, D.C.

February 4-5, 1946 — Auditorium, Hartford, CT

February 6, 1946 — Metro Theatre, Providence, RI

February 7, 1946 — Plymouth Theatre, Worcester, MA

February 8, 1946 — Lawlor Theatre, Greenfield, MA

February 9, 1946 — Academy of Music, Northampton, MA

February 11-16, 1946 — Royal Alexandra Theatre, Toronto, Ontario

February 18-23, 1946 — Hanna Theatre, Cleveland, OH

February 24-March 2, 1946 — American Theatre, St. Louis, MO

March 4, 1946 — Orpheum Theatre, Davenport, IA

March 5, 1946 — Iowa Theatre, Cedar Rapids, IA

March 6-May 25, 1946 — Harris Theatre, Chicago, IL

NOTES: The play had a tryout on August 13-18, 1945, at the Montclair Theatre in Montclair, New Jersey. Judy Holliday was in this cast. Other cast members included Bruce Covert, Ruth Conley, Eulabelle Moore, Robert Stewart, Louis Lytton, John E. Wilson, Ann Lawrence, and Jetti Preminger. Kay had an affair with fellow actor Roger Pryor during the run.

REVIEWS: "The combination of a personal appearance by a movie star and a premier performance of a play, risking pre–Broadway panning, last night brought out the best first night audience enjoyed by the Montclair Theater since its inception. Obviously the main drawing card in the deck was Kay Francis, since the play, 'Windy Hill,' was an unknown parvenu.... Miss Francis deserved the clapped palms she received loudly last night." (*Newark Evening News*)

"Miss Francis has her good moments; but the other moments probably make little difference. I'm not fooling myself that capacity audiences in Montclair last week were on hand to cheer Eulabelle

Moore as Arabella the Maid." (*Newark Sunday Call*, Aug. 19, 1945)

"Miss Francis, first time in legit in about 15 years and handicapped by a laryngitis attack, nevertheless handles her playwright assignment well. She looks very smart and attractive." (*Variety*, August 22, 1945)

"The play is rather loosely constructed and the first act in particular gets off very slowly. The second act climax is well timed, however, even though it is a little startling.... Miss Francis is a glamorous and intense stage personality and her work last night was watched with interest." (*New Haven Courier-Journal*)

"The plot is strictly formula.... This is all the more disappointing, because of the excellent performance given by the star, who is as much home on the stage as if she had never left it, and is obviously worthy of a more substantial vehicle." (*Baltimore Sun*)

"Miss Francis portrays the author's feminine protagonist with a brash sort of impertinence that is discreetly forceful and decidedly on the nimbly comic side. Her mellow, throaty voice is given many effective shadings." (*Washington Post*)

"The whole performance is easy and natural.... In all this Miss Francis and Mr. Pryor are admirable. The handsome Miss Francis has about her a gaminesque quality to match her husky contralto." (*Detroit Free Press*)

"...wry, intelligent, unaffected, he [Pryor] can't steal scenes outright from Miss Francis, because of her radiant looks and natural magnetism ... Miss Francis the woman correspondent is handicapped by not having a straight, true emotional course to sail." (*Buffalo Evening News*, December 26, 1945)

"Miss Francis is something of a rara avis, an actress who has built up a remarkable reputation as a film star and does not lose in effectiveness on the stage proper. Her voice ... is clearly produced and most pleasing ... to listen to. She is at graceful ease in moving about the stage." (*Toronto Evening Telegram*)

"Miss Francis handled her role with the skill that everyone expected and was just as appealing as she has been in her screen appearances." (*Reading Call*, January 10, 1946)

"A light, fluffy comedy. It's amusing but artificial. The act one curtain line by Miss Francis is one of the better bits of dialogue in the show. Incidentally, her wardrobe is all one would expect from a visiting film star. Miss Francis is properly glamorous in her role which lacks real acting demands." (*The Wilmington Morning News*, January 12, 1946)

"Kay Francis has a restless, uninhibited manner of acting, lacking subtlety of effect, but rich in vitality, warmth and high spirits. She has personal distinction, a vibrant melodious voice, and she suggests the intelligence and the volcanic temperament essential to the role she plays. She also knows what to do with a comedy line." (*Cleveland Plain Dealer*, February 19, 1946)

"It really was a pleasure to see Kay Francis in person. Kay Francis's presence adds a great deal to the play. Miss Francis, moreover, is one of our most pleasing theatrical personalities." (*Cleveland Press*, February 19, 1946)

"Miss Francis, obviously handicapped by a cold, exhibited much of the youthful glamour that won her fame on the screen years ago." (*Cedar Rapids Gazette*, March 5, 1946)

"'Windy Hill' ... isn't too bad if you don't expect too much.... No great shakes as an actress, she [Kay Francis] at least seems at home on the stage, and she has moments of considerable charm." (*Chicago Tribune*)

September 2, 1946—Kay Francis first appeared in "State of the Union" at the Hudson Theatre, NY, replacing Ruth Hussey in the role of Mary Matthews. The Pulitzer Prize winning play opened on November 14, 1945. Produced by Leland Howard. Written by Howard Lindsay and Russel Crouse. Cast included Hussey, Kay Francis (replacing Ruth Hussey), Minor Watson, Myron McCormick, Margalo Gillmore, Ralph Bellamy, Helen Ray, John Rowe, Howard Graham, Robert Toms, Herbert Heyes, Fred Ayers Cotton, G. Albert Smith, Maidel Turner, Madeleine King, Aline McDermott, Victor Sutherland, George Lessey. Staged by Bretaigne Windust. Settings by Raymond Sovey. Costumes by Emeline Roche. Gowns by Hattie Carnegie.

September 2, 1946–November 30, 1946—Hudson Theatre, New York, NY

January 20–May 17, 1947—Hudson Theatre, New York, NY

June 16–September 16, 1947—Hudson Theatre, New York, NY

September 18–20, 1947—Playhouse, Wilmington, DE

September 22, 1947—Karlton Theatre, Williamsport, PA

September 23–24, 1947—Rajah Theatre, Reading, PA

September 25–26, 1947—Lyric Theatre, Allentown, PA

September 27, 1947—Mosque Theatre, Harrisburg, PA

September 29–October 4, 1947—Opera House, Newark, NJ

October 6–7, 1947—Erie Theatre, Schenectady, NY

October 8, 1947—Empire, Syracuse, NY

October 9, 1947 — Strand Theatre, Ithaca, NY
October 10–11, 1947 — Auditorium, Rochester, NY
October 13, 1947 — Avon Theatre, Utica, NY
October 14–15, 1947 — Strand Theatre, Elmira, NY
October 16–18, 1947 — Erlanger Theatre, Buffalo, NY
October 20–22, 1947 — Town Hall, Toledo, OH
October 23, 1947 — Michigan Theatre, Ann Arbor, MI
October 24, 1947 — Palace Theatre, Flint, MI
October 25, 1947 — Temple Theatre, Saginaw, MI
October 27, 1947 — Michigan Theatre, Jackson, MI
October 28, 1947 — Michigan Theatre, Lansing, MI
October 29, 1947 — Bijou Theatre, Battle Creek, MI
October 30, 1947 — State Theatre, Kalamazoo, MI
October 31–November 1, 1947 — Keith's Theatre, Grand Rapids, MI

November 3–9, 1947 — Davidson Theatre, Milwaukee, WI
November 10–11, 1947 — Parkway Theatre, Madison, WI
November 13, 1947 — Auditorium, LaCrosse, WI
November 14–15, 1947 — Auditorium, St. Paul, MN
November 17, 1947 — Coliseum, Sioux Falls, SD
November 18, 1947 — Orpheum Theatre, Sioux City, IA
November 19, 1947 — KRNT, Des Moines, IA
November 20–22, 1947 — Music Hall, Kansas City, MO
November 24, 1947 — Auditorium, St. Joseph, MO
November 25, 1947 — Municipal Auditorium, Topeka, KS
November 26, 1947 — Majestic Theatre, Wichita, KS
November 27, 1947 — Convention Hall, Tulsa, OK
November 28–29, 1947 — Home Theatre, Oklahoma City, OK
December 1, 1947 — Paramount Theatre, Amarillo, TX
December 2, 1947 — Majestic Theatre, Wichita Falls, TX
December 3–4, 1947 — Melba Theatre, Dallas, TX
December 5, 1947 — Paramount Theatre, Austin, TX
December 6, 1947 — Texas Theatre, San Antonio, TX
December 8–9, 1947 — Music Hall, Houston, TX
December 10, 1947 — Auditorium, Beaumont, TX
December 12–16, 1947 — Poche Theatre, New Orleans, LA
December 18–20, 1947 — Erlanger Theatre, Atlanta, GA
December 25–27, 1947 — Auditorium, Louisville, KY
December 29, 1947 — Coliseum, Evansville, IN
December 30–January 3, 1948 — English Theatre, Indianapolis, IN
January 5–6, 1948 — Shrine Mosque, Peoria, IL
January 7, 1948 — Fischer Theatre, Springfield, IL
January 8, 1948 — Palace Theatre, Rockford, IL
January 9, 1948 — Palace Theatre, South Bend, IN

Kay and Ralph Bellamy on a *State of the Union* playbill.

January 10, 1948—University Theatre, Lafayette, IN

January 12–17, 1948—Shubert Lafayette, Detroit, MI

January 18–23, 1948—Hartman Theatre, Columbus, OH

NOTES: Helen Hayes provided the playwrights with the idea for the play in 1945. She suggested a play based on a candidate much like Wendell Wilkie, but when the play was finished she turned it down, deeming it too political. Kay Francis replaced Ruth Hussey when Hussey became pregnant. Kay left the show in November to undergo abdominal surgery. She was replaced by Edith Atwater until her return in January 1947. The show also closed from May 18 to June 15, 1947. The play finally closed at the Hudson Theatre on September 16, 1947 after 765 productions. It then went on a successful road tour. Lindsay and Crouse kept the material fresh by frequently rewriting to include current events. For example the candidate, played by Ralph Bellamy, read a newspaper excerpt—and the line was changed in almost every performance. In other productions, Kay was supported by Forrest Orr, Ben Lackland, Eleanor Wilson, K. Elmo Lowe, Ruth Rickaby, Henry Craig Neslo, Will Scholz, Donald McClelland, Sanford McCauley, Marion Green, Dorothy Paxton, Adnia Rice, Ruth Conley, Will Scholz, and Robert Strange. Kay was hospitalized on January 23, 1948, when she received a serious burn in a well-publicized incident involving her stage manager and lover, Hap Graham. Erin O'Brien-Moore replaced her for the rest of the tour, including the Hartman Theatre, Columbus, OH; Ohio Theatre, Lima, OH (January 26); Ohio Theatre, Mansfield, OH (January 27); Auditorium, Newark, OH (January 28); and Virginia Theatre, Wheeling, WV (January 29–30). The tour closed on February 7 in Pittsburgh, PA. The Hudson Theatre is located at 139 West 44th Street. It opened on October 19, 1903. The architect was J. B. McElfatrick and Co. It is no longer in use. It was also known as the Savoy. The play was made into a 1948 movie, directed by Frank Capra, titled *State of the Union* (the British title was *The World and His Wife*). The cast included Spencer Tracy and Katharine Hepburn (playing Kay's role).

REVIEWS: "We've seen it with our own eyes—Kay Francis' performance in 'State of the Union' at the Hudson—and it's good!... We liked, too, the marital relationship she and Bellamy established. Though the Matthews' marriage has slipped from its firm foundation, Miss Francis and Mr. Bellamy make the audience feel that the old flame still burns. To the ladies: Kay Francis can still wear clothes. She's handsome ... lovely ... striking ... sensational ... her black dinner dress, and a DRU-EAM in her third act white crepe with sequins evening dress." (*New York Post*, September 29, 1946)

"Her appearance and performance delighted a capacity audience. Miss Francis was beautifully gowned, and the stage settings were of first order. The audience demanded four curtain calls." (*Ithaca Journal*, October 10, 1947)

"One of Hollywood's and the stage's loveliest ladies, Kay Francis acquitted herself admirably. Miss Francis was every bit the star of the production." (*Kalamazoo Gazette*, October 31, 1947)

"Miss Francis, veteran of stage and screen, satisfactorily displayed her beauty and modeled some very lovely suits and gowns, including a green ensemble, a gray suit, a chartreuse negligee, and a svelte black evening frock." (*Grand Rapids Herald*, November 1, 1947)

"She makes a stunning looking heroine, but she insists on portraying her as a Great Lady." (*Wisconsin State Journal*, Madison, WI, November 1, 1947)

"Miss Francis, one of Hollywood's most glamorous stars of the 30s, has a great deal of charm which compensates for her tendency to over-dramatize her role. In the costumes she wears, she obtains her right to the title of one of the 10 best-dressed women in the country. As a matter of interest to the fashion-minded, the hemline of her suits is not too low, a becoming 14 inches." (*Houston Chronicle*, December 9, 1947)

"Miss Francis, an accomplished actress, seemed not to be getting the most out of her part. Perhaps it was the small and not too responsive audience. The topical laugh lines which usually pull down the house were getting over just about half way, and the whole cast seemed a little disappointed." (Norton Spayde, *Amarillo Daily News*, December 2, 1947)

"Miss Francis, beautifully gowned, proved herself as capable an actress on stage as she so often revealed on screen. Her low, vibrant voice is her greatest asset. She comes through in her big moments, does a drinking scene admirably and her big speech, her plea for the next generation, was acting of high caliber." (*South Bend Tribune*, January 10, 1948)

"Miss Francis makes of the cooled wife of the man persistently nibbled by the presidential bug a gay and humorous person, bearing with rueful laughter the attitude of compromise of a husband troubled not only by the impact of practical politics but by the interference of another woman. The cast is uniformly excellent." (*Detroit Free Press*, January 13, 1948)

"Miss Francis' husky voice—and the ladies in the audience will insist, her gowns and dresses—make her an especially regal potential first lady. She handled the sharp lines of Mary Matthews exceedingly well." (*Detroit Times*, January 13, 1948)

"Kay Francis plays the wise wife, Mary Matthews, and brings much more than a handsome appearance to the role, although her stunning gowns occasionally lure the feminine portion of the audience, and the male, too, away from the business at hand." (*Detroit News*, January 13, 1948)

"Miss Francis is an attractive Mary Matthews through most of the play." (*Columbus Dispatch*, January 19, 1948)

"Miss Francis managed to give all the speeches of Mary Matthews with the right emphasis. Entirely at home in the role, she set the tempo for the play." (*Wilmington Journal*)

"It was Kay Francis all the way.... True, the supporting cast was of exceptional caliber, but the success of the ... production can be attributed directly to the star headliner. Miss Francis, as charming and graceful as ever, may be remembered best from her motion picture appearance for sophistication and her well-chosen wardrobe." (*Syracuse Herald-Journal*)

"Her appearance and performance delighted a capacity audience.... Her personal triumph, set off by sparkling performances by the featured players and other members of the cast, was achieved in spite of a heavy cold.... Miss Francis was beautifully gowned." (*Ithaca Journal*)

"That outstanding example of an American play which says something, 'State of the Union,' returned to the Auditorium last evening, and it struck this three-time onlooker as being as glittering and effective as ever.... Kay Francis acted Mary in tiptop style." (*Rochester Democrat and Chronicle*)

"An appreciative audience applauded Miss Francis' performance, and, we suspect, her costumes, for she has a model's figure and wears her clothes well.... Although Miss Francis obviously made a hit with the audience, she seemed less convincing to us than she had in the New York production." (*Rochester Times-Union*)

"The current company headed by the handsome and well-groomed ex–Hollywoodian, Kay Francis, was quite acceptable.... Miss Francis and her associates employ ... the road show style.... This is broad, expansively dramatic, heavily underscored.... Miss Francis, looking as everyone remembers her from the screen, played with charm, dignity and force." (*Dallas Morning News*)

"The fashion show was staged by lovely brunette Kay Francis, who displayed both her dramatic and physical charm.... As for the play, it is still as funny as anything on the boards.... It is frothy, smart, fast and satirical.... Miss Francis acted rings around Irene Hervey [in a previous performance]. " (*Atlanta Constitution*)

June 7, 1948—"The Last of Mrs. Cheyney" opened at the McCarter Theatre, Princeton, NJ. Written by Frederick Lonsdale. Cast included Fredd Wayne, Wendy Atkin, Mary Fickett, Oliver Thorndike, Mabel Taylor, Nancy Clark, Joel Ashley, Jack Hartley, Kay Francis, Frances Brant, Arthur Marsh, Harold Kennedy, Paul Hennesy. Kay played Mrs. Cheyney. Staged by Jerome Shaw. Scenery and Lighting by Francis M. Mahard, Jr.

Week of:

June 7, 1948—McCarter Theatre, Princeton, NJ

June 14, 1948—Kenley Players, Deer Lake Theatre, Orwigsburg, PA

June 28, 1948—Cape Playhouse, Dennis, MA

July 5, 1948—Summer Theatre, Boston, MA

July 12, 1948—Playhouse, Ivoryton, CT

July 19, 1948—Lake Whalom Playhouse, Fitchburg, MA

July 26, 1948—North Shore Players, Marblehead, MA

August 3, 1948—Spa Theatre, Saratoga Springs, NY

August 10, 1948—Windsor Theatre, Bronx, NY

August 17, 1948—Flatbush Theatre, Brooklyn, NY

August 23, 1948—Crest Theatre, Long Beach, NY

August 30, 1948—Auditorium Theatre, Atlantic City, NJ

September 6, 1948—Brighton Theatre, Brooklyn, NY

September 20, 1948—Montclair Theatre, Montclair, NJ

January 9–14, 1950—Penthouse Theatre, Atlanta, GA

NOTES: Kay began an affair with Joel Ashley after auditioning him for this role. In other productions, Kay was supported by Stiano Braggiotti, William Weaver, Peter Dane, Dorothy Elder, Priscilla Weaver, Jerome Shaw, Jean Arden Cobb, Elizabeth Ayers, David White, Myrtle Tannahill, E. Earle Mayo, Carl Betz, Joe Starr, Jean Barnes, Jane Norvell, Ken Brunner, Elsbeth Hofmann, Barbara Holloran, Frank Lyon, Pamela Simpson, Robert Fisher, and James Reese. The concerto "played" by Kay in the first scene was composed for her by Phil Saltman of the Saltman School of Music in Boston, Massachusetts. "The Last of Mrs. Cheyney" was made into a film in 1929, which starred Norma Shearer, along with Basil Rathbone, Hedda Hopper, and Maude Turner Gordon. It was directed by Sidney Franklin. A 1937 film, directed by Richard Boleslawski and Dorothy Arzner, starred Joan Crawford, Robert Montgomery, William Powell, and Frank Morgan. *The Law and the Lady* (1951) was also loosely based on this play. This version, directed by Edwin Knopf, starred Greer Garson,

Michael Wilding, Fernando Lamas, Marjorie Main, and Margalo Gillmore.

REVIEWS: "Beautiful Kay Francis needs no introduction to playgoers....'The Last of Mrs. Cheyney,' a comedy with an English background ... gives ample chance for her to wear smart clothes with the inimitable Francis chic...." (*Princeton Packet*, June 14, 1948)

"She ably acted the part of Mrs. Cheyney, but her scene before the final curtain, during which her voice was choked with emotion and her eyes were filled with tears, made the spectator wish that she had attempted a straight dramatic role." (*Fitchburg Sentinel*)

"Miss Francis, in addition to an aura of Hollywood glamour, can act, and what more need to be said in her praise? If she fails to stir any particular emotions—and who on a warm summer night wants emotions stirred—it is because the playwright doesn't permit it." (*The Falmouth Enterprise*)

"Kay Francis is stunning as Mrs. Cheyney, and she is ably supported particularly by the men of the cast." (*Boston Globe*)

"Kay Francis, the attractive screen star who has never played on the stage in this city, was well advised to select 'The Last of Mrs. Cheyney' for her tour of the strawhat circuit this summer.... It is a well turned piece, well suited to Miss Francis' personality, good looks, and unfailing sense of style." (*Boston Herald*)

"It is always a pleasure to see a gracious and beautiful star, famous for the most part through the Hollywood medium, step forth behind the footlights and prove that she is every bit as skilled and effective on the legitimate stage.... Miss Francis gives a poised and completely satisfying performance." (*The Shore Line Times*, Ivoryton, CT)

"The star injects more than considerable warmth into the current Mrs. Cheyney, and there was no doubt as to what the local customers thought about her at the opening night curtain. She got a small ovation from subway circuit clients." (*Billboard Magazine*, Brooklyn, NY)

"Kay Francis and Joel Ashley got an enthusiastic reception at the Flatbush Theater last night, when 'The Last of Mrs. Cheyney' opened for a week's run. Miss Francis, a popular screen as well as stage star, appeared in a series of stunning gowns, which were of particular interest to the women of the audience.... Joel Ashley and Miss Francis made an excellent team." (*Brooklyn Daily Eagle*)

"There they will see Kay Francis radiantly traversing one of the thinnest and at the same time one of the most beguiling presentations of many a season.... Miss Francis, as charmingly assured and stylishly gowned as ever, appears as Mrs. Cheyney." (*Newark Evening News*)

December 25, 1948—"Favorite Stranger" opened at the Strand Theatre in Elmira, NY. Produced by Jules J. Leventhal. Written by Eleanore Sellars. Cast included Joel Ashley, Kay Francis, Gordon Mills, Paul Langton. Kay played Chalice Chadwick. Directed by Leon Michel. Setting by Louis Kennel.

December 25, 1948—Strand Theatre, Elmira, NY

December 27–January 1, 1949—Hanna Theatre, Cleveland, OH

January 3–8, 1949—Royal Alexandria Theatre, Toronto, Ontario

January 10, 1949—Shea's Theatre, Erie, PA

January 11, 1949—Park Theatre, Youngstown, OH

January 12, 1949—Colonial Theatre, Akron, OH

January 13–15, 1949—Town Hall, Toledo, OH

January 17–29, 1949—Shubert Lafayette Theatre, Detroit, MI

January 31–February 5, 1949—American Theatre, St. Louis, MO

February 7, 1949—Shrine Mosque, Peoria, IL

February 8, 1949—Palace Theatre, Rockford, IL

February 9, 1949—Parkway Theatre, Madison, WI

February 10–12, 1949—Davidson Theatre, Milwaukee, WI

February 14, 1949—Auditorium, St. Paul, MN

February 15, 1949—Chateau Theatre, Rochester, MN

February 16–19, 1949—Lyceum, Minneapolis, MN

February 20, 1949—Virginia Theatre, Wheeling, WV

February 21, 1949—Hippodrome, Marietta, OH

February 24, 1949—Oklahoma City, OK

February 25, 1949—Auditorium, Louisville, KY

February 26, 1949—Auditorium, Lexington, KY

February 28, 1949—Auditorium, Ponca City, OK

March 1–2, 1949—Arcadia Theatre, Wichita, KS

March 3, 1949—Memorial Hall, Indianapolis, IN

March 4–5, 1949—Music Hall, Kansas City, MO

March 7–8, 1949—Majestic Theatre, Fort Worth, TX

March 9–10, 1949—Melba Theatre, Dallas, TX

March 11, 1949—Paramount Theatre, Austin, TX

March 12, 1949—Music Hall, San Antonio, TX

March 15, 1949—Municipal Auditorium, Shreveport, LA

March 16–23, 1949—Poche Theatre, New Orleans, LA

March 24, 1949—Auditorium, Jackson, MS

March 25–26, 1949—Auditorium, Memphis, TN

March 27, 1949—Louisville, KY (cancelled)

March 28–April 2, 1949—Nixon Theatre, Pittsburgh, PA

April 3–4, 1949—Wheeling, WV (cancelled)

NOTES: An advertising flyer described the plot in this way: "A Wise & Witty Comedy on Love Affairs & Marriage." The play's premiere, at the Strand Theatre in Elmira, New York, on Christmas Day 1948 was attended by the author, producer, and director. The publicity materials described the play in this way: "'Favorite Stranger' is a gay comedy which handles the modern problem of love affairs and divorce with consummate tact and humor. Chalice Chadwick (Kay Francis) is the long neglected wife of a man who has forgotten to return from Paris at the war's end. A handsome bachelor moves in next door and, being a doctor, prescribes a more interesting social life. But a naval commander moves faster than the doctor and Chalice finds herself in the enjoyable position of breakfasting with two charming men every Sunday morning. When her husband returns unexpectedly, ready to resume his marriage but with one eye cast wistfully toward the delights of love in Paris, Chalice is truly in a dilemma. When any woman has only one man in love with her, life can get pretty complicated. And, even with the best of intentions, the three men in love with Chalice cause her a great deal of trouble ... all of it handled with such underlying sympathy and humor that the net result of 'Favorite Stranger' is sheer entertainment." This was Eleanore Sellars' first play. A journalist and short story writer, the Pittsburgh native won an award for her first mystery novel, *Murder a la Mode*. She worked on this play while recovering from spinal surgery. It was hoped the play would move on to Broadway, but the lukewarm response led to its closing.

Kay's wardrobe included outfits totaling $3,500. The clothing was custom-designed for her by Bergdorf Goodman, Fifth Avenue in New York.

REVIEWS: "Kay Francis and three talented supporting players last night tendered Elmira a splendid Christmas gift." The review further described the cast as "a live and competent quartet of players in a better-than-average comedy. The company didn't have to do any milking to get a nice run of curtain calls." (*Star Gazette*, December 26, 1948)

"Even the glamorous Kay in black taffeta dress with two red roses on the behind hardly make an evening in the theatre. Miss Francis tries very hard.... She gives her character a lot of charm and vivacity. But the dialogue and the character delineation just aren't there." (*Cleveland Press*, Dec. 28, 1948)

"Kay Francis is potentially a great actress. She has a lovely appearance, a musical voice, and an arresting individuality. Her whole composition is essentially theatrical.... Now and then she will hit a line exactly right, or create a striking effect of mood and character, and you can see the fine actress shining through the restlessness and overemphasis." (*Cleveland Plain Dealer*, Dec. 28, 1948)

"Kay Francis, in her own special way, convinced a Monday Majestic audience that strangers really are 'The Nicest People' with a frothy comedy. The dialogue is spicy and just right for Miss Francis. Women in the audience were anxious, and well pleased, to see Miss Francis' $3500 wardrobe." (Fort Worth, March 8, 1949)

"The handsome brunette Miss Francis has a tailor-made vehicle. She is decoratively gowned in a number of changes of costumes with a nice run of moods to match.... Miss Francis tosses off her lines for the laughs with an eye to timing." (*Dallas Morning News*, March 11, 1949)

"The female part of the audience seemed as much impressed with her stunning wardrobe as the main part was with her alluringly feminine smoothness. She has a sort of adult sex appeal without vulgarity, that seems to have become a lost art in recent years." (*Toronto Globe and Mail*)

"The play's only merit as entertainment lies in the fact that it does provide Miss Francis with an opportunity to wear some very becoming garments, to be coy as all get out, to play a little ping-pong with philosophy, and finally to wind up in the arms of a handsome actor called Joel Ashley." (*Milwaukee Journal*)

"The Eleanore Stellars comedy, which has given Miss Kay Francis another fashion show, and little else, has the look and feel of the sleek magazine stories... Miss Francis has, of course, walked through this type of stuff so often that she could do it with her eyes shut." (*Pittsburgh Sun-Telegraph*)

June 3, 1949—"Let Us Be Gay" opened at the Bucks County Playhouse, New Hope, PA. Written by Rachel Crothers. Cast included St. Clair Bayfield, Ruth White, Viola Roache, June Dayton, Joel Ashley, Kay Francis, Lewis Martin, Michael Sivy, Dorothy Elder, Henry Jones. Kay played Kitty Brown. Staged by Gerald Savory. Settings by Paul Morrison.

Week of:

June 3, 1949—Bucks County Playhouse, New Hope, PA

June 13, 1949—Lake Whalom Playhouse, Fitchburg, MA

June 21, 1949—Drama Festival, Worcester, MA

June 27, 1949—Westchester Playhouse, Mt. Kisco, NY

July 4, 1949—Pocono Playhouse, Mountain Home, PA

July 11, 1949—Berkshire Playhouse, Stockbridge, MA

July 18, 1949—Summer Theatre, Boston, MA

July 25, 1949—Olney Theatre, Olney, MD

August 3, 1949—Kenley Players, Lakewood Theatre

August 11, 1949—Spa Theatre, Saratoga Springs, NY

August 15, 1949—Country Playhouse, Fayetteville, NY

August 22, 1949—Summer Theatre, Sea Cliff, NY

August 29, 1949—John Drew Theatre, East Hampton, NY

September 6, 1949—Maryland Theatre, Baltimore, MD

October 22, 1949—Penthouse Theatre, Atlanta, GA

November 7, 1949—Greater Hartford Drama Festival, Hartford, CT

March 8, 1950—Sombrero Playhouse, Phoenix, AZ

March 27, 1950—Penthouse Theatre, Jacksonville, FL

June 19, 1951—Bill Green's Arena Theatre, Pittsburgh, PA

June 26, 1951—The Play House, Sharon, CT

NOTES: The film version of Rachel Crothers' play was directed by Robert Z. Leonard. The 1930 film featured dialogue by Frances Marion and Lucile Newmark, and a cast headed by Norma Shearer; other cast members included Marie Dressler, Sally Eilers, Rod La Rocque, Gilbert Emery, and Hedda Hopper.

REVIEWS: The *Fitchburg Sentinel* was very impressed with Kay, finding her role "tailor-made for her talents," and noting, "The selection of Rachel Crothers' sprightly comedy and Kay Francis as its star was a happy combination.... Her flair for comedy was apparent throughout the production, but her characterizations during the dramatic episodes on the balcony and in the last act constituted the high spots of the play." (June 14, 1949)

"Let Us Be Gay' is the type of vehicle in which Miss Francis is at her best. It shows her vivacious character, the clever manner in which she can read lines with that peculiar but effective voice.... This sterling actress has lost none of her charm, nor poise, nor those fetching mannerisms made so telling in screen close-ups." (*Worcester Telegram*, June 22, 1949)

"The major portion of her career has been before the camera. Such a history, in general, does not forecast stage success, the techniques being considerably at variance. Miss Francis, however, carries it off with a high degree of credit." (*Berkshire Eagle*, Stockbridge, MA)

"Miss Francis is most wholeheartedly in favor of making the evening crackle if possible. She bounces into every line and situation with the fervor of a true summer theatre star, a woman who chose her vehicle and never distrusts her judgment." (*Washington Star*, Olney, MD)

"Histrionically and sartorially resplendent, Miss Francis dominates the stage every moment she graces it. She is alternately gay and romantic.... Miss Francis turns on the floodgates of her very complete emotional nature for audience sympathy and admiration." (*Albany Times Union*, Saratoga Springs, NY)

"The entire company rates an 'A' for accomplishment in putting the play over with a bang.... Miss Francis, who appeared in Syracuse last season in 'State of the Union,' is an accomplished actress, and adept at tossing a smart line with maximum effect. Also, she is extremely easy to look at." (*Syracuse Herald-Journal*, Fayetteville, NY)

"Miss Francis postures, poses and glitters her way through her part." (*The Saratogian*, August 9, 1949)

"Miss Francis set the stage for the play with her performance. She was never lovelier, or more enthusiastic about a part in the movies or on the stage. She had the audience on the tip of their seats with her every line, her every move." (*Atlanta Constitution*)

"The comedy again affords theatergoers an opportunity to see Kay Francis, the charming star of both stage and screen, who gives another flawless performance as Kitty Brown." (*Knickerbocker News*, Saratoga Springs, NY)

"The Country Playhouse had the largest Monday night attendance since its initial opening.... The play is distinctive for the brilliance, comedy and forthrightness of its script both for the lead and supporting cast. There was constant laughter and applause throughout the amusing and complicated story ... 'Let Us Be Gay' sparkles from start to finish, direction is speedy, never a dull moment, and costuming definitely on the elegant side." (*Syracuse Post-Standard*, Fayetteville, NY)

"Miss Crothers is no Noël Coward and some of the dialogue sounds like the *Cosmopolitan* magazine issue of December 1926 but there is some humor in the situation and the acting is ... acceptable. Miss Francis—bless her—is as attractive as ever. She looks like the proverbial million (only a half million in 1926) and makes an effective characterization as she weaves and bobs in a dusty situation." (*Pittsburgh Post Gazette*)

May 23, 1950—"Goodbye, My Fancy" opened at the Flatbush Theatre in Brooklyn, NY. A Comedy by Fay Kanin. Cast included Joel Ashley, Alison Prescott, Jane Wurster, Marie Phillips, Aline McDermott, Harold Walters, Alfred Garr, JoAnne Flanigan, Haila Stoddard, Kay Francis, Florence Sundstrom, Fay Sappington, Isobel Robins, Jane Owen, Josef Draper, Al Boylen, Frank Albertson,

Guy Arbury. Kay played Agatha Reed. Staged by Tom Donovan. Settings by Donald Oenslager.

Week of:

May 23, 1950— Flatbush Theatre, Brooklyn, NY

May 30, 1950— Windsor Theatre, Bronx, NY

June 6, 1950— Central Theatre, Passaic, NJ

June 13, 1950— Brighton Beach Theatre, Brooklyn, NY

June 27, 1950— Strand Theatre, Rockville Centre, NY

July 3, 1950— Summer Theatre, Norwich, CT

July 10, 1950— Summer Theatre, Somerset, MA

NOTES: "Goodbye, My Fancy was made into a film in 1951. Kay's part was played by Joan Crawford, and supported by Robert Young, Frank Lovejoy, Eve Arden, and Janice Rule. The director was Vincent Sherman.

REVIEWS: "Kay Francis is an extremely agreeable substitute for her predecessors in the shoes of the congresswoman who returns to her alma mater for an honorary degree and an effort to recapture a lost love of 25 years, and opening night left no doubt as to her draw with the customers." (*Billboard Magazine*, Brooklyn, NY)

"Kay Francis failed to recapture the fancy of her college days last night, but won a lot of new friends and influenced an opening night audience at the Norwich summer theatre. To the play has good dialogue, contains a deft balance of comedy and pathos, and in general provides an amusing evening.... Miss Francis skillfully handles the difficult assignment in the production." (*New London*, Norwich CT)

"Miss Francis captured her audience with her dynamic personality and portrayal of congresswoman, Agatha Reed. The part is ideally suited for the exotic star, giving her ample opportunity to display her talents as a comedienne and an emotional actress. The audience, estimated at 300, applauded her frequently during the performance and enthusiastically at curtain calls when the production ended." (*Falls River Herald News*, Somerset, MA)

August 14, 1950—"The Web and the Rock" opened in Saratoga Springs, NY. Produced by John Huntington. Written by Lester Cohen. Based on novel by Thomas Wolfe. Cast included Joel Ashley, Kay Francis, Robert Gallagher, Kenneth Rosen, Virginia Colt, Dana Kraus, Roderick Winchell, Katherine Jones, John Huntington, Frank Myers, Betty Shannon, Ruth Saville, George Snowden, Gwyneth Dunn, Clyde Waddell, David Roykoff, Mina Barstow, John Elbert, Kathleen Borzani, Gerry Lockerty, Jerry Hackady. Kay played Mrs. Esther Jack. Staged by Richard Barr. Settings designed by Donald Shirely.

Week of:

August 14, 1950— Spa Theatre, Saratoga Springs, NY

August 21, 1950— North Shore Players, Marblehead, MA

NOTES: Kay's character, Esther Jack, was based on Aline Bernstein, a New York costume and set designer, who met writer Thomas Wolfe in 1925 and became his mentor and lover. Bernstein, married and Jewish, remained with Wolfe until their affair ended in the early 1930s. Coincidentally, Kay worked with Bernstein in "Hamlet," Kay's first Broadway play.

REVIEWS: "Mr. Cohen has done remarkably well in capturing the feeling of the story and transferring it to dialogue and action.... Miss Francis is convincing as the married career woman who finds that a great love can mean heartbreak." (*Saratogian*, August 15, 1950)

"Miss Francis has an admirable opportunity to display her talent for dramatic characterization." (*Albany Times Union*, August 16, 1950)

"Lovely Kay Francis gives the play what realism and convincing notes it has. Miss Francis is always a delight to see." (*Boston Traveler*)

"Miss Francis seems a little lost in a role calling for more of the earth mother than she is capable of." (*Salem News*)

"A sketchy characterless character who lacks conviction. It is not entirely Miss Francis' fault that this is so for the part has been written without a real grasp of the character." (*Boston Evening American*, August 23, 1950)

"Kay Francis in the part of Esther Jack, costume designer, underplays her role with the result that in several scenes of tumultuous overtones she appears to be overacting. Further playing will undoubtedly correct this, as the role is one of great possibilities." (*Variety Magazine*)

"Though limited in emotional scope, Miss Francis is attractive as Esther, and plays the big fight scene with conviction.... 'The Web and the Rock' has two interesting characters and a certain rugged honesty, but if Broadway is the goal, major surgery is indicated." (*Boston Globe*)

"'The Web and the Rock' is currently a tiresome, exhausting lovers' quarrel with heavy overtones of mother-fixation, sordidness and wholly objectionable racial references. Miss Francis plays a two-edged role with some skill, but certain aspects of it are too complicated even for her." (*Lynn Daily Evening Item*)

July 9, 1951—"Mirror, Mirror" opened at the Westhampton Playhouse, Long Island, NY. A Comedy by George Oppenheimer. Based on the novel 'The Back Seat' (1923) by G.B. Stern. Cast included Joel Ashley, Jeanne Flanigan, Patricia Miller, Ronald

Telfer, Kay Francis, Gene Blakely, Ruth White, Ruth Hammond, Carl White. Kay played Leonora Barton.

Week of:

July 9, 1951— Westhampton Playhouse, Westhampton, LI, NY

July 16, 1951— Spa Theatre, Saratoga Springs, NY

July 23, 1951— Boston Summer Theatre, Boston, MA

July 30, 1951— The Theatre-by-the-Sea, Matunuck, RI

August 6, 1951— The Playhouse, Ivoryton, CT

August 13, 1951— The Playhouse, Marblehead, MA

August 20, 1951— Summer Theatre, Olney, MD

August 27, 1951— Kenley Players, Barnesville, PA

September 3, 1951— Bucks County Playhouse, New Hope, PA

NOTES: The intention was that the play would get a tryout and then move on to Broadway, but reviews helped close it. The play was described as "a sophisticated comedy about a glamorous stage actress suddenly facing middle age and the competition of her young stage-struck daughter."

REVIEWS: "Kay Francis ... glided through 'Mirror, Mirror.'... [She] is the experienced actress, happy when she is in the midst of performances, benefits, dinners and attention but uneasy when she is just a fortyish wife." (*The Saratogian*, July 17, 1951)

"The beauteous Miss Francis accomplishes a fine job." (*Albany Times Union*, July 19, 1951)

"Her performance suggest an uneasy blend of Tallulah Bankhead and Ian Claire. But she is much better when she gets down to business in the meaty scenes of the second act, and reasonably believable in the third." (*Variety*)

"Miss Francis, slim and dark, looked charming in a series of attractive costumes, and Joel Ashley ... is tall and handsome. But that's about all there is to praise as 'Mirror, Mirror' stands right now." (*Boston Globe*)

"Kay Francis, elegantly gowned and charming to look at, does a great deal to build something with Mr. Oppenheimer's largely strawless bricks. She has sincerity, pleasant humor, and she knows how to listen well." (*Boston Herald*)

"Their [Francis and Ashley] interpretation in 'Mirror, Mirror' is possibly their best performances.... [The play] has sufficient plot to hold interest, but it is not involved enough to become wearisome on a summer night. It offers good entertainment, and it is likely that the play will draw large audiences." (*The Saratogian*)

"George Oppenheimer, an observer of the passing human comedy who knows this business of luring laughter upon a stage, has done it again. His new play ... described ... as a 'sophisticated comedy' is certainly pleasant diversion ... Kay Francis does a good job in the lead role." (*Billboard Magazine*)

"A clever comedy with sparkling lines.... A splendid vehicle for the superb performance by Miss Francis as the actress, wife, and mother.... A fast and witty show." (*Shore Line Times*)

March 5, 1952— "Theatre" opened in Winter Park, FL. Directed by William Miles. Adapted by Guy Bolton from the novel by Somerset Maugham. Cast included Audrey Ridgwell, John W. Austin, Howard Bailey, Kay Francis, Dennis Allen, William Swan, Gaye Jordan, Deirdre Owens, Stuart Germain. Kay played Julia Lambert. Staged by Dennis Allen. Settings designed by William Roberts. Miss Francis' gowns by Bernard Newman of Bergdorf Goodman.

Week of:

March 5, 1952— Central Florida Drama Festival, Winter Park, FL

March 15, 1952— Playgoers Guild, Richmond, VA

May 19, 1952— Bermudiana Theatre, Hamilton, Bermuda

June 23, 1952— Pocono Playhouse, Mountain Home, PA

June 30, 1952— Berkshire Playhouse, Stockbridge, MA

July 7, 1952— Sacandaga Park, Sacandaga, NY

July 14, 1952— Newport Casino Theatre, Newport, RI

July 21, 1952— Marblehead Playhouse, Marblehead, MA

July 28, 1952— Bar Harbor Playhouse, Bar Harbor, ME

August 4, 1952— Lakes Region Playhouse, Gilford, NH

August 11, 1952— Lakewood Theatre, Skowhegan, ME

August 18, 1952— Ogunquit Playhouse, Ogunquit, ME

August 25, 1952— Spa Theatre, Saratoga Springs, NY

September 1, 1952— Bucks County Playhouse, New Hope, PA

September 8, 1952— Kenley Players, York, PA

January 6, 1953— Empress Playhouse, St. Louis, MO

February 2, 1953— Capitol Theatre, St. Petersburg, FL

February 17, 1953— Memphis Arena Theatre, Memphis, TN

March 2, 1953— Sombrero Playhouse, Phoenix, AZ

August 4, 1953 — Lakewood Playhouse, Skowhegan, ME

May 25, 1954 — Biltmore Playhouse, Miami, FL

July 12, 1954 — Pickwick Players, Birmingham, AL

July 27, 1954 — Town and Country Playhouse, Indianapolis, IN

August 9, 1954 — Grove Theatre, Lake Nuangola, PA

NOTES: Kay began a long-term affair with Dennis Allen after meeting him while working on this production. "Theatre" appeared at the first season of the Central Florida Drama Festival in Winter Park, FL. In the Grove Theatre production, Kay was supported by Dan Rubinate, Jorg Jackson, Tom Troupe, Katherine Kingston, Valerie Hopkins, Sally Singer and Milton Jacobson. In the St. Petersburg performance, Kay was supported by Hal Thompson, Brent Sargent, Tom Raynor, Ethel Britton, Maude Brooks, Gloria Jones and Len Wayland. She also appeared in a production with Anthony Perkins at the Spa Theatre. There was a German television adaptation of the play that was broadcast in 1960. In 1962, the play was made into a French movie, *Julia, Du bist zauberhaf* (1962), starring Lilli Palmer and Charles Boyer. *Teatr* was yet another film version, produced in the Soviet Union in 1978. *Being Julia*, starring Annette Bening and Jeremy Irons, was released in 2005.

REVIEWS: "By the time the final curtain dropped, it was evident from the insistent applause that Kay Francis had scored something of a victory. And indeed she had, over the most unpredictable enemy; for if the hero of this play was the Theatre itself, the villain was opening night nerves. As a result, Miss Francis' initial scenes were somewhat uneven. Let us say she portrayed an actress in the first act and was an actress in the last two. Dark, elegant and smokey-voiced, she is best known for her deft light comedy. It was, however, in her dramatic scenes that she appeared to particular advantage in this play. The twilight loneliness with which she closed her second act, for instance, could not possibly have been better. The play itself is fun. It is not top-drawer Maugham, but it is definitely fun. His expose of the foibles and fables of a far-famed theatrical team is gay rather than malicious, tender rather than incisive, and he has tempered his wit with poignancy. He is dealing with people he knows and loves and consequently, for all their absurdities, their postures and fashionable infidelities, there are moments when you, too, will care very much about them. 'Theatre' may not be a great play. It is, however, very good theatre." (*Winter Park Topics*)

"Miss Francis's first appearance in Richmond should prove a thrill to theater-goers. Her charm and personality suit the role of Julia perfectly and she is certainly as glamorous on stage as on the screen. She reads her line with an intriguing voice and with the understanding of long experience on the stage. (*Richmond News Leader*)

"Miss Francis brings off the triple-threat characterization in high style, supplementing her capable performance with her own good looks and a handsome wardrobe.... Her second-act finale, incidentally, proves that Miss Francis can shed honest tears without the aid of the tricks of the movie trade." (*Richmond Times Dispatch*)

"Miss Francis is magnificent in the second act dramatic scene when she discovers the lesson life teaches." (*Bermuda Mid-Ocean News*)

"Maugham's somewhat synthetic heroine was brought to life by Kay Francis, who enacted her perpetual self — dramatization and tragic-comic posings with zestful variety without overplaying, or burlesquing her — an everpresent danger in such a part." (*Hamilton Royal Gazette*)

"Miss Francis, every inch an actress, has here a part she can get her teeth into, and she makes the most of it from beginning to end. Playgoers are given a chance ... to watch a polished dramatic performance take shape in her skillful hands." (*Newport News*)

"Her role is a difficult one, but well suited to her talents. She runs the gamut of emotions—from disarming coquetry to pain of disappointment and loss of affection. Miss Francis' performance reveals the clever, versatile actress that she is, and she is lovely to look at in the numerous chic gowns she wears." (*Boston Globe*)

"... one of her best performances. Very much at home in highly dramatic roles, Miss Francis also proves herself adept as a comedienne in several scenes.... Miss Francis, who has a reputation as a well dressed woman, is beautifully gowned." (*Saratogian*, August 26, 1952)

"She [Kay] uses her throaty voice with notable range, expressiveness and effect. She is mistress of a thousand-and-one gestures, expressions, and bits of subtle stage business which comprise a finished performance of the glossy smoothness she displayed her last night." (*The Commercial Appeal*)

June 22, 1954 — "Black Chiffon" opened at the Biltmore Playhouse in Miami, FL. It closed July 4, 1954. Produced by Sam Hirsch. Written by Lesley Storm. Cast included Cliff Gould, Yvonne Clifford, Charlotte Frank, Doreen O'Neill Curtis, Kay Francis, John Behney and Frank Schofield. Kay played Alicia Christie. Directed by Dennis Allen.

REVIEWS: A critic described Kay's performance as "almost flawless. The rest of the cast suffers somewhat in comparison to her smoothly professional job. She manages to raise the script to some degree of importance and creates a sympathetic character." (*Miami Daily News*, June 23, 1954)

"Kay Francis was welcomed joyously back to Miami. The play is a sort of theatrical dress creation for a competent actress and Miss Francis 'wears' it becomingly and with fine dramatic flair. Miss Francis brings to the role of Alicia Christie, the wife, the charm, and dramatic depth which are the wondrous attributes of an accomplished professional actress." (*The Miami Herald*, June 24, 1954)

Appendix B:
Major Radio Appearances

January 4, 1935. Hollywood Hotel. CBS. Kay Francis and George Brent reenact scenes from *Living on Velvet*. Hosted by Dick Powell. Interviewer: Louella O. Parsons. 60 minutes.

November 1, 1935. Hollywood Hotel. CBS. Kay Francis, Ian Hunter, and Baby Sybil Jason reenact scenes from *I Found Stella Parish*. Hosted by Dick Powell. Interviewer: Louella O. Parsons. 60 minutes.

May 29, 1936. Hollywood Hotel. CBS. Kay Francis, Ian Hunter, and Donald Woods reenact scenes from *The White Angel*. Hosted by Dick Powell. Interviewer: Louella O. Parsons. 60 minutes.

September 25, 1936. Hollywood Hotel. CBS. Kay Francis and George Brent reenact scenes from *Give Me Your Heart*. George Burns and Gracie Allen sub for Dick Powell. Interviewer: Louella O. Parsons. 60 minutes.

November 26, 1937. Hollywood Hotel. CBS. Kay Francis, Preston Foster, and Verree Teasdale reenact scenes from *First Lady*. Hosted by Ken Murray. Interviewer: Louella O. Parsons. 60 minutes.

May 13, 1938. Hollywood Hotel. CBS. Kay Francis, Bonita Granville, and John Litel reenact scenes from *My Bill*. Hosted by Frank Parker. Interviewer: Louella O. Parsons. 60 minutes.

March 6, 1939. Lux Radio Theatre. *One Way Passage*. CBS. 60 minutes.
Based on the 1932 Warner Bros. film screenplay by Wilson Mizner and Joseph Jackson. Original story by Robert Lord. Hosted by Cecil B. DeMille. Music by Louis Silvers. Announcer: Melville Ruick.
Cast: William Powell (Dan Hardesty), Kay Francis (Joan Ames), William Gargan (Steve Burke), Marjorie Rambeau (Countess/Barrel House Betty), John Fee (Dr. Bolton), Ross Forrester (Skippy), Lee Millar (Mike/Pursar), Lou Merrill (Dick/Steward), David Kerman (Captain Mallory/Officer), Bobby Larson (Child), Myron Gary (Coolie/Mexican Bartender), Raymond Lawrence (Second Steward/Sailor Number Three), Charles Emerson (Tours/Sailor), Gaughan Burke (Sailor Number Two/Man), Geraldine Peck (Woman in Act 1/Woman in Act 3), Frank Nelson (Barman/Man in Singapore).
Notes: Norma Shearer was the announced female lead, but Kay replaced her when illness prevented Shearer's appearance. This was Kay's first *Lux* appearance. Intermission guest was Commander Carl A. Allen of the steamship *Calvin Coolidge* of the American Presidents Line.
Reviews: According to Connie Billups and Arthur Pierce, "Both stars give touching performances in this famed story ... and the second leads are capably handled by William Gargan (a more serious detective than Warren Hymer of the film) and Marjorie Rambeau (taking Aline MacMahon's movie role). Frank Woodruff called the show "excellent," noting "Kay Francis proves great value as [a] radio personality."

March 26, 1939. Gulf Screen Guild Show. *Never in This World*. CBS. 30 minutes.
Cast: Kay Francis (Martha Sheldon), Leslie Howard (Paul Dodd), Virginia Weidler (Susan). With Mary Nash, Irving Pichel, Morgan Wallace. CBS. Host: George Murphy. Director: Sidney Franklin. Writer: Stephen Morehouse Avery. Musical Director: Oscar Bradley.
Synopsis: "Tonight's play, 'Never in This World,' is a fantasy, a strange story of a child who lives in an enchanted world, created for her by her father."

July 30, 1939. The Chase and Sanborn Hour, Starring Edgar Bergen and Charlie McCarthy. NBC. 60 minutes. Guests: Kay Francis, Luis Alberni.

December 11, 1939. Lux Radio Theatre. *In Name Only*. CBS. 60 minutes. Hosted by Cecil B. DeMille.
Cast: Cary Grant (Alec Warren), Carole Lombard (Julie Eden), Kay Francis (Maida Warren), Julie Bannon (Suzanne), Jean Arden (Laura), Peggy

Ann Garner (Ellen), Clara Blandick (Mrs. Warren), Wright Kramer (Dr. Grayson), Lou Merrill (Mr. Warren), Wheaton Chambers (Dr. Muller), Harry Walker (Hotel Manager), Gil Patric (Groom). Music by Louis Silvers.

NOTES: Character names were changed in this adaptation. In the film, Alec and Maida's last name is Walker, but it was changed to Walter in the radio version. Dr. Gateson became Dr. Grayson.

REVIEWS: According to Connie Billups and Arthur Pierce, "Grant, Lombard, and Francis repeat their memorable portrayals."

December 17, 1939. The Silver Theatre. *Twice Upon a Time*. CBS. 30 minutes. Sponsor: International Silver. Host: Conrad Nagel. Announcer: John Conte. Music: Felix Mills.

March 3, 1940. The Silver Theatre. *A Lady By Preference*. CBS. 30 minutes. Sponsor: International Silver. With Ned Le Fevre. Host: Conrad Nagel. Announcer: John Conte. Music: Felix Mills.

March 18, 1940. Lux Radio Theatre. *The Rains Came*. CBS. 60 minutes. Hosted by Cecil B. DeMille. Musical director: Louis Silvers. Announcer: Melville Ruick.

CAST: Kay Francis (Lady Esketh), George Brent (Tom Ransome), Jean Parker (Fern), Jim Ameche (Major Safti), Martha Wentworth (The Maharani), Verna Felton (Mrs. Simon), Lou Merrill (Smiley), Jack Lewis (Lord Esketh), Lal Chand Mehra (Rashid/Messenger), Wyndham Standing (The Maharajah), Thomas Mills (Bates), John Fee, James Eagles, and Melville Ruick (Ad Libs).

NOTES: George Brent repeated the role he played in the 1939 20th Century–Fox film version, which also starred Myrna Loy as Lady Esketh. Jean Parker played Brenda Joyce's role, and Jim Ameche replaced Tyrone Power as the Indian doctor. Lal Chand Mehra replaced William Royle (Mehra had a small role in the film as a chant singer). Myrna Loy wrote about the film role in her autobiography. According to her, "Marlene Dietrich, Kay Francis, Tallulah Bankhead, and Ina Claire, among others, campaigned for Lady Esketh in *The Rains Came*. For months Roz Russell kept telling me I'd be a fool to change my type for the part, freely admitting that she wanted it for herself. I was surprised when Darryl Zanuck asked to borrow me for that role." It was based on Louis Bromfield's 1937 bestseller; the author sold the movie rights for $55,000, and then sent three identical telegrams to Kay Francis, Marlene Dietrich, and Constance Bennett telling each woman she would be perfect as Lady Esketh. Zanuck, however, decided on Loy. A 1955 remake, *The Rains of Ranchipur*, starred Lana Turner, Fred MacMurray, Joan Caulfield, and Michael Rennie.

REVIEWS: "Even though the vivid earthquake and flood sequences ... are de-emphasized in the Lux production, the dramatic situations in the story of an English lady's doomed love for an Indian physician make for an interesting broadcast." Billups and Pierce applaud the "fine cast."

December 15, 1940. The Silver Theatre. *Four on a Match*. CBS. 30 minutes. Sponsor: International Silver. Set in Havana, two friends vie for a woman's affections. Host: Conrad Nagel. Announcer: John Conte. Music: Felix Mills.

March 3, 1941. Lux Radio Theatre. *My Bill*. CBS. 60 minutes. Hosted by Cecil B. DeMille. Musical director: Louis Silvers. Announcer: Melville Ruick.

CAST: Kay Francis (Mary Colbrook), Warren William (John Rudlin), Dix Davis (Bill), Clare Verdera (Aunt Caroline), Janet Waldo (Muriel), Sidney Miller (Reggie), Barbara Jean Wong (Gwen), Verna Felton (Mrs. Crosby), Edward Arnold Jr. (Linn), Bernice Pilot (Beulah), Lou Merrill (Truck Driver/Prospective Employer), Ferdinand Munier (Doctor/Jenner), Shirley Ward (Woman), Alair Omstead (Miss Kelly), James Reed (Barnes), Tommy Lane (Mike).

REVIEWS: According to Billups and Pierce, "Francis gives a fine performance, as do Warren William as the man in her life and Dix Davis as her fiercely loyal son."

May 18, 1941. Jack Benny Program. NBC Red. 30 minutes. Sponsored by: Jell-O. A visit to the set of *Charley's Aunt*. Guests are Kay and director Archie Mayo. With Don Wilson, Frank Nelson, Mary Livingstone, Dennis Day, and Phil Harris and His Orchestra.

October 13, 1941. The Cavalcade of America. *Waters of the Wilderness*. NBC Red. 30 minutes. A radio play based on the 1941 novel by Shirley Seifert. Adapted by Robert L. Richards and William Johnstone. Produced and directed by Homer Fickett.

CAST: Kay Francis (Teresa), Gale Gordon (Col. Clark), Lou Merrill (Fernando/First Settler/Voice One), Gerald Mohr (Liard), Agnes Moorehead (Female Homesteader/Suzette; Voice Three), Bea Benaderet (Indian Woman/Maria/Voice Five), Jack Mather (Voice Two/Tom Pace/Second Homesteader/Second Settler); Pat McGeehan (Third Settler/Voice Four/First Homesteader); Earle Ross, Grace Leonard, Catherine Cragen, Jerry Gale (Supernumeraries); Gayne Whitman (Servant). Musical composer and conductor: Robert Armbruster. Announcer: John Heistand. Commercial Announcer: Gayne Whitman.

NOTES: This broadcast (Episode #248) was the first produced in Hollywood. Previously set in New York, the program moved to California to make it more convenient for stars to appear.

SYNOPSIS: A biography of Colonel George Rogers Clark, it's also "a romantic love story of a daring colonel of the continental army and the beautiful sister of a Spanish governor."

February 11, 1943. Stage Door Canteen. CBS. 30 minutes. Kay was a guest star.

March 1, 1943. Lux Radio Theatre. *The Lady Is Willing.* CBS. 60 minutes. Hosted by Cecil B. DeMille. Musical director: Louis Silvers. Announcer: John Kennedy.

CAST: Kay Francis (Liza Madden), George Brent (Dr. Corey McBain), Arthur Q. Bryan (Ken), Ann Doran (Buddy), Lillian Randolph (Mary Lou), Leone Ledoux (Baby Corey/Nurse), Verna Felton (Mrs. Cummings), Norman Field (Dr. Gohling/Workman), Marla Shelton (Frances), Fred MacKaye (Clerk/Victor), Eddie Marr (Newsboy), Wally Maher (Sergeant Bonds), Charles Seel (Manager/Doorman).

NOTES: DeMille announces at the beginning of the show that Kay has been back in the United States for only a week since ending her tour of North Africa. At the conclusion of the radio play, Brent and DeMille interview Kay about her trip. **The Lady Is Willing** was filmed in 1942 with Marlene Dietrich and Fred MacMurray in the lead roles. The supporting cast included Aline MacMahon, Stanley Ridges, and Arline Judge.

SYNOPSIS: A stage actress finds an abandoned baby. Since the only way she can keep the infant is to marry, she weds the child's physician, Dr. McBain. The marriage of convenience turns romantic—until McBain's ex-wife shows up. The baby's illness brings Liza and Dr. McBain back together again.

REVIEWS: According to Billups and Pierce, "Neither the story ... nor the dialogue is as humorous as it tries to be, but it makes a pleasant *Lux* vehicle for Kay Francis and George Brent."

March 24, 1943. Stage Door Canteen. CBS. 30 minutes. Kay was a guest star.

April 5, 1943. Great Gildersleeve. *Rabbits.* NBC. 30 minutes. Kay makes a War Bond speech during the intermission. Here's her introduction: "Ladies and gentlemen, we're going to interrupt here for just a moment in order to present a very charming and courageous lady who has something to say to you. That she is charming is no secret to her thousands of admirers and the proof of her courage is her four months expedition across the Atlantic this past winter to entertain our troops in England, Ireland, Scotland, and North Africa. Ladies and gentlemen, Miss Kay Francis...."

"Thank you. Ladies and gentlemen, I ask your attention for one minute [the sound of a clock ticking]. One minute isn't very long, but in this very brief minute that you hear my voice, men are dying for you. Dying on distant battlefields, in strange waters. Men from Nebraska, Illinois, Texas, boys from across the street, boys that you know. Right now while I speak to you, sixty seconds in a minute, how many times sixty men are dying for you ... and as they die they are remembering home, remembering us, wanting to come home, knowing they never will. Are we worth remembering? Are we worth coming home to? No. Not unless we do all we possibly can to win this war, and our possible all is so little compared to what they give. We are not asked to give but to lend our dollars to our government, to carry our share of the 15 million dollars needed in the second war loan. Lend your dollars. Right now. Right this minute. While those men are giving their lives for you. You'll get your dollars back."

"Thank you, Miss Francis! Now let's get back to Summerfield and the Great Gildersleeve. It's Easter Morning, and the great man...."

May 3, 1943. Cavalcade of America. *Soldiers in Greasepaint.* NBC. 30 minutes. Starring Kay Francis, Mitzi Mayfair, and Martha Raye. Written by George Corey. Produced and directed by Homer Fickett.

CAST: Wally Maher (Bob/Another Soldier); Hans Conried (Charlie/Another Soldier); Hal Gerard (Soldier/Another Soldier); Virginia Gordon (Nurse); Joseph Kearns (Colonel); Bob Bruce (Sergeant/Corporal); Frank Graham (Hotel Man/Paratrooper); Eustace Wyatt (Guardsman); Sheila Sheldon (Princess); Frank Nelson (Another Soldier); Joe Granby (Commanding Officer). Announcer: Jim Bannon. Commercial Announcer: Georgia Backus. Music composer and conductor: Robert Armbruster.

NOTES: Carole Landis was supposed to appear but canceled. The broadcast (Episode #329) included skits that Francis, Mayfair, Raye, and Landis performed while entertaining the troops in North Africa and Europe.

July 4, 1943. The Silver Theatre. *Murder Unlimited.* CBS. 30 minutes. Sponsor: International Silver. Host: Conrad Nagel. Announcer: Henry Charles. Music: Felix Mills.

November 25, 1943. Soldiers in Greasepaint. NBC. 45 minutes. Hosted by Jack Benny & Bob Hope. Appearances by Al Jolson, Fredric March, Jascha Heifetz, Martha Raye, Kay Francis, Carole Landis, Judith Anderson, Merle Oberon, Jerry Colonna, Andy Devine, Jinx Falkenberg, Fay MacKenzie, Anna Lee, John Garfield, Frances Langford. 45 minutes.

NOTES: Kay briefly spoke before introducing Mitzi Mayfair, Carole Landis, and Martha Raye. Her voice, much huskier and deeper than usual, suggests she might have been suffering from a cold or even more serious illness.

Bob Hope: "Here is the feminine task force who entertained not only our boys overseas, but also appeared before Queen Elizabeth and the royal family. Led by the lovely Kay Francis, they did a bang-up job, and here she is to present them — Kay Francis!

Kay: Thank you. Thank you very much. Now all I can say is that, well, we had a wonderful time, and you'll hear our story in song from Martha Raye, Carole Landis, and Mitzi Mayfair. Girls! If you please!

Raye, Landis, and Mayfair sang "Sunday, Monday, and Always."

November 28, 1943. The Silver Theatre. *The Lady Grew Up.* CBS. 30 minutes. Sponsor: International Silver. Host: Conrad Nagel. Announcer: Henry Charles. Music: Felix Mills.

December 11, 1943. Command Performance. AFRS. 30 minutes. The program is dedicated to the AFRS North African Network, with "The North African Follies." Martha Raye sings, "Mr. Paganini." Kay Francis, Raye, Carole Landis, and Mitzi Mayfair play the roles of G. I.'s. Announcer: Ken Carpenter. With The 370th Army Air Force Band, Skinnay Ennis, Anna Lee, Bob Hope, Arvin Dale.

April 9, 1944. The Globe Theatre. *Strange Victory.* CBS. 30 minutes. After losing her fortune, a woman finds employment as a governess. Written by Franklin Maloney. Host: Herbert Marshall. With Walter Pidgeon, Kay Francis, Gloria McMillan. Conductor: Alfred Newman.

August 21, 1944. Hollywood's Open House. Paramount Weekly Show. KNX, Los Angeles. Kay guest stars as a movie producer who meets an amnesiac (Jim Ameche) on a train. Announcer: Dick Wesson. With Enric Madriguera and His Orchestra, Gene Wesson, Jerry Cooper. 30 minutes.

December 16, 1944. Don McNeill and the Breakfast Club. Chicago. ABC. This series first came on the air on June 23, 1933, and its final show was December 27, 1968, making it radio's longest running variety show.

January 8, 1945. Hildegarde's Raleigh Room. NBC. Though born in Wisconsin, Hildegarde spoke with a slight European accent. After her hit song "I'll Be Seeing You" made her a household name, she was given a radio show. It started in 1943 and ran for three years.

January 16, 1945. Hollywood's Open House.

January 26, 1945. Stage Door Canteen. ABC. With Bob Hope, Vera Vague, Jerry Colonna, and the Raymond Paige Orchestra.

February 1, 1945. Morton Downey Show.

March 25, 1945. Melody Lane. Chicago.

September 5, 1946. Kate Smith Chat. ABC.

September 9, 1946. Martin Deane Wickett Show. WOR.

September 15, 1946. Exploring the Unknown. WOR. How Not to Worry. This science fiction program featured Hollywood stars.

September 29, 1946. Warriors of Peace.

October 17, 1946. USO Appeal.

November 10, 1946. Sammy Kaye's Serenade. ABC.

March 24, 1947. Army Show. NBC.

Appendix C:
Television Appearances

May 14, 1950 — This Is Show Business. Sunday, 7:30 P.M. CBS. 30 minutes.

NOTES: This variety show first aired July 15, 1949. In 1950 it was shown on Sundays (7:30–8:00 P.M.). The emcee was Clifton Fadiman. Panelists included George S. Kaufman and Abe Burrows. Its last telecast was September 11, 1956. Stars appeared on the show to ask for advice from the panelists. In her television debut, Kay appeared with Herb Shriner and Patrice Munsel.

November 7, 1950 — The Prudential Family Playhouse. Tuesday, 8:00 P.M. CBS. 60 minutes. Episode #3. *Call It a Day*.

CAST: Kay Francis, Peggy Ann Garner, John Loder, John McQuade, Kyle MacDonnell, Peggy French, Frances Ingalls, Robert Pastene, Joan Lazar. Adapted from a play by Dodie Smith.

NOTES: *The Prudential Family Playhouse* was a live one-hour anthology series. It first aired October 10, 1950 and was shown every other Tuesday (8:00–9:00 P.M.). The show featured popular stage play adaptations. Unfortunately, it was scheduled opposite the ratings hit *Milton Berle's Texaco Star Theatre*, and was taken off the air in March 1951. *Call It a Day*, written by Dodie Smith, is set in London on the first day of spring. A romantic comedy, it was also adapted into a 1937 film starring Ian Hunter, Olivia de Havilland, Anita Louise, Roland Young, and Alice Brady. Alfred Lunt and Lynn Fontanne starred in a *Theater Guild* radio version on June 2, 1946.

January 8, 1951 — Hollywood Screen Test. Monday, 7:30 P.M. ABC. 30 minutes.

NOTES: This talent show first aired April 15, 1948, and last aired May 18, 1953. Hosted by Neil Hamilton in 1951, it was shown on Mondays (7:30–8:00 P.M.). The contestants were paired with stars in various scenes and skits. Kay appeared in a skit titled "The Long Way Round."

May 24, 1951 — Betty Crocker Show. Thursday, 3:30 P.M. CBS. 60 minutes. This daytime variety show, hosted by Adelaide Hawley, included cooking and household tips.

June 4, 1951 — Lux Video Theatre. Monday, 8:00 P.M. CBS. 30 minutes. Episode #36. *Consider the Lilies*. Lawrence Du Pont (Writer), Richard Goode (Director).

CAST: Kay Francis (Alice), Jerome Cowan (Alfred Bragg), Joel Ashley (Myles), Olive Templeton Flannery (Agnes), Marlene Cameron (Barbara), Arthur Jarrett (Hardwicke).

NOTES: *Lux Video Theatre* first aired on October 2, 1950, and last aired September 12, 1957. The show was a spin-off from *Lux Radio Theatre*.

October 20, 1951 — Beat the Clock. Saturday, 7:30 P.M. CBS. 30 minutes. Host: Bud Collyer. Assistant: Roxanne Arlen. Other guests included Ilka Chase, Peter Donald, and John Murray.

NOTES: This game show aired from the 58th Street Theatre. It premiered on March 23, 1950. Contestants from the studio audience were required to perform a variety of activities within a certain time limit.

October 31, 1951 — The Frances Langford–Don Ameche Show. 10:30 AM. ABC. 60 minutes.

NOTES: This daytime variety series was sponsored by the Richard Hudnut hair products company. Frances Langford and Don Ameche, known as *The Bickersons* on radio, were joined by regulars Jack Lemmon and Cynthia Stone, along with the Tony Romano Orchestra. The show premiered on September 10, 1951, and was last broadcast on March 14, 1952.

November 11, 1951 — Celebrity Time. Sunday, 10 P.M. CBS. 30 minutes.

NOTES: Hosted by Conrad Nagel, the panelists on this quiz-talk show included Kitty Carlisle, Ilka

Chase, John Daly, Mary McCarty, Herman Hickman, Jane Wilson, Kyle MacDonnell, and Martha Wright. The show first aired January 23, 1949, and its last broadcast was September 21, 1952. Kay appeared with Red Smith. The topic was sports.

April 22, 1952 — The Stork Club. Tuesday, 7:45–8:00 P.M. CBS. 15 minutes.

NOTES: Hosted by Stork Club owner Sherman Billingsley, this variety-interview show was set at the legendary nightclub. During the time Kay appeared, the show was broadcast on Tuesdays and Thursdays.

May 10, 1952 — The Ken Murray Show. Saturday, 8:00 P.M. CBS. 60 minutes.

NOTES: Hosted by Ken Murray, this variety show first aired on January 7, 1950, and was last telecast on June 21, 1953. It also featured Art Lund, Laurie Anders, Pat Conway, Jane Bergmeier, Lillian Farmer, and Anita Gordon. Kay appeared in a skit with Lola Albright. Other guests included Victor Borge, Fayne and Foster, Mrs. Arthur Murray, and Bill Callahan.

September 1, 1953 — Anyone Can Win. Tuesday, 9:00 P.M. CBS. 30 minutes.

NOTES: Hosted by Al Capp, this short-lived game show was first broadcast on July 14, 1953. Kay appeared on its last broadcast. The Light Brigade consisted of a disguised star, hiding behind Hairless Joe's mask, and three celebrity panelists. On this episode, the panelists were Patsy Kelly, Ilka Chase, and Jimmy Dykes. Audience members aligned themselves with a panelist before the show started. If their star answered the most questions, the group got to divide $2,000. Then at the conclusion of the show, Hairless Joe drew a viewer's name, and that person was phoned and given the opportunity to guess who was behind the mask.

Appendix D: Selected Memorabilia

During Kay Francis' movie career, there were literally thousands of products and advertisements that used Kay's likeness. The following list includes magazine covers, tobacco cards, sheet music, recordings, and other interesting memorabilia.

Movie Magazine Covers

(The name of the artist, when known, is in parentheses. If the publication is not American, the country is in brackets.)

July 1930, *Motion Picture* (Marland Stone)
December 1930, *Modern Screen*
December 1930, *Photoplay* (Earl Christy)
December 1930, *Screenland*
February 1931, *Screen Play Secrets* (Henry Clive)
March 1931, *Silver Screen*
April 1931, *The New Movie Magazine*
May 1931, *Screen Book*
May 2, 1931, *Film Weekly* [Great Britain]
May 9, 1931, *Picture Show* [Great Britain], Kay Francis / Ronald Colman
August 1, 1931, *Picture Show* [Great Britain]
September 1931, *Cinlandia*
December 1931, *Movie Classic*
February 6, 1932, *Film Weekly* [Great Britain]
February 20, 1932, *Film Favourite* [Great Britain], Kay Francis / Ricardo Cortez
April 2, 1932, *Picture Show* [Great Britain], Kay Francis / Alan Mowbray
June 3, 1932, *Pelicula* [Uruguay]
July 1932, *Photoplay* (Earl Christy)
August 1932, *Movie Mirror*
September 2, 1932, *Film Weekly* [Great Britain]
September 3, 1932, *Film Pictorial* [Great Britain]
October 1932, *The New Movie Magazine* (McCelland Barclay)
October 15, 1932, *Picture Show* [Great Britain], Kay Francis / Fredric March
November 1932 *Screen Book*
December 9, 1932, *Film Weekly* [Great Britain]
January 1933, *Movie Classic*
March 3, 1933, *Film Weekly* [Great Britain]
March 25, 1933, *Picture Show* [Great Britain], Kay Francis / William Powell
April 1933 *Screenland*
April 15, 1933, *Picture Show* [Great Britain], Kay Francis / Ronald Colman
April 28, 1933, *Film Weekly* [Great Britain], Kay Francis / Herbert Marshall
May 6, 1933, *Picture Show* [Great Britain], Kay Francis / Herbert Marshall
July 28, 1933 *Ciné-Miroir* [France]
August 1933, *Movie Mirror*
September 29, 1933, *Film Weekly* [Great Britain]
October 21, 1933, *Picture Show* [Great Britain], Kay Francis / George Brent
December 1933, *Modern Screen*
December 30, 1933, *Picturegoer* [Great Britain]
February 1934, *Photoplay*
February 1934, *Picture Play*
March 1934, *Screenland*
March 26, 1934, *Entertainment*
April 1934, *Photoplay*
May 1934, *Movie Classic*
June 10, 1934, *Screen and Radio Weekly Magazine* [supplement to *The Detroit Free Press*]
July 1934, *Modern Screen*
August 1934, *Cinelandia* [Spain]
August 1934, *Modern Screen*
August 1934, *Silver Screen*
August 3, 1934, *Family Circle*, Kay Francis / Richard Barthelmess
November 1934, *Screen Play Magazine*
January 1935, *Woman's Filmfair*
April 1935, *Movie Classic*
May 1935, *Modern Screen*
June 4, 1935 *Ecran* [Chile]
June 22, 1935, *Film Pictorial* [Great Britain]
August 1935, *Photoplay*
August 16, 1935, *Film Weekly* [Great Britain], Kay Francis / Leslie Howard

Left: Kay on the cover of the Chilean magazine *Ecran* (1935). *Right:* Kay often looked more ethnic in international magazines as seen here on the cover of *Ciné-Miroir* (July 1933).

August 24, 1935, *Picture Show* [Great Britain], Kay Francis / Leslie Howard
December 1935, *Romantic Movie Stories*
January 1936, *Picture Play*
April 1936, *Movie Mirror*
June 1936, *Screenland*
August 1936, *Lecturas*
August 29, 1936, *Film Pictorial* [Great Britain]
November 21, 1936, *Film Weekly* [Great Britain]
February 1937, *Picture Play*
March 1937, *Silver Screen*
March 20, 1937, *Picture Show* [Great Britain]
July 24, 1937, *Picturegoer* [Great Britain]
August 1937, *Lecturas*
October 2, 1937, *Picturegoer* [Great Britain]
November 1937, *Picture Play*
December 13, 1937 *Cinefilio*
February 1938, *Cinelandia* [Spain]
March 26, 1938, *Film Weekly* [Great Britain]
June 11, 1938, *Film Pictorial*, [Great Britain], Preston Foster / Kay Francis
June 25, 1938, *Picturegoer* [Great Britain]
July 1940, *Cinelandia*
January 4, 1941, *Picturegoer* [Great Britain]

Miscellaneous

The Art of Society Make-Up. Max Factor Makeup for the Stars Booklet. 1928.
Breyers ice cream lid.
Brody Novelty Candy Co. Big Stars collecting card. Brody Novelty Candy Package Co., 676 Broadway, New York, New York.
Butterick Pattern Book.— describes the new patterns and a special page which shows Kay from the movie *The Keyhole*, dressed in two of the completed outfits. 1933.
Dixie ice cream lid for Supplee features Warner Bros. actress Kay in *Stranded.*
Faccino's Reel-Star Chocolate Wafers. Series of 50 photographs of various stars.
Favorite Recipes of the Movie Stars. Tower Books, 1931.
Photo. Distributed by *New York Mirror.* Special Edition Print Collection of Movie Stars from 1937. *I Found Stella Parish.* 1937.
1932 Olympic Games/Movie Star Playing Cards Xth Olympiad, Los Angeles. Copyrighted 1932 by P. J. Wenger Co, 3440 South Hope Street, Los Angeles, California.

230 Appendix D: Selected Memorabilia

Pinback button. Pender Grocery, Norfolk, Virginia.
Regent cigarette advertisement. "What do you know about Monroe ... Francis ... Kruger? ... Quality tobacco ... Multiple Blended make Regent the milder better tasting cigarette!"
1847 Rogers Bros. Silver advertisement. "'See if my taste is yours,' suggests Kay Francis."

Recordings

Another Dawn (Soundtrack). Korngold: *Another Dawn, Escape Me Never*. Marco Polo #223871. [This is a double compact disc, featuring soundtracks for *Another Dawn* and *Escape Me Never*. Composed by Erich Wolfgang Korngold.

The Cocoanuts (Soundtrack). Marx Brothers: *The Cocoanuts/Monkey Business*. Soundtrack Factory.
Four Jills in a Jeep (Soundtrack). *Lady Be Good—Four Jills in a Jeep*. Original Soundtracks. Great Movie Themes. Compact Disc. CD 60029. Cedar. [This is a double compact disc, featuring soundtracks for *Lady Be Good* and *Four Jills in a Jeep*.]
Four Jills in a Jeep (Soundtrack). *Four Jills in a Jeep*. Original soundtrack. Hollywood Soundstage no. 407. [33 rpm vinyl LP]

Sheet Music

"Home on the Range." W.M. Goodwin. From *I Loved a Woman*, 1933.
"When Tomorrow Comes." Sammy Fain and Irving Kahal. From *Mandalay*, 1934.
"Don't Say Goodnight." From *Wonder Bar*, 1934.
"Going to Heaven on a Mule." Al Dubin and Harry Warren. From *Wonder Bar*, 1934.
"Why Do I Dream These Dreams." Al Dubin and Harry Warren. From *Wonder Bar*, 1934.
"Living on Velvet." Al Dubin and Harry Warren. From *Living on Velvet*, 1935.
"Jealous." Tommy Malie, Dick Finch, and Jack Little. From *The Feminine Touch*, 1941.
"Always in My Heart." Kim Gannon and Ernesto Lecuonoa. From *Always in My Heart*, 1942.
"How Many Times Do I Have To Tell You." From *Four Jills in a Jeep*, 1944.

Tobacco Cards

Bridgewater Film Stars. 1932. Stars of the Screen Set. Godfrey Phillips.
Film Stars. Carreras Personality Series. Turf Cigarettes. Australia. 1933.
Stage and Cinema Beauties, Series A. Godfrey Phillips. 1933.
Shots from the Films. Printed by Godfrey Phillips. 1934
Famous Film Stars . Printed by Ardath. England. 1934.
Film Stars. John Player and Sons. Great Britain. 1934. Card #14 of 50 Movie Legends.

KAY FRANCIS
So much of her childhood was spent in boarding schools and hotels that Miss Francis never learned how to cook, but she keenly appreciates the value of good home cooking.

Kay was one of the featured stars in a booklet titled "Favorite Recipes of the Movie Stars." The information was concocted by publicity writers.

Appendix D: Selected Memorabilia

Signed Portraits of Famous Stars. Gallaher Ltd.
Stage and Radio Stars. Ardath. 1935. Card #9 of 25.
Nestle Stars of the Silver Screen, Vol. I. 1936.
Who Is This? (Film Stars). Ardath. 1936.
Film Stars. Carreras. Commentary by Florence Desmond. 1936.
Film Episodes. Gallaher. 1936.
Film Favourites. International Tobacco Ltd. 1937.
Characters Come to Life. Godfrey Phillips Tobacco. 1938
Modern Beauties, 5th Series. British American Tobacco Co. Ltd (BAT). 1938.
My Favourite Part. Gallaher. 1939. Card #9.

Videos & DVDs

The Cocoanuts. Universal Studios. VHS, DVD. 1995.
Four Jills in a Jeep. 20th Century–Fox. VHS. 1995.
Greatest Moments in TV & Movies: Classic Bloopers. Brentwood Home Video. VHS BC812. 1990.
Hidden Hollywood II: More Treasures From the 20th Century–Fox Vaults. DVD. 1997. Also available on VHS.
Hollywood Goes to War. Video Yesteryear. VHS. 1999.
Hollywood Out-Takes & Rare Footage. RCA/Columbia Pictures Home Video. VHS. 1982.
In Name Only. VHS. Turner Home Entertainment. 1995.
It's a Date. Warner Studios. VHS. 1991.
Little Men. Timeless Video. VHS. 1994.
Movie Bloopers, Vol. 1. Viking Video Classics. VHS VCC812. 1988.
Raffles. HBO Studios. VHS. 1999.
Showbiz Ballyhoo. USA Home Video. VHS. 1984.
Trouble in Paradise. Criterion Collection. DVD. 2003.
When the Daltons Rode. DVD. 2004.
Wonder Bar. Warner Home Video. VHS. 1997.
WW II America At War: Show Business in War. Bridgestone Multimedia. VHS. ISBN 1–56371–196–6. 1995.

Left: Kay's image was often used to advertise products as seen in this makeup booklet. Here she poses with Max Factor in the early 1930s. *Right:* The New Art of Society Make-Up by Max Factor booklet. 1932. This 4¼ × 5½ booklet was included with Max Factor makeup products.

Kay Francis on a British cigarette card.

Websites

Kayfrancis.com. This is the official site for our Kay Francis books. You'll find links, information

Soundtrack for *Four Jills in a Jeep*.

about the books, and be able to view Kay's movie bloopers.

Kayfrancis.net. This is a fan site that offers photographs, slideshows, wallpaper, and more.

TCM.com. The site for Turner Classic Movies includes trailers for Kay's films as well as oddities like the "Movies on Sunday" short. In it, Kay speaks out for a bill to allow movies to be shown on Sunday. We see her in her home (most likely a movie set), sitting comfortably on a sofa while reading. The telephone rings, and her maid answers it. Kay is then interviewed via telephone about her views on the bill. Both the "maid" and "reporter" appear to be from Central Casting. Notice how Kay, perhaps two feet or so from the ringing telephone, makes no effort to answer it — or even glance at it! Apparently movie stars never answered their own telephones. The short was probably made around 1936.

APPENDIX E: RESIDENCES

April 14, 1922: Moved from 55th Street to unknown address.

August 31, 1922: 224 East 49th Street

December 4, 1922: 41 West 54th Street

December 17, 1922: 21 West 49th Street

New York Social Register: Winter 1924 Edition
Mr. and Mrs. James Dwight Francis
(Katharine E. Gibbs)
61 West 10th Street   Chelsea 5770
[Moved there on October 1, 1923]

New York Social Register: Summer 1924 Edition
Mr. and Mrs. James Dwight Francis
(Katharine E. Gibbs)
South Street Inn   Tel. No. 2078
Pittsfield, MA [April 9, 1924]

New York Social Register: Winter 1925 Edition
Mrs. James Dwight Francis
(Katharine E. Gibbs)
150 East 54th Street   Plaza 0758
[Moved there on November 7, 1924]

New York Social Register: Winter 1926 Edition
Mrs. Katharine G. Francis
(Katharine E. Gibbs)
37 East 60th Street   Regent 7155
[Moved there on October 1, 1925]

[Moved to 381 Park Avenue on October 14, 1926]

[Moved to 3 West 8th St. on November 1, 1926]

New York Social Register: Winter 1927 Edition
Mrs. Katharine G. Francis
(Katharine E. Gibbs)
140 East 39th Street   CA 4235
[Moved there on November 29, 1926]

New York Social Register: Winter 1928 Edition
Mrs. Katharine G. Francis
(Katharine E. Gibbs)
137 East 58th Street   Regent 6480
[Moved there on October 1, 1927]

New York Social Register: Winter 1929 Edition
Mrs. Katharine G. Francis
(Katharine E. Gibbs)
137 East 58th Street   Regent 6480

Kay left New York for Los Angeles on April 11, 1929

April 15, 1929: Roosevelt Hotel (Hollywood), 7000 Hollywood Boulevard

July 12, 1929: 8401 Fountain Avenue (West Hollywood)

February 21, 1931: 8487 Franklin Avenue (Hollywood Hills)

November 1932: 1117 North Alta Loma Road

November 1933: 8218 DeLongpre Avenue (West Hollywood)

August 22, 1935: 8341 DeLongpre Avenue (West Hollywood)

December 16, 1937: 9033 Briar Crest Lane (Hollywood Hills)

December 1938: An apartment in Beverly Hills, address unknown.

June 2, 1939: Moved back to 9033 Briar Crest Lane

October 31, 1941: 1735 Angelo Drive (Beverly Hills)

June 20, 1942: 1010 Benedict Canyon Drive (Beverly Hills)

July 7, 1946: Hotel Gotham, 2 West 55th Street

July 13, 1946: Hotel Drake, 440 Park Avenue

August 1, 1946: Hotel New Weston, 34 East 50th Street

May 4, 1948: 31 East 61 Street (northwest corner of Madison Avenue)

January 15, 1952: 32 East 64th Street (northwest corner of Madison Avenue)

Appendix F:
Katherine Clinton's Selected Stage Appearances

This is not a complete list of Katherine Clinton appearances— only ones for which we found information. Reviews are from the Robinson Locke Collection, New York Public Library for the Performing Arts, New York, unless otherwise noted.

September 1898—"A Runaway Girl" opened. Written by George Edwardes. Clinton was listed as one of the Postillions.

November 10, 1898—"The Merchant of Venice" opened. It closed on January 2, 1899. Written by William Shakespeare. Cast included Sidney Herbert, Ada Rehan, and Clinton played (in role of Jessica).

1898/1899?—"The Taming of the Shrew." Cast included Ada Rehan. Clinton played the role of Bianca.

February 1900—"The Great Ruby" opened at the Boston Theatre. Clinton played the role of the Honorable Moya Denzil. A reviewer remarked that Clinton "acted very well last season in 'The Great Ruby' and has certainly advanced in her art."

October 8, 1900—"Marcelle" opened at the Broadway Theatre. Written by Eugene W. Presbrey. Cast also included Emily Baker, Dustin Farnum, George Foster, Robert Gemp, Fred Harris, Joseph Kilgour, Thomas Lawrence, Emma Maddern, Frederick Perry, Katherine Power, Harold Russell, Ellis Ryse, Frank Sheridan, Algernon Tassin, Blanche Walsh. Clinton played Mira.

1901?— Clinton toured with the Daly Company, performing with Blanche Walsh. Clinton also toured with Maude Adams in "Little Minister."

June 2, 1902—"The Two Orphans" opened at the Castle Square Theatre in Boston. Written by Mons. D'Ennery. Cast included Hallett Thompson, Edward Wade, James L. Seeley, Robert Elliott, Charles Mackay, James A. Keane, Lindsay Morison, William J. Hasson, Louis Thiel, Warren Cook, Frank Minzey, B.F. Duffy, George Siegman, Frank McHardy, Nelson Lewis, George Simpson, Lavinia Shannon, Mary Sanders, Fanny Addison Pitt, Izetta Jewel, Cordelia MacDonald, Sadie Galloupe, Katharine Kent, Alexia Durant, Sarah Kingsley, Grace Olin. Clinton played Countess De Linieres.

The theatre was built by E.M. Maynard in 1894. Castle Square's best-known member was Alfred Lunt, who was with them from 1912 to 1914. The building was renamed the Arlington in 1918 and torn down in 1932.

June 9, 1902—"The Iron Master" opened at the Castle Square Theatre in Boston. Written by J.V. Prichard. Cast included Hallett Thompson, Robert Elliot, John T. Craven, James L. Seeley, James A. Keane, Charles Mackay, William J. Hasson, Edward Wade, Louis Thiel, Frank Minzey, Lavinia Shannon, Fanny Addison Pitt, Mary Sanders, Izetta Jewel, Alexia Durant. Clinton played Athenais Moulinet.

June 16, 1902—"The Colleen Bawn" opened at the Castle Square Theatre in Boston. Written by Dion Boucicault. Cast included John T. Craven, Charles Mackay, Hallett Thompson, Robert Elliot, James L. Seeley, William J. Hasson, Lindsay Morison, Edward Wade, Louis Thiel, Frank Minzey, Mary Sanders, Lavinia Shannon, Fanny Addison Pitt, Izetta Jewel, Alexia Durant. Clinton played Mrs. Cregan.

June 23, 1902—"The Rivals" opened at the Castle Square Theatre in Boston. Written by Richard Brinsley Sheridan. Cast included James L. Seeley, Charles Mackay, Edward Wade, John T. Craven, Robert Elliot, William J. Hasson, Lindsay Morison, Louis Thiel, Frank Minzey, Fanny Addison Pitt,

Izetta Jewel, Mary Sanders. Clinton played Lydia Languish.

June 30, 1902—"The Corsican Brothers" opened at the Castle Square Theatre in Boston. Written by M.M. Grange and X. De Montepin. Cast included Hallett Thompson, Edmund Breese, James L. Seeley, James A. Keane, Edward Wade, Lindsay Morison, John T. Craven, George R. Simpson, W. Paul Linton, William J. Hasson, Warren Cook, Louis Thiel, B.F. Duffy, Nelson Duffy, Nelson Lewis, W.C. Mason, H.C. Wetherbee, Fanny Addison Pitt, Izetta Jewel, Cordelia MacDonald, Sarah Kingsley, Alexia Durant. Clinton played Emilie De Lespare.

July 7, 1902—"The Lost Paradise" opened at the Castle Square Theatre in Boston. Cast included James L. Seeley, Hallett Thompson, Edmund Breese, James A. Keane, John T. Craven, Edward Wade, Louis Thiel, Lindsay Morison, Warren Cook, Frank Minzey, B.F. Duffy, George R. Simpson, William J. Hasson, Fanny Addison Pitt, Mary Hall, Izetta Jewel, Mary Sanders, Sarah Kingsley, Alexia Durant. Clinton played Nell.

July 14, 1902—"She Stoops to Conquer" opened at the Castle Square Theatre in Boston. Cast included Lindsay Morison, Hallett Thompson, James L. Seeley, Charles Mackay, James A. Keane, William J. Hasson, B.F. Duffy, W.C. Mason, George R. Simpson, Edward Wade, Warren Cook, John J. Geary, John C. Hinds, Louis Thiel, Frank Minzey, W. Paul Linton, Master Louis Moscowitz, Fanny Anderson Pitt, Mary Hall, Izetta Jewel, Alexia Durant. Clinton played Constance Neville.

July 21, 1902—"Dora" opened at the Castle Square Theatre in Boston. Cast included Edmund Reese, Edward Wade, Charles Mackay, Louis Thiel, B.F. Duffy, Little Blanche Winters, Mary Hall. Clinton played Mary Morrison.

July 28, 1902—"Romeo and Juliet" opened at the Castle Square Theatre in Boston. Cast included Hallett Thompson, Charles Mackay, James A. Keane, Edward Wade, Lindsay Morison, Edmund Breese, E.D. Denison, John T. Craven, Frank Minzey, B.F. Duff, George R. Simpson, William J. Hasson, Alexia Durant, Mary Hall, Fanny Addison Pitt. Clinton played Lady Capulet.

August 4, 1902—"Engaged" opened at the Castle Square Theatre in Boston. Cast included James A. Keane, Hallett Thompson, John T. Craven, Edmund Breese, Lindsay Morison, Mary Hall, Izetta Jewel, Fanny Addison Pitt, Alexia Durant. Clinton played Maggie.

August 18, 1902—"Ours" opened at the Castle Square Theatre in Boston. Cast included Edmund Breese, John T. Craven, Edward Wade, Thomas MacLarnie, Hallett Thompson, Lindsay Morison, Louis Thiel, Frank Minzey, W. Paul Linton, C.R. Foster, Fanny Addison Pitt, Mary Hall. Clinton played Blanche Haye.

August 25, 1902—"Pygmalion and Galatea" opened at the Castle Square Theatre in Boston. Cast included Hallett Thompson, Edmund Breese, John T. Craven, Edward Wade, William J. Hasson, Mary Hall, Jane Irving, Fanny Addison Pitt. Clinton played Myrine.

1903?— Katherine Clinton was employed by the Jessie Bonstelle Stock Company in Rochester, New York. Several years later, Katharine Cornell became Miss Bonstelle's protégée.

October 5, 1904—"Two Hours of Oblivion." Oklahoma City, Oklahoma. Presented by the Ladies Guild of the Episcopal Church, and Staged Under the Personal Direction of Mrs. Joseph S. Gibbs (Katherine Clinton).

October 5, 1904—"A Happy Pair." Oklahoma City. Cast included Katherine Clinton and Nels Darling. *The Daily Oklahoman* described Clinton's performance as having "airy grace and perfection of acting."

April 14, 1905—"Sense and Nonsense." Overholser Opera House, Oklahoma City, Oklahoma. Clinton and Nels Darling appeared in a sketch in this vaudeville-like show.

April–May 1905— Katherine Clinton was hired by C.W. Stater to be the leading lady at the Delmar Garden theatre company. She appeared in "Woman's Sacrifice," "Three of a Kind," "Union Forever," and "Brother John." *The Daily Oklahoman* reviews were always positive. Comments included: "an actress of exceptional ability" and "exceptionally strong in her part." Despite the excellent reviews, Stater apparently ran out of money, and the company closed after only a brief time.

1909–?— Clinton toured with the Lindsay Morison Stock Company. In "Home Folks," Clinton was lauded for her performance; the critic described her acting as "effective and highly dramatic." Clinton played the unpleasant Madeline Gray in "The Bingville Bugel." According to a reviewer, "Miss Clinton is to be congratulated on the way she acted it."

1914?–?— Katherine Clinton toured with vaudeville performer Harry Brooks in "The Old Minstrel Man." Although the dates are uncertain, Kay reportedly told friends that her mother toured with Brooks for ten years.

November 28, 1921—"The Wife With the Smile" and "Bourbouroche" opened at the Garrick Theatre. "The Wife With the Smile" was produced by the Theatre Guild. Written by Denys Amiel and Andre Obey. Staged by Frank Reicher. Cast included Willard Bowman, Maud Brooks, Arnold

Daly, Philip Loeb, Catherine Proctor, Jeanne Wainwright, Edwin R. Wolfe, Blanche Yurka. Clinton played Mme. Lebas.

"Bourbouroche" was produced by The Theatre Guild. Written by Georges Courteline. Book adapted from the French by Ruth Livingstone. Staged by Philip Moeller. Cast included Carl Anderson, Willard Bowman, J. Monte Crane, Arnold Daly, Robert Donaldson, Philip Loeb. Clinton played the Cashier.

This was part of the fourth season of the legendary Theatre Guild, later known for their frequent collaboration with Alfred Lunt and Lynn Fontanne.

October 22, 1923—"Open Road" was produced at the Stamford Theatre, Stamford, Connecticut. Written by Clifford Pember and Barry Macollum. Directed by Albert Bannister. Cast included George Duryea, Barry Macollum, Vivara, Frances Verdi, Lionel Pape, Gaspaer Mangione. Clinton played Madre. *Variety* panned the play: "Three acts and seven scenes are required to unfold the story that could be told in two" (November 1, 1923). The reviewer adored actress Vivara, writing, "There is action when Vivara is on the stage and the force of her personality is evident from the lagging dullness when others are entrusted to carry on the dialog." Unfortunately Clinton didn't fare as well: "A continuity writer wouldn't waste any time pondering on eliminating Katherine Clinton from the cast. As a time filler she isn't a success. The bits she contributes may be intended for atmosphere but even this has to be gathered from the gaudy clothes and the bracelet she affects. Grease paint helps the gypsy makeup but otherwise you wouldn't suspect it."

August 29, 1928—"Caravan" opened at the Klaw Theatre. It ran for 29 performances. Produced by Richard Herndon. Written by Clifford Pember and Ralph Cullinan. Cast included Mildred Byron, Jerome Daley, Edmund Forde, Robert Hyman, Leo Kennedy, Barry Macollum, Louise Mainland, Kate Mayhew, H. H. McCollum, George Neville, Virginia Pemberton, Michael Rice, Elsa Shelley, Edwin Thompson, George Thornton, Joseph Casey, and Jethro Warner. Clinton played Madre Layet.

APPENDIX G: THE PLAYERS

Brief biographies for selected cast who worked with Katherine Clinton and Kay Francis.

Iris Adrian was born Iris Adrian Hostetter in Los Angeles in 1912. A former Ziegfeld dancer, she went on to appear in more than 100 films. She also performed on television in the 1950s, 60s, and 70s, on *The Beverly Hillbillies*, *The Munsters*, and *The Ted Knight Show*. She died in 1994 from injuries she received during the Los Angeles earthquake.

Brian Aherne, born in England in 1902, received an Oscar nomination for *Juarez* (1939). Aherne, brother of Patrick — and ex-husband of Joan Fontaine — began his career in silents. He appeared in more than 50 films and numerous TV shows, and also wrote a biography of actor George Sanders. Aherne died in 1986.

Frank Albertson, born in Fergus Falls, Minnesota, in 1909, appeared in silent films in the 1920s. His credits include more than 100 films, but he is perhaps best known as Donna Reed's annoying boyfriend (Sam Wainwright) in *It's a Wonderful Life* (1946). He also appeared in *Psycho* (1960) and *Johnny Cool* (1963). Albertson died in 1964.

Hardie Albright, born in Pennsylvania in 1903, was part of his parents' vaudeville act when he was growing up. After a Broadway stint, he made his film debut in 1931. Albright taught drama at UCLA and wrote books on acting. He died in 1975.

Lola Albright was born in Akron, Ohio in 1925. She first appeared on film in *Easter Parade* (1948). Albright won an Emmy for her role in the television series *Peter Gunn* (1958). She appeared in more than 30 films and made many television appearances, including *Burke's Law*, *Branded*, and *Hollywood Squares*.

Dennis Allen studied acting at the Mohawk Drama Festival, and later toured with Diana Barrymore. He eventually became a stage director.

Don Ameche, born in Kenosha, Wisconsin, in 1908, was the brother of Jim, and a successful leading man for decades. He performed on radio and stage and appeared in more than 70 films, beginning in the 1930s, but won his first Oscar in 1986 for *Cocoon*. Ameche died in 1993.

Jim Ameche was born in Kenosha, Wisconsin, in 1915. Brother of Don, Jim was a radio star for many years, appearing on *Jack Armstrong, The All-American Boy* and many other shows. Ameche died in 1983.

Adrienne Ames, born in Texas in 1907, began her career as a stand-in for Pola Negri. Sister of Gladys MacClure and divorced from Bruce Cabot, Ames died of cancer in 1947.

Stage, film, TV, and radio star **Eve Arden**, born Eunice Quedens in California in 1908, received an Oscar nomination for *Mildred Pierce* (1945). She made her film debut in 1929 and worked steadily through the decades. She had stints on such TV shows as *Our Miss Brooks*, *The Mothers-In-Law*, and *Faeirie Tale Theatre*. Arden died in 1990.

Born Cornelius Richard Van Mattemore in Charlottesville, Virginia, in 1898, **Richard Arlen** literally crashed into Paramount's gates on a motorcycle. While he was recovering from a broken leg, the studio gave him a contract. He worked as an extra on several films before finding success in *Wings* (1927), a World War I film with Buddy Rogers and Clara Bow which won the first Academy Award for Best Picture. He ended his career by appearing in westerns and also performing on television in the 1950s and 1960s, including a stint on *Petticoat Junction* where he played himself. He died in 1976.

Armida, born in Mexico in 1911, appeared in more than 25 films, mostly in the 1930s and 1940s. She died in 1989.

One of Hollywood's greats, **Jean Arthur** was born Gladys Greene in New York in 1900. Her first film was *Cameo Kirby* (1923). She was possessed of a unique voice and undeniable charm, and her best known film roles include *Mr. Deeds Goes To Town* (1936), *Mr. Smith Goes to Washington* (1939), and *Shane* (1953). Arthur was nominated for an Oscar for *The More the Merrier* (1943), and appeared on her own television series in 1966. Arthur also taught acting at Vassar for a number of years. Never comfortable in the limelight, Arthur died on June 19, 1991.

Joel Ashley was born in Atlanta in 1919. He appeared in many television shows, especially westerns, and died in 2000.

Earl Askam was born in 1909 in Seattle. *Let's Go Native* was his first film. He's best known for playing Officer Torch in the *Flash Gordon* movies. He died of a heart attack in 1940.

Nils Asther, born in Denmark in 1897, began in Swedish silent films, under the direction of Mauritz Stiller. He became a silent star in Hollywood, but had trouble with his accent when talkies replaced silents. He eventually moved back to Sweden and died there in 1981.

Gertrude Astor, born in Lakeland, Ohio, on November 9, 1897, was a former riverboat trombonist who signed with Universal in 1915. The tall actress (5' 7") was known as one of Hollywood's best dressed. Astor appeared in more than 250 films, including several with Laurel and Hardy, and retired in the 1960s. She died on her birthday in 1977.

Stage actor **Hooper Atchley**, born in Tennessee in 1887, made his film debut in 1929 and appeared in more than 180 films until his suicide in 1943.

Mischa Auer, born in Russia in 1905, appeared in more than 150 films, beginning in 1928. Auer was nominated for an Oscar for his work in *My Man Godfrey* (1936). His last film was *For Love ... For Magic* in 1967. He died in Rome in 1967.

William Austin was born in 1884 in what is now known as British Guyana. His first film was *Common Sense* (1920). He died in 1975.

Irving Bacon, born in 1893 in St. Joseph, Missouri, made more than 300 film and television appearances. His first film was *California or Bust* (1927). His brother was director Lloyd Bacon, and his father was writer-director Frank Bacon. Irving Bacon died in 1965.

Raymond Bailey, born in San Francisco in 1904, is best known for playing Mr. Drysdale on TV's *The Beverly Hillbillies*. He also appeared in more than 50 movies and dozens of other TV shows before his death in 1980.

Sherwood Bailey, born in California in 1923, was Spud in the *Our Gang* serials. He died in 1987.

George Bancroft, born in Philadelphia in 1882, was a major silent film star, who continued to be quite popular into the 1930s. Nominated for an Oscar for his acting in *Thunderbolt* (1929), he retired in 1942 to become a rancher. Bancroft died in 1956.

Phyllis Barry, born in London in 1909, made her debut in *Cynara* (1932). She appeared in films until 1947, mostly in small roles.

Diana Barrymore, born in New York in 1921, was the daughter of John Barrymore and writer Michael Strange (aka Blanche Oelrichs). A stage star, she made only ten films before her death in 1960 (probably a suicide). Married and divorced from Bramwell Fletcher, she wrote an autobiography, *Too Much, Too Soon*, which detailed her alcoholism, romances, and difficult relationship with her father. She was Lionel and Ethel Barrymore's niece — and Drew Barrymore's aunt.

Actor-director-writer-composer-painter **Lionel Barrymore**, born in Philadelphia in 1878, won an Oscar for *A Free Soul* (1931) and received a nomination for best director for *Madame X* (1929). He made his film debut in 1908, and appeared in more than 200 films. Brother of Ethel and John, he was Diana Barrymore's uncle and Drew Barrymore's great-uncle. Barrymore died in 1954.

Anne Baxter, born in Indiana in 1923, was the granddaughter of architect Frank Lloyd Wright. As a child she studied with Marie Ouspenskaya, and as a teenager performed on Broadway. Her film career began in 1940, and she won an Oscar for *The Razor's Edge* (1946) and was nominated for *All About Eve* (1950). A regular on TV's *Hotel*, she died in 1985.

Louise Beavers, born in Ohio in 1902, was Leatrice Joy's maid when she began her film career. Her best known role was in *Imitation of Life* (1934). Beavers also appeared on such TV shows as *Beulah* and *Make Room for Daddy*. She died in 1962.

Scotty Beckett, born in 1929, began his film career in 1933 and appeared in the *Our Gang* comedies. He also played Winky in the *Rocky Jones* movies. He died from a drug overdose in 1968.

Character actor **Janet Beecher**, born Janet Meysenburg in Jefferson City, Missouri, in 1884, appeared in more than 40 films and was also a stage actor. She retired from film in 1943, and died in 1955. Her sister was actor Olive Wyndham.

Ralph Bellamy, born in Chicago in 1904, was a stage, radio, and film star for many years. Bellamy received an Oscar nomination for his work in *The Awful Truth* (1937), and he received an honorary Oscar in 1987. He also received Emmy nominations for *The United States Steel Hour* (1953), *The Missiles of October* (1974), and *The Winds of War* (1983). Bellamy died in 1991.

Bea Benaderet was born in New York in 1906. A radio and stage star early in her career, she appeared in many films and countless television shows. She was nominated for Emmys, for her appearances on *The George Burns and Gracie Allen Show* (1950), but she's best known for *Petticoat Junction*. She also provided voice work on many cartoons, including *The Flintstones*, *Bugs Bunny*, and *The Roadrunner*. She died in 1968.

Wilson Benge was born in London in 1875. His long film career began with an appearance in *Robin Hood* (1922). Often cast as the butler, Benge was also a stage actor and producer. He died in 1955.

Jack Benny was born Benjamin Kubelsky in Illinois in 1894. Benny enjoyed a long and successful career in vaudeville, radio, film, and television. His first film appearance was *The Hollywood Revue of 1929* (1929). In later years he was often seen on television, both on his own show (he received an Emmy nomination in 1956) and as a guest on such programs as *Make Room For Daddy*, *The Lucille Ball Show*, and *Rowan & Martin's Laugh-In*. Benny, a comedy legend, died in 1974.

Sara Berner, born in Albany, New York, in 1912, appeared as Mabel on *The Jack Benny Show*, and also did voices for such cartoons as *Life Begins for Andy Panda*, *The Henpecked Duck*, and *The Bashful Buzzard*. She was also a regular on the *Hank McCune Show*. Berner died in 1969.

Charles Bickford was born in 1891 in Cambridge, Massachusetts. He appeared in *Dynamite* (1929), *Anna Christie* (1930), and *Little Miss Marker* (1934). Bickford was almost killed by a lion during the filming of *East of Java* (1935). He received Oscar nominations for *The Song of Bernadette* (1943), *The Farmer's Daughter* (1947), and *Johnny Belinda* (1948). In his later years, he worked in television on such shows as *Dr. Kildare*, *The Virginian*, and *The Dick Powell Show*. He died in 1967.

Clara Blandick, born on a ship in Hong Kong in 1881, is best known for her portrayal of Auntie Em in *The Wizard of Oz* (1939). This legendary character actor had a distinguished stage and film career. She began her career in silent films in 1914 with *Mrs. Black Is Back* and appeared in more than 100 films. She committed suicide at the age of 80.

Humphrey Bogart, born in New York in 1899, won an Oscar for *The African Queen* (1951) and received nominations for *Casablanca* (1942) and *The Caine Mutiny* (1954). His mother was an illustrator and his father a successful surgeon. Wives included Helen Menken, Mary Philips, Mayo Methot, and Lauren Bacall. He died in 1957.

John Boles, born in Texas in 1895, began his film career in silents. He was a spy during World War I. Boles appeared in more than 50 films before his death in 1969.

Symona Boniface, born in New York in 1894, appeared in more than 100 films, beginning in 1925. She began her career as a playwright-producer-actor. Boniface, who often appeared in *Three Stooges* and other comedy shorts, died in 1950.

Veda Ann Borg, born in Boston in 1915, modeled in the 1930s before becoming an actor. A serious car accident in 1939 required extensive plastic surgery, but she successfully resumed her career, though she often appeared in low-budget pictures. She was at one time married to director Andrew McLaglen, and she died in 1973. Her children are producers Mary McLaglen and Josh McLaglen.

Clara Bow, born in Brooklyn in 1905, endured a horrible childhood marked by poverty and an unstable mother who attempted to kill her. After winning a beauty contest, Clara was signed to a movie contract. One of Hollywood's first sex symbols, Clara was known as the "It Girl," following her appearance in the 1927 film *It*, which referred to that wonderful quality in women that makes men do foolish things. Scandals, the coming of sound, and weariness led to her retirement in 1933 after her final appearance in *Hoopla*. She married cowboy film star Rex Bell in 1931. Bow died in 1965.

William Stage Boyd, often confused with the cowboy actor who shared the same name, was known mostly for his stage acting. Born in New York in 1889, he died March 20, 1935, of a liver ailment.

Walter Brennan, born in Massachusetts in 1894, won Oscars for *Come and Get It* (1936), *Kentucky* (1938), and *The Westerner* (1940). Brennan, who appeared in more than 200 films, beginning in the 1920s, is probably best known for his regular role on TV's *Real McCoys*. He died in 1974.

Born in Tampa in 1895, **Evelyn Brent** was a silent film actor whose first film was *The Shooting of Dan McGrew* (1915). She began working as an extra in her teens and appeared in more than 100 films and several television shows before retirement. Brent died in 1975.

George Brent was born George Brendan Nolan in Ireland in 1904. While in Ireland, he was active in the Irish Republican Army. His first film appearance was *Under Suspicion* (1930). Brent had three brief marriages to Ruth Chatterton, Constance Worth, and Ann Sheridan. He made several television appearances in the 1950s, including *Wire Service* and *Rawhide*, and died in 1979.

Mary Brian was born Louise Byrdie Dantzler in Texas in 1908. She made her first film appearance in the 1924 silent version of *Peter Pan*, playing Wendy. One of Hollywood's most popular leading ladies in the 1920s and 1930s, Brian appeared in 80 films, retiring after 1947's *Dragnet*. Mary died at the age of 96 in 2003.

Sheila Bromley, born in San Francisco in 1911, made her first film appearance in 1930 billed as Sheila Le Gay. She also appeared in films, usually westerns or serials, under the names Sheila Manners, Sheila Manors, and Sheila Mannors. She continued to appear in films throughout the 1960s, and made numerous television appearances in the 1950s and 1960s on such shows as *I Love Lucy*, *Rawhide*, and *Adam-12*. She played the role of Janet Tobin on the *I Married Joan* TV series. Bromley died in 2003.

Clive Brook, born in England in 1887, began his film career in 1920 with *Trent's Last Case* and was perhaps best known for playing Sherlock Holmes in two film versions. Married to Mildred Evelyn, his children were Lyndon and Faith Brook. He died in 1974.

Harry Brooks, actor, banjo player, and minstrel, was a popular vaudeville performer. Best known for creating the title role in *Peck's Bad Boy*, he died in 1942 at the age of 72.

Nigel Bruce, born in Mexico in 1897, was best known for playing Dr. Watson to Basil Rathbone's Sherlock Holmes. He died in 1953.

Virginia Bruce, born in Minnesota in 1910 but raised in North Dakota, began her film career in 1929. She, along with Lucille Ball, Betty Grable, and Paulette Goddard, was one of the original Goldwyn Girls. Bruce was a star in the 1930s and 1940s, appearing in such films as *Jane Eyre* (1934), *Shadow of a Doubt* (1935), and *Hired Wife* (1940). Married to screen legend John Gilbert from 1932 to 1934, she died in 1982.

Arthur Q. Bryan was born in Brooklyn in 1899. A popular radio actor, Bryan provided the voice of Elmer Fudd, the cartoon character — and nemesis of Bugs Bunny — who shared Kay Francis' speech impediment. Bryan died in 1959.

Gertrude Bryan, born around 1892, was a society beauty who had a huge hit with the musical "Little Boy Blue" in 1911. One of her final roles was an appearance with Gertrude Lawrence in "Skylark."

Jane Bryan, born Jane O'Brien in Hollywood in 1918, made only fourteen films before retiring at 21 to marry millionaire Justin Dart, president of Rexall Drug Company and eventual owner of Dart Industries, makers of Tupperware. She was discovered while appearing in "Green Grows the Lilacs," a play produced by Jean Muir at her experimental theatre. Dart, a staunch conservative, was a longtime friend of Ronald Reagan and became part of his 'kitchen cabinet' during his first term. Justin and Jane Dart were also art collectors who donated a large collection to the Monterey Museum of Art.

Edgar Buchanan was born in Missouri in 1903. A former dentist, he appeared in many films, often westerns, but is best known to TV fans as Uncle Joe on *Petticoat Junction*. Buchanan died in 1979.

Mae Busch, born in Australia in 1891, had once been a silent film star nicknamed the Versatile Vamp. Best known for playing Oliver Hardy's wife in the *Laurel and Hardy* films, she died in 1946.

Bruce Cabot, born Etienne Pelissier Jacques de Bujac in New Mexico in 1904, appeared in almost 100 films until his death in 1972. Probably best known for playing the hero in *King Kong* (1933), Cabot was once married to Adrienne Ames.

Nancy Carroll, born in New York in 1904, was often teamed with Buddy Rogers. Carroll, who became one of Hollywood's biggest stars in the 1930s and was a singer and dancer, began her film career in the 1927 silent *Ladies Must Dress*. Her popularity soared with the coming of sound. She received an Oscar nomination in 1930 for *The Devil's Holiday*. Carroll retired from the screen in the late 1930s, but did television work in the 1950s and 1960s, including playing Alice Aldrich in *The Aldrich Family*. She died in 1965.

Paul Cavanagh, born in England in 1888, made his film debut in *Two Little Drummer Boys* (1928). His career lasted well into the 1950s, and included television appearances on such shows as *Perry Mason* and *The Adventures of Superman*. He died in London in 1964.

Helen Chandler, born in New York in 1906, began her film career in 1927 with appearances in *The Music Master* and *The Joy Girl*. She also appeared in *Dracula* (1931), *Christopher Strong* (1933), and others until her career ended in the late 1930s. She married and divorced Bramwell Fletcher, Kay's co-star in *Raffles* (1930). Chandler died in obscurity in 1965, with no one to claim her ashes.

Lane Chandler, born in Montana in 1899, was a silent film star whose long career continued well into the 1960s and included many western films and TV shows. He died in 1972.

Spencer Charters, born in Pennsylvania in 1875, made his film debut in 1920, and appeared in more than 200 films. He committed suicide in 1945.

Ruth Chatterton had a remarkable career and life. Born in New York on December 24, 1893, she became a chorus girl when she was 14 and a stage star with her Broadway appearance in *Daddy Long Legs* in 1914. Eventually lured to Hollywood in 1925, Chatterton became one of Hollywood's highest paid actors. She was twice nominated for Oscars for acting–*Madame X* (1929) and *Sarah and Son* (1930). Her last television appearance was in a 1953 version of *Hamlet* for Hallmark Hall of Fame. A brilliant woman, she was a successful author, an accomplished pilot, as well as a play producer. She died in Connecticut in 1961. Chatterton's husbands included Ralph Forbes and George Brent, both of whom appeared in films with Kay.

Maurice Chevalier, born in Paris in 1888, was one of Kay's lovers in the 1930s. An agile performer, he was an acrobat in his early career until an injury led him into singing and acting. Chevalier was wounded and imprisoned during World War I. After the war, he arrived in Hollywood, where he was often teamed with Jeanette MacDonald. He was twice nominated for Oscars—*The Love Parade* (1929) and *The Big Pond* (1930). His other notable films include *Love Me Tonight* (1932), *The Merry Widow* (1934), and *Gigi* (1958). He died in 1972.

Jack Clifford, born in Italy in 1880, had a long film career, beginning with an appearance in *Threads of Destiny* (1914). He appeared in many westerns, usually as an extra. He also made several appearances on the *Lone Ranger* television show. Once married to the legendary (and scandalous) Evelyn Nesbitt, he died in 1956.

Charles Coburn, born in Savannah, Georgia, in 1877, won an Oscar for *The More the Merrier* (1943), and received two other nominations for *The Green Years* (1946) and *The Devil and Miss Jones* (1941). A stage actor, he and his wife started the Coburn Players. He died in 1961.

Irene Coleman, born in New Hampshire in 1913, was Miss Chicago of 1931. She died in 1975.

Mildred Coles, born in Los Angeles in 1920, was a beauty contest winner who appeared in more than 20 films, mostly westerns. She died in 1995.

Lois Collier was born Madelyn Jones in South Carolina in 1919. Her name came from a character she played on a radio program. Collier appeared in many low-budget films and also had a role in the *Boston Blackie* TV show. She died in 1999.

Patricia Collinge, born in Ireland in 1892, appeared in several films, including *The Little Foxes* (1941), *Shadow of a Doubt* (1943), and *The Nun's Story* (1959). She also made guest television appearances on *Studio One*, *Alfred Hitchcock Presents*, and *The Alfred Hitchcock Hour*. She died in 1974.

Cora Sue Collins, born in West Virginia in 1927, was a child actor who made her film debut in 1932. She made her last film in 1945.

June Collyer was born in New York in 1906. She married Stuart Erwin in 1931, and was the sister of TV's Bud Collyer. She was born Dorothea Heermance, but used her mother's maiden name. Her first film was a silent picture made in 1927, *East Side, West Side*. She retired from films in the late 1930s, but made a comeback on her husband's television show, *The Stu Erin Show*, in the 1950s. She died in 1968, just a few months after Stuart's death.

Charming, debonair **Ronald Colman** was born in Richmond, Surrey, England, in 1891. Wounded at the Battle of Messines in World War I, he began his entertainment career on stage. By 1919 he was appearing in silent films, and in 1920 he moved to New York. He became a popular silent star after being signed by Samuel Goldwyn. His wonderful speaking voice made it easy for him to make the transition to sound films. Notable film roles include *Beau Geste* (1926), *Lost Horizon* (1937), and *A Double Life* (1947), for which he won an Academy Award. Colman was also nominated for *Condemned* (1929), *Bulldog Drummond* (1929), and *Random Harvest* (1942). Active in radio and television, he appeared on *The Halls of Ivy*, *Four Star Playhouse*, and *The Jack Benny Show*. Wife Benita Hume often worked with him in the latter part of his career. Colman died in 1958.

Dorothy Comingore, born Linda Winters in Los Angeles in 1913, is best known for playing Susan Kane in *Citizen Kane* (1941). Blacklisting in the 1950s ended her career. She died in Connecticut in 1971.

Joyce Compton, born in Kentucky in 1907, specialized in dumb blonde roles, which she played to perfection in *The Awful Truth* (1937). A former Kentucky beauty contest winner, she started in silent pictures but turned to a nursing career when her career faltered in the 1950s. She died in 1997.

Juliette Compton, born in Columbus, Georgia, in 1899, was a former Ziegfeld Girl who appeared in silent films, including *The Wine of Life* (1924), *White Heat* (1926), and *Nell Gwynne* (1926). Her last film was *That Hamilton Woman* (1941). Involved in a messy divorce with James Bartram in the 1940s, Compton died in 1989.

Hans Conried, born in Baltimore in 1917, enjoyed a long, successful career on stage, and in radio, film, and television. He was also much in demand for cartoon work — he was the voice for Snidely Whiplash on *Dudley Do-Right*. His best known film appearance was probably *The 5,000 Fingers of Dr. T.* (1953). Conried died in 1982.

Gary Cooper, born Frank James Cooper in Montana in 1901, appeared in many of Hollywood's greatest films, including *Wings* (1927), *Morocco* (1930), and *Meet John Doe* (1941). His Oscar nominations include *Mr. Deeds Goes to Town* (1936), *The Pride of the Yankees* (1942), and *For Whom the Bell Tolls* (1943). He won Academy Awards for *Sergeant York* (1941) and *High Noon* (1952). Cooper died in 1961.

Ricardo Cortez, born Jacob Krantz in Austria in 1899, was the brother of cinematographer Stanley Cortez. Groomed as a successor to Valentino, he first appeared in silent films, and eventually appeared in more than 100 films and directed seven.

Cortez became a successful stock broker when he retired. He was married to Alma Rubens until her death in 1931. He died in 1977.

Jerome Cowan was born in 1897 in New York. One of the great B movie actors, he appeared in his first film, *Beloved Enemy*, in 1936, following a successful stage career. Other credits include *The Maltese Falcon* (1941), *Mr. Skeffington* (1944), and several *Blondie* films in the 1940s. Cowan also made many television appearances, including *The Twilight Zone*, *Perry Mason*, and *Bonanza*. He died in 1972.

Broderick Crawford, born in Philadelphia in 1911, won an Oscar for *All the King's Men* (1949). The son of Helen Broderick and Lester Crawford, he got his start on Broadway before going on to have a long film and TV career, which included a starring role on TV's *Highway Patrol*. He died in 1986.

Laird Cregar, born in Philadelphia in 1914, appeared in only 16 films before his death in 1944, the result of a crash weight loss diet.

Stage actor **Laura Hope Crews**, born in San Francisco in 1879, appeared in silent films and later became a legendary character actor. Notable films included *The Age of Innocence* (1934), *Camille* (1936), and *Gone with the Wind* (1939) She died in 1942.

Donald Crisp, born in Scotland in 1880, won an Oscar for *How Green Was My Valley* (1941). A silent screen director and star, he was once married to writer Jane Murfin, Jane Cowl's co-writer. Crisp died in 1974 after working in film for seven decades.

Robert Cummings, born in Joplin, Missouri, in 1908, was a pilot (godson of Orville Wright) and health food fan who died in 1980. Cummings began his long film career in the early 1930s, but he is best known for his TV series *The Bob Cummings Show*. Married for many years to Mary Elliott, he married four other times.

Cecil Cunningham was born in St. Louis in 1888. *Paramount on Parade* (1930) was her second film. Cunningham appeared in many films through the 1940s. She died in 1959.

Frances Dade was born in Philadelphia in 1910. Her short career included only eleven films. Her best known role was Lucy Weston in *Dracula* (1931). She died in 1968 in Philadelphia.

Emmett Dalton, born in Missouri in 1861, was the youngest Dalton brother. He appeared in a movie version of his book *Beyond the Law* (1918). Dalton died in 1937.

Henry Daniell, who specialized in slimy sophisticates, was born in England in 1894. He began his career on stage and appeared in more than 60 films. Daniell also made numerous TV appearances on shows including *Wagon Train*, *Thriller*, and *Lights Out*. He died in 1963.

Alexander D'Arcy, born in Egypt in 1908, died in 1993. Married at one time to Arleen Whelan, he appeared in more than 30 films and also appeared on TV in the 1960s.

Frankie Darro, born in Chicago in 1917, began his long career in 1924. The son of circus performers, he also was a stuntman. Darro also appeared on many TV shows including *The Red Skelton Show* and *Public Defender*. He died in 1976.

Jane Darwell, born in Missouri in 1879, won an Oscar for *Grapes of Wrath* (1940). A stage and silent film actor, she enjoyed a long career which included her role as the Bird Woman in *Mary Poppins* (1964). She died in 1967.

Philippe De Lacy was born in France in 1917. His mother was killed in an air raid, and Phillippe was adopted by Edith De Lacy, a worker with the Women's Overseas Hospital. His modeling career led to his first film appearance in *A Doll's House* (1922). His last acting appearance was in 1930, after which he became a producer-director for Cinerama Corporation. De Lacy died in 1995.

Mexican-born **Dolores Del Rio** was Ramon Novarro's cousin, and was at one time married to Cedric Gibbons. She also appeared in the first Fred Astaire–Ginger Rogers film, *Flying Down to Rio*, in 1933. She returned to Mexico in the 1940s and became one of her country's biggest movie stars. Born in 1905, she died in 1983.

Veteran character actor **William Demarest**, born in St. Paul, Minnesota, in 1902, was nominated for an Oscar for *The Al Jolson Story* (1946) and an Emmy for *My Three Sons*. The former vaudevillian died in 1983.

Katherine DeMille, born in Canada in 1911, was adopted by Cecil B. DeMille and his wife. She was married to Anthony Quinn from 1937 to 1963.

Andy Devine, born Jeremiah Schwartz in Arizona in 1905, was a college football star before he turned to acting. His distinctive raspy voice was the result of a childhood accident. Devine, a popular actor who appeared in numerous films and TV shows, died in 1977.

Gloria Dickson, born Thais Dickerson in Idaho in 1916, made her film debut in 1937. Divorced from Perc Westmore, she appeared in around 20 films until her tragic death in a house fire in 1945.

Alan Dinehart, born in St. Paul, Minnesota, in 1889, died in 1944. Dinehart, who specialized in villains, was the father of Alan Dinehart III. He began his film career in 1931 and appeared in 90 films.

Claire Dodd, born in Iowa in 1908 and raised in Arkansas, was a one-time member of the Ziegfeld Follies. Nicknamed "Ice Bucket" because people perceived her as aloof, she made her film debut in

1930 and retired in 1942 to raise a family — she had her last child at the age of 47. Dodd died in 1973.

Brian Donlevy was born in Ireland in 1901. He appeared in almost 100 films, including Oscar-nominated *Beau Geste* (1939), *The Great McGinty* (1940), and *The Miracle of Morgan's Creek* (1944). *Gentlemen of the Press* was his first sound film. His last wife was Bela Lugosi's widow. He died in 1972.

Ruth Donnelly, born in New Jersey in 1896, was a stage and silent film actor who began her film career in 1914. Before she died in 1982, she'd appeared in more than 90 films, and was a popular character actor. Donnelly was also a regular on the *Imogene Coca* TV series.

Ann Doran was born in Texas in 1911. Her long career began with appearances in silent films when she was four. She appeared in literally hundreds of films and television shows and steadily worked well in the 1980s. A regular on *Longstreet* and *Shirley*, her last film appearance was *Wildcats* (1986). Doran died in 2000.

Adrienne Dore was Miss America in 1925. Born in Idaho in 1910, she appeared in 19 films, beginning in 1928. She died in 1992.

Fifi D'Orsay, born in Canada in 1904, made her film debut in 1929. Nicknamed the French Bombshell, she was a vaudeville star who went on to film and TV. D'Orsay died in 1983.

Billie Dove, born in New York in 1904, was a very successful silent film star. Her first film was *Get-Rich-Quick Wallingford* (1921). She retired in the 1930s and lived with Howard Hughes for several years. Nicknamed "The American Beauty," she was also a writer, pilot, and painter. Dove died in 1997.

Elspeth Dudgeon, born in England in 1871, was on the British stage until she made her film debut in 1932. While appearing in James Whale's *The Old Dark House* (1932), she played Sir Roderick Femm — and was credited as John Dudgeon. She died in 1955.

Douglass Dumbrille, born in Canada in 1889, appeared in more than 180 film and TV shows. His second wife was Patricia Mowbry, 28-year-old daughter of actor Alan Mowbry. They married in 1960 when Dumbrille was 70. He died in 1974.

Margaret Dumont was born in Brooklyn in 1889. A stage actor, her first film appearance was in a silent version of *A Tale of Two Cities* (1916). She appeared in seven Marx Brothers films. *The Cocoanuts* (1929) was her first teaming with Groucho Marx. The ideal straight woman, it's been said that Groucho's jokes went over her head, and she never understood why they were funny. Dumont was married to millionaire businessman John Moller. She died in 1965.

Deanna Durbin, born Edna Mae Durbin in Winnipeg, Canada, in 1921, won a Juvenile Oscar with Mickey Rooney in 1939. Her Hollywood debut was *Three Smart Girls* (1936). Henry Koster and Universal helped make her star, but at the age of 27 she retired from films. She has not given an interview since 1949. She moved to France with husband Charles David, who died in 1999.

Mary Eaton was born in Norfolk, Virginia, in 1901. The first of her five films was *His Children's Children* (1923). Sisters Pearl and Doris were also performers. Eaton was divorced from director Millard Webb. She later married actor Eddie Laughton. Eaton died in 1948.

Gordon "Wild Bill" Elliott, a noted cowboy actor, also appeared under the name of William Elliott. He appeared in *The Great Adventures of Wild Bill Hickok* and many Republic and Monogram westerns. Born in 1903, he died in 1965.

Patricia Ellis, born in Michigan in 1915, made her film debut in 1932 and appeared in more than 40 films before her retirement in 1940. Her stepfather was actor-producer Alexander Leftwich. Ellis died in 1970.

James Ellison, born in Iowa in 1910, was raised in Montana. He often appeared in westerns, but when his career never really took off he retired to go into real estate. He died in 1983.

Leon Errol, born in Australia in 1881, appeared in vaudeville, burlesque, and the Ziegfeld Follies before becoming a film actor. His first film was *Yolanda* (1924). He continued working until his death in 1951; he had appeared in more than 150 films. He's perhaps best known for his work with Lupe Velez in the *Mexican Spitfire* films.

Stuart Erwin enjoyed a long Hollywood career. He was born in Squaw Valley, California, in 1903. His first film appearance was *Mother Knows Best* (1928) and is familiar to people today through his work in such films as *Son of Flubber* (1963) and *The Misadventures of Merlin Jones* (1964), as well as his appearances on *Perry Mason*, *Green Acres*, and *Wagon Train*. He was nominated for an Oscar for his work in *Pigskin Parade* (1936). Erwin, who married June Collyer in 1931, appeared on the *Trouble with Father* television series with Collyer in the 1950s. He died in 1967.

Charles Esmond, born in Austria in 1908, also used the name Carl Esmond. He appeared in more than 50 films and numerous TV shows, including *Lux Video Theatre* and *The Hardy Boys/Nancy Drew Mysteries*. Esmond died in 2004.

Madge Evans, born Margherita Evans in New York in 1909, died in 1981. A child actor, she made her film debut in 1914, and appeared in more than 100 films and TV shows. Married to writer Sidney

Kingsley, she often appeared on stage and TV after she retired from films in 1938.

Paul Everton, born in New York in 1868, began his film career in 1915. He worked steadily during the silent film era and then became an extra when talkies arrived. He died in 1948.

Clifton Fadiman was born in Brooklyn in 1904. The host of *Information Please, What's in a Word, The Name's the Same*, and other game shows, he was a brother of story editor William and film producer Edwin Miles. He died in 1999.

Dustin Farnum, born in New Hampshire in 1874, was a successful silent film actor, particularly in westerns. He appeared in *The Squaw Man*, the legendary western directed by Cecil B. DeMille, in 1914. Farnum retired from films in 1926 and died in 1929 in New York. His brothers were actors William and Marshall Farnum.

Fast-talking **Glenda Farrell** (clocked at 390 words a minute) appeared as Torchy Blaine in the popular movie series. She later guested on TV shows, including *Bewitched, The Fugitive*, and *Ben Casey*. Born in 1904, she died in 1979. She was divorced from Thomas Richards. Her son was Tommy Farrell.

Louise Fazenda, a former Mack Sennett silent screen comedienne, was married to producer Hal Wallis. Fazenda was born in Indiana in 1895 and died in 1962. She made her film debut in 1913 and retired in 1939.

Fritz Feld, born in Berlin in 1900, appeared in more than 130 films, beginning in the silent era. He also played dozens of roles on TV shows. Feld, who often played waiters and was known as the guy who made the popping sound with his hand over his mouth, died in 1993.

Verna Felton was born in Salinas, California, in 1890. Felton was a notable radio performer, and she appeared often on TV, including *The Jack Benny Show* and *I Love Lucy*. She was nominated for an Emmy for *December Bride* (1954). She provided the voice of Wilma's mother on TV's *The Flintstones*, but she is best known for providing voices in several Disney films: *Dumbo* (1941), *Lady and the Tramp* (1955), *Sleeping Beauty* (1959), and *The Jungle Book* (1967). Married to radio actor Lee Millar, she died in 1966.

Mary Fickett, born in Bronxville, New York, in 1932, has won an Emmy for her acting on TV's *All My Children*. She was nominated for a Tony in 1958 for *Sunrise at Campobello*, and she also appeared on *The Edge of Night* and guested on episodes of *Studio One, Kraft Television Theatre, The Defenders*, and others.

James Finlayson, born in Scotland in 1887, began his long film career in 1919 in *The Dentist*. A popular comedian, he was best known for his "slow burn," often opposite *Laurel and Hardy*. He is also reportedly the inspiration for Homer Simpson's "D'oh!" Finlayson died in 1953.

Cissy Fitzgerald, born in England in 1873, was nicknamed "The Girl with the Wink." She made her film debut in a 1896 film short — showing said wink. A stage and vaudeville performer, she later became a silent film star. Fitzgerald died in 1941.

Paul Fix, born in New York in 1901, was a friend of John Wayne's. He appeared in more than 200 films and dozens of TV shows. Fix, who was a regular on *The Rifleman* and played Dr. Piper on the *Star Trek* pilot, died in 1983.

Bramwell Fletcher was born in Yorkshire, England, in 1904. His first film was *Chick* (1928). He also appeared on many television shows in the 1940s and 1950s, including *The Philco Television Playhouse, Kraft Television Theatre*, and *Studio One*. Fletcher was married and divorced from Helen Chandler, who appeared with Kay in the 1925 "Hamlet" play in New York. He was also married and divorced from Diana Barrymore, who appeared with Kay in *Between Us Girls*. He died in 1988.

Stage actor **Helen Flint**, born in Chicago in 1898, appeared in more than 20 films between 1931 and 1944. She died in a car accident in Washington, D.C., in 1967.

Handsome, scandal-ridden **Errol Flynn** was born in Australia in 1909, but raised in England. He made his film debut in 1933 and became a Hollywood star until his hard living took its toll. His wives included Lili Damita, Nora Eddington, and Patrice Wymore. He died in 1959.

Ralph Forbes, born in London in 1896, began his career in the silent film era. He was the son of Mary Forbes and the brother of Brenda Forbes. Forbes' ex-wives included Heather Angel and Ruth Chatterton. He died in 1951.

Norman Foster was born in Richmond, Indiana, in 1900. He married Claudette Colbert (divorced in 1935) and later Sally Blane (Loretta Young's sister). A film actor in the early 1930s, he turned his attention to writing and directing in 1936. Best known for directing several *Mr. Moto* serials, his TV credits include *Zorro, The Green Hornet*, and *Batman*. Foster returned to acting in television movies and shows in the 1970s. He died in 1976.

Preston Foster, born in New Jersey in 1900, was an opera singer and Broadway actor before he appeared on film. Foster, who appeared in more than 100 films, sometimes in lead roles, also appeared as detective Bill Crane in several Universal Crime Club movies and was a regular on TV's *Waterfront*. He died in 1970.

Eddie Foy, Jr., born in New York in 1905, was one of the Seven Little Foys, a vaudeville act that was started by father Eddie Foy after the death of wife Madeline Morando. He appeared in his first film in 1915 and continued acting into the 1970s in film and on television. Foy, brother of Mary Foy, died in 1983.

Betty Francisco, born Elizabeth Bartman in Little Rock, Arkansas, in 1900, made her first film appearance in *Broadway Cowboy* (1920). She appeared in almost 60 films. However, only a few of these were after sound. Francisco died in 1950.

Vaudeville star **Richard "Skeets" Gallagher** was born in Indiana in 1891. His first film was *The Daring Years* (1923). Before his death in 1955, he appeared in more than 50 films.

Edward Gargan, brother of William Gargan (they appeared together in 1942's *Miss Annie Rooney*), was born in Brooklyn in 1902. A character actor, he appeared in more than 200 films, often as a policeman, and died in 1964.

William Gargan was born in Brooklyn in 1905. He was nominated for an Oscar in 1941 for *They Knew What They Wanted*. Executive producer and star of the TV show *The New Adventures of Martin Kane*, Gargan played Ellery Queen in the movies. After losing his voicebox to cancer, he became an antismoking advocate. Gargan, brother of Edward Gargan, died in 1979.

Peggy Ann Garner was born in Canton, Ohio, in 1932. A child star, she is best known for her performance in *A Tree Grows in Brooklyn* (1945), for which she won an Academy Award. Garner married and divorced actor Albert Salmi and made many television appearances in the 1960s and 1970s. Her credits include *The Loveboat*, *Ironside*, *Batman*, and *Bonanza*. She died in 1984.

Pauline Garon, born in Canada in 1901, began her film career in 1920. She appeared in more than 80 films, though most of her roles were before talkies. She died in 1965.

Louis Gasnier, who co-directed *The Virtuous Sin* (1930) with Cukor, was born in France in 1875. He started his career in Paris where he directed comedian Max Linder. After coming to the United States, Gasnier directed several serial movies, including *The Perils of Pauline* (1914). Unable to successfully make the transition to sound films, Gasnier often required a co-director to help with dialogue. He's also known as the director of the cult hit *Reefer Madness* (1936). Gasnier died in 1963.

Marjorie Gateson, born in Brooklyn in 1891, enjoyed a long career. *The False Madonna* (1931) was her second film. She ended her career as a regular (Grace Harris Tyrell) on TV's *The Secret Storm*. She died in 1977.

Margalo Gillmore, born in London in 1897, was a stage star who also appeared in film and on television. Her father was actor Frank Gillmore. Gossips claimed author Jacqueline Susann was an admirer. Gillmore died in 1986.

Lucile Gleason, born in Pasadena, California in 1888, began her film career in 1929. She was married to actor-writer James Gleason; their son was Russell Gleason. Sometimes credited as Lucille, she died in 1947.

Gale Gordon, son of Gloria Gordon, was born in New York in 1906. He appeared in several films, but is best known for his radio and television work. Gordon received Emmy nominations for his work on *Our Miss Brooks* and *The Lucille Ball Show*. He also played Mr. Wilson on the *Dennis the Menace* television show. A member of the Radio Hall of Fame, Gordon died in 1995.

Julia Swayne Gordon, born Sarah Victoria Swayne, in Columbia, Ohio, in 1878, was a silent screen star who began her film career in 1908 with a series based on Shakespeare. She made the transition to sound pictures with some degree of success. She died on May 28, 1933, in Los Angeles, after appearing in almost 200 films.

Mary Gordon, born in Scotland in 1882, began her career in silent films, appearing in more than 250 pictures before her death in 1963. She's best known for playing Sherlock Holmes' housekeeper on radio and in film.

Howard Graham, stage manager for "State of the Union," was an actor and associate director at the famed Pasadena Playhouse in 1943–1945. He was assistant stage manager for *Two's Company* in 1952–1953.

Cary Grant was born Archibald Leach in Bristol, England, in 1904. His first show business work was in British music halls as an acrobat who was also adept at pantomime. He began his film career in 1932, and received Oscar nominations for *Penny Serenade* (1940) and *None But the Lonely Heart* (1944). In 1970 Grant received an Honorary Oscar. Married five times—Virginia Cherrill, Barbara Hutton, Betsy Drake, Dyan Cannon, Barbara Harris—he's the father of Jennifer Grant. His longtime housemate was actor Randolph Scott. Grant died in 1986 in Davenport, Iowa, where he was performing his one-man show.

Bonita Granville, born in Chicago in 1923, is best known for playing Nancy Drew in the movie serials. She received an Oscar nomination for *These Three* (1936). Granville married oilman-movie producer Jack Wrather and eventually bought the rights to *Lassie* and *The Lone Ranger*. She died in 1988.

Harry Green was born in New York in 1892. A lawyer before becoming an actor, he first appeared in film in 1929, with roles in *Close Harmony*, *The Man I Love*, and *Why Bring That Up?* He died in 1958.

Mitzi Green was Paramount's first major child star. Born in the Bronx in 1920, she was billed as "Little Mitzi." She also appeared in TV's *So This Is Hollywood* series in 1955 as Queenie Dugan. Green died at 48 of cancer in 1969.

Edmund Gwenn, born in Wales in 1875, won an Oscar for *Miracle on 34th Street* (1947) and received a nomination for *Mister 880* (1950). He died in 1959.

Sara Haden, born in Texas in 1899, appeared in more than 80 films, beginning in 1934. Daughter of Charlotte Walker, Haden was Richard Abbott's ex-wife. She died in 1981.

Jonathan Hale, born in Canada in 1891, appeared in more than 200 films, beginning in 1934. A former diplomat, he's best known for playing Mr. Dithers in the *Blondie* serials. He committed suicide in 1966.

Stage actor-writer **Louise Closser Hale**, born in Chicago in 1872, died in 1933 of heat stroke.

Patti Hale, also known as Patty Hale, appeared in only four films from 1942 to 1943. *Always in My Heart* was her debut.

Thurston Hall, born in Boston in 1882, was best known for playing the boss on TV's *Topper*. A former stage actor-producer, he made his film debut in the silent era. Hall died in 1958.

John Hamilton, born in Pennsylvania in 1897, began his film career in 1927. A former stage actor, he's best known for playing Perry White on TV's *The Adventures of Superman*. He died in 1958.

Margaret Hamilton, born in Cleveland in 1902, is best known for playing the Wicked Witch in *The Wizard of Oz* (1939). The former kindergarten teacher had a long career, which included a stint as Cora on TV's Maxwell House coffee commercials in the 1970s. She died in 1985.

John Harron, born in New York in 1903, began his career in the silent era. Brother of tragic silent star Bobby Harron, who committed suicide, John, too, died young in 1939.

Richard Haydn, born in London in 1905, made his film debut in *Charley's Aunt* (1941). Haydn, who also directed three films, appeared in such films as *Cluny Brown* (1946), *Alice in Wonderland* (1951), and *Young Frankenstein* (1974). He played Stephen Spettigue on *Playhouse 90's* version of *Charley's Aunt* in 1956, and also appeared on the *The Dick Van Dyke Show*, *Bewitched*, and other TV shows. Haydn died in 1985.

George "Gabby" Hayes was born George Francis Hayes in Wellsville, New York, in 1885. A circus worker and baseball player, he acted in vaudeville and on stage before entering film. His first film was *The Rainbow Man* (1929). Hayes was a cowboy sidekick to Hopalong Cassidy, John Wayne, Roy Rogers, and Randolph Scott, and eventually hosted his own television show. A refined, dignified gentleman off the set, he died in 1969.

Susan Hayward, born Edythe Marriner in Brooklyn in 1918, won an Oscar for *I Want to Live* (1958), and received four other nominations. She died in 1975.

Harold Healy appeared in *Enemies of the Law* (1931) and *Sign of the Cross* (1932). His other film appearances were bit parts. A stage actor, he appeared in the 1922 and 1924 productions of "Rain" with Jeanne Eagels.

Eileen Heckart, born in Columbus, Ohio, in 1919, began her entertainment career on stage in summer stock. She won many awards before her death from cancer in 2001, including an Oscar for *Butterflies Are Free* (1974) and an Emmy for *Love and War* (1992). She was also nominated for the movie *The Bad Seed* (1956) and the television shows *The Mary Tyler Moore Show*, *Backstairs at the White House*, *F.D.R.: The Last Year*, and *The Cosby Show*. She continued acting on stage and received Tony nominations and awards throughout her long career.

Van Heflin, born in Oklahoma in 1910, won an Oscar for *Johnny Eager* (1942). A radio and stage performer, he died in 1971. His sister was soap actor Frances Heflin.

Character actor **Halliwell Hobbes** reportedly had his molars removed to further increase the look of his sunken cheeks. Born in England in 1877, he began his film career in 1929, and appeared in more than 100 films and TV shows until his death in 1962.

Judy Holliday, born Judith Tuvim in New York in 1921, tragically died of cancer in 1965. A truly gifted actor and singer, she won an Oscar for *Born Yesterday* (1950). She also appeared in *Adam's Rib* (1949), *The Solid Gold Cadillac* (1956), and *Bells Are Ringing* (1960).

Sterling Holloway, born in Cedartown, Georgia, in 1905, enjoyed a long film and TV career. He began in the silent film era, but is probably best known as the voice of Winnie the Pooh, as well as many Disney characters. He died in 1992.

Phillips Holmes was born in Grand Rapids, Michigan, in 1907. His parents were actors Taylor Holmes and Edna Phillips, and his brother was actor Ralph Holmes. Holmes died in a plane crash in Canada in 1942.

Miriam Hopkins, born in Bainbridge, Georgia, in 1902, received an Oscar nomination for *Becky Sharp* (1935). Her long career began on stage and ended in film and TV shows in the 1960s. She was known for her feud with Bette Davis. Her ex-husbands included Anatole Litvak and Austin Parker. A true original, she died in 1972.

William Hopper, born William De Wolf Hopper, Jr., in New York in 1915, was the son of gossip columnist Hedda Hopper and actor De Wolf Hopper, Sr. He later played Paul Drake on the *Perry Mason* TV series. Hopper died in 1970.

Edward Everett Horton, born in Brooklyn in 1886, began his long career on stage in 1906. He entered films in 1922 and quickly became a popular character actor. Narrator of TV's *Fractured Fairy Tales*, he made many TV appearances on such shows as *Love, American Style* and *Nanny and the Professor*. He was the grandson of writer Edward Everett Hale, and he died in 1970.

Esther Howard, born in Montana in 1892, made her film debut in 1929, and appeared in almost 100 films. Widow of silent film star Arthur Albertson (he committed suicide in 1926), she died in 1956.

Gertrude Howard, born in Hot Springs, Arkansas, in 1892, made her film debut in 1925, and appeared in 22 films until her death in 1934.

Leslie Howard, born in London in 1893 to Hungarian parents, went into acting as therapy for World War I shell shock. Howard received Oscar nominations for *Berkeley Square* (1933) and *Pygmalion* (1938). Best known for playing Ashley to Vivien Leigh's Scarlett in *Gone with the Wind*, he was killed June 1, 1943, when his plane was shot down by Germans during World War II. His son was actor Ronald Howard.

Jobyna Howland, born in Indianapolis in 1880, was a six-foot stage beauty before she made her film debut in *Her Only Way* (1918). A wonderful character actor who stole every scene she appeared in, she was actor Olin Howlin's sister, and the wife of writer Arthur Stringer, though she lived for many years with writer Zoë Akins. Her last film was *The Story of Temple Drake* (1933). She died in 1936.

Ian Hunter was born in Cape Town, South Africa, in 1900. His film career began in the silent film era, and he appeared in more than 90 films until his death in 1975.

Walter Huston was born Walter Houghston in Canada in 1884. His acting career started on stage, and he, along with Kay Francis, went from Broadway to film stardom. He's the father of director John Huston, and the grandfather of Anjelica, Tony, and Danny. He won an Oscar for a film directed by his son, *The Treasure of Sierra Madre* (1948), and was nominated for *Dodsworth* (1936), *The Devil and Daniel Webster* (1941), and *Yankee Doodle Dandy* (1942). In *Yankee Doodle Dandy* he played the father of his one-time producer George M. Cohan. Huston died in 1950.

Warren Hymer was born in New York in 1906 and died in 1948. The son of writer John Hymer and actress Eleanor Kent, he made his film debut in 1929 and appeared in more than 120 films.

Scottish-born **Frieda Inescort**, daughter of Elaine Inescort, was born in 1901. Diagnosed with multiple sclerosis in 1932, she eventually died from its complications in 1976 after numerous film and TV appearances.

Selmer Jackson, born in Iowa in 1888, began his film career in the 1920s and appeared in more than 300 roles before his death in 1971. His many TV credits included *The Green Hornet*, *The Life and Legend of Wyatt Earp*, and *Bonanza*.

Thomas E. Jackson, born in New York on July 4, 1886, began his acting career on Broadway. He often played tough detectives, beginning with his first film appearance in *Broadway* (1929) in a role he'd played on stage. Jackson's film career continued well in the 1950s, and he also guested on TV shows, including *Dragnet* and *The Adventures of Superman*. He died in 1967.

Child actor **Sybil Jason**, born in South Africa in 1929, appeared in less than 20 films.

Isabel Jeans, born in England in 1891, began her film career during the silent era. Her more than 30 films included *Suspicion* (1941), *Gigi* (1958), and *The Magic Christian* (1969). Married to Claude Rains from 1913 to 1915, she died in 1985.

Isabell Jewell, born in Wyoming in 1907, was a Broadway star who appeared in many Hollywood films, including *A Tale of Two Cities* (1935), *Lost Horizon* (1937), and *Gone with the Wind* (1939). Jewell died in 1972.

Kay Johnson was born Catherine Townsend in Mount Vernon, New York, in 1904. A stage actor, her first film was *Dynamite* (1929). She also appeared in *Madam Satan* (1930), *Thirteen Women* (1932), and *Of Human Bondage* (1934). Mother of actor James Cromwell, she was divorced from director John Cromwell. She died in 1975 in Waterford, Connecticut.

William Johnstone was a noted radio, film, and television actor. He played Judge Lowell on TV's *As the World Turns*, but is perhaps best known for portraying radio's *The Shadow*.

Actor-composer **Al Jolson**, born in Lithuania in 1886, appeared in less than 20 films. The son of a cantor, he started as a minstrel and later became a stage sensation. Divorced from Ruby Keeler, he died in 1950.

Henry Jones, born in Philadelphia in 1912, was a distinctive character actor who appeared in more than 50 movies and dozens of television programs. His credits include *Vertigo* (1958), *Butch Cassidy and the Sundance Kid* (1969), *Alfred Hitchcock Presents*, and *Falcon Crest*. He died in 1999.

Jane Jones, born in Pennsylvania in 1888, appeared in nine films, almost always playing a singer. *One Way Passage* (1932) was her film debut. She died in 1962.

Bobby Jordan, born in New York in 1923, was one of the *Dead End Kids*. He died in 1965 at the age of 42 of cirrhosis of the liver.

Victor Jory, born in Canada in 1902, was the father of noted director and playwright Jon Jory. He began his career in 1930s films, and continued to make numerous television and film appearances up through 1980. Jory died in 1982.

Helen Kane never lost her Bronx accent. Born in 1903, she was reportedly the model for Betty Boop. Although she made less than ten films, she will be remembered for singing "I Want To Be Loved By You" in her unique style. Kane died in 1966 in New York.

Roscoe Karns was born in California in 1891 and died in 1970. He made his film debut in 1915 and appeared in more than 150 films and TV shows. He and son Todd Karns appeared together on TV's *Rocky King, Inside Detective*.

Joseph Kearns, born in 1907 in Salt Lake City, Utah, was the voice of an angel in *It's a Wonderful Life* (1946), but is best known for portraying Mr. Wilson on TV's *Dennis the Menace*. Kearns was also a successful pipe organist. He died in 1962.

Stage actor **Ian Keith**, born in Boston in 1899, began his film career in silent films and ended it on television. His ex-wives included Blanche Yurka and Ethel Clayton. He died in 1960.

Paul Kelly, born in Brooklyn in 1899, was involved in one of Hollywood's most sordid scandals when, in the midst of an affair with Dorothy MacKaye, he killed her husband Ray Raymond. The April 1927 murder was initially covered up. However, an investigation led to manslaughter charges against Kelly, who served a little more than two years in prison. MacKaye, found guilty of compounding a felony, was imprisoned for less than a year. In 1931 the couple married, and Kelly resumed his acting career. MacKaye died in a car accident on January 5, 1940. A former child actor who started his film career in 1911, Kelly won a Tony Award in 1948. He died in 1956 of a heart attack.

Merna Kennedy, born in Kankakee, Illinois, in 1908, was a film star in the late 1920s and early 1930s. Briefly married to Busby Berkeley, she retired in 1934 and died in 1944.

Frederick Kerr, born in London in 1858, is best known for playing Baron Frankenstein in the 1931 film version of *Frankenstein*. He died in 1933.

Guy Kibbee, born in Texas in 1882 and died in 1956, appeared in more than 100 films, beginning in the 1930s. Brother of Milton Kibbee.

Milton Kibbee, born in Santa Fe, New Mexico, in 1896, appeared in more than 300 films, beginning in the early 1930s. Brother of Guy Kibbee, he died in 1970.

Victor Kilian was born in New Jersey in 1891. He made his first acting appearance in *Gentlemen of the Press* (1929). His long career culminated in a recurring role as the Fernwood Flasher (Raymond Larkin) on *Mary Hartman, Mary Hartman*. He was murdered in 1979 in his Hollywood home during a burglary.

Shakespearean actor **Dennis King**, born in England in 1897, was a stage star who continued to make Broadway, film, and television appearances into the 1960s. He made several appearances on TV's *The Philco Television Playhouse* and *The Chevrolet Tele-Theatre*. King died in 1971.

Leonid Kinskey, born in Russia in 1903, appeared in more than 100 film and TV shows. Nicknamed the "Mad Russian," he was a regular on TV's *The People's Choice*. Kinskey died in 1998.

Handsome actor **Patric Knowles**, born in Yorkshire, England, in 1911, made many film and TV appearances, beginning in 1933. He died in 1995.

Scott Kolk, born in Baltimore in 1905, made his first film appearance in *Marianne* (1929). He appeared as an extra in several other films in the 1930s, sometimes using the name Scott Colton. He died in 1993.

Henry Kolker, born in Quincy, Illinois, in 1870, was a silent film director before turning to acting full-time. Kolker, who made more than 160 films, died in 1947 after a fall.

Otto Kruger, born in Toledo, Ohio, in 1885, began his silent film career in 1915. A matinee idol for a time, he eventually became a character actor, often appearing on such TV shows as *Suspense*, *Perry Mason*, and *Science Fiction Theatre*. He hosted TV's *Lux Video Theatre*. Kruger died in 1974.

Ben Lackland played Commissioner Carey on *Captain Video and His Video Rangers*. He made additional television appearances in the 1940s and 1950s until his death in 1959.

Carole Landis, born Frances Lillian Mary Ridste in Wisconsin on January 1, 1919, made her screen debut in 1937. Married at 15, she married three other times, and had lesbian affairs. Nicknamed the Ping Girl, she committed suicide on July 5, 1948, after a failed romance with actor Rex Harrison.

Allan Lane, born in Indiana in 1909, appeared in more than 100 films and TV shows, beginning in 1929. The voice of TV's *Mister Ed*, he died in 1973.

Character actor **Charles Lane**, born in San Francisco in 1899, appeared in more than 240 films, and numerous TV shows. He played Homer Bedloe on TV's *Petticoat Junction*, and was also a regular on *The Real McCoys*.

Elaine Lang, born in Indiana in 1919, made her film debut in *The Man From Oklahoma* (1945). She also appeared on the TV show *Life with Father*. Lange died in 1963.

John Langan, born in 1917 in Denver, is remembered by sci-fi fans for his portrayal of *The Amazing Colossal Man* (1957). He also appeared in many television shows in the 1950s and 1960s, including *Hondo* and *Letter to Loretta*. Married to former showgirl and actress Adele Jergens, Langan died in 1991.

Paul Langton, born in Salt Lake City, Utah, in 1913, was in many B-films in the 1940s and 1950s before becoming a prolific television performer. He made many guest appearances on *Perry Mason*, *Leave it To Beaver* and other shows, and was a regular on *Peyton Place*. Langton died in 1980.

Bobby Larson was born in Los Angeles in 1930. He began his career in 1939 when he appeared in *Down the Wyoming Trail*. He appeared in more than 30 films before he retired in 1950 and became an elementary school teacher. Larson died in 2002.

Jack La Rue was born Gaspere Biondolillo in New York in 1902. He began appearing in films in 1930 and enjoyed a long career, often playing villains in more than 100 pictures, including *42nd Street* (1933), *The Story of Temple Drake* (1933), and *Robin and the Seven Hoods* (1964). He was the father of actor Jack La Rue, Jr., and died in 1984.

Lucille La Verne, born in Memphis, Tennessee, in 1869, made her film debut in 1915. A stage star who had her own repertory company, she was the voice of the evil Queen in *Snow White and the Seven Dwarfs* (1937). She died in 1945.

Betty Lawford, born in England in 1910, was Peter Lawford's cousin. She married and divorced producer Monta Bell. Her father was English actor Ernest Lawford, who appeared with Kay in the 1925 production of "Hamlet" in New York. *Gentlemen of the Press* (1929) was her first major role. Her last film was *The Devil Thumbs a Ride* (1947). She died in 1960.

Ernest Lawford was born in England in 1870. His first film appearance was in the silent *The On-The-Square Girl* (1917), which was directed by George Fitzmaurice, who would later direct Kay in *Raffles* (1930). Primarily a stage actor, he made only three other films. His daughter was Betty Lawford, who would appear with Kay in the film *Gentlemen of the Press* (1929). He died in 1940.

Anderson Lawler, born in Russellville, Alabama, in 1902, made his film debut in 1929. He produced *Somewhere in the Night* (1946) and appeared in 39 films. He died in 1959.

Lillian Lawrence was born in West Virginia in 1868. A successful stage and silent screen actor, she died in 1926. Her films included *The Galley Slave* (1915), *A Fallen Idol* (1919), and *Stella Maris* (1925). Her daughter was actor Ethel Grey Terry.

Marc Lawrence, born in New York in 1910, specialized in playing bad guys. Lawrence, who studied with Eva La Gallienne, enjoyed a long career, which included more than 200 films and numerous TV shows, despite his being blacklisted in the 1950s. He's also been a writer and producer. His daughter is Toni Lawrence, ex-wife of Billy Bob Thornton.

Rosina Lawrence, born in Canada in 1912, is best known for her appearances in several *Our Gang* and *Laurel and Hardy* films. Upon her marriage to Juvenal Marchisio in 1939, she retired from films. She died in 1997.

Harry Lee was born William Henry Lee in Richmond, Virginia, in 1872. His first film was *Destiny's Toy* (1916), and his last was *The Animal Kingdom* (1932). He committed suicide on December 8, 1932, when he jumped from a fire escape at the Hollywood Roosevelt Hotel.

Hal LeRoy, born in Ohio in 1913, died in 1985. A former vaudevillian, he and dance partner Mitzi Mayfair starred in *Ziegfield Follies of 1931*. He appeared in several film shorts but few feature films.

Lawrence Leslie was born in 1908. He appeared in only one other film, *Why Bring That Up?* (1929), before his death on July 15, 1930, at the age of 22. Ward Morehouse described him as "red-thatched [and] a brilliant young actor who died just as his career was beginning."

Vera Lewis, born in New York in 1873, was a stage actor who became a popular silent screen star. Her credits included *Intolerance* (1916) and *Peg O' My Heart* (1922). She died in 1956.

Margaret Lindsay, born Margaret Kies in Iowa in 1910, made her film debut in 1932, and appeared in more than 100 films and TV shows, including *Ellery Queen* serials and such TV shows as *Take a Guess* and *The Chadwick Family*. Sister of Jane Gilbert, she died in 1981. Lindsay has long been rumored to have been part of a lesbian scandal at Warner Bros.

John Litel, born in Wisconsin in 1892, began his film career in 1929 after success on the stage. He appeared in more than 100 films and dozens of TV shows, and had a regular role on *Zorro*. Litel died in 1972.

Lucien Littlefield, born in Texas in 1895, began in the silent film era and appeared in more than 250 films and TV shows. Littlefield, who played Mr. Beasley on TV's *Blondie*, died in 1960.

Doris Lloyd, born Hessy Doris Lloyd in Liverpool, England, in 1896, began her film career in 1920. She appeared in more than 170 films and made many TV appearances on such shows as *Alfred Hitchcock Presents* and *Thriller*. She died in 1968.

John Loder was born in 1898 in England. The son of a British general, he began his film career as an extra in a German film, *Madame Wants No Children* (1926). He had a long career, often as a character actor in film and television. He married and divorced Hedy Lamarr in the 1940s, and died in 1988.

Philip Loeb, born in Philadelphia in 1894, played Jake Goldberg in the movie and TV series *The Goldbergs*. His other credits include *Room Service* (1938) and the "Dinner At Eight" episode of *The Philco Television Playhouse* (1948). He committed suicide in 1955.

Scottish-born **Cecilia Loftus**, born in 1876, appeared in two silent pictures, *A Lady of Quality* (1913) and *Diana of Dobson's* (1917), as well as several sound films in the 1930s and early 1940s. Loftus, nicknamed "Cissie," also appeared in a one-woman show at the Vanderbilt Theatre in 1938. She died in 1943.

Carole Lombard was born Jane Alice Peters in Fort Wayne, Indiana, in 1908. Her first film work was in silent movies, and she used the name Carol Lombard. She was nominated for an Oscar for *My Man Godfrey* (1936), a film on which Carole worked with her ex-husband, William Powell. She was married to Clark Gable when she died January 16, 1942, in a Nevada plane crash.

Tom London, born in Louisville, Kentucky, in 1889, amassed more than 500 film credits, beginning in the silent film era. He appeared in hundreds of westerns in film and on TV, and was Sunset Carson's sidekick in many films. London, who was listed in the Guinness Book of World Records for most film appearances, died in 1963.

Richard Loo, born in Hawaii in 1903, began his long film career in 1931, and appeared in more than 100 films and TV shows until his death in 1983. He also appeared in a Toyota automobile commercial in the 1980s.

Teala Loring, born in Denver in 1924, is the sister of Debra Paget, Lisa Gaye, and Ruell Shayne. Sometimes credited as Judith Gibson, she retired from films in 1950 after appearing in 25 films.

Child actor **Anita Louise** was born Anita Fremault in New York in 1915. She began her career at the age of 6 in a Broadway production of "Peter Ibbetson." Louise had a long career, winding up in television, including a role on *My Friend Flicka* and guest spots on *Mod Squad* and *Mannix*. She was also an accomplished harpist. Louise died in 1970.

Montagu Love, born in 1877 in England, appeared in almost 200 films. An illustrator before he became an actor, Love first appeared in *The Suicide Club* (1914). Often cast as a villain, he died in 1943.

Dorothy Lovett was born in Rhode Island in 1915. She's best known for playing Judy Price in Dr. Christian movie series, beginning with *Meet Dr. Christian* (1939). Lovett died in 1998.

Edith Luckett, born in 1896 in Washington, D.C., appeared in several silent pictures, including *The Coming Power* (1914). She was the mother of Nancy Davis, wife of Ronald Reagan. Luckett died in 1987.

Troubled **Jack Luden**, born in Pennsylvania in 1902, was the nephew of the founder of Luden's Cough Drops. He died in San Quentin Prison in 1951 after convictions for heroin possession and check fraud. A contract player, he appeared in more than 60 films.

Paul Lukas was born in Hungary in 1887. He arrived in Hollywood in 1927, after a very successful European acting career. He won an Academy Award for his performance in *Watch on the Rhine* (1943). Lukas also appeared on television shows, including *It Takes a Thief*, *The F.B.I.*, and *Studio One*. He died in Morocco in 1971.

Jimmy Lydon, born in New Jersey in 1903, began his acting career on stage. Son-in-law of actors Bernard Nedell and Olive Blakeney (he played her son in the Henry Aldrich serials), he went from film acting to numerous TV appearances, including *The New Daughters of Joshua Cabe*, *The Real McCoys*, and *Love That Jill*. Lydon also directed for TV's *The Six Million Dollar Man* and wrote for *Hawaii Five-O*.

A true Hollywood legend, **Jeanette MacDonald** is still popular today. Born in Philadelphia in 1903, she will forever be remembered for her performances with co-star Nelson Eddy. Her first film was *The Love Parade* (1929) with Maurice Chevalier. She continued performing in concerts and on television into the 1950s. MacDonald died in 1965.

Helen Mack, born in Illinois in 1913, was a child actor who started her film career in 1923. After retiring from film in 1946, Mack became a radio writer and producer. She died in 1986.

Kenneth MacKenna was born Leo Melziner, Jr., in Canterbury, New Hampshire, in 1899. His first film was *Miss Bluebird* (1925). His brother was stage designer Jo Mielziner and his father artist Leo Mielziner. Married to Kay Francis from 1931 to 1933, he married Mary Philips in August 1938. MacKenna directed six films from 1931 to 1934, and then became a studio story editor. He returned to acting in the 1960s and died in 1962.

Barton MacLane was born in South Carolina in 1902. *The Cocoanuts* was his second film appearance. A star football player at Wesleyan University, MacLane co-starred with Glenda Farrell in the 1930s *Torchy Blane* serials. He also appeared in many movies, including *The Treasure of Sierra Madre* (1952), *The Maltese Falcon* (1945), and *A Pocketful of Miracles* (1965). He may best known, however, as General Peterson on TV's *I Dream of Jeannie* in the 1960s. He died in 1969.

Mary MacLaren, born Mary MacDonald in Pittsburgh in 1896, was a silent film star who ended up dying in poverty in 1985. In the 1950s she wrote an unsuccessful lesbian novel, *Twisted Heart*, that is now rare and valuable.

Stage actor **Aline MacMahon**, born in Pennsylvania in 1899, received an Oscar nomination for *Dragon Seed* (1944). She made her film debut in 1931, and appeared in more than 50 films and TV shows. She died in 1991.

Paul M. MacWilliams, who appeared in only two films (in both cases playing a doctor) supposedly dated Elizabeth Short, the infamous Black Dahlia, who was murdered in 1947.

Anna Magruder also played the fat lady in *Two Flaming Youths* (1927), *Three-Ring Marriage* (1928), and *Side Show* (1931).

David Manners was born Rauff de Ryther Duan Acklom in Canada in 1901. Manners was his mother's maiden name. He's best known for his work in horror films, including *The Mummy* (1932) and *Dracula*. (1931). After 1936, Manners retired from film and spent his time painting, stage acting, and writing books. He died in 1998.

Fredric March, born Ernest Bickel in Wisconsin in 1897, began his film career as an extra in 1921. He became successful on stage in 1926, and was soon one of Hollywood's most popular leading men. March was nominated for Oscars for *The Royal Family of Broadway* (1930), *A Star Is Born* (1937), and *The Death of a Salesman* (1951). He won Academy Awards for *Dr. Jekyll and Mr. Hyde* (1931) and *The Best Years of Our Lives* (1946). March acted into the 1970s, often with wife Florence Eldridge, until his death from cancer in 1975.

Eddie Marr was born in New Jersey in 1900. He appeared in more than 50 films and also was seen on such television shows as *The Munsters*, *Leave It To Beaver*, and *The Addams Family*. Marr died in 1987.

Charles Marsh, born in Wisconsin in 1893, enjoyed a long career as an extra. He was also Mickey Rooney's whistling double in *The Courtship of Andy Hardy* (1942). He died in 1953.

Herbert Marshall, born in London in 1890, often appeared on stage and occasionally on film with wife Edna Best. They divorced in 1940. Another ex-wife was Boots Mallory. His first big movie hit was *The Letter* (1940) with Jeanne Eagels. Marshall, who lost a leg in World War I, died in 1966. His daughter was actor Sarah Marshall.

Actor **Alphonse Martell**, born in France in 1890, began his film career in 1924. He also wrote and directed *Gigolettes of Paris* (1934) and appeared on such TV shows as *Climax!* and *Mission Impossible*. He died in 1976.

Chris-Pin Martin, born Ysabel Ponciana Chris-Pin Martin Piaz in Arizona in 1893, made his film debut in 1925. He died in 1953 after appearing in more than 100 films, including several *Cisco Kid* and *Zorro* films.

Lewis Martin, born in California in 1894, appeared in many films and television programs, especially in the 1940s and 1950s. His credits include *The War of the Worlds* (1953), *Rockabilly Baby* (1957), and *Perry Mason*. Martin died in 1969.

Nino Martini was born in Italy in 1905. *Paramount on Parade* (1930) was the first of his five films. He died in Italy in 1976.

Chico Marx, born Leonard Marx in New York in 1891, replaced mother Minnie as manager of the Marx Brothers. His nickname was actually Chicko, in honor of his womanizing. He died in 1961.

Groucho Marx, the best known Marx Brother, was born Julius Henry Marx in New York in 1890. He also became a popular television performer on his own show *You Bet Your Life*, and through numerous guest appearances. He died in 1977.

Harpo Marx was born Adolph Marx in New York in 1888. The mute, but definitely noisy Marx Brother, was also an accomplished harpist. He died in 1964.

Zeppo Marx was born Herbert Marx in New York in 1901. He left the troupe after *Duck Soup* (1933) to become a talent agent and inventor — he's credited with developing a wrist watch designed to monitor pulse for cardiac patients. He died in 1979.

Billy Mauch, born in Peoria, Illinois, in 1924, made his film debut in 1936. Mauch, who often co-starred with twin brother Bobby, became an editor after his film career ended.

Mitzi Mayfair, born in Kentucky in 1914, was a Broadway dancer who made only a few film appearances, including some Vitaphone shorts. She traveled with Kay, Martha Raye, and Carole Landis on a USO tour during World War II. Mayfair retired in 1944 after her marriage to 20th Century–Fox studio executive Charles Henderson. She died in 1976 in Arizona.

Frank Mayo, born in 1886 in New York, was a silent screen star who began his career in 1911. He appeared in more than 250 films before his death in 1963.

Lon McCallister, born Herbert Alonzo McCallister in 1923 in Los Angeles, started as a child actor. He appeared in *Stage Door Canteen* (1943), *Winged Victory* (1944), *The Red House* (1947), and many others. In the 1950s he retired to sell real estate. McCallister died in 2005.

Myron McCormick, a popular character actor who appeared on stage, in radio, film, and television, was born in New Albany, Indiana, in 1908. He won a Tony for *South Pacific* (1950). McCormick, a former New York roommate of Henry Fonda, James Stewart, and Joshua Logan, died in 1962.

Joel McCrea, born in California in 1905, appeared in more than 100 films and TV shows in his long career. Long associated with westerns, he appeared on TV's *Wichita Town* with son Jody. Married for more than 50 years to Frances Dee, he died in 1990.

Sam McDaniel, born in Kansas in 1886, appeared in almost 200 films, beginning in 1929. Brother of Hattie and Etta McDaniel, he died in 1962.

Colonel G. L. McDonnell was born in England in 1881. He also played a butler in *Dr. Jekyll and Mr. Hyde* (1931). McDonnell died in 1976.

Claire McDowell, born in New York in 1877, was a silent film actor who made her film debut in 1908. She appeared in more than 250 films and was married to actor Charles Hill Mailes. She died in 1966.

Radio actor **Pat McGeehan**, also known as Patrick McGeehan, had a wonderful voice, which was used for narration in such films as *The Dark Past* (1948), *Challenge the Wild* (1954), and *Okeefenokee* (1958).

Frank McHugh was born in Pennsylvania in 1898 and died in 1981. A child actor whose parents owned a stock company, he was in vaudeville before he entered films in 1930. Brother of actor Matt McHugh, he also appeared on TV's *Bing Crosby Show*.

Character actor **Donald Meek**, born in Scotland in 1878, had extensive stage experience before he became a popular Hollywood actor in more than 100 films. He died in 1946.

Character actor **George Meeker**, born in Brooklyn in 1904, went from the stage to film in 1928. He appeared in such films as *Gone with the Wind* (1939), *Casablanca* (1942), and *The Ox-Bow Incident* (1943). Meeker, an expert polo player, also appeared in the *Superman* and *Invisible Monster* serials. He died in California in 1984.

Lal Chand Mehra was born in India in 1897. He appeared in more than 37 films, including the film version of *The Rains Came* (1939) (he also helped with the music soundtrack). Television credits include a *Bewitched* episode. Mehra died in 1980.

Emilie Melville was born in 1852. Primarily a stage actor in New York, she died in 1932. She appeared in the 1912 production of *Peg O' My Heart* at the Cort Theatre, along with Laurette Taylor.

Una Merkel began her long career as a stand-in for silent star Lillian Gish. She won a Tony in 1956 for "The Ponder Heart," and was nominated for an Oscar in 1961 for *Summer and Smoke*. Born in Covington, Kentucky, in 1903, she died in 1986.

Charlotte Merriam, born in Sheridan, Illinois, in 1906, made her film debut in 1919 and quickly became a star. Most of her 60 films were silent pictures. She died in 1972.

Lou Merrill was born in Canada in 1912. Sometimes billed as Louis Merrill, he appeared in 19 films and an episode of *I Love Lucy* before his death in 1963.

Torben Meyer was born in Denmark in 1884. His first film appearances were in Denmark, beginning in 1912. His career, which included more than 150 films, lasted into the 1960s. He also appeared on the television shows *I Dream of Jeannie*, *Burke's Law*, and others. Meyer died in 1975.

Gertrude Michael, born in Alabama in 1911, appeared in many films in the 1930s, but might be best known for singing "Marijuana" in *Murder at the Vanities* (1934). Boyfriend Paul Cain (aka George Ruric) wrote about her legendary drinking in the novel *Fast One*. An alumni of the Stuart Walker Company, she died in 1965.

Ray Milland was born Reginald Alfred Truscott-Jones in Wales in 1907. He was an extra in British films in 1929, but he quickly graduated to speaking roles. He won an Oscar for *The Lost Weekend* (1945), and also starred in *The Uninvited* (1944), *Till We Meet Again* (1944), and *Dial M for Murder* (1954). Milland's television appearances include *Meet Mr. McNutley*, *Death Valley Days*, *The Love Boat*, and *Hart to Hart*. He also directed several films and television episodes. Milland died in 1986.

Lee Millar, born in Canada in 1888, was a well known radio actor who appeared in only one film—*Nobody's Children* (1940). Married to Verna Felton, he died in 1941.

Patsy Ruth Miller was born in St. Louis, Missouri, in 1904. A silent film star before she became a playwright, she appeared in *The Sheik* (1922), *Camille* (1922), and *The Hunchback of Notre Dame* (1924).

Married to director Tay Garnett from 1929 to 1933, she died in 1995.

Gordon Mills was a B movie and TV actor. He appeared in *Kronos* (1957) and on television in *Gunsmoke* and *Captain Video and His Video Rangers*.

Borrah Minevitch, born in Russia in 1902, appeared in several films. He died in Paris in 1955.

Gerald Mohr was born in New York in 1914. A radio, film, and television actor, he appeared in the television show *Foreign Intrigue*, and was the voice of *The Lone Ranger* and *Phillip Marlowe* on the radio. His last film was *Funny Girl* (1968). He died in Sweden in 1968.

Douglass Montgomery, born in Los Angeles in 1907, appeared in several films, most notably as Laurie in *Little Women* (1933). He died in 1966.

Clayton Moore, born in Chicago in 1914, is best known for playing the *Lone Ranger* on TV. He was a circus performer and model before he made his film debut in 1937. He appeared in more than 70 films and died in 1999.

Dickie Moore was born in Los Angeles in 1925. A child star, his first film was *The Beloved Rogue* (1927). By the age of 10, he'd already amassed more than 50 credits. Moore also appears in *Oliver Twist* (1933), *Miss Annie Rooney* (1942), in which he gave Shirley Temple her first on-screen kiss, and *Out of the Past* (1947). In addition, Moore worked on the TV series *Captain Video and His Video Rangers*. He retired from acting in the 1950s and went into public relations. Moore married actor Jane Powell in 1988.

Eulabelle Moore, a longtime stage actor, was born in 1903 and died in 1964.

Agnes Moorehead was born in Clinton, Massachusetts, in 1900. A stage, radio, film, and television performer, she received Oscar nominations for *The Magnificent Ambersons* (1942), *Mrs. Parkington* (1944), *Johnny Belinda* (1948), and *Hush ... Hush, Sweet Charlotte* (1964). Best known for her Emmy-nominated role as Endora on TV's *Bewitched*, she won an Emmy for a guest appearance on *The Wild, Wild West*. She died in 1974.

Peggy Moran, born in Clinton, Iowa, in 1918, made her film debut in 1938 and retired from films in 1943 after marrying producer Henry Koster. Her mother was a dancer with the Denishawn Dance Company and her father was famed pin-up artist Earl Moran. Peggy died in 2002 from injuries received in an automobile accident.

Polly Moran, born in Chicago in 1883, made her film debut in 1915, and appeared in almost 100 films. She died in 1952.

Adrian Morris, born in New York in 1907, was the brother of Chester Morris. He died in 1941, after appearing in more than 60 films, beginning in 1931.

Chester Morris was born John Chester Brooks Morris in New York in 1901. The son of actor William Morris and brother of Adrian Morris, he appeared in several silent pictures, but is best known as Boston Blackie, a role he played first in 1941 and then throughout the 1940s. He was also nominated in 1930 for an Oscar for his performance in *Alibi*. Morris worked in horror pictures in the 1950s as well as making television appearances on such shows as *Robert Montgomery Presents*. He returned to the stage in the 1960s with an appearance in "The Subject Was Roses." He died of a drug overdose in 1970.

Frances Morris, born in Massachusetts in 1908, appeared as an extra in more than 100 films, but received bigger roles on TV in such shows as *Perry Mason, The Virginian,* and *Wagon Train*.

Adrienne Morrison was born in New York in 1883. The mother of Constance, Barbara, and Joan Bennett, she divorced husband Richard in April 1925. A stage actor, she made only six films—all were silent. The first was *Damaged Goods* (1914), which was directed by—and starred—her husband. She died in 1940.

Maurice Moscovich, born in Odessa, Russia, in 1871, was a veteran of New York's Yiddish stage. He was the father of actor Noel Madison. Sometimes billed as Maurice Moscovitch, he died in 1940.

Alan Mowbray, born in London in 1896, made his film debut in 1931 and appeared in more than 180 films and TV shows. He was a regular on such TV shows as *Colonel Humphrey Flack*, *The Mickey Rooney Show*, and *The Best in Mystery*. Mowbray died in 1969.

Jean Muir, accused of being a Communist in the 1950s, retired to become a drama professor. She made occasional TV appearances on such shows as *Route 66* and *The Naked City*. Born in New York in 1911, she died in 1996.

Herbert Mundlin, born in England in 1898, made his film debut in 1931 and appeared in more than 50 films until he died in a car accident in 1939.

Patrice Munsel was born in Spokane, Washington, in 1925. A panelist on *To Tell the Truth* in the 1950s, she also appeared on *Your Show of Shows*, *The Alcoa Hour*, and *The Wild, Wild West*.

George Murphy was born in New Haven, Connecticut, in 1902. He received an Honorary Oscar in 1951, and was the host of TV's *The M-G-M Parade* in the 1950s. A dancer and actor, he retired from show business and went into politics, eventually becoming a United States senator. Murphy died in 1992.

Ken Murray was born in New York in 1903. A ubiquitous performer, he appeared in nightclubs, films, and television. Murray died in 1988.

J. Carrol Naish, born in New York in 1897, played a variety of ethnic roles, including Italian, Japanese, and Native Americans, but rarely an Irishman, though he was of Irish descent. He died in 1973.

Mary Nash was born in Troy, New York, in 1885. The sister of actor Florence Nash, she appeared in a few silent films and then became a character actor in sound pictures. She died in 1976.

Frank Nelson was born in 1911 and died in 1986. He's best known for his appearances on *The Jack Benny Show*. His catchphrase was a long drawn out "Yeeeeeeees." Nelson appeared in more than 30 films and countless TV shows. He also provided voice work in films and television, notably *The Jetsons* and *The Flintstones*.

David Newell was born in Carthage, Missouri, in 1905. A Paramount contract player, he became a makeup artist for Walt Disney after a disfiguring automobile accident. His TV credits included *The Mickey Mouse Club* and *Lassie*. Newell died in 1980.

Theodore Newton, born in New Jersey on August 4, 1904, died in Hollywood in 1963. A stage actor, he made his film debut in 1933 and appeared in almost 30 films. He also made numerous TV appearances, including *Wagon Train*, *Alfred Hitchcock Presents*, and *Rawhide*.

Jack Oakie was born Louis Delaney Offield in Sedalia, Missouri, in 1903. His mother was actor Evelyn Oakie. He was a great character actor, and his career began in the 1920s and lasted through the early 1960s. Nominated for an Oscar for his acting in *The Great Dictator* (1941), he also made many television appearances, including *Bonanza* and *Night Gallery*. Oakie died in 1978.

Writer-director-composer-actor-stuntman **Dave O'Brien** was born in Texas in 1912 and died in 1969. Sometimes credited as David Barclay, he began his acting career in 1940, and is probably best known as the hapless guy in the Pete Smith shorts.

Fast talking **Pat O'Brien**, born in Milwaukee in 1899, began his acting career on stage. A popular leading actor in the 1930s and 1940s, he enjoyed a long career in film and TV. He died in 1983.

Frank O'Connor was born in Lorain, Ohio, in 1897 and died in 1979. He met Ayn Rand on a movie set and eventually married her in 1929. O'Connor made 11 films between 1927 and 1934, and then left film acting.

Character actor **Una O'Connor**, born in Ireland in 1880, was memorable in *Witness for the Prosecution* (1957), her last film, as well as *The Bride of Frankenstein* (1935) and many others. She died in 1959.

George O'Hanlon, born in Brooklyn in 1912, enjoyed a long film and TV career. He played the doofus Joe McDoakes in the 1940s and 1950s film shorts and was also the voice of George Jetson on TV. He died in 1989.

Dennis O'Keefe, born in Iowa in 1908, died in 1968. Sometimes billed as Bud Flanagan, he started in vaudeville as a child. After appearing in many films, he had his own TV show in the 1950s.

Swedish-born **Warner Oland** is best known for his portrayal of Charlie Chan and Dr. Fu Manchu in countless movies. Purportedly discovered by Alla Nazimova, his long career began in 1915 with *The Romance of Elaine*. Born in 1880, he died in 1938.

Pat O'Malley, born in Pennsylvania in 1890, began his film career in 1915 and amassed more than 300 film and TV credits. He died in 1966.

Nance O'Neil, born in Oakland, California, in 1874, made her film debut in 1915 and appeared in 33 films. Although married to Alfred Hickman, she had a close friendship with accused ax murder Lizzie Borden. O'Neil died in 1965.

Zelma O'Neil was born Zelma Schrader in Rock Falls, Illinois, in 1903. *Paramount on Parade* (1930) was her first film. A stage star, she made only a few films before retiring in the late 1930s to marry actor Patrick O'Moore. O'Neil died in 1989.

Rafaela Ottiano, born in Italy in 1888, appeared in more than 40 films until her death in 1942.

English actor **Reginald Owen**, born in England in 1887, enjoyed a long career. He first appeared in silent films and ended his career in such films as *Mary Poppins* (1964), *Bedknobs and Broomsticks* (1971), and *Tammy and the Doctor* (1963), and with TV appearances on *Bewitched*, *It Takes a Thief*, and *Maverick*. He died in 1972.

Born Signe Auen in Spokane, Washington, in 1894, **Seena Owen** was a silent screen star as well as a film writer. She made her first film appearance in the 1915 production of *A Day That Is Gone*, and also appeared in D. W. Griffith's *Intolerance* (1916). She retired from acting in 1932, and died in 1966.

Monroe Owsley, born in Atlanta, Georgia, in 1900, made his film debut in 1928. He appeared in 30 films until his death from a heart attack in 1937.

Sarah Padden, born in England in 1881, appeared in more than 150 films and numerous TV shows until her death in 1967.

Short, squat, froggy-voiced character actor **Eugene Pallette** was born in 1889 in Kansas. He made more than 200 film appearances in his long film career, which began in 1913 with *When the Light Fades*. He died in 1954.

Paul Panzer, born in Germany in 1872, was a silent

film star whose career began in 1905. He appeared in more than 250 films and died in 1958.

Jean Parker was born Lois Mae Green in Montana in 1915. She was discovered by Louis B. Mayer's personal assistant, Ida Koverman, after posing as Father Time in a poster contest. Her first film appearance was *Divorce in the Family* (1932), and she appeared in more than 70 films and several television shows. Divorced four times, her husbands included George McDonald, Douglas Dawson, Curtis Grotter, and Robert Lowery.

Elizabeth Patterson, daughter of a Confederate soldier, had a long career, beginning in silent film and ending on television with appearances on *I Love Lucy* and *Alfred Hitchcock Presents*. Born in Savannah, Tennessee, in 1875, she died in 1966.

Sally Payne, born in Chicago in 1912, appeared in more than 40 films, beginning in 1936. Payne, who was a regular on the TV show *I Married Joan*, died in 1999.

Shelby Payne was one of the Goldwyn Girls. She appeared in very few films, usually as a cigarette girl. *Wife Wanted* was her last film.

Joan Peers, born in Chicago in 1909, appeared in less than ten films. Her last film was *Over the Hill* (1931). She died in 1975.

Duncan Penwarden, born in 1880 in Canada, also played the realtor in the stage version of *Gentlemen of the Press*. He appeared in the film *The Lady Lies* (1929) and died in 1930.

Anthony Perkins, born in New York in 1932, was nominated for an Oscar for *Friendly Persuasion* (1956), but is best known for playing Norman Bates in Alfred Hitchcock's *Psycho* (1960). His father was actor Osgood Perkins, and he married Berry Berenson. Perkins died of AIDS-related pneumonia in 1992.

Irving Pichel was born in Pittsburgh in 1891. He was also a director and is credited with "discovering" Natalie Wood. One of his last films—which he acted in and directed—was *Martin Luther* (1953). He died in 1954.

Walter Pidgeon, born in Canada in 1897, received Oscar nominations for *Mrs. Miniver* (1943) and *Madame Curie* (1943). After studying voice at the New England Conservatory of Music, he became a stage actor, and then appeared in silent films before becoming a leading man, often co-starring with Greer Garson. He died in 1984.

Bernice Pilot appeared in more than 20 films, almost always as a maid. Her film debut was *Hearts in Dixie* (1929).

ZaSu Pitts was born Eliza Susan (named after two aunts) Pitts in Parsons, Kansas, in 1898. She was a silent film star who became a character actor with the advent of sound. Her first credit was *Uneasy Money* (1917). A notorious scene stealer, she appeared in more than 200 films, including *Greed* (1925), *The Squall* (1929), and *Life with Father* (1947). Pitts also worked on many television shows, including *Perry Mason*, *The Gale Storm Show*, and *Burke's Law*. She was the model for Popeye's Olive Oyl. She died in 1963.

Paul Porcasi, born in Italy in 1879, appeared in more than 130 films, beginning in the silent era. He died in 1946.

Victor Potel, born in Lafayette, Indiana, in 1889, also dabbled in writing and directing. His long career began with a silent short comedy, *Hank and Lank: Joyriding* (1910), the first of the Hank and Lank comedy serials. Potel played Lank, and Augustus Carney played Hank. Potel's career ended with a bit role in *The Shocking Miss Pilgrim* (1947). He also appeared in several *Alkali Ike* and *Broncho Billy* shorts. Potel died March 8, 1947, in Hollywood.

Singer **Dick Powell** became a tough guy detective in such 1940s film roles as *Farewell, My Lovely* (1944). He ended his career by producing and directing as well as making TV appearances and serving as host of *The Dick Powell Show*, *Zane Grey Theater*, and *The Four Star Playhouse*. Born in Arkansas in 1904, he died in 1963. Divorced from Joan Blondell, he was married to June Allyson when he died.

Richard Powell, born in 1896, began his film career in 1931, and died in a car accident in 1937. *Another Dawn* (1937) was his last film.

Character actor **Russ Powell**, born in Indianapolis in 1875, appeared in more than 100 films, beginning in 1915 and ending in the 1940s. He died in 1950.

William Powell, born in Pittsburgh in 1892, was one of Hollywood's most charming male leads, especially in the 1930s and 1940s *Thin Man* films with Myrna Loy. A brilliant actor, he was equally adept at comedy and drama. His first film was *When Knighthood Was in Flower* (1922). Powell was nominated for Oscars three times—*The Thin Man* (1935), *My Man Godfrey* (1937), and *Life with Father* (1947). Divorced from Carole Lombard, he married Diana Lewis in 1940. He died in 1984.

Tyrone Power, Sr., father of film star Tyrone Power, Jr., was born in London in 1869. His grandfather, also named Tyrone Power, was a famous Irish actor, and his father, Harold Power, a concert pianist. He was a popular actor, appearing in many silent films, including *Where Are My Children?* (1916), *Fury* (1923), and *The Truth About Wives* (1923). He married three times, first to Edith Crane in 1898. The marriage ended with her death in 1912. The second marriage was to Patia Reaume, who took the name Mrs. Tyrone Power. She was the mother of Tyrone Power, Jr., born in 1914. They divorced in 1916.

Aileen Pringle, born in San Francisco in 1895, was a silent film star before becoming a character actor. She appeared in more than 70 films. Once married to writer James M. Cain, she died in 1989.

Herbert Prior, born in England in 1867, made his film debut in 1907, and appeared in more than 215 films. He was married to silent film star Mabel Trunnelle.

Catherine Proctor was born in Canada in 1879. Her film appearances include *Without Hope* (1914), *The Foolish Virgin* (1917), and *Youth Takes A Fling* (1938). Her New York stage credits include "A Midsummer Night's Dream" in 1906.

Roger Pryor was born in New York in 1901. He was a hit in the Broadway play, "Saturday's Children," in which he appeared with Ruth Gordon. He was also an orchestra leader and worked on the radio program "Gulf Screen Guild Theatre of the Air." He appeared in more than 50 films, and died in 1974.

Claude Rains, born in England in 1889, received four Oscar nominations. Rains started his career on stage and enjoyed a long film and TV career. Married seven times, his wives included Isabel Jeans, Marie Hemingway, and Beatriz Thomas. Rains died in 1967.

Marjorie Rambeau was born in San Francisco in 1889. Her film career began in 1917 with an appearance in *The Greater Woman*. Nominated for Oscars for *The Primrose Path* (1940) and *Torch Song* (1953), she died in 1970.

Lillian Randolph was born in Louisville, Kentucky, in 1898. Best known for playing Madam Queen on the radio and television versions of *Amos 'n' Andy*, Randolph enjoyed a long career up until her death in 1980. Her sister was Amanda Randolph, and her daughter was Barbara Randolph.

Basil Rathbone, born in South Africa in 1892, is perhaps best known for his portrayal of Sherlock Holmes. Rathbone's wife, Ouida, who socialized with Kay, has been quoted as saying, "In many ways she was a lonely lady. People were afraid to approach her." Rathbone's first film was *Innocent* (1921). He was nominated twice for Oscars: *Romeo and Juliet* (1936) and *If I Were King* (1938). Often cast as a villain in the early part of his career, his final appearances were on television and in low-budget films. Rathbone died in 1967, and Ouida in 1974.

Herbert Rawlinson, born in England in 1885, was a silent film star who began his career in 1911. Rawlinson, who died in 1953, appeared in more than 330 films.

Martha Raye, born Margaret Teresa Yvonne Reed in Butte, Montana, in 1916, worked in vaudeville as a child and then became a big band singer before making her film debut in 1936. She was married seven times; her husbands included David Rose and Bud Westmore. She died in 1994.

Frances Raymond was born in Massachusetts in 1869. She first appeared on film in 1915 as Frankie Raymond in *The Fable of the Home Treatment and the Sure Cure*. Appearing in more than 70 films, she made her last appearance in *Ladies' Man* in 1947 — not a remake of the 1931 William Powell-Kay Francis film. She died in 1961.

Gene Raymond, born Raymond Guion in New York in 1908, was a child actor on Broadway. He made his film debut in 1931. He and his wife Jeanette McDonald appeared together in *Smilin' Through* in 1941. Raymond died in 1998.

Phillip Reed, born in New York in 1908, made occasional TV appearances in the 1950s and 1960s, including one on *Alfred Hitchcock Presents*, and his last film appearance was in 1965's *Harum Scarum*. He died in 1996.

George Regas, born in Greece in 1890, appeared in more than 80 films, beginning in 1921. Regis, who was married to Marion Davies' sister Reine, died in 1940.

Ada Rehan, born Ada Crehan in Limerick, Ireland, in 1860, was a popular stage actor known for her Shakespearean roles. She died in 1916.

Frank Reicher, born in Germany in 1875, was a prolific actor, writer, director, and producer. His film credits alone total more than 200 appearances. He helped write the German screenplay for *Anna Christie* (1930), and directed more than 40 films. His sister was actress Hedwiga Reicher. He died in 1965.

James Rennie, born in Canada in 1890, began his film career in *Remodeling Her Husband* (1920). He also appeared in *The Girl of the Golden West* (1930), *Now, Voyager* (1942), and others. He was married to Dorothy Gish from 1920 to 1935. He died in 1965.

Craig Reynolds, born in California in 1907, began his film acting career in the 1920s. He appeared in more than 60 films, often crime dramas, before he was killed in a motorcycle accident in 1947.

Ila Rhodes, once engaged to Ronald Reagan, appeared in five films.

Adnia Rice was born in 1923 in Fayetteville, Tennessee. After studying at Sullins College, Vanderbilt University, and the Pasadena Playhouse, she played the role of Jennie in "State of the Union" and was also listed as assistant stage manager. By 1952 she was described as Kay's "comedienne protégée," and later appeared on television and in several Broadway shows, including *The Music Man* and

Little Me. A theatre in her hometown is named in her honor. She died in 1987.

Sam Rice, born in New York in 1874, was a former burlesque performer who appeared in more than 50 films. He died in 1946.

Addison Richards, born in Ohio in 1887, enjoyed a long career beginning in 1933. He worked in film and television until his death in 1964, amassing more than 300 credits.

Kane Richmond was born Fred Bowditch in Minneapolis in 1906. He appeared in more than 80 films in the 1930s and 1940s, often in B films. Richmond also played the Shadow in *Behind the Mask* (1946) and *The Shadow Returns* (1946). He died in 1973.

John Ridgely, born in Chicago in 1909, appeared in more than 150 films, beginning in the 1930s. He died in 1968.

Cyril Ring was born in Massachusetts in 1892. He was married to dancer and comedienne Charlotte Greenwood from 1916 to 1922. His sister was actor Blanche Ring, and his brother-in-law was actor Thomas Meighan. He appeared in almost 200 films, mostly as an extra, and died in 1967.

Elizabeth Risdon, born in England in 1887, was a British silent film star who became a Hollywood character actor. She made her film debut in 1913 and appeared in more than 140 films until her death in 1958.

Bert Roach, born in Washington, D.C., in 1891, appeared in more than 280 films, beginning in 1914. He died in 1971.

Edward G. Robinson, born in Bucharest in 1893, never received an Oscar nomination, though he did receive a lifetime award in 1973. Robinson, a stage actor before coming to Hollywood in 1923, also cowrote a play with Jo Sperling, "The Kibitzer." He died in 1973.

Viola Roche, born in London in England in 1885, appeared in *Royal Wedding* (1951) and the film version of *Goodbye, My Fancy* (1951). She died in 1961.

Buddy Rogers, born in Olathe, Kansas, in 1904, was nicknamed "America's Boyfriend." He was a bandleader and actor who married Mary Pickford, "America's Sweetheart," in 1937. Though eleven years separated them, they remained married for more than four decades until Pickford's death in 1979. Rogers played himself in a couple episodes of *Petticoat Junction* in 1963. He died in 1999.

Sometimes known as "Pegleg" Rogers, **John Rogers** was born in Manchester, England, in 1888. He appeared as an extra in more than 50 films. He died in 1963.

Professional wrestler **Constantine Romanoff** made his film debut in the 1920s and appeared in more than 70 films.

TV fans know **Cesar Romero** for his work as the Joker on *Batman*. *British Agent* (1934) was his second film appearance. Born in New York in 1907, he appeared in more than 115 films and dozens of TV shows. Grandson of Cuban hero Jose Marti, Romero died in 1994.

Henry Roquemore, born in Texas in 1886, appeared in more than 200 films, beginning in the 1920s. Married to Fern Emmett, he died in 1943.

Maxie Rosenbloom, born in New York in 1904, was the world light heavyweight boxing champion from 1930 to 1934. Nicknamed "Slapsie Maxie," he appeared in many films and made TV appearances in the 1960s on such programs as *I Dream of Jeannie* and *The Munsters*. He died in 1976.

Earle Ross, born in Illinois in 1888, was a TV and radio actor who appeared on *The Great Gildersleeve* and *Meet Millie*. He died in 1961.

Lillian Roth was born in Boston in 1910. *Illusion* (1929) was her feature talkie debut. Her biography, *I'll Cry Tomorrow*, was made into a feature film with Susan Hayward playing Roth. She was married and divorced eight times, and she struggled with alcoholism. Roth died in New York in 1980.

Christian Rub, born in Austria in 1887, appeared in more than 100 films until his death in 1956. Although he played many janitors, Rub is most recognized for providing the voice of Geppetto in *Pinocchio* (1940).

Charles Ruggles, born in Los Angeles in 1886, was the brother of director Wesley Ruggles. Charles won a Tony in 1959 for "The Pleasure of His Company." He appeared in dozens of movies, including Disney films in the 1960s. He also appeared often on stage and made numerous television appearances, which included providing the voice of Aesop on *The Bullwinkle Show*. Like Kay Francis, Ruggles was a dog lover who opened the Terrier Store, selling food and supplies, and a kennel (See-Are Kennels). Many stars, including Kay, used the kennel to board their dogs when they were out of town. Amenities included a "warm bath and a rubdown at a balmy temperature," along with a "private, long screened exercise run with pepper trees for shade." Ruggles died in 1970.

Melville Ruick was born in Idaho in 1898. A character actor who had an extensive career in radio and television, his former wife was actress Lurene Tuttle, and his daughter was Barbara Ruick.

Sig Ruman, born in Germany in 1884, appeared in more than 100 films. His long film and TV career included such gems as *A Night at the Opera* (1935), *Ninotchka* (1939), and *To Be Or Not To Be* (1942). He died in 1967.

Rosalind Russell, born in Connecticut in 1907, attended the American Academy of Dramatic Art and went on to become one of America's classiest stage and screen stars. She received four Oscar nominations and received the Jean Hersholt Humanitarian Award in 1973. Her best roles were in *His Girl Friday* (1940), *The Women* (1939), and *My Sister Eileen* (1942). She died in 1976.

Basil Ruysdael was born in New Jersey in 1888. *The Cocoanuts* (1929) was his first film. He also appeared in *Pinky* (1949), *The Blackboard Jungle* (1955), and did voice-over work for Disney's *One Hundred and One Dalmatians* (1961), his last film. He died in 1960.

Robert Ryan, born in Chicago in 1911, received an Oscar nomination for *Crossfire* (1947). He steadily worked in film and TV until his death in 1973.

Tim Ryan, born in New Jersey in 1899, appeared in more than 130 films, beginning in 1936, and was a writer on more than 40 pictures. He died in 1956.

Sally Sage, born in Milwaukee, Wisconsin, in 1914, appeared in nine films between 1938 to 1941. She was Betty Davis' stand-in on many films. Sage died in 2000.

S.Z. Sakall, born in Budapest, Hungary, in 1884, was nicknamed "Cuddles." Unable to speak English when he arrived in Hollywood, he learned his lines phonetically. Sakall died in 1955.

Fay Sappington, born in Galveston, Texas, in 1906, appeared in several movies, including *The Owl and the Pussycat* (1970), and guested on television programs, such as *Tales From The Darkside*. She died in 1984.

Syd Saylor, born in Chicago in 1895, began his acting career with a number of 1926 film appearances. By the time he died in 1962, he'd appeared in more than 300 movies and on such television shows as *Buffalo Bill Jr.*, *Maverick*, and *Perry Mason*.

Frank Schofield appeared in several films and was a regular on *The Secret Storm*, *Dark Shadows*, *Days of Our Lives*, and other television programs.

Producer and actor **Randolph Scott** was born in Virginia in 1898. He appeared in more than 100 films, including many westerns. Scott, who made a fortune investing, was not known as a great actor, but nevertheless enjoyed a long career. Scott, a longtime friend of Cary Grant, died in 1987.

Child actor **Jackie Searl**, sometimes billed as Jackie Searle, was born in California in 1920. His first film was *Daughters of Desire* (1929). Searl, in many films in the 1930s, ended his career on television shows such as *Perry Mason*, *Gunsmoke*, and *The High Chaparral*. He died in 1991.

George Seaton, born in Indiana in 1911, won Oscars for *The Miracle on 34th Street* (1947) and *The Country Girl* (1954) and received three other nominations. He won the Jean Hersholt Humanitarian Award in 1962. Radio's first Lone Ranger, he died in 1979.

Child actor **Billy Seay** was born in Chicago in 1922. His sister Dorothy was also a child actor in the 1920s. Seay appeared in five films between 1928 and 1934.

Rolfe Sedan, born in New York in 1896, began his long career as an extra in the early 1920s. His last film was *Love At First Bite* (1979), and he also appeared in numerous television shows including *Maude*, *Petticoat Junction*, and *The Addams Family*. Sometimes billed as Ralph Sedan, Rolf Sedan, and Rolphe Sedan, he died in 1982.

Charles Seel was born in New York in 1897. *Comet Over Broadway* (1938) was his first film, but his long career included more than 30 films and countless television shows, including *Gunsmoke*, *Night Gallery*, and *The Twilight Zone*. His last film was *Westworld* (1973), and he died in 1980.

Louise Seidel, born in 1947, was married to writer and Dartmouth film professor Maurice Rapf, son of producer Harry Rapf.

Stage actor **Janet Shaw**, born Ellen Stuart in Nebraska in 1919, signed a seven-year Warner Bros. contract in 1937. She died in 2001.

Robert Shayne, born in Yonkers, New York, in 1900, enjoyed a long stage film, and TV career. He appeared in more than 100 films, but is probably best known for TV roles on *Navy Log*, *The Lone Ranger*, and *The Adventures of Superman*. Shayne died in 1992.

John Shelton, born in Los Angeles in 1915, made his film debut in 1936. Divorced from actor Kathryn Grayson, he died in 1972.

Marla Shelton was a songwriter and actor. She appeared in more than 20 films and also supplied songs for *A Song for Miss Julie* (1945), *Crime, Inc.* (1945), and *Breakfast in Hollywood* (1946).

Ann Shoemaker, born in Brooklyn in 1891, was married to actor Henry Stephenson. She died in 1971.

Sylvia Sidney, born Sophie Kosow in the Bronx in 1910, began acting on stage at a young age, and made her first film, *Broadway Nights*, in 1927; she played herself, a successful theatre star. She was only 17 years old. During her years at Paramount she was the mistress of producer B.P. Schulberg. Her long career included many films and television appearances, along with numerous stage plays. Her TV credits include *The Defenders*, *Eight Is Enough*, *An Early Frost*, and *Fantasy Island*. She also was seen in *Beetlejuice* (1988), *Sabotage* (1936), and *Madame Butterfly* (1932). Sidney died in 1999.

Penny Singleton, born Mariana Dorothy Agnes Letitia McNulty in Philadelphia in 1908, is best known for her role as *Blondie* in the serial. Her brother was Barney McNulty, inventor of TV cue cards.

Hal Skelly was born in Pennsylvania in 1891. His first film was *The Dancing Town* (1928). He was a dancer who also worked in circus and vaudeville. He died in 1934 in a car-train collision.

Alison Skipworth, born Alice Groom in 1863 in London, was a wonderful character actor who made several films with W.C. Fields. Her first film was *39 East* (1920), her last *Wide Open Faces* (1938). She died in 1952.

C. Aubrey Smith was one of the first actors to be knighted. Upon his arrival in Hollywood from his native England, he started the Hollywood Cricket Club, which also included Boris Karloff, Ronald Colman, Cary Grant, David Niven, Errol Flynn, Basil Rathbone and others. He also co-founded the Screen Actors Guild, which often met in secret in its earliest days. Smith considered himself psychic, and some believe he made his presence felt to family and friends following his death. He was born in London in 1863, and he died in 1948.

Oscar Smith, an African American contract player, was born in Kansas in 1885. He died in 1956.

Born in 1903 in Kansas City, Missouri, **Stanley Smith** made 21 films between 1929 and 1943. He began his career on stage and eventually played several lead roles in the early 1930s. Smith died in 1974.

Stage actor-producer-director **George Somnes** died in 1956.

John Graham Spacey, born in England in 1897, made his film debut in 1935, appearing in 19 films until his death in 1940. Spacey was Kevin Spacey's great-great uncle.

Gordon Standing was born in London in 1887. He died in 1927 following a lion attack at Selig Zoo in Los Angeles. His last film was *King of the Jungle* (1927). Standing's cousin, Wyndham Standing, appeared with Kay in *British Agent* (1934).

Joan Standing was born in England in 1903. Her first film was *The Loves of Letty* (1919). Her last film was *Lil' Abner* (1940). Standing died in 1979 in Houston, Texas.

Wyndham Standing was born in London in 1880. Cousin of actor Gordon Standing, brother of Guy Standing, and son of Herbert Standing, Wyndham appeared in more than 100 films, beginning in 1915. Although he played leads in silent films, his later career was usually as an extra. Standing died in 1963.

Will Stanton, born in England in 1885, appeared in his first film in 1927. He often played a drunk, and his credits included more than 80 films. He died in 1969.

Henry Stephenson, born in the West Indies in 1871, began his film career as Harry Stephenson in *The Spreading Dawn* (1917). Married to character actor Ann Shoemaker, he appeared in almost 100 films, and died in 1956.

James Stephenson, born in England in 1889, received an Oscar nomination for *The Letter* (1940). He appeared in 39 films until his death in 1941.

Houseley Stevenson, born in England in 1879, began his film career in 1936. He later taught and directed at the famed Pasadena Community Playhouse. The father of Edward, Houseley Jr., and Onslow Stevenson, he died in 1953.

Carl Stockdale, born in Minnesota in 1874, became involved in one of Hollywood's most famous murder mysteries when he provided an alibi for Charlotte Selby (Mary Miles Minter's mother) in the shooting death of William Desmond Taylor. Stockdale's career began in the silent era, and he appeared in more than 225 films before his death in 1953.

Haila Stoddard, born in Montana in 1914, played Aunt Pauline on TV's *The Secret Storm*. She also made guest appearances on *Studio One*, *Suspense*, and other television programs.

Lewis Stone was best known for his role as Judge Hardy in the Andy Hardy films with Mickey Rooney. He was born in Worcester, Massachusetts, in 1879. His first film credit was *The Man Who Found Out* (1915). A successful silent and sound film star, he received an Oscar nomination for *The Patriot* (1928). He also appeared in *The Prisoner of Zenda* (1922), *The Lost World* (1925), *A Woman of Affairs* (1928), *Grand Hotel* (1932), and *Red-Headed Woman* (1932). He died in Beverly Hills in 1953, after suffering a heart attack chasing hooligans out of his garden.

Gloria Stuart retired from movies for several decades only to return with her Academy Award–nominated role in *Titanic* (1997). Born in California in 1910, she was married to writer Arthur Sheekman. *Street of Women* (1932) was her film debut.

Florence Sundstrom appeared in such movies as *The Rose Tattoo* (1955) and *Bachelor in Paradise* (1961). Her career has also included many television appearances, including spots on *Gloria* and *Roseanne*.

Grady Harwell Sutton was born in Chattanooga, Tennessee, in 1906. His long career began with silent screen appearances in the mid–1920s and concluded with the role of the school board president in *Rock 'n' Roll High School* (1979). His career also included television shows including *The Egg and I*, *The Pruitts of Southampton*, and *Petticoat Junction*. Sutton, who never lost his southern accent, died in 1995.

William Swan, born in Buffalo, New York, in 1928, has appeared on such television programs as *The Avengers*, *The Twilight Zone*, and *The Streets of San Francisco*.

Basil Sydney, born in England in 1894, made his first film appearance in the silent film *Romance* (1920). He was sometimes credited as Basil Sidney. His career continued into the 1960s, and he died in 1968.

Lyle Talbot, born in Pittsburgh in 1902, enjoyed a long career, even after he stopped playing romantic leads. He started his own repertory company before entering films in the early 1930s. He appeared in several Ed Wood, Jr., films and made appearances on such shows as *Newhart*, *The Beverly Hillbillies*, and *The Adventures of Ozzie and Harriet*. Father of actor/filmmaker Stephen and editor David, Talbot died in 1996.

Akim Tamiroff, born in Russia in 1889, received Oscar nominations for *The General Died at Dawn* (1936) and *For Whom the Bell Tolls* (1943). He died in 1972.

Lilyan Tashman, born in Brooklyn in 1899, first appeared on film in a 1921 silent picture, *Experience*. She made almost 70 films before her death at the age of 34, following unsuccessful cancer surgery. Her last film, *Frankie and Johnny*, was released in 1936. Although married to Edmund Lowe, she was one of Hollywood's most notorious lesbians.

Viva Tattersall, born in 1898, made her film debut in *Cynara* (1932). Married to actor Sidney Toler, she appeared in only a few other films before she retired in the 1930s. She died in 1989.

Kent Taylor, born in Iowa in 1907, began his film career in 1931. He appeared in more than 130 films and TV shows, including *Boston Blackie*, *Zorro*, and *Rough Riders*.

Phil Tead, born in Massachusetts in 1893, died in 1974. Tead played Professor Pepperwinkle on TV's *The Adventures of Superman*.

Conway Tearle was born in New York in 1878 and died in 1938. He appeared in almost 100 films, beginning in 1914.

Stage actor **Verree Teasdale**, born in Spokane, Washington, in 1904, was Edith Wharton's cousin and the wife of Adolphe Menjou. She began her film career in 1929 and made 25 films before retiring in 1941. She died in 1987.

Olive Tell was born in New York in 1894 and died in 1951. She made her film debut in 1915, and appeared in almost 50 films. Her sister was Alma Tell.

Shirley Temple began her acting career at the age of three and became a star and box-office champion in the mid–1930s. She won a special Oscar in 1935. Born in Santa Monica in 1928, she entered government public service after retiring from show business and eventually became Ambassador to Ghana and Czechoslovakia.

Sheila Terry, born Kay Clark in Minnesota in 1910, first appeared in films as an extra in 1932. She appeared in *The Lawless Frontier* (1934), *A Scream in the Night* (1935), and *The Fury Below* (1938), which was her last film. She died in New York in 1957.

Frankie Thomas, born in New York in 1921, was the son of actors Frank M. Thomas and Mona Bruns. He's best known for his TV appearances on *Tom Corbett, Space Cadet* and *First Love*. Thomas died in 2006 and was buried in his space cadet uniform.

Duane Thompson was born in Iowa in 1903. Her first film was *Up and At 'Em* (1921). She appeared in more than two dozen silent films. Her last film was *Hollywood Hotel* (1938). She died in 1970.

Kenneth Thomson, born in Pennsylvania in 1899, began his film career in *Risky Business* (1926). Between 1926 and the late 1930s, he appeared in more than 60 films. Thomson died in 1967.

Oliver Thorndike, born in Boston in 1918, appeared on several early television programs, including *The Ford Theatre Hour*, *Starring Boris Karloff*, and *Kraft Television Theatre*. He died in 1954.

Genevieve Tobin, born in New York in 1899, was a child actor who began her career in the silent film era. Married to William Keighley, she retired from films in 1940 and died in 1995. Siblings included Vivian and George.

Vivian Tobin, born in New York in 1902, was the younger sister of Genevieve and George Tobin. She made her film debut in 1915, then went on the stage until her film career resumed in 1932. Her last film was in 1942. She died in 2002.

Thelma Todd, born in Lawrence, Massachusetts, in 1905, died suspiciously in 1935. A beauty contest winner, she made her film debut in 1926 and appeared in more than 100 films. Nicknamed "The Ice Cream Blonde" and "Hot Toddy," she also appeared in a number of comedy shorts with ZaSu Pitts and Patsy Kelly. Her mysterious death from carbon monoxide has been variously described as suicide, murder, or accident.

Sidney Toler, born in Missouri in 1874, is best known for his work in the Charlie Chan serials. In 1943, he married Viva Tattersall, and died in 1947.

Regis Toomey was born in Pittsburgh in 1898. This hard-working actor appeared in more than 100 films and countless television shows. He played Dr. Stuart on TV's *Petticoat Junction*. His last film was *Evil Town* (1987). He died in 1991.

David Torrence was born in Scotland in 1864 and died in 1951. He appeared in the first filmed version of *The Prisoner of Zenda* (1913). His career included more than 100 films. His brother was actor Ernest Torrence.

June Travis, born in Chicago in 1914, made her film debut in *Stranded* (1935). She appeared in only two films after 1939.

Dorothy Tree, born in 1906 in Brooklyn, was a founding member of the Screen Actors Guild. She appeared in more than 40 films—and also designed the costumes for *The Trial of Mary Dugan* (1941). She died in 1992.

Mary Treen, born in St. Louis in 1907, had a long career, beginning in vaudeville. She appeared in numerous films and on TV before her death in 1989.

Harland Tucker, born in Ohio in 1893, was married to silent screen star Marie Walcamp (she committed suicide in 1936). He began his career in silent films, and appeared in more than 35 films until his death in 1934.

Ellinor Vanderveer, born in New York in 1886, made her first appearance in *The Red Kimono* (1925). Often cast as a party guest or dowager, she was known as the "queen of the dress extras." Sometimes billed as Elinor Vandivere, she died in 1976.

Helen Vinson, was born Helen Rulfs in Beaumont, Texas, in 1907. She appeared in 40 films before retiring in 1945. Married at one time to tennis player Fred Perry, she died in 1999.

Janet Waldo enjoyed a long career. A child actor, her film career began with *Cocoanut Grove* (1938). Since then she has appeared in more than 70 films and countless television shows. She provided the voice of Judy Jetson in *The Jetsons* TV series, as well as voices on *The Atom Ant Show*, *Tom and Jerry*, and *King of the Hill*.

Blanche Walsh, born in Boston in 1873, was a popular stage star around the turn of the century. Her best known role was Katusha in "Resurrection," which opened February 17, 1903. She died in 1915.

John Ward appeared in his first Hollywood film in 1936—*Headline Crasher*. He appeared in several other pictures, usually as an extra. He married and divorced Athole Shearer, sister of Norma and Douglas.

Anthony Warde, born in Pennsylvania in 1906, appeared in more than 100 films, ending his career in low-budget science fiction pictures. Sometimes credited as Anthony Ward, he died in 1975.

Helen Ware, born in San Francisco in 1877, began her film career in 1914. A well known stage actor, she appeared in more than 40 films before her death in 1939.

Gloria Warren, born in Delaware in 1926, appeared in five films before her career ended. Her last film was *Bells of San Fernando* (1947).

Blue Washington, born Edgar Washington Blue in Los Angeles in 1898, died in 1970. He made his film debut in the 1920s, and appeared in more than 40 films.

Pierre Watkin, born in Iowa in 1889, appeared in more than 300 films until his death in 1960. One of the hardest working character actors, he also made numerous TV appearances.

Minor Watson, born in Marianna, Arkansas, in 1889, appeared in more than 100 films, including *A Brother's Loyalty* (1913). He died in Alton, Illinois, in 1965.

Fredd Wayne appeared on numerous television shows, including *Maverick*, *Perry Mason*, and *The Rockford Files*, He played Benjamin Franklin on TV's *Bewitched*.

Virginia Weidler was born in Eagle Rock, California, in 1926. A child actor, her first film was *After Tonight* (1933). Her brother was actor George Weidler. Weidler, whose last film was in 1943, died in 1968.

Ben Welden, born in Ohio in 1901, began his long career in 1930. His TV appearances included several roles on *The Adventures of Superman* and Foo Young on *Batman*. Welden, who also owned a Beverly Hills candy store, died in 1997.

Marie Wells, born in Mississippi in 1894, made her film debut in 1915, billed as Marie Edith Wells. She committed suicide in 1949.

Martha Wentworth was born in New York City in 1889. Known as "The Actress of 100 Voices," Wentworth was a popular radio performer for many years. She also appeared in more than 30 films and provided voices for *One Hundred and One Dalmatians* (1961) and *The Sword in the Stone* (1963). She appeared on many TV shows, including *Perry Mason*. Wentworth died in 1974.

Charles West was born in Pennsylvania in 1885. He began his film career in a 1908 silent film, *The Christmas Burglars*. Most of his 180 film credits were silent films. He died in 1943.

Pat West, born in Paducah, Kentucky, in 1888, began his film career in 1929. Before turning to film, he and wife Lucille were a popular vaudeville team. West died in 1944.

Arleen Whelan was born in Utah in 1916 and died in 1993. She was at one time married to Alexander D'Arcy. Her career began in 1938 and ended in 1957.

Ruth White appeared on stage, film, and television. Her credits include *Captain Video and His Video Rangers* (1949), *Edge of the City* (1957), and *The Defenders*. She also played Sally Buck in *Midnight Cowboy* (1969). She died in 1969.

Writer/actor **Gayne Whitman**, born in Chicago in 1890, was the voice of TV's *The Masked Marvel*. He was also the narrator for the *Strange as it May Seem*, *Unusual Occupations*, *Adventures By Morse*, and *Popular Science* series. He died in 1958.

Warren William, the "poor man's John Barrymore," replaced William Powell as Philo Vance and also played the screen's first Perry Mason. Born Warren William Krech in Minnesota in 1894, William studied at the American Academy of Dramatic Arts, and first appeared in *The Town That Forgot God* (1922). William appeared in more than 70 films before his death in 1948.

Guinn "Big Boy" Williams, born in Texas in 1899, was a pro baseball player before appearing in more than 200 films. His nickname was attributed to Will Rogers. Williams died in 1962.

Eleanor Wilson appeared in several television series in the 1940s and 1950s. She was a regular on *Love of Life*.

Tom Wilson, born in Montana in 1880, made his film debut in *The Birth of a Nation* (1915). He appeared in more than 200 films before his death in 1965.

Barbara Jean Wong was born in Los Angeles in 1924. She's best known for playing Arbedella Jones on the radio program *Amos 'n' Andy*. Wong died in 1999.

Judith Wood, born in New York in 1906, appeared in *The Gold Diggers of Broadway* (1929), *The Divorcee* (1930), and *Children of Pleasure* (1930). Although promising, her career largely ended in the early 1930s. Her last appearance was in a small role in *The Asphalt Jungle* (1950). Wood died in 2002.

Barbara Woodell, born in Lewistown, Illinois, in 1910, began her film career in the 1940s. She also made numerous TV appearances on shows including *Wagon Train*, *Rough Riders*, and *The Lone Ranger*. Woodell died in 1997.

Donald Woods, born in Canada in 1906, appeared in many films and TV shows, and hosted the TV series *Hotel Cosmopolitan* and *Damon Runyan Theater*. He died in 1998.

Harry Woods, born in Cleveland in 1889, specialized in playing villains. He made his film debut in 1923 and appeared in more than 225 films and TV shows until his death in 1968.

Director-actor **William Worthington**, born in New York in 1872, was a silent film star who became a character actor later in his career. He died in 1941.

Fay Wray, memorable for her role as the gorilla's love interest in *King Kong* (1933), was born in Canada in 1907. Her first film was *Gasoline Love* (1923). In 1926 she was chosen by the Western Association of Motion Picture Advertisers (WAMPUS), along with other young actors, as most likely to succeed in Hollywood. This group also included Janet Gaynor and Mary Astor. She retired from movies in the 1940s, but made a comeback that included television appearances on such programs as *Perry Mason* and *Alfred Hitchcock Presents*. Wray died in 2004.

Eustace Wyatt, born in England in 1882, was a radio and film actor who appeared in *Journey Into Fear* (1942), *Nightmare* (1942), and *Ministry of Fear* (1944). He died in 1944.

Barton Yarborough, born in Texas in 1900, went from the circus to radio, where he worked on *Dragnet*, *I Love a Mystery*, and *One Man's Family*. He appeared in two *Dragnet* TV episodes before his sudden death in 1951.

Duke York, born in New York in 1908, was a stuntman and actor who appeared in more than 120 films. He committed suicide in 1952.

Stage actor **Roland Young**, born in London in 1887, was best known for his *Topper* movies—he received an Oscar nomination for *Topper* (1937). He died in 1953.

Blanche Yurka was born in St. Paul, Minnesota, in 1887. She had a long stage, film, and television career. Her film debut was in *National Red Cross Pageant* (1917), and she also appeared in *A Tale of Two Cities* (1935), *A Night to Remember* (1943), *The Song of Bernadette* (1943), and others. She made several guest appearances on *Kraft Television Theatre* in the 1950s. Yurka died in 1974.

NOTES

Abbreviations:
MCNY = Museum of the City of New York
NYPL = Robinson Locke Collection, New York Public Library for the Performing Arts, New York
WCA = Wesleyan Cinema Archives–Kay Francis diaries

1. "The notorious character type," Joshua Zeitz, *Flapper: A Madcap Story of Sex, Style, Celebrity, and the Women Who Made America Modern*, pp. 5–6.
2. "On a typical evening," Joshua Zeitz, *Flapper: A Madcap Story of Sex, Style, Celebrity, and the Women Who Made America Modern*, pp. 90–91.
3. Personal email interview with Harold Sunners, January 15, 2006.
4. Personal interview with Charles Stumpf, August 13, 2006.
5. "Many people jeered," Dan Callahan, "Kay Francis: Secrets of an Actress," *Bright Lights Film Journal* 52.
6. American-born illustrator Gordon Conway was also a costume and set designer for British films in the late 1920s up until the mid–1930s. See Raye Virginia Allen's book *Gordon Conway: Fashioning a New Woman* for more information about this fascinating woman.
7. "that bad posture," Angela J. Latham, *Posing a Threat: Flappers, Chorus Girls, and Other Brazen Performers of the American 1920s*, pp. 20–21.
8. "The principal character, Wick Snell," Ward Morehouse, *Forty-Five Minutes Past Eight*, p. 73.
9. "unfolded near a microphone," Joe Adamson, *Groucho, Harpo, Chico, and Sometimes Zeppo*, p. 84.
10. "Whatever happened," Joe Adamson, *Groucho, Harpo, Chico, and Sometimes Zeppo*, p. 82.
11. "Each week Hale devised," Ben M. Hall, *Best Remaining Seats*, pp. 225–26.
12. "During the shooting of one especially talky scene," David Stenn, *Clara Bow Runnin' Wild*, p. 170.
13. "my first really personal film," Ronald Haver, *David O. Selznick's Hollywood*, p. 60.
14. "Every contract player in the studio," Jack Oakie, *Jack Oakie's Double Takes*, p. 51.
15. "There was a roster of stars," Fay Wray, *On the Other Hand*, p. 104.
16. The film was released in English, French, German, Japanese, Spanish, and Swedish versions.
17. "I never said anything," William M. Drew, *At the Center of the Frame*, p. 49.
18. "was not at his best," Michael B. Druxman, *Basil Rathbone*, p. 123.
19. "'You and I don't speak the same language,'" Jon Tuska, *The Detective in Hollywood*, p. 276.
20. "'What are you guys,'" Arthur Marx, *Goldwyn: A Biography of the Man Behind the Myth*, p. 280.
21. "her pop-eyed looks," Arthur Marx, *Goldwyn: A Biography of the Man Behind the Myth*, p. 280.
22. "It was made purely as a star vehicle," Sam Frank, *Ronald Colman*, p. 88.
23. "Whenever we made a musical picture," Jack Oakie, *Jack Oakie's Double Takes*, p. 91.
24. "When the studios finally stopped," Jack Oakie, *Jack Oakie's Double Takes*, p. 93.
25. "Its origin was a play," Ivor Montagu, *With Eisenstein in Hollywood*, pp. 55–56.
26. "Huston, an oldish actor," Montagu, *With Einstein in Hollywood*, p. 59.
27. "'Kay Francis is wrong," Montagu, *With Einstein in Hollywood*, p. 60.
28. "rediscovered ... the film's slow pacing," Gene D. Phillips, *Cukor*, p. 28.
29. "This little dilly," Charles Bickford, *Bulls Balls Bicycles & Actors*, pp. 253–54.
30. "'I was what we'd now call,'" Richard Lamparski, *Whatever Became Of... Ninth Series*, pp. 198–199.
31. "As a result, these girls," Gene D. Phillips, *Cukor*, p. 33.
32. "'That studio seemed to me like an absolute sea of short men,'" Richard Lamparski, *Whatever Became Of... Ninth Series*, p. 182.
33. "was absolutely the wrong dress," unidentified clipping, MCNY.
34. "I thought I had never seen a lady," Gloria Swanson, *Swanson on Swanson*, p. 437.
35. "One of the loveliest gowns I wore,' unidentified clipping, MCNY.
36. "As to pure style," Scott Eyman, *Ernst Lubitsch*, p. 354.
37. "It was just another job," Scott Eyman, *Ernst Lubitsch*, p. 200.
38. "No matter what you thought," Scott Eyman, *Ernst Lubitsch*, pp. 195–96.
39. "Jones sat there amiably," Scott Eyman, *Ernst Lubitsch*, p. 190.

40. "He wouldn't be content," Scott Eyman, *Ernst Lubitsch*, p. 190.
41. "Chaplin and Goldwyn were part of United Artists," Dowd & Shepard, *King Vidor*, p. 135.
42. "I think Goldwyn was always striving for very high quality," Dowd & Shepard, *King Vidor*, p. 134.
43. "I particularly leaned toward the unknown young girl," Dowd & Shepard, *King Vidor*, p. 135.
44. "The director's chair was upturned," Sara Hamilton, "Eddie Goes Spanish," in *The Movie Musical*, p. 27.
45. "Not many actors could talk," David Zinman, *Saturday Afternoon at the Bijou*, p. 442.
46. "I saw it the other night," Edward G. Robinson, *All My Yesterdays*, p. 142.
47. "By the time you read this," Elsie Janis, "Class With a Capital Kay," *The New Movie Magazine*, p. 50.
48. "*Mandalay* was a steamy," Shirley Temple, *Child Star*, pp. 28–29.
49. "this unlikely tale of a mistreated lady's survival," Jerry Vermilye, *The Films of the Thirties*, p. 119.
50. "a revolutionary show," Michael Freedland, *Jolson*, p. 138.
51. "I had them build me sixty tall white movable columns," Tony Thomas, *The Busby Berkeley Book*, p. 75.
52. "The huge set of a London nightclub," Wallis & Higham, *Starmaker*, p. 34.
53. "A lesson in patience," William R. Meyer, *Warner Brothers Directors: The Hard-Boiled, the Comic, and the Weepers*, p. 249.
54. "Mary: This is hideous," Mark A. Vieira, *Sin in Soft Focus*, p. 177.
55. Some film collectors insist there are prints that retained the abortion dialogue.
56. "During the premiere," "Good News," *Modern Screen Magazine*, August 1934.
57. "that glorious, creamy beauty," William Gargan, *Why Me?*, p. 163.
58. "There are not so many things," Grace Wilcox, "The Best Dressed Woman in Pictures," *Screen & Radio Weekly*, p. 9.
59. "'For once,'" Wilcox, "The Best Dressed Woman in Pictures," *Screen & Radio Weekly*, p. 9.
60. "Up to Jack Warner's office," Sara Hamilton, "Okay Kay!" *Photoplay*, March 1936, p. 104.
61. "Plans had to be drawn," Rose Pelswick, "Section of Golden Gate Span Reproduced for Kay Francis Picture," unidentified clipping, NYPL.
62. "The railway terminal," Rose Pelswick, "Section of Golden Gate Span Reproduced for Kay Francis Picture," unidentified clipping, NYPL.
63. "We cabled London," Wallis & Higham, *Starmaker*, p. 57.
64. "objected to Dieterle's old trick of cutting in the camera," Wallis & Higham, *Starmaker*, p. 57.
65. "Aren't they pitiful?" Harrison Carroll, *Los Angeles Evening Herald Express*, March 28, 1936.
66. "When the picture was released," Pola Negri, *Memoirs of a Star*, pp. 374–75.
67. "The original German version," Druxman, *Basil Rathbone*, p. 183.
68. "ridiculous," Druxman, *Basil Rathbone*, p. 183.
69. "the difference between you and a good actress," "It's K.O. Francis Now," *Picturegoer*, October 2, 1937.
70. "the best dialogue," "It's K.O. Francis Now," *Picturegoer*, October 2, 1937.
71. "So many pictures," Harrison Carroll, *Los Angeles Evening Herald Express*, May 22, 1937.
72. "Miss Francis is the screen's tallest actress," Erskine Johnson, "Behind the Makeup," *Los Angeles Examiner*, June 14, 1937.
73. "One of the most glamorous leading ladies," Pat O'Brien, *The Wind At My Back*, p. 260.
74. "The performances in *Courage*," Nowlan & Nowlan, *Cinema Sequels*, p. 172.
75. "The performances were good," Vincent Sherman, *Studio Affairs*, p. 76.
76. "old-fashioned dribble," Bette Davis with Whitney Stine, B*ette Davis Mother Goddam*, p. 104.
77. "I would hear my father," Leon Calanquin, "The Tragedy of Kay Francis," *The World of Yesterday*, p. 15.
78. "A number of years ago," Sybil Jason, *My Fifteen Minutes*, p. 192.
79. "I felt that we could not," Vincent Sherman, *Studio Affairs*, p. 77.
80. "I made *Women in the Wind*," Eve Arden, *Three Phases of Eve*, p. 49.
81. "Cary Grant and I," "Free! By Kay Francis," unidentified source, MCNY.
82. "Every tendency," "Free! By Kay Francis," unidentified source, MCNY.
83. "You rarely see stagecoach chases," Bill Collins, *Bill Collins Book of Movies*, p. 125.
84. "The two film versions," Nowlan & Nowlan, *Cinema Remakes*, p. 432.
85. "Kay was a wonderful gal," Daniel Bubbeo, *Women of Warner Brothers*, p. 96.
86. "She never caught on," Nowlan & Nowlan, *Cinema Remakes*, p. 193.
87. "I had worked hard," Diana Barrymore, *Too Much Too Soon*, p. 211.
88. "introduces a new method," Lee Mortimer, "Starring Diana Barrymore *Between Us Girls* Is Exciting Escapism," *Sunday Mirror Magazine Section*, September 27, 1942.
89. "'Now, every time we make a suggestion,'" E. J. Fleming, *Carole Landis: A Tragic Life in Hollywood*, p. 158.
90. "I've had enough," Kirk Crivello, *Fallen Angels*, p. 97.
91. "This is a special Booking," Fleming, *Carole Landis: A Tragic Life in Hollywood*, p. 248.
92. "was a surprisingly good crime melodrama," John Cocchi, *Second Feature*, p. 138.
93. "It's surprising that Francis," Mick LaSalle, "Dark Side of the 20th Century," *San Francisco Chronicle*, April 30, 2000, p. 58.
94. "qualifies as a major rediscovery," Mick LaSalle, "B Movie Bad Girls," *San Francisco Chronicle*, May 9, 1999, p. 51.
95. "One would be hard-pressed," Ted Okuda, *Monogram Checklist*, p. 6.

BIBLIOGRAPHY

Adamson, Joe (1973). *Groucho, Harpo, Chico, and Sometimes Zeppo: A Celebration of the Marx Brothers.* New York: Simon & Schuster.

Allotment Wives, Inc. (November 1945). *Screen Romances,* pp. 52–53, 113–20.

The Amateur Cracksman Again (1930, July 25). [Review of *Raffles*]. *The New York Times,* 20:2.

Arce, Hector (1979). *Gary Cooper: An Intimate Biography.* New York: William Morrow & Co.

Arden, Eve (1985). *Eve Arden: Three Phases of Eve.* New York: St. Martin's Press.

Atkinson, J. Brooks (1927, February 23). Crook Drama, Modern Style [Review of *Crime*]. *The New York Times,* 27:3.

An Attorney Confesses (1930, July 19). [Review of *For the Defense*]. *The New York Times,* 27:7.

Barbour, Alan G. (1973). *Humphrey Bogart: The Pictorial Treasury of Film Stars.* New York: Gallahad Books.

Barrymore, Diana (1957). *Too Much Too Soon.* New York: Henry Holt & Co.

Basinger, Jeanine (1993). *A Woman's View: How Hollywood Spoke to Women 1930–1960.* New York: Alfred A. Knopf.

Behlmer, Rudy (1985). *Inside Warner Bros. 1935–1951: The Battles, Brainstorms, and the Bickering— From the Files of Hollywood's Greatest Studio.* New York: Fireside.

Bergman, Ingrid, and Alan Burgess (1980). *Ingrid Bergman: My Story.* New York: Delacorte Press.

Bernard, April (January 1990). "Screen Gem." [Interview with Sylvia Sidney]. *Interview,* pp. 54–56, 104.

Berry, Sarah (2000). *Screen Style: Fashion and Femininity in 1930s Hollywood.* Minneapolis: University of Minnesota Press.

Bickford, Charles (1965). *Bulls Balls Bicycles & Actors.* New York: Paul S. Eriksson.

Billups, Connie, and Arthur Pierce (1995). *Lux Presents Hollywood: A show-by-show history of the Lux Radio Theatre and the Lux Video Theatre, 1934–1957.* Jefferson, N.C.: McFarland.

Black, Shirley Temple (1988). *Child Star.* New York: McGraw-Hill.

Bradshaw, Jon (1985). *Dreams That Money Can Buy: The Tragic Life of Libby Holman.* New York: William Morrow & Co.

Brief Reviews of Current Pictures (October 1934). *Photoplay,* p. 6, 110, 115.

Brief Reviews of Current Pictures (March 1936). *Photoplay,* p. 5.

Brooks, Tim, and Earle Marsh (1979). *The Complete Directory to Prime Time Network TV Shows 1946–Present.* New York: Ballantine Books.

Brown, Gene (1995). *Movie Time: A Chronology of Hollywood and the Movie Industry from its Beginnings to the Present.* New York: Macmillan.

Bryce, Robert (October 1999). Without a Net. *Polo Magazine.*

Bubbeo, Daniel (2002). Kay Francis: "Trouble in Paradise." In Bubbeo, *The Women of Warner Brothers: The Lives and Careers of 15 Leading Ladies.* Jefferson, N. C.: McFarland. pp. 86–101.

Calanquin, Leon V. (April 1980). "The Tragedy of Kay Francis." *The World of Yesterday,* pp. 15–19.

Callahan, Dan (May 2006). "Kay Francis: Secrets of an Actress." *Bright Lights Film Journal,* issue 52.

Carey, Gary (1988). *Anita Loos: A Biography.* London: Bloomsbury.

Cheatham, Maude (March 1934). "Not What She Seems To Be — That's Kay." *Motion Picture,* pp. 59, 82–83.

Chevalier, Maurice (1960). *With Love.* Boston: Little, Brown.

Chierichetti, David (2003). *Edith Head: The Life and Times of Hollywood's Celebrated Costume Designer.* New York: HarperCollins.

Cocchi, John (1991). *Second Feature: The Best of the "B" Films.* New York: Citadel Press.

Coffee, Frank (1991). *Always Home: 50 Years of the USO: The Official Photographic History.* Washington: Brassey's.

Collins, Bill (1977). *Bill Collins Book of Movies.* Australia: Cassell.

Collins, Bill (1974, June 8). "Kay Francis, Hollywood's Fallen Angel." *TV Times,* pp. 16–18.

Considine, Shaun (1989). *Bette & Joan: The Divine Feud.* New York: E.P. Dutton.

Corliss, Rae S. (1986, June 14). "Kay Francis Visited Ill Father in Albion Hospital." *Journal of Albion,* pp. 1, 5.

Cosio, Robyn (2000). *The Eyebrow.* New York: ReganBooks.

Crivello, Kirk (1988). *Fallen Angels: The Lives and Untimely Deaths of 14 Hollywood Beauties*. New Jersey: Citadel Press.

Cruikshank, Herbert (October 1931). "Lucky Thirteen." *Modern Screen*, unknown page numbers.

Daniel, Clifton, ed. (1989). *Chronicle of America*. Mount Kisco, N.Y.: Chronicle Publications.

Davis, Bette, with Whitney Stine (1975). *Bette Davis Mother Goddam*. New York: Berkley Medallion.

Denver City Directories, 1906–1909.

Deschner, Donald (1973). *The Complete Films of Cary Grant*. Secaucus, N.J.: Citadel Press.

Direct from Hollywood (November 1941). [Review of *Charley's Aunt*]. *Silver Screen*, p. 80.

Dooley, Roger (1981). *From Scarface to Scarlett: American Film in the 1930s*. New York: Harcourt Brace Jovanovich.

Dowd, Nancy, and David Shepard (1988). *King Vidor*. Metuchen, N.J.: Scarecrow Press.

Drew, William M. (1999). *At the Center of the Frame: Leading Ladies of the Twenties and Thirties*. Lanham, MD: Vestal Press.

Druxman, Michael B. (1975). *Basil Rathbone: His Life and His Films*. New York: A.S. Barnes.

Edelson, Edward (1976). *Funny Men of the Movies*. Garden City, N.Y.: Doubleday & Co.

Edwards, Anne (1988). *Shirley Temple: American Princess*. New York: William Morrow & Co.

Eells, George (1976). *Ginger, Loretta and Irene Who?* New York: G.P. Putnam's Sons.

Emerson, Dorothy (March 1931). "Reading Their Writing." *Silver Screen*, pp. 28–29, 60–61.

Engstead, John (1978). *Star Shots: Fifty Years of Pictures and Stories by One of Hollywood's Greatest Photographers*. New York: E.P. Dutton.

Evans, Harry (1934, August 3). "The Personal Touch: Chats with Kay Francis, Jessie and Dick Barthelmess, Louella Parsons, and Countess Frasso at Bert Taylor's Party." *Family Circle*, pp. 10–11, 22.

Eyman, Scott (1993). *Ernst Lubitsch: Laughter in Paradise*. New York: Simon & Schuster.

Eyman, Scott (1990). *Mary Pickford: America's Sweetheart*. New York: Donald I. Fine, Inc.

Eyman, Scott (1997). *The Speed of Sound*. New York: Simon & Schuster.

Farrar, Rowena Rutherford (1982). *Grace Moore and Her Many Worlds*. New York: Cornwall Books.

A Fashionable Rogue (1931, May 1). [Review of *Ladies' Man*]. *The New York Times*, 30:3.

Felheim, Marvin (1956). *The Theater of Augustin Daly: An Account of the Late Nineteenth Century American Stage*. Cambridge: Harvard University Press.

Fidler, James M. (August 1934). "Spiking the Rumors: Kay Francis Answers the Gossips." *Silver Screen*, pp. 61–62.

A Film of the Circus (1929, July 15). [Review of *Dangerous Curves*]. *The New York Times*, 25:1.

"Film Stars Flee on Yacht: Kay Francis and Kenneth MacKenna Silent on Marriage Plans" (January 17, 1931). *The New York Times*, p. 23.

First Lady [review]. (November 1937). *Silver Screen*, p. 58.

Fleming, E.J. (2005). *Carole Landis: A Tragic Life in Hollywood*. Jefferson, N.C.: McFarland.

Ford, Hugh (1975). *Published in Paris: American and British Writers, Printers, and Publishers in Paris, 1920–1939*. New York: Macmillan.

Francis, Kay (January 1937). "Don't try your luck out here!" *Pictorial Review*, 16–17, 50.

Frank, Sam. (1997). *Ronald Colman: A Bio-Bibliography*. Westport, CT: Greenwood Press, 1997.

Franks, Norman, Frank Bailey, and Rick Duiven (1996). *The Jasta Pilots*. London: Grub Street.

Freedland, Michael (1972). *Jolson*. New York: Stein and Day.

Freedland, Michael (1979). *The Two Lives of Errol Flynn*. New York: William Morrow & Co.

French, William Fleming (August 1936). "Kay Francis Says: Give Yourself a Break." *Woman's World*, pp. 12–13, 16.

Frick, John W., and Carlton Ward (1987). *Directory of Historic American Theatres*. Westport, CT: Greenwood Press.

Frischauer, Willi (1974). *Behind the Scenes of Otto Preminger: An Unauthorized Biography*. New York: William Morrow & Co.

Gallagher, Brian (1987). *Anything Goes: The Jazz Age Adventures of Neysa McMein and Her Extravagant Circle of Friends*. New York: Times Books.

Gargan, William (1969). *Why Me?* Garden City, N.Y.: Doubleday & Co.

Garnett, Tay (1973). *Light Your Torches and Pull Up Your Tights*. New Rochelle, N.Y.: Arlington House.

Geist, Kenneth L. (1978). *Pictures Will Talk: The Life & Films of Joseph L. Mankiewicz*. New York: Da Capo Press.

A General Falls in Love (1930, November 2). [Review of *The Virtuous Sin*]. *The New York Times*, 5:2.

Graham, Sheilah (1970). *The Garden of Allah*. New York: Crown.

Grams, Jr., Martin (1998). *The History of the Cavalcade of America*. Kearney, NB: Morris Publishing.

Gray, Sonya F. (July 9, 2002). "Making a Difference: Katharine Ryan Gibbs." http://www.projo.com/specials/women/94root13.htm.

Green, Abel, and Joe Laurie, Jr. *Show Biz: From Vaude to Video*. New York: Henry Holt & Co.

Greene, Graham (1980). *The Pleasure-Dome: The Collected Film Criticism 1935–40*. Edited by John Russell Taylor. Oxford: Oxford University Press.

Griffith, Richard (1971). *The Talkies: Articles and Illustrations from a Great Fan Magazine 1928–1940*. New York: Dover Publications.

Grobel, Lawrence (1989). *The Hustons*. New York: Charles Scribner's Sons.

Guest, Val (1933, December 30). "Oh Kay — That's Francis." *Film Pictorial*, p. 10.

Guiles, Fred Lawrence (1975). *Hanging on in Paradise*. New York: McGraw-Hill.

Hadleigh, Boze (1996). *Bette Davis Speaks*. New York: Barricade Books.

Hall, Ben M. (1988). *The Best Remaining Seats: The*

Golden Age of the Movie Palace. New York: Da Capo Press.

Hall, Leonard (October 1929). "Vamping with Sound." *Photoplay*, pp. 51, 126.

Hall, Leonard (October 1932). "Just Three Years." *Photoplay*, pp. 48, 112–113.

Hall, Mordaunt (1929, December 14). The Children [Review of *The Marriage Playground*]. *The New York Times*, 22:4.

Hall, Mordaunt (1929, December 22). Children of Divorce: Edith Wharton's Novel Makes an Interesting Talker—"This Thing Called Love" [Review of *Marriage Playground*]. *The New York Times*, 1.

Hall, Mordaunt (1931, November 2). Gold-Diggers on Parade [Review of *Girls About Town*]. *The New York Times*, 27:1.

Hall, Mordaunt (1929, May 25). Groucho and His Brethren [Review of *The Cocoanuts*]. *The New York Times*, 17:3.

Hall, Mordaunt (1931, February 9). Hoist with His Own Petard [Review of *Scandal Sheet*]. *The New York Times*, 25:4.

Hall, Mordaunt (1930, April 21). A Hollywood Studio Frolic [Review of *Paramount on Parade*]. *The New York Times*, 20:4.

Hall, Mordaunt (1930, January 18). The Lout [Review of *Behind the Make-Up*]. *The New York Times*, 21:1.

Hall, Mordaunt (1930, December 22). Love and Infatuation [Review of *Passion Flower*]. *The New York Times*, 16:2.

Hall, Mordaunt (1930, August 30). Merry Tomfoolery [Review of *Let's Go Native*]. *The New York Times*, 7:4.

Hall, Mordaunt (1931, June 15). The Missing Letter [Review of *Transgression*]. *The New York Times*, 23:3.

Hall, Mordaunt (1931, August 29). Murder as an Art [Review of *Guilty Hands*]. *The New York Times*, 16:3.

Hall, Mordaunt (1930, April 26). A Notorious Affair Given [Review of *A Notorious Affair*]. *The New York Times*, 11:2.

Hall, Mordaunt (1929, September 28). Queer Happenings [Review of *Illusion*]. *The New York Times*, 17:3.

Hall, Mordaunt (1930, February 3). A Rothstein Shadow [Review of *Street of Chance*]. *The New York Times*, 17:1.

Hall, Mordaunt (1931, October 3). A Sinister Record [Review of *Twenty-Four Hours*]. *The New York Times*, 20:2.

Hall, Mordaunt (1931, June 6). The Stool Pigeon [Review of *The Vice Squad*]. *The New York Times*, 15:5.

Hamann, G.D. (2003). *Kay Francis in the 30's*. Hollywood: Filming Today Press.

Hamilton, Sara (1975). "Eddie Goes Spanish." In *The Movie Musical: From Vitaphone to 42nd Street As Reported in a Great Fan Magazine*. Edited by Miles Kreuger. New York: Dover Publications.

Hamilton, Sara (March 1936). "Okay Francis!" *Photoplay*, pp. 30–31, 104–05.

Hamlet Modishly (1925, November 10). *The New York Times*, p. 23.

Haver, Ronald (1980). *David O. Selznick's Hollywood*. New York: Bonanza Books.

Haynes, Marjorie (November 1936). "The Untold Love Stories of Kay Francis." *Movie Mirror*, pp. 26–27, 98–99.

Heffernan, Harold (1938, May 11). "Quickie Plans Fail to Upset." *The Daily Oklahoman*, p. 9.

Henderson, Mary C. (2001). Mielziner: *Master of Modern Stage Design*. New York: Watson-Guptill Publications.

Herlin, Hans (1960). *Udet: A Man's Life*. Translated by Mervyn Savill. London: MacDonald.

Higham, Charles, and Roy Moseley. *Cary Grant: The Lonely Heart*. New York: Harcourt Brace Jovanovich.

Hill, Beverly (December 1932). "Keep This Under Your Hat." *Screen Book Magazine*, p. 32.

Hollywood Newsreel (June 1937). "Okay, Kay!" *Hollywood*, p. 11.

Hopper, Hedda (1952). *From Under My Hat: The Fun and Fury of a Stage, Screen and Column Career*. Garden City, N.Y.: Doubleday & Co.

House, Marie (March 1931). "Tips on Tempting from Kay Francis." *Screenland*, pp. 23, 107.

"The House of Gibbs: History of One of Homer's Oldest Families" (October 16, 1901). *The Homer Index*, p. 1.

"How the Stars Rate in Popularity" (December 1932). *Screen Book Magazine*, p. 38.

Howard, Jean, with James Watters (1989). *Jean Howard's Hollywood: A Photo Memoir*. New York: Harry N. Abrams.

Hudson, Derek (1975). *For Love of Painting: The Life of Sir Gerald Kelly, K.C.V.O., P.R.A.* London: Peter Davies.

Hulse, Ed (1996). *The Films of Betty Grable*. Burbank: Riverwood Press.

Hunt, Marsha (1996). *The Way We Wore: Styles of the 1930s and '40s and Our World Since Then*. Fallbrook, CA: Fallbrook.

Illustrated Atlas and Directory of Free Holders of Calhoun County Michigan Including Brief Biographical Sketches of Enterprising Citizens: Compiled and Published from Official Records and Personal Examinations (1894). Fort Wayne, IN: The Atlas Publishing Co.

"It's K.O. Francis Now" (October 2, 1937). *Picturegoer*.

Janis, Elsie (March 1934). "Class with a Capital Kay." *The New Movie Magazine*, pp. 50–51, 84.

Jason, Sybil (2005). *My Fifteen Minutes: An Autobiography of a Child Star of the Golden Era of Hollywood*. Boalsburg, PA: BearManor Media.

Jerome, Stuart (1983). *Those Crazy Wonderful Years When We Ran Warner Bros*. Secaucus, N.J.: Lyle Stuart, Inc.

Johnston, Alva (1962). "Hollywood's Ten Per Centers." In *Hello Hollywood!*, pp. 193–205. Originally published in *The Saturday Evening Post* August 8, 1942, and August 22, 1942.

Jones, Jennifer (1998). "Rebels of Their Sex: Nance

O'Neil and Lizzie Borden." In R.A. Schanke & K. Marra (eds.), *Passing Performances: Queer Readings of Leading Players in American Theater History*, pp. 83–103. Ann Arbor: The University of Michigan Press.

Karney, Robyn (1997). *Chronicle of the Cinema.* New York: DK Publishing.

"Kay Francis, Actress, Dies at 63; Epitome of Glamour in the 30s" (August 27, 1968). *The New York Times*, p. 41.

"Kay Francis Back from S. American Army Tour" (May 1, 1945). *Hollywood Reporter*.

"Kay Francis Lives Here" (October 1939). *House and Garden*, pp. 52–53.

"Kay Francis Parts from Her Husband" (December 20, 1933). *The New York Times*, 27.

Kear, Lynn, and John Rossman (2006). *Kay Francis: A Passionate Life and Career.* Jefferson, N.C.: McFarland.

Keats, Patricia (January 1934). "Kay Francis 'as 'eard the East A'Callin.'" *Silver Screen*, pp. 49, 63–64.

Kellum, Frances (December 1936). "The Men in Kay Francis' Life!" *Screen Book*, pp. 34, 86–87.

Kennedy, Harold J. (1978). *No Pickle, No Performance: An Irreverent Theatrical Excursion from Tallulah to Travolta.* Garden City, N.Y.: Doubleday & Co.

Kennedy, Matthew (2004). *Edmund Goulding's Dark Victory: Hollywood's Genius Bad Boy.* Madison: The University of Wisconsin Press.

Lambert, Gavin (1997). *Nazimova.* New York: Alfred A. Knopf.

Lamparski, Richard (1985). *Whatever Became Of ... Ninth Series.* New York: Crown Publishers.

Lane, Jerry (March 1935). "Kay Francis' Amazing Secret." *Screen Play*, pp. 23, 80.

Langner, Lawrence (1951). *The Magic Curtain: The Story of a Life in Two Fields, Theatre and Invention by the Founder of the Theatre Guild.* New York: E.P. Dutton & Co.

LaSalle, Mick (1999, May 9). "B Movie Bad Girls," *San Francisco Chronicle*, p. 51.

LaSalle, Mick (2000). *Complicated Women: Sex and Power in Pre-Code Hollywood.* New York: St. Martin's Press.

LaSalle, Mick (2000, April 30). "Dark Side of the 20th Century." *San Francisco Chronicle*, p. 58.

Lasky, Bessie Mona (1957). *Candle in the Sun.* Los Angeles: DeVorss.

Lasky, Jesse L. (1975). *Whatever Happened to Hollywood?* New York: Funk & Wagnalls.

Latham, Angela J. (2000). *Posing a Threat: Flappers, Chorus Girls, and Other Brazen Performers of the American 1920s.* Hanover, N.H.: University Press of New England.

Lawrence, Greg (May 2001). "Ballets Over Broadway." *Vanity Fair*, pp. 122–48.

Leff, Leonard J., and Jerold L. Simmons (2001). *Dame in the Kimono: Hollywood, Censorship, and the Production Code.* Lexington: University Press of Kentucky.

Leonard, William (1946). Chicago Season. In *Theatre World Season, 1945–1946*, Daniel Blum, ed. New York: Guide Printing Co.

"Let's Talk About Hollywood: More News and Chit-Chat about the Film City and Its Folks" (June 1933). *Modern Screen*, p. 80.

Levin, Martin (1970). *Hollywood and the Great Fan Magazines.* New York: Castle Books.

LoMonaco, Martha Schmoyer (2004). *Summer Stock! An American Theatrical Phenomenon.* New York: Palgrave Macmillan.

Loy, Myrna, and James Kotsilibas-Davis (1987). *Being and Becoming.* New York: Alfred A. Knopf.

McGilligan, Patrick (1997). *Fritz Lang: The Nature of the Beast.* New York: St. Martin's Press.

McNeil, Alex (1984). *Total Television: A Comprehensive Guide to Programming from 1948 to the Present.* New York: Penguin.

Maddox, Ben (September 1934). "Kay Francis Wants Life." *Movie Mirror*, pp. 31, 76–77.

Maddox, Ben (November 1937). "Pets for Pals." *Silver Screen*, pp. 30–31, 66–68.

Maltin, Leonard (1985). *Movie Comedy Teams.* New York: New American Library.

Maltin, Leonard (1995). *1996 Movie & Video Guide.* New York: Plume.

Mandelbaum, Howard, and Eric Myers. *Screen Deco: A Celebration of High Style in Hollywood.* New York: St. Martin's Press, 1985.

Mann, Carol (1996). *Paris: Artistic Life in the Twenties & Thirties.* London: Laurence King.

Mann, William J. (2001). *Behind the Screen: How Gays and Lesbians Shaped Hollywood 1910–1969.* New York: Viking.

Mann, William J. (1998).*Wisecracker: The Life and Times of William Haines: Hollywood's First Openly Gay Star.* New York: Penguin Books.

Mantle, Burns, ed. (1945). *Best Plays of 1925–1926.* New York: Dodd, Mead, & Co.

Mantle, Burns, ed. (1945). *Best Plays of 1926–1927.* New York: Dodd, Mead, & Co.

"Marsha Hunt Home with Report on Troops in Arctic." *Hollywood Reporter*, March 20, 1944.

Martin, Charlotte, ed. (1901). *The Stage Reminiscences of Mrs. Gilbert.* New York: Charles Scribner's Sons.

Martin, Mart (1996). *Did She or Didn't She? Behind the Bedroom Doors of 201 Famous Women.* New York: Citadel Press.

Marx, Arthur (1976). *Goldwyn: A Biography of the Man Behind the Myth.* New York: W.W. Norton & Co.

Mattfield, Julius (1968). *Variety Music Cavalcade 1620–1961: A Chronology of Vocal and Instrumental Music Popular in the United States.* Englewood Cliff, N.J.: Prentice-Hall.

Maxwell, Elsa (May 1938). "It's Romance Again for Kay Francis." *Photoplay*, pp. 24–25, 71.

Maxwell, Virginia (June 1933). "Just 'Life and Love.'" *Photoplay*, pp. 76, 85.

Meryman, Richard (1978). *Mank: The Wit, World, and Life of Herman Mankiewicz.* New York: William Morrow & Co.

Meyer, William R. (1978). *Warner Brothers Directors: The Hard-Boiled, the Comic, and the Weepers.* New Rochelle, N.Y.: Arlington House Publishers.

Miles, Mary (Spring 2001). "Life Before Nantucket: Never Bored, Always busy." http://www.yesterdaysisland.com/spring_01/lifebefore/bored.html.

Miller, Patsy Ruth (1988). *My Hollywood: When Both of Us Were Young: The Memories of Patsy Ruth Miller.* O'Raghailligh Ltd. Publishers.

Mills, Brian (1991). *Movie Star Memorabilia: A Collector's Guide.* London: B. T. Batsford.

The Modern Screen Directory of Pictures ... These brief reviews are to serve as a guide when you do your movie shopping. From them you can get an idea whether the picture is good or bad and whether it is the sort of story you go for (June 1933). *Modern Screen*, p. 90.

Montagu, Ivor (1967). *With Eisenstein in Hollywood: A Chapter of Autobiography Including the Scenarios of Sutter's Gold and An American Tragedy.* New York: International Publishers.

Mook, Dick (April 1941). "Pictures on the Fire." *Silver Screen*, pp. 66–72, 98.

Mook, Dick (April 1941). "She Wanted to Be Forgotten." *Silver Screen*, pp. 46–47, 91–92.

Mook, S. R. (March 1939). "'I Can't Wait to be Forgotten'—Kay Francis Looks Ahead." *Photoplay*, pp. 32, 72.

Mook, S.R. (November 1934). "Unguarded Moment." *Picture Play*, pp. 26–28, 54.

Moore, Grace (1944). *You're Only Human Once.* Garden City, N.Y.: Country Life Press.

Mordden, Ethan (1983). *Movie Star: A Look at the Women Who Made Hollywood.* New York: St. Martin's Press, 1983.

Morehouse, Ward (1939). *Forty-five Minutes Past Eight.* New York: Dial Press.

Morella, Joe, and Edward Z. Epstein (1986). *Loretta Young: An Extraordinary Life.* New York: Delacorte Press.

Morrow, Lee Alan (1998). Elsie Janis: "A Comfortable Goofiness." In R.A. Schanke and K. Marra (eds.), *Passing Performances: Queer Readings of Leading Players in American Theater History,* pp. 151–72. Ann Arbor: The University of Michigan Press.

Moses, Robert (1999). *American Movie Classics Classic Movie Companion.* New York: Hyperion.

Munn, Michael (1999). *X-Rated: The Paranormal Experiences of the Movie Star Greats.* London: Robson Books.

Negri, Pola (1970). *Memoirs of a Star.* Garden City, N.Y.: Doubleday & Co.

New York City Directories, 1921–1922.

New York Social Register, 1922–1929.

A Newspaper Play (May 13, 1929). [Review of *Gentlemen of the Press*]. *The New York Times,* 27:2.

Norman, Barry (1987). *The Story of Hollywood.* New York: New American Library.

Nowlan, Robert A., and Gwendolyn Wright Nowlan (1989). *Cinema Sequels and Remakes, 1903–1987.* Jefferson, N.C.: McFarland.

Oakie, Jack (1980). *Jack Oakie's Double Takes.* San Francisco: Strawberry Hill Press.

Oakie, Victoria Horne (2001). *Life with Jack Oakie.* Waterville, ME: Five Star.

O'Brien, Pat (1964). *The Wind at My Back: The Life and Times of Pat O'Brien.* New York: Doubleday & Co.

O'Brien, Scott (Winter 1995/1996). "Kay Francis: Portrait on Silk." *Films of the Golden Age,* pp. 56–62.

Okuda, Ted (1987). *The Monogram Checklist: The Films of Monogram Pictures Corporation, 1931–1952.* Jefferson, N.C.: McFarland.

Oller, John (1999). *Jean Arthur: The Actress Nobody Knew.* New York: Limelight Editions.

O'Toole, Lawrence (October 1989). "New York Story: The Blockbuster saga of a filmmaker's dream — one hundred years in the making." *American Film* (62–74).

Palmer, Gretta (1970). "This Year's Love Market." In *Hollywood and the Great Fan Magazines,* p. 115.

Parish, James Robert (1978). *The Hollywood Beauties.* New Rochelle, N.Y.: Arlington House.

Parish, James Robert (2002). *Hollywood Divas: The Good, the Bad, and the Fabulous.* Chicago: Contemporary Books.

Parish, James Robert (1980). *The Hollywood Reliables.* Westport, CT: Arlington House.

Parish, James Robert (1977). *Hollywood's Great Love Teams.* New York: Arlington House.

Parish, James Robert (1976). *The Jeanette MacDonald Story.* New York: Mason/Charter.

Parish, James Robert, and Gene Ringgold (February 1964). "Kay Francis." *Films in Review.*

Pegolotti, James A. (2003). *Deems Taylor: A Biography.* Boston: Northeastern University Press.

Petaja, Emil (1975). *Photoplay Edition.* San Francisco: SISU Publishers.

Peters, Margot (1990). *The House of Barrymore.* New York: Touchstone.

Phillips, Gene D. (1982). *George Cukor.* Boston: Twayne Publishers.

Pitrone, Jean Maddern (1999). *Take It from Big Mouth: The Life of Martha Raye.* Lexington: University of Kentucky Press.

Pizzitola, Louis (2002). *Hearst Over Hollywood.* New York: Columbia University Press.

"Plus Fours 'Hamlet' Here: Erlanger Production to Observe Dry Law in Modernist Effort" (August 28, 1925). *The New York Times,* 8:5.

Pratley, Gerald (1971). *The Cinema of Otto Preminger.* New York: A.S. Barnes.

Preminger, Otto (1977). *Preminger: An Autobiography.* New York: Doubleday.

Prestholdt, Torben (1947). Summer Theatre Circuit. In *Theatre World, 1946–1947.* Daniel Blum, ed. New York: Stuyvesant Press Corp.

Pyle, E. (March 29, 1943). "Four Good Soldiers." *Senior Scholastic,* p. 2

Quirk, Lawrence J. (1990). *Fasten Your Seat Belts: The Passionate Life of Bette Davis.* New York: William Morrow & Co.

Quirk, Lawrence J. (1971). *The Films of Fredric March*. New York: Citadel Press.

Quirk, Lawrence J. (1974). *The Great Romantic Films*. Secaucus, N.J.: Citadel Press.

Reviews — A Tour of Today's Talkies (June 1933). *Modern Screen*, p. 82.

Rich, Sharon (1994). *Sweethearts: The Timeless Love Affair — On Screen and Off — Between Jeanette MacDonald and Nelson Eddy*. New York: Donald I. Fine, Inc.

Riley, Sidney (February 1937). "It's Never Been Told." *Picture Play*.

Roberts, Katharine (March 16, 1935). "Acting in a Business Way." *Colliers*, pp. 14, 32.

Roberts, Kay (December 1932). "They hope to stay married." *Photoplay*, pp. 34, 119–20.

Robinson, Edward G. (1973). *All My Yesterdays*. New York: Signet.

Rogers, Ginger (1991). *Ginger: My Story*. New York: HarperCollins.

Rosen, Marjorie (1974). *Popcorn Venus: Women, Movies and the American Dream*. New York: Avon Books.

Roth, Andrew (1996). *Infamous Manhattan*. New York: Citadel Press.

Rubin, Hanna, and Cynthia Grisolia (October 1989). "Star quality." *American Film*, pp. 58–61, 76–89.

Rush, Dana (February 1932). "The aristocrat of the screen: Kay Francis lives in a thoroughbred world." *Silver Screen*, pp. 41, 77.

St. Johns, Adela Rogers (March 1931). "Working Girl." *New Movie Magazine*, pp. 84–86, 124.

Savages and Ink (May 19, 1929). [Review of *Gentlemen of the Press*]. *The New York Times*, 7:2.

Schapiro, Amy (2003). *Millicent Fenwick: Her Way*. New Brunswick, N.J.: Rutgers University Press.

Schatz, Thomas (1988). *The Genius of the System: Hollywood in the Studio Era*. New York: Pantheon Books.

Schickel, Richard (1983). *Cary Grant: A Celebration*. Boston: Little, Brown.

Screen Parliament (December 30, 1933). [Letters to the editor]. *Film Pictorial*, p. 31. "Presentable — Kay Francis has a dignity and a 'presence' lacking entirely in any other film star on the screen to-day." John Hiddy, Bournemouth.

Selznick, David O. (2000). *Memo from David O. Selznick*. Edited by Rudy Behlmer. New York: Modern Library.

Sennett, Ted (1973). *Lunatics and Lovers*. New Rochelle, N.Y.: Arlington House.

Sennett, Ted (1971). *Warner Brothers Presents*. New York: Arlington House.

Service, Faith (November 1932). "Did $26,000 Outweigh a Honeymoon Trip for Kay Francis?" *Motion Picture*, pp. 51, 78.

Shadow Stage: A Review of the New Pictures (October 1934). *Photoplay*, p. 53.

Sherman, Vincent (1996). *Studio Affairs: My Life as a Film Director*. Lexington: University Press of Kentucky.

Shipman, David (1979). *The Great Movie Stars: The Golden Years*. New York: Da Capo Press.

Silver, Gordon R. "Their Favourite Rooms: Did You Know Stars Have Favourite Rooms — Pet Nooks and Corners in their Luxurious Mansions? They do!" *The Film-Lovers' Annual*. London: Dean & Son Ltd., pp. 27–30.

Silvers, Phil (1973). *This Laugh Is On Me: The Phil Silvers Story*. Englewood Cliffs, N.J.: Prentice-Hall.

Skinner, Cornelia Otis (1976). *Life with Lindsay & Crouse*. Boston: Houghton Mifflin Co.

Smith, Geraldine (November 2, 1941). "Triple Failure to Break Love Jinx." *Philadelphia Inquirer*.

Smith, Jewel (1970). "Kay's Dream of Romance: Kay Francis Outlines Her Conception of an Ideal Honeymoon." In *Hollywood and the Great Fan Magazines*, pp. 58, 182. Edited by Martin Levin. New York: Castle Books.

Spergel, Mark (1993). *Reinventing Reality — The Art and Life of Rouben Mamoulian*. Metuchen, N.J.: The Scarecrow Press.

Stenn, David (2000). *Clara Bow Runnin' Wild*. New York: Cooper Square Press.

Stewart, Donald Ogden (1975). *By a Stroke of Luck!* New York: Paddington Press.

Stewart, Roy P. (1974). *Born Grown: An Oklahoma City History*. Oklahoma City: Fidelity Bank.

Stine, Whitney (1985). *Stars & Star Handlers: The Business of Show*. Santa Monica: Roundtable.

Stuart, Gloria (1999). *I Just Kept Hoping*. Boston: Little, Brown.

Tague, William H., Robert B. Kimball and Richard V. Happel (1961). *Berkshire: Two Hundred Years in Pictures: 1761–1961*. Pittsfield, MA: The Eagle Publishing Co.

Tapert, Anne (1998). *The Power of Glamour*. New York: Crown.

Teichmann, Howard (1972). *George S. Kaufman: An Intimate Portrait*. New York: Atheneum.

Thomas, Tony (1973). *The Busby Berkeley Book*. New York: A & W Visual Library.

Thoughts, Some Sad, on New Films (July 21, 1929). [Review of *Dangerous Curves*]. *The New York Times*, p. 3.

Tierney, Tom (1974). *Thirty from the 30s*. Englewood Cliffs, N.J.: Prentice-Hall.

Turk, Edward Baron (2000). *Hollywood Diva*. Berkeley: University of California Press.

Tuska, Jon (1978). *The Detective in Hollywood*. Garden City, N.Y.: Doubleday & Co.

Udet, Ernst (1970). *Ace of the Iron Cross: The Autobiography of the Red Baron's Leading Ace*. New York: Ace Books.

Underwood, Peter (1992). *Death in Hollywood*. London: Clio Press.

Van Ishoven, Armand (1977). *The Fall of an Eagle: The Life of Fighter Ace Ernst Udet*. Translated by Chaz Bowyer. London: William Kimber.

Vermilye, Jerry (1982). *The Films of the Thirties*. Secaucus, N.J.: Citadel Press.

Vieira, Mark A. (1999). *Sin in Soft Focus: Pre-Code Hollywood*. New York: Harry N. Abrams.

Walker, Alexander (1979). *Shattered Silents*. New York: William Morrow & Co.

Walker, Helen Louise (September 1930). "How Men Annoy Us: Kay Francis Gives the Woman's Side." *Motion Picture*, pp. 71, 98.

Wallace, David (2001). *Lost Hollywood*. New York: St. Martin's Press.

Wallis, Hal, and Charles Higham (1980). *Starmaker: The Autobiography of Hal Wallis*. New York: Macmillan.

Weibel, Kathryn (1977). *Mirror Mirror: Images of Women Reflected in Popular Culture*. New York: Anchor Books.

Westmore, Frank, and Muriel Davidson (1976). *The Westmores of Hollywood*. New York: J. B. Lippincott Co.

Wilcox, Grace (June 10, 1934). "The Best Dressed Woman in Pictures." *Screen and Radio Weekly*.

Wilkerson, Tichi, and Marcia Borle (1984). *The Hollywood Reporter: The Golden Years*. New York: Arlington House.

Williams, Whitney (November 1937). "Which Will Win the Golden Apple of Success?" *Silver Screen*, pp. 24–25, 80–81.

Wilson, Elizabeth (March 1937). "Projections." *Silver Screen*, pp. 26–27, 80–82.

Winecoff, Charles (1996). *Split Image: The Life of Anthony Perkins*. New York: Dutton.

Wise, James E. Jr., and Paul W. Wilderson III (2000). *Stars in Khaki: Movie Actors in the Army and the Air Services*. Annapolis: Naval Institute Press.

Wray, Fay (1989). *On the Other Hand: A Life Story*. New York: St. Martin's Press.

Yurka, Blanche (1970). *Bohemian Girl: Blanche Yurka's Theatrical Life*. Athens: Ohio University Press.

Zeitz, Joshua (2006). *Flapper: A Madcap Story of Sex, Style, Celebrity, and the Women Who Made America Modern*. New York: Crown.

Zinman, David (1973). *Saturday Afternoon at the Bijou*. New Rochelle, N.Y.: Arlington House.

INDEX

Abbott, George 18, 65, 180
Abel, David 45, 51
Acuff, Eddie 124, 166, 188
Adams, Ernest 38
Adams, Lowden 128
Adams, Maude 5
Adams, Tommye 185
Adamson, Harold 188
Adamson, James 162
Adolphson, Edvin 47
Adrian 48, 93, 180
Adrian, Iris 32, 42, 237
The Adventuress 90, 92
The Affairs of Monica 112
Aherne, Brian, 176, 177, 178, 237
Aiken, Joseph E. 178
Ainslee, Mary 168
Akins, Zoe 65, 67
Akst, Albert 180
Alberni, Luis 83, 222
Albert, Eddie 187
Albertson, Frank 168, 169, 218, 237
Albright, Hardie 76, 101, 237
Albright, Lola 227, 237
Alcott, Louisa May 13, 171, 173, 174
Alden, Bob 199
Alden, Marian 160
Alderson, Erville 168
Alexander, J. Grubb 35
Alexander, Katharine 162, 174
Alexis, Demetrius 107
All Woman 182
Allan K. Foster Girls 20
Alleborn, Al 138, 141
Allen, Dennis 15, 87, 165, 219, 220, 237
Allen, Gracie 222
Allen, Harry 125, 128
Allen, Joel 188
Allister, Claud 178
Allotment Wives 13, 195–199
Allotment Wives, Inc. 198
Alper, Murray 158
Always in My Heart 13, 182–182
Alyn, Kirk 188
Amateur Anne 7, 208
Ameche, Don 180, 181, 182, 226, 237
Ameche, Jim 223, 225, 237
American Film Institute 35
Amersteth, Gwendolyn 42
Ames, Adrienne 63, 65, 86, 237

Ames, Jean 183
Amy, George 107
Anders, Merry 170
Anderson, Doris 25
Anderson, Wesley 95, 122, 141
Anderson, William 107
Andre, Tom 180
Andren, Jean 195
Andrews, Stanley 174
Andrieu, L. 60
Angel of Mercy 132
Animal Crackers 20, 21
Another Dawn 11, 78, 138–141
Anthony, Mark 166
Anthony, Stuart 169
Anyone Can Win 15, 227
Apfel, Oscar 45, 90
Applegate, Fred 141
Arden, Eve 160, 161, 162, 237, 218
Arden, Mary 195
Ardis, Valerie 199
Ardizoni, Louis 107
Arledge, John 166
Arlen, Harold 133
Arlen, Richard 22, 23, 32, 34, 237
Arliss, George 119
Armida 182, 237
Armitage, Walter 114
Arms, Russell 183
Armstrong, Margaret 176
Army Show 225
Arnold, Jessie 120
Arnold, William 51, 56
Arnt, Charles 171, 174
Arrowsmith 90
Arthur, Jean 29, 30, 31, 32, 33, 34, 238
Arville, Dorothy 128
Arzner, Dorothy 27, 28, 32, 214
Ash, Sam 142
Ash, Warren 188
Asher, Irving 35
Ashley, Joel 14, 214, 215, 217, 218, 219, 226, 238
Askam, Earl 42, 238
Askey, Arthur 179
Astaire, Marie 160
Asther, Nils 10, 93, 94, 95, 176, 178, 238
Astor, Gertrude 178, 195, 238
Astoria, New York 7, 21
Atchley, Hooper 83, 238
Athena 199

Atkinson, Frank 53
Aubrey, Jimmy 128
Auer, Mischa 32, 93, 238
Augustin Daly Company 5, 234
Austa 117
Auster, Islin 190
Austin, Charles 138
Austin, William 24, 25, 32, 42, 44, 123, 178, 195, 238
Axt, William 60, 93, 95
Aylesworth, Arthur 114, 158, 162

Baby LeRoy 106
Bacon, Irving 29, 51, 56, 90, 107, 185, 238
Bacon, Lloyd 35, 95
Baer, Abel 32
Bailey, Raymond 160, 238
Bailey, Sherwood 158, 238
Bailey, William 117
Bainter, Fay 182
Baker, Frank 103, 128
Baker, Graham 171, 172
Baker, Joe Don 27
Bakewell, William 60
Baldwin, Earl 107
Baldwin, Faith 155
Bancroft, George 9, 32, 33, 34, 35, 51, 52, 53, 69, 168, 169, 171, 172, 173, 238
Bankhead, Tallulah 141, 219, 223
Banks, Polan 73, 75
Banton, Travis 29, 64, 65, 83, 178
Barber, Bobby 185
Barbier, George 63, 65, 70
Barnekow, Erik 11, 13, 158
Barnes, Binnie 82
Barnes, George S. 40
Barnes, T. Roy 22
Barnett, Vince 51
Barrat, Robert 98, 107, 120, 141
Barrows, Henry 60
Barry, Fern 155
Barry, Phyllis 88, 89, 90, 238
Barry, Tom 150, 152
Barrymore, Diana 13, 185, 186, 187, 188, 238
Barrymore, John 42, 187
Barrymore, Lionel 9, 60, 61, 62, 63, 238
Barthelmess, Richard 119
Bartlett, Bennie 185
Basevi, James 188

Baskerville, Charles 6
Bastian, Jesse 188
Bates, Granville 19
Bates, Louise 133
Bauchens, Anne 60
Baum, Lew 148
Baxter, Alan 162
Baxter, Anne 178, 238
Baxter, Warner 145
Beat the Clock 15, 226
Beatty, May 117, 128
Beau Geste 58
Beavers, Louise 65, 67, 74, 111, 238
Beck, John 168
Beckett, Scotty 185, 238
Beecher, Janet 152, 176, 238
Beery, Noah, Jr. 170
Beery, Wallace 95
Behind the Make-Up 8, 27–29
Belasco, Leon 166, 182, 185
Bell, James 93
Bell, Monta 17, 19, 20
Bell, Rex 152
Bellamy, Ralph 211, 212, 213, 238
Belle Starr 180
Bellew, Kyrle 42
Belmondo, Jean-Paul 138
Belmore, Daisy 128
Belmore, Lionel 128
Benaderet, Bea 223, 239
Bender, Dawn 142
Benedict, Brooks 29, 31
Benedict, William (Billy) 176
Benge, Wilson 35, 40, 88, 176, 239
Bening, Annette 220
Bennett, Belle 152
Bennett, Constance 61, 223
Bennett, David 32, 42
Bennett, Dorothy 182, 184
Bennett, Hugh 88
Bennett, Joan 42
Bennett, Les 195
Benny, Jack 178, 179, 180, 223, 224, 239
Beranger, George 136
Beresford, Harry 51, 125
Bergen, Edgar 222
Bergman, Gustaf 47
Berkeley, Busby 21, 107, 108, 109, 110, 155, 157
Berlin, Irving 20, 22, 88
Berman, Pandro S. 162
Bernard, Harry 42
Bernard, Joseph E. 95
Berner, Sara 199, 239
Bernerd, Jeffrey 192, 195, 199, 203
Bernstein, Aline 205, 218
Bernstein, G.W. 103
Bertine, E.K. 18
Bessier, Eugenie 24
The Betty Crocker Show 15, 226
Between Us Girls 13, 185–188
Bevan, Billy 38, 138
Bevans, Clem 155, 158
Beyond the Law 170
Bickford, Charles 48, 49, 50, 51, 239
Billingsley, Sherman 227
Bing, Herman 76, 103

Bischoff, Robert 178
Bischoff, Sam 120
Bjerring, Frank 65
Black, Martin 188
Black, Maurice 29, 90
Black, Ralph 165
Black Chiffon 15, 220–221
Black Fury 122
The Black Robe see *Strangers in Love*
Black-Stemmed Cherries 93, 95
Blackmer, Sidney 180, 182, 184
Blackwell, Carlyle 123
Blackwood, George 98
Blandick, Clara 223, 239
Blanke, Henry 110, 113, 128, 141, 144, 145
Bloch, Bertram 75, 78
Blondell, Joan 154
The Blue Lagoon 178
Blumenstock, Morton 17
Blystone, Stanley 171
Boardman, True 185
Bogart, Humphrey 92, 158, 159, 239
Bolder, Robert 128
Boles, John 69, 185, 186, 187, 188, 239
Boleslavsky, Richard 93, 95, 214
Boley, May 22
Bolger, Ray 179, 180
Bolton, Guy 219
Bond, Richard 158, 160
Bonestell, Chesley 178
Boniface, Symona 101, 142, 148, 239
Bonstelle, Jessie 235
Booker, Phillip W. Booker 188
Booth, Margaret 93
Borden, Lizzie 60
Borg, Veda Ann 141, 145, 199, 200, 201, 202, 239
Borgato, Agostino 28, 58
Borrah Minevitch and His Rascals 182, 185
Borzage, Frank 109, 116, 120, 122
Borzage, Lew 116, 120
Boteler, Wade 63, 117, 123, 185
Bourne, George 65
Bow, Clara 11, 22, 23, 32, 34, 239
Boy Meets Girl 187
Boyd, William (stage) 67, 68, 69, 101, 102, 103, 239
Boyer, Charles 110, 220
Boyer, Hal 93
Bracey, Sidney *see* Bracy, Sidney
Bracy, Sidney 150, 155, 158, 160
Bradley, Harry 103, 117, 120, 148
Bradley, Paul 195
Brady, Edward 168
Brahm, John 188
Braidon, Thomas 114
Branch, Bill 16
Brannigan, Thomas 95
Brecher, Egon 128, 136
Breeden, John 67, 68, 69
Breen, Joseph 112, 165
Brenda, Brenda 223
Brennan, Walter 90, 239

Brenon, Herbert 58, 60
Brent, Evelyn 32, 33, 209, 239
Brent, George 10, 11, 82, 90, 91, 92, 93, 97, 106, 116, 117, 118, 119, 120, 121, 122, 123, 124, 133, 134, 135, 136, 137, 138, 150, 152, 153, 154, 222, 223, 224, 239
Brent, Lynton 56
Brereton, Tyrone 138
Bretherton, Howard 101
Breuer, Bessie 162
Brian, Mary 25, 26, 32, 34, 239–240
Bricker, George 158
Brierre, Maurice 142
Briggs, Harlan 124
Brissac, Virginia 166
British Agent 1, 10, 113
Broadley, Edward 148
Brock, J.K. 48
Brock and Thompson 69
Brodel, Mary 183
Brodie, Don 76
Bromfield, Louis 63, 65, 223
Bromley, Sheila 65, 160, 240
Brook, Clive 9, 32, 33, 51, 52, 53, 63, 64, 65, 240
Brook, Tyler 83
Brooks, Harry 5, 235, 240
Broughton, George 128
Brower, Otto 32
Brown, Bernard B. 166, 168, 176, 185
Brown, Charles D. 22, 63, 67
Brown, Everett A. 158
Brown, Harry Joe 124, 136, 138, 145
Brown, Martin 45
Brown, Raymond 155, 158
Brown, W.S. 103
Browne, Lucille 65
Browne, Michael 195
Bruce, Nigel 128, 174, 175, 240
Bruce, Virginia 24, 32, 40, 42, 240
Bruce, Warren 133
Bruno, Frank 158
Bryan, Arthur Q. 224, 240
Bryan, Gertrude 7, 208, 240
Bryan, Jane 141, 142, 143, 144, 145, 240
Bryar, Paul 176
Buchanan, Edgar 168, 240
Buchanan, Elsa 124
Buckinham, Jane 123
Buckland, Veda 65
Buckner, Robert 155
Bulldog Drummond 42
Bullet Scar 159
Bumbaugh, Hal 176
Bunny, George 128
Bunston, Herbert 111
Bupp, Tommy 150
Burgess, Francis 70
Burke, Frankie 93, 160
Burke, Johnny 171
Burnett, Carol 82
Burnett, Paul 141
Burnett, W.R. 158
Burns, George 222

Burress, William 74
Burris, Walter 141
Burroughs, Russell 178
Burton, Bernard W. 166
Burton, David 65
Burton, Frederick 79, 176
Burton, Martin 53
Busch, Mae 120, 240
Bushman, Ralph 125
Busley, Jessie 158
Butler, Roy 195
Buy Your Woman 55
Byrd, Ralph 174, 188
Byron, Walter 114

Cable, Paul 67
Cabot, Bruce 192, 193, 194, 195, 240
Cady, Jerry 174, 176
Caesar, Arthur 171
Caesar's Wife 138, 141
Cagney, Jimmy (James) 78, 122
Caine, Georgia 128, 148
Caldwell, Edgar 195
Calihan, William 199
Calkins, Johnny 192, 195
Call It a Day 226
Callahan, Dan 16
Callahan, Robert E. 199, 202
Callender, Romaine 166
Calvert, E.H. 28, 42
Camp Show 189
Campbell, Mrs. Patrick 47
Cannon, William H. 124
Cantor, Eddie 89-90
Cape Playhouse 1-2
Capp, Al 227
Carey, Joyce 133, 134
Carleton, George 199
Carlyle, Rita 124, 128
Carney, Art 180
The Carol Burnett Show 82
Caron, Patricia 65
Carr, Albert H.Z. 148, 150
Carr, Nat 155, 158, 160
Carr, Trem 192, 195
Carroll, Georgia 174
Carroll, John 182
Carroll, Nancy 24, 32, 34, 240
Carruth, Milton 176
Carson, James B. 153
Carson, Renee 188
Carter, Audrey 35
Carter, Monte 56
Carter, Waverly 35
Carthew, Margaret 154
Caruso, Anthony 182
Caruth, Burr 120
Cass, Maurice 142, 178
Cassidy, Mary 168
Cast Iron see *The Virtuous Sin*
Castle Square Company 5, 234, 235
Cathedral School of St. Mary's 5, 205
Catlett, Walter 185, 186
The Cavalcade of America 223, 224
Cavan, Allan 148, 160
Cavanagh, Paul 45, 58, 59, 60, 199, 200, 201, 202, 240
Cavanaugh, Hobart 95, 103, 107

Cavanaugh, Stan 120
Cavender, Glen 80, 120, 123, 142, 150, 155, 183
Cavett, Frank 155
Cecil, Nora 171
Ceiling Zero 122
Celebrity Time 15, 226
Chaldecott, Fay 128
Chandler, Eddy 117, 123
Chandler, George 90
Chandler, Helen 205, 240
Chandler, Lane 142, 240
Chanel, Coco 138
Chaney, Lon 59, 170
Chapin, Charles 53
Chapin, Jack 162
Chaplin, Charlie 88, 89
Chaplin, Geraldine 27
Chaplin, Sidney 179
Chapman, Janet 157
Charles, Glenn 195
Charley's (Big Hearted) Aunt 179
Charley's Aunt 13, 178-180, 223
Charley's Aunt in a Mini-Skirt 180
Charley's Tante 180
Charters, Spencer 76, 107, 120, 123, 160, 162, 240
Chase, Ilka 226, 227
Chase, Newell 27
The Chase and Sanborn Hour, Starring Edgar Bergen and Charlie McCarthy 222
Chatterton, Ruth 2, 32, 34, 61, 93, 97, 103, 106, 112, 124, 210, 240-241
Chautard, Emile 107
Cheaney, Loia 148, 155
Chefe, Jack 185
Cheron, Andre 95
Chevalier, Maurice 8, 10, 32, 33, 34, 35, 112, 113, 241
The Children 27
Chodorov, Edward 116
Cimarron 50
Citizen Kane 100
Claire, Ina 219, 223
Clark, Bob 195
Clark, Davison 51, 56, 98, 123, 158
Clark, Frank 160
Clark, Harvey 148
Clark, Roger 188
Clark, Wallis 98
Clemens, William 110, 124
Clement, Clay 107
Cleopatra 112
Clifford, Jack 168, 241
Clifton, Ethel 176
Clinton, Katherine 3, 5-6, 15-16, 234-236
Clive, E.E. 128
Club Alabama 6
Clute, Chester 155
Clyde, David 138, 180
Clyde, June 26-27
Clyde, Walter 120
Coburn, Charles 162, 163, 164, 165, 241
Cochi, John 198
Coco, James 82

The Cocoanuts 8, 20-22, 178
Coffee, Lenore J. 29
Coghlan, Frank, Jr. 120
Coghlan, Junior 72
Coghlan, Phyllis 125
Cohen, Lester 22, 218
Colbert, Claudette 11, 110, 135
Cole, Lester 169
Coleman, Caryl 199, 203
Coleman, Charles 76, 98, 123, 162, 185
Coleman, Claudia 120
Coleman, Irene 176, 241
Coles, Mildred 174, 175, 176, 241
Collinge, Patricia 208, 241
Collings, Pierrre 113, 116
Collins, Arthur Greville 90
Collins, Bill 100, 169
Collins, Cora Sue 95, 241
Collins, G. Pat 56
Collins, Monte 51
Collyer, June 24, 25, 241
Colman, Ronald 8, 10, 18, 40, 41, 42, 88, 89, 90, 241
Columbo, Russ 78
Comandini, Adele 182
Comet Over Broadway 13, 155-158
Comingore, Dorothy 155, 241
Command Performance 225
Command Performance U.S.A. 189
Compton, Joyce 22, 23, 148, 241
Compton, Juliette 56, 70, 71, 241
Conan Doyle, Arthur 42
Confession 2, 11, 16, 141-145
Conklin, Heinie 79, 90
Conlin, Jimmy 155
Connolly, Myles 185
Connolly, Walter 145, 146
Connors, Alice 155, 160
Conried, Hans 224, 241
Conroy, Frank 93, 128, 136
Consider the Lilies 226
Conti, Albert 136
Conway, Bob 178
Conway, Gordon 18, 263
Cook, Clyde 128, 138
Cook, Edward 131
Cook, Glenn 195, 199
Cooper, Bobbie 171
Cooper, Edward 125
Cooper, Gary 32, 34, 241
Cooper, George 95
Cooper, Georgie 120
Cooper, John 117
Cooper, Melville 148, 155
Copeland, Nick 120, 123, 125
Copping, Cecil 35
Corbay, Laura 195
Corday, Marcelle 195
Cording, Harry 128, 168
Cormack, Bartlett 17
Cornell, Bob 178
Cornell, Katharine 6, 155, 235
Corrado, Gino 35, 90, 137, 180
Corrigan, Douglas (Wrong Way) 162
Cortez, Ricardo 9, 31, 53, 59, 60, 101, 102, 103, 104, 105, 106, 107, 108, 109, 110, 241-242

Coslow, Sam 27, 32, 45
Cosmopolitan 135
Cossart, Ernest 178
Courage 150, 152
Cowan, James R. 20
Cowan, Jerome 192, 226, 242
Cowan, Robert 155
Cowl, Jane 147
Cram, Mildred 27, 29
Cramer, Richard 24, 53, 93
Crawford, Broderick 168, 169, 242
Crawford, Joan 16, 154, 198, 199, 214, 218
Cregar, Laird 178, 180, 242
Crehan, Joseph 120
Crews, Laura Hope 141, 242
Crime 7, 82, 207–208
Cripps, Kernan 168
Crisp, Donald 114, 128, 141, 145, 182, 242
Crockett, Charles 60
Croker-King, Charles 128
Crompton, Owen 114
Cromwell, John 8, 9, 19, 29, 30, 31, 38, 39, 51, 52, 53, 56, 58, 162, 164
Crosby, Bing 78
Crosby, Percy 195
Cross, Oliver 174
Crothers, Rachel 208, 216, 217
Crouse, Russel 211, 213
Crowley, Earl 70, 83
Cruze, Warner 70
Cukor, George 9, 45, 47, 65, 67
Cummings, Robert, 185, 186, 187, 188, 242
Cummings, Robert, Sr. 145
Cunningham, Cecil 32, 34, 174, 242
Cunningham, Joe 160
Curci, Elvira 182
Curci, Gennaro 142
Currier, Richard 192
Curtain Call 157
Curtiss, Ed 168
Curtiss, Ray 90, 95, 188
Curtiz, Michael 90, 92, 103, 113, 116, 136, 184
Curzon, George 128, 132
Cynara 10, 88–90

Dade, Frances 40, 242
D'Agostino, Albert 174
Daheim, John 166
Dalmatoff, Michael 107
Dalton, Emmett 168, 170, 242
Dalton, Mrs. Emmett 169
The Dalton Girls 170
The Daltons Ride Again 170
D'Ambricourt, Adrienne 51, 58
Damn the Tears 7, 206–207
A Dangerous Brunette see *Man Wanted*
Dangerous Curves 8, 22–24
Daniell, Henry 180, 242
Daniels, Bebe 23, 103
D'Arcy, Alexander 136, 242
Darien, Frank 101
The Dark Page see *Scandal Sheet*

D'Arrast, Harry 40, 41
Darrell, Steven 160
Darro, Frankie 120, 242
Darwell, Jane 107, 242
Da Silva, Howard 159
Daughters Courageous 184
Daumery, John 35
Davenport, Harry 145
Daves, Delmer 11, 120, 121
Davidson, John 76, 142
Davidson, William B. 38, 56
Davies, Marion 100, 135
Davis, Alan 158
Davis, Bette 41–42, 109, 135, 141, 145, 154, 157
Davis, Bob 114
Davis, Dix 152
Davis, Donald 22
Davis, George 76, 101
Davison, Tito 82
Dawson, Hal K. 171
Dawson, Ralph 75, 79, 138, 145
Day, Doris 92
Day, Richard 88, 89, 178
Dayton, Katharine 145, 147
Deane, Linda 166
De Angelis, L. 107
Dearing, Edgar 168, 185
De Briac, Jean 28
Debutantes, Inc. 176
de Casalis, Jeanne 179
de Cordova, Arturo 82
De Cruz, Alphonse 58
De Curtis, Ernesto 32
Dee, Frances 69
de Havilland, Olivia 42, 187, 226
De Lacy, Philippe 25, 27, 242
Del Rio, Dolores 10, 107, 108, 109, 110, 154, 242
De Main, Gordon 25, 107
Demarest, William 171, 209, 242
Demetrio, Anna 166
DeMille, Cecil 50, 112, 222, 223, 224
DeMille, Katherine 65, 242
deMille, William C. 48, 50
DeMond, Albert 160
De Never, Lucille 160
Denni, Lucien 165
De Packh, Maurice 188
Destry Rides Again 170
Devine, Andy 71, 73, 168, 169, 185, 188, 242
Devlin, Joe 158
Dew, Edward (Eddie) 138, 174
Dewar, Frank 158
Dewey, Earle 185
Dickerson, Dudley 155
Dickson, Gloria 152, 153, 154, 209, 242
Dieterle, Charlotte 73
Dieterle, William 71, 73, 75, 78, 79, 110, 128, 131, 132, 138, 141
Dietrich, Marlene 143, 144, 154, 223, 224
di Frasso, Dorothy 11
Digges, Richard H., Jr. 24
Dilson, John 124, 160, 162
Dinehart, Alan 65, 74, 242

Dirman, Rose 100
Divorce 13, 192–195
Dr. Jekyll and Mr. Hyde 70
Dr. Monica 10, 78, 110–113
Dr. Socrates 158
Dodd, Claire 65, 71, 122, 242–243
Dodd, Frank 117
Dodd, Neal 117
A Dog's Life 88, 89
Doll, Alice 61
Don McNeill and the Breakfast Club 225
Donlan, James 98
Donlevy, Brian 17, 19, 168, 169, 243
Donlin, Mike 79
Donnelly, Ruth 76, 103, 104, 105, 107, 243
Doran, Ann 224, 243
Dore, Adrienne 74, 243
Dorr, Lester 101, 155, 188
D'Orsay, Fifi 107, 243
Dorsey, Jimmy 188, 189
Douglas, Maria 82
Douglas, Melvyn 178
Dove, Billie 35, 37, 243
Downen, Don 120, 142
Downing, Vernon 125
Dowson, Ernest 89
Doyle, Laird 113, 116, 138, 141
Dreir, Hans 83, 86
Dressler, Marie 217
Drew, Norma 111
Dreyer, Dave 32
Drought, Doris 27
Druxman, Michael 37
Dubin, Al 79, 107, 116, 136
Dudgeon, Elspeth 124, 133, 243
Dudley, Robert 51, 168
Duff, Warren 136
du Maurier, Gerald 42
Dumbrille, Douglass 98, 243
Dumont, Margaret 20, 22, 243
Dunn, Emma 111
Dunn, Ralph 120, 158, 160
Dunne, Elizabeth 145
Dunne, Irene 154
DuPar, Edwin A. 182
Duperey, Anny 138
Durbin, Deanna 13, 166, 167, 168, 184, 187, 188, 243
Durkin, James 56
Dvorak, Ann 109, 159

Eagan, Raymond B. 32
Eaton, Evelyn 195
Eaton, Jay 117
Eaton, Mary 20, 22, 243
Eckhardt, William 188
Eddy, Helen Jerome 111
Edginton, May 67, 69
Edwards, Anne 106
Edwards, Eddie 124
Edwards, Edgar 155, 160
Edwards, Penny 170
Edwards, Sarah 148, 171, 195
Eells, George 157
Ehlers, Donald J. 171
Eichberg, Richard 187
Eilers, Sally 217

Eisenstein, Sergei 95
Ekland, Britt 27
Ekszerrablas a Vaci-uccaban 75, 78
Eldredge, John 122, 145, 158
Elliott, Gordon (Wild Bill) 76, 90, 107, 111, 117, 123, 125, 243
Elliott, John 38, 42, 195
Ellis, Patricia 120, 209, 243
Ellis, Robert 188
Ellison, Edith 128
Ellison, James 174, 178, 180, 243
Elmer the Great 7, 18, 209–210
Elsie 171, 172, 173
Emanuel, Demetrius 133
Emerson, Emmett 141
Emery, Gilbert 51, 53, 217
Eminent Victorians 128
Emmett, Fern 162
Engels, Virginia 166, 185
Enger, Willard Van 124, 138
Engle, Billy 176
Epstein, Julius J. 116, 141, 152
Erickson, Carl 120
Erickson, Knute 24
Errol, Leon 32, 33, 243
Erwin, Stuart 22, 23, 32, 34, 70, 168, 169, 243
Escapade 144
Esmond, Carl (Charles) 171, 172, 173, 243
Essex, David 188
Estabrook, Howard 27, 29, 31
Estes, Paull 171
Ethier, Alphonse 58, 114
Evans, Charles 124
Evans, Douglas 174
Evans, Helena Phillips 150
Evans, Madge 60, 61, 62, 63, 243–244
Evanson, Edith 188
Everson, William K. 47–48
Everton, Paul 199, 244
Every Woman's Life 152
Exploring the Unknown 225

Fadiman, Clifton 226, 244
Fain, Matty 195, 198
Fain, Sammy 103, 106, 109
Fair, Florence 120
Fair, G.M. 208
Fairbanks, Douglas, Jr. 164–165
Falkenstein, Fritz 155
Fallon, William 39
False Idol see *The False Madonna*
The False Madonna 9, 67–69
Famous Player 7
Fanchon & Marco 69
Fanning, Frank 117
Fapp, Daniel 67
Farkas, Karl 107
Farley, Jim 101
Farnum, Dustin 234, 244
Farrell, Glenda 90, 91, 92, 93, 95, 96, 97, 243
Farrington, Betty 72
Farrow, John 150, 152, 157, 160, 162
Farrow, Mia 162
Fast Company see *Elmer the Great*
Fatal Attraction 89

Fausset, Hudson 160
Faversham, Philip 101
Faversham, William 178
Favorite Stranger 14, 215–216
Faye, Alice 31, 188, 189
Faylen, Frank 160
Fazenda, Louise 107, 145, 146, 147, 244
Fehr, Rudi 141
Feld, Fritz 166, 244
Felker, Ruby 138, 141, 155
Fellowes, Rockliffe 56
Fellows, Robert 79
Felton, Verna 223, 224, 244
Female of the Species 182
The Feminine Touch 13, 180–182
Fenwick, Hugh 13
Fenwick, Jean 192
Ferguson, Perry 162
Ferrer, Jose 179
Fickett, Mary 214, 244
Field, Mary 188
Fields, Stanley 29, 31, 79
Films in Review 2
Finch, Dick 180
Fine, Budd 199
Fink, Henry 32
Finlayson, James 38, 244
Finnerman, Perry 71
First Lady 2, 11, 145–148, 222
First National Pictures 35
Fischbeck, Harry 22, 24, 32
Fisher-Smith, E.L. 138
Fitzgerald, Cissy 58, 60, 244
Fitzgerald, Edith 48
Fitzgerald, F. Scott 42
Fitzgerald, Geraldine 82
Fitzgerald, Neil 128
Fitzmaurice, George 40, 41
Fix, Paul 117, 244
Flanagan, Fionnula 107
Flavin, James 168, 188
Flavin, Martin 48
Fletcher, Bramwell 40, 187, 244
Fletcher, Jerry 153, 155, 158
Fliegle, Edward 162
Flint, Helen 19, 133, 134, 244
Florey, Robert 20, 21, 101
Flowers, Bess 53, 72, 125, 133
Fly Away Home 182, 184
Flynn, Charles 174
Flynn, Errol 138, 140, 141, 244
Fodor, Ladislaus 75, 78
Folsey, George J. 17, 20, 93
Fontanne, Lynn 226, 236
For the Defense 8, 38–40
Forbes, Mary 114, 120, 138
Forbes, Ralph 123, 124, 148, 149, 150, 244
Forbstein, Leo S. 35, 71, 74, 75, 79, 90, 95, 98, 101, 103, 107, 110, 113, 116, 120, 122, 124, 128, 133, 136, 138, 141, 145, 148, 150, 152, 155, 158, 160, 182
Forrest, Dave 114
Forst, Willi 144
Foster, Arthur Turner 128
Foster, Eddie 136
Foster, Norman 17, 244

Foster, Phoebe 89, 128
Foster, Preston 145, 146, 147, 222, 244–245
Foulger, Byron 162
Four Jills in a Jeep 13, 188–192
Four on a Match 223
Fowler, Almeda 67
Fox, Allan 93
Fox, Frank 182
Fox, Lawrence W., Jr. 176, 178
Fox, Paul Hervy 103
Foxe, Earle 70
Foy, Bryan 150, 155, 158, 160
Foy, Charley 158
Foy, Eddie, Jr. 160, 162, 245
Foy, Mary 51
Framed 203
Francis, James Dwight 6
The Francis Langford–Don Ameche Show 15, 226
Francisco, Betty 29, 245
Franklin, David 32
Franks, Katherine Clinton see Clinton, Katherine
Frederici, Blanche 35
Fredericks, Ellsworth 65, 101
Freed, Ralph 166
French, Dick 120, 133
French, Park 40
Friedhofer, Hugo 128, 138
Friend, Bud 155
Frisco, Otto 103
Frost, Terry 195
Fruchtchen 187
Le Fruit Vert 185
Frye, Louise 195
Fuller, Sammy 58
Fulton, John P. 176
Fung, Willie 79
The Furies 67
Furthman, Julius 38

Gaal, Frankziska 187
Gabel, Martin 179
Gabrielle, Iris 160
Galas de la Paramount 35
Gallagher, Richard (Skeets) 32, 33, 34, 42, 209, 245
Gallaudet, John 199
Gamby-Hale Girls 20, 21
Gannon, John 195
Garbo, Greta 95, 150, 154
Gardner, Jack 160
Garfield, John 184
Gargan, Edward (Ed) 95, 100, 185, 245
Gargan, William 82, 100, 114, 115, 116, 160, 161, 162, 222, 245
Garner, Peggy Ann 162, 222–223, 226, 245
Garnett, Tay 79, 82
Garon, Pauline 107, 135, 245
Garralaga, Martin 138
Garretson, Oliver S. 35, 71, 141
Garrett, Oliver H.P. 29, 31, 38, 51, 56
Garson, Greer 214
Gasnier, Louis 45, 47, 245
Gaston, William 6, 7, 206, 207

Gates, Harvey H. 192, 195
Gates, John 116
Gateson, Marjorie 67, 68, 69, 74, 145, 245
Gaudio, Frank 138
Gaudio, Tony 103, 128, 138
Gausman, R.A. 166, 168, 176, 182
Gay, Joan 120
Gaye, Gregory 114, 145
Gaynor, Janet 106
Geary, Bud 117
Gee, Parker 195
Gelsey, Erwin 75
Generalen 47
Gentlemen of the Press 5, 7, 8, 17–20, 47, 140
Geraghty, Gerald 29
Gerald, Ara 128
Gering, Marion 63
Gerrard, Douglas 72, 79
Gerstad, Merritt B. 60
Gibbon, James 71, 74, 133, 138, 141, 155
Gibbons, Cedric 48, 60, 180
Gibbs, Helen 5
Gibbs, Joseph 5
Gibbs, Mary 5
Gibbs, Minnie 5
Gibbs, Virginia 5
Gibney, Sheridan 101
Gibson, Wynne 65
Gignoux, Regis 185
Gilbert, Jody 142
Gilbert, L. Wolfe 32
Giller, Walter 180
Gillingwater, Claude 98
Gillis, Ann 171
Gillmore, Margalo 215, 245
Ginger, Loretta, and Irene Who? 157
Girardot, Etienne 93, 103, 180
Girls About Town 9, 65–67
Gish, Lillian 89
Give Me Your Heart 11, 132–136, 138, 222
Glassmire, Gus 162
Gleason, Lucile Webster 65, 145, 245
Gleason, Pat 195
Glickman, Larry 195
Globe Theatre 225
Godfrey, Phyllis 133
Godfrey, Sam 98
Goff, Ivan 13
The Golden Widow 86
Goldwyn, Samuel 40, 41, 42, 88, 89
Gombell, Minna 155, 156, 157
Good, Dick 107
Goodbye, My Fancy 14, 217–218
Goodrich, J.A. 51
The Goose and the Gander 11, 122–124
Gordon, C. Henry 93
Gordon, Douglas 162
Gordon, Gale 223, 245
Gordon, Gavin 120
Gordon, Harris 170
Gordon, Huntley 25, 27
Gordon, Julia Swayne 67, 245

Gordon, Kay 155
Gordon, Mary 63, 101, 168, 169, 192, 245
Gordon, Maude Turner 24, 25, 26, 53, 117, 214
Gore-Brown, Robert 88, 89
Gorman, Buddy 199
Gottschalk, Ferdinand 90
Gould, William 80, 150, 158, 160, 168, 176
Goulding, Edmund 32, 82, 157
Grable, Betty 188, 189
Graham, Eddie 123, 160
Graham, Howard (Hap) 14, 211, 213, 245
Graham, Jo 160, 182, 184–185
Grand Hotel 109
Granger, Dorothy 168
Granger, William 107
Grant, Cary 13, 86, 162, 163, 164, 165, 178, 222, 223, 245
Grant, Helena 133
Grant, Lawrence 76, 128, 142
Granville, Bonita 150, 151, 152, 222, 245–246
Granville, Charlotte 63
Graves, Robert 107
Gray, Eden 176
Gray, Jennifer 166
Great Gildersleeve 224
The Great Lie 145
Green, Alfred E. 98, 122
Green, George 171
Green, Harry 32, 34, 35, 246
Green, Little Mitzi 25, 26, 32, 34, 35, 246
Green Fruit 187
The Green Hat 6
Greene, Harrison 120
Greene, Joseph J. 199
Greenfield, Ida 138, 141
Gregg, Alan 142
Greig, Robert 32, 72, 76, 83
Grey, Shirley 120
Griffies, Ethel 185
Griffith, D.W. 7, 78
Griffith, Raymond 65
Groesse, Paul 180
Gross, Frank 185
Grot, Anton 35, 37, 71, 74, 79, 90, 92, 103, 110, 113, 120, 128, 131, 136, 141, 152
Grove, Gerald 40
Guhl, George 160, 168, 183
Guilaroff, Sydney 180
Guilty Hands 9, 60–63
Gulf Screen Guild Show 115, 222
Gunn, Herbert 178, 182
Gwenn, Edmund 178, 246

Haade, William 150
Haas, Robert 75, 98, 116, 122, 124, 138
Haden, Sara 145, 246
Hageman, Marshall 160
Haight, George 162
Hajos, Karl 45, 51
Hale, Chester 21
Hale, Dorothy 89

Hale, Jonathan 162, 192, 195, 199, 246
Hale, Louise Closser 93, 246
Hale, Patty 182, 184, 185, 246
Hall, Charles 188
Hall, Charlie 42, 88
Hall, James 32, 34, 42, 44
Hall, Jane 165
Hall, Jon 187
Hall, Thurston 148, 246
Hall, Winter 48, 114
Haller, Ernest 35, 37, 63, 65, 74, 101, 114
Halliday, John 101
Halligan, William 79
Halton, Charles 93, 136
Hamilton, Chuck 95
Hamilton, Hale 111
Hamilton, John 182, 199, 246
Hamilton, Margaret 174, 175, 176, 246
Hamilton, Ward 138, 141
Hamilton, William 162
Hammond, Virginia 111
Hand, Herman 67
Hansen, Chuck 95, 122, 152
Harburg, E.Y. 133
Harding, Ann 58, 135
Harford, Alec 138, 188
Harlan, Richard 192, 195
Harland, Russell 56
Harling, W. Franke 22, 27, 51, 67, 74, 79, 83, 90, 101, 133
Harmer, Lillian 103, 120, 145, 148
Harmon, John 158
Harmon, Marie 195
Harmon, Pat 42
Harper's Bazaar 6
Harrigan, William 120
Harris, Glen 138
Harris, Ray 67
Harris, Sam (Major) 125, 138, 162
Harris, Theresa 95, 153
Harris, Winifred 188
Harron, John 142, 145, 150, 153, 158, 160, 246
Harry Owens and His Royal Hawaiians 166, 168
Hart, Gordon 160
Hartley, Esdras 95, 101
Hartmann, Edmund L. 180, 182
Harvey, Forrester 60
Harvey, John 188
Harvey, Lew 114, 125, 158
Harvey, Paul 188
Harwood, E.M. 88, 89
Haskin, Byron 110, 182
Haworth, Joe 188
Haydn, Richard 178, 180, 246
Hayes, Edgar 199
Hayes, George (Gabby) 38, 246
Hayes, Helen 213
Hayes, Sam 117
Hayle, Grace 95, 107, 117, 153
Haymes, Dick 188, 190
Hays Office 67, 86, 112, 131, 165, 191
Hayward, Susan 155, 246
Healy, Harold 209, 210, 246

Hearn, Edward 53
Hearn, Sam 69
Hearst, Brandon 136
Hearst, William Randolph 135
The Heart Is Young 69
Heartburn 182
Heath, Frank 138, 158
Heath, Percy 42
Heaven Can Wait 86
Hecht, Ben 29, 31
Heckart, Eileen 210, 246
Heerman, Victor 32
Heflin, Van 180, 181, 182, 187, 246
Hegland, Phil 195
Heindorf, Ray 79, 90, 155
Heisler, Stuart 40
Hellinger, Mark 155, 160
Hell's Angels 37
Heman, Roger 178
Hemingway, Mariel 172
Henderson, Charles 188
Henderson, Dell 125
Henderson, Jack 171
Hepburn, Katharine 187, 213
Herbert, Holmes 136
Herbert, Hugh 107
Herbert, Victor 20
Herczeg, Geza 107
Herman, Ace 199
Herman, Al 171
Herrera, George 103
Hersch, Ben 176
Hersholt, Jean 172
Hervey, Irene 214
Heyes, Herbert 185
Heymann, Werner R. 136
Heywood, Herbert 142, 158, 183
Hickman, Howard 98, 171
Hickox, Sid 95, 116, 120, 122, 124, 133, 136, 141, 145, 148, 150, 152, 158, 160, 182
Hicks, Russell 117, 176
Hickson, E.R. 195
Hiestand, John 160
Higgs, Stuart 103
Hildegarde 225
Hildegarde's Raleigh Room 225
Hill, Al 76
Hiller, Wendy 178
The Hillsboro Story 195
Hinds, Samuel 101, 116, 166
Hively, George 171
Hobbes, Halliwell 88, 103, 114, 128, 133, 246
Hodgson, Leyland 142, 153
Hoff, Harold 162
Hoffman, Max, Jr. 158
Hogan, Dick 174
Hogsett, Albert 188
Holden, Fay 128
Holland, John 53
Holliday, Judy 210, 246
Holloway, Sterling 171, 246
Hollywood Dog High School 33
Hollywood Hotel 119, 128, 132, 135, 147, 152, 222
Hollywood Screen Test 15, 226
Hollywood's Open House 225
Holm, Jan 150, 155

Holman, Harry 117
Holmes, Brown 74
Holmes, Phillips 24, 32, 86, 93, 246
Holmes, Stuart 142, 150, 158
Holmes, William 116, 120
Holtz, Tenen 114
Homans, Robert 38, 63, 180
Homer, Michigan 5, 128
The Honest Finder 82, 86
Hope, Bob 179, 180, 224, 225
Hopkins, Keneth 192
Hopkins, Miriam 9, 10, 63, 64, 65, 83, 84, 85, 87, 88, 100, 157, 247
Hopper, Hedda 178, 214, 217
Hopper, William 148, 247
Hornblow, Arthur, Jr. 89
Hornung, Ernest William 40, 42
Horton, Edward Everett 83, 84, 85, 86, 88, 124, 247
The Hours Between see *24 Hours*
The House on 56th Street 2, 10, 16, 101–103
Housman, Arthur 153
Hovey, Ann 95
How Not to Worry 225
Howard, Anne 171
Howard, Esther 56, 247
Howard, Gertrude 70, 247
Howard, Hazel 65
Howard, Kathleen 136
Howard, Leslie 10, 114, 115, 116, 178, 222, 247
Howard, Lewis 166
Howard, Sidney 40
Howe, James Wong 155
Howell, John 40
Howland, Jobyna 45, 47, 247
Hoyt, Julia 205, 206
Hubbard, Lucien 93
Huber, Harold 95
Hubert, Rene 60
Hugh, R.L. 188
Hughes, Charles Anthony 160
Hughes, Diana 160
Hughes, Rupert 53, 54
Hultman, Rune 195
Humberstone, H. Bruce 40
Humbert, George 83, 90, 148
Hunt, J. Roy 162
Hunter, Ian 124, 126, 127, 128, 128, 132, 136, 137, 138, 140, 141, 142, 143, 144, 145, 152, 153, 154, 155, 156, 157, 205, 222, 226, 247
Hunter, Kenneth 138
Huntley, G.P., Jr. 138
Huntley, George P. 174
Huntley, Hugh 125
Hunyady, Sandor 93, 95
Hurst, Brandon 178
Hussey, Ruth 14, 211, 213
Huston, Walter 7, 10, 17, 18, 19, 45, 46, 47, 48, 93, 94, 95, 182, 183, 184, 185, 209, 210, 247
Hutchinson, Claude 114
Hutchinson, Josephine 132
Hyams, Leila 50
Hymer, John B. 82, 207
Hymer, Warren 79, 80, 81, 82, 207, 222, 247

Hytten, Olaf 101, 103, 114, 124, 145, 153

I Found Stella Parish 1, 11, 124–128, 135, 157, 222
I Gave My Heart 135
I Give My Heart 135
I Have Been Faithful 89
I Loved a Woman 10, 98–100
I Was Faithless 89
Ichioka, Mia 107
Illusion 3, 8, 24–25, 57
An Imperfect Lover 88, 89
In Name Only 13, 78, 162–165, 222–223
Inescort, Frieda 133, 134, 138, 140, 141, 247
Ingraham, Amo 107
Ingraham, Lloyd 95, 162
Ingraham, Mitchell 133, 155
Insull, Samuel 100
Intimate see *Strangers in Love*
Irene 162
Irons, Jeremy 220
Irving, Bill 171
Irving, George 107, 171
Irwin, Boyd 174
Irwin, Carlotta 19
Irwin, Charles 125, 128, 138
Irwin, Lew 190
Isle of Fury 92
It Happened in Kaloha 168
It's a Date 13, 14, 165–168
Ivans, Perry 51, 83

Jack Benny Program 223
Jackman, Fred 124, 128, 136
Jackson, Horace 148
Jackson, Howard 32, 45, 150
Jackson, Jessie Mae 155
Jackson, Joseph 79
Jackson, Selmer 117, 153, 174, 176, 195, 198, 199, 247
Jackson, Thomas E. 38, 63, 247
Jacobs, William 182
Jacoby, John 185
Jacoby, Michael 128
Jaffee, Sam 44
James, Alfred 107
James, Rian 95
Jamerson, Peter 185
Jamison, Bud 107, 171
Janis, Elsie 32, 106
Janney, Leon 152
Jason, Sybil 124, 126, 127, 128, 155, 156, 157, 158, 222, 247
Jeans, Isabel 152, 153, 154, 247
Jenkins, Allen 90, 91, 92, 93
Jennings, DeWitt 98
Jensen, Eulalie 179
Jerome, M.K. 155
Jessel, George 188, 189
Jessie Bonstelle Stock Company 5, 235
Jewel Robbery 1, 9, 13, 16, 75–79
Jewell, Isabel 171, 247
Jimmy Dorsey & His Band 188, 189
Johnson, Casey 171
Johnson, Helen see Wood, Judith

Johnson, Kay 9, 30, 48, 49, 50, 51, 207, 247
Johnson, Laurence E. 48
Jolson, Al 10, 107, 108, 109, 110, 191, 247
Jones, Gordon 180
Jones, Grover 70, 82–83, 86
Jones, Henry 216, 248
Jones, Jane 80, 248
Jones, Olive 123
Jones, Ray 56
Jones, Stanley 148
Joos, Doc 199
Jordan, Bobby 150, 151, 152, 248
Jordan, Jewell 142
Jordan, Kate 58, 59
Jory, Victor 145, 160, 161, 248
Joy, Leatrice 67
Joyce, Mike 107
The Judas Tree 127
Julian, Mac 103
June, Ray 88, 180
Jungmeyer, Jack 168
Juran, Nathan 178

Kahal, Irving 103, 106, 109
Kahlo, Frida 89
Kahn, Gus 93, 95
Kaliz, Armand 25
Kalkhurts, Eric 45
Kane, Eddie 24, 76, 107
Kane, Helen 32, 34, 248
Kane, Joseph J. 195
Kanin, Fay 217
Kaplan, Dora 116
Karlson, Phil 199, 202–203
Karlstein, Philip P. 185, 187
Karns, Roscoe 79, 248
Karsner, David 98
Kate Smith Chat 225
Katherine Gibbs School of Secretarial Training 6
Katscher, Robert 107
Katz, Lee 110, 116, 160
Kaufman, Albert S. 32
Kaufman, George S. 20, 21, 145, 147, 148, 226
Kaun, Bernhard 67, 71, 75, 79, 95, 101, 113, 116, 120, 122
Kay, Edward J. 192, 195, 199
Kay, Erna 20
Kay Francis: A Passionate Life and Career 3
Keane, Edward 98, 107, 120, 142
Kearns, Joseph 224, 248
Keating, Alice 124
Keats, Patricia 106
Keays, Vernon 168
Keeler, Ruby 109
Keighley, William 75, 95, 101, 110, 152, 154, 157
Keith, Ian 155, 248
Keithley, Jane 32
Kelley, Mary 166
Kellogg, Virginia 95, 136
Kellum, Theron O. 174
Kelly, Gerald 6
Kelly, John 120
Kelly, Lew 160, 171

Kelly, Mark 171
Kelly, Patsy 227
Kelly, Paul 195, 196, 197, 198, 199, 248
Kelsie, James 51
Kemble-Cooper, Lillian 128
The Ken Murray Show 15, 227
Kendis, James 82
Kenley Players 14
Kennedy, Edgar 117
Kennedy, Merna 107, 109, 248
Kennedy, Neal 138
Kent, Crawford 125, 188
Kenyon, Charles 71, 74, 98, 103, 110, 122
Kerman, David 160
Kerr, Frederic 40, 248
Keyes, Don 65
The Keyhole 10, 90–93
Keys, Peggy 142
Kibbee, Guy 107, 248
Kibbee, Milton 95, 98, 120, 123, 124, 160, 248
The Kid from Spain 89–90
Kidd, Michael 138
Kilian, Victor 17, 248
Killian, Mike 188
Kilpatrick, Reid 160, 192, 195
The Kind Men Marry 162
King, Dennis 32, 34, 248
King, Jack 32
King, Joe 120, 166
King, Matty 142
King, Owen 155
King, Stanley 117
King, Walter Woolf 185
King of the Underworld 13, 158–160
Kingsford, Walter 124, 136
Kingsley, Ben 27
Kinnell, Murray 98
Kinskey, Leonid 83, 248
Kirby, George 88, 128
Kisloff, Lou 69
Klein, Lou 82
Knight, Karen 195
Knopf, Edwin H. 32
Knowles, Patric 133, 248
Knox, Elyse 176
Kober, Arthur 67
Kobliansky, Nicholas 63, 114
Kohlmar, Lee 76
Kohner, Frederick 165
Kolk, Scott 38, 39, 248
Kolker, Henry 76, 90, 91, 92, 98, 107, 108, 109, 176, 248
Kopp, Rudolph G. 56, 70
Korngold, Erich Wolfgang 138
Kortman, Bob 63
Koster, Henry 185, 187, 188
Krasna, Norman 165
Kreuder, Peter 141
Krims, Milton 152
Kruger, Otto 195, 196, 197, 198, 199, 248
Kurrle, Robert 75, 79

Lackland, Ben 213, 248
Lackteen, Frank 114, 183
Lacy, Madison 138, 141, 155

Ladies' Man 9, 53–56
A Lady by Preference 223
The Lady Grew Up 225
The Lady Is Willing 224
Lady with a Badge 120
The Lady with the Lamp 132
Lagerstrom, Oscar 40, 42
Laidlaw, Ethan 22
Laing, John 162
Lake, Arthur 26–27
Lamas, Fernando 215
Lambert, Tom 192, 195, 199
Lancaster, Betty 19
Landi, Elissa 69
Landis, Carole 13, 148, 150, 188, 189, 190, 191, 192, 224, 225, 248–249
Lane, Allan 80, 249
Lane, Arthur 67
Lane, Charles 166, 249
Lane, Lola 145
Lane Sisters 184
Lang, Charles 27, 29, 38, 56, 150, 152, 155, 160
Langan, Glenn 188, 191, 249
Lange, Elaine 199, 249
Langford, Frances 187, 226
Langton, Paul 215, 249
Lapis, Joseph 166, 185
Lardner, Ring 209
La Rocque, Rod 217
Larson, Bobby 222, 249
Larson, Vernon 141
La Rue, Danny 180
LaRue, Frank 120
LaRue, Jack 207, 249
LaSalle, Mick 198–199
Lasky, Jesse 18, 20, 22, 24, 25, 27, 29, 32
The Last of Mrs. Cheyney 1, 14, 214–215
Laszlo, Aladar 82, 86
Laszlo, Robert 185
Lauder, Harry 67
La Verne, Lucille 63, 65, 249
The Law and the Lady 214
Lawford, Betty 17, 19, 136, 249
Lawford, Ernest 205, 249
Lawler, Anderson 65, 66, 141, 148, 153, 249
Lawrence, Lillian 249
Lawrence, Marc 176, 249
Lawrence, Rosina 32, 249
Lawrence, Vincent 51
Laye, Evelyn 134
Layson, Lorena 98, 103
Leary, Nolan 195
LeBaron, William 58
LeBorg, Reginald 170
Lederman, D. Ross 159
Lee, Eddie 166
Lee, Harry 17, 249
Lee, Jocelyn 25
Lee, Robert B. 95, 124, 133, 138
Lee, Rowland V. 32, 47
Lee, Ruth 192
Lee, Sylvan
Leftwich, Alexander 160
Lehmann, Vela 195

Index

Leigh, Rowland 145, 152
Leipold, John 27, 29, 67, 70
Lenardi, Bert 122
Lengle, William C. 63
Lenhart, Billy 185
Leon, Peggy 195
Leonard, Barbara 128
Leonard, Gus 83
Leong, James 103
LeRoy, Hal 107, 190, 249
LeRoy, Mervyn 124, 127
Le Saint, Edward 38
Leslie, Lawrence 17, 249
Lessing, Marion 111
Let Us Be Gay 14, 216–217
Let's Go Native 8, 42–44
Let's Not and Say We Did 205
Levenson, Lew 63
Levering, Otto 29, 49
LeVino, Margaret 141
Levy, Benn 58
Levy, Hubert 98
Lewis, David 152
Lewis, Harold C. 70
Lewis, Harry 182
Lewis, Vera 155, 158, 160, 249
Licho, Edgar 185
Lindau, Rolf 142
Lindgren, Harry M. 24, 53
Lindsay, Howard 211, 213
Lindsay, Margaret 101, 102, 154, 249
Lindsay Morison Company 5, 234, 235
Linow, Ivan 76
Lipstick see Long, Lois
Lissner, Ray 58
Litel, John 150, 151, 152, 155, 156, 157, 222, 250
Little, Jack 180
Little, Thomas 178, 188
The Little Foxes 42
Little Men 13, 171–174
Littlefield, Lucien 51, 70, 103, 250
Litvak, Anatole 110
Liu, Lotus 124
Liu, Mia 120
Living on Velvet 11, 116–120, 222
Lloyd, Al 158, 160
Lloyd, Albert 141
Lloyd, Alma 128
Lloyd, Doris 58, 114, 131, 179, 195, 250
Locke, William J. 70
Lockhart, R.H. Bruce 113, 116
Loder, John 187, 226, 250
Loeb, Philip 236, 250
Loesser, Frank 180
Loftus, Cecilia 166, 167, 168, 208, 250
Logan, Helen 188
Logan, Stanley 128, 136, 138, 141, 145, 147
Lombard, Carole 9, 13, 53, 162, 163, 164, 165, 222, 223, 250
London, Tom 168, 250
The Long Way Round 226
Long, Lois 7
Long, Louise 45

Long, Walter 168
Longmire, Adele 159
Longworth, Alice Roosevelt 145
Longworth, B. 107
Longworth, Nicholas 145
Loo, Richard 120, 250
Loper, Don 188
Lorch, Theodore 142
Lord, Robert 71, 79, 82, 95, 107, 133, 148
Loring, Teala 195, 196, 197, 198, 199, 200, 201, 202, 250
Los Angeles Illustrated Daily News 52
Loshak, Rydo 141
Louise, Anita 25, 78, 145, 150, 151, 152, 226, 250
Love, Montagu 35, 37, 128, 250
Love and Kisses 187
Love Is Like That 37
The Love Parade 86
Lovejoy, Frank 218
Lovely Lady 152, 154
Lovering, Otto *see* Levering, Otto
Lovett, Dorothy 250
Low, Warren 114, 128
Lowell, Helen 116, 122, 123, 124
Lowry, Morton 178
Loy, Myrna 182, 223
Lubitsch, Ernst 10, 22, 23, 32, 33, 78, 79, 82, 83, 84, 85, 86, 87, 88
Lucas, Wilfred 95, 101, 120, 125, 160
Luce, Clare Boothe 89
Luckett, Edith 209, 250
Luden, Jack, 23, 32, 250
Ludwig, Edward 176
Lueker, Arthur 101
Luguet, Andre 76
Luick, Earl 71, 98, 101
Lukas, Paul 9, 24, 28, 55, 56, 57, 58, 124, 125, 126, 127, 250
Lunt, Alfred 226, 234, 236
Lux Radio Theatre 82, 152, 165, 222, 223, 224, 226
Lux Video Theatre 15, 82, 226
Lydon, Jimmy 171, 172, 173, 250
Lyle, Bessie 24
Lyman, Abe 24, 32, 34
Lynch, Bert 67
Lynch, Warren 70
Lynn, Basil 114

Macalpin, Frederic 119
MacArthur, Charles 29, 31
MacDonald, Ballard 32
MacDonald, J. Farrell 98
MacDonald, Jeanette 8, 32, 35, 42, 43, 44, 150, 180, 250
MacDonald, Wallace 95, 98
MacEwen, Walter 182
Mack, Charlie 34
Mack, Helen 192, 193, 194, 195, 250
Mack, Stanley 111
Mack, Wilbur 53, 74, 199
Mackaill, Dorothy 60
MacKenna, Kenneth 8, 45, 46, 47, 48, 251

MacLane, Barton 20, 120, 125, 251
MacLaren, Mary 162, 251
MacLean, Lorraine 192, 195, 199
MacMahon, Aline 79, 222, 224, 251
MacMurray, Fred 224
MacWilliams, Paul 158, 251
Magee, Frank 150
Magruder, Anna 24, 251
Maguire, Mary 141
Maher, Frank 88
Main, Marjorie 215
Malatesta, Fred 83
Maley, Keefe 101
Malie, Tommie 180
Mallory, Jay 133, 134
Malyon, Eily 120, 125, 128, 138
Mamoulian, Rouben 13, 14
Man Wanted 1, 9, 71–73, 78
The Man Who Lost Himself 13, 176–178
Manatt, James 124
Mandalay 10, 103–107
Mander, Myles 188
Mankiewicz, Herman J. 53, 56
Mankiewicz, Joseph L. 32, 180
Mann, Hank 182
Mann, Stanley 178
Manners, David 1, 9 71, 72, 73, 251
Manolescu, George 86
March, Fredric 25, 26, 27, 32, 34, 70, 71, 145, 251
Marcin, Max 51
Marcus, Lee 174
Margetson, Arthur 103
Marical, Leona 155
Marion, Frances 88, 217
Marion, George F. 42
Marion, George, Jr. 22, 42
Marion Morgan Dancers 32, 33
Mark, Michael 141
Marks, Owen 152
Marley, J. Peverell 178, 188
Marlin, Miriam 107
Marlow, Brian 65
Marlowe, Frank 120
Marlowe, John 107
Marr, Eddie 224, 251
Marr, Patsy 69
La Marraine de Charley 180
The Marriage Playground 8, 25–27, 44, 67, 203
Marsh, Charles 199, 251
Marshall, George 168, 169
Marshall, Herbert 10, 83, 84, 85, 87, 88, 225, 251
Marston, John 95, 101
Marston, Theodore 170
Martell, Alphonse 107, 125, 133, 142, 251
Martin, Chris-Pin 53, 251
Martin, Lewis 216, 251
Martin Deane Wickett Show 225
Martini, Nino 32, 33, 35, 251
Marx, Chico 20, 251
Marx, Groucho 20, 21, 251
Marx, Harpo 20, 251

Marx, Zeppo 20, 251
Marx Brothers 8, 20–22, 47
Mary Stevens, M.D. 10, 95–98, 106
Maschmeyer, Dudie 141
Mashmeyer, Rudy 124
Maskerade 144
Mason, Reginald 95
Massey, Raymond 184
Mather, John 142
Matthews, Harriet 162
Matthews, Lester 188
Matthews, Paul 171
Mauch, Billy 128, 251
Maugham, W. Somerset 138, 219, 220
Maxwell, Edwin 98
May, James 128
May, Joe 141, 144
Mayer, Laura Walker 110, 112
Mayer, Louis B. 50, 103
Mayer, Ray 155
Mayfair, Mitzi 13, 32, 188, 189, 190, 191, 192, 224, 225, 251–252
Mayo, Archie 73, 133, 135, 152, 178, 179, 180, 223
Mayo, Frank 160, 182, 195, 252
Mazurka 141, 144, 145
McCall, Mary, Jr. 74, 127
McCallister, Lon 183, 252
McCall's 6
McCallum, John 138
McCarey, Leo 42, 43, 44
McCormick, Myron 211, 252
McCrea, Joel 9, 65, 66, 112, 252
McDaniel, Sam 60, 120, 148, 252
McDonald, Frank 114
McDonell, (Colonel) G.L. 24, 252
McDowell, Claire 111, 114, 252
McDowell, Hugh, Jr. 162
McDowell, Nelson 128
McGeehan, Pat 223, 252
McGill, Barney 90
McHugh, Frank 79, 82, 101, 209, 252
McHugh, Jimmy 188
McIntyre, Leila 111
McKee, Lafe 168
McKenzie, Eva 83
McKenzie, Fay 166, 168
McKenzie, Robert (Bob) 60, 168
McKim, Sammy 171
McKinney, Florine 88
McLaughlin, William 24
McLeod, Gordon 45
McLeod, Norman Z. 171, 172–173
McManus, George 30
McNally, William 103
McNiff, Harold M. 38, 45
McNutt, William Slavens 70
McWade, Edward 111, 120, 123, 155
McWade, Robert 65, 98
Meade, Claire 199
Meehan, Elizabeth 58
Meehan, John 8, 17, 103
Meehan, John, Jr. 103
Meek, Donald 180, 252
Meeker, George 206, 252
Mehra, Lal Chand 223, 252
Melody Lane 225

Melville, Emilie 24, 252
Memoirs 86
Memory of Love 162, 164
Mendes, Lothar 22, 23, 24, 25, 27, 32, 53, 54, 55, 70
Menjou, Adolphe 103, 109
Menzies, William Cameron 40
Meredith, Frank 174
Meredith, John 178
Merkel, Una 71, 73, 252
Merlo, Tony 162
Merriam, Charlotte 72, 252
Merrill, Lou 222, 223, 224, 252
Merrill, Martha 117
Merrivale, Philip 89, 90
Meyer, Torben 28, 103, 252
MGM (Metro-Goldwyn-Mayer) 9, 48, 50, 60, 93, 180, 182
Michael, Gertrude 195, 198, 252
Midnight Club 78
Mildred Pierce 198–199
Milland, Ray 48, 252
Millar, Lee 252
Miller, Alice D.G. 90, 92
Miller, Harold 162
Miller, Patsy Ruth 14, 210, 252–253
Miller, Sidney 95
Miller, Walter 117
Miller, William 83
Millhauser, Bertram 93
Mills, Frank 162
Mills, Gordon 215, 253
Mills, Harry D. 27, 29, 42
Milner, Victor 25, 32, 42, 53, 83, 176
Milton, Dave 192, 195, 199
Milton, Robert 27, 29
Minevitch, Borrah 182, 185, 253
Minjir, Harold 76, 180
Miranda, Carmen 168, 188, 189
Mirror, Mirror 14, 218–219
The Mistress of Fashion 138
Mitchell, Grant 145, 148, 180
Mitchell, Howard M. 155
Mitchum, Robert 198
Mizner, Wilson 79
Mohr, Gerald 223, 253
Mohr, Hal 168
Mong, William V. 98
Monogram Pictures 13, 14, 100, 192, 195, 199, 202
Montagu, Ivor 47
Montgomery, Douglass 207, 253
Montgomery, Robert 58, 214
Moore, Carlyle, Jr. 133, 160
Moore, Clayton 153, 253
Moore, Dennie 152
Moore, Dickie 48, 150, 151, 152, 172, 253
Moore, Dorothy 168
Moore, Emily 101
Moore, Eulabelle 210, 211, 253
Moore, Scotty 114
Moorehead, Agnes 223, 253
Moorhouse, Bert 107, 162
Moraine, Lyle 141
Moran, Eddie 176
Moran, Peggy 153, 158, 253

Moran, Polly 60, 253
Moran and Mack 34
Mordant, Edwin 120
Moreau, Marie 107
Morehouse, Ward 7, 18, 19
Moreno, Antonio 92
Moreno, Rosita 35
Morgan, Clive 162
Morgan, Frank 214
Morgan, Ralph 172
Morgan, Sandra 162
Morgan, Will 160
Moriarty, Pat 120
Moritz, Stefan 138
Morozowicz-Szczepkowska, Maria 110, 112
Morris, Adrian 120, 253
Morris, Chester 207, 253
Morris, Frances 188, 253
Morris, McKay 6, 206
Morrison, Adrienne 205, 253
Morrow, Jackie 145
Morse, N. Brewster 155
Morse, Terry 136
Mortimer, Edmund 133
Morton, James C. 168
Morton Downey Show 225
Moscovich, Maurice 162, 253
Mowbray, Alan 60, 61, 62, 76, 253
Mower, Jack 117, 145, 153, 155, 158, 160, 183
Mudie, Leonard 103, 136, 138, 192
Muir, Jean 110, 110, 111, 112, 113, 253
Mulhall, Evelyn 142
Mulhall, Jack 185
Mundin, Herbert 79, 138, 253
Muni, Paul 78, 132, 133, 159
Munier, Ferdinand 93, 124, 128, 141–142
Munroe, Warren 182
Munsel, Patrice 226, 253
Murder Unlimited 224
Murphy, Dudley 63, 65
Murphy, George 222, 253
Murphy, Maurice 150
Murray, Ken 222, 227, 253–254
Musuraca, Nicholas 171, 174
My Bill 13, 150–152, 222, 223
Myers, Harry 95
Myrtil, Odette 192, 195

Nagel, Conrad 223, 224, 225, 226
Naish, J. Carrol 114, 254
Nancy Goes to Rio 168
Nard, Winnie 195
Nash, J.E. 24
Nash, Mary 222, 254
Nash, Ogden 180, 182
Natheaux, Louis 166
Nazimova, Alla 112
Neagle, Anna 132
Neal, Siri 27
Nedell, Bernard 180, 195, 198
Negri, Pola 144
Neil, Tony 171
Nelson, Frank 222, 223, 224, 254
Nelson, Harold 117
Nervig, Conrad A. 48

Neumann, Harry 192, 195, 199
Never in This World 222
New York Evening World 53
The New Yorker 7
Newcombe, Warren 180
Newell, David 22, 23, 25, 32, 33, 42, 117, 123, 160, 254
Newman, Alfred 88, 178
Newman, Emil 188
Newton, Theodore (Ted) 209, 254
The Next Corner 59
Niblo, Fred, Jr. 188
Nichols, George, Jr. 24, 38, 51
Nichols, Richard 171
Nicklin, Al 195
Nigh, William 192, 195
Nightingale, Florence 11, 100, 128–133
Ninotchka 86
Niven, David 42
Nixon, Marian 152
Norman, Al 32
Norris, Kathleen 48, 50
North, Robert 35
North, Mrs. Wilfrid 117
Norton, Barry 35
Norton, Edgar 133
Norton, Jack 180
Norvell, Mahlon 107
A Notorious Affair 8, 35–38
Novak, Kim 27, 58
Novi, C.M. (Charles) 133, 155, 158
Now I'll Tell 31
Nowell, Wedgwood 125, 136, 145, 153, 160
Nowlan, Robert and Gwendolyn 152
Noyer, C. 88
Nuit d'Espagne 60

Oakie, Jack 8, 32, 33, 34, 42, 44, 171, 172, 173, 190, 192, 209, 254
Oberon, Merle 82, 191
O'Brien, Bill 53
O'Brien, Dave 107, 254
O'Brien, Eloise 150
O'Brien, Pat 13, 82, 122, 148, 149, 150, 254
O'Brien-Moore, Erin 172, 213
Obzina, Martin 166, 168
O'Connell, Hugh 148
O'Connor, Frank 53, 155, 176, 254
O'Connor, Una 95, 97, 182, 184, 254
O'Daveren, Vesey 114, 120, 124, 128
O'Donnell, Spec 153, 183
O'Driscoll, Martha 170
O'Farrell, Broderick 51
O'Gatty, Jimmy 158
O'Hanlon, George 160, 254
O'Hanson, George 153
O'Keefe, Dennis 101, 107, 254
Okey, Jack 107
Okuda, Ted 202
Oland, Warner 32, 33, 103, 254
Oliver, David 166
Oliver, Gordon 148
Olsen, Larry 192

O'Malley, Pat 160, 183, 254
One Hour of Romance 145
One Hour to Live 145
One Way Passage 1, 9, 13, 16, 79–82, 207, 222
O'Neal, Anne 180
O'Neal, Nance 58, 60, 254
O'Neal, Zelma 32, 33, 254
O'Neill, Henry 98, 101, 107, 116, 120, 128, 145
Oness, Randy 166
Oppenheimer, George 180, 182, 218, 219
Orenbach, Al 188
Orry-Kelly 79, 90, 95, 101, 103, 107, 110, 114, 116, 118, 120, 122, 124, 125, 127, 128, 133, 135, 136, 137, 138, 141, 145, 146, 148, 150, 152, 155, 158, 160, 182
Orth, Frank 155
Ossining School 5
O'Sullivan, Maureen 78
Otho, Henry 95, 103, 107, 120, 150, 155
Otterson, Jack 166, 168, 176, 185
Ottiano, Rafaela 103, 254
Owen, Reginald 103, 178, 180, 254
Owen, Seena 25, 26, 254
Owsley, Monroe 90, 91, 92, 93, 254

Padden, Sarah 120, 176, 254
Paggi, M.M. 25, 83
Palange, Inez 95
Pallette, Eugene 32, 33, 42, 65, 66, 67, 93, 166, 254
Palmer, Leslie 51, 70
Palmer, Lilli 220
Palmer, Tony 27
Panzer, Paul 120, 142, 158, 160, 254–255
Pape, Lionel 178
Paramount 5, 7, 8, 9, 10, 11, 13, 17, 18, 20, 21, 22, 23, 24, 25, 27, 29, 31, 32, 33, 38, 42, 43, 44, 45, 50, 51, 53, 56, 58, 60, 63, 65, 67, 70, 73, 82, 86, 87
Paramount on Parade 8, 32–35, 190
Pardee, Ida 170
Parker, Austin 101, 103
Parker, Frank 222
Parker, Jean 93, 223, 255
Parker, Max 133, 145, 148, 150
Parrish, Imboden 63
Parrish, Robert 51
Parsley, Ruby 25
Parsons, Louella 141, 222
Pasch, Reginald 111
Passion Flower 9, 48–51, 52, 207
Pasternacki, Stephan 70
Pasternak, Joseph 165, 168
Patrick, Gail 31
The Patriot 86
Patterson, Elizabeth 71–72, 73, 255
Patterson, Pat 133, 138
Payne, Sally 168, 255
Payne, Shelby 199
Pearce, George 114
Pearce, Guy 188

Peers, Joan 32, 255
Pegler, Arthur James 19
Pegler, Westbrook 19
Penley, W.S. 180
Pennick, Jack 32
Pennington, Ann 26–27
Penwarden, Duncan 17, 19, 255
Pereda, Ramon 35
Perier, Francois 138
Perkins, Anthony 220, 255
Perkins, Frank 182
Perlberg, William
Perry, Bob 28
Perry, Gene 107
Pertwee, Roland 113
Peters, House 42
Petersen, Dorothy 141
Peterson, Elsa 133, 142
Phelps, Lee 53, 72, 95, 125, 160
Pichel, Irving 86, 114, 255
Pickering, Virginia 63
Pickfair 121
Pickford, Mary 121
Pidgeon, Walter 166, 167, 168, 169, 225, 255
Pierce, Jack 185
Pierce, Otto 67
Pigott, Tempe 124, 128
Pilot, Bernice 148, 150, 255
Pine, Virginia 111
Pink Tights see *Dangerous Curves*
Pittack, Robert 56
Pitts, ZaSu 48, 50, 51, 255
Pittsfield, Massachusetts 6
Platt, Mrs. Thomas 85
Playgirl 13, 174–176
Pleasure First see *Man Wanted*
Pogany, Willy 107
Pokrass, Samuel 32
Polglase, Van Nest 162, 171
Polito, Sol 107, 109, 110
Pollard, Alex 162, 188
Polo, Eddie 166
Porcasi, Paul 88, 98, 114, 255
Potel, Victor 45, 51, 255
Powell, Dick 107, 108, 109, 222, 255
Powell, Jane 168
Powell, Richard 138, 255
Powell, Russ 22, 32, 93, 101, 133, 168, 171, 255
Powell, William 8, 9, 18, 27, 28, 29, 30, 31, 32, 33, 38, 39, 40, 53, 54, 55, 56, 58, 76, 78, 79, 80, 81, 82, 92, 192, 214, 222, 255
Power, Paul 107, 111
Power, Tyrone 179, 180, 223
Power, Tyrone, Sr. 208, 255–256
Pratt, Thomas 103, 160, 182
Preminger, Otto 13
Presbrey, Eugene Wiley 40
Presnell, Robert 90, 103
Preston, Kiki Whitney 5
Previn, Charles 165, 168, 176, 185
Price, Edward 141
Prince, Maurice 199
Pringle, Aileen 185, 256
Pritchard, Robert 168
Prival, Lucien 93

Proctor, Catherine 236, 256
Prudential Family Playhouse 15, 226
Pryor, Roger 210, 211, 256
Puglia, Frank 162, 182
Pulido, Juan 35
Pulley, B.S. 188
Pursley, Ruth 103

Quigley, Charles 174
Quine Richard 158
Quinn, Phil 182
Quintana, Rosita 82

Rabbits 224
Rabinowitz, Max 141
Rackerby, Donald 171
Raffles 8, 40–42, 90
Raft, George 78
Rainger, Ralph 45, 56
Rains, Claude 136, 137, 138, 184, 256
The Rains Came 223
Ralph, Jessie 124, 125, 126, 127
Rambeau, Marjorie 82, 145, 222, 256
Rameau, Hans 141
Ramsey, Quen 168
Randolf, Anders 22
Randolph, Lillian 171, 224, 256
Raphaelson, Samson 82, 86
Rasch Albertina
Ratcliffe, E.J. 98
Rathbone, Basil 35, 36, 37, 141, 142, 143, 144, 145, 187, 206, 214, 256
Rathbone, Ouida 187
Rau, Neil 198
Raw Meat 100
Rawlinson, Herbert 148, 153, 256
Ray, Charles 178
Ray, Joey 174
Rayan, Amy 98
Raye, Martha 13, 188, 189, 190, 191, 192, 224, 225, 256
Raymond, Frances 24, 256
Raymond, Gene 101, 102, 103, 256
Reagan, Nancy Davis 209
Red Cross 13
Red Meat 100
Ree, Max 58
Reed, George 101
Reed, Phillip 101, 111, 114, 256
Reefer Madness 47
Reeves, Bob 168
Regas, George 138, 256
Rehan, Ada 5, 234, 256
Reicher, Frank 114, 136, 235, 256
Reid, Cliff 174
Remley, Ralph 158
Rennie, James 207, 256
Resnais, Alain 138
Reticker, Hugh 120, 182
Return from Limbo 148
The Return of Carol Deane 103
Reyher, Ferdinand 120
Reynaud, Fernand 180
Reynolds, Craig 192, 256
Rhapsody 95

Rhodes, Ila 160, 256
Riano, Renie 148
Rice, Adnia 213, 256–257
Rice, Edward 171
Rice, Sam 111, 141, 257
Rich Man's Folly see *Scandal Sheet*
Richards, Addison 114, 192, 257
Richards, Thomas 114, 148
Richardson, Jack 51, 117, 120, 138, 141, 153, 158
Richmond, Kane 38, 174, 257
Ridgely, John 150, 158, 160, 257
Riedel, Richard H. 176, 185
Ring, Cyril 20, 21, 176, 257
Ringgold, Gene 1, 2
Risdon, Elisabeth 132, 150, 151, 152, 257
Risso, John 29, 31
RKO 58, 162, 171, 172, 173, 174, 180
Roach, Bert 199, 257
Roadman, Betty 188
Roberts, Al 114
Roberts, Arthur 58
Roberts, Desmond 103
Robin, Leo 27, 32, 45, 83, 188
Robinson, Ann 158
Robinson, Casey 124, 127, 133, 136
Robinson, Dewey 79
Robinson, Edward G. 10, 98, 99, 100, 172, 257
Roche, Viola 216, 257
Roder, Milan 138
Roe, Guy 83
Roemheld, Heinz 103, 110, 113, 116, 120, 122, 124, 128, 133, 136, 141, 148, 152, 155, 158, 182
Rogan, Barney 20
Rogers, Charles (Buddy) 24, 25, 32, 33, 257
Rogers, Ginger 187
Rogers, John 40, 257
Rolf, Ernst 32
Romaine, Jane 124
Romance on the High Seas 92
Romanoff, Constantine 95, 257
Romantini, Joseph 145
Romero, Cesar 114, 257
Roosevelt, Eleanor 147
Roosevelt, Teddy 98, 99, 147
Roquemore, Henry 142, 176, 257
Rosenbloom, Maxie 160, 257
Rosener, George 162
Rosing, Bodil 103
Rosley, Adrian 120
Ross, Earle 223, 257
Rosson, Hal 48
Roth, Lillian 24, 32, 33, 257
Rothstein, Arnold 30
Roy, Rosalie 107
Rozelle, Rita 120
Rub, Christian 95, 257
Ruben, J. Walter 25
Rucker, Douglas 171
Ruggles, Charles 17, 83, 88, 179, 257
Ruhl, William 166
Ruick, Melville 222, 223, 257
Rule, Janice 218

Ruman, Sam 171, 174
Ruman, Sig 176, 257
Russell, Rosalind 180, 181, 182, 223, 258
Ruth, Phyllis 166
Ruysdael, Basil 20, 258
Ryan, Allan A., Jr. 7
Ryan, Robert 180, 258
Ryan, Sheila 176
Ryan, Thomas Fortune 7
Ryan, Tim 199, 258
Ryerson, Florence 22
Ryskind, Morrie 20, 22, 178

S.S. Atlantic see *One Way Passage*
Sage, Sally 160, 258
St. Mauer, Adele 142
St. Polis, John 58
Sakall, S.Z. 166, 176, 178, 258
Salt, Waldo 190
Salter, Hans J. 165, 176
Sammy Kaye's Serenade 225
Sand, Froma 188
Santley, Joseph 20, 21, 101
Santoro, Francesca 171
Sappington, Fay 217, 258
Sardo, Cosmo 195
Sarno, Hector 83
Saulter, William 20, 21
Saum, Cliff 123, 142, 153, 158, 160, 182
Saunders, John Monk 124, 127
Saunders, Russell 101, 150, 155
Savino, Domenico 60
Sawtell, Paul 174
Sawyer, Joseph 124
Sayles, Francis 158
Saylor, Syd 38, 51, 258
Sayre, George 198
Sayre, Jeffrey 142
Scandal Sheet 9, 51–53, 202
Scheid, Francis J. 182
Schertzinger, Victor 32
Schindell, Cy 120
Schofield, Frank 220, 258
Scholl, Jack 141
The School of Scandal 6
Schubert, Marina 114
Schubert, Mel 188
Schulberg, B.P. 24, 47
Schulman, Leo 158
Schumann-Heink, Ferdinand 142
Scott, Margaretta 180
Scott, Randolph 168, 169, 170, 180, 258
Scott, Victoria Elizabeth 155
Seager, Gwen 174
Searl, Jackie 32, 51, 258
Seaton, George 178, 180, 258
Seaver, Edwin 189
Seay, Billy 25, 258
Secrets of an Actress 13, 152–154
Sedan, Rolfe 32, 58, 83, 107, 258
Seeing Eye 16
Seel, Charles 155, 224, 258
Seidel, Louise 120, 258
Seiler, Lewis 158
Seipp, Hilde 144
Seiter, William A. 165, 188

Sell, Bernie 188
Sellars, Eleanore 215, 216
Sellon, Charles 42
Selwyn, Edgar 6
Selwyne, Clarissa 88
Selznick, David O. 8, 29, 30
Semels, Harry 93, 142
Sennett, Mack 147
Sergova, Kathryn 106, 107
Sersen, Fred 188
Servoss, Mary 188
Seven Arconis 69
Seymour, Harry 80, 95, 111
Seymour, James 101, 122
Shadow of Blackmail 202
Shadows on the Wall see *Guilty Hands*
Shairp, Mordaunt 128
Shakespeare's Hamlet 6, 205, 218
Shannon, Mary 166
Sharp, Henry 67, 70
Sharpe, Lester 182
Shaw, C. Montague 88, 178
Shaw, Frank 103, 166
Shaw, Janet 142, 155, 158, 258
Shaw, Oscar 20, 22
Shayne, Robert 199, 200, 201, 202, 258
Shearer, Douglas 48, 60, 90, 180
Shearer, Norma 2, 85, 147, 154, 214, 217, 222
Sheehan, John 90, 123
Sheffield, Reginald 138
Sheldon, E. Lloyd 24
Shelton, John 142, 258
Shelton, Marla 224, 258
Shenberg, Al 60
Sheridan, Frank 120
Sheridan, Richard Brinsley 205
Sherlock, Charles 80
Sherman, Richard 162
Sherman, Vincent 150, 152, 158, 159, 218
Sherry, J. Barney 42
Sherwood, York 138
Shipman, Bert 71
Shipman, Samuel 207
Shirpser, Cliff 56
Shoemaker, Ann 111, 120, 258
The Shop Around the Corner 86
Shore, Viola Brothers 22
The Shorn Lamb 70
Shourds, Sherry 88, 133, 141, 145
Shubert, Eddie 123
Shumate, Harold 168
Sidney, Basil 205
Sidney, Sylvia 207, 258
Siegel, Bernard 142
The Silver Theatre 223, 224, 225
Silvera, Darrell 162, 171, 174
Silvers, Phil 188, 190, 191
Simon, Arlette 138
Simpson, Ivan 114
Simpson, Napoleon 192
Simpson, Robert M. 138
Simpson, Shirley 124
Sinclair, Betty 195
Singleton, Penny 152, 259
Skelly, Hal 27, 28, 29, 259

Skinner, Frank 165, 168, 176
Skipworth, Alison 40, 136, 137, 138, 259
Slausson, Dudley 101
Sloane, W.& J. 74
Smalley, Al 70
Smith, C. Aubrey 60, 61, 62, 83, 87, 259
Smith, Donald 25
Smith, Jaclyn 132
Smith, Kate 225
Smith, Oscar 22, 42, 259
Smith, Red 227
Smith, Stanley 32, 34, 259
Snegoff, Leonid 114
Soderling, Walter 168
Soldiers in Greasepaint 224, 225
Somnes, George 206, 259
Sothern, Ann 168
Spacey, John Graham 125, 259
Sparks, William N. 93
Spier, Larry 24
Spiker, Harriet 24
Spivack, Murray 188
Stack, William 107
Stacpoole, H. De Vere 176, 178
Stage Door Canteen 224, 225
Standing, Gordon 205, 259
Standing, Joan 25, 29, 259
Standing, Wyndham 114, 259
Standish, Schuyler 171
Stanley, Edwin (Ed) 98, 120, 155, 158
Stanley, Eric 145
Stanton, Will 125, 138, 178, 199, 259
Stanwyck, Barbara 109, 112, 115, 198
Stark, Juanita 183
Starkey, Dewey 162
Starling, Lynn 88
Starr, Irving 188
Starrett, Charles 86
State of the Union 14, 172, 211–214
Stavisky 138
Stavisky, Serge Alexandre 138
Stedman, Myrtle 142
Steele, Vernon 125
Steers, Larry 83, 174, 195
Steiner, Max 58, 145
Stephens, Harvey 168
Stephens, Landers 166
Stephenson, Henry 88, 134, 166, 176, 259
Stephenson, James 158, 159, 259
Stevenson, Bob 183
Stevenson, Edward 35, 162, 171, 174
Stevenson, Houseley 136, 259
Stewart, Kattie (Katherine) 5, 205
Stockdale, Carl 158, 259
Stoddard, Haila 217, 259
Stolen Holiday 11, 136–138
Stone, Doc 158
Stone, Lewis 48, 50, 259
The Stork Club 15, 227
Storm, Lesley 220
Storm, Rafael 42
Storm at Daybreak 10, 93–95

The Story of Louis Pasteur 132
Strachey, Lytton 128
Straight, Clarence 188
Stranded 11, 120–122
Strang, Harry 188
Strange, Philip 35
Strange, Robert 124, 136, 162
Strange Rhapsody 95
Strange Victory 225
Strangers in Love 9, 70–71
Street of Chance 8, 29–32, 37, 40
Street of Women 9, 73–75
Strohbach, William 192
Stromberg, Hunt 60
Stuart, Donald 88, 188
Stuart, Gilchrist 178
Stuart, Gloria 74, 259
Stuart, Nick 51
Stuart Walker Company 6, 23, 37, 73, 198, 205–206
Stumpf, Charles 14–15
El Suicidio de Dorothy Hale 89
Sullivan, Charles 38, 158
Sullivan, E. 56
Sullivan, Elliott 158
Sullivan, Frederick 51
Sullivan, John M. 70
Sunderland, Nan 209, 210
Sundstrom, Florence 217, 259
Sunkist Beauties 69
Sunners, Harold 14
Sutherland, A. Edward 32, 209
Sutherland, Sidney 98, 100, 192, 195, 199, 203
Sutton, Grady 42, 162, 259–260
Sutton, John 190
Swan, William 219, 260
Swanson, Gloria 85
Sweet, Lavonne 69
Sweet Alice 135
Sweet Aloes 133, 34
Sydney, Basil 205, 260
Sykes, Ethel 133

Taggart, Ben 63, 70
Tailspin 162
Talbot, Lyle 95, 96, 97, 103, 104, 105, 106, 260
Talmadge, Norma 109
Tamiroff, Akim 93, 260
Tanina, Zozia 114, 116
Tanned Legs 26–27
Tashman, Lilyan 2, 9, 25, 27, 58, 65, 66, 67, 260
Tattersall, Viva 88, 260
Taylor, Don 103
Taylor, Kent 67, 170, 260
Taylor, Vin 192, 195
Tead, Phil 56, 98, 260
Teakle, Spencer 138
Tearle, Conway 59, 67, 68, 69, 260
Teasdale, Verree 111, 113, 145, 146, 147, 148, 222, 260
Teddington Studios 103
Teeple, Perc 141
Tell, Olive 53, 260
Temple, Shirley 103, 106, 260
Tenbrook, Harry 120
Terr, Max 45

Terry, Sheila 76, 101, 260
Teske, Charles 133
Texas Guinan's 6
Thalberg, Irving 50
Theatre 15, 219–220
Theatre Guild 235–236
Theek, Ingeborg 144
Thery, Jacques 185
Thieves and Lovers 86
Thimig, Hermann 187
Thin Man 182
This Is Show Business 15, 226
This Woman Is Dangerous 150
Thomas, Brandon 178, 180
Thomas, Frankie 182, 184, 260
Thompson, Charles 195
Thompson, Larry 188
Thompson, Lotus 124
Thomson, Kenneth 35, 71, 260
Thorndike, Oliver 214, 260
Three Smart Girls 187
Thursby, David 125
Tidblad, Inga 47
Tilbury, Zeffie 120, 133
Till We Meet Again 82
Titus, Frank 56, 65
Tobias, Harry 165
Tobin, Genevieve 98, 99, 100, 109, 122, 123, 124, 260
Tobin, Vivian 206, 260
Todd, Mabel 199
Todd, Thelma 95, 97, 260
Toland, Gregg 40, 71, 73
Toler, Sidney 70, 260
Toluhoff, Alexander 93
Tombes, Andrew 185, 186
Tomlin, Pinky 165
Tone, Franchot 58
Tony's 6, 7
Toomey, Regis 24, 29, 31, 51, 63, 159, 260–261
Torrence, David 40, 103, 261
Tours, Frank 20
Tovarich 11, 110
Tover, Leo 58
Towne, Gene 171, 172, 173
Towne, Rosella 160
Tozier, Joseph 138
Tracy, Spencer 31, 213
Tragedy with Music 118
Train, Arthur Cheney 24
Transgression 9, 58–60
Travis, Dennis 180
Travis, June 120, 122, 261
Tree, Dorothy 176, 261
Treen, Mary 125, 185, 261
Tribby, John E. 58, 171
Trigg, Tockie 133
Troubetzkov, Youcca 45
Trouble in Paradise 2, 10, 13, 16, 82–88
Trowbridge, Charles 158
True, Pauline 111
Tucker, Harland 158, 261
Turk, Edward Baron 35
Turner Classic Movies (TCM) 1, 16, 232
Turner, Don 142
Tuttle, Frank 32

Twelvetrees, Helen 31
Twentieth Century-Fox 13, 178, 179, 188
24 Hours 9, 16, 63–65, 85
21 Club 7
Twice Upon a Time 223
Tyler, Fred 141
Tyne, George 188

UCLA Film and Television Archive 24, 32
Unfit to Print see *Scandal Sheet*
The Unholy Garden 42
United Artists 8, 10, 40, 88, 89, 170
Universal 165, 168, 176, 178, 185, 187
Unlawful 159
Usher, Guy 123
USO 13, 188, 189, 190, 191, 192
USO Appeal 225

Valentine, Joseph 166, 185, 187
Valkis, Helen 141
Vallee, Rudy 78
El Valor de vivir 82
van der Osten, Paul 47
Van Dyke, W.W. 60, 63, 180, 182
Van Pelt, Homer 71, 114
Van Sickel, Dale 142
Van Sloan, Edward 72
Van Trees, James 98
Vanaire, Jacques 28, 76
Vanderveer, Ellinor 35, 48, 261
Vaughan, Silvia 128
Veiller, Bayard 60, 208
Venturini, Edward D. 67
Venus 7, 208–209
Verdera, Claire 138
Vermilye, Jerry 106
Vernon, Billy 195
Verrill, Virginia 106
A Very Private Scandal 86
The Vice Squad 9, 56–58
Vidor, King 88, 89
Viera, Mark A. 112
Vilches, Ernesto 35
Villarreal, Julio 82
Vincent, Allen 74
Vinson, Helen 76, 77, 78, 79, 162, 163, 164, 261
The Virtuous Sin 8, 45–48
Visaroff, Michael 24
Vitaphone 190
Vogan, Emmett 117, 120, 125, 142, 153, 155, 160
von Brincken, Wilhelm 93
von Eltz, Theodore 174
Vroom, Henry 195

Waite, Malcolm 35, 63
Wald, Jerry 116
Waldo, Janet 223, 261
Waldorf Astoria 6
Waldridge, Harold 76
Wales, Wally 120
Walker, Basil 178
Walker, Harry 38, 98
Walker, Nella 83, 101, 162, 171
Walker, Stuart 6, 67, 69, 73, 198

Walker, Vernon 162, 171, 174
Walker, Walter 95, 98, 101
Walking Tall 203
Wallace, Catherine 24
Wallace, Milton 93
Wallace, Morgan 98
Wallace, Thomas C. 191, 192
Wallis, Hal 73, 79, 95, 110, 122, 130–131, 133, 136, 138, 141, 145, 147, 155
Walsh, Blanche 5, 227, 261
Walthall, Patricia 142
Walton, Francis 160, 162
Walton, Fred 114
Wanger, Walter 20
Ward, John 207, 261
Ward, Kathrin Clare 128
Warde, Anthony 195, 198, 199, 261
Ware, Frank 35
Ware, Helen 90, 91, 261
Ware, Virginia 192
Warner, Jack 92, 110, 115, 118, 119, 122, 133, 138, 141, 145, 158
Warner Bros. 2, 9, 10, 11, 13, 56, 58, 69, 71, 72, 73, 75, 78, 79, 82, 89, 90, 92, 95, 97, 98, 101, 103, 110, 112, 113, 116, 119, 120, 122, 124, 128, 132, 133, 135, 136, 136, 141, 144, 145, 148, 150, 152, 154, 155, 158, 159, 160, 161, 174, 179, 182, 184, 185, 187, 222
Warren, Eda 22
Warren, Gloria 182, 183, 184, 185, 261
Warren, Harry 107, 116, 136, 188, 191–192
Warriors of Peace 225
Washington, Blue 60, 261
Waters of the Wilderness 223
Watkin, Pierre 142, 158, 192, 261
Watson, Minor 63, 211, 261
Watson, Ralph J. 188
Watters, George Manker 27
Waxman, Franz 180
Way of a Lancer 89
Wayne, Billy 150
Wayne, Fredd 214, 261
Wayne, Velma 133
Wayne, William 117
Wead, Frank 120
The Web and the Rock 14, 218
Webb, Ira 185
Webb, Millard 5, 8, 17, 19
Webb, Roy 162, 171
Webb, Seward 176
Weenie 145
Weidler, Virginia 222, 261
Weiss, Pinky 95
Welbourne, Charles Scott 101
Welch, Niles 117, 120
Welden, Ben 138, 141, 261
Wells, Marie 125, 261
Weltzenkorn, Louis 63
Wenger, John 32
Wentworth, Martha 223, 261
Werris, Snag 188
Wesselhoeft, Eleanor 120
West, Charles 38, 261
West, Henry 138

West, Mae 107
West, Pat 168, 261
West, Vera 166, 168, 176, 185
Westmore, Bud 185
Westmore, Perc 127, 154, 182, 187
Weston, Ruth 58, 60
Weyl, Carl Jules 160
Wharton, Carly 179
Wharton, Edith 25, 26, 27
What Happened, Caroline? 187
Whelan, Arleen 178, 261
When the Daltons Rode 13, 168–170
When Tomorrow Comes 112
Where's Charlie 180
White, Irving 182, 184
White, Leo 76, 90, 101, 136, 153, 183
White, Merrill B. 32
White, Robertson 150
White, Ruth 216, 219, 262
The White Angel 11, 78, 100, 128–133, 222
Whiting, Richard A. 32, 42, 45
Whitlock, Lloyd 117, 176
Whitman, Gayne 174, 223, 262
Whitney, John 188
Whitney, Renee 90, 101, 107
Whittell, Josephine 148
Wife Wanted 13, 145, 199–203
Wife Wanted: An Unusual Human Story 199, 202
Wilber, Robert 114
Wilcox, Frank 188
Wilde, Cornel 190
Wilding, Michael 215
Wilkins, June 168
William, Warren 110, 111, 112, 116, 117, 118, 119, 152, 223, 262
Williams, Corinne 116

Williams, Guinn (Big Boy) 185, 262
Williams, Lottie 103, 158, 183
Willis, Edwin B. 93, 180
Willock, Dave 188
Wilmarth, William H. 195
Wilson, Charles C. 95
Wilson, Clarence 53, 76, 90, 93, 171
Wilson, Eleanor 213, 262
Wilson, Kathryn 162
Wilson, Tom 56, 120, 123, 142, 150, 158, 160, 262
Wilton, Eric 72, 103, 111, 117, 128, 133
Windheim, Marek 174
Windy Hill 14, 210–211
Wing, Pat 101
Wise, Jack 142, 150, 155, 160
Wix, Florence 162
Wolfe, Thomas 218
Wolffe, Albert 24
The Woman Habit 154
Woman in the Case 198
The Women 47
Women Are Like That 13, 148–150
Women in the Wind 13, 160–162
Wonder Bar 1, 10, 107–110
Wong, Barbara Jean 223, 262
Wood, Allan 162
Wood, Helen 123
Wood, Judith 56, 57, 58, 65, 66, 262
Wood, Sam 59
Wood, Yvonne 188
Woodell, Barbara 199, 262
Woodruff, Frank 174, 176
Woods, Al 123
Woods, Donald 106, 120, 128, 132, 222, 262

Woods, Harry 107, 262
Woods, Lottie 107
Woods, Margo 199
Working Wives see *Man Wanted*
Worth, Lillian 120
Worthington, William 98, 148, 262
Wray, Fay 28, 29, 32, 34, 42, 58, 262
Wray, John 120
Wright, Elizabeth 195
Wright, Marbeth 120
Wright, Tenny 138
Wyatt, Eustace 224, 262
Wynn, Gordon 188
Wynn, R.C. 58
Wynyard, Diana 134

Yance, Luis 35
A Yank in the R.A.F. 180
Yaple, Warren 155
Yarbo, Lillian 185
Yarborough, Barton 199, 262
Yarus, Buddy 188
York, Duke 171, 262
You Never Can Tell 205
Young, Emma 120
Young, Loretta 154
Young, Robert 218
Young, Roland 74, 75, 133, 134, 262
Yurka, Blanche 236, 262

Zaner, Jimmy 171
Zanuck, Darryl F. 78, 178, 223
Zeidman, B.F. 22
Zeisler, Alfred 195
Zellner, Arthur J. 141
Zilahy, Lajos 45, 47
Zukor, Adolph 32, 42

www.ingramcontent.com/pod-product-compliance
Ingram Content Group UK Ltd.
Pitfield, Milton Keynes, MK11 3LW, UK
UKHW050540150426
5217IPUK00026B/2018